MYTH AND LITERATURE

MYTH AND LITERATURE

Contemporary Theory and Practice

Edited by

JOHN B. VICKERY

A
BISON
BOOK

UNIVERSITY OF NEBRASKA PRESS

LINCOLN

Acknowledgments for permission to reprint copyrighted
material appear on page 383

First Bison Book printing: August, 1969

Most recent printing shown by first digit below:

4   5   6   7   8   9   10

Manufactured in the United States of America

To Olga and Ann

CONTENTS

INTRODUCTION

One of the most distinctive trends in contemporary literary study is that of myth criticism. To provide an introduction to its theories, methods, and problems is the purpose of this volume. For a variety of reasons myth criticism has aroused a great deal of discussion, not a little of it acrimonious. The details of its battle for recognition, however, need not concern us here. Suffice it to say, as one scholar has, that myth criticism "is a committed point of view and so cantankerous, obstreperous, irritating, wrong on details, and dictatorial, but it is passionate and alive and has something to say."

Obviously it is the second part of his statement that provides the warrant for the present collection of essays. But to state briefly and precisely what myth criticism has to say is difficult, for it has more than its share of antagonistic sub-groups, internecine rivalries, and just plain mavericks. Nevertheless, most myth critics would probably subscribe to the following as general principles. First, the creating of myths, the mythopoeic faculty, is inherent in the thinking process and answers a basic human need. Second, myth forms the matrix out of which literature emerges both historically and psychologically. As a result, literary plots, characters, themes, and images are basically complications and displacements of similar elements in myths and folktales. How myth gets into literature is variously explained by the Jungian racial memory, historical diffusion, or the essential similarity of the human mind everywhere. Third, not only can myth stimulate the creative artist, but it also provides concepts and patterns which the critic may use to interpret specific works of literature. Knowing the grammar of myth, it is argued, gives a greater precision and form to our reading of the language of literature. In recognizing that mythic features reside beneath as well as on the surface of a work, myth criticism differs substantially from earlier treatments of the mythological in literature. Fourth and last, the ability of literature to move us profoundly is due to its mythic quality, to its possession of *mana*, the *numinous*, or the mystery in the face of which we feel an awed delight or terror at the world of man. The real function of literature in human affairs is to continue myth's ancient and basic endeavor to create a meaningful place for man in a world oblivious to his presence.

The question of what myth criticism is leads logically to what it can do. Foremost is the capacity it shares with all good criticism, to materially sharpen our perception of theme, structure, and character in specific works. Recognition of the sacrificial myth in *Tender is the Night*, the rites of passage in *The Plumed Serpent*, or the divine king-scapegoat in Joyce's HCE uncovers significant aspects of these works that other types of criticism have slighted. The myth critic isolates latent elements, which, like those of dreams, possess the force that vitalizes the manifest pattern. Myths and rituals also help him gauge the unique features of literary works. For instance, identifying Dick Diver and Joe Christmas as sacrificial scapegoats is but the first step. In terms of his myth-model, the critic also asks such questions as why they were chosen, what communal sins they are to remove, what form the expulsion takes, and what view of the myth is implicit. And in the process he learns how individual dynamics shape the character's fulfilment of his mythic role. This approach further leads to a comparative method that uses myth and archetype as the ground for comparison and differentiation. To follow the arc of the Promethean myth from Aeschylus to Saul Bellow's *Herzog* or the permutations of the trickster through Mann as well as Melville enriches our understanding of artist and age alike. Such a concern for the emotional patterning resident in myth is peculiarly appropriate to the twentieth century and its struggle to achieve a viable mode of psychic order.

An equally important facet of this criticism is that it affords a unifying point of view which more nearly than any other derives from literature itself. Its key terms—myth and ritual—encompass that out of which literature emerged; therefore, it is aligned with literature essentially, not accidentally, and in a way that social, political, philosophical, and religious concepts are not. Its terminology, perspective, and values are inherently and radically literary; to this extent, myth criticism is non-ideological. Thus, whatever anthropologists may say about the meaning of the word "myth," critics legitimately extend or alter its sense subject to the needs of their own discipline. For instance, one speaks of the myth in Kafka's work and refers to a projection of its author's psychoses. Used of *Ulysses* or *Joseph and His Brothers*, myth means a formal extrapolation of an ancient story. And in *Darkness at Noon*, *Light in August*, or *Lord of the Flies* it describes what F. M. Cornford called the writer's "mythistoria," that is, "the circumambient atmosphere of his place and time." For the myth critic, then, the term may refer to the author, to his work, or to the society which attends to both. Accordingly, it acquires manifold dimensions: psychological, rhetorical or semantic, and ideological or sociological. What is essential is not reduction to a single definition but skill in discriminating the meaning relevant to the occasion. Through extended and sensitive development of these various dimensions—as *Anatomy of Criticism* shows us—myth criticism may help to close the gap between formal analysis, whether semantic, rhetorical, or archetypal, and the functional, genetic concerns of the literary historian, biographer, and psychoanalyst.

While myth criticism endorses the autonomy of literature and its study, it does not consign the critic to the vacuum-sealed container of his own brain. Instead it links him to other disciplines, notably anthropology and psychology, and so broadens his approach to reality and the modes of experiencing it. In this it aspires to reverse the practical achievement of the New Criticism which was largely to cut off the critic from direct, explicit access to the resources of science, sociology, and philosophy. By espousing the necessity of extra-literary knowledge for the critic while reserving the right to adapt that knowledge in accord with the needs of literary study, myth criticism makes a third contribution of considerable importance. It serves as a reminder of the dangers of concentrating too narrowly upon limited areas and approaches, as past philological, historical, and rhetorical studies have done. To avoid its own form of narrowness is the challenge confronting myth criticism.

From the foregoing one might think a critical millennium is at hand. But as someone once remarked, intelligent theory always holds out the possibility of unintelligent practices. When inverted Persephones materialize out of thin air and Grail quests replace the original plot, this possibility seems to have been realized. Such aberrations are, however, inevitable considering the many critics interested in the subject. They range from the devout to the unbelieving, from Eastern mystagogues to Freudian apologists, from those conversant with myth to those with only a glancing knowledge of it. Inevitably misreadings, distortions, and oversimplifications result and they are, of course, regrettable, but they do not constitute the really significant feature of myth criticism. What does is that there should be so much responsible, illuminating, and exciting criticism in a field whose boundaries, principles, and methods are just beginning to be explored.

Why this kind of critical interest should have arisen when it did is a complex and as yet incompletely understood matter. But even now three factors stand out. The earliest is nineteenth-century symbolism with its serious attention to arcane subjects, irrational states, and hermetic meanings. It encouraged in the succeeding age a climate of opinion receptive to an interest in myth, primitive life, and unfamiliar religious modes. To take but obvious instances. Baudelaire's absorption in the esoteric specula-tions of Swedenborg yielded to Yeats' fascination with Madame Blavatsky. Rimbaud's hallucinatory derangement of the senses is followed by Hart Crane's effort to attain poetic vision through jazz-ridden intoxication. And Mallarmé's reliance on what has been described as "a belief that a primitive language, half-forgotten, half-living, exists in each man" finds an echo in the art of T. S. Eliot. Underlying these different interests is a sense of the vital importance of literature to the spiritual or psychological state of man. It is this sense which historically provided the initial impetus for myth criticism.

A second contributory factor was the development of anthropology and psychology and their use in comparative religion during the early years of this century. Psycho-analysis and the Cambridge school of anthropology were from the beginning the dominant intellectual forces in this movement, however much it was also indebted to Bergson, Durkheim, Lévy-Bruhl, and others. Crucial insights were drawn largely from Frazer's *The Golden Bough*, Jane Harrison's *Themis*, Freud's *Totem and Taboo*, and Jung's *Psychology of the Unconscious*, a fact which led Stanley Edgar Hyman to call 1912 a watershed year in the growth of this critical interest. Out of these and similar books came the controlling ideas of myth criticism, such as the dying and reviving god, the hero's quest, ritual drama, the scapegoat, and the cyclical nature of existence. The continuing adaptation of these and related concepts to the particular demands of literary study make up the subsequent history of myth criticism. Landmarks in this history are the psychoanalytically oriented studies of Maud Bodkin and Joseph Campbell as well as the works of Philip Wheelwright, Francis Fergusson, and Northrop Frye, which employ related but distinctive approaches.

The third factor in the emergence of myth criticism was the situation created by the New Criticism of Empson, Blackmur, and Brooks. Halting the retreat into an ever-receding study of prompt books and climates of opinion, the New Criticism focused attention on the full significance inherent in the language of literature. Its intense semantic concentration on the problems of meaning, however, led readers to see more than its advocates bargained for, namely, that the meaning of a work extends far beyond questions of paradox and ambiguity. This together with the difficulty of applying its techniques to fiction and the long poem explains the critical shift in the last decade or so from rhetoric to myth. For not only does myth criticism deal with the macroscopic meanings provided by symbol and cumulative tradition, it also is a means of coping with such extended and complex narrative patterns as the epic and the novel. Thus the truly historical role of myth criticism may lie in its endeavor to deal with all literary modes and in a manner appropriate to each.

Note on the Text and Arrangement

The essays are arranged to lead from general issues, providing a background in depth, to analyses of specific works and authors. In Part I the selections (Bidney, Campbell, Roheim, and Kluckhohn) constitute an informal survey of the views of myth and ritual taken by disciplines other than literature—anthropology, philosophy, comparative religion, and psychoanalysis. Of the nine essays in Part II, the first six (Hyman, Wheelwright, Chase, Watts, Frye, and Lytle) relate the concept of myth and ritual to general literary issues, while the concluding group of three (Rahv, Douglas, and Block) seeks to evaluate the uses of myth in critical theory and practice. The twenty-one essays in Part III apply myth criticism to individual literary works or authors and afford a representative sampling of the mythopoeic patterns critics have traced in literature from Homer to Faulkner.

The principal criteria in selection were intrinsic merit and diversity of subject, but I have also tried to present self-contained essays rather than portions of generally well-known and accessible books. Thus, excerpts from such noted and influential theoreticians as Ernst Cassirer and Carl Jung are omitted on the assumption that their views, which do not readily lend themselves to piecemeal presentation, would be either familiar or easily available. The omission of these and other authors has, to some extent, been compensated for by the inclusion of a reasonably full bibliography of books in English which provides an introduction to the scholarly literature on the subject.

Bibliographical data on the essays appear in the source notes following each selection. Obvious typographical and punctuation errors have been corrected and some spellings have been changed to ensure consistency of usage throughout the volume. In the interest of economy some of the original footnotes have been omitted either in whole or in part. Where an English translation of a foreign language passage has not been given in the original, it has been supplied. In such cases the translation appears in the text while the foreign language passage is given in a footnote. Three asterisks (* * *) indicate that a portion of the original text has been omitted.

Part One

THE NATURE OF MYTH

Since myth is rooted in language, human behavior, and society, it commands the attention of a variety of intellectual disciplines, each of which looks at it from a slightly different perspective. The four essays comprising Part I represent approaches to the problem of myth in which philosophical, anthropological, humanistic, and psychoanalytic interests merge and sometimes clash.

David Bidney, whose survey of western man's attitude toward myth opens this volume, is primarily concerned with the philosophy of culture. His views are most fully embodied in Theoretical Anthropology (*1953*). *In the following selection the emphasis is on the modern status of myth, particularly as it figures in the philosophy of culture developed by Ernst Cassirer (1874–1945), whose neo-Kantian views on myth are among the most influential in contemporary thought. Students of literature will be quick to note the analogies between the New Criticism and Cassirer's idea that through the image, myth fuses the real and the ideal. Similarly, what Cassirer calls myth's "law of metamorphosis" will be recognized as a principle modified and put to brilliant use in Northrop Frye's* Anatomy of Criticism (*1957*).

Mr. Bidney's essay introduces the inevitable question of the kind of interpretation to be applied to myth. Is it to be interpreted literally or symbolically? Is it to be regarded from a secular, scientific point of view or from a religious, metaphysical standpoint? Does its value reside in its historical occurrence or in its intuitive truth? A related question—the connection of belief and myth—also comes into the discussion. According to Cassirer, myth implies a belief in the reality of the object; Bidney suggests that a myth is not a myth unless it is disbelieved. Joseph Campbell and Suzanne Langer, among others, take a more Coleridgean tack by stressing the make-believe, play quality of the mythic response. The problem is a crucial one since it affects our estimate of the relations between myth and literature.

MYTH, SYMBOLISM, AND TRUTH

David Bidney

The problem of myth is one that has concerned Western philosophers from the time of Plato and the Sophists. In Greek thought the problem was to explain the relation of rational, philosophical truth to traditional, religious beliefs. The Sophists of the Greek Enlightenment attempted a reconciliation by interpreting the traditional myths or theogonic tales as allegories revealing naturalistic and moral truths. This allegorical mode of interpretation was criticized by Plato but found continuous favor among the Neo-Platonic and Stoic philosophers of the Hellenistic period who saw in it a method of preserving the authority of tradition as well as the religious prerogatives of the state. The emperor Julian and the philosopher Sallustius regarded myths as divine truths and mysteries hidden from the foolish crowd and apparent only to the wise. By contrast, the Epicurean philosophers since the time of Democritus and Lucretius, the so-called atheists of the ancient world, sought to explain away and get rid of the traditional tales on the ground that they were fabrications which concealed purely naturalistic and historical events at best but were introduced primarily to bolster the authority of the priests and the rulers. Euhemerus in the third century B.C. gave classic expression to this trend of thought and Euhemerism has since become a symbol for all purely historical explanations of myth. In an age which witnessed the deification of actual rulers such as Alexander the Great, it seemed obvious to some philosophers that the traditional myths of gods and heroes concealed no supernatural mysteries but only the prosaic events of actual history at most.

Both the Neo-Platonists and Stoics, as well as the Epicureans, agreed that the myths were not to be taken literally, but the tender-minded conservatives saw in them eternal, allegorical, religious, and philosophical truths, while the tough-minded reformers explained them away as fictions designed to mislead the credulous, superstitious multitude. In the early Christian era, the Christian theologians were glad to avail themselves of the arguments of the Epicureans against the pagan myths while the Stoic and Neo-Platonic philosophers and rulers contended against the Christian claim to exclusive divine revelation. Christian and Hebrew theologians, such as Philo and Saint Augustine, were prepared to interpret the Old Testament narratives allegorically as well as literally but were not willing to acknowledge the same authority to the pagan myths. It is owing largely to Christian influence and intolerance that the pagan religious scriptures have since been regarded in the West as "myths" in the sense of discredited and incredible narratives.

With the advent of the European Renaissance in the fifteenth and sixteenth centuries there was a revival of interest in Greek letters and art. Christian humanism could tolerate an interest in the classic Greek and Roman myths provided they did not compete with the Christian religion. Hence, to the extent that myths could be interpreted as moral allegories or purely poetic or artistic representations of human emotions and aspirations, they were tolerated by the Catholic Church. This tolerance was facilitated by the artistic tradition of the early Church itself which permitted symbolical representation of Christian ideals. The symbol of the Cross and the monogram of Christ, together with such emblems as the Good Shepherd, the Vine, and the Fish, were popularly accepted. During the later Middle Ages Catholic painters were occupied with the representation of subjects of the Old and New Testament history. It was an easy step, therefore, for Renaissance artists to utilize afresh those figures of Greek and Roman mythology which enabled them to express symbolically new secular ideas as, for example, in the work of Titian, Tintoretto, Leonardo, and Michelangelo. Renaissance art gave symbolic expression to Greek ideals of beauty in the context of Christian culture. Among philosophers, Francis Bacon's attempt in his *The Wisdom of the Ancients* to revive a purely allegorical interpretation of the classic myths as repositories of esoteric philosophical wisdom was not in accord with the culture of the times and received little serious encouragement. The Christian artist could accept Greek ideals of beauty but the Christian philosopher could hardly derive inspiration from their myths.

During the second European Age of Enlightenment in the eighteenth century the typical attitude of the rationalistic philosophers such as Voltaire was to discredit the classic myths either as irrational superstitions or as deliberate fictions foisted upon the multitude by the crafty priests. The point of the attack was to discredit the Hebrew-Christian Scriptures together with the pagan tales as equally untrustworthy. The rationalists were not anti-religious; they sought a religion of reason to replace the religion of faith.

The work of Giovanni Battista Vico stands out as a unique monument of protest against the predominant rationalism of the eighteenth century, which in turn owed so much to the Cartesianism and mathematicism of the seventeenth century. Vico's *New Science* was a seminal work which had substantial influence outside Italy, particularly in Germany, where it was appreciated by men of the stature of Herder and Goethe and influenced the Romantic movement. Vico's method of mythological interpretation may be characterized as "allegorical Euhemerism" since he attempted to reduce the culture heroes of myth to class symbols of society. Vico's method combines an element of allegory together with historic reductionism; myths are taken symbolically as well as literally. He appreciated the ethnological value of myths as containing significant historic records of the cyclical evolution of human thought and social institutions. But the myths were significant not only as ethnological records; they were thought to be originally "true and severe narrations," expressed in poetic language, of actual historical events. In the course of time, Vico held, as later generations failed to understand the true symbolical meaning of these poetic narratives they were altered and finally regarded as incredible.

In the Romantic movement of the late eighteenth century and early nineteenth century, poetic myth became a subject of veneration and was regarded as the mainspring of human culture. In the work of Schelling myth received philosophical justification as an essential element in the philosophy of religion. As Cassirer has observed, Schelling's *Philosophy of Mythology* discards the allegorical interpretation of myth and replaces it by a "tautegorical interpretation" of mythical figures as "autonomous configurations of the human spirit." Myth is said to have its mode of necessity and its own mode of reality. The very intensity with which myth is believed by its adherents excludes any rationalistic theory of pure invention. Myth is not something freely invented but a necessary mode of feeling and belief which appears in the course of history and seizes upon human consciousness. In accordance with Schelling's philosophy of absolute idealism, the mythological process is fundamentally a "theogonic process," that is, a process in which God or the Absolute reveals Himself historically through human consciousness. Man's consciousness had to pass through the mythological stage of polytheism before the true God could be known as such. Mythology is a necessary stage in the self-revelation of the Absolute.

In the Neo-Kantian philosophy of Ernst Cassirer we have the most significant attempt of moden times to construct a philosophy of myth as an integral part of a philosophy of culture. Cassirer's *Philosophy of Symbolic Forms* is an attempt to utilize the positive insights of Schelling while transferring them from a philosophy of absolute idealism to that of the Kantian critical philosophy. Myth is thought of as an autonomous form of the human spirit and hence is not reducible to the play of empirical-psychological forces governing the production of representations. Unlike Schelling, however, Cassirer seeks to explain myth through "the unity of a specific structural form of the spirit," rather than as a theogonic phase of the "absolute process." He is concerned to inquire into the essential character of the mythical function and to contrast this function with that of linguistics, aesthetics, and logic. As he puts it, "A critical phenomenology of the mythical consciousness will start neither from the godhead as an original metaphysical fact nor from mankind as an original empirical fact but will seek to apprehend the subject of the cultural process, the human spirit, solely in its pure actuality and diverse configurations whose immanent forms it will strive to ascertain."[1] Myth creates a world of its own in accordance with a spiritual principle, a world which discloses an immanent rule, a characteristic necessity. The objectivity of myth consists in its being a concrete and necessary mode of spiritual formation, "a typical mode of formation in which consciousness disengages itself from and confronts the mere receptivity of the sensory impression."

Cassirer observes that for Schelling all mythology was essentially the theory and history of the gods. Schelling's philosophy of myth, like the ethnological theories of Andrew Lang, Wilhelm Schmidt, and Wilhelm Koppers, presupposes a primary original monotheism followed by a mythological polytheism. Cassirer, however, is inclined to accept the views of Preuss, Vierkandt, and Marett, that primitive religion began with an entirely undifferentiated intuition of a magical, extraordinary power inherent in things. The primitive, mythopoeic mind, he maintains, is to be studied empirically and functionally without any preconceived metaphysical notions.

According to Cassirer, mythical thinking is a unitary form of consciousness with its specific and characteristic features. There is no unity of object in myth but only a unity of function expressed in a unique mode of experience. Hence he is opposed to all forms of "nature mythology" which would explain the origin of myth by reference to some particular class of natural objects, such as astral mythology. Unity of explanation is to be sought only in unity of function, in unity of cultural sphere and structured form.

Ultimately the unity of myth is to be sought not in a genetic and causal explanation but in a teleological sense as a direction followed by consciousness in constructing spiritual reality. It is Cassirer's self-imposed task to inquire into the nature of that formal unity through which the infinitely multiform world of myth constitutes a characteristic spiritual whole. Myth is an autonomous cultural form and must not be "explained" by reduction to some other symbolic form, such as language. Max Müller's attempt to explain the origin of myth in linguistic ambivalence as a kind of "disease of language" is a case in point. Not unity of origin, whether in language or natural object, but unity of structure and function, as revealed in the end or final product, is the true objective. Myth is not a reflection of an objective reality independent of it, but is rather the product of true creative, spiritual actions, an independent image world of the spirit as well as an active force of expression. Myth is the first expression of a spiritual process of liberation which is effected in the progress from the magical-mythical world view to the truly religious view. Myth is the first step in "the dialectic of bondage and liberation which the human spirit experiences with its own self-made image worlds."

In the beginning of human culture myth is not yet sharply differentiated from other cultural forms. Thus language, like myth, preserves a complete equivalence of world and thing and only gradually acquires its own spiritual form and significatory function. Similarly in art there is at first no sharp differentiation between the real and

1. Ernst Cassirer, *The Philosophy of Symbolic Forms*, II (New Haven: Yale University Press, 1955), p. 13.

the ideal. Art also is embedded at first in magical representations, and the image has no purely aesthetic significance. Thus, although myth, language, and art interpenetrated one another originally in primitive culture, there is a progressive development to the point where the human spirit becomes conscious of the diversity and relative autonomy of its self-created symbols. Science is distinguished from other forms of cultural life in that through science the human mind knows its symbols as symbols distinct from sense impressions. But this spiritual freedom of self-consciousness is the result of a long process of critical endeavor.

According to Cassirer's Neo-Kantian approach, we must understand the mythical symbol, not as a representation concealing some mystery or hidden truth, but as a self-contained form of interpretation of reality. In myth there is no distinction between the real and the ideal; the image is the thing and hence mythical thinking lacks the category of the ideal. This is true in all stages of mythical thinking and is expressed most clearly in mythical action. In all mythical action the subject of the rite is transformed into a god or demon whom he represents. Hence Cassirer is prepared to admit with Robertson Smith that rites precede myth and that the narrative of myth is a mediate interpretation of the immediately given rite. This explains why rites are taken so seriously in primitive religion and why it is constantly believed that the continuance of human life and the very survival of the world depend on the correct performance of rites. Nature is thought to yield nothing without ceremonies. Thus in the dance as well as in fertility rites the human actor does not regard himself as engaging in mere imitative representation but as becoming identified momentarily with the person of the mythical drama and exercising his powers. Similarly, word and name do not merely designate and signify objects; they are the essence of the thing and contain its magical powers. In like manner, the image of a thing is endowed with its active force and what happens to the image happens also to the object—a basic assumption of much of primitive magic. Thus in primitive language, art, and magic, mythical thinking uses symbolic representations but without differentiating the symbols from their objects.

This would seem to imply that the Neo-Kantian theory of the constitutive character of symbolism is in accord with the practice of primitive culture and would be valid for us *if* we adhered to primitive rites and mythical beliefs. Cassirer himself arrived at the "astonishing conclusion" that David Hume, in attempting to analyze the causal judgment of science, rather revealed a source of all mythical explanation of the world. One feels tempted to say that Cassirer, in attempting to analyze the constructive functions of cultural symbols in constituting objective reality, succeeded only in revealing an implicit assumption of all mythological thought but *not* of critical philosophical and scientific thought, as he thought he had done.

According to Cassirer, myth has a truth of its own distinct from that of other cultural forms since the mythical mind is creative and gives expression to its own form of objective reality. That is why he insists that myth is to be interpreted literally and is opposed to allegorical interpretation on the ground that the latter reduces myth to some other mode of cultural truth such as philosophy, religion, or history, and does not account for the unique and irreducible element in mythical expression.

We are then faced with the problem: what is this ideal, distinctive function of myth? What is myth apart from its expression in primitive word-magic, ritual-magic, and image-magic? If myth as narrative is merely the mediate interpretation of the immediately given rite, in what sense is myth an autonomous expression with a truth of its own? Since all mythical thinking is said to confuse the ideal and the real, the symbol and its object, in what sense then does myth convey a truth of its own through its autonomous symbolic forms?

Cassirer has demonstrated how language gradually frees itself from the mythological context, and how the notion of language as a distinct symbolic form emerges. There is a crisis or breaking point in the development of language at which the symbolic, semantic function of language becomes clearly differentiated from its objects. Similarly, religion breaks away from its mythical foundations and assumes its own form. Religious dogma is said to be the form assumed by pure religious meaning when men seek to express this meaning in terms of objective representations. In religious mysticism both the mythical and the dogmatic elements of faith are rejected and the incarnation of God is understood as a process which operates continuously in human consciousness. In the religious consciousness, however, the conflict between the pure meaning and the mythical image is never really resolved. Only in the sphere of art, Cassirer maintains, does the opposition between image and meaning become resolved, for only in the aesthetic consciousness is the image recognized as such. The aesthetic consciousness which gives itself over to pure contemplation finally achieves a pure spiritualization of symbolic expression and a maximum of freedom.

One is compelled to conclude reluctantly that in his *Philosophy of Symbolic Forms* Cassirer has not demonstrated his thesis that myth is an autonomous form of symbolism. For him, as for the ethnologists and philosophers whom he criticized, myth is a stage in the development of culture. Far from being an autonomous and integral segment of universal human culture, it is rather a mode of thought based on the confusion of the symbolic ideal and the existential real which manifests itself historically at a given stage of cultural evolution. In the progressive development of human conciousness the symbolic functions of language, art, religion, and science are gradually differentiated from the mythological-magical complex, though traces of their mythic origin remain. At most it may be said that for Cassirer myth is a necessary stage in the creative expression and self-liberation of the human spirit. But since Cassirer acknowledges no metaphysical Absolute as does Schelling, the mythic symbols may not be said to express an implicit religious truth, but only the delusions of the primitive human consciousness as it struggles to interpret the world of experience and reality. Ironically, it may be said that Cassirer's Neo-Kantian vision of a synthesis of symbolic forms each of which is constitutive of objective reality is in agreement with the implicit assumptions of mythological thought, but fails to account for the critical, transcultural validity and objectivity of philosophical and scientific thought which he himself sought to establish.

In his later works, notably in the *Essay on Man* and his posthumous *The Myth of the State*, Cassirer returned to the problem of myth, apparently feeling dissatisfied with his treatment in the earlier work. In his *Essay* he stated that in myth one observes not objective but "physiognomic characters." The world of myth is said to be a dramatic world, a world of conflicting powers, and mythical perception is impregnated with these emotional qualities. While all efforts of scientific thought are directed towards eliminating the subjective, physiognomic perception of nature, the "anthropological value" of the data of physiognomic experience remains unchanged. "Science delimits their objectivity, but it cannot completely destroy their reality." The mythic perception is just as real as the scientific since every feature of our human experience has a claim to reality. Thus myth may be said to contribute a truth of its own as a distinct, qualitative way of envisaging reality through its own symbolic forms and categories.

It is important to note here that myth has no explanatory value as an interpretation of nature. The nature myths with their poetic language and physiognomic characterizations comprise a record of uncritical human experience and constitute "a step on our way to reality." The "truth" of myth is a purely subjective, psychological truth and expresses how reality appears in terms of our human feeling-qualities. In this sense myth is real, just as every psychological experience is real to the subject.

On this evaluation, the "truth" of myth is then purely subjective and differs in no significant way from the purely subjective "truth" of a delusion. This is hardly an argument for the autonomy of myth as a distinct symbolic form with an objective validity comparable to that of science. To argue for the reality of mythical experience in the minds of certain believers is not to establish its autonomy as a distinct symbolic form. The significant question is whether myth may be said to have an objective truth and value of its own, and Cassirer's argument, so far, suggests that it has none. If it be true that "in the new light of science mythical perception has to fade away,"[2] and that myths have no cosmological value, then their so-called "anthropological value" is of no significance other than as a record of precritical human experience.

Far from denying that myths have no objective explanatory value, Cassirer makes a special point of admitting it. The unity of myth is said to consist in a unity of function rather than of object, but this function is not that of explanation. In *The Myth of the State* he develops the thesis that myths are primarily emotional in origin, and that their function is essentially practical and social, namely, to promote a feeling of unity or harmony between the members of a society as well as a sense of harmony with the whole of nature or life. This theory of the pragmatic function of myth is one which Cassirer admittedly derived in large measure from Malinowski, to whom he often refers.

Here we must differentiate between Cassirer's views as to the psychological motivation of the mythopoeic mind and his evaluation of the sociological function of myth. The psychological motivation of myth-making explains the origin of this activity as a direct expression of human feeling rather than of intellectual thought. "The real substratum of myth is not a substratum of thought but of feeling."[3] Religion and myth are said to give us a "unity of feeling," whereas art provides a unity of intuition, and science comprises a unity of thought. On this psychological premise, myth provides a

2. Ernst Cassirer, *Essay on Man* (New Haven: Yale University Press, 1944), p. 77.
3. Cassirer, *Essay on Man*, p. 81.

rationalization and validation of human emotions rather than an objective explanation of nature. In this respect Cassirer's position is anti-intellectual since it reduces the function of thought in primitive culture to a secondary position and gives the primacy to feeling and action. Man acts first and rationalizes his conduct later. This is the psychological basis for Cassirer's acceptance of the historical priority of ritual to myth.

The notion of a "unity of feeling" turns out to be rather complex. First, it refers to the fact that myth and religion have a common origin in human feeling considered as a separate mental faculty. Second, "unity of feeling" has an ontological import and refers to "the solidarity of life." This renders intelligible the outstanding feature of the mythical world, "the law of metamorphosis" in virtue of which everything may be turned into everything. Hence primitive man's view of nature is said to be neither theoretical nor practical, but sentimental and "sympathetic." Primitive man has a deep immediate feeling of the fundamental solidarity of life that underlies the multiplicity of its forms. "To mythical and religious feeling nature becomes one great society, the society of life."[4] When, therefore, Cassirer speaks of the sociological function of myth he finds it easy to make the transition from this metaphysical principle of cosmic sympathy to the notion of the solidarity of human society. With Durkheim and Malinowski he maintains that the pragmatic function of myth is to promote social solidarity as well as solidarity with nature as a whole in time of social crises. Mythical thought is especially concerned to deny and negate the fact of death and to affirm the unbroken unity and continuity of life.

I would differentiate, therefore, the *unity of feeling* considered as a mental faculty from the *feeling of unity* which is a metabiological assumption of the indestructible unity of life. One may maintain the theory that mythical thought implicitly presupposes the latter metaphysical assumption without affirming the former psychological thesis that myth originates in the faculty of feeling rather than of thought. Cassirer, however, does not make this distinction clear and speaks as if unity of feeling and feeling of unity were identical.

Cassirer makes the point in his *Myth of the State* that he does not wish to maintain the thesis that myth originates solely in emotion. "Myth," he states, "cannot be described as bare emotion because it is the *expression* of emotion. The expression of a feeling is not the feeling itself—it is emotion turned into image."[5] Mythical symbolism leads to an objectification of feelings; myth objectifies and organizes human hopes and fears and metamorphosizes them into persistent and durable works. Myth is then a symbolic expression of emotion and instinct with an objective character of its own and it is this symbolic expression which differentiates the work of myth from animal reactions.

On the other hand, man's metabiological impulse to identify himself with, and participate in, the life of nature as a whole leads him to express himself directly in symbolic rites of a religious-magical character in order to ensure his survival and well-being. In myth these ritual acts are "explained" and validated. Thus myth is a unique form of symbolism which supervenes upon the symbolism of ritual in order

4. Cassirer, *Essay on Man*, p. 83.
5. Cassirer, *Essay on Man*, p. 75.

to validate and perpetuate it. It is not at all clear from Cassirer's account why myth may not be a direct symbolic expression of human emotion without prior reference to ritual. In any event, myth is not a conscious creation or invention of individuals but is rather a product of man's spontaneous expression of emotion and feeling of unity with nature as a whole. Myth differs from art precisely in the fact that the mythical imagination and intuition imply a *belief* in the reality of its object. The mythopoeic mind does not regard myth merely as a symbolic expression or representation of some independent reality; the mythic symbols are identical with the reality. Hence mythical reality is accepted as given and is not subjected to critical evaluation.

Here I would distinguish further two distinct points which are implicit in Cassirer's argument: first, myth is said to be *based on belief* in the reality of its objects and the truth of its intuitions of the unity of nature and solidarity of life; second, myth is said to have the pragmatic function of *promoting belief* in the solidarity of life and society and in overcoming the fear of death. According to the first argument, ritual acts already presuppose an intuition of cosmic unity of life and a feeling of identity of man with nature. On the other hand, if the function of myth is to promote belief in the solidarity of life then this mythic belief is independent of ritual and the latter becomes intelligible only as a function or consequent of myth. There is, it seems to me, a real issue here which Cassirer did not resolve. He tended to agree with Malinowski in stressing the social and pragmatic function of myth in the crises of life and with Robertson Smith in granting the priority of ritual to myth. He did not realize that his pragmatic, utilitarian approach to myth failed to account for the *fact of belief* which is presupposed in myth but which the myth itself does not produce. Malinowski's pragmatic theory implies the notion of myth as a kind of unconscious, or conscious, fiction which supervenes upon institutional rites—a thesis which Cassirer himself rejects as incompatible with his evolutionary approach to symbolic forms.

To my way of thinking, the central and inescapable issue is the relevance of the question of truth to mythic belief. If myth be conceived as an intrinsically subjective mode of experience, then it may be said to have a purely psychological and ethnological value as a record and expression of uncritical, "physiognomic" emotional experience. The "truth" of myth would then lie in its factual and historical subjectivity. But if the mythic and religious intuition of the solidarity and continuity of cosmic life be accepted as true in the sense of being in accord with a non-mythic reality, then myth may be interpreted allegorically. Since Cassirer does not acknowledge any reality other than symbolic reality, the idea of a non-symbolic reality as a referent for myth is precluded. His only alternative is to suggest, following Durkheim, that myth has a sociological or anthropological value. Not nature but society is the model of myth. Myth refers to a social reality, to the rites and institutions of society, and hence the truth of myth consists in its symbolic representation of social rites. In this way Cassirer thought to avoid an allegorical interpretation of myth while providing an objective social referent for mythic symbolism.

Cassirer saw no contradiction in following simultaneously both a metaphysical and a sociological approach. According to his metaphysical approach, myth is based on a primitive intuition of the cosmic solidarity of life and hence he affirms that myth is potential religion. In so far as he follows the sociological approach of Durkheim and Malinowski myth is said to rationalize and validate ritual and metamorphose human hopes and fears, especially the fear of death.

The truth of myth is then a function of the interpretation of myth. If one accepts the truth of the original intuition of the solidarity of life and the dramatic character of its underlying forces then myth symbolizes allegorically a fundamental metaphysical and religious truth. For the sociological approach, however, the truth of myth consists in its symbolic expression of ritual and has no cosmic reference. Cassirer, it appears, was not prepared to acknowledge the rational validity of the primitive intuition of the organic and cosmic solidarity of all life. His only alternatives were to accept either a purely subjective truth of the reality of mythic experience, or else an objective sociological truth which reduced myth to the secondary role of symbolizing ritual. In either case, it is difficult to see how he could defend his original thesis that myth is an autonomous form of symbolism comparable to language, art, and science.* * *

The history of mythological theory demonstrates that there have been two basic approaches to the interpretation of myth, the literal and the symbolic. On the whole, ethnologists have tended to interpret myth literally as an expression of primitive thought but have differed in their evaluation of myth. Evolutionary, positivistic ethnologists, such as Tylor, have regarded myth negatively as a mode of explanatory thought destined to be superseded by scientific thought. Functionalistic ethnologists, such as Malinowski, have evaluated myth in terms of its pragmatic function in resolving critical problems which affect the welfare and destiny of the individual and his society. Myths are then said to validate institutions and rites. They are rationalizations introduced to justify established social facts. Pragmatic philosophers and sociologists, such as Sorel and Pareto, have recognized cynically the fictional character of myth but have nevertheless justified its use as an instrument of policy and social control. Bergson * * * saw in myth an expression of the cunning of nature and intelligence designed to counteract the excesses of intelligence in alienating man from society and nature. So understood, myth has a limited biological value which may be superseded in so far as man is motivated to act by his supra-rational intuitions and aspirations.

On the other hand, idealistic philosophers and theologians have, from ancient to modern times, interpreted myth allegorically as symbolizing some transcendental, timeless truth but have differed among themselves as to the nature of the object and truth so symbolized. In contemporary thought, myth has been evaluated positively owing in large measure to the influence of psychoanalytical theory, especially that of Jung. In philosophy and religion, Neo-Kantian philosophers, such as Cassirer and Urban, and theologians of the stature of Nicolas Berdyaev and Richard [Reinhold?] Niebuhr, have advocated a positive evaluation of myth. In the sphere of literary criticism, scholars such as Northrop Frye, Maud Bodkin, and most recently Philip Wheelwright, have taken myth seriously as symbolizing universal archetypes and "primordial images" emerging from the collective unconscious. The positive value of myth is affirmed by those who are skeptical of the power of reason to comprehend reality, or the revelations of intuition, as well as by those who accept the position of linguistic and symbolic relativism and adhere to the theory that symbols have no truth-value but only a moral, poetic value as regulative ideals.

My own thesis is that a scientific study of myth should be concerned with the comparative and historical analysis of myth and that myth should be interpreted literally. Myth has a positive value for the ethnologist and folklorist as a record of man's culture history and as a means of establishing universal patterns of thought. Myth, like great art and dramatic literature, may have profound symbolic or allegorical value for us of the present, not because myth necessarily and intrinsically has such latent, esoteric wisdom, but because the plot or theme suggests to us universal patterns of motivation and conduct.

Journal of American Folklore, LXVIII (1955), 379–392. Some of the reference notes have been omitted.

Joseph Campbell, one of America's best-known writers on myth and ritual, is the author of The Masks of God *(1964) and the extremely influential* The Hero with a Thousand Faces *(1949). Although he relies heavily on psychoanalytic ideas in interpreting myth, he is also well informed about folklore, literature, anthropology and comparative religion. Where David Bidney, in the preceding essay, calls for a literal, scientific approach to the study of myth, Campbell argues that the historian and the anthropologist have not really treated the primary problem, which is psychological. Moreover, by claiming myth as an educative cultural force, he diverges sharply from Bidney's stress upon its capacity for deluding man.*

Mr. Campbell raises two points of particular interest. The first is his distinction between homology and analogy, which recognizes similarity of function as more significant than identity of content, thus providing myth critics with a useful way of looking at plots, scenes, and characters. The other intriguing notion is that of myth and ritual as a second womb, a concept which derives from Géza Róheim's theory of man's delayed infancy. Myth and ritual are embodiments of civilization which protect the individual while he matures psychologically and socially. His maturation is equivalent to rebirth ; he is released from his community's myths without recoiling from them as frauds. Such an idea has a variety of applications : for instance, it may explain homogeneous, conservative societies of the past or it may illuminate certain modern writers, especially those from the South like Andrew Lytle, Caroline Gordon, and Eudora Welty.

BIOS AND MYTHOS:
PROLEGOMENA TO A SCIENCE OF MYTHOLOGY

Joseph Campbell

I

The archetypes of mythology are constant enough for sixteenth and seventeenth century Roman Catholics, adequately trained in their own symbology, to have regarded the myths and images, sacraments and temples of the New World as diabolical mockeries of the one True Church.∗ ∗ ∗ The Mexican symbols and myths of Quetzalcoatl so closely resemble those of Jesus that the Padres in that area supposed that Saint Thomas' legendary mission to India must have reached Tenochtitlan, where, cut off from the pure source of Rome, the Waters of Redemption were muddied by Fallen Angels. Three centuries later, Adolf Bastian (1826–1905), voyaging in China and Japan, India, Africa, and South America, also recognized the uniformity of mankind's "Elementary Ideas" (*Elementargedanke*), but took a scientifically maturer view of the implicit problem. Instead of attributing the local variations to the distorting power of a devil, he considered the force of geography and history in the processing of the "Folk Ideas" (*Völkergedanke*), that is to say, in the shaping of the local manifestations of the universal forms. "First," he writes, "the idea as such must be studied . . . and as a second factor, the influence of climatic-geological conditions must be studied."[1] A

---

1. Adolf Bastian, *Das Beständige in den Menschenrassen und die Spielweite ihrer Veränderlichkeit* (Berlin: Dietrich Reimer, 1868), p. 88. (Author's translation.)

third factor, to which he devotes many chapters of his innumerable volumes, is that of the influence upon each other of the various "folk" traditions throughout the course of history. Bastian's insight is basic, and has not yet been supplanted.

Tylor, Frazer, and the other comparative anthropologists, likewise recognized the obvious constancy in mankind's Elementary Ideas. Even Franz Boas, in the first edition of his *The Mind of Primitive Man*, stated without qualification that "in the main the mental characteristics of man are the same all over the world"; and that "Certain patterns of associated ideas may be recognized in all types of culture."[2] But these avowals were expunged from his second, "revised" (actually, recomposed) edition; for the vogue had begun of stressing the differences between the dialects of the common human language.

We owe this new tendency in large measure to the muddle-headed Émile Durkheim. Read his confused discussion of Kant's *a priori* forms of sensibility, and his quackery about the distinction between the Zuñi and European experiences of space, and the shallowness of his whole parody of profundity will be apparent! The entire culturalist movement in our contemporary Anglo-American anthropological literature is touched with this Durkheimian myopia. Bronislaw Malinowski's misreading of Sigmund Freud's technical term *oedipus complex* and his refutation, then, of his own misconception added new dignity to the movement, which now has culminated in a kind of *curia*, dedicated to the proposition that mankind is not a species but an indefinitely variable dough, shaped by a self-creating demiurge, "Society." The idea that man may have a psychological as well as physical character is anathematized as "mystical."[3]

The *curia*'s characteristic mistake, specifically, is that of confusing function with morphology—as though a congress of zoologists, studying the wing of the bat, flipper of the whale, foreleg of the rat, and arm of man, should not know that these organs, though shaped to differing functions, are structurally homologous, and were to suppose that the wing of the bat might be compared, morphologically, with that of a butterfly, the flipper of a whale with the fin of a trout, the leg of a rat with that of a beetle, and the arm of man with that of a lobster. Skipping the first task of a comparative science— that, namely, of distinguishing precisely the sphere of analogy from that of homology—these students of mankind have proceeded to the second task—that of the monograph. The result has been a complete dismemberment of what, forty years ago, promised to become a science.

In contrast, we have the sundry schools of the diffusionists, stressing cultural affinities that obviously unite vast portions of the human race. The philologists of the nineteenth century (Bopp, Grimm Brothers, Max Müller, etc.) studied the wide diffusion of the verbal roots and deities of the Indo-Europeans. Hugo Winckler and his school then indicated Mesopotamia as the area from which the world image and concomitant social structure that we find in all the high cultures of the planet must have been diffused; James H. Breasted, G. Elliot Smith and W. J. Perry spoke for Egypt;

2. Franz Boas, *The Mind of Primitive Man* (New York: Macmillan, 1911), p. 228.
3. The denotation of this neologism in the polemical literature of the social sciences, where it is employed as a term of abuse, is obscure. It seems to mean, roughly, "unscientific."

Harold Peake and Herbert John Fleure tentatively championed Syria; V. Gordon Childe makes it evident that somewhere in the area between the Nile and the Indus, ca. 5000 B.C., the great step was taken from Paleolithic food gathering to Neolithic food production which underlies the structure of settled civilizations throughout the world. Sylvanus G. Morley, on the other hand, held out for an independent origin of the agricultural civilizations in Middle America, thus maintaining the traditional isolationism of the American Anthropological Society, whereas Leo Frobenius long ago detected the evidence of a diffusion across the Pacific. Ad. E. Jensen has recently supported Frobenius' view with his study of the trans-Pacific diffusion of the mythological complex of an early gardening culture; G. F. Scott Elliot thought it probable that fugitives from Japan, ca. 1000 B.C., were responsible for the Middle American development; Robert von Heine-Geldern shows us that late Chou art motifs were diffused from China to Indonesia and Middle America: and we know that the sweet potato, which was called *kumar* in Peru, is *kumara* in Polynesia. C. C. Uhlenbeck points to a fundamental affinity between the Western Eskimo languages, the Uralo-Altaic, and the so-called "A" complex of the Indo-European tongues, and there is, moreover, increasing evidence of some kind of Semitic Indo-European continuity. There can be no question but that vast areas of culture diffusion have been distinguished, and that these represent not only late diffusions but also very ancient ones. We cannot but be impressed, moreover, by the clean-cut definition and self-consistency of many of these culture spheres, as well as by the tenacity with which their fundamental patterns of mythology have been retained in differing landscapes and even in spite of greatly varying economic conditions.

However, it is important not to lose sight of the fact that the mythological archetypes (Bastian's Elementary Ideas) cut across the boundaries of these culture spheres and are not confined to any one or two, but are variously represented in all. For example, the idea of survival after death seems to be about coterminous with the human species; so also that of the sacred area (sanctuary), that of the efficacy of ritual, of ceremonial decorations, sacrifice, and of magic, that of supernal agencies, that of a transcendental yet ubiquitously immanent sacred power (mana, wakonda, śakti, etc.), that of a relationship between dream and the mythological realm, that of initiation, that of the initiate (shaman, priest, seer, etc.), and so on, for pages. No amount of learned hairsplitting about the differences between Egyptian, Aztec, Hottentot, and Cherokee monster killers can obscure the fact that the primary problem here is not historical or ethnological but psychological—even biological; that is to say, precedent to the phenomenology of the culture styles; and no amount of scholarly jargon or apparatus can make it seem that the mere historian or anthropologist is dealing with the problem at all.

In this sensitive and trickish field (Goethe's wondrous realm of "The Mothers") the poet, the artist, and a certain type of romantic philosopher (Emerson, Nietzsche, Bergson, for example) are more successful; for, since in poetry and art, beyond the learning of rhetorical and manual techniques, the whole craft is that of seizing the idea and facilitating its epiphany, the creative mind, adequately trained, is less apt than the analytic to mistake a mere trope or concept for a living, life-awakening image. Poetry and art, whether "academic" or "modern," are simply dead unless informed by Elementary Ideas: ideas not as clear abstractions held in the mind, but as cognized, or rather re-cognized, vital factors of the subject's own being. Though such living ideas become manifest only in the terms and style of some specific historical moment, nevertheless their force lies not in what meets the eye but in what dilates the heart, and this force, precisely, is their essential trait. Since mythology is the compendium of such ideas effective at any given moment, the historian or anthropologist proud of his objective eye has been gelded of the organ that would have made it possible for him to distinguish his materials. He may note and classify circumstances, but can no more speak authoritatively of mythology than a man without taste buds of taste. On the other hand, however, though the poet or the artist, with immediate recognition, experiences the idea and grows to meet it; though it thus affects him as initiatory to his own nature, and in such a way that through it he comes into possession of himself and simultaneously into increased understanding of the Elementary Idea—he is finally an amateur in the fields of history and ethnology. There is certainly no comparison between the profundity of Wagner's masterful realization of the import of Germanic mythology in his *Ring of the Nibelungs* and Max Müller's sentimental theory about solar allegories; nevertheless, for detailed information concerning the materials involved, one would properly turn to the unilluminated philologist, not to the genius of Bayreuth.

Is it then impossible to have a science of myth?

Since Wagner's and Max Müller's day, Sigmund Freud has opened the way to the new prospect. With his recognition in *Totem and Taboo* that ceremonial and neurosis are homologous—with his psychological analysis of the phenomena of magic, sorcery, and theology, demonstrating the identity of the mythological realm and age with the unconscious, and the relationship, consequently, of myth to dream—a total transformation of our control of the problem of the Elementary Idea has taken place. Freud, stressing the parallelism to neurosis, and C. G. Jung, shortly following, recognizing the educative (in the primary sense of the term *e-ducere*) power of the images, have laid the foundations of a possible science of the universals of myth. Bastian's order of study was correct: 1. the Elementary Idea 2. the influence of local climatic-geological factors in the processing of the folk ideas, and 3. the impact upon each other of the varying local traditions in the course of history. Psychoanalysis now makes it possible to go beyond Bastian's mere listing and description of the Elementary Ideas to a study of their biological roots. To criticize the method as unscientific is ridiculous, since objective scholarship, in this particular field, has shown itself helpless—and absolutely so; helpless by definition; for the materials are not optically measurable, but must, on the contrary, be experienced: if not as in the craftsmanship of the poet and the artist, then somehow in life.

There is no need to rehearse the demonstration by psychoanalysis of the parallelism of dream and myth, and the consequent theory of the possibility of mythology developing spontaneously, along traditional lines, wherever mankind may be nesting. "Anyone who really knows what a dream is will agree," writes Róheim, "that there cannot be several 'culturally determined' ways of dreaming just as there are no two ways of sleeping. . . . The dream work is the same for everybody although there are differences in the degree and technique of secondary elaboration."[4] The relationship of dream and vision to mythological symbolism from Dante to the dreamers (*oko-jumu*) of the Andamanese, is too well known, now, to require demonstration. There is a close relationship between the protective, ego-defending religious symbolism of any people and the dreams of its most talented dreamers. The medicine men, as Róheim so aptly phrases it, are "the lightning conductors of common anxiety. They fight the demons so that others can hunt the prey and in general fight reality."[5] They fight the demons and, while doing so, achieve a measure of psychological wisdom that is denied their extraverted, pig-hunting fellows. They are, in fact, the forerunners of those really great dreamers, whose names are the names of the pedagogues of the race: Gilgamesh, Ptahhotep, Akhnaton, Jacob, Socrates, Plato, Laotze, Confucius, Vyāsa, Homer, Buddha, Jesus, Quetzalcoatl and Mohammed. The intentional fathoming of the interior darkness of the psyche in the long tradition of the disciplines of yoga has perhaps given India a larger share than other lands of the wisdom bestowed by the Eternal Ones of the Dream; nevertheless, some portion of that wisdom is shared by all the world. Hence Ananda K. Coomaraswamy could demonstrate that the metaphysics taught through the dreamlike images of myth in India is the same as that of mythology everywhere. "All mythology," he writes, "involves a corresponding philosophy; and if there is only one mythology, as there is only one 'perennial philosophy,' then that 'the myth is not my own, I had it from my mother' (Euripides) points to a spiritual unity of the human race already predetermined long before the discovery of metals. It may be really true that, as Jeremias said, the various cultures of mankind are no more than the dialects of one and the same spiritual language."[6]

"Myth," he writes again, "is the penultimate truth, of which all experience is the temporal reflection. The mythical narrative is of timeless and placeless validity, true nowever and everywhere";[7] precisely, one might add, as the dream is the penultimate truth about the dreamer, of which all his experience is the temporal reflection.

A serious science of mythology must take its subject matter with due seriousness, survey the field as a whole, and have at least some conception of the prodigious range of functions that mythology has served in the course of human history. It is dreamlike and, like dream, a spontaneous product of the psyche; like dream, revelatory of the psyche and hence of the whole nature and destiny of man; like dream—like life— enigmatic to the uninitiated ego; and like dream, protective of that ego. In the simplest human societies mythology is the text of the rites of passage; in the writings of the Hindu, Chinese, and Greek philosophers (as of all who have ever read them) mythology is the picture language of metaphysics. The first function is not violated by the

4. Géza Róheim, "Dream Analysis and Field Work in Anthropology," *Psychoanalysis and the Social Sciences*, I (1947), 90.

5. Géza Róheim, *The Origin and Function of Culture* (New York: Nervous and Mental Disease Monographs, 1943), p. 51.

6. Ananda K. Coomaraswamy, *Recollection, Indian and Platonic*, Supplement to the Journal of the American Oriental Society, Number 3, April–June 1944, p. 18.

7. Ananda K. Coomaraswamy, *Hinduism and Buddhism* (New York: Philosophical Library, n.d.), p. 6.

second, but extended; both harmoniously bind man, the growing animal, to his world, simultaneously in its visible and in its transcendent aspects. Mythology is the womb of mankind's initiation to life and death.

II

How mythology functions, why it is generated and required by the human species, why it is everywhere essentially the same, and why the rational destruction of it conduces to puerility, become known the moment one abandons the historical method of tracing secondary origins and adopts the biological view (characteristic of the medical art of psychoanalysis), which considers the primary organism itself, this universal carrier and fashioner of history, the human body. As Róheim states in his brilliant monograph on *The Origin and Function of Culture*: "The outstanding difference between man and his animal brethren consists in the infantile characters of human beings, in the prolongation of infancy. The prolonged infancy explains the traumatic character of sexual experiences which do not produce the like effect in our simian brethren or cousins, and the existence of the oedipus complex itself which is partly a conflict between archaic and recent love objects. Finally, the defence mechanisms themselves owe their existence to the fact that our Soma (Ego) is even more retarded than the Germa (Id) and hence the immature Ego evolves defence mechanisms as a protection against libidinal quantities which it is not prepared to deal with."[8] "Man," as Adolf Portmann of Basel vividly phrases it, "is the incomplete creature whose style of life is the historical process determined by a tradition."[9] He is congenitally dependent on society and society, commensurably, is both oriented to and derived from the distinctive psychosomatic structure of man. This structure, furthermore, is rooted not in any local landscape, with its economic-political potentials, but in the Germa of a widely distributed biological species. Whether on the ice of Baffin Land or in the jungles of Brazil, building temples in Siam or cafés in Paris, "civilization," as Dr. Róheim shows, "originates in delayed infancy and its function is security. It is a huge network of more or less successful attempts to protect mankind against the danger of object-loss, the colossal efforts made by a baby who is afraid of being left alone in the dark."[10] In such a context, the symbolical potentialities of the various environments are at least as important as the economic; symbolism, the protection of the psyche, no less necessary than the nourishment of the soma. Society, as a fostering organ is thus a kind of exterior "second womb," wherein the postnatal stages of man's long gestation —much longer than that of any other placental—are supported and defended.* * *

George Bernard Shaw played on this anomaly in his biological fantasy, *Back to Methuselah*, where he viewed man, in Nietzsche's manner, as a bridge to the superman. Looking forward to the year 31,920 A.D., he showed us the birth from a huge egg of a pretty girl, who, in the twentieth century, would have been thought to be about seventeen. She had been growing within the egg for two years: the first nine

8. Róheim, *The Origin and Function of Culture*, p. 17.

9. Adolf Portmann, "Das Ursprungsproblem," *Eranos-Jahrbuch 1947* (Zurich: Rhein-Verlag, 1948), p. 27. (Author's translation.)

10. Róheim, *The Origin and Function of Culture*, p. 100.

months, like the nine of the present gestation period of the human embryo, recapitulated the biological evolution of man; the remaining fifteen then matured the organism, briefly but securely, to the condition of the young adult. Four years more, spent among youthful playmates in the sort of childhood that we remain in today until seventy, would terminate when her mind changed and the young woman, tiring suddenly of play, became wise and fit for the wielding of such power as today, in the hands of children, is threatening to wreck the world.

Human adulthood is not achieved until the twenties: Shaw put it in the seventies: not a few look ahead to Purgatory. Meanwhile, society is what takes the place of the Shavian egg.

Róheim has indicated the problem of man-growing-up everywhere, namely, defense against libidinal quantities with which the immature ego is not prepared to deal; and he has analyzed the curious "symbiotic mode of mastering reality," which is the very fashioner, the master builder, of all human societies. "It is the nature of our species," he writes, "to master reality on a libidinal basis and we create a society, an environment, in which this and only this is possible." "The psyche as we know it, is formed by the introjection of primary objects (super-ego) and the first contact with environment (ego). Society itself is knitted together by projection of these primary introjected objects or concepts followed by a series of subsequent introjections and projections."[11] This tight-knitting of defensive fantasy and external reality is what builds the second womb, the marsupial pouch that we call society. Hence, though man's environment greatly varies in the corners of the planet, there is a marvelous monotony about his ritual forms. Local styles of the century, nation, race, or social class obviously differ; yet what James Joyce calls "the grave and constant in human experience" remains truly constant and grave. It arrests the mind, everywhere, in the rituals of birth, adolescence, marriage, death, installation and initiation, uniting it with the mysteries of eternal recurrence and of man's psychosomatic maturation. The individual grows up, not only as a member of a certain social group, but as a human being.

<h1 style="text-align:center">III</h1>

Rites, then, together with the mythologies that support them, constitute the second womb, the matrix of the postnatal gestation of the placental *Homo sapiens*. This fact, moreover, has been known to the pedagogues of the race, certainly since the period of the Upanishads, and probably since that of the Aurignacian caves.* * *

In India the objective is to be *born* from the womb of myth, not to remain in it, and the one who has attained to this "second birth" is truly the "twice born," freed from the pedagogical devices of society, the lures and threats of myth, the local *mores*, the usual hopes of benefits and rewards. He is truly "free" (*mukti*), "released while living" (*jivan mukti*); he is that reposeful "superman" who is man perfected—though in our kindergarten of libidinous misapprehensions he moves like a being from another sphere.

11. Róheim, *The Origin and Function of Culture*, pp. 80, 81, 82. (This reference includes the two immediately preceding quotations from Róheim.)

The same idea of the "second birth" is certainly basic to Christianity also, where it is symbolized in baptism. "Except a man be born of water and of the spirit, he cannot enter into the kingdom of God. That which is born of the flesh is flesh; and that which is born of the Spirit is spirit." One could ask for no more vivid rendition of the doctrine of the two wombs: the womb of the mammal and the womb of perfected man.

Within the Christian Church, however, there has been a historically successful tendency to anathematize the obvious implications of this idea, and the result has been a general obscuration of the fact that regeneration means going beyond, not remaining within, the confines of mythology. Whereas in the Orient—India, Tibet, China, Japan, Indo-China and Indonesia—everyone is expected, at least in his final incarnation, to leave the womb of myth, to pass through the sun-door and stand beyond the gods, in the West—or at least throughout the greater part of the Judaeo-Christian-Mohammedan development—God remains the Father, and none can step beyond Him. This accounts, perhaps, for the great distinction between the manly piety of the Orient and the infantile of the recent Occident. In the lands of the truly "twice born" man is finally superior to the gods, whereas in the West even the saint is required to remain within the body of the Church and the "second birth" is read rather as being born into the Church than born out of it. The historical result was a shattering of this particular marsupial pouch in the fifteenth century.* * *

Whether, in any given culture, the individual is enabled to be really born again or required to remain spiritually foetal until released from purgatory, myth is everywhere the womb of man's specifically human birth: the long-tried, the tested matrix within which the unfinished being is brought to maturity; simultaneously protecting the growing ego against libidinal quantities which it is not prepared to deal with and furnishing it with the necessary foods and saps for its normal, harmonious unfoldment. Mythology fosters a balanced intuitive and instinctive, as well as rational, ontogenesis, and throughout the domain of the species the morphology of this peculiar spiritual organ of *Homo sapiens* is no less constant than that of the well-known, readily recognizable physique itself.

IV

Misbirth is possible from the mythological womb as well as from the physiological: there can be adhesions, malformations, arrestations, etc. We call them neuroses and psychoses. Hence we find today, after some five hundred years of the systematic dismemberment and rejection of the mythological organ of our species, all the sad young men, for whom life is a problem. Mythology leads the libido into ego-syntonic channels, whereas neurosis (to cite, once again, Róheim) "separates the individual from his fellows and connects him with his own infantile images." Psychoanalysis and certain movements in contemporary art and letters represent an effort to restore the biologically necessary spiritual organ. Blake, for example, Goethe and Emerson, saw the need for it. Their effort was to restore the poet to his traditional function of seer and mystagogue of the regenerative vision. James Joyce has supplied the whole blueprint.

The morphology of the organ will remain the same as ever, but the materials of which it is composed and the functions served will have to be those of the new world: the materials of the machine age and the functions of the world society that is today in its throes of birth—as myth.

Psychoanalysis and Culture, edd. G. B. Wilbur and W. Muensterberger (New York: International Universities Press, 1951), pp. 329-343. Some of the reference notes have been omitted.

Géza Róheim (1891–1953) was one of the great pioneers in the joint exploration of cultural anthropology and psychoanalysis. As early as 1911 he had recognized that "the key to the data furnished by anthropology was in the unconscious or primary process," and shortly thereafter published the first articles by a trained anthropologist wholly committed to psychoanalysis. His major contributions to the enrichment of both disciplines lie in such works as Animism, Magic and the Divine King *(1930),* The Riddle of the Sphinx *(1934),* The Origin and Function of Culture *(1943), and* Psychoanalysis and Anthropology *(1950).*

Like Joseph Campbell in the preceding essay, Róheim accepts fully such Freudian ideas as the similarity of myth and dream and of ritual and neurosis, but his position is by no means identical with Campbell's. Although he essays a psychoanalytic explanation of the difference between myth and folktale, he does so in terms of specific myths and folktales which he himself collected on anthropological field expeditions in central Australia. Thus Róheim finds the crux of myth in the death and apotheosis of the Primal Father, and he distinguishes between myth and folktale in terms of their different relations to the Super-Ego. Since mythic and folktale elements can be traced in literature (see, for example, Francis Fergusson's essay, pp. 139 ff.), it would seem that a similar classification of literary themes in terms of ego psychology might be possible.

Whatever the merits of such a view for literature, it raises some difficulties for mythology. Put in its simplest terms, the problem is to explain how such tales can be defined through their authors' mental state when, by general agreement, their origin is largely anonymous and collective. Another question implicitly raised here is how far Róheim's definition is applicable to tales other than those in his collection. Can it embrace all those narratives ordinarily called myth and folktale or is it meaningful only for the specific kinds of tale he cites?

MYTH AND FOLKTALE

Géza Róheim

A psychological explanation of myth and folktale must start out with a definition, and the difficulty that arises here is that the theory should not be implicit in the definition. Therefore the safe way would be to differentiate what is generally known as a myth from what is generally known as a folktale.

In a myth the actors are mostly divine and sometimes human. In a folktale the *dramatis personae* are mostly human and especially the hero is human, frequently with supernatural beings as his opponents. In a myth we have definite locality; in a folktale the actors are nameless, the scene is just anywhere. A myth is part of a creed; it is believed by the narrator. The folktale is purely fiction, and not intended to be anything else. According to a method of interpretation which is now (luckily) extinct a myth always deals with natural phenomena, while according to another view which had advocates among the anthropologists of the previous generation and also has many influential representatives today, a myth is always connected with a ritual. In these views we have the elements of a theory and they go beyond what we should call a definition. Wundt and von der Leyen thought that the myth and the "Märchen," which are so similar to each other in certain ways and yet so different, must have had one common origin, a type of narrative from which both have developed in the course of evolution (Mythen-märchen).

I have collected myths and folktales in many areas, and if I just make a hasty mental survey of my own collections I find that in some areas a clear line of distinction runs between the two, while in others matters seem to be more confused. Now considering the magnitude of the task and the avowedly preliminary nature of this effort I will make matters easy for myself and consider the situation only in central Australia. Here we have a very clear distinction between a folktale and a mythological narrative so that at least our starting point seems secure.

Before I went out to the field very little was known about folktales in central Australia. The narratives recorded by Spencer and Gillen and Strehlow were pure myths and more than that they were *esoteric myths*, that is, they were only known to the initiated. I wondered whether women and children had no narratives of their own; it did not seem probable to me that this type of sublimation should be absent. I never found it by looking for it; I found it by pure chance. One of the old women who used to come and tell me her dreams launched out into a long narrative that did not sound like a dream at all. "Did you really dream this?" I asked her. No, this is not something she dreamt last night, it is an old altjira (dream). Then I found out that the Aranda word Altjira meant both dream and folktale. In the western (Luritja) dialects the situation is the same: tukurpa means myth and folktale.

Once I knew what to ask for there was no difficulty in collecting more than a hundred folktales from this area. The interesting thing in these folktales is that they are of a type that is utterly unknown from any other primitive area. Primitive folktales, including other narratives of this type from Australia, are more varied than my collection. Many of them are on the lines familiar to students of folklore from Dänhardt's *Naturmärchen*. They are explanatory narratives which end up with some peculiarity of an animal species or some phenomenon in nature. Therefore they are hardly "Märchen" at all in our sense of the word, because the ending indicates a certain claim to be believed, an attempt at connecting the fable with reality.

My collection is quite different. They are variations of one constant theme: the struggle of human beings against the demons. The hero of a story is always an indatoa (L. kuninjatu), which translated literally means a good-looking man. The heroine is a tneera, i.e. a beauty. In a sense it does not really mean beautiful, it is just normal healthy, not monstrous. On the other hand, however, sometimes it is stressed that the indatoa is really a beautiful man, big and strong, with fair skin and fair hair, and he is a skilled hunter. His wife the tneera (L. aneera) is fair and beautiful like her husband. Some of the full-blooded natives actually have fair hair.

As antagonists we have the nanananas, and bankalangas. They are hairy giants with big penises and testicles, with some of the characteristics of the "stupid devils" of European folklore. The females of the species have big breasts and genitals, sometimes they are superhuman in size. Besides these two opposing groups there is a third actor on the scene, the malpakara, who seems to be halfway between the hero and the villain of the melodrama. The malpakara is always a young man with an unbridled craving for intercourse. This is about the only thing he can do, but the folktales give hyperbolistic description of his sexual prowess. He will go on having intercourse for several days and nights or he will push a woman along with his penis inserted into her vagina. Moreover, the malpakara is always represented as thin, ugly, and a very poor hunter. After his initiation he becomes a real human being, a kuninjatu.

The kulaia (L. muruntu), a fabulous serpent—who rises out of the waterholes right up to the sky in a whirlwind and swallows people—may be on either side; he may appear in the role of a demon or of a normal human being who has been transformed into a serpent by evil magic.

But the most outstanding feature of all these narratives is cannibalism. The war between human beings and ogres is being waged with equal ruthlessness on both sides but whereas the ogres always eat the indatoas, human beings never retaliate in kind. Neither do they bury the body of the ogre or put it up on a kind of scaffold, which would be the two ways these tribes have of disposing of their dead. The ogre is always burnt at the end and the human beings are always victorious. Besides cannibalism the other outstanding feature of these narratives is the happy end.

The story starts with a sentence like this:

"An indatoa lived with a tneera" or "an old man lived with his grandson" and ends with the formula "then they came to a big camp and lived there for ever." It is quite striking that while most primitive folktales have no such beginning and end formulas, the beginning and the end of an Australian folktale finds its closest parallels in Europe, "Once upon a time"—and "they lived happily ever afterwards." The other striking analogy with European Märchen is the transformation motive in its particular setting. Just as in the European folktale, the animal metamorphosis of the hero is frequently the result of a curse of an injured person; there the serpent form is due to the evil magic of a man whose wife the other man has captured.

When taken in conjunction with another feature of these folktales, their peculiar and sometimes even weird archaism and savagery, one is certainly tempted to believe that here "our plummets have touched bottom"[1] and that we have here actually a type of narrative which is the fore-runner of folktales.* * *

Our Central Australians are "savage" enough from a European point of view, but the folktales are far more so. There is less native culture in them, some institutions like the marriage classes are completely absent, others like totemism barely mentioned. And there is more "savagery," more sadism, more unbridled lust and aggression. Perhaps they actually reflect a phase of culture that is more primitive than that of the Central Australians as we find them today. Some of the customs described by D. Bates certainly give me the impression of a society far more savage than any I have known among the Aranda or Yumu or Pitjentara. I have heard nothing like her account of the Koogurda who hunted and ate kangaroo, and emu, and human flesh on much the same level, or the Kaalurwonga who pursued fat men, women, and girls and ate

1. Sir James G. Frazer, *Totemism and Exogamy* (London: Macmillan, 1910), I, 161.

them. Or the account of Dowie who was given four baby sisters to eat and was rubbed over with their fat to make him grow big and strong. He hated his mother, Bildana, and his other mothers and his sisters and his brothers. He would have eaten them all but they were older than he was, and so they could not be given to him to eat. At the blood drinking he drank greedily and swallowed the big pieces of raw liver at initiation. He brought home many human bodies, for he would stalk human game in murderer's slippers and he loved the flesh of man, woman and child. More than this even; he killed and ate his own four wives.

Dowie is certainly behaving like the bankalangas and nanananas of our folktales and one possible explanation of these narratives would therefore be *historical*. They represent the past of native civilization, social and cultural conditions that antedate those we find at the present time. Then we should also have to assume that they are accounts of warfare between two tribes, one of them cannibalistic (the bankalangas) and the other not cannibalistic. Since Central Australian tribes are actually in the habit of confusing their concepts of a demon with those of the neighboring tribe, since there is in their minds not much difference between the leltja (avenger, human being), the ltana (ghost), and the erintja (demon) such a theory would seem quite plausible. Yet, while admitting that some of the features of the folktale in Central Australia might well be accounted for on these lines, there are some obvious difficulties. Why is the folktale called a dream? Why does it usually end with marriage? What is the role of the malpakara, who becomes a normal person after initiation? What is the explanation of the demons' huge genital organs? If the narrative is historical we should expect names and localities, especially the latter since we see that locality is such an important factor in their myths.

I think we can account for these aspects of the story from a different angle. The prevailing form of cannibalism in central, south and western Australia is "baby-eating." The Pitjentara eat every second child. The infant is knocked on the head by the father and then eaten by the mother and the siblings who are supposed to acquire double strength by this proceeding. With the Pindupi Yumu and Ngali the proceeding is more irregular; they seem to eat the babies whenever they are hungry and especially when the mother gets a strong craving to do so. They even go to the length of pulling the foetus out of the womb and eating it—which is exactly the practice ascribed to the demons in the story.

The cannibal demons represent the cannibal parents. The Australian child has to face a peculiar difficulty in his attitude towards his parents, that is, in growing up. He has really loving parents who grant him nearly everything. His mother and the other mothers of the tribe never refuse their nipple; both parents are always ready to play with him and they rarely restrict even his aggression against their own person. Yet these same parents have eaten his siblings and therefore might have eaten him also. Now compare the motives of some of my folktales to this situation.

1. A manatatai (another name for the cannibal demon) steals a boy and takes him to his camp to be eaten.

2. The father follows on the track and attacks the giants with his magic stick.

3. The giants kill each other. Father and son go home.

The paternal imago has undergone a fission. The kind, loving father of everyday life is the one who protects and rescues his son while the cannibal father appears in the guise of the cannibal giant. The giants fighting against each other represents this ambivalence of the father-imago. The next story shows this process of fission quite clearly.

1. A boy lives with his grandfather who is half a demon.

2. The grandfather has a mate in a cave who is a real demon.

3. The old man and the boy hunt wallabies; the old man is always trying to entice the boy into the cave.

4. He lights a fire at the entrance of the cave and kills both old men. The boy goes to another camp.

A favorite trick of the demons in these stories again reminds us of European folklore. In European "Märchen" we find the episode in the following form. The hero meets an old witch whose jaws reach to the sky and who is otherwise as hideous as she can be. He says, "Good morning, grandmother," and the witch says, "It's lucky you called me grandmother, otherwise I would have killed you." In my Australian collection the male or female demon always poses as some relation of the unsuspecting human being in order to eat him afterwards.

A bankalanga lived with his wife and with them lived a human (kuninjatu) child whom they had stolen. They had a big hut with a partition in it. The bankalanga slept on the partition and his wife and the child slept on the ground. The child thought he was alone in the hut with his mother because he never saw the bankalanga. She sent him out for rats and when he brought them in she passed them to her husband who was hidden behind the partition. One day the child said, "It is raining into the hut." But it was not rain; it was the bankalanga's urine. The old woman said, "Make a big fire and dry yourself." He did this but next day he could still smell the wet sand. "This is not water, it is urine," he says. He called the old woman to go hunting but he stayed at home and hid. Then he saw the male bankalanga coming out of the hut and going back again. He set fire to the hut and burnt it with the bankalanga in it and he went to the real people. When the old woman returned she found the husband dead and followed the boy's footsteps, weeping. The real people killed her too and burnt her with her husband. The boy was initiated and lived there always.

The child transforms the "bad parents" into demons; he is not their child at all, they have stolen him from his real parents. In the beginning there is no such thing as a father, the world for the infant consists in himself and his mother. But father and mother are doing something mysterious in the hut and finally the father's presence becomes obvious and emotionally significant through his sexual activity (primal scene). The father's urine stands for his semen and we know that enuresis or in general urinating is an infantile form of rivalry with the father's sexual activity.

Fire and water, as in this narrative, are exactly the most widespread symbols for urine; and if the bankalanga is regularly burnt, in the end this might well mean that the father conflict is here fought out on the urethral level. The end of the story is that the boy gets initiated or marries and lives happily ever afterwards. It is a young child's dream about growing up.* * *

Now something about the myth, again from a central Australian point of view. The mythical heroes have definite names and their wanderings take place in definite localities. Indeed the myth is mainly concerned with explaining these localities, it is definitely trying to link up phantasy and reality. The map is marked by ceremonies and the rites of the present day are merely repetitions of the rites celebrated by the primeval ancestors.

All these rites form a part of the initiation ritual and the ancestors seem to have nothing else to do than to initiate their young men. But the story is not about the young people, not about the initiated but about the initiators. The difference in the final sentence is significant. In the folktale it is the central Australian equivalent of "they were married and lived happily ever afterwards." In the myth it is *borkerake tjurungeraka*: he was tired and became transformed into a tjurunga, i.e. he died. Becoming a tjurunga ends the story and the career of the hero, *it is death and apotheosis. A folktale is a narrative with a happy end, a myth is a tragedy; a god must die before he can be truly divine.*[2]

A detailed analysis of my myth material reveals that certain heroes of the altjiranga mitjina (the eternal ones of the dream) are merely adjectives of the one great hero Malpunga, the phallic originator of the tjurunga cult. Malpunga is often called the great father and he is the leader of a group of young men. The significant thing is, however, that these mythical personages who are derived from adjectives originally applied to Malpunga always have names that imply a curse (like "Rough anus," etc.), i.e. that the names represent the aggression of the brothers against the Primal Father. In a version collected by Strehlow subincision is performed on the Father by his son out of jealousy. Some of the tribes in Western New Guinea have myths of the Australian type in which the wanderings of a totemistic ancestral hero are told ending with his death and apotheosis. After finishing their life on earth these ancestors become petrified or changed into trees and they are honored as the patron spirits of certain localities and groups. In these narratives the Oedipus and Primal Horde theme is strongly marked.* * *

The Kiwai myth of Marunogere is very instructive. Marunogere, the great leader, swallows a lump of sago like a cassowary and defecates it back unchanged, but the sago is then rapidly transformed into a pig which he names after himself, Marunogere. All the people hunt the pig and his youngest son shoots it so he dies but comes to life again for a short time. He opens the vulva of the women and teaches people to have intercourse. Then he dies again and after his death people cut up and preserved his flesh as strong "medicine" and in some places they have preserved small pieces of dried human flesh which is said to be that of Marunogere's body. So far we see a clear Oedipus and Primal Horde myth. It starts with a phantasy, frequently found in our analysis, and the enhanced magical power of the father who has become a representative of both parents in the anal delivery phantasy. Then we have the attack of the group, the youngest son as murderer of the Primal Father, the death of the latter as origin of death in general. When the father is dead human beings grow up; they have

2. This hypothesis aims at what I have come to regard as the kernel of the folktale and of the myth; it cannot account for every narrative which, according to our definition, should be called a myth.

intercourse. If the youngest son were the hero of the narrative and the story were to end at this point, we should have what I regard as the kernel of all "Märchen" plots. However, the hero in this narrative is the father and the revolt is regarded as a crime and an outrage. The psychological background of the story is a strong father identification. The sequel of the narrative is that besides Marunogere there was another great man called Gibogu. This chief wanted everybody to take part in the *moguru*. (The *myth is the first moguru and the prototype of all subsequent rites*.) Marunogere wished to keep the ceremony secret and to give prominence to the sexual aspects which were to take place in the dark. On account of the quarrel Gibogo and his followers left the rest and went up into the sky where they cause the thunder to frighten Marunogere and his people. The second chief, introduced at the end of Marunogere, is the part that opposes sexuality and frightens people from the sky by his thunder. Like so many of his thunder wielding colleagues he represents law and order, the Super-Ego.

If we believe that the nucleus of myth is the death and apotheosis of the Primal Father we support a theory once so very popular among anthropologists according to which the *gods are the dead*. If at the same time we assume as a regular or at least frequent phase of evolution the type of totemistic myth found in Australia and New Guinea in which mythological ancestors are identified with an animal species or natural phenomena, this would be one of the channels through which a "nature mythology" could develop. Whereas some of these myths may be handed down directly as oral tradition from the Primal Horde period[3] others may have been created by later generations on the old lines, and in these we may find the marks left on myth by history. Others may have stepped into the Primal Father's shoes. But the main thing is that this type of narrative is only conceivable on a super-ego level, that is, it must be based on a strong father identification. This is the "tragic conflict" of the hero-rebel. And this difference in ontogenetic stage, the folktale with its fight against "Super-Ego precursors," "wicked parent" imagos, and the myth with its roots in the fully fledged super-ego, may account for the different attitude to reality that we find in myth. The fully developed super-ego represents the real father or at least the real father enters into the picture beside the phantasy image of infancy. Moreover in the overlying, conscious strata, the super-ego also stands for society. Myths in the "Primal Horde style," that is, myths that represent the brothers revolting against a single father, might very well arise later, not by inherited memory but by the idea of shared responsibility and identification as defences against super-ego anxiety. It is too much to be against the father and against the group at the same time; therefore by introducing the device of representation by the opposite, the father becomes the Lone Hero and the enemy of society. The son becomes part of the group, and by this *fission in the super-ego* his anxiety is reduced and revolt becomes imaginable. As this conflict is partly real, as it is a more adult form of the same conflict which we find in "Märchen" on a more infantile level, myth is a phantasy that demands to be believed and is bound up with group activity in the form of ritual.

3. I again emphasize that I am trying to give an explanation which does not necessitate the assumption of an "inherited unconsciousness."

In the folktale we relate how we overcome the anxiety connected with the "bad parents" and grow up; in myth we confess that only death can end the tragic ambivalence of human nature. Eros triumphs in the folktale, Thanatos in the myth.

American Imago, II (1941), 266–279. Some of the reference notes have been omitted; also some parenthetical native phrases. Obvious typographical errors have been corrected and the punctuation regularized.

Clyde Kluckhohn (1905–1960) was one of the most eminent of American anthropologists, as books like The Navaho *(1946) and* Mirror For Man *(1949) attest. Although basically he held to a "functionalist" theory, his functionalism was modified by a receptivity to psychoanalytic insights that pointed toward a synthesis of the two approaches. This attitude compels him, in the present essay, to criticize both anthropological failures and psychoanalytic excesses.*

Apart from the general cogency of Kluckhohn's ideas, which serve as an admirable coda to those of Bidney, Campbell, and Róheim, several of his points have a special relevance for students of literature. For instance, by showing that neither myth nor ritual can claim universal priority, he implicitly qualifies Stanley Hyman's Cambridge-influenced insistence on the primary character of ritual (pp. 47 ff.). Also, his differentiation of cultures by the relative richness or poverty of their mythological and ritualistic forms suggests that the homologue of a poem or novel may lie in myth or in ritual as well as in a combination of both. Thus, there is no point in looking for complex myths in, for example, Hemingway or Ionesco when their work is predominantly ritualistic. Finally, by his detailed exploration of myth's role as a symbolic expression of society's unconscious desires and attitudes, we see more clearly the close relation literature has to myth.

MYTHS AND RITUALS: A GENERAL THEORY

Clyde Kluckhohn

I

Nineteenth century students strongly tended to study mythology apart from associated rituals (and indeed apart from the life of the people generally). Myths were held to be symbolic descriptions of phenomena of nature. One prominent school, in fact, tried to find an astral basis for all mythic tales. Others, among whom Andrew Lang was prominent, saw in the myth a kind of primitive scientific theory. Mythology answered the insistent human HOW? and WHY? How and why was the world made? How and why were living creatures brought into being? Why, if there was life must there be death? To early psychoanalysts such as Abraham and Rank myths were "group phantasies," wish-fulfillments for a society strictly analogous to the dream and daydream of individuals. Mythology for these psychoanalysts was also a symbolic structure par excellence, but the symbolism which required interpretation was primarily a sex symbolism which was postulated as universal and all-pervasive. Reik recognized a connection between rite and myth, and he, with Freud, verbally agreed to Robertson Smith's proposition that mythology was mainly a description of ritual. To the psychoanalysts, however, mythology was essentially (so far as what they did with it is concerned) societal phantasy material which reflected impulse repression. There was no attempt to discover the practical function of mythology in the daily behaviors of the members of a society nor to demonstrate specific interactions of mythology and ceremonials. The interest was in supposedly pan-human symbolic meanings, not in the relation of a given myth or part of a myth to particular cultural forms or specific social situations.

To some extent the answer to the whole question of the relationship between myth and ceremony depends, of course, upon how wide or how restricted a sense one gives to "mythology." In ordinary usage the Oedipus tale is a "myth," but only some Freudians believe that this is merely the description of a ritual! The famous stories of the Republic are certainly called "$\mu\hat{\upsilon}\theta\sigma$," and while a few scholars believe that Plato in *some* cases had reference to the Orphic and/or Eleusinian mysteries there is certainly not a shred of evidence that all of Plato's immortal "myths" are "descriptions of rituals." To be sure, one may justifiably narrow the problem by saying that in a technical sense these are "legends," and by insisting that "myths" be rigorously distinguished from "legends," "fairytales," and "folktales." If, however, one agrees that "myth" has Durkheim's connotation of the "sacred" as opposed to the "profane" the line is still sometimes hard to draw in concrete cases. What of "creation myths"? In some cases (as at Zuni) these are indeed recited during ritual performances (with variations for various ceremonies). In other cases, even though they may be recited in a "ritual" attitude, they do not enter into any ceremonial. Nevertheless, they definitely retain the flavor of "the sacred." Moreover, there are (as again at Zuni) exoteric and esoteric forms of the same myth. Among the Navaho many of the older men who are not ceremonial practitioners know that part of a myth which tells of the exploits of the hero or heroes but not the portion which prescribes the ritual details of the chant. Granting that there are sometimes both secular and sacred versions of the same tale and that other difficulties obtrude themselves in particular cases, it still seems possible to use the connotation of the sacred as that which differentiates "myth" from the rest of folklore. At least, such a distinction appears workable to a rough first approximation and will be followed throughout this paper.

But defining "myth" strictly as "sacred tale" does not carry with it by implication a warrant for considering mythology purely as a description of correlative rituals. Rose quite correctly says "among myths there are many whose connection with any rite is a thing to be proved, not assumed." What is needed is a detailed comparative analysis of actual associations. Generally speaking, we do seem to find rich ritualism and a rich mythology together. But there are cases (like the Toda) where an extensive ceremonialism does not appear to have its equally extensive mythological counterpart and instances (like classical Greece) where a ramified mythology appears to have existed more or less independent of a comparatively meagre rite-system. For example, in spite of the many myths relating to Ares the rituals connected with Ares seem to have been few in number and highly localized in time and space. The early Romans, on the other hand, seemed to get along very well without mythology. The poverty of the ritual which accompanies the extremely complex mythology of the Mohave is well known. Kroeber indeed says "Public ceremonies or rituals as they occur among almost all native Americans cannot be said to be practised by the Mohave."[1] The Bushmen likewise had many myths and very little ritual. On the other hand, one can point

1. A. L. Kroeber, *Handbook of the Indians at California* (Washington: Goverment Printing Office, 1925), p. 755.

to examples like the Central Eskimo, where every detail of the Sedna myth has its ritual analogue in confessional, other rites, or hunting taboos, or, for contrast, to the American Indian tribes (especially some Californian ones) where the creation myth is never enacted in ceremonial form. In different sectors of one culture, the Papago, all of these possibilities are represented. Some myths are never ceremonially enacted. Some ceremonies emphasize content foreign to the myth. Other ceremonies consisting only of songs have some vague place in the mythological world; between these and the myths "there is a certain tenuous connection which may be a rationalization made for the sake of unity. . . ."[2]

The anthropology of the past generation has tended to recoil sharply from any sort of generalized interpretation. Obsessed with the complexity of the historical experience of all peoples, anthropologists have (perhaps over-much) eschewed the inference of regularities of psychological reaction which would transcend the facts of diffusion and of contacts of groups. Emphasis has been laid upon the distribution of myths and upon the mythological patterning which prevailed in different cultures and culture areas. Study of these distributions has led to a generalization of another order which is the converse of the hypothesis of most nineteenth century classical scholars that a ritual was an enactment of a myth. In the words of Boas: "The uniformity of many such rituals over large areas and the diversity of mythological explanations show clearly that the ritual itself is the stimulus for the origin of the myth. . . . The ritual existed, and the tale originated from the desire to account for it."[3]

While this suggestion of the primacy of ritual over myth is probably a valid statistical induction and a proper statement of the modal tendency of our evidence, it is, it seems to me, as objectionably a simple unitary explanation (if pressed too far) as the generally rejected nineteenth century views. Thus we find Hocart recently asking: "If there are myths that give rise to ritual where do these myths come from?"[4] A number of instances will shortly be presented in which the evidence is unequivocal that myths did give rise to ritual. May I only remark here that—if we view the matter objectively— the Christian Mass, as interpreted by Christians, is a clear illustration of a ritual based upon a sacred story. Surely, in any case, Hocart's question can be answered very simply: from a dream or a waking phantasy or a personal habit system of some individual in the society. The basic psychological mechanisms involved would seem not dissimilar to those whereby individuals in our own (and other) cultures construct private rituals or carry out private divination—e.g. counting and guessing before the clock strikes, trying to get to a given point (a traffic light, for instance) before something else happens. As DuBois has suggested, "the explanation may be that personal rituals have been taken over and socialized by the group."[5] These "personal rituals" could have their genesis in idiosyncratic habit formations (similar to those of obsessional neurotics in our culture) or in dreams or reveries. Mrs. Seligman has

2. Personal communication from Dr. Ruth Underhill.
3. F. Boas et al., *General Anthropology* (New York: D. C. Heath, 1938), p. 617.
4. A. M. Hocart, "Myth and Ritual," *Man*, XXXVI (1936), 167.
5. C. DuBois, "Some Anthropological Perspectives on Psychoanalysis," *Psychoanalytic Review*, XXIV (1937), 254.

convincingly suggested that spontaneous personal dissociation is a frequent mechanism for rite innovations. The literature is replete with instances of persons "dreaming" that supernaturals summoned them, conducted them on travels or adventures, and finally admonished them thereafter to carry out certain rites (often symbolically repetitive of the adventures).

Moreover, there are a number of well documented actual cases where historical persons, in the memory of other historical persons, actually instituted new rituals. The ritual innovations of the American Indian Ghost Dance cult and other nativistic cults of the New World provide striking illustration. In these cases the dreams or phantasies—told by the innovators before the ceremonial was ever actualized in deeds—became an important part of traditionally accepted rite-myths. Lincoln has presented plausible evidence that dreams are the source of "new" rituals. Morgan, on the basis of Navaho material, says:

> ... delusions and dreams ... are so vivid and carry such conviction that any attempt to reason about them afterwards on the basis of conscious sense impressions is unavailing. Such experiences deeply condition the individual, sometimes so deeply that if the experience is at variance with a tribal or neighborhood belief, the individual will retain his own variation. There can be no doubt that this is a very significant means of modifying a culture.[6]

Van Gennep asserts that persons went to dream in the sanctuary at Epidaurus as a source for new rites in the cult of Asclepius. To obtain ceremony through dream is, of course, itself a pattern, a proper traditional way of obtaining a ceremony or power. I do not know of any cases of a society where dreaming is generally in disrepute, as at Zuni, and where ceremony has yet demonstrably originated through dream. But where dreaming is accepted as revelation it must not be assumed that the content (or even, entirely, the structure) of a new myth and its derived ceremony will be altogether determined by pre-existent cultural forms. As Lowie has remarked, "That they themselves (dreams) in part reflect the regnant folklore offers no ultimate explanation."[7] Anthropologists must be wary of what Korzybski calls "self-reflexive systems"— here, specifically, the covert premise that "culture alone determines culture."

The structure of new cultural forms (whether myths or rituals) will undoubtedly be conditioned by the pre-existent cultural matrix. But the rise of new cultural forms will almost always be determined by factors external to that culture: pressure from other societies, biological events such as epidemics, or changes in the physical environment. Barber has recently shown how the Ghost Dance and the Peyote Cult represent alternative responses of various American Indian tribes to the deprivation resultant upon the encroachment of whites. The Ghost Dance was an adaptive response under the earlier external conditions, but under later conditions the Peyote Cult was the more adaptive response, and the Ghost Dance suffered what the stimulus-response psychologists would call "extinction through non-reward." At any rate the

6. William Morgan, *Human Wolves Among the Navaho* (New Haven: Yale University Press, 1936), p. 40.

7. R. H. Lowie, *The History of Ethnological Theory* (New York: Farrar & Rinehart, 1937), p. 264.

Ghost Dance became extinct in some tribes; in others it has perhaps suffered only partial extinction.

There are always individuals in every society who have their private rituals; there are always individuals who dream and who have compensatory phantasies. In the normal course of things these are simply deviant behaviors which are ridiculed or ignored by most members of the society. Perhaps indeed one should not speak of them as "deviant"—they are "deviant" only as carried to extremes by a relatively small number of individuals, for everyone probably has some private rituals and compensatory phantasies. When, however, changed conditions happen to make a particular type of obsessive behavior or a special sort of phantasy generally congenial, the private ritual is then socialized by the group, the phantasy of the individual becomes the myth of his society. Indeed there is evidence that when pressures are peculiarly strong and peculiarly general, a considerable number of different individuals may almost simultaneously develop substantially identical phantasies which then become widely current.

Whether belief (myth) or behavior (ritual) changes first will depend, again, both upon cultural tradition and upon external circumstances. Taking a very broad view of the matter, it does seem that behavioral patterns more frequently alter first. In a rapidly changing culture such as our own many ideal patterns are as much as a generation behind the corresponding behavioral patterns. There is evidence that certain ideal patterns (for example, those defining the status of women) are slowly being altered to harmonize with, to act as rationalizations for, the behavioral actualities. On the other hand, the case of Nazi Germany is an excellent illustration of the ideal patterns ("the myth") being provided from above almost whole cloth and of the state, through various organizations, exerting all its force to make the behavioral patterns conform to the standards of conduct laid down in the Nazi mythology.

Some cultures and sub-cultures are relatively indifferent to belief, others to behavior. The dominant practice of the Christian Church, throughout long periods of its history, was to give an emphasis to belief which is most unusual as seen from a cross-cultural perspective. In general, the crucial test as to whether or not one was a Christian was the willingness to avow belief in certain dogmas. The term "believer" was almost synonymous with "Christian." It is very possibly because of this cultural screen that until this century most European scholars selected the myth as primary.

II

To a considerable degree, the whole question of the primacy of ceremonial or mythology is as meaningless as all questions of "the hen or the egg" form. What is really important, as Malinowski has so brilliantly shown, is the intricate interdependence of myth (which is one form of ideology) with ritual and many other forms of behavior. I am quite aware that I have little to add conceptually to Malinowski's discussion in *Myth in Primitive Psychology*. There he examines myths not as curiosa taken out of their total context but as living, vitally important elements in the day to day lives of his Trobrianders, interwoven with every other abstracted type of activity. From this point of view one sees the fallacy of all unilateral explanations. One also sees the aspect of truth in all (or nearly all) of them. There are features which seem to be explanatory of natural phenomena. There are features which reveal the peculiar forms of wish fulfillments characteristic of the culture in question (including the expression of the culturally disallowed but unconsciously wanted). There *are* myths which are intimately related to rituals, which may be descriptive of them, but there are other myths which stand apart. If these others are descriptive of rituals at all, they are, as Durkheim (followed by Radcliffe-Brown and others) suggested, descriptions of rituals of the social organization. That is, they are symbolic representations of the dominant configurations of the particular culture. Myths, then, may express not only the latent content of rituals but of other culturally organized behaviors. Malinowski is surely in error when he writes ". . . myth . . . is not symbolic. . . ."[8] Durkheim and Mauss have pointed out how various non-literate groups (notably the Zuni and certain tribes of south-eastern Australia) embrace nature within the schema of their social organization through myths which classify natural phenomena precisely according to the principles that prevail in the social organization. Warner has further developed this type of interpretation.

Boas, with his usual caution, is sceptical of all attempts to find a systematic interpretation of mythology. But, while we can agree with him when he writes ". . . mythological narratives and mythological concepts should not be equalized; for social, psychological, and historical conditions affect both in different ways,"[9] the need for scrupulous inquiry into historical and other determinants must not be perverted to justify a repudiation of all attempts to deal with the symbolic processes of the all-important covert culture. At all events, the factual record is perfectly straightforward in one respect: neither myth nor ritual can be postulated as "primary."

This is the important point in our discussion at this juncture, and it is unfortunate that Hooke and his associates in their otherwise very illuminating contributions to the study of the relations between myth and ritual in the Near East have emphasized only one aspect of the system of interdependences which Malinowski and Radcliffe-Brown have shown to exist. When Hooke points out that myths are constantly used to justify rituals this observation is quite congruent with the observed facts in many cultures. Indeed all of these data may be used toward a still wider induction: man, as a symbol-using animal, appears to feel the need not only to act but almost equally to give verbal or other symbolic "reasons" for his acts. Hooke rightly speaks of "the vital significance of the myth as something that works," but when he continues "and that dies apart from its ritual"[10] he seems to imply that myths cannot exist apart from rituals and this, as has been shown, is contrary to documented cases. No, the central theorem has been expressed much more adequately by Radcliffe-Brown: "In the case of both ritual and myth the sentiments expressed are those that are essential to the existence of the society."[11] This theorem can be regarded as having been well

8. B. Malinowski, *Myth in Primitive Psychology* (London: Kegan Paul, Trench, Trubner, 1926), p. 19.

9. F. Boas, *Race, Language, and Culture* (New York: Macmillan, 1940), p. 450.

10. S. H. Hooke, ed., *The Labyrinth* (New York: Macmillan, 1935), p. ix.

11. A. R. Radcliffe-Brown, *The Andaman Islanders* (Cambridge: Cambridge University Press, 1933), p. 405.

established in a general way, but we still lack detailed observations on change in myths as correlated with changes in ritual and changes in a culture generally. Navaho material gives certain hints that when a culture as a whole changes rapidly its myths are also substantially and quickly altered.

In sum, the facts do not permit any universal generalizations as to ritual being the "cause" of myth or vice versa. Their relationship is rather that of intricate mutual interdependence, differently structured in different cultures and probably at different times in the same culture. As Benedict has pointed out, there is great variation in the extent to which mythology conditions the religious complex.* * * Both myth and ritual satisfy the needs of a society and the relative place of one or the other will depend upon the particular needs (conscious and unconscious) of the individuals in a particular society at a particular time. This principle covers the observed data which show that rituals are borrowed without their myths, and myths without any accompanying ritual. A ritual may be reinforced by a myth (or vice versa) in the donor culture but satisfy the carriers of the recipient culture simply as a form of activity (or be rationalized by a quite different myth which better meets their emotional needs). In short, the only uniformity which can be posited is that there is a strong tendency for some sort of interrelationship between myth and ceremony and that this interrelationship is dependent upon what appears, so far as present information goes, to be an invariant function of both myth and ritual: the gratification (most often in the negative form of anxiety reduction) of a large proportion of the individuals in a society.

If Malinowski and Radcliffe-Brown (and their followers) turned the searchlight of their interpretations as illuminatingly upon specific human animals and their impulses as upon cultural and social abstractions, it might be possible to take their work as providing a fairly complete and adequate general theory of myth and ritual. With Malinowski's notion of myth as "an active force" which is intimately related to almost every other aspect of a culture we can only agree. When he writes: "Myth is a constant by-product of living faith which is in need of miracles; of sociological status, which demands precedent; of moral rule which requires sanction,"[12] we can only applaud. To the French sociologists, to Radcliffe-Brown, and to Warner we are indebted for the clear formulation of the symbolic principle. Those realms of behavior and of experience which man finds beyond rational and technological control he feels are capable of manipulation through symbols. Both myth and ritual are symbolical procedures and are most closely tied together by this, as well as by other, facts. The myth is a system of word symbols, whereas ritual is a system of object and act symbols. Both are symbolic processes for dealing with the same type of situation in the same affective mode.

But the French sociologists, Radcliffe-Brown, and—to a lesser extent—Malinowski are so interested in formulating the relations between conceptual elements that they tend to lose sight of the concrete human organisms. The "functionalists" do usually start with a description of some particular ritualistic behaviors. Not only, however, do the historical origins of this particular behavioral complex fail to interest them.

12. Malinowski, *Myth in Primitive Psychology*, p. 92.

Equally, the motivations and rewards which persons feel are lost sight of in the pre-occupation with the contributions which the rituals make to the social system. Thus a sense of the specific detail is lost and we are soon talking about myth in general and ritual in general. From the "functionalist" point of view specific details are about as arbitrary as the phonemes of a language are with respect to "the content" of what is communicated by speech. Hence, as Dollard says, "What one sees from the cultural angle is a drama of life much like a puppet show in which 'culture' is pulling the strings from behind the scenes."[13] The realization that we are really dealing with "animals struggling in real dilemmas" is lacking.

From this angle, some recent psychoanalytic interpretations of myth and ritual seem preferable. We may regard as unconvincing Róheim's attempts to treat myths as historical documents which link human phylogenetic and ontogenetic development, as we may justly feel that many psychoanalytic discussions of the latent content of mythology are extravagant and undisciplined. Casey's summary of the psychoanalytic view of religion ". . . ritual is a sublimated compulsion; dogma and myth are sublimated obsessions"[14] may well strike us as an over-simplified, over-neat generalization, but at least our attention is drawn to the connection between cultural forms and impulse-motivated organisms. And Kardiner's relatively sober and controlled treatment does "point at individuals, at bodies, and at a rich and turbulent biological life"—even though that life is admittedly conditioned by social heredity: social organization, culturally defined symbolic systems, and the like.[15] * * *

IV

The inadequacy of any simplistic statement of the relationship between myth and ritual has been established. It has likewise been maintained that the most adequate generalization will not be cast in terms of the primacy of one or the other of these cultural forms but rather in terms of the general tendency for the two to be inter-dependent. This generalization has been arrived at through induction from abstractions at the cultural level. That is, as we have sampled the evidence from various cultures we have found cases where myths have justified rituals and have appeared to be " after the fact" of ritual; we have also seen cases where new myths have given rise to new rituals. In other words, the primary conclusion which may be drawn from the data is that myths and rituals tend to be very intimately associated and to influence each other. What is the explanation of the observed connection?

The explanation is to be found in the circumstance that myth and ritual satisfy a group of identical or closely related needs of individuals. Thus far we have alluded only occasionally and often obliquely to myths and rituals as cultural forms defining

13. John Dollard, "Culture, Society, Impulse, and Socialization," *American Journal of Sociology*, XLV (1939), 52.

14. R. P. Casey, "The Psychoanalytic Study of Religion," *Journal of Abnormal and Social Psychology*, XXXIII (1938), 449.

15. A. Kardiner, *The Individual and His Society* (New York: Columbia University Press, 1939), esp. pp. 182–194, 268–270.

individual behaviors which are adaptive or adjustive[16] responses. We have seen how myths and rituals are adaptive from the point of view of the society in that they promote social solidarity, enhance the integration of the society by providing a formalized statement of its ultimate value-attitudes, afford a means for the transmission of much of the culture with little loss of content—thus protecting cultural continuity and stabilizing the society. But how are myth and ritual rewarding enough in the daily lives of individuals so that individuals are instigated to preserve them, so that myth and ritual continue to prevail at the expense of more rational responses?* * *

We can profitably begin by recurring to the function of myth as fulfilling the expectancy of the familiar. Both myth and ritual here provide cultural solutions to problems which all human beings face. Burke has remarked, "Human beings build their cultures, nervously loquacious, upon the edge of an abyss." In the face of want and death and destruction all humans have a fundamental insecurity. To some extent, all culture is a gigantic effort to mask this, to give the future the simulacrum of safety by making activity repetitive, expective—"to make the future predictable by making it conform to the past." From one angle our own scientific mythology is clearly related to that motivation as is the obsessive, the compulsive tendency which lurks in all organized thought.

When questioned as to why a particular ceremonial activity is carried out in a particular way, Navaho singers will most often say "because the diɣin diné—the Holy People—did it that way in the first place." The *ultima ratio* of non-literates strongly tends to be "that is what our fathers said it was." An Eskimo said to Rasmussen: "We Eskimos do not concern ourselves with solving all riddles. We repeat the old stories in the way they were told to us and with the words we ourselves remember."[17] The Eskimo saying "we keep the old rules in order that we may live untroubled" is well-known. The Navaho and Eskimo thus implicitly recognize a principle which has been expressed by Harvey Ferguson as follows:

> . . . man dreads both spontaneity and change, . . . he is a worshipper of habit in all its forms. Conventions and institutions are merely organized and more or less sanctified habits. These are the real gods of human society, which transcend and outlive all other gods. All of them originate as group expedients which have some social value at some time, but they remain the objects of a passionate adoration long after they have outlived their usefulness. Men fight and die for them. They have their high priests, their martyrs, and their rituals. They are the working gods, whatever the ostensible ones may be.[18]

These principles apply as well to standardized overt acts as to standardized forms of words. Thus Pareto considered the prevalence of ritual in all human cultures as

16. This useful distinction I owe to my colleague, Dr. Hobart Mowrer. "Adaptation" is a purely descriptive term referring to the fact that certain types of behavior result in survival. "Adjustment" refers to those responses which remove the motivation stimulating the individual. Thus suicide is adjustive but not adaptive.

17. Knud Rasmussen, *Intellectual Culture of the Hudson Bay Eskimos* (Copenhagen: Gyldendal, 1938), p. 69.

18. Harvey Ferguson, *Modern Man* (New York: Knopf, 1936), p. 20.

perhaps the outstanding empirical justification for his thesis of the importance of non-logical action. Merton writes:

> ... activities originally conceived as instrumental are transmuted into ends in themselves. The original purposes are forgotten and ritualistic adherence to institutionally prescribed conduct becomes virtually obsessive. ... Such ritualism may be associated with a mythology which rationalizes these actions so that they appear to retain their status as means, but the dominant pressure is in the direction of strict ritualistic conformity, irrespective of such rationalizations. In this sense ritual has proceeded farthest when such rationalizations are not even called forth.[19]

Goldstein, a neurologist, recognizes a neurological basis for the persistence of such habit systems and writes: "The organism tends to function in the accustomed manner, as long as an at least moderately effective performance can be achieved in this way."[20]

Nevertheless, certain objections to the position as thus far developed must be anticipated and met. It must be allowed at once that the proposition "man dreads both spontaneity and change" must be qualified. More precisely put, we may say "most men, most of the time, dread both spontaneity and change in most of their activities." This formulation allows for the observed fact that most of us *occasionally* get irked with the routines of our lives or that there are certain sectors of our behavior where we fairly consistently show spontaneity. But a careful examination of the totality of behavior of any individual who is not confined in an institution or who has not withdrawn almost completely from participation in the society will show that the larger proportion of the behavior of even the greatest iconoclasts is habitual. This must be so, for by very definition a socialized organism is an organism which behaves mainly in a predictable manner. Even in a culture like contemporary American culture which has made an institutionalized value of change (both for the individual and for society), conformity is at the same time a great virtue. To some extent, this is phrased as conformity with the latest fashion, but Americans remain, by and large, even greater conformists than most Europeans.

Existence in an organized society would be unthinkable unless most people, most of the time, behaved in an expectable manner. Rituals constitute a guarantee that in certain societally organized behaviors touching upon certain "areas of ignorance" which constitute "tender spots" for all human beings, people can count upon the repetitive nature of the phenomena. For example, in Zuni society (where rituals are highly calendrical) a man whose wife has left him or whose crops have been ruined by a torrential downpour can yet look forward to the Shalako ceremonial as something which is fixed and immutable. Similarly, the personal sorrow of the devout Christian is in some measure mitigated by anticipation of the great feasts of Christmas and Easter. Perhaps the even turn of the week with its Sunday services and mid-week prayer meetings gave a dependable regularity which the Christian clung to even more in disaster and sorrow. For some individuals daily prayer and the confessional gave

19. R. K. Merton, "Social Structure and Anomie," *American Sociological Review*, III (1938), 673.
20. K. Goldstein, *The Organism* (New York: American Book Co., 1939), p. 57.

the needed sense of security. Myths, likewise, give men "something to hold to." The Christian can better face the seemingly capricious reverses of his plans when he hears the joyous words "lift up your hearts." Rituals and myths supply, then, fixed points in a world of bewildering change and disappointment.

If almost all behavior has something of the habitual about it, how is it that myths and rituals tend to represent the maximum of fixity? Because they deal with those sectors of experience which do not seem amenable to rational control and hence where human beings can least tolerate insecurity. That very insistence upon the minutiae of ritual performance, upon preserving the myth to the very letter, which is characteristic of religious behavior must be regarded as a "reaction formation" (in the Freudian sense) which compensates for the actual intransigeance of those events which religion tries to control.

To anticipate another objection: do these "sanctified habit systems" show such extraordinary persistence simply because they are repeated so often and so scrupulously? Do myths and rituals constitute repetitive behavior par excellence not merely as reaction formations but because the habits are practiced so insistently? Perhaps myths and rituals perdure in accord with Allport's "principle of functional autonomy" —as interpreted by some writers? No, performances must be rewarded in the day to day lives of participating individuals. Sheer repetition in and of itself has never assured the persistence of any habit. If this were not so, no myths and rituals would ever have become extinct except when a whole society died out. It is necessary for us to recognize the somewhat special conditions of drive and of reward which apply to myths and rituals.

It is easy to understand why organisms eat. It is easy to understand why a defenceless man will run to escape a charging tiger. The physiological bases of the activities represented by myths and rituals are less obvious. A recent statement by a stimulus-response psychologist gives us the clue: "The position here taken is that human beings (and also other living organisms to varying degrees) can be motivated either by organic pressures (needs) that are currently felt *or* by the mere anticipation of such pressures and that those habits tend to be acquired and perpetuated (reinforced) which effect a reduction in either of these two types of motivation."[21] That is, myths and rituals are reinforced because they reduce the anticipation of disaster. No living person has died—but he has seen others die. The terrible things which we have seen happen to others may not yet have plagued us, but our experience teaches us that these are at least potential threats to our own health or happiness.* * *

V

* * *The specific adaptive and adjustive responses performed by myth and ritual will be differently phrased in different societies according to the historical experience of these societies (including the specific opportunities they have had for borrowing from other cultures), in accord with prevalent configurations of other aspects of the

21. O. H. Mowrer, "A Stimulus-Response Analysis of Anxiety and its Role as a Reinforcing Agent," *Psychological Review*, XLVI (1939), 561.

culture, and with reference to pressures exerted by other societies and by the physical and biological environment. But the general nature of the adaptive and adjustive responses performed by myth and ritual appears very much the same in all human groups. Hence, although the relative importance of myth and of ritual does vary greatly, the two tend universally to be associated.

For myth and ritual have a common psychological basis. Ritual is an obsessive repetitive activity—often a symbolic dramatization of the fundamental "needs" of the society, whether "economic," "biological," "social," or "sexual." Mythology is the rationalization of these same needs, whether they are all expressed in overt ceremonial or not. Someone has said "every culture has a type conflict and a type solution." Ceremonials tend to portray a symbolic resolvement of the conflicts which external environment, historical experience, and selective distribution of personality types have caused to be characteristic in the society. Because different conflict situations characterize different societies, the "needs" which are typical in one society may be the "needs" of only deviant individuals in another society. And the institutionalized gratifications (of which rituals and myths are prominent examples) of culturally recognized needs vary greatly from society to society. "Culturally recognized needs" is, of course, an analytical abstraction. Concretely, "needs" arise and exist only in specific individuals. This we must never forget, but it is equally important that myths and rituals, though surviving as functioning aspects of a coherent culture only so long as they meet the "needs" of a number of concrete individuals, are, in one sense, "supra-individual." They are usually composite creations; they normally embody the accretions of many generations, the modifications (through borrowing from other cultures or by intra-cultural changes) which the varying needs of the group as a whole and of innovating individuals in the group have imposed. In short, both myths and rituals are cultural products, part of the social heredity of a society.

Harvard Theological Review, XXXV (1942), 45–79. Part III of the original article and some of the reference notes have been omitted.

Part Two

MYTH AND LITERATURE

The nine essays in Part II all come from men whose primary interest is literature and who are seeking to determine in what ways the concepts of myth and ritual may contribute to the understanding and appreciation of literature. The essays are divided into two groups: the theories and observations set forth in the first six are subjected to a critical scrutiny in the concluding group of three, which mirrors, at least approximately, the current range of attitudes toward archetypal or myth criticism.

As in Part I, we open with a historical essay, but of a more restricted order than Mr. Bidney's. Stanley Edgar Hyman is chiefly concerned here with the work of the so-called Cambridge group—Frazer, Jane Harrison, Gilbert Murray, and F. M. Cornford. After tracing the intellectual origins of the ritual view of myth, he outlines the ritual theory as it was formulated by the Cambridge group, discusses its applications in a variety of contexts (children's lore, fairy tales, and Biblical, classical, and literary studies), and identifies the problems and opportunities confronting its supporters. Mr. Hyman's essay affords the reader an invaluable supplementary reading list as well as a historical introduction to the movement most responsible for mythic analyses of literature.

THE RITUAL VIEW OF MYTH AND THE MYTHIC

Stanley Edgar Hyman

The ritual approach comes directly out of Darwin, and thus, I suppose, ultimately from Heraclitus, whose *panta rei* seems to be the ancestor of any dynamic account of anything. When Darwin concluded *The Origin of Species* (1859) with a call for evolutionary treatment in the sciences of man, he opened the door to a variety of genetic studies of culture, and when he showed in *The Descent of Man* (1871) that human evolution was insignificant organically although vastly speeded up culturally (we might not be so quick to say "ethically" as he was), he made cultural studies the legitimate heirs of evolutionary biology. The same year as *The Descent*, in response to *The Origin*, E. B. Tylor's *Primitive Culture* appeared, drawing an immediate fan letter from Darwin. It staked off quite a broad claim to cultural studies in its subtitle "Researches into the Development of Mythology, Philosophy, Religion, Language, Art, and Custom." Tylor's general principle, almost his law, is that survivals are significant because they embody, sometimes in trivial or playful form, the serious usages of earlier stages. In material culture, it meant that such important tools as the bow and arrow, the fire drill, and the magician's rattle evolved into the toys of children; in non-material culture, it meant that myths were based on rites, although, like many rationalists before him, Tylor believed that they had been consciously devised as explanations.

Tylor's evolutionary anthropology, carried on by such successors as R. R. Marett and Henry Balfour, became the central tradition of British anthropology, but the emphasis gradually shifted from Tylor's concern with belief and custom to the more tangible areas of social organization, economics, and material culture. Meanwhile, at Cambridge, a classicist named James G. Frazer had found *Primitive Culture* a revelation, and his interest in ancient survivals was broadened and extended by his friend William Robertson Smith's studies of religion, in which Smith made use of the comparative method, invented by Montesquieu and developed by German philology. Weaving together the two main strands of Tylor's evolutionary survivals and Smith's comparative method, in 1885 Frazer began publishing a series of periodical articles on custom. When one of them, on a curious priesthood at Nemi in Italy, tied in with

Smith's ideas about the slain god and outgrew article size, he kept working on it and in 1890 published it as the first edition of *The Golden Bough* in two volumes, dedicated to Smith. For Frazer in *The Golden Bough*, myth is still Tylor's rationalist "a fiction devised to explain an old custom, of which the real meaning and origin had been forgotten,"[1] and the evolution of custom is still Tylor's "to dwindle from solemn ritual into mere pageant and pastime,"[2] but Frazer constantly approaches, without ever quite stating, a synthesis of the two, with myths not consciously-devised rational explanations, but the actual dwindling or later form of the rite. Long before 1915, when the third and final edition of *The Golden Bough* appeared, that synthesis had been arrived at.

Since 1882, Jane Ellen Harrison, Frazer's contemporary at Cambridge, had been writing on Greek mythology and art, and in 1903, after she had seen a clay seal at Cnossos with its sudden revelation that the Minotaur was the king of Crete in a bull mask, she published *Prolegomena to the Study of Greek Religion*, which clearly stated the priority of ritual over myth or theology. Her book acknowledged the cooperation of Gilbert Murray at Tylor's Oxford, and Frazer, F. M. Cornford, and A. B. Cook at Cambridge. Cook, whose book, *Zeus*, did not begin to appear for another decade, began publishing parts of it in periodicals about that time, and his important series "Zeus, Jupiter, and the Oak" in the *Classical Review* (1903) took an approach similar to Harrison's. By the time Murray published *The Rise of the Greek Epic* (1907), reading such mythic figures as Helen and Achilles as ritual concretizations, he was able to draw on some of this Cambridge work his earlier writings had influenced. By 1908, when the Committee for Anthropology at Oxford sponsored six lectures, published under Marett's editorship later that year as *Anthropology and the Classics*, with the aim of interesting students of the humanities in "the lower culture,"[3] students of the humanities at the sister university had been turning their attention to the lower cultures for two decades, and the seed Tylor planted had flowered elsewhere.

The watershed year was 1912, when Harrison published *Themis*, a full and brilliant exposition of the chthonic origins of Greek mythology, including an excursus on the ritual forms underlying Greek tragedy by Murray (to whom the book is dedicated), a chapter on the ritual origin of the Olympic Games by Cornford, and copious material from Cook's forthcoming work. (Curiously, this book too had been inspired by a visit to Crete, where Harrison encountered the "Hymn of the Kouretes," which suggested that ritual magic, specifically the rite of a year-daimon, was the central element in early Greek religion.) In *Themis*, Harrison made three important points with great clarity: that myth arises out of rite, rather than the reverse;[4] that it is "the spoken correlative of the acted rite, the thing done; it is *to legomenon* as contrasted with or rather as related to *to dromenon*"[5] (a Greek definition of myth is *ta legomena*

1. J. G. Frazer, *The Golden Bough* (London: Macmillan, 1915), IV, 153.
2. Frazer, *The Golden Bough*, IV, 214.
3. *Anthropology and the Classics*, ed. R. R. Marett (Oxford: Oxford University Press, 1907), p. 5.
4. J. E. Harrison, *Themis* (Cambridge: Cambridge University Press, 1912), p. 13.
5. Harrison, *Themis*, p. 328.

epi tois dromenois 'the things said over a ritual act'); and that it is not anything else nor of any other origin.[6]

Basic to this view, as Harrison makes clear, is a dynamic or evolutionary conception of process whereby rites die out, and myths continue in religion, literature, art, and various symbolic forms with increased misunderstanding of the ancient rite, and a compensatory transformation for intelligibility in new terms. Thus myths are never the record of historical events or people, but freed from their ritual origins they may attach to historical events or people (as Alexander was believed to be, or claimed to be, a god and the son of a snake, because mythic Greek kings like Cecrops had been ritual snake gods); they never originate as scientific or etiological explanations of nature, but freed from their ritual origins may be so used (as stars have their positions in the sky because the mythic hero threw them there, but *his* origin is in rite, not primitive astronomy).

The ritual approach to mythology, or any form based on myth, thus cannot limit itself to genetic considerations. In the artificial division I have found most handy, it must deal with the three related problems of Origin, Structure, and Function. If the origin is the ancient anonymous collective one of ritual, the structure is intrinsically dramatic, the *dromenon* or thing done, but that form ceaselessly evolves in time in the chain of folk transmission. Here the considerations are not historic nor anthropological, but formal in terms of literary structure, principles of *Gestalt* organization, and dynamic criteria. In folk transmission, the "folk work" involves operations comparable to those Freud found in the "dream work"—splitting, displacement, multiplication, projection, rationalization, secondary elaboration, and interpretation—as well as such more characteristically aesthetic dynamics as Kenneth Burke's principle of "completion" or the fulfillment of expectations, in the work as well as in the audience. In regard to function, as the myth or text alters, there is at once a changing social function, as the work satisfies varying specific needs in the society along Malinowskian lines, and an unchanging, built-in function best described by Aristotle's *Poetics* and Freudian psychology, carrying with it its own context, taking us through its structural rites. In other words, the book of Jonah in the reading satisfies our need to be reborn in the belly of the great fish as efficiently as the initiatory rites from which it presumably derived satisfied the same need in the initiates. If these are now as then "fantasy gratifications," they are the charismatic experiences of great art now, as they were the charismatic experiences of organic religion then.

In a relatively short time, the ritual approach to folk study has met with remarkable success. There had of course been individual ritual studies in various areas long before 1912. Most of them were in the field of children's lore, where ritual survivals, after Tylor had called attention to them, were readily apparent. Some of the earliest studies were William Wells Newell's *Games and Songs of American Children* (1883), Henry Carrington Bolton's *The Counting Out Rhymes of Children* (1888), Alice Gomme's *The Traditional Games of England, Scotland and Ireland* (1894), and Lina Eckenstein's *Comparative Studies in Nursery Rhymes* (1906). Much of this work has never been

6. Harrison, *Themis*, p. 331.

superseded, and similarly, the most impressive ritual studies we have of the Bible appeared at the turn of the century: for the Old Testament, William Simpson's *The Jonah Legend* (1899), and for the New, John M. Robertson's series of books on the mythic Jesus, beginning with *Christianity and Mythology* (1900). All of these people seem to have operated in relative isolation, independently working through to conclusions about their own material without knowing what was going on in other areas or recognizing the general application of their conclusions.

With the appearance of *Themis*, a powerful general statement of the theory buttressed by a prodigy of scholarship in several complicated areas of Greek culture, a "Cambridge" or "ritual" approach became generally available. Within a few years, its application to Greek studies had been enormously widened: Cornford's *From Religion to Philosophy* (1912) traced the ritual origins of some basic philosophic ideas; Harrison's *Ancient Art and Ritual* (1913) turned her theory on Greek plastic and pictorial arts; Murray tested his ritual forms on one tragic dramatist in *Euripides and His Age* (1913), (both it and *Ancient Art and Ritual* are popularizations for the Home University Library); Cornford tested the same forms on Greek comedy in *The Origin of Attic Comedy* (1914); and the first volume of Cook's enormous storehouse of ritual interpretation, *Zeus*, appeared (1914).

The first application of the theory outside Greek studies was Murray's 1914 Shakespeare Lecture, "Hamlet and Orestes,"[7] a brilliant comparative study in the common ritual origins of Shakespeare and Greek drama. 1920 saw the appearance of Jessie Weston's *From Ritual to Romance*, treating the Grail romances as the "misinterpreted" record of a fertility rite, and Bertha Phillpotts' *The Elder Edda and Ancient Scandinavian Drama*, tracing the ritual sources of Northern epic poetry. The next year Margaret Murray's *The Witch-Cult in Western Europe* appeared, claiming a real "Dianic cult," the survival of the old pagan religion, persecuted by Christianity as witchcraft, the book constituting the first substantial excursion of the theory into history. In 1923, the widening ripples took in fairy tales, in P. Saintyves' *Les Contes de Perrault et les Récits Parallèles*; folk drama, in R. J. E. Tiddy's editing *The Mummers Play*; and law, in H. Goitein's *Primitive Ordeal and Modern Law*. In 1927, A. M. Hocart's *Kingship* appeared, tracing a great variety of material to a basic royal initiatory ceremony, and in 1929 Scott Buchanan's *Poetry and Mathematics* (the first American work along these lines in the third of a century since Bolton) boldly proposed a treatment of experimental science in ritual terms, and imaginatively worked some of it out.

In the thirties, S. H. Hooke edited two important symposia, *Myth and Ritual* (1933) and *The Labyrinth* (1935), in which a number of prominent scholars studied the relationships of myth and ritual in the ancient Near East; Lord Raglan published *Jocasta's Crime*, a ritual theory of taboo (1933), and his enormously influential *The Hero* (1937), which broadly generalized the ritual origins of all myth, as against the historical; Enid Welsford investigated the sources of an archetypal figure in *The Fool* (1935); Allen, Halliday, and Sikes published their definitive edition of *The Homeric Hymns* (1936), extending previous considerations of Greek epic and dra-

---

7. In Gilbert Murray, *The Classical Tradition in Poetry* (Cambridge: Harvard University Press, 1927), pp. 205–240.

matic poetry into sacred lyric; and in the late thirties William Troy began publishing his as yet uncollected ritual studies of such writers as Lawrence, Mann, and Fitz-gerald.

By the forties, old subjects could be gone back over with greatly augmented in-formation. George Thomson combined a ritual and Marxist approach in *Aeschylus and Athens* (1941) and *Studies in Ancient Greek Society* (the first volume of which appeared in 1949); Rhys Carpenter amplified Murray's earlier treatment of Homer in *Folk Tale, Fiction and Saga in the Homeric Epics* (1946); Lewis Spence brought Newell, Bolton, and Lady Gomme somewhat up to date in *Myth and Ritual in Dance, Game, and Rhyme* (1947); and Hugh Ross Williamson expanded Margaret Murray's brief account (in *The God of the Witches*, 1933) of the deaths of Thomas à Becket and William Rufus as Dianic cult sacrifices in *The Arrow and the Sword* (1947). Venturing into fresh fields, Gertrude Rachel Levy in *The Gate of Horn* (1948), traced some ritual sources of culture down from the stone age, paying con-siderable attention to plastic and pictorial art; and in 1949 there were two important literary applications: Francis Fergusson's *The Idea of a Theater*, a reading of modern drama in terms of the ritual patterns exemplified in Sophocles' *Oedipus the King*, and John Speirs' "Sir Gawain and the Green Knight," in *Scrutiny*, Winter 1949, the first of an important series of ritual studies of medieval English literature.

So far in the fifties half a dozen new territories have been explored and to some extent colonized. Theodor H. Gaster's *Thespis* (1950) generalized a ritual origin for the whole body of Near East sacred literature; Gertrude Kurath's articles on dance in the Funk and Wagnalls' *Dictionary of Folklore* the same year embraced a body of primitive and folk dance forms in the same approach; Cornford's luminous "A Ritual Basis for Hesiod's *Theogony*" was published posthumously in *The Unwritten Philosophy* (1950, although it had been written in 1941); and C. L. Barber published an ambitious exploration of Shakespeare in "The Saturnalian Pattern in Shakespeare's Comedy" in *The Sewanee Review*, Autumn 1951. Since then we have had the publication of Levy's second volume, *The Sword from the Stone* (1953), a ritual genesis of epic; Herbert Weisinger's *Tragedy and the Paradox of the Fortunate Fall* (1953), a similar treatment of tragedy; and Margaret Murray's third book on the Dianic cult, *The Divine King in England* (1954). In this listing I have made no attempt at completeness, confining it to those writers with whose work I am most familiar, and only one or two titles by each (Murray, Cornford, and Harrison have written about a dozen books each), but the breadth and variety of even this truncated list should make it obvious that the "Cambridge" view has gone far beyond the confines of Greek mythology, and that it is apparently here to stay.

Since the ritual approach to myth and literature does not claim to be a theory of ultimate significance, but a method of study in terms of specific significances, it can cohabit happily with a great many other approaches. If its anthropology has histori-cally been Frazerian, the comparative generalization across many cultures, many of its most successful works, from *Themis* to Speirs on Gawain, have stayed narrowly within one area, and where it deals with social function, its anthropology is most profitably Malinowskian (if an unusually historical Malinowskian). The Boas tradition in American anthropology, with its bias against cross-cultural generalization and evolutionary theory, in favor of empirical cultural studies and known history, has often seemed inimical to the ritual approach at those key points. Many of the Boas rigidities, however, seem to have softened in the decade since his death: the new culture and personality anthropology from Ruth Benedict's *Patterns of Culture* (1934) to E. Adamson Hoebel's *The Law of Primitive Man* (1954) seems as cheerfully comparative as *The Golden Bough*; we are all neo-evolutionists once again; and *Primitive Heritage* (1953), Margaret Mead's anthology with Nicholas Calas, calls for "the restoration of wonder," and means, apparently, let us take Frazer and Crawley more seriously. If out of this comes a neo-Frazerian generalizing anthropology, based, not on dubious material wrenched out of its configuration, but on detailed and accurate field studies done with Boasian rigor, no one would welcome it more than the ritualists.

In regard to psychology, the ritual approach can draw centrally on Freudian psychoanalysis, informed by new knowledge and less circumscribed by ethnocentric patterns. This requires modernization without the loss of Freud's central vision, which is tragic where such rebels as Adler and Jung and such revisionists as Fromm and Horney are cheery faith-healers; unshrinking where they bowdlerize; stubbornly materialist where they are idealist and mystic; and dynamic, concerned with process, where they are static and concerned with one or another variety of timeless *élan vital*. After we have brought the Frazerian anthropology of *Totem and Taboo* up to date and restored Freud's "vision" of the Primal Horde, in Burke's terms, to its place as "essence" rather than "origin," the book remains our most useful and seminal equation of primitive rite with neurotic behavior, and thus the bridge to Burke's own "symbolic action," the private, individual symbolic equivalent for the ancient collective ritual. In the form of "symbolic action," psychoanalytic theory gives us the other dimension of function, the wish-fulfillment or fantasy gratification, and can thus answer some of our questions about the origins of origins.

As Jung's work increasingly seems to move toward mystic religion and away from analytic psychology, it appears to be of increasingly little use to a comparative and genetic approach. Strong as Jungian psychology has been in insisting on the universal archetypal identity of myth and symbol, its explanation of this identity in terms of the collective unconscious and innate awareness militates directly against any attempt to study the specific forms by which these traits are carried and transmitted in the culture (as did Freud's own "memory traces"). As Jung is used in the work of Maud Bodkin[8] or Joseph Campbell, as a source of suggestive insights, it seems far more to our purposes, and we can readily utilize Campbell's universal "great myth" or "monomyth," a concept itself derived from Van Gennep's *rites de passage*: "a separation from the world, a penetration to some source of power, and a life-enhancing return."[9] We must first, however, put the Jungian myth back on its roots,

8. Maud Bodkin, *Archetypal Patterns in Poetry* (London: Oxford University Press, 1934), and *Studies of Type-Images in Poetry, Religion, and Philosophy* (London: Oxford University Press, 1951).
9. Joseph Campbell, *The Hero with a Thousand Faces* (New York: Pantheon, 1949), pp. 10, 35.

either a specific myth and text (literary study) or a specific culture and rite (anthropology). The ritual approach is certainly compatible with varieties of mysticism, as the conclusions of Weston's *From Ritual to Romance* or Harrison's *Epilegomena to the Study of Greek Religion* (1921) make clear, and Harrison was herself strongly drawn to Jung as well as to Bergson. Despite their examples, and the opinions of even so impressive a ritual poet as William Butler Yeats, the job of mythic analysis would seem to require a basic rational materialism, and a constant pressure in the direction of science and scholarship, away from mysticism and the occult. Within these limits of naturalism, and on the frame of this central concern with ritual, all possible knowledge and all approaches to myth, from the most meticulous motif-classification to the most speculative reconstruction of an *ur*-text, can be useful, with pluralism certainly the desirable condition.

There are only two varieties of approach, I think, with which the ritual view cannot usefully coexist. One is the euhemerist, the idea that myths are based on historic persons or events. This theory has been driven back from rampart to rampart over the years, but it stubbornly holds to each new defensive position: if it is forced to give up a historic William Tell, it retreats to a historic Robin Hood; if the historic Orpheus even Harrison's *Prolegomena* accepted in 1903 seems no longer tenable, perhaps Moses is; if there was no Leda and no egg, could there not have been a real Helen? By now, in regard to the greath myths, we know that none of these is possible, even at those key points the Trojan War and the figure of Jesus. With stories unquestionably made up about real people, whether fictions about Napoleon or Eleanor Roosevelt jokes, it becomes a simple matter of definition, and if the euhemerists of our various schools want to call those stories myths, they are welcome to them. We find it more useful to apply some other term, insofar as the distinction between myth and history is a real and a basic one.[10]

The other approach to mythology that seems to offer no point of juncture with the ritual view is the cognitionist idea that myths derive from a quest for knowledge. In its nineteenth century forms, the theories that myths were personifications of nature, or the weather, or the sun and moon, it seems substantially to have died out; in various insidious twentieth century forms, the theories that myths are designed to answer etiological questions about how death came into the world or how the bunny got his little furry tail, or that taboo is primitive hygiene or primitive genetics, it is still pervasive. Again, all one can say is that myths do not originate in this fashion, that primitive peoples are speculative and proto-scientific, surely, but that the lore they transmit is another order of knowledge. If they knew that the tabooed food carried trichinosis or that the tabooed incestuous marriage deteriorated the stock, they would not save the first for their sacred feasts and the second for their rulers. Once more, if our various cognitionists want to call myth what is unquestionably primitive proto-science, like techniques for keeping a pot from cracking in the firing or seasonal lore for planting and harvesting, that is their privilege. The Alaskan Eskimos who took the Russian explorers for cuttlefish "on account of the buttons

10. Myth must also be distinguished from all the other things we loosely call by its name: legend, tale, fantasy, mass delusion, popular belief and illusion, and plain lie.

on their clothes," as Frazer reports,[11] obviously had speculative minds and a sense of continuity between the animal and human orders not unlike that informing Darwin's theory, but the difference between their myth of "The Great Cuttlefish That Walks Like a Man" (if they had one) and *The Origin of Species* is nevertheless substantial.

If we keep clearly in mind that myth tells a story sanctioning a rite, it is obvious that it neither means nor explains anything; that it is not science but a form of independent experience, analogous to literature. The pursuit of cognition in myth or folk literature has led to all the worst excesses of speculative research, whether the political slogans and events Katherine Elwes Thomas found hermetically concealed in nursery rhymes in *The Real Personages of Mother Goose* (1930), the wisdom messages, deliberately coded and jumbled, that Robert Graves uncoded in *The White Goddess* (1948), or, most recently, the secret fire worship Flavia Anderson discovered hidden behind every myth in *The Ancient Secret* (1953).

Among the important problems facing the ritual view at present is an adequate working-out of the relationship between ritual, the anonymous regular recurrence of an action, and history, the unique identifiable experience in time. The problem is raised dramatically in the latest book by Margaret Murray, one of the pioneers of ritual studies. Called *The Divine King in England*, it is the third in her series on the Dianic cult and easily her wildest. Where *The Witch-cult in Western Europe* named two historical figures, Joan of Arc and Gilles de Rais, as voluntary sacrificial figures in the cult, and her second book, *The God of the Witches*, added two more, Thomas à Becket and William Rufus, the new book makes the bold claim on English history that "at least once in every reign from William The Conqueror to James I the sacrifice of the Incarnate God was consummated either in the person of the king or in that of his substitute,"[12] generally in a regular seven-year cycle. Since I have already reviewed the book at length for a forthcoming issue of *Midwest Folklore*, I can here only briefly summarize the problem. Murray's historical excursion is not only dubious history (as reviewers have pointed out, showing the errors of dates and durations by which she gets her seven-year victims, the number jugglery by which she gets her covens of thirteen), it is totally unnecessary history. She is certainly right about survivals of the old religion into modern times, but she seems to be basically in error about the manner in which it survives, to be confusing origins with events. As the ancient rites die out in literal practice, their misunderstood and transformed record passes into myth and symbol, and that is the form in which they survive and color history, without being themselves the events of history. In English history, assuming as she does that the primitive divine king was once slain every seven years, the monarch and his subjects might very well feel an ominousness about each seventh anniversary, and might welcome the death of the king or some high personage, but the step from that to the idea that the dead man was therefore the voluntary victim

11. J. G. Frazer, "Some Primitive Theories of the Origin of Man," *Darwin and Modern Science*, ed. A. C. Seward (Cambridge: Cambridge University Press, 1909), p. 159.

12. M. A. Murray, *The Divine King in England* (London: Faber & Faber, 1954), p. 13.

of a sacrificial cult is the unwarranted one. Murray's witch cult was a genuine worship of the old gods, surviving into modern times in a distorted form, but her Royal Covens are only the travesty of historical scholarship.

If the fallacy of historicity is still with us, the fallacy of etiology may finally be on its way out. In *Themis*, as far back as 1912, Harrison wrote:

> The myth is not at first etiological, it does not arise to give a reason; it is representative, another form of utterance, of expression. When the emotion that started the ritual has died down and the ritual though hallowed by tradition seems unmeaning, a reason is sought in the myth and it is regarded as etiological.[13]

In his recent posthumous volume edited by Lord Raglan, *The Life-Giving Myth* (1952), A. M. Hocart finally shows the process whereby myth goes beyond explaining the ritual to explaining other phenomena in nature, thus functioning as general etiology. In Fiji, he reports, the physical peculiarities of an island with only one small patch of fertile soil are explained by a myth telling how Mberewalaki, a culture hero, flew into a passion at the misbehavior of the people of the island and hurled all the soil he was bringing them in a heap, instead of laying it out properly. Hocart points out that the myth is used etiologically to explain the nature of the island, but did not originate in that attempt. The adventures of Mberewalaki originated, like all mythology, in ritual performance, and most of the lore of Hocart's Fijian informants consisted of such ritual myths. When they get interested in the topography of the island or are asked about it, Hocart argues, they do precisely what we would do, which is ransack their lore for an answer. Our lore might include a body of geological process, and we would search through it for an explanation; theirs has no geology but tells the acts and passions of Mberewalaki, and they search through it similarly and come up with an explanation. It should take no more than this one pointed example, I think, to puncture that last survival of the cosmological origin theories, the etiological myth, except as a category of function.

After the relationship to history and to science or cognition, we are left with the relationship of ritual theory to belief. For Harrison, as for Frazer, ritual studies were part of comparative religion, and a hoped-for result, if not the ultimate aim, was finding a pattern in which a person of sense or sensibility could believe. Harrison concludes her essay in the Darwin centenary volume: "It is, I venture to think, towards the apprehension of such mysteries, not by reason only, but by man's whole personality, that the religious spirit in the course of its evolution through ancient magic and modern mysticism is ever blindly yet persistently moving."[14] In the course of his researches, Darwin himself lost most of his faith, but for Asa Gray, as for some Darwinians since, the doctrine of evolution celebrated God's powers and strengthened Christian faith. For John M. Robertson, the demolition of the historicity of Jesus was a blow against Christianity on behalf of free-thought; for W. B. Smith and Arthur Drews it was a way of purifying Christianity by purging it of legendary accretions.

13. Harrison, *Themis*, p. 16.

14. Harrison, "The Influence of Darwinism on the Study of Religions," *Darwin and Modern Science*, ed. A. C. Seward, p. 511.

William Simpson seems to have hit on the idea of Jonah as an initiation ritual because he was preoccupied with such matters as a Freemason. There is apparently no necessary correlation between knowledge and belief; to know all is to believe all, or some, or none.

Most contemporary ritual students of myth, I should imagine, are like myself unbelievers, and it would seem to get progressively more difficult to acknowledge the essential identity of religious myths, and their genesis from the act of worship itself, the god out of the machinery, while continuing to believe in the "truth" of any one of them (or of all of them, except in the woolliest and most Jungian fashion). On the other hand, in *Cults and Creeds in Graeco-Roman Egypt* (1953), we saw Sir Harold Idris Bell, a professional papyrologist, produce a learned and impressive study of the pragmatic competition of religions in Hellenistic Egypt, with the constant proviso that one of those systems, Christianity, was not only morally superior to the others, but was the divinely inspired true faith. So perhaps to know all *is* to believe all.

Finally, then, a number of technical problems remain. In its brief history, the ritual view has illuminated almost the whole of Greek culture, including religion, philosophy, art, many of the forms of literature, and much else. It has done the same for the games, songs, and rhymes of children; the Old and New Testaments, epic and romance, edda and saga, folk drama and dance, folktale and legend, Near East religion, modern drama and literature, even problems in history, law, and science. A few forms of folk literature have not yet been explored in ritual terms, prominent among them the English and Scottish popular ballads (the present writer has made a tentative foray in that direction)[15] and the American Negro blues. A ritual origin for the ballads presumes a body of antecedent folk drama, from which they evolve as narrative songs (as it in turn derives from ritual sacrifice), which hardly exists except in a few late poor fragments such as Robin Hood plays, and which must consequently be conjectured. Such conjecture is not impossible, but it is a hard job involving heavy reliance on that frail reed analogy, and it still awaits its doer. The blues raise serious problems. If they are a true folksong of ancient anonymous collective ritual origin, rather than a folk-transmitted song of modern composition, then they precede any American conditions experienced by the Negro and must have an African source. No trouble here, except that nothing like them has ever been found in Africa, perhaps because it does not exist, perhaps because it would look so different before its sea change that no one has yet identified it. In any case, a ritual origin for the blues constitutes a fascinating problem, although not a critical issue (too much obviously convincing ritual interpretation has been produced for the theory to stand or fall on any single form). A ritual account of the ballads and the blues would close two large chinks, and might keep out drafts even in the coldest climate of opinion.

The relationship of ritual and ritual myth to formal literature has hardly yet been touched. The brilliant work that should have inaugurated such a movement in literary criticism was Murray's 1914 Shakespeare Lecture, "Hamlet and Orestes," in which he showed the essential identity of the two dramatic heroes, not as the result of any

15. S. E. Hyman, "The Raggle–Taggle Ballads O," *The Western Review*, XV (1951), pp. 305–313.

direct linkage between the two, but because Shakespeare's Hamlet, through a long Northern line of Amlethus, Amlodi, and Ambales, derived from precisely the same myth and rite of the Winter King—cold, mad, death-centered, bitter, and filthy—that Orestes derived from in his warmer clime. The plays are neither myth nor rite, Murray insists, they are literature, but myth and rite underly their forms, their plots, and their characters. (Greek drama itself represents a fusion of two separate derivations from ritual: the forms of Attic tragedy arise out of the sacrificial rites of tauriform or aegiform Dionysos, the plots of Attic tragedy come mostly from Homer; and the bloody plots fit the ritual form so well, as Rhys Carpenter showed most fully, because the Homeric stories themselves derive from similar sacrificial rites far from Mount Olympus.) In the four decades since Murray's lecture, literary criticism has scarcely noticed it. A student of Murray's, Janet Spens, published a ritual treatment of Shakespeare, *An Essay on Shakespeare's Relation to Tradition* (1916), which I have never seen, but which Barber describes with serious reservations, and until his own essay almost nothing had been done along that line. Troy and Fergusson have dealt with a handful of novels and plays in ritual terms, Carvel Collins has written several essays on Faulkner, and the present writer has similarly tackled Thoreau and a few others, but there has been very little else.

The chief difficulty seems to lie in the need to recognize the relationship of literature to folk tradition, while at the same time drawing Murray's sharp line between them. Literature is analogous to myth, we have to insist, but is not itself myth. There has been a great deal of confusion on this point, best exemplified by Richard Chase's *Quest for Myth* and *Herman Melville* (both in 1949). Chase simply equates the two, defining myth in the former as "the aesthetic activity of a man's mind,"[16] turning Melville's works in the latter into so many myths or mythic organizations. Here we ought to keep in mind a number of basic distinctions. Myth and literature are separate and independent entities, although myth can never be considered in isolation, and any specific written text of the protean myth, or even fixed oral text, can fairly be called folk literature. For literary purposes, all myths are not one, however much they may be one, the monomyth or ur-myth, in essence or origin. What such modern writers as Melville or Kafka create is not myth but an individual fantasy expressing a symbolic action, equivalent to and related to the myth's expression of a public rite. No one, not even Melville (let alone Moritz Jagendorf) can invent myths or write folk literature.

The writer can use traditional myths with varying degrees of consciousness (with Joyce and Mann perhaps most fully conscious in our time), and he often does so with no premeditated intention, working from symbolic equivalents in his own unconscious. Here other arts closer to origins, like the dance, where the ritual or symbolic action is physically mimed, can be profoundly instructive. Just as there are varying degrees of consciousness, so are there varying degrees of fruitfulness in these uses of traditional patterns, ranging from dishonest fakery at one extreme to some of the subtlest ironic and imaginative organizations in our poetry at the other. The aim of a ritual literary

16. Richard Chase, *Quest for Myth* (Baton Rouge: Louisiana State University Press, 1949), p. vii.

criticism would be the exploration of all these relations, along with missionary activity on behalf of some of the more fruitful ones.

What begins as a modest genetic theory for the origin of a few myths thus eventually comes to make rather large claims on the essential forms of the whole culture. If, as Schroedinger's *Nature and the Greeks* (1954) shows, the patterns of Greek myth and rite have been built into all our physics until the last few decades, perhaps ritual is a matter of some importance. Raglan and Hocart argue that the forms of social organization arise out of it, Goitein throws in the processes of law, Cornford and Buchanan add the forms of philosophic and scientific thinking (perhaps all our thinking follows the ritual pattern of *agon* or contest, *sparagmos* or tearing apart, then *anagnorisis* or discovery and *epiphany* or showing-forth of the new idea). Even language itself suggests at many points a ritual origin. From rites come the structures, even the plots and characters, of literature, the magical organizations of painting, the arousing and fulfilling of expectation in music, perhaps the common origin of all the arts. If ritual is to be a general theory of culture, however, our operations must get more tentative and precise in proportion as our claims become more grandiose. We then have to keep distinctions even clearer, know so much more, and use every scrap of fact or theory that can be used. Having begun so easily by explaining the myth of the Sphinx, we may yet, working humbly in cooperation with anyone who will and can cooperate, end by reading her difficult riddle.

Myth: A Symposium, ed. T. A. Sebeok (Bloomington: Indiana University Press, 1958), pp. 84–94.

Philip Wheelwright is a philosopher who, in such works as The Burning Fountain (*1954*) *and* Metaphor and Reality (*1962*), *has contributed notably to the contemporary dialogue on the nature of poetic language, myth, and symbolism. The following essay explores the symbolic role of ritual and myth as it operates both in the primitive world-view (see Géza Róheim's essay, pp. 25 ff.)and in sophisticated literary questions of structure and metaphor. Its implicit opposition to a purely naturalistic treatment of myth aligns it with the essays of Joseph Campbell (pp. 15 ff.) and Harold H. Watts (pp. 75 ff.). In addition, Mr. Wheelwright's comments on the rhythmic and cyclic character of nature and ritual can be compared with Northrop Frye's discussion of myth and archetype (pp. 87 ff.).*

NOTES ON MYTHOPOEIA

Philip Wheelwright

How far can we divest ourselves of paleface preconceptions and enter imaginatively into the primeval world-view from which, by successive refinements, disavowals, and reorientations, the later phenomena of human thought have lumberingly evolved? The divestment will be partial and dubious at best; for when once the virus of civilization has thoroughly infected us—for better *and* for worse—our tribal habits of conceptualization stubbornly assert themselves as of universal validity. The result is an ingrained partisanship, which renders myopic the backward look, and encourages a sort of snobbery toward earlier peoples in proportion as their ways of thinking, feeling, and behaving differ radically from our own. The bare fact that undergraduate courses in "primitive cultures" have come to occupy a strategic place in modern college curricula is no guarantee that our understanding of the primitive condition has been correspondingly deepened.

What is meant by "primitive"? Do we prejudge important issues by playing fast and loose with the word? Is it simply a verbal stopgap of ignorance, an omnibus-symbol for societal types on which it pleases our pride to look with condescension? Admittedly there are real obstacles to an objective study of cultural primitivity. If we collect data from among proto-civilized peoples of today, there is first the difficulty of finding tribal specimens any longer uncontaminated by civilizing influences; second, the difficulty of overcoming radical language barriers and sly native reticence to achieve real communication regarding perennial matters; and third, the unanswerable doubt whether these contemporary so-called primitives—even where we can find them and understand them—are truly primitive in the sense of preserving custom and belief intact since before the beginning of recorded history. If, on the other hand, our data are taken from the earliest literary remains of ancient peoples, there are (besides interpretative difficulties of another kind) haunting indications of long prior ages, of which even the most venerable writings are late after-products and therefore imperfect records.

Such obstacles, faced candidly, would be formidable if the object of search were the primitive in a strictly chronological sense. There is no real knowledge of how men thought, felt, and acted ten thousand or fifty thousand years ago. Fortunately, however, there does not need to be. Any such time-spans are arbitrary. Mankind's primitive condition had no assignable beginning and end. Besides, an interest in what the *earliest* men were like, even if it could be satisfied, is more antiquarian than philosophical. Primitivity in its most relevant sense is a character to be recognized not by its *when* but by its *what*. Out of both of the two great systems of evidence conjoined—those furnished by "uncivilized" peoples of today, or rather of two or three generations ago before their molestation had proceeded to such destructive lengths, and those furnished by ancient documents and supplemented by archeological exhumations—there emerges a picture of the human condition which, regardless of how far back into pre-history it may or may not refer, is firmly significant both because, with abundant deviations, it is so well-nigh universal, and because it stirs even in our minds today some dim response of recognition.

The primitive world-view has so many facets—magic and legend, totem and taboo, initiation ceremonies and death chants, worship of gods and ghosts, and many others—that anything like full treatment here is out of the question. A simplification is required, and it must be one that without distorting the main data and main emphases which anthropological science discloses as typically primitive, will be sufficiently relevant to our present semantic inquiry to throw light upon the nature of the expressive symbol. Such a simplification is found in the fundamental pair of cultural phenomena: *ritual* and *myth*. Ritual connotes a way of doing, and myth a way of envisaging; but the doing and the envisaging are of a special, not of an everyday sort, and imply in their turn a belief in a penumbral reality, something extending beyond yet interpenetrating with the affairs of mortal men.

Now doing and envisaging bring into play the two most basic types of imagery contributing to human experience—namely, the kinaesthetic and the visual. By these the substance of our world is largely given. Discovery and interpretation play back and forth through them both, in varying combination, as the case of an infant exploratively exercising its muscular reflexes to reach toward an object which it sees will conform. Kinaesthesis and vision—the Nietzschean Dionysus and Apollo—are the two most indispensable and typical ingredients of the human situation at whatever level of advancement. If Hindu seer or Christian saint can sometimes virtually subdue his motor-impulses to emancipate the beatific vision in its purity, that is a brilliant exception which does not invalidate the rule. Again, if an occasional creative musical genius can experience pure tone as the main area of reference in his world (analogously, perhaps, to a dog's reliance upon odors), still for most persons musical sounds are adjectival appendages of "the real world" rather than its very substance. The eye and the muscle normally come first. And when they function on the human as distinguished from the merely animal level they tend to assume (as Susanne K. Langer has persuasively argued) a *symbolic* role in addition to their practical one. In man qua animal, sight and behavior are little more than phases of a predictable reflex-circuit: they simply *are*. But in man qua man, vision and action become enjoyed, furthered, and controlled for their own sake; developed into visual imaginings, story-telling, legend and myth on the one hand, and into gesture and ritual on the other.

The mythopoeic vision involves a certain idea of nature; for a myth, whatever its undertones of psychic extrapolation, tells a story whose locale is the world "out there." What is the primitive world-out-there? The answer must reckon on ambivalence. In part the primitive man's world is an extension of his community-sense, which is to say it is continuous with his own tribal existence and therefore something familiar, with which he is in congenital attunement; in part it is starkly and awefully different from himself, and potentially hostile. The distinction marks roughly a difference between two kinds of ritual: celebrative or sacramental, and magical— ritual expressing joy in the attunement, and ritual seeking to exploit the otherness or defend against the hostility. But no sooner is the distinction made than qualifications suggest themselves. In many instances of ritual the elements of sacrament and of magic are so closely joined as to be hardly distinguishable; and both elements lose their proper character as ritual lapses into rote. Moreover, while magic is primarily a technique of controlling—i.e., either exploiting or exorcising—the otherness of nature, the operation involves (as Frazer and others have shown) a strong sense of affinity, an effective identity of life-power, between the operator and the portion of nature to be magically controlled.

For nature, mythopoeically envisaged, is subject to what Lévy-Bruhl has called "the law of participation." Admitting the difficulty of formulating the law adequately, he suggests that "in the collective representations of primitive mentality, objects and phenomena can be, though in a manner incomprehensible to us, at once themselves and not themselves." Thus when the Bororo tribe of northern Brazil declare that they are red parakeets, they are not merely taking a name or claiming a relationship; they are asserting positive identity with the species of red parakeet. On the basis of our accustomed logic—the logic of Literal Discourse—it is paradoxical to regard them as human beings and as birds of scarlet plumage at the same time, but "to the mentality that is governed by the law of participation there is no difficulty in the matter." Lévy-Bruhl characterizes such mentality as "pre-logical": not implying that it is necessarily antecedent in time to the birth of logical thought, but merely "that it does not bind itself down, as [logical] thought does, to avoiding contradiction." In practical situations, he observes, a primitive man reasons much as we would do: seeking shelter in a storm and a way of escape on encountering a wild beast—where he has to think and act as an individual. Typically primitive "pre-logical" ideas do not depend on the individual but on the group: "they present themselves in aspects which cannot be accounted for by considering individuals merely as such; they cannot be deduced from the laws of a psychology based upon the analysis of the individual subject." Lévy-Bruhl calls them "collective representations."

Now the law of participation operates not only in combining concepts, but—when they are collective representations—in the very manner of their formation. Our familiar concepts—man, animal, organism, and the like—involve judgmental operations of which we are scarcely aware: in particular, the operations of remembering similar instances, of judging what similarities are relevant, and of grouping the instances into classes on the basis of those similarities. Collective representations, too, involve mental selection and synthesis, but along different lines from such concepts as we call logical. The collective representations "contain, as integral parts, affective and motor elements, and above all they imply, in the place of our conceptual inclusions or exclusions, participations which are more or less clearly defined, but as a general rule, very vividly sensed." Thus a portrait to the primitive mind is different from what it is to ours. The Sioux chieftains would not let Catlin take their portrait, fearing that whatever happened to their likenesses, delivered over into strange hands, would equally happen to themselves. But how interpret this well-known sort of native shyness? Frazer's learned but comparatively superficial analysis assumes that a primitive man sees a portrait just as we do but holds different beliefs about its magical efficacy, and therefore has different feelings about it. Lévy-Bruhl's analysis is more adequate. He understands that feelings and beliefs, when they go deep, affect the nature of the seeing; and that to the primitive consciousness a portrait is not a distinct thing related to its original by similarity, but actually participates in its nature, properties, and life. The unwillingness to have the chieftains' picture taken was shared equally by all the tribe; for by virtue of the same law of participation the tribe's welfare and very existence depend upon the condition of its chieftains, living or dead. The chieftains merge ontologically with their portrait on the one hand and with their human subjects on the other: in mythopoeic perspective there are no clear-cut atoms of existence. Things flow, in varying degrees and according to the emotional character of each occasion, into other things. Participation implies a partial but thoroughly real identity, a transcendence of either-or, an ontological tangency by which things empirically distinct blend into oneness.

Sociologists have usefully popularized the Melanesian word *mana* to denote the mysterious and potent vital force which primitive man accepts as present to different degrees in all things. But the sociological interpretation makes mana something purely fictional—"mythical" rather than "mythic"—representing a mistaken belief about the nature of things, which produces the pseudo-utilitarian form of behavior which is magic. But if with a patient effort of empathetic imagination we are willing to think ourselves into the primitive milieu, we must renounce, at least temporarily, our all too smug assurance of knowing where fact leaves off and fiction begins. The effort must be one of intellectual hospitality, a willingness to explore the hypothesis that mana may be not just a fanciful (i.e., "mythical") superstition of ignorant primitives, but something absolutely primal, which (paraphrasing J. S. Mill) I may define functionally as *the permanent possibility of genuinely mythic experience*. It is as open today as ever before; but only to those with the knack of "becoming as little children"; and the childlike perspective suffers doubly from dispersion by the engines of technological living and from ridicule by the snobbery of sophisticated thinking. Mana is a borderland idea, whose mode of existence lies between the personal and impersonal, between the natural and supernatural, and between the subjective and objective. That is not to say, of course, that primitive man first thinks these antitheses and then compromises between them, but simply that he does *not* make the distinctions which appear logically and experientially axiomatic to us moderns. By virtue of the last of the three borderland characteristics that I have mentioned, i.e., its undifferentiated hovering between subjective and objective actuality (if such philosophical language is not indeed grossly inappropriate to so primitive a situation), mana is at once the agency and the expression (I do not see how the paradox can be avoided) of man's participation in living nature.

Vital force communicates itself—that is to say, the law of participation, or of natural sympathy, is at work—in three principal ways. Frazer discusses two of them, similarity and previous contact, but he overlooks, or at least does not explicitly classify, a third: the power of complementaries. Daily experience testifies that we are not only stirred by similars, we can be challenged by contraries. Mozart wrote some of his gayest melodies when suffering from penury, illness, and depression; and it is said that Wagner was in a more cheerful mood when he wrote *Tristan* than when he composed his one comedy, *Die Meistersinger*. The human tendency to be moved by opposition is not merely behavioral; it enters deeply into the human epistemic, which is to say, it is constitutive of man's basic ways of envisaging reality.

Now this tendency toward association by complementaries, or opposites, throws light upon a pervasive element in man's primal relationship with nature. The element of participation and sympathy, of kinship between society and nature, is not the whole story. It is complemented by a lurking sense of nature's otherness, strangeness, and lurking hostility. The typically primitive attitude toward nature is largely a tension between familiarity and watchfulness. The former gives stability and confidence, a feeling of membership, of at-homeness, of being comfortably rooted in Mother Earth. The security of the cave, of the family, and subconsciously perhaps of the womb, supplies the primordial ground-plan of human living. Familiar localities, persons, objects, and events confirm the basic sense of belonging; as do the patterned festivities of seasonal and tribal occurrence. But the familiar is not all of life, and to bask in it exclusively is to approach the condition of vegetable. Man encounters also, and develops a readiness to encounter, the strange; and this readiness in turn has a double aspect. For the strange can alarm and it can fascinate: it is likely to do both at once, and the two emotions in combination—terror subdued by wonder—produces awe. Where the effect is more intriguing than frightening, men see fetishes in pebbles, spirits in rocks and rivers, totem-brothers in beasts, and gods in the sun and mountain-tops. Where the note of alarm predominates, and where it is not definite enough to arouse the self-preservative instincts by suggesting particular measures of defense—the unguessable menace of hurricane and earthquake, of black night and bottomless pool, of the snake's beady stare and the tiger's sinewy power—in such cases man's imaginative awareness falls into a primal terror of the strange as such, i.e., of the Wholly Other.

The primordial awe and sometimes dread of nature in its guise of the Wholly Other, which a highly intellectualized version of the world allows a majority of contemporary men to escape or ignore, is at the very heart of the primitive world-view. The tension which it creates in the primitive psyche, and less consciously but still effectively in the psyche of everyone, demands release. There are uncontrolled forms of release, such as hysteria, trances, and running amok: disturbances which it is the business of the medicine man, the shaman, to cure—perhaps by some transference of mana, perhaps by exorcism of the evil spirit causing the disturbance. But far more significant is the substitution of tribally shared rhythms for individual anarchic ones.

Effective defense against alien reality is communal; only where there is vigorous imaginative independence combined with tough moral courage can it be individual. Submersion in tribal ways of thinking, feeling, speaking and doing have always been man's handiest remedy for cosmic loneliness and terror of the dark unknown.

Even today communal response tends to involve an element of "throbbing together" —whether to the same journalistic clichés or to the same juke-box syncopations. In primitive society the collective throbbing is more deliberately stylized, and man's instinctive defense against the Wholly Other finds embodiment in ceremonial. Because the throbbing together of primitive ceremonial represents not only an experiential togetherness of man with man but also of man taken collectively with his world, and because Praxis and Theoria, the way of doing and the way of envisaging, are inextricable at bottom and mutually interacting, the primitive world has for its primitive observer a more strongly rhythmic time-character than our world has for us. Time, in modern perspective, splits into subjective and objective—into the freely flowing *durée* of private reverie and the postulated uniform time by which we set our watches and mark our calendars. Utilitarian necessities dichotomize it. Moreover, our public and measurable time, as Bergson has demonstrated, is inescapably space-oriented—the more so in proportion as it is conceived with scientific rigor. Whatever surrealist realignments and combinations of the space and time categories may be found in post-Einsteinian physics, the unassailable evidence of the Instrument proves that space and not time is the ultimate fulcrum of physico-scientific reference. For even the time-hypotheses of physics are tested by "readings" on some kind of chronometer, and the readings are visual—which is to say, what they immediately report are discriminations of space, which can be seen, and not of time, which cannot. The primitive, by contrast, assigns equal ontologic reality to time as experienced—in the succession of day and night and the cycle of the seasons, in the progress from childhood to maturity and from maturity to old age and death, and in the tribal calendar of ceremonies appropriate to planting, reaping, feasting, war, the hunt, adolescent initiation, marriage, sacrifice, and the like. Nature, in mythopoeic perspective, is cyclical; it exhibits vitally periodic, as opposed to mechanically regulated, becoming.

Mythopoeic periodicity is more richly qualitative than the periodicities recognized by the scientizing mind of today. It takes many forms, of which anthropologists have sometimes singled out one or another for special attention. In my review in the Spring [1951] issue of [the *Sewanee Review*] I outlined Theodor Gaster's theory of the four phases of seasonal ritual, and of the importance of seasonal ritual as the matrix of drama. His analysis is highly pertinent, and neither anthropologists nor dramatologists can afford to ignore it. Nevertheless there is, I judge, a more general character of primitive ritual, of which the drama of the death and rebirth of the vegetation god is a particular though very basic exemplification. That character, in the theory of the anthropologist Arnold van Gennep, is the total experience, in which man and nature harmoniously join, of *transition*. (Van Gennep uses the French word *passage*.) Every change of human condition—birth, puberty, initiation, betrothal, marriage, pregnancy, paternity, specialization of occupation, death—is mythopoeically regarded as a passage from a state of self that is dying to a state of self newly born. Such events do not merely happen to an individual on the outside, they change the very thing he *is*. Again and again primitive literature draws an analogy between an individual's passage from state to state and a worm's metamorphosis into a moth. In the world of physical nature, too, there are demarcations and periods of passage—steps forward and relatively static periods of suspension. Moreover, such alternations of movement and rest as there may be are accentuated and dramatized by ritual so that mythopoeically they stand out as fundamental characteristics of the primitive world—as happens particularly in the ceremonies of the full moon celebrating the passage from month to month, in those of the solstices and equinoxes celebrating the passage from season to season, as well as in vegetation ceremonies, which are frequently timed according to astronomical phenomena. Primitive ceremonies of human transition have a tendency to blend with those pertaining to cosmic transition: another working of the "law of participation." Consequently it is often impossible to say, without falsifying the situation, whether a given ceremonial pertains to a change in human state or to a recurrent change in nature, just as it is often impossible to say how far it is magical and how far celebrative. Here again the logical "either-or" cannot be pressed too far.

Instead of Gaster's four, van Gennep distinguishes three stages in the typical "ceremonies of transition" (*rites de passage*): the rites of separation, those of "the margin" when the celebrant finds himself in the darkness and anonymity of "between two worlds," and those of attainment. Here, for instance, is the probable sequence of rites of initiation at ancient Eleusis, which van Gennep bases largely upon the Eleusinian researches of Foucart:

1. The candidates and the hierophant are separated by a taboo from those who have impure hands and who talk in an unintelligible manner—i.e., unintelligible by the standards of the new light of wisdom that is to be won.

2. The neophytes are introduced into the Eleusinion, but before penetrating the enclosure (*l'enceinte*) they must purify themselves with a vase of holy water placed next to the door.

3. The neophytes are led to the shore of the sea, wherein, accompanied by Demeter's sacred animal the pig, they take a ritual bath, to be washed clean of their earlier "profane" and impure life.

4. They return to Eleusis in a holy procession, carrying the Bacchus figure and other sacred objects to various places of agrarian worship en route.

5. Re-entering into the enclosure of the Eleusinion they undergo the ceremony of initiation, which, although not known to us in full detail, appears to have included at least the following steps: traveling across a hall divided into dark compartments representing the regions of Hades; climbing a stair; entry into the great hall where the *sacra* (among which the sacred ear of corn had prominence) were exhibited; a representation of the abduction of Kore (both in her general aspect of untarnished maidenhood and in her particular aspect as Persephone, whose mother the grain goddess Demeter was the patron deity of Eleusis).

6. Finally there were dances, processions, and other ceremonial forms of rejoicing.

Although I have slightly simplified van Gennep's account, I have kept the order of events as he gives it, and his interpretation of the testimony of ancient writers appears to be sound. Evidently the first three stages represent rites of separation, probably the fourth and certainly the fifth are rites of the margin, and the sixth comprises rites of attainment. But a different light is thrown upon the relationship when Gaster's categories are substituted: Stage 1 then represents Mortification, Stages 2 and 3 Purification, Stages 4 and 5 presumably Reinvigoration, and Stage 6 Jubilation.

Some of the ceremonies at Eleusis—the washing, wandering in the dark, climbing the stair, and processional rejoicing—are found in different religions all over the world. The ritual display of a sacred animal and a sacred fruit of the earth are universal in general character and intent, although local conditions and traditions dictate what specific objects shall be used. But why the rape of Persephone? It is not enough to reply that Persephone was the daughter of Demeter and that Demeter was the goddess chiefly worshipped in the Eleusinian mysteries. Such an explanation makes the dubious assumption that the myth preceded the ritual, and does not explain how the myth itself arose. The real answer must be sought in the meaning of the archetype of the *Kore* (Divine Maiden) and of the myth of Persephone's rape. Let it be recalled that in the well-known myth the rape was followed by a famine, caused by Demeter's maternal grief which, by magical "participation," discouraged all crops from growing; but that by virtue of Demeter's descent into Hades an arrangement was effected with Dis, lord of the underworld, whereby Persephone could sojourn on the upper earth during certain months of the year, in which months thereafter growth could be restored. Of course the etiological aspect of the myth is clear and has often been re-marked: as explaining allegorically why the earth is fruitful during some months and barren during others. That aspect is too unmistakable to be denied, but it is hardly the entire story. If it comprised the total meaning, any other incident provoking Demeter's grief or petulance might have served equally well. But why specifically a rape? Evidently because rape symbolizes one of the most important and emotionally arresting "passages" in human experience—the passage from the pure state of virginity through the shock of violation and attaining to the happy issue of periodic motherhood. Demeter's descent into Hades connects symbolically the rape archetype with the even more universal archetype of death and life in alternation.* * *

I have intended in these notes to bring together scattered data which might assist in an understanding of the mythopoeic outlook. The study of the mythos can contribute to the problems of literature—I mean its *Urprobleme*—in two ways. The interrelation of mythos with ritual (as Nietzsche and Gaster have shown) points to the development of dramatic structure, and can furnish a useful commentary on such basic dramaturgical analyses as Aristotle's *Poetics* and Francis Fergusson's *The Idea of a Theatre*. The other way, the study of how images and image-clusters function within a mythic context * * * leads to a study of metaphor and hence to the very heart of poetic meaning. But both the one and the other of those investigations reach far beyond the appointed limits of this propaedeutic essay.

Sewanee Review, LIX (1951), 574–591.

Richard Chase (1914–1962) contributed to myth studies in two ways. His Quest for Myth *(1949) explored a part of the intellectual background for the modern literary interest in myth; and his subsequent studies of Emily Dickinson, Melville, and Whitman showed ways in which myth criticism might be used. In "Notes on the Study of Myth"—which may be regarded as a companion piece to Mr. Wheelwright's preceding examination of the general relations between myth and literature—Mr. Chase concentrates on what he believes to be the nature of myth, its relation to certain other cultural expressions, its functions, and its proper interpretative uses in the modern world. Like Wheelwright and Campbell (pp. 59 ff. and pp. 15 ff.) he emphasizes the imaginative power and suasiveness shared by myth and literature, but he also strikes a cautionary note—like Kluckhohn (pp. 33 ff.) and Wallace W. Douglas (pp. 119 ff.) he is wary of the multiple and often contradictory modern senses of "myth." This problem and others related to it ultimately led Mr. Chase to disavow myth criticism in* The American Novel and Its Tradition *(1957), his last book.*

NOTES ON THE STUDY OF MYTH

Richard Chase

For twenty years or more there has been a general feeling that creative literature should be brought closer to myth. The resources of naturalism, aestheticism and symbolism have come to seem insufficient for modern literature, and these disciplines have been superseded, or at least modified, by the search for myth. I say "the search for myth" because the new mythological literature—the work of Eliot, Yeats, Mann, Joyce, Toynbee, Freud and others—has been able to make only a few tentative steps. I should like to say at the outset that I agree with the general opinion: our creative literature *should* be brought closer to myth.

In this short essay I do not intend to offer a theory of myth but only to suggest some restrictions on such a theory. These days the word "myth" is thrown about as cavalierly as is any word which the cultural climate envelops with glamor and charges with an emotional voltage. It is a powerful word, but not precise. Let me set down some of the more serious remarks about myth which I have encountered recently. In an essay on Mann and his use of myth (*Partisan Review*, V, June–July, 1938) and in a subsequent controversy with James Burnham, William Troy wrote that myth is "a mode of cognition," that "myth, like science, is at once a method and a body of ordered experience." We need a new myth, he wrote in effect, to replace the narrow and now harmful nineteenth century world-view of science and progress; especially as a method of criticizing and creating literature is myth far superior to science. In retrospect, Troy's account of myth seems gratifyingly sensitive, but it was excessively metaphysical. His loose phraseology allowed Burnham to leap in with the accusation that Troy, and Mann, were proposing that we "revert" to a primitive dogma or absolute world-view which would smother science. Burnham held that science was the best weapon with which to attack those basic dilemmas of modern culture posed by Mann himself. More recently Mark Schorer, in the *Kenyon Review* (Autumn,

1942) wrote that "a myth is a large controlling image . . . which gives philosophic meaning to the facts of ordinary life." Myth, he says, is the "indispensable substructure" of poetry, an opinion which I take it he shares with T. S. Eliot. Joseph Campbell, in his appendix to the recent edition of *Grimm's Fairy Tales*, supposes that myth is a system of metaphysics: it is a "revelation of transcendental mysteries"; it is "symbolic of the spiritual norm for Man the Microcosm." These are ideas which at least have the advantage of being as old as the Stoics, or older. Finally, the surrealist Jacques B. Brunius, writing in the Spring, 1945, *Partisan Review*, tells us that "the creation of a modern myth coincides with the problem of knowledge," and he contrasts the modern myth which he hopes to see created with the "myths" of "Egypto-Graeco-Roman paganism," Christianity and contemporary Statism. I do not propose to criticize these writers separately—they are all suggestive in varying degrees. But I do feel that one ought to object to the assumption they all explicitly or implicitly make: namely, *that myth is philosophy—that it is a system of metaphysical or symbolic thought, that it is a theology, a body of dogma, or a world-view, that it is in direct opposition to science, is indeed the other side of the scientific coin.* To make these assumptions, or any one of them, is to make of myth something it has never been; to make them is to commandeer the word "myth" and apply it to something for which there are more exact, though less fashionable words. To make them is to burden myth with a task it cannot by itself perform. If we persist in this interpretation we are bound for another huge disappointment: "myth" will become as empty a word as some of those for which we now substitute it. Our pretensions will have to be more modest, our conclusions more tentative if there is to be any pungency in our understanding and use of myth.

The fact is that the simplest meaning of the Greek word "myth" is the right one: *a myth is a story, myth is narrative or poetic literature.* It need be no more philosophic than any other kind of literature. Myth is therefore art and must be studied as such. Myth is a mode of cognition, a system of thought, a way of life, only as art is. It can be opposed to science only as art is opposed to science. There is no question of one defeating the other. They are complementary and fulfill different needs. The romantic fear that science may destroy myth betrays an acquiescence in the misinterpretation of myth which science sometimes gives us: namely, that it is frivolous or delicate nonsense. There are no eras in recorded history when science has banished myth: though there *are* eras when human thought in general has become superficial. When science is psychologically adequate, it can be shown to have much in common with myth. The best modern proof of this is Freud's reassertion of the natural validity of myth.[1]

1. Nothing could more palpably suggest the complementary functions myth and science may assume than the fact that Freud became a myth-maker and a profound student of myth *reluctantly*. His scientific temperament rebelled at every step; yet it forced him into the realm of myth. Jung, for whom mythology is a welcome escape from the rigors of science, is, compared with Freud, a vaporous and fruitless mythologist. (When I speak of Freud as a mythologist, I do not refer to the arbitrary collection of symbols which he erroneously supposed to be common to myths and dreams; I refer rather to his treatment of psychic forces and his reconstructions of the tensions, displacements, and conceptualizations which make images in both myths and dreams.)

The definition of myth as art will be disappointing only to those who refuse to grant art a primary function and efficacy in human thought but must always make it dependent on something else—theological dogma, religion, the State, economics, science. Myth is not the "indispensable substructure" of poetry. Poetry is the indispensable substructure of myth. Myth is a less inclusive category than poetry. Poetry *becomes* myth when it performs a certain function, an idea which Vico entertained and one which, as I shall at least hint, is abundantly affirmed by modern anthropology.

The Relevance of Primitive Myth. We often confuse myth with those hypostatized versions of myth which have come down to us in European literature, "mummified in priestly wisdom," says Malinowski, and "enshrined in the indestructible but lifeless repository of dead religions." We have thus gained the impression that myth is more systematic, less naïve and functional than it is. Those writers who tell us that myth is a system of recondite symbols, that it is a pseudo-scientific explanation of nature or that it describes the sun and the moon, reaffirm this impression. We must study myth as it works in primitive society, before it is overlaid with interpretation.

In primitive culture myth is a relatively clearly definable activity instead of being diffused and obscured by other activities as it is in our culture. Nevertheless we usually overestimate the difference between primitive culture and our own. It is perhaps trite to observe that we are more like primitive men than we once thought, but not so trite to observe that primitive men are more like *us* than we once thought. Only one specific point can be made here: The idea of a primitive "mythopoeic age" in which all thought was mystic or symbolic and in which all literature was equally and completely mythical must be abandoned. All the primitive peoples who have been studied by anthropologists have treated a part of their experience matter-of-factly, just as we do. Primitive thought is in some ways *more* mythical than civilized thought. But the psychoanalyst's analogy with the development of the individual does not hold. We do not simply "revert" to an outgrown stage of fantasy by trying to make our literature more mythical. This is also a problem of maturity, of living better in the present, and of going on to the future. All cultures are capable of making myth. We study primitive culture because it clarifies certain psychological processes of concentration and revivification upon which depends our proceeding into the future.

Vico tells us that he thought of myth as a clear, deep river which in modern times flows into the ocean but retains its purity for a certain distance before being swallowed up. We should rather think of myth as a river which flows eternally; sometimes it is clear and deep but sometimes it becomes shallow and muddy by having to flow over broad flatlands.

Myth and Religion. If we mean by "religion" the whole magico-religious complex of primitive culture then myth is indeed closely allied with religion. If on the other hand we mean moral theism or dogmatic theology, or even a pantheon of gods, myth must be recognized as the enemy of religion. The clear-cut, powerful god, the celestial abstraction, the theological synthesis have always been subverted by the humanizing leaven of myth. The gods of myth, as Herbert Spencer observed, are always "running down from Olympus." The grandiose South Seas and Greek myths about the sky and the earth being separated by their divine sons are not religious philosophy—they are tales of men tearing their parents apart.

Myth and Magic. Myth is much more akin to the naïve assumptions and techniques of magic than to religion. Magic does not of itself imagine discrete spirits or deities, but only efficacious preternatural forces residing in objects, animals and men, which can be manipulated by human compulsion. Myth should be thought of as a dramatic picturization of magical forces as they clash, interact or harmonize with each other.

Myth and Folktale. The traditional idea that myths were primeval philosophies of nature and that the folktales of wonderful animals and birds, magical objects, lost children, young heroes, enchanted forests and so on were degenerate or misread popular versions of the myths was accepted down to the last years of the nineteenth century. The theory of evolution, on the other hand, led to the conclusion that myths had developed out of folktales in accordance with the general evolutionary process. The American anthropologists accept neither of these views. In the writings of Boas, for example, we learn that the folktale is a permanent and universal form of literature and that what are usually called myths are to be thought of as folktales which have been elaborated upon by specially gifted individuals. Several formal distinctions have been made between myth and folktale; but these distinctions are almost completely confounded by the literature of primitive peoples as it actually exists. Primitive literature should be thought of primarily as folktale; once this has been grasped we are in a position to observe that folktales have sometimes been remodeled by story-tellers of religious or philosophic temperament. By far the most useful definition of myth is one which cuts across formal distinctions and says, Myth is any kind of literature which functions in a certain way to the fulfilment of certain ends.

Some Functions of Myth. In what follows I shall try to do two things at once: show how literature becomes myth in primitive culture and suggest how our literature, especially our poetry, may become mythical. Obviously I shall have to leave several large questions unanswered. What I say is suggestion only.

Myth must always discover and accept preternatural forces; it must always re-affirm the efficacy of the preternatural and insulate it from the ordinary world. Here a note of definition: the word "supernatural" is often used in discussions of myth, sometimes with the necessary qualifications, oftener without. But there are at least two objections to "supernatural": it implies a philosophical distinction between two realms of being which are unknown to the myth-maker and it has certain misleading theological overtones. I therefore use the word "preternatural," by which I mean to indicate no more or less than is conveyed by the Melanesian word *mana*; whatever has impersonal magic force or potency and is therefore extraordinarily beautiful, terrible, dangerous, awful, wonderful, uncanny or marvelous has *mana* and is, in our sense of the word, preternatural. Myth shows us reality set afire with our own emotions. In this sense myths do not show us what is *less* than ordinarily natural; they show us what is *more* than ordinarily natural. This function may be regarded as a given fact which holds true of all myth and of much poetry. But not all literature which deals with the preternatural is myth.

Literature becomes mythical by suffusing the natural with preternatural force toward certain ends, by capturing the impersonal forces of the world and directing them toward the fulfilment of certain emotional needs. Within this broad definition, we may notice three functions of myth.

1. In his *Myth in Primitive Psychology* Malinowski discusses especially those serious primitive tales which include statements about the origin of man or which comment on his rituals and social institutions. These commonly invoke what the savage conceives as a primeval period of the world. This was a time of wonderful magic; it is a special projection into the past of the preternatural forces which in other stories (particularly those usually labelled folktales) are represented as ever present and capable of effective interference in the life of man. The serious myth, says Malinowski, is "a narrative resurrection of a primeval reality." This primeval reality is for the moment more relevant to human problems than the reality of the ordinary world; and the myths are told in order to preserve the meaningfulness and purposefulness of social customs and institutions. They "come into play when rite, ceremony, or a social or moral rule demands justification, warrant of antiquity, reality, and sanctity." There can be no doubt that these myths sometimes have the efficacy of dogma. But unlike dogma they are plastic and dynamic. They look to the present and the future. As Malinowski says, they are made *ad hoc* and are "constantly regenerated." No one deduces a way of life from the myths; they are not a canon of behavior or thought. The way of life is given; the myths are life grown literary.

The myths discussed by Malinowski, however, have mostly social and moral functions. Myths, both serious and playful, have a more purely psychological function.

2. Our culture provides innumerable substitutes for what William James called "the pungent sense of effective reality," the sense of "the possibilities of nature." Much of primitive man's life—like much of ours—is spent in apathy and routine; yet primitive man is capable of a precise and dynamic attention which we can equal only with great difficulty. Primitive culture, writes Goldenweiser, is "dynamic and vibrant"; it has to be, like any other organism for which survival is a perpetual ordeal. Our society allows us to let the world run down, grow cold and inoperative, without exposing ourselves to danger. But to primitive man a vibrant sense of present reality is vitally necessary. Paul Radin shows in his *Primitive Man as Philosopher* that to the savage reality is pragmatic. The world is not a museum of objects or a textbook of science; it is a theater of dynamic activities, of richly mysterious powers, of ends accomplished by forces analogous to human emotions and subject to partial control by magic compulsion. To most savages, gods and spirits exist only in an end accomplished; the spirits become brightly real or fade into impersonality as a desired effect is more or less successfully brought about. The world becomes vibrant in an end accomplished: as Radin says, the savage's world then becomes "a blaze of reality."

The idea of discrete spirits inhabiting and motivating objects is not primary as E. B. Tylor and Herbert Spencer thought; it is secondary and does not take into account the universal practice of magic. To the savage, *mana* or preternatural power is impersonal; he apprehends it as an immediate quality of things, just as color, sound, size, shape and motion are immediate qualities. As the savage envelops the world in his own emotions, things assume dramatic qualities: they are, in the words of Dewey, "poignant, tragic, beautiful, humorous, settled, disturbed, comfortable, annoying, barren, harsh, consoling, splendid, fearful; are such immediately and in their own right and behalf." Magic, and all the benefits it is supposed to bring, depends upon this fusion of power, quality and object: without it "things fall apart"; the world becomes chaotic and dangerous when it can no longer be enveloped in the tissue of human emotion. When objects and qualities become efficacious by being fused with power, they are subject to the compulsive techniques of magic. Besides being a compulsive technique—a pseudo-science as Frazer says—magic is obviously an aesthetic activity. Magic is immediately available to art, and art to magic. Primitive literature is shot through with magic and we may regard it as mythical when it fortifies the magical view of things, when it reaffirms the vibrant dynamism of the world, when it fortifies the ego with the impression that there is a magically potent brilliancy in the world. Myth is not vaporous, abstract, or unreal; it is a "blaze of reality."

3. Like other kinds of literature, myth performs the cathartic function of dramatizing the clashes and harmonies of life in a social and natural environment. But myth can be understood as the aesthetic leaven which heals or makes tolerable those deep neurotic disturbances which in primitive culture are occasioned by the clashing attitudes of magic and religion. This collision of forces, as Radin points out in his *Primitive Religion*, is partly the result of the priest's struggle to achieve a dominant economic position. Coincident with his war upon the people is his war against magic. For magic is the prerogative of mankind in general; it exalts human power; it places the world and the gods at the disposal of mankind. The priest's task is to transmute magic into religion, to overcome the subjectivism on which magic depends, to present spirits and gods as clearly conceived objective beings, to transfer magical power to the gods and make men obeisant before them. Mythology is full of the tensions created by this universal struggle, and many myths may be said to array the propaganda of men, animals, and magical beings against the propaganda of the gods. But art is constructive where life is destructive. Myth keeps the dilemma operative and resolves the contesting forces into useful experience.

Stated in somewhat abstract terms, magic, as Radin says, is the coercion of the objective world by the ego; religion is the coercion of the ego by the objective world, or by the powers and beings in the objective world. Now I suggest that when literature brings these opposing forces together so that they interact coercively toward a common end, literature has become mythical. This interpretation of myth, as it seems to me, is less immediately valuable to us than are the two interpretations I have offered above; it requires more thorough translation before it can be applied to our own problems. Yet the war between magic and religion still goes on, though sometimes under different names. Certain terms in which this "cathartic function" of myth might be restated will doubtless occur to any student of Freud.

Myths and Paramyths. I am aware that what has been said here cannot fully elucidate those processes of amalgamation by which the symbols, images, concepts and personified beings of myth are made—though a complete elaboration of what I have said would lead us a long way in that direction.

I am aware too that no complete account of myth can be undertaken without wider references to human needs and aspirations than those I have chosen here. The method of pragmatic naturalism seems to me the only fruitful method of studying myth—yet that method leaves us, as it often does, with the feeling that we have made art too resolutely functional, too outward looking, too optimistic. Psychoanalysis may be misleading as psychology, but "the pleasure principle" and the desperate "instincts" of sex and death give myth a dramatic richness unknown to contemporary pragmatism, or at least not yet assimilated by it.

I do not mean, either, to reduce the latitude of reinterpretation unduly. Those ever recurring writers who find the study of primitive thought somehow degrading or irrelevant are right at least when they say that the tales of the folk are often vague, dull or childish. We must be free, as was the primitive intellectual (who may be studied in Radin's *Primitive Man as Philosopher*), so to interpret a myth that it comes alive for us in the moral and intellectual context of our culture—as we have in our time interpreted the myths of Oedipus, Joseph and Philoctetes. This may require symbolism or allegory, certainly conscious intelligence. But we cannot assume a symbol, an allegory or a concept to be the same as the myth itself, or to be the only interpretation of the myth. Apart from the dictates of parochial cultural necessity, there remain constant human needs against which we must measure the adequacy of our interpretations.

Myth has often been philosophical, frequently in advanced cultures, less frequently in primitive cultures. We should not care, for example, to ignore the philosophical aspects of the Oedipus, Joseph or Philoctetes myths or of the myths which we find in the poems of Eliot or Yeats. These myths offer us patterns of feeling and thought. But we are likely to find in them not philosophy but (as Eliot says) the "emotional equivalent" of philosophy. We may be sure at least that the myth is never philosophical without being something else. Myth is, in the phrase of Renan, "simultaneous humanity."

And we have to remember that all myths begin with the apprehension of some marvelous activity or potentiality. Magic and literature meet in myth. An unusual stone, a strange animal, a witch doctor have *mana* for the savage just as do Oedipus for Sophocles or Freud, Joseph for Mann, the "great tomb-haunter" for Yeats, or Mme Sosostris for Eliot. Those concepts, allegories, symbols and theologies which are loosely called mythical are so only so long as they are still faithful to the emotional complexity of literature; for only literature can perform the mythical function of preserving and giving significance to the sensation of *mana*. Once disinherited from their literary matrix concepts are not, properly speaking, myths. I propose (following Herder) disinherited "mythical ideas" called *paramyths*.

Poetry as Myth. A myth is not "a large controlling image." The future of mythical poetry does not depend upon reconciling poetry with an image. It depends rather upon making of poetry something it is always striving against human bias and superficiality to become. The poetical imagination when it attains any consistent fire and efficacy is always displacing the texture of the mind into the external world so that it becomes a theater of preternatural forces. A certain control and direction given the poetical emotions, and poetry, as it always has, becomes mythical.

Partisan Review, XIII (1946), 338–346.

The three remaining essays in this group are concerned with specific literary or critical adaptations of myth to literature: thus in the essay immediately following, Harold H. Watts centers his discussion on the drama, while the next two consider respectively criticism and the creative process itself.

Among the topics introduced by Mr. Watts, the most important is his discovery of a general analogy between tragedy and comedy and certain kinds of religious myth. His remarks on the relation of genre to myth open up a subject that is treated more concretely by Herbert Weisinger (pp. 149 ff.) and Louis Crompton (pp. 289 ff.) in essays on Shake-speare and Hardy.

MYTH AND DRAMA

Harold H. Watts

IV

Let us, as lovers of drama or as esteemers of the *effects* of drama, seek to be instructed by the two uses of myth that we can observe in developed religions. For in these two uses are both the roots of comedy and tragedy and the rationale of their persisting appeal.

If religion has any distinguishing mark, it is this: it is an all-over assertion about the existence in which man is involved. (Magic is no such all-over assertion. It is not so much science before science as pragmatics before pragmatics.) Logically, one would expect that there would be, in religion, only one all-over assertion. But logic is a minor though not utterly absent element in religion and in drama; whatever their differences, both religion and drama must be faithful to existence first and only secondarily faithful to a pursuit of order. Thus, from the point of view of logic, a religious state-ment about the complete nature of reality, a statement made in terms of myth and cherished by cult, "ought" to make other statements of a similar nature impossible of assertion. Logic would suggest this question: if existence "at its heart" is thus and so, is it likely that the very same existence is "at its heart" something quite different? Yet developed religions make two such assertions, not one—assertions logically opposed to each other and cancelling.

One must, however, insist that religion does not proliferate uselessly contradictory statements about what is the total existence (its nature, its place for man) which we experience. But most developed religions find place for the following two (and con-tradictory) statements about existence. Logic would cancel one or the other, and we indeed find that systematizers of religion and secular systematizers of insights that have a religious origin if not at present a religious context struggle to cancel one of the two all-over statements as false or as an obscure form of the other statement. But these efforts overlook this truth: that both religion and drama are primarily records of man existing rather than of man trying to put his existence into comprehensible order. Religion and drama share this function; they enable man to *endure* existing, whereas

75

philosophy and (in an often delusive way) science offer man the prospect of *comprehending* existence. Religion and drama are not interchangeable, despite certain present hopes. But one of the signs that they address themselves to the same task is that both are involved in advancing, at the same time, contradictory assertions about man and his existence. (That is, portions of a religious ritual make assertions that later portions cancel, logically. Comedy makes assertions about existence which tragedy always casts doubt on.)

Religion rests on a narrative. From the narrative may be drawn doctrines exceedingly abstract and indeed opposed to an esteem for narrative, for time-contained event, as the primary means of revelation (e.g., Buddhism). But what religion latterly becomes (and not all developed religions become the same thing) is not our interest here. Our interest must concern itself with how religion "began"—at least, "began" when it reached a point at which it supplemented its direct perceptions of numen—the wonderful, the pervasively compulsive—with narrative. The contrast between Greek religion, which richly supplemented its perceptions of the numinous with narrative and Latin religion which simply preserved, for several historical centuries, the perception of numen suggests that man did—at some unrecorded time in some civilizations— build into the structure of religion key-narratives that came to bear the great weight of religious superstructure—the weight of cult, rite, and dogma.

What were the two uses to which narrative was put at this point in the growth of religion—a point early, real, but mostly unrecoverable? They are sharply contrasting uses. They are uses that record two logically opposed insights which man came to have about his position in the world. Both insights are valid and real; they may be incompatible with each other, but they are not, by that circumstance, either to be disregarded or discredited. Man created and used mythological narrative for these two purposes: he asserted that existence, in its root organization, was *cyclic*; he asserted that existence—and this was an unconscious criticism of his cyclic assertion— was not what he had at first thought it but was, instead, *linear*.

We shall presently define and distinguish these two assertions. Let us grant at once the logical contradiction—indeed, to many, the puerility—involved in entertaining these two assertions simultaneously. It is plain that once the opposition between these two assertions is clearly perceived, many persons will judge that they have one more reason to dismiss the authority of religious experience. One may concede that such persons move in intellectual regions that are less demanding on the sympathetic imagination—regions that have their own sort of profit. But such persons are cut off from the profit that is the gift to man of religion and myth, and they are also in a poor position to measure the conflicting endowments, to man, of tragedy and comedy. These persons are not likely to see the significance of the likewise perplexing fact that tragedy and comedy are also logical incompatibles that coexist and that are intimately related in ways that vex and elude. Both tragedy and comedy are representations of experience; both mediate comprehension of experience. Are these two acts of comprehension so opposed to each other as to coexist only senselessly, as do random acts? Or do they have a supplementing function as they present their opposed visions of the universe? One form gives us the universe as a place suffused with laughter (*sustained* by laughter, we shall see); the other gives us the universe as a place falling in pieces, all props awry, "all coherence gone." Tragedy and comedy—the preliminary answer must be—constitute an uneasy unity: drama. But their coexistence *is* a unity and not an accident, not "random" coexistence, as above. And we can best understand the supplementary functions of these humanly contrived narratives—narratives that constantly vary on the surface—by seeking the analogy that links them with the two *uses* of myth that we discover in many developed religions.

As noted, what we present is an analogy only. Yet it is an analogy that (I believe) puts our ideas about comedy and tragedy in better order. Yet it is an analogy valid at only one point; it concerns only the two contrasting *uses* to which myth is put in religion and the two contrasting trains of reaction, of sensibility and induced comment, which the two forms of drama can stir in men. To make no mystery: comedy has its religious analogue in the *cyclic* assertions that myth enables religion to make, and tragedy finds its analogue in the non-cyclic, *linear* assertions that myth sometimes supports. I would deny utterly the truth or usefulness of the analogy were it pushed beyond this point—were it argued that the myth that "asserts cycle" is comic *in substance* and the myth that asserts the linear perception tragic in substance. There is no comedy-tragedy contrast by which one can divide the abundance of myth. The *story* of Osiris and the *story* of Jesus—it has often been observed—resemble each other. Certainly the story of Osiris, a story that is the vehicle of a cyclic assertion, is not comic; it is quite as grim as the story of Jesus which, I judge, mediates a linear assertion. The story of Osiris "happened" to be "captured" by a religion which, at a particular time, needed to "assert cycle"; and the story of Jesus happened to be put to use as a narrative support to a linear, non-cyclic insight about existence. (The bulk of myth—of narrative that exists and functions to some degree in a religious context—asserts cycle. But the normal is not a binding norm; there is nothing abnormal about a story that a religion uses to express a linear insight about man's life. To my mind, the story of the "white god" Quetzalcoatl—the god who abandons his people *once* and promises a single return—asserts the linear almost as forcefully as does the narrative about Jesus.)

Deeper in drama, then—if the analogy I am drawing has real power to cast light—than the contrast between the laughable and the "weepable" is this one: comedy is a representation of life that asserts cycle (as does the bulk of myth), and tragedy is that representation of life that asserts the linear, the non-cyclic. The laughter that, rightly, we associate with comedy is important but surface testimony to the fact that we have cause to rejoice when we contemplate the totality of existence as cycle; the tears that we shed for tragedy, the qualm that tragedy is said to stir, is a natural by-product of the perception that total existence is not cyclic at all—at least, not cyclic when it concerns us most intimately.

Comedy and tragedy, then, are secular purveyors—I mean no disrespect by the word—of two all-over assertions about the root-nature of existence as man must experience it. (In *one* of these two ways he must experience it; he has no further choice.) The *materials* of comedy and tragedy do often differ much more than do the narrative materials that constitute the two sorts of myth. But, as often observed, what really distinguishes comedy from tragedy is the treatment accorded the materials that come to hand. It would not be impossible to alter *Oedipus Rex* into a knock-about farce, nor would it be difficult to transform Malvolio into a figure of devastating import, particularly were one writing a naturalistic or sociological tragedy. The imperfect religious analogue to all this is what we have already noted: that the narrative that becomes myth does not automatically proclaim whether it will be cyclic or linear; *that* is determined by the kind of existence it takes on in a specific religious context.

V

What are the distinguishing marks of these two all-over assertions, the cyclic and the linear?

Let us begin their precise definition thus. When we say that myth asserts two all-over insights into existence, we are concerned with existence collectively perceived and *not* discriminated. "Early man" had many of the powers of discriminatory judgment that we have; that is, he could look sensibly at *portions* of existence. Aspects of his arts, the bulk of his "civil law," and the conduct of his economy are sufficient records of this. But he—no more than can we—could not escape making a collective or all-over assertion about the world in which he was immersed. Nor is the "advance of human thought"—as modern drama, for one, obliquely testifies—from collective assertions to assertions that are more modest, more discriminated. Indeed, without a collective assertion of some kind, discrimination itself ceases; and this is just as true in a secular context as in a religious one. What we regard as the "advance of human thought" is simply a substitution of a later and more logically defensible collective assertion for an earlier one. The later assertion may be more valid, more soundly based. But that is not the point here. What we must perceive is that our "advance" has not freed our thought from the task of making total assertions not completely unlike the early religious cyclic and linear assertions.

Respect for them established, one may attempt a genetic explanation of the two mythological assertions that (I believe) casts great light on the way tragedy and comedy still function for us. A genetic explanation is not exhaustive; and, in this instance, it involves this bold hypothesis: that we can reproduce the intellectual and emotional growth of early man. What we say firmly on such a topic, we should also say modestly. But we need not abandon the effort; it is no more bold than the genetic efforts of literary scholars who speak of the formative attention of "Shakespeare's audience"—it is no more risky than the discourses on medieval piety that "explain" certain beautiful tensions at Chartres.

Man was first aware—and to this ancient scriptures are witness—of that which bore in on him from outside. He was aware of the great forces of nature as he saw them in wind and wave and weather; he was aware of his terrible dependence on the fertility of grass-land and arable field. And he was just as deeply impressed by the social forces that weighed on him: his family, his tribe, his tribal enemies. To assume as early man did that these outside forces—nature and the collective groups—made up each man's existence is to assume truly; it is also to assume incompletely, as religion after religion discovered at some point in its course.

Yet this incomplete assumption—that man's existence is composed of the awful natural and social forces that toss man about—"created" as its corollary an assertion made in terms of myth rather than, as here, in terms of abstract concept. Man employed myth for this reason: man must be more than the victim of the forces that are outside him; he must be their *imaginative* master. It is not enough to discriminate these external forces and come to a competent control of *some* of them. The nascent arts of agriculture did not free man from the need of myths about the forces of growth; the early and perhaps relatively satisfactory codes of law did not obviate the preservation of myths about the "origin" of law; and successful magic and medicine was never a threat to the inclusive assertions of religion. In short, all the practical control and knowledge of what bore in on man had to be supplemented by assertions that provided man *imaginative* all-over control. This control was provided by myths that, whatever their variety, were put to one task, the task of asserting cycle; they were man's warrant over and above his own observation for the recurrence of season and crop and for the persistence (despite the aging of all men and the death of leaders) of a given and experienced social form. It was myth and rite that could assure men that what man could not control was, in the long run, as much to be depended on as what he could control; natural and social phenomena would be exactly what man already knew them to be. Nature and society, myth testified, would always come full circle, would offer apprehensive man familiarity and not novelty. Man used, for example, the myth of Osiris to give himself this cyclic assurance. Osiris, we know, dies not once but many times; his scattered members are gathered by Isis in a basket again and again—in fact, year after year, so long as the society that uses the myth of Osiris persists. Mr. Joseph Campbell, in *The Hero with a Thousand Faces*, has revealed to us the impressive and yet monotonous use to which certain narrative materials were once put; the "thousand faces" are really the face of one hero. Beneath surface variety, the hero offers man the assurance of a *recurrent* salvation, of security in nature and in society that can never be really threatened by natural catastrophe or military invasion. The myth always repeats itself and is *cyclic*. If Osiris eternally dies and eternally is brought back to life, each man can feel secure: his plot of land will bear again, and the tribe or society to which he belongs will survive any temporary perils. Thanks to the myth, man is in calm imaginative control of what actually is beyond his just-nascent science and his non-existent sociology.

Is Christ Osiris? Is he too a vegetation god, a supporter of cycle? Not to those who cherished his story. Yet the bold outlines of his story are similar to the Osiris narrative; for this, some persons call him the last and most triumphant of the Asia Minor vegetation deities. On the basis of narrative materials, there is no utterly conclusive way of repudiating the similarity. But what one may deny—concerning Christ, concerning Quetzalcoatl as well—is that the Christ-story was put to the use the Osiris story was put to. A central Christian phrase refers to Christ as "our sacrifice once offered"; whatever the contradictory implications of certain Christian rituals, a sense that Christ did indeed die only once and rise only once remains at the heart of the Christian assertion and is opposed to the sense that lies at the heart of the Osiris mystery and similar mysteries.

Genetically speaking, what "begot" the Christian assertion? It was a second total perception of what existence was. After he had gained imaginative control of what lay outside him, man became aware of himself. He could express this awareness of himself only by uttering—with the aid of some myth—a total assertion that, logically but not actually, cancelled the cyclic assertion. (There are few developed religions in which the two assertions do not persist as peers.) When man turns to himself, he "knows" that what myth and cult have, to that point, told him either is not true or is very incompletely true. Nature and society are eternally dying and eternally reborn: let that stand. But man himself—man apart from the great processes that very nearly have him at their utter mercy—man is eternally dying and he never will be reborn.[1]

What is the second total assertion which the story of Christ, as well as other stories, implements? The assertion that man's existence is in time, historical. The assertion that to man *as man* (as opposed to man when he is plainly the creature of natural and social forces) the same event, the same choice, never comes round again. Man as man makes a choice among a series of events that follow each other in a non-repeating sequence; he has only one chance to make a certain choice since the time for a certain choice comes only once. As man, his experience is basically linear however much he may be, as an object, subject to the effects of natural and social cycle. As a cyclically oriented creature, man plants a crop at a certain time of the year and rethatches his house against the monsoons, and also prepares himself for the public fasts and the public rejoicings peculiar to his society. These come round again and again. But man comes to see that such preparations are not *all* his destiny or even a finally distinguishing part. He is, at the center of his nature, a creature of time, of *line*; and he and his forebears were, at the least, misled when they found the clue to human nature in what, in some sense, lay outside each separate man: in nature and the social group. The essential lies inside each man, in his experience of choice, of sequence; hence, the second total assertion, the one we have called the *linear* one.

The essential—we should observe when we watch *Hamlet* or *Oedipus* as well as when we savor the impact of the Christ-story—lies inside each man; it lies in man's experience of a horrid, sheerly linear necessity which no man, once he is aware of it, is ever able to evade. This is the necessity of choice; it is a necessity that gets no comforting "moral support" from the phases of the moon or the return of a season. Each human choice, at a certain time in a non-repetitive sequence of events, projects into future time only a certain portion of the past; each choice denies to the future significant developments of other portions of the past. This is human choice; it is also existence conceived in a linear fashion.

This all-over perception sought—and, of course, found—an august warrant. Not

1. It is beside the point to appeal to the developed dogma of Eastern religions which "work" this non-cyclic insight into the continuing assertion of cycle by elaborating theories of reincarnation and karma—and then absorb both the awareness of cycle and the "illusion" of linear existence into a superior awareness: nirvana. That these complex adjustments had to be made is at least testimony to the existence and power, over man's will, of the insights that we now reconstitute. The synthesis called Nirvana is a witness to the painful tension created by the coexistence, in religious life, of the two ancient assertions that concern us. And Nirvana, as a theory, does not concern us, for it casts little light on either comedy or tragedy.

just the Jesus-myth itself but the whole body of what used to be called "sacred history" constituted a widely embracing myth that detached itself from the bulk of ancient myth and its cyclic assertions. The bulk of story that we may call the Christian myth—as well as groups of story that have some resemblance to it—braced man for the assertion that is just as essential to his health as is the earlier assertion of cycle. The linear assertion is, I believe, a record of a later, a more subtle, and certainly a more intimate reading of man's position in the world since it sees that man as a person, an individual, has an "economy" for which there are very few clues and models outside man. Why was this insight comparatively late in coming? Because what was outside man first rushed in on human awareness promising inclusive instruction. (And the cyclic instruction is one that man has never been able to dispense with.) But insofar as man has discovered individuality and personality, he has involved himself in myths that limit if they do not cancel the assurances of cyclic legend. A god that dies only once "answers" to man's more subtle analysis of the conditions of human action (as opposed to the conditions of natural event to which man was first eager to assimilate human action). A god that dies only once, a god that does not enjoy the easy luxury of dying again and again, a god that traces the arc of choice only once—that god is a human god. His myth is a warrant for our most painful perceptions about what it is to be a human being rather than a tide that rushes up the shore or a society that persists even though its members unimportantly perish.

VI

The point of the analogy between cyclic and linear myth on the one hand and comedy and tragedy on the other now shapes up. Comedy, on a non-religious level, offers man the assurance that he can bank on the universe and its laws and, more importantly, on society and its structure. As does the myth that asserts cycle, comedy offers the individual the illusion that he exists and moves in a universe he can count on. This illusion, when it is effectively held, is a cause for rejoicing; it is a cause for *laughter*. It was in this sense that Dante wrote a *Comedy*; his poem was, at the last, an assurance of order—to be sure, an order of a complex kind. Even more ordinary comedy makes available to man some of the comforts that early man drew from religiously "asserting cycle." The comic narrative—in materials gulfs apart from the Osiris legend but in effect quite close to it—must, like *all* narratives, embody an upset, a threat to our sense of certainty. Farce or high comedy—the effect is the same. What is the archetypical plot? A shift of forces, a social realignment, threatens the security of the chief persons on the stage—threatens *our* security. Comedy, its appears, has its qualm as well as tragedy. But the qualm is allayed by a combination of strategies that dissociates comedy from tragedy. For it is soon clear that the threat is neither serious nor permanently effective. It is a trivial threat, no more, to the status quo—to what we would call in religious terms the continuance of cycle. And it is also soon clear that the persons involved are not full, real persons like ourselves. They are "comic"; in religious language, they have only that degree of reality that marks a cyclic interpretation of man's experience—they are not sufficiently alive to qualify or even shatter that view.

Since the characters in a comedy are incomplete, they easily loom before us as quasi-ritual figures who march through the events of the comic play as unconcernedly as did the King of Egypt when he performed his yearly role of Osiris in the New Year festivals.

What is all that comedy offers us? It is certainly not a contemptible "all." It is simply an "all" that is inferior to the "all" that tragedy offers us, just as the "all" of Egyptian religion is at once valid and yet distinctly inferior to the gifts of a religion that has strong linear marks. In fact, all that comedy offers us is *a sense of regain*. The comic "qualm"—the "situation," the misunderstanding, the threat to someone's security—threatens the status quo in a way that is sometimes playful and sometimes serious. But very few comedies leave us with anything but a sense that the status quo has been essentially reestablished. The happy ending reasserts the security of the important characters; much more important, their individual security amounts to a promise that well-known social forms will persist. The effect of cycle, put slightly in doubt, has, with the descent of the last curtain, been established more firmly than ever.

And as audience we have *regained* the security, personal and social, that the initial dramatic situation playfully threatened. We are, as characters, where we were at the commencement of the play, or where we deserved to be. The society to which we, as audience, imaginatively belong has been "established" more firmly than ever. In a popular farce, it is the most obvious sort of conventional standards which have been threatened by (say) adultery or sharp business practice and which are, in the last insincere minutes of the play, refounded; in a play of Shaw's like *Candida* it is the society of the Shavian elect. The differences are there, but they do not, in our connection, count. *Parlor, Bedroom, and Bath* and *Candida* function for their different audiences in exactly the same way. They mediate—in an obscure secular way, I admit—a counterpart of the cyclic religious assurance. They tell us that there is a secure, predictable, and even recurrent place provided for man in the universe. Further, they tell us that man can exercise imaginative control over this universe. The threats to this control—the situation that troubles Act I—always turn out to be delusive; and the comic drama always terminates with man more in imaginative command of his universe than before.

Not so tragedy. Tragedy, like the linear total assertion which it resembles, is no play for imaginative control of the world; it is a confession, sometimes noble and sometimes desponding, that man's "game"—the "game" utterly proper to him—lies somewhere else. It is a perception that, for man, imaginative control of the world that is distinctly external to him is beside the point. And when we regard comedy from the vantage-point of tragedy, we see that what it offers man is not so much a sense of regain as an *illusion* of regain. Comedy keeps man domiciled—and fairly securely domiciled—in a world that he does not live in properly unless he wills to live in a contradictory world at the same time. Comedy offers man an illusory paradise: the paradise of imaginative control of what is outside man. But man is driven from this paradise by his dismaying discovery that he does not entirely belong there. He is driven out not by any flaming sword but by his own nature whose destiny it is to exercise choice and thus deny or qualify all cyclically-based perceptions. For the reassuring continuum of cycle external to man, tragedy puts before us a discontinuity: man that chooses not to repeat, man that by his choice wills the unknown. Such a being is, from the cyclic point of view, a *lusus naturae*, one that taints and distorts the secure universe for which both Osiris and comedy stand. Were we to pair phrases, we might say that tragedy offers us a gift as permanent and pervasive as the comic sense of regain; it is a sense of loss, an awareness that man, in his most intimate activities, follows a line that leads only to darkness and an enigma—a line that will never curve back upon itself and so in the future confirm what it has been. The characteristic human act—that of choice— is closely allied with loss, even though we seem to choose to win something, to gain something. Choice, the specific linear activity, the activity that we see brought to sharp focus in Gethsemane and in the palace at Elsinore, always has for its ground-bass the note of loss. We turn our back on the joys we are certain of and might like to repeat, and we put ourselves in the trust of the future: a moment or an hour that we do not know but yet must count on—and we have willed to lose, if we must, the profit that can come to us from past moments: moments we have savored and could—did not choice intervene with its crucial break—still count on. Agony and death at some future time are but incidental marks of tragedy. The real agony, the real death, come at the moment when we choose; when, willing loss, we trust ourselves to an enigma; when we abandon the comic vein and cease counting on limited certainties. Not only is the crucifixion "a sacrifice once offered"; each crucial choice that marks a tragic drama is such a sacrifice, for it is loss of the world that the cyclic temper would preserve as man's great comfort and support. Whatever the upshot of tragic choice, whatever temporary palliatives and patent compensations may move toward us, the fact persists: we have given up or, at the least, qualified a very useful insight into man's experience, the comic insight, the insight that we have compared with the cyclic assertions certain myths have made. In comedy the world we inhabit is but playfully threatened; by the end of the play, it is refounded more firmly than before. But in tragedy, as if in accord with its linear, non-reversible nature, choice threatens the world, the status quo, in deadly earnest. In choice, we do not know with much confidence what it is we shall create; we know with grim certainty what it is that we destroy: our happiness, our security—in short, our confidence in a future that follows— or seems to follow—cyclic laws.

Both tragic insight and the religious assertion that we call linear are not easy to endure, whether we arrogate to them exclusive truth or confess sadly that the comic or the cyclic insights are true also. Christians have permitted themselves the alleviation of encrusting their linear faith with recurrent ritual that prolongs, throughout the "Christian year," a necessary minimum of cyclic illusion. And, when we draw back from the blank that is choice and act in time, in linear succession, we may turn back to comedy which, in its way, represents our human lot if not our essential human lot. One way to endure tragedy, on the stage and off, is to listen to some of the things that comedy tells us when it speaks of "fundamental decency" and the recurrence of events and their correspondence to an understandable, definable order.

It is plain that there is nothing "wrong" with a penchant for comedy; tragedy is "truer" than comedy (it is a more penetrating comment on our lot) but it is less endurable. This relation between the truth of the two dramatic forms also gains light from the comparable religious tension. There is nothing "wrong" about the persistence of cyclic insights in a religion basically linear (e.g., the Christian). A perception that, at the centers of our being, we exist linear-wise can never cancel the truth that in relation to external forces we live under a cyclic dispensation. What is perhaps "wrong" is a reworking of the two religious insights that deprives either of its proper authority. This is the chief heresy that Western eyes find in Buddhism: the denial that both recurrence and unique event have high significance in man's life.

Finally, all that tragedy offers us in the audience is loss or deprivation: the possibility of becoming something that we have not yet been. If tragedy offers us a gain, it is a gain that is, unlike the comic gain, incalculable. If the tragedy we watch is real tragedy and not deterministic tragedy, which has the *events* of tragedy but the *certainty* of comedy, we live for a while lives from which the cyclic effects have fallen away or have receded into the background. Comedy occurs at any moment (it has the effect, if not the actuality, of being repeatable); tragedy occurs at only one moment: a moment that has come *this time* and that will never come again. It presents us with the spectacle of ourselves urged by the logic inherent in once-occurring events to make a choice. We cannot escape choice and responsibility for the choice which we make. Yet we make the choice without a full knowledge of the consequences. How can we, in a universe conceived in a linear way, have such knowledge? It is only in a cyclically conceived universe that we seem to have such knowledge. It is a knowledge which the other sort of drama strips from us.

For this reason, the tragic qualm—however purgation be explained—is never really purged. When we watch the acts of Oedipus and Hamlet and the results of those acts, the only comfort we draw is analogous to that which we get from a myth aligned with linear perceptions. Christ on the cross or Quetzalcoatl on his raft of serpents wrenches our eyes from a flattering and comforting view of our destinies as men. As men, we are apart from mountain and stream, we are apart from society collectively considered; we are—in all conventional or comic sense—apart from each other. We can find union only in the insight given to us by linear myth or by its analogue in tragic drama: that every moment is a crucifixion if we face it seriously. To do this we are most of the time incompetent. We would like to deny that we are Prince Hamlet. We would rather, along with Eliot's Prufrock, go to swell a crowd and there take refuge in sententious and (in our sense) "comic" remarks.

If we are correct, if the similarities between drama and religion are indeed striking, are we correct to oppose those who, directly or covertly, treat drama as a full surrogate for religious assertion? I think we are. The basic dissimilarity persists although it is not our duty here to study it. The religious context provides fixity and hence authority as the companions of the opposed total assertions, and drama provides a context of constant variety and change. This latter context will seem the correct and perhaps the only one to those who doubt that even the most sensitive and analytical attention to experience can win to binding answers. Such doubt is not hampering provided the doubter does not take the final step and observe that religion is really about the same thing as that which drama treats in two logically opposed ways. Religion, we should repeat, is "about" that which is sensed as permanently true; drama handles the permanently uncertain in what we see and recollect. All that the similarities we have traced here support is this observation: there are two sovereign ways of naming the impermanent and the fixed. Since these ways belong to both religion and drama, we are tempted to identify religion and drama. This we must refuse to do, for when we say "the same" we offer up, in the name of system and simplicity, discriminations rich, suggestive, and illogical that are a large part of the treasure that has been put into our hands.

Cross Currents, V (1955), 154–170. Parts I, II, and III of this five-part article have been omitted.

Northrop Frye's Fearful Symmetry *(1947),* Anatomy of Criticism *(1957), and* Fables of Identity *(1963) have enormously stimulated the present interest in myth. While other of his essays may present his views on myth and literature in more detail, the following selection is unique in that as well as revealing his interest in placing myth criticism within a larger critical theory it forecasts his more recent concentration on the educational problems of criticism and literature. At the same time, it is relevant to other essays in the collection, in particular to Mr. Watts's treatment of genre in the preceding study and to the discriminations between myth, legend, and folktale in the essays by Richard Chase and Francis Fergusson (pp. 67 ff. and pp. 139 ff.).*

Here we have the total absorption of myth and ritual into literary criticism that we saw Mr. Chase inaugurating. For not only does Mr. Frye systematize the familiar aspects of the critical process, he also extends that process to the study of archetypes, a study involving the way in which literature contains pre-literary categories such as ritual, myth, and folktale. In addition, he argues that by beginning from the concepts of narrative and pattern one may deductively arrive at the centrality of the quest-myth and its archetypal significance for literature.

THE ARCHETYPES OF LITERATURE

Northrop Frye

Every organized body of knowledge can be learned progressively; and experience shows that there is also something progressive about the learning of literature. Our opening sentence has already got us into a semantic difficulty. Physics is an organized body of knowledge about nature, and a student of it says that he is learning physics, not that he is learning nature. Art, like nature, is the subject of a systematic study, and has to be distinguished from the study itself, which is criticism. It is therefore impossible to "learn literature": one learns about it in a certain way, but what one learns, transitively, is the criticism of literature. Similarly, the difficulty often felt in "teaching literature" arises from the fact that it cannot be done: the criticism of literature is all that can be directly taught. So while no one expects literature itself to behave like a science, there is surely no reason why criticism, as a systematic and organized study, should not be, at least partly, a science. Not a "pure" or "exact" science, perhaps, but these phrases form part of a nineteenth century cosmology which is no longer with us. Criticism deals with the arts and may well be something of an art itself, but it does not follow that it must be unsystematic. If it is to be related to the sciences too, it does not follow that it must be deprived of the graces of culture.

Certainly criticism as we find it in learned journals and scholarly monographs has every characteristic of a science. Evidence is examined scientifically; previous authorities are used scientifically; fields are investigated scientifically; texts are edited scientifically. Prosody is scientific in structure; so is phonetics; so is philology. And yet in studying this kind of critical science the student becomes aware of a centrifugal movement carrying him away from literature. He finds that literature is the central division of the "humanities," flanked on one side by history and on the other by philosophy. Criticism so far ranks only as a subdivision of literature; and hence, for the systematic mental organization of the subject, the student has to turn to the conceptual framework of the historian for events, and to that of the philosopher for ideas. Even the more centrally placed critical sciences, such as textual editing, seem to be part of a "background" that recedes into history or some other non-literary field. The thought suggests itself that the ancillary critical disciplines may be related to a central expanding pattern of systematic comprehension which has not yet been established, but which, if it were established, would prevent them from being centrifugal. If such a pattern exists, then criticism would be to art what philosophy is to wisdom and history to action.

Most of the central area of criticism is at present, and doubtless always will be, the area of commentary. But the commentators have little sense, unlike the researchers, of being contained within some sort of scientific discipline: they are chiefly engaged, in the words of the gospel hymn, in brightening the corner where they are. If we attempt to get a more comprehensive idea of what criticism is about, we find ourselves wandering over quaking bogs of generalities, judicious pronouncements of value, reflective comments, perorations to works of research, and other consequences of taking the large view. But this part of the critical field is so full of pseudo-propositions, sonorous nonsense that contains no truth and no falsehood, that it obviously exists only because criticism, like nature, prefers a waste space to an empty one.

The term "pseudo-proposition" may imply some sort of logical positivist attitude on my own part. But I would not confuse the significant proposition with the factual one; nor should I consider it advisable to muddle the study of literature with a schizophrenic dichotomy between subjective-emotional and objective-descriptive aspects of meaning, considering that in order to produce any literary meaning at all one has to ignore this dichotomy. I say only that the principles by which one can distinguish a significant from a meaningless statement in criticism are not clearly defined. Our first step, therefore, is to recognize and get rid of meaningless criticism: that is, talking about literature in a way that cannot help to build up a systematic structure of knowledge. Casual value-judgments belong not to criticism but to the history of taste, and reflect, at best, only the social and psychological compulsions which prompted their utterance. All judgments in which the values are not based on literary experience but are sentimental or derived from religious or political prejudice may be regarded as casual. Sentimental judgments are usually based either on non-existent categories or antitheses ("Shakespeare studied life, Milton books") or on a visceral reaction to the writer's personality. The literary chit-chat which makes the reputations of poets boom and crash in an imaginary stock exchange is pseudo-criticism. That wealthy investor Mr. Eliot, after dumping Milton on the market, is now buying him again; Donne has probably reached his peak and will begin to taper off; Tennyson may be in for a slight flutter but the Shelley stocks are still bearish. This sort of thing cannot be part of any systematic study, for a systematic study can only progress: whatever dithers or vacillates or reacts is merely leisure-class conversation.

We next meet a more serious group of critics who say: the foreground of criticism is the impact of literature on the reader. Let us, then, keep the study of literature centripetal, and base the learning process on a structural analysis of the literary work itself. The texture of any great work of art is complex and ambiguous, and in unravelling the complexities we may take in as much history and philosophy as we please, if the subject of our study remains at the center. If it does not, we may find that in our anxiety to write about literature we have forgotten how to read it.

The only weakness in this approach is that it is conceived primarily as the antithesis of centrifugal or "background" criticism, and so lands us in a somewhat unreal dilemma, like the conflict of internal and external relations in philosophy. Antitheses are usually resolved, not by picking one side and refuting the other, or by making eclectic choices between them, but by trying to get past the antithetical way of stating the problem. It is right that the first effort of critical apprehension should take the form of a rhetorical or structural analysis of a work of art. But a purely structural approach has the same limitation in criticism that it has in biology. In itself it is simply a discrete series of analyses based on the mere existence of the literary structure, without developing any explanation of how the structure came to be what it was and what its nearest relatives are. Structural analysis brings rhetoric back to criticism, but we need a new poetics as well, and the attempt to construct a new poetics out of rhetoric alone can hardly avoid a mere complication of rhetorical terms into a sterile jargon. I suggest that what is at present missing from literary criticism is a co-ordinating principle, a central hypothesis which, like the theory of evolution in biology, will see the phenomena it deals with as parts of a whole. Such a principle, though it would retain the centripetal perspective of structural analysis, would try to give the same perspective to other kinds of criticism too.

The first postulate of this hypothesis is the same as that of any science: the assumption of total coherence. The assumption refers to the science, not to what it deals with. A belief in an order of nature is an inference from the intelligibility of the natural sciences; and if the natural sciences ever completely demonstrated the order of nature they would presumably exhaust their subject. Criticism, as a science, is totally intelligible; literature, as the subject of a science, is, so far as we know, an inexhaustible source of new critical discoveries, and would be even if new works of literature ceased to be written. If so, then the search for a limiting principle in literature in order to discourage the development of criticism is mistaken. The assertion that the critic should not look for more in a poem than the poet may safely be assumed to have been conscious of putting there is a common form of what may be called the fallacy of premature teleology. It corresponds to the assertion that a natural phenomenon is as it is because Providence in its inscrutable wisdom made it so.

Simple as the assumption appears, it takes a long time for a science to discover that it is in fact a totally intelligible body of knowledge. Until it makes this discovery it has not been born as an individual science, but remains an embryo within the body of some other subject. The birth of physics from "natural philosophy" and of sociology from "moral philosophy" will illustrate the process. It is also very approximately true that the modern sciences have developed in the order of their closeness to mathematics. Thus physics and astronomy assumed their modern form in the Renaissance, chemistry in the eighteenth century, biology in the nineteenth, and the social sciences in the twentieth. If systematic criticism, then, is developing only in our day, the fact is at least not an anachronism.

We are now looking for classifying principles lying in an area between two points that we have fixed. The first of these is the preliminary effort of criticism, the structural analysis of the work of art. The second is the assumption that there is such a subject as criticism, and that it makes, or could make, complete sense. We may next proceed inductively from structural analysis, associating the data we collect and trying to see larger patterns in them. Or we may proceed deductively, with the consequences that follow from postulating the unity of criticism. It is clear, of course, that neither procedure will work indefinitely without correction from the other. Pure induction will get us lost in haphazard guessing; pure deduction will lead to inflexible and oversimplified pigeon-holing. Let us now attempt a few tentative steps in each direction, beginning with the inductive one.

II

The unity of a work of art, the basis of structural analysis, has not been produced solely by the unconditioned will of the artist, for the artist is only its efficient cause: it has form, and consequently a formal cause. The fact that revision is possible, that the poet makes changes not because he likes them better but because they are better, means that poems, like poets, are born and not made. The poet's task is to deliver the poem in as uninjured a state as possible, and if the poem is alive, it is equally anxious to be rid of him, and screams to be cut loose from his private memories and associations, his desire for self-expression, and all the other navel-strings and feeding tubes of his ego. The critic takes over where the poet leaves off, and criticism can hardly do without a kind of literary psychology connecting the poet with the poem. Part of this may be a psychological study of the poet, though this is useful chiefly in analysing the failures in his expression, the things in him which are still attached to his work. More important is the fact that every poet has his private mythology, his own spectroscopic band or peculiar formation of symbols, of much of which he is quite unconscious. In works with characters of their own, such as dramas and novels, the same psychological analysis may be extended to the interplay of characters, though of course literary psychology would analyse the behavior of such characters only in relation to literary convention.

There is still before us the problem of the formal cause of the poem, a problem deeply involved with the question of genres. We cannot say much about genres, for criticism does not know much about them. A good many critical efforts to grapple with such words as "novel" or "epic" are chiefly interesting as examples of the psychology of rumor. Two conceptions of the genre, however, are obviously fallacious, and as they are opposite extremes, the truth must lie somewhere between them. One is the pseudo-Platonic conception of genres as existing prior to and independently of creation, which confuses them with mere conventions of form like the sonnet. The other is that pseudo-biological conception of them as evolving species which turns up in so many surveys of the "development" of this or that form.

We next inquire for the origin of the genre, and turn first of all to the social conditions and cultural demands which produced it—in other words to the material cause of the work of art. This leads us into literary history, which differs from ordinary history in that its containing categories, "Gothic," "Baroque," "Romantic," and the like are cultural categories, of little use to the ordinary historian. Most literary history does not get as far as these categories, but even so we know more about it than about most kinds of critical scholarship. The historian treats literature and philosophy historically; the philosopher treats history and literature philosophically; and the so-called "history of ideas" approach marks the beginning of an attempt to treat history and philosophy from the point of view of an autonomous criticism.

But still we feel that there is something missing. We say that every poet has his own peculiar formation of images. But when so many poets use so many of the same images, surely there are much bigger critical problems involved than biographical ones. As Mr. Auden's brilliant essay *The Enchafèd Flood* shows, an important symbol like the sea cannot remain within the poetry of Shelley or Keats or Coleridge: it is bound to expand over many poets into an archetypal symbol of literature. And if the genre has a historical origin, why does the genre of drama emerge from medieval religion in a way so strikingly similar to the way it emerged from Greek religion centuries before? This is a problem of structure rather than origin, and suggests that there may be archetypes of genres as well as of images.

It is clear that criticism cannot be systematic unless there is a quality in literature which enables it to be so, an order of words corresponding to the order of nature in the natural sciences. An archetype should be not only a unifying category of criticism, but itself a part of a total form, and it leads us at once to the question of what sort of total form criticism can see in literature. Our survey of critical techniques has taken us as far as literary history. Total literary history moves from the primitive to the sophisticated, and here we glimpse the possibility of seeing literature as a complication of a relatively restricted and simple group of formulas that can be studied in primitive culture. If so, then the search for archetypes is a kind of literary anthropology, concerned with the way that literature is informed by pre-literary categories such as ritual, myth and folktale. We next realize that the relation between these categories and literature is by no means purely one of descent, as we find them reappearing in the greatest classics—in fact there seems to be a general tendency on the part of great classics to revert to them. This coincides with a feeling that we have all had: that the study of mediocre works of art, however energetic, obstinately remains a random and peripheral form of critical experience, whereas the profound masterpiece seems to draw us to a point at which we can see an enormous number of converging patterns of significance. Here we begin to wonder if we cannot see literature, not only as complicating itself in time, but as spread out in conceptual space from some unseen center.

This inductive movement towards the archetype is a process of backing up, as it were, from structural analysis, as we back up from a painting if we want to see composition instead of brushwork. In the foreground of the grave-digger scene in *Hamlet*, for instance, is an intricate verbal texture, ranging from the puns of the first clown to the *danse macabre* of the Yorick soliloquy, which we study in the printed text. One step back, and we are in the Wilson Knight and Spurgeon group of critics, listening to the steady rain of images of corruption and decay. Here too, as the sense of the place of this scene in the whole play begins to dawn on us, we are in the network of psychological relationships which were the main interest of Bradley. But after all, we say, we are forgetting the genre: *Hamlet* is a play, and an Elizabethan play. So we take another step back into the Stoll and Shaw group and see the scene conventionally as part of its dramatic context. One step more, and we can begin to glimpse the archetype of the scene, as the hero's *Liebestod* and first unequivocal declaration of his love, his struggle with Laertes and the sealing of his own fate, and the sudden sobering of his mood that marks the transition to the final scene, all take shape around a leap into and return from the grave that has so weirdly yawned open on the stage.

At each stage of understanding this scene we are dependent on a certain kind of scholarly organization. We need first an editor to clean up the text for us, then the rhetorician and philologist, then the literary psychologist. We cannot study the genre without the help of the literary social historian, the literary philosopher and the student of the "history of ideas," and for the archetype we need a literary anthropologist. But now that we have got our central pattern of criticism established, all these interests are seen as converging on literary criticism instead of receding from it into psychology and history and the rest. In particular, the literary anthropologist who chases the source of the Hamlet legend from the pre-Shakespeare play to Saxo, and from Saxo to nature-myths, is not running away from Shakespeare: he is drawing closer to the archetypal form which Shakespeare recreated. A minor result of our new perspective is that contradictions among critics, and assertions that this and not that critical approach is the right one, show a remarkable tendency to dissolve into unreality. Let us now see what we can get from the deductive end.

III

Some arts move in time, like music; others are presented in space, like painting. In both cases the organizing principle is recurrence, which is called rhythm when it is temporal and pattern when it is spatial. Thus we speak of the rhythm of music and the pattern of painting; but later, to show off our sophistication, we may begin to speak of the rhythm of painting and the pattern of music. In other words, all arts may be conceived both temporally and spatially. The score of a musical composition may be studied all at once; a picture may be seen as the track of an intricate dance of the eye. Literature seems to be intermediate between music and painting: its words form rhythms which approach a musical sequence of sounds at one of its boundaries, and form patterns which approach the hieroglyphic or pictorial image at the other. The attempts to get as near to these boundaries as possible form the main body of what is called experimental writing. We may call the rhythm of literature the narrative, and the pattern, the simultaneous mental grasp of the verbal structure, the meaning or significance. We hear or listen to a narrative, but when we grasp a writer's total pattern we "see" what he means.

The criticism of literature is much more hampered by the representational fallacy than even the criticism of painting. That is why we are apt to think of narrative as a sequential representation of events in an outside "life," and of meaning as a reflection of some external "idea." Properly used as critical terms, an author's narrative is his linear movement; his meaning is the integrity of his completed form. Similarly an image is not merely a verbal replica of an external object, but any unit of a verbal structure seen as part of a total pattern or rhythm. Even the letters an author spells his words with form part of his imagery, though only in special cases (such as alliteration) would they call for critical notice. Narrative and meaning thus become respectively, to borrow musical terms, the melodic and harmonic contexts of the imagery.

Rhythm, or recurrent movement, is deeply founded on the natural cycle, and everything in nature that we think of as having some analogy with works of art, like the flower or the bird's song, grows out of a profound synchronization between an organism and the rhythms of its environment, especially that of the solar year. With animals some expressions of synchronization, like the mating dances of birds, could almost be called rituals. But in human life a ritual seems to be something of a voluntary effort (hence the magical element in it) to recapture a lost rapport with the natural cycle. A farmer must harvest his crop at a certain time of year, but because this is involuntary, harvesting itself is not precisely a ritual. It is the deliberate expression of a will to synchronize human and natural energies at that time which produces the harvest songs, harvest sacrifices and harvest folk customs that we call rituals. In ritual, then, we may find the origin of narrative, a ritual being a temporal sequence of acts in which the conscious meaning or significance is latent: it can be seen by an observer, but is largely concealed from the participators themselves. The pull of ritual is toward pure narrative, which, if there could be such a thing, would be automatic and unconscious repetition. We should notice too the regular tendency of ritual to become encyclopedic. All the important recurrences in nature, the day, the phases of the moon, the seasons and solstices of the year, the crises of existence from birth to death, get rituals attached to them, and most of the higher religions are equipped with a definitive total body of rituals suggestive, if we may put it so, of the entire range of potentially significant actions in human life.

Patterns of imagery, on the other hand, or fragments of significance, are oracular in origin, and derive from the epiphanic moment, the flash of instantaneous comprehension with no direct reference to time, the importance of which is indicated by Cassirer in *Language and Myth*. By the time we get them, in the form of proverbs, riddles, commandments and etiological folktales, there is already a considerable element of narrative in them. They too are encyclopedic in tendency, building up a total structure of significance, or doctrine, from random and empiric fragments. And just as pure narrative would be unconscious act, so pure significance would be an incommunicable state of consciousness, for communication begins by constructing narrative.

The myth is the central informing power that gives archetypal significance to the ritual and archetypal narrative to the oracle. Hence the myth *is* the archetype, though it might be convenient to say myth only when referring to narrative, and archetype when speaking of significance. In the solar cycle of the day, the seasonal cycle of the year, and the organic cycle of human life, there is a single pattern of significance, out of which myth constructs a central narrative around a figure who is partly the sun, partly vegetative fertility and partly a god or archetypal human being. The crucial importance of this myth has been forced on literary critics by Jung and Frazer in particular, but the several books now available on it are not always systematic in their approach, for which reason I supply the following table of its phases:

1. The dawn, spring and birth phase. Myths of the birth of the hero, of revival and resurrection, of creation and (because the four phases are a cycle) of the defeat of the powers of darkness, winter and death. Subordinate characters: the father and the mother. The archetype of romance and of most dithyrambic and rhapsodic poetry.

2. The zenith, summer, and marriage or triumph phase. Myths of apotheosis, of the sacred marriage, and of entering into Paradise. Subordinate characters: the companion and the bride. The archetype of comedy, pastoral and idyll.

3. The sunset, autumn and death phase. Myths of fall, of the dying god, of violent death and sacrifice and of the isolation of the hero. Subordinate characters: the traitor and the siren. The archetype of tragedy and elegy.

4. The darkness, winter and dissolution phase. Myths of the triumph of these powers; myths of floods and the return of chaos, of the defeat of the hero, and Götterdämmerung myths. Subordinate characters: the ogre and the witch. The archetype of satire (see, for instance, the conclusion of *The Dunciad*).

The quest of the hero also tends to assimilate the oracular and random verbal structures, as we can see when we watch the chaos of local legends that results from prophetic epiphanies consolidating into a narrative mythology of departmental gods. In most of the higher religions this in turn has become the same central quest-myth that emerges from ritual, as the Messiah myth became the narrative structure of the oracles of Judaism. A local flood may beget a folktale by accident, but a comparison of flood stories will show how quickly such tales become examples of the myth of dissolution. Finally, the tendency of both ritual and epiphany to become encyclopedic is realized in the definitive body of myth which constitutes the sacred scriptures of religions. These sacred scriptures are consequently the first documents that the literary critic has to study to gain a comprehensive view of his subject. After he has understood their structure, then he can descend from archetypes to genres, and see how the drama emerges from the ritual side of myth and lyric from the epiphanic or fragmented side, while the epic carries on the central encyclopedic structure.

Some words of caution and encouragement are necessary before literary criticism has clearly staked out its boundaries in these fields. It is part of the critic's business to show how all literary genres are derived from the quest-myth, but the derivation is a logical one within the science of criticism: the quest-myth will constitute the first chapter of whatever future handbooks of criticism may be written that will be based on enough organized critical knowledge to call themselves "introductions" or "outlines" and still be able to live up to their titles. It is only when we try to expound the derivation chronologically that we find ourselves writing pseudo-prehistorical fictions and theories of mythological contract. Again, because psychology and anthropology are more highly developed sciences, the critic who deals with this kind of material is bound to appear, for some time, a dilettante of those subjects. These two phases of criticism are largely undeveloped in comparison with literary history and rhetoric, the reason being the later development of the sciences they are related to. But the fascination which *The Golden Bough* and Jung's book on libido symbols have for literary critics is not based on dilettantism, but on the fact that these books are primarily studies in literary criticism, and very important ones.

In any case the critic who is studying the principles of literary form has a quite different interest from the psychologist's concern with states of mind or the anthropologist's with social institutions. For instance: the mental response to narrative is mainly passive; to significance mainly active. From this fact Ruth Benedict's *Patterns of Culture* develops a distinction between "Apollonian" cultures based on obedience to ritual and "Dionysiac" ones based on a tense exposure of the prophetic mind to epiphany. The critic would tend rather to note how popular literature which appeals to the inertia of the untrained mind puts a heavy emphasis on narrative values, whereas a sophisticated attempt to disrupt the connection between the poet and his environment produces the Rimbaud type of *illumination*, Joyce's solitary epiphanies, and Baudelaire's conception of nature as a source of oracles. Also how literature, as it develops from the primitive to the self-conscious, shows a gradual shift of the poet's attention from narrative to significant values, this shift of attention being the basis of Schiller's distinction between naive and sentimental poetry.

The relation of criticism to religion, when they deal with the same documents, is more complicated. In criticism, as in history, the divine is always treated as a human artifact. God for the critic, whether he finds him in *Paradise Lost* or the Bible, is a character in a human story; and for the critic all epiphanies are explained, not in terms of the riddle of a possessing god or devil, but as mental phenomena closely associated in their origin with dreams. This once established, it is then necessary to say that nothing in criticism or art compels the critic to take the attitude of ordinary waking consciousness towards the dream or the god. Art deals not with the real but with the conceivable; and criticism, though it will eventually have to have some theory of conceivability, can never be justified in trying to develop, much less assume, any theory of actuality. It is necessary to understand this before our next and final point can be made.

We have identified the central myth of literature, in its narrative aspect, with the quest-myth. Now if we wish to see this central myth as a pattern of meaning also, we have to start with the workings of the subconscious where the epiphany originates, in other words in the dream. The human cycle of waking and dreaming corresponds closely to the natural cycle of light and darkness, and it is perhaps in this correspondence that all imaginative life begins. The correspondence is largely an antithesis: it is in daylight that man is really in the power of darkness, a prey to frustration and weakness; it is in the darkness of nature that the "libido" or conquering heroic self awakes. Hence art, which Plato called a dream for awakened minds, seems to have as its final cause the resolution of the antithesis, the mingling of the sun and the hero, the realizing of a world in which the inner desire and the outward circumstance coincide. This is the same goal, of course, that the attempt to combine human and natural power in ritual has. The social function of the arts, therefore, seems to be closely connected with visualizing the goal of work in human life. So in terms of significance, the central myth of art must be the vision of the end of social effort, the innocent world of fulfilled desires, the free human society. Once this is understood, the integral place of criticism among the other social sciences, in interpreting and systematizing the vision of the artist, will be easier to see. It is at this point that we can see how religious conceptions of the final cause of human effort are as relevant as any others to criticism.

The importance of the god or hero in the myth lies in the fact that such characters, who are conceived in human likeness and yet have more power over nature, gradually build up the vision of an omnipotent personal community beyond an indifferent nature. It is this community which the hero regularly enters in his apotheosis. The world of this apotheosis thus begins to pull away from the rotary cycle of the quest in which all triumph is temporary. Hence if we look at the quest-myth as a pattern of imagery, we see the hero's quest first of all in terms of its fulfillment. This gives us our central pattern of archetypal images, the vision of innocence which sees the world in terms of total human intelligibility. It corresponds to, and is usually found in the form of, the vision of the unfallen world or heaven in religion. We may call it the comic vision of life, in contrast to the tragic vision, which sees the quest only in the form of its ordained cycle.

We conclude with a second table of contents, in which we shall attempt to set forth the central pattern of the comic and tragic visions. One essential principle of archetypal criticism is that the individual and the universal forms of an image are identical, the reasons being too complicated for us just now. We proceed according to the general plan of the game of Twenty Questions, or, if we prefer, of the Great Chain of Being:

1. In the comic vision the *human* world is a community, or a hero who represents the wish-fulfillment of the reader. The archetype of images of symposium, communion, order, friendship and love. In the tragic vision the human world is a tyranny or anarchy, or an individual or isolated man, the leader with his back to his followers, the bullying giant of romance, the deserted or betrayed hero. Marriage or some equivalent consummation belongs to the comic vision; the harlot, witch and other varieties of Jung's "terrible mother" belong to the tragic one. All divine, heroic, angelic or other superhuman communities follow the human pattern.

2. In the comic vision the *animal* world is a community of domesticated animals, usually a flock of sheep, or a lamb, or one of the gentler birds, usually a dove. The archetype of pastoral images. In the tragic vision the animal world is seen in terms of beasts and birds of prey, wolves, vultures, serpents, dragons and the like.

3. In the comic vision the *vegetable* world is a garden, grove or park, or a tree of life, or a rose or lotus. The archetype of Arcadian images, such as that of Marvell's green world or of Shakespeare's forest comedies. In the tragic vision it is a sinister forest like the one in *Comus* or at the opening of the *Inferno* or a heath or wilderness, or a tree of death.

4. In the comic vision the *mineral* world is a city, or one building or temple, or one

stone, normally a glowing precious stone—in fact the whole comic series, especially the tree, can be conceived as luminous or fiery. The archetype of geometrical images: the "starlit dome" belongs here. In the tragic vision the mineral world is seen in terms of deserts, rocks and ruins, or of sinister geometrical images like the cross.

5. In the comic vision the *unformed* world is a river, traditionally fourfold, which influenced the Renaissance image of the temperate body with its four humors. In the tragic vision this world usually becomes the sea, as the narrative myth of dissolution is so often a flood myth. The combination of the sea and beast images gives us the leviathan and similar water-monsters.

Obvious as this table looks, a great variety of poetic images and forms will be found to fit it. Yeats's "Sailing to Byzantium," to take a famous example of the comic vision at random, has the city, the tree, the bird, the community of sages, the geometrical gyre and the detachment from the cyclic world. It is, of course, only the general comic or tragic context that determines the interpretation of any symbol: this is obvious with relatively neutral archetypes like the island, which may be Prospero's island or Circe's.

Our tables are, of course, not only elementary but grossly over-simplified, just as our inductive approach to the archetype was a mere hunch. The important point is not the deficiencies of either procedure, taken by itself, but the fact that, somewhere and somehow, the two are clearly going to meet in the middle. And if they do meet, the ground plan of a systematic and comprehensive development of criticism has been established.

Kenyon Review, XIII (1951), 92–110.

Andrew Lytle is the editor of the Sewanee Review *and the author of three novels including* The Velvet Horn *(1957), whose genesis he describes here. Unlike the other contributors, he reports from the inside on one writer's experience with the mythopoeic process, and in so doing corroborates many of the views advanced in this volume, principally in the essays by Frye and Wheelwright. The impulse of creation leads him to compare his chosen society, the South of 1880–1910, to others and to see the cyclic character of their growth and decline, the relevance of the myth of Adam and Eve, the possible symbolic dimensions of incest, and the archetypal qualities of his protagonist. The true artist, Mr. Lytle suggests, is an inveterate symbolizer, a seeker of the archetypal who presents myth through images which focus "the essence of meaning."*

THE WORKING NOVELIST AND THE MYTHMAKING PROCESS

Andrew Lytle

When I first began thinking about the book which was to become *The Velvet Horn*,[1] I was thinking consciously: that is, rationally. I could almost say falsely, except that the creative act uses all the mind's faculties. I thought I wanted to do a long piece of fiction on a society that was dead. At the time I saw the scene as the kind of life which was the Southern version of a life that, discounting the sectional differences, had been common everywhere east of the Mississippi and east of the mountains. That life seemed to me to be what was left of the older and more civilized America, which as well retained the pattern of its European inheritance. The Civil War had destroyed that life; but memory and habit, manners and mores are slow to die.

As a boy I had witnessed its ghostly presence, and yet the people which this presence inhabited were substantial enough. They were alive in their entire being. They seemed all the more alive because their culture was stricken. The last active expression of this society seemed to fall somewhere between 1880 and 1910. Those decades seemed the effective turning point of the great revolution which was to diminish a Christian inheritance. The mechanics of the change are obvious to all; the most effective was the automobile, since it uprooted the family by destroying its attachment to place. In the South, certainly, family was the one institution common to all its parts. There was great variety to the South's homogeneity, which the false myths about it never understood. There has been no part of this country so afflicted with "galvanized" myths which presumed to interpret it, but it was family as institution which best expressed its culture. By family, I mean all the complex interrelationships of blood and kin, the large "connections" which extended to the county lines and by sympathy overlapped the states.

1. *The Velvet Horn* (New York: McDowell, Obolensky Inc., 1957), is set in the Cumberland hill country in the nineteenth century, and revolves round the passionate-natured Cropleigh family. Besides its poetic descriptions and its sensitivity to speech rhythms, the novel, marked for its use of symbolism, is rich in metaphor and allusiveness.—Editor [H. A. Murray].

I take the automobile as the supreme agency in the destruction of attachment to place, since the railroads did not destroy the communities; they merely connected them more readily. Family and place, as I said, go together. It was the sense of both which set the South apart in this country, but too much was asked of the family as institution. It should have been one among many institutional expressions of culture; it was called upon to do more than its form allowed. But the artist works by means of such limitations. So it seemed to me as I began. I had no intention, no sense of dealing with a myth which forever recurs within the human scene.

This conscious approach is merely one way in, or down. The writer may begin with anything, a mood, a scene, an idea, a character, a situation. Whatever sets him going generally appears suddenly in that suspension of attention which is like the after-effect of shock. It is a condition of the psyche when it finds itself outside time. This condition may be the occasion for vision or dream. In the Middle Ages any man might know it. Dreams remain, but vision commonly fails us today. We are helpless before the condition in which dreams appear; but vision strikes the state of consciousness. This stroke and that mysterious sense of being possessed largely remain for the artist, the point being that presumably he suffers this intrusion when he is conscious. Presumably, because the aftereffect of shock allows for a certain awareness of what is going on around outside, but the consciousness does not respond in action. It is suspended before the intuitive and instinctive action taking place within the mind. Somehow, through a fissure, the unconscious pierces the consciousness, and from below streams the image, or whatever it is, that sets the artist to work. The shock is a true shock. It paralyzes the rational mind momentarily. It is mysterious. The cause, the source, can in no way be discovered by natural or positive means. But the experience is true, and forever denies to mere formula a rendition of the knowledge which is experience.

The creative act is, then, both a rational and an intuitive performance. What comes up from below through this fissure generally relates to the subject, but for me at least it always seems at first to be the essence of the subject. It can be this, but it rarely is. It must contain the essence, however; and it is just here that the conscious use of the craft of fiction comes in. The craft is the lesser part, but nevertheless crucial. Without its procedure of arranging, finding relationships between structural parts, and all such matters, as well as the tedious search for the right word or phrase, there would be no art of language as fiction.

It is curious, but for as long as I have written, I am always surprised afresh, after much sorrow and trouble to get a story going, that the idea may merely be related to, not be, the subject. Each time I have to learn afresh that it is either a segment of a larger idea or an idea too big for the action, as it shows itself. The resistance to its dissolution in the action is enormous, partly because it retains the excitement of the moment of inspiration. This inspiration is a momentary vision of the whole. It quickly sinks into the abyss from which it arose, leaving the idea as a kind of clue, the end of the thread which leads into the labyrinth. No matter how firmly the critical sense has explored the idea's limitations, the moment the artist engages himself, he cannot but take it to mean more than it does. An idea is so inflexible; it tends so easily toward the conceptual. It *must* turn flesh before it is fiction. Fiction above all should give the illusion of life, of men and women acting out some one of the eternal involvements we all know, resolving, not solving. Only God may solve. A character or a situation would be the simpler way to begin. It would lead more directly into the conflict. It is rarely my way.

I feel there is an advantage to beginning with an idea rather than a situation or a mood. This advantage is suggested by its very irrefrangibility. If the idea is universal, in action it becomes archetypal. Therefore, to render it describes more nearly a whole action; and the artist must not tell any story but the *one* story which the people and situation demand. I would like to distinguish at this point between an opinion about behavior and archetypal representation. Opinion is the vulgarity of taste. It is never a true idea, because it is either topical or partial. It distorts any action, since it is blind to the fullest complexity of that action. No matter how disguised, opinion always has a "message," it always wants to prove something instead of making experience show itself. Its selection of incidents, therefore, is often obviously arbitrary. This is the failure of the realistic school of fiction, if school it is.

To begin by wanting to resuscitate a dead society, it seems to follow, involves the writer in a great risk. It gets in the way of bringing his people alive. For the first hundred pages or so he is in danger of being misled by opinion. He is saved by the creative act; that is, he is saved by his people showing life. The moment comes when the actors in the stress of the situation will come "alive," will make a response that reveals them. In the light of this response the writer can go back and rectify, revise, remove the scaffolding. Then he is able to examine, to criticize the impulse which set him going. He can do this without impairing the life evoked. He can do it because life is there. It is at this point that the conscious and the intuitive practice of the craft work most easily together. The mechanics for this is cleaning up as you go along. Ford Madox Ford taught me this method. Many practice it, but not all. You do the day's stint, let it set, and next morning look at it again. Tighten it up, change things about, and then proceed. As the action grows, each day's work moves closely out of what has gone before. In the beginning it is not always clear which of the threads of complication holds the center. Cleaning up at last shows it. This is a decisive moment. Such a process simulates natural growth most unnaturally: that is, it has about it the mystery of all growth, and yet is artificial. The common miracle of life is the seasonal change. It is so common, and of necessity must be so, else we would be too aware of living in a state of constant miracle. This would strain the amenities. So it is in the practice of a craft. But there are moments when the craft is overborne by the stroke of life. This is the flash of miracle. This is the artist's reward, almost the only lasting reward, for it is an assurance that the work is moving as it should. Perhaps it was of this that Blake was thinking when he said the artist continues the act of God.

How gradually does this bemusement with the strict idea lift. I do not now remember at what stage it became clear again that you do not write about a society living or dead. You write about people who live within the constraint of some inherited social agreement. They are already involved when you take them up, for there is no natural man. He has never anywhere been seen, certainly not within historic time. But what is natural or common to all men has been changed from birth by manners and mores, institutions, all the conventions and laws of a given society. It is the restraint of decorum, propriety, taste, the limits of estates and classes—all such which distort, repress, guide the instincts, impulses, passions, the unruly demands of the blood toward the multifold kinds of behavior. All forms of intercourse rely upon faith and belief. This is a platitude of statement, but as working knowledge for the author it shows itself with the fresh light of truth.

And this working knowledge was already informing, changing from a concept to the movements of life, the idea of a dead society. I was not only rationally seeing fuller implications; that is, I was not only seeing of what this society was composed as action, which had already taken it out of a conceptual stage; I was comparing it to the cycles which other societies go through. The decline of civilizations, for example, of necessity follows the failure of belief, the cultural forces gradually withdrawing made manifest in the hardening of traditional laws and forms, foreshadowing rigidity: that is, death. But out of death comes life, as appositely death is the conclusion to life. Within the circling spiral of such change lies the belief in immortality and continuance. At some point it came to me that it is the archetypes which forever recur, are immortal, timeless; it is only the shapes in which these appear that seem to harden and die, that is, the manners and mores that are unique to a given society; and these shapes are the appearances of reality, the world's illusion moving within the illusion of time. What a shock this was to my partial and emotional view of the South!

Now the South was a mixed society, and it was a defeated society; and the defeated are self-conscious. They hold to the traditional ways, since these ways not only tell them what they are but tell them with a fresh sense of themselves. Only defeat can do this. It is this very self-consciousness which makes for the sharpened contemplation of self. It is comparable to euphoria. The sudden illumination made life fuller and keener, as it made life tragic. But it stopped action. The very heightening of self-awareness made for a sudden withdrawal of the life force. What was left of it remained in the surface forms. The forms were shattered, but because of this force they held their shape briefly. The shed skin for a while shines with life, but the force of life is already on its night sea journey. I did not know how to define this force at the time; I only felt it vaguely, as I felt the vacuum beneath, which is the atmosphere of chaos. I was slow to connect this basic energy with the repetitive thrust out of chaos into the surrounding void, but I felt I knew that chaos is the underlying condition of any artifice, whether it was the state or the family or a work of art. Mythically, for so far only did I read the myth, it seemed the state Adam and Eve found themselves in after Eve had been taken from Adam's side. Their expulsion from the earthly paradise seemed to put them into the disorder of chaos. Actually, they were confronted by a natural order which was a multiplicity of the conflicts of opposites. This is not chaos but life as we suffer it, and we fall into it as the child falls into the world. Continuance depended upon the exercise of the will and especially the crafts, not only to survive but to try to restore, to bring together the two halves which make a whole. Together, man and woman serve as the basic symbol for the life drama. How old is the sentence we hear every day, "This is my better half."

It was some years after I had been working on the as yet unnamed *The Velvet Horn* that I realized I was treating an aspect of this ancient drama. The brothers and sister, under the guidance of the eldest, withdrew from the stresses of formal society in an effort to return to the prenatural equilibrium of innocence and wholeness. This is an habitual impulse, the refusal to engage in the cooperating opposites that make life. It is also as illusory as any Golden Age, and forbidden by divine and human law. Therefore, it is the grounds for one of the oldest forms of search and conflict. The symbol for this is incest. It need not be fact; but it is symbol, also one having a literal counterpart; in one instance in the story it happened as fact as well.

For many years it has seemed to me that incest was a constant upon the Southern scene. There was plenty of circumstantial evidence. The boys' and girls' rooms seemed too obviously separated. I remember in old houses the back stairs with solid paneling to hide ankles and lower legs as the girls came down. Call it prudery, but what is prudery? The fear of incest, if incest it was, was perhaps not overt, but I knew of whore houses where too many of the girls had been ravished by fathers and brothers. Even if these were extreme instances—I had no way to know how general they may have been—still they were indicative. But the actual union between close kin was not my interest. It was the incest of the spirit which seemed my subject, a spiritual condition which inhered within the family itself. I did not have to look very far, no farther than both sides of my own house, to know this. It was clearest in the county family, where the partial isolation meant an intimacy and constancy of asso-ciation in work and play which induced excessive jealousy against intrusion from the outside. Often enough a partiality for one child went beyond the needs of parental care, bringing about all kinds of internal stresses within the family circle. This jealousy, this love, extended to the land and to natural objects with a possessiveness lasting even generations. I know of a family that today will engage in ritualized quarrels for hours on end over whether a field has been let grow up in sprouts, while the guests sit as at a play. These are all love quarrels, and the land is as much subject as object.

But to return: once I had got well into the first section of the novel, I had completely forgotten that I had wanted to bring a dead society to life. What part incest would play had, as well, moved to the edge of my attention. I was involved in the first pressures of making a world, peopling this world into which the young nephew, Lucius, would be guided by his uncle. The surface action seemed to be the initiation of the boy, cul-minating in his first sexual experience, although this was by no means his only ad-venture. The world he was entering, I felt, must seem out of the world, withdrawn, mysterious, of a strange look to him and refreshing, since in climbing the Peaks of Laurel, he left behind a dry and sterile place, burning under excessive drought. Of course he was climbing into his entanglement with life, which his father's suicide would rebegin. The seeming accidental reason for the climb was to witch a well: find water. It bore a literal as well as symbolical meaning.

Gradually I became aware of the need for this double usage as far as fiction is con-cerned. The symbol should always have its literal or natural counterpart. It should never rely upon the Platonic ideal image; this is a concept. Since fiction is an action in which nothing must be left inert, a concept of perfection, say, cannot be known actively. Perfection can only be sought out of imperfection, out of the fallen state of man represented by the cooperating forces of good and evil. The reinterpretation of myth by such people as Jung and Zimmer has done much to make this clear, but I think it has always been known by a certain kind of artist, if only intuitively. It was the yeast which worked the dough. An image seemed, then, not an imperfect reflection of perfection, but an action derived from the shattering of a whole into parts, which in all myths of origin begins the world drama. The end of this would be a reunion of the parts into a whole, but a whole no longer innocent. But this reunion never takes place in the world, else the drama would end. Here was the clue to the end of my novel, however, although I in no way saw it. The action had not moved sufficiently to inform me.

Anyway, the action itself must be symbolic of the archetypal experience. This, I consider, was the most important thing *The Velvet Horn* taught me. The symbol must be more than an inert sign or emblem. Where symbols appear—and there will be one to contain them all in their relationships—they represent the entire action by compressing into a sharp image or succession of images the essence of meaning. For example, in animal nature, the horn stands for both the masculine and feminine parts of being, the two aspects of the opposites which make a whole: the two in one contained by a single form. Add the velvet to this and you posit the state of innocence, that suspension before the act which continues the cycle of creation. At a certain moment the buck, out of the mystery of instinct, rubs the velvet off against the tree, and then he is ready for the rutting season. The velvet grows about the feminine end of the horn, and it bleeds as it is rubbed away. The blood is real, but the act symbolizes what the other end of the horn will do. In human nature the horn's counterpart would be the hermaphrodite, Hermes and Aphrodite contained within the one form. Their separation, Eve taken from Adam's side, at another level continues the cycle of creation. Both forms exist within the constancy of the seasonal turn of nature. The entire range of imagery relates to these.

So used, the image as symbol becomes the clue to reading, the means by which all the parts are related to the structure. It is not inert but active, being both root and crown of a particular living experience. This is technically called the controlling image; and once discovered, it allows the reader to read, not read *into* a book his own preconceptions and preoccupations. It also guides the judgment as it analyzes the rendition. When an action eschews the partial or topical, it is always symbolic, that is archetypal, whether the author knows it or not. To see a fiction either as so-called realism or symbolism is to commit the literal error, either as writing or reading. Realism distorts or diminishes the full action by plotting beforehand a beginning, middle, and end. How can this be done without inhibiting the creative act? How can a writer know beforehand what his people will do, until he has put them into action and so let the kind of thing they do show them for what they are; and upon this ground proceed partly creatively and partly deliberately? I rather imagine that when such fiction is successful, the author allows his creative sense to abandon the rigid plotting or the parts of it which get in the way. On the other hand you find the symbol misused as sign. Sign as symbol will be inserted in place of the concretion, the motion of action. It will be made to stand for the action instead of the actors in conflict showing it. To let the bare boards of the Cross stand for the Crucifixion is one thing; the Cross as image releasing the action of the Passion in the mind and heart is the other, the fictive way.

The writer working out of some form of myth will accept the supernatural as operating within nature. He does not take the world as the end in itself. His form will be some form of myth. Myth: symbol: archetype—the structure: the image: the conflict of the ever recurring human experience. In the Garden of Eden section of *The Velvet Horn* ("The Water Witch") there are three parts that represent the three stages of Eden as symbol of the world drama. Adam alone, the hermaphrodite, is the entire creature isolated within himself, the stasis of innocence, the loss of which is the beginning of action. When the woman is taken out of his side (symbolic: not according to nature as we know it), the separation begins the perpetual conflict. Incest is the symbol for this next stage. The third is the continuing action of the drama, the effort to fuse the parts into a wholeness which is complete knowledge. The symbol for this is the serpent, the old intruder. But there is another symbol for wholeness, the *uroboros*, the serpent eating its tail, lying about the waters of chaos. This is one of the oldest symbols, and out of it comes the only perfect figure, the circle. You will find it all over the world. In our hemisphere it encircles the Mexican calendar stone. To shift the image, Adam within his form contains the *uroboros*, both the masculine and feminine parts. Once separated, the feminine in Adam becomes Eve, the masculine the Serpent. All the goods and evils grow out of this separation, and one of the images of it is the caduceus, the two serpents entwining sickness and health. There are numerous forms of the separation, the dragon fight, where destructive nature take its fire-breathing, scaly shape without the human creature; or the Medusa; or Moses' staff. This, I should think, is repeated endlessly in myth.

Of course reading has helped me tremendously, but I read not as a scholar but as an artist. The wonder of it is its accidental nature. I did not look to books for help. I happened to be reading certain authors at the time of writing—some even before I began, Frazer years ago, more recently Zimmer, Jung, particularly *Psychology and Alchemy*, and Neumann's *Origin and History of Consciousness*. This accidental reading comes close to mystery, but anyway the first real surge of conscious direction and awareness came out of it. The curious part is that, as I looked back over what already had been done, I found little to change. The action was doing its own work. Whether it would have continued or not I cannot say. Of course there was rearrangement but the intrusion from the depths, where the subject lay, had already painfully and haltingly been moving in its own direction, its own autonomous way. The conscious help from me was ambiguous. I thought I was helping another kind of story; then at a certain moment I took hold consciously. The invisible form showed only streaks of substance, but I was able to *feel* the subject shaping its form. And I had my controlling image well fixed in the top part of my head: incest, the act symbolic of wholeness, not the wholeness of innocence but the strain toward a return to this state of being. Was not the brotherhood of man most supremely defined by the love of brother and sister, at least in symbolic terms? If they represented the two parts of the whole of experience, the effort to become one again must contain every kind of love which the separation had scattered throughout the world as man struggled to escape his fallen condition.

Through love and the act of will he could escape it, but only temporarily as far as the flesh was concerned. The irony of the central conflict lay just here. It is most surely known in the act of love, when flesh and spirit surcharge each other, in that brief annihilation of every separate faculty, the annihilation being the act of fusion, the disembodiment within the body, which was the suspension in chaos before the fall. The moment in which this could be felt had nothing to do with time, but with its opposite, the knowing of eternity which under-stands, that is stands under or outside time, the brief insight into the unmoving Mover.

I now saw my two working parts of the structure: the moving present tense which is the world's illusion, and the eternal present tense which knows nothing of past or future but always is. We know it best in the images of dreams. But the myth and fairy tale all operate through and represent this sense of the eternal. *Once upon a time; Long, long ago in a far kingdom*—these beginnings by their tone and meaning speak of no time, no country. They are outside time; they are always and forever about what is constant in human experience. The seeming tone of the far past is the announcement of the timeless held within the point of a moment. To emphasize this, there is little or no natural landscape, no recognizable cities, in myth or fairy tale. This is a crucial distinguishing feature between myth and fiction which deals with myth. They have the archetypes in common, but in fiction the action must be put in a recognizable place and society. The moment I say this, Kafka appears. Except for the intrusion of his moral rage, he more nearly approaches the ideal form of myth. But morality as we know it has little to do with myth.

As soon as I began to feel the right limits of the structure, I could deal with its formalities. Within the various levels and distinctions of the mind, especially where it oscillates between conscious and unconscious, I could put the sense of eternity, the images of the past which are not past but forever quivering with immediacy. Opposed to this, by closing the mind and letting the action take place as upon a stage, I could use the moving present tense, the action in time. But this last was not to proceed in a continuous movement of surface beginning, middle, and end. Each of the five sections was to be nearly complete within itself, the tensions of the action evoked by eternal knowledge acting against time's knowledge. The movement in time would allow the sections to be dramatically connected, each showing a whole but differently, involving, I hoped, the fullest possibilities of the central image: incest. Not until the end of the book would the shock of meaning connect all the parts and the action be complete. There would be no way to turn to the end of the book and find out what had happened. This puts a handicap upon reading, this juxtaposition and accumulation rather than the steady advance of a conflict, which is the way of naturalism and the oldest form of all, the simple art of narrative.

By now I also had a firm grasp upon the point of view, and I knew who the protagonist was. Everybody was the hero and heroine, but only Jack Cropleigh, the brother and uncle, could represent them, for Jack, the spiritual hermaphrodite, contained them all in his mind. He alone could suffer the entire myth. The point of view would therefore be that of the Roving Narrator, where the variety of the action might lie within the levels of his consciousness as it met the unconscious: time and eternity. Having set him apart with no life of his own, other than his entanglement with all life viewed by family and community, he was best suited to control as central intelligence, and his office as victim-savior could bring it all to a focus by his death. The irony I intended, or recognized when it happened, lay in how little his victimage could offer. He could save nobody, not even his beloved nephew, by proxy. He could only save his nephew from running away from life. All he could tell him was that no matter how far you run you are always there. As archetype of victim-savior, Jack, I'm afraid, denies the efficacy of the Mass. His death implies that for heroes, at any rate, the sacrifice must be forever repeated, actually as well as symbolically. This perhaps is theological heresy but mythical truth, and certainly fictional truth. The feeling and knowledge he suffers throughout pass progressively through the three phases of the Garden's drama, renewing through the nephew, the inheritor, the same perpetual cycle.

The nephew Lucius, the bastard child of incest, is in a sense then the youthful counterpart of Jack, or if you like of all his uncles and mother. I think this was the reason I was so long in finding the protagonist. I had begun with Lucius so the tale opens out of his eyes and mind. Jack takes over in the next section, and the view remains with him throughout for the reasons given, in spite of the fact that it roves again to Lucius and even to Pete Legrand, the old intruder. In the roving point of view it is only necessary, I feel, for one mind to dominate throughout the story, so that no matter where the view shifts, it might seem to belong to one central intelligence, that intelligence and sensibility alone equal to the fullest knowledge. The success of this depends upon how you write it, and especially upon the transitions from section to section. (The roving is no good written in chapters.) For example, although the view is with Lucius at the beginning, Jack so fills the pages, especially toward the end, that when he takes over in the next section the reader should feel no jar and without question follow, as he was now entering a fuller complexity of the complication. If he did not feel that what had gone before was actually in Jack's mind, he could feel that it might have been. This was tricky, I know, but if it could be made to go smoothly, then what follows could also seem an extension of the central intelligence, as every mind is equal to the total experience, the difference being that only one can know the fullest meaning in suffering for all. Anyway, this is how it worked out—how successfully, it is not the author's place to say.

I can only feel that it comes off. My pace of writing is generally very slow, with constant cleaning up and structural revisions. Too often I will spend a day on a paragraph; a page is a good day's work. But as I drew toward the end, the last thirty pages or so, the artifice completely usurped my mind. It possessed me. There is no other word for it, and I've never quite felt it before. I became merely an instrument. I wrote three or four pages a day, scarcely changing a word. It was as if I had divided myself into two persons, one watching and one doing. The physical presence seemed a shadow. I felt disgust for its demands, and appetite had lost its savor. My impulse was to remain at the typewriter and not get up until the book was done, but this would be too long for my strength. Food and sleep were necessary, and the tactical considerations of how much changed from day to day. I could not bear to be touched or noticed. My nerves had drawn into the tissue of the skin. I forced myself to eat as in a dream. I would go to bed at seven or eight o'clock and rise each morning earlier, until I was getting up at two. In a kind of half-awareness I knew that I had to watch this expense of energy, or I would give out before the end. I sensed that if I did, I would lose it, that once this possession of me by the actors was broken, it would never return. It was as if there were only so many words left, and each had its place, if I could hold out to receive them. The last day my breath was all in the front part of my mouth, and each word had weight. Then in the final hour or so they began to fade, the substance of meaning growing lighter. When it was all done, the final period made a final expulsion of breath. I leaned back in the chair. I felt that all that had gone before was right, or the illusion of the last acts being not fiction but life would not have seized me.

This is the way it was done, to the best of my recollection. There is such cunning in the way the creative part uses the conscious craft that it is hard to follow the twisted windings of the journey. It seems just that. You must act as if it is real, and yet know you are acting; but the acting is lost in the act. How it is sustained over so long a time, in this instance over nine years, is a mystery and a cause for shame, as is the setting down of what seems to be the procedure.

This fresh interest in myth derives, perhaps, from a weakening of the formal authority of the Church. Everywhere the Satanic acceptance of matter as the only value, the only fulfillment, has been shaken. We sense again that people cannot live, except in some belief outside themselves. The cycles of cultures seem to show that when belief hardens into formalism, leaving the center dry and hollow, it is a time, as Yeats says, of the trembling of the veil of the temple. But before some new faith breaks through, there is a withdrawal into the source. This I believe to be the archetypal conflicts of myth which precede the formalized rituals and dogmas of institutional religion. This is a statement only an artist can make. And he can make it only vaguely, as it affects his work, for the artist is a cannibal of Gargantuan appetite who does not exclude himself, if he is lucky.

Daedalus, LXXXXVIII (1959), 326–338.

Scattered throughout the preceding Part I and Part II essays have been a number of warnings, qualifications, and criticisms alerting the reader to the difficulties inherent in the problem of myth and literature. The following three essays consider in depth the possible weaknesses of this alliance.

Although Philip Rahv begins as though he wishes only to correct excesses in the literary interest in myth, he quickly mounts a full-scale attack on what he calls the current "cultic interest in myth." For him, it is a revival or a persistence of romanticism and conservatism occasioned by the fear of history and freedom, of change and making choices. Such an intellectual or ideological analysis joins issue sharply with apologists for myth like Philip Wheelwright and Joseph Campbell. This is particularly apparent when Rahv discusses the role of belief in myth and literature and the impossibility of a return to genuine mythic consciousness.

THE MYTH AND THE POWERHOUSE

Philip Rahv

> *One must know how to ask questions: the question is who was Ariadne and which song did the sirens sing?*—FRIEDRICH GEORG JUENGER.

Much has been written of late about myth. What it is and what it will do for us has been widely debated, yet I cannot see that any clear statement of the intrinsic meaning of present-day mythomania has emerged from the discussion. The exponents of myth keep insisting on its seminal uses, appealing indiscriminately to Yeats and Joyce and Mann and other exemplars of the modern creative line, while the opponents point to the regressive implications of the newfangled concern with myth, charging that at bottom what it comes to is a kind of nebulous religiosity, a vague literary compromise between skepticism and dogma, in essence a form of magico-religious play with antique counters in a game without real commitments or consequences.

To be sure, not all exponents of myth are of one type. Some make no excessive claims; others have turned into sheer enthusiasts who blow up myth into a universal panacea, proclaiming that the "reintegration of the myth" will not only save the arts but will lead to no less than the cure of modern ills and ultimate salvation. So extravagant have been their claims that even Jacques Maritain, who is hardly to be accused of a naturalistic view of myth, has been moved to rebuke them, primarily for confusing metaphysical and poetic myths, that is confusing the fictions composed by the poet *qua* poet (which may be called myths, if at all, only in a loose analogical sense) with the great myths deriving their power solely from the belief that men have in them. For myth actually believed in is not understood as a symbolic form, competing with other such forms, but as truth pure and simple.

Now why should a distinction so elementary be generally overlooked by the cultists of myth? For the very good reason, obviously, that it is this very cultism which enables them to evade the hard choice between belief and unbelief. After all, now that the idea of myth has been invested in literary discourse with all sorts of intriguing suggestions of holiness and sacramental significance, one can talk about it as if it were almost the same thing as religion, thus circumventing the all-too-definite and perhaps embarrassing demands of orthodoxy even while enjoying an emotional rapport with it. At the same time, myth having been somehow equated with the essence of poetry, it becomes possible to enlist its prestige along with that of religion. The mythomaniac puts himself in the position of speaking freely in the name both of poetry and religion without, however, making himself responsible to either. But it should be evident that in the long run neither benefits from so forced a conjunction. It deprives them equally of specific definition and commitment; and this, I take it, is the implicit point of M. Maritain's critical remarks.

The discussion of myth has led some literary men to undertake interpretations of it in terms of its origins and fundamental import in the history of culture. Such interpretations are in the main more wishful than accurate, running counter to the findings at once of such noted philosophical students of myth as Ernst Cassirer and anthropologists and ethnologists like Malinowski, Jane Harrison, Lord Raglan, A. M. Hocart, S. H. Hooke, et al. The fact is that the current literary inflation of myth is not in the least supported by the authoritative texts in this field of study. Typical is the approach of a distinguished literary critic, who on the subject of myth proceeds entirely without discretion. Myth is for him "the cartograph of the perennial human situation," and he contends that in myth alone can we hope to encounter "a beckoning image of the successful alliance of love and justice, the great problems of the race from its dark beginnings." In other words: Back to myth if you want to be saved! It leaves one wondering how that sort of thing can possibly be squared with anything to be found, for instance, in the late Professor Cassirer's numerous, painstaking, and truly imaginative inquiries into myth. What we do realize in reading Cassirer, however, is that contemporary mythomania makes for the renewal in our time of the symbolic-allegorical treatment of myth favored by the romantics, who saw in myth a source of higher teachings and ultra-spiritual insights, converting it into a magic mirror that reflected their heart's desire. As Cassirer observes, the romantic philosophers and poets in Germany were the first to embrace myth with rapture, identifying it with reality in the same way as they identified poetry with truth: from then on "they saw all things in a new shape. They could not return to the common world—the world of the *profanum vulgus*."[1] The cultism of myth is patently a revival of romantic longings and attitudes.

It seems as if in the modern world there is no having done with romanticism—no having done with it because of its enormous resourcefulness in accommodating the neo-primitivistic urge that pervades our culture, in providing it with objects of nostalgia upon which to fasten and haunting forms of the past that it can fill with its own content. And the literary sensibility, disquieted by the effects of the growing division of labor and the differentiation of consciousness, is of course especially responsive to the vision of the lost unities and simplicities of times past. Now myth, the appeal of which lies precisely in its archaism, promises above all to heal the wounds of

1. Ernst Cassirer, *The Myth of the State* (New Haven: Yale University Press, 1946), p. 5.

time. For the one essential function of myth stressed by all writers is that in merging past and present it releases us from the flux of temporality, arresting change in the timeless, the permanent, the ever-recurrent conceived as "sacred repetition." Hence the mythic is the polar opposite of what we mean by the historical, which stands for process, inexorable change, incessant permutation and innovation. Myth is reassuring in its stability, whereas history is that powerhouse of change which destroys custom and tradition in producing the future—the future that at present, with the fading away of the optimism of progress, many have learned to associate with the danger and menace of the unknown. In our time the movement of history has been so rapid that the mind longs for nothing so much as something permanent to steady it. Hence what the craze for myth represents most of all is the fear of history. But of that later. First let us turn to the genetic approach to myth developed by the scholars in this field, comparing it with some of the literary notions which, by infusing myth with the qualities that properly belong to art, have brought about widespread confusion as to the differences between the mythic and the aesthetic mode of expression.

The most commonly accepted theory among scholars is the so-called ritual theory defining myth as a narrative linked with a rite. The myth describes what the ritual enacts. A mode of symbolic expression objectifying early human feeling and experience, the myth is least of all the product of the reflective or historical consciousness, or of the search for scientific or philosophical truth. Though satisfying "the demands of incipient rationality . . . in an unfathomed world,"[2] it arises, basically, in response to ever-recurrent needs of a practical and emotional nature that are assumed to require for their gratification the magical potency of a sacral act. Its originators, as S. H. Hooke writes, "were not occupied with general questions concerning the world but with certain practical and pressing problems of daily life. There were the main problems of securing the means of subsistence, of keeping the sun and moon doing their duty, of ensuring the regular flooding of the Nile, of maintaining the bodily vigor of the king who was the embodiment of the prosperity of community. . . . In order to meet these needs the early inhabitants of Egypt and Mesopotamia developed a set of customary activities directed toward a definite end. Thus the coronation of a king . . . consisted of a regular pattern of actions, of things prescribed to be done, whose purpose was to fit the king completely to be the source of the well-being of the community. This is the sense in which we shall use the term 'ritual.'"[3] Cassirer uses the term in much the same sense, as for example, in his comment on the mythic tale of Dionysus Zagreus: "What is recalled here is neither a physical nor historical phenomenon. It is not a fact of nature nor a recollection of the deeds or sufferings of a heroic ancestor. Nevertheless the legend is not a mere fairy tale. It had a *fundamentum in re*; it refers to a certain 'reality.' . . . It is *ritual*. What is seen in the Dionysiac cult is explained in the myth."[4] As for the Greek myths with which we are most familiar, Hooke sees them as the frag-

2. F. S. C. Northrop and Mason Gross (edd.), *Alfred North Whitehead: An Anthology* (New York: Macmillan, 1953), p. 475.
3. S. H. Hooke in *Myth and Ritual* (London: Oxford University Press, 1933), p. 6.
4. Cassirer, *The Myth of the State*, p. 42.

ments of a very antique pattern that in becoming separated from ritual gradually acquired an independent life through poetic formulation. Thus both the Minotaur and Perseus myths manifestly involve an underlying ritual pattern of human sacrifice developed in a stage when myth and ritual were still one. And to comprehend that unity one must keep in mind, as Lord Raglan puts it, that "in the beginning the thing said and the thing done were inseparably united, although in the course of time they were divorced and gave rise to widely differing literary, artistic and religious forms." It is clear that both *epos* and *logos* evolved out of *mythos*. But that this evolution is irreversible the literary expatiators of myth fail to grasp.

The primitive significance of myth is not to be disclosed by scrutinizing ancient poetry. "It is as vain to look to Homer for the primitive significance of myth," writes A. M. Hocart, "as it would be to seek it in Sir Thomas Malory." The epic, though a medium of mythological lore, is at the same time, as Susanne M. Langer observes, "the first flower, or one of the first, of a new symbolic mode—the mode of art. It is not merely a receptacle of old symbols, namely those of myth, but is itself a new symbolic form, great with possibilities, ready to take meaning and express ideas that have had no vehicle before."[5] Poetic structure transforms the mythic material, disciplining and subjecting it to logical and psychological motives that eventually alienate it from its origins. To take the fact that myth is the common matrix of many literary forms as an indication that myth is literature or that literature is myth is a simple instance of the genetic fallacy. Myth is a certain kind of objective fantasy to which literature has had frequent recourse for its materials and patterns; but in itself it is not literature. The literary work is mainly characterized by the order and qualitative arrangement of its words; myths, on the other hand, as Miss Langer notes, are not bound to "any particular words, nor even to language, but may be told or painted, acted or danced, without suffering degradation or distortion. . . . They have no meter, no characteristic phrases, and are just as often recorded in vase-paintings and bas-reliefs as in words. A ballad, however, is a composition. . . ."[6] We know that *Oedipus Rex* is based on a mythic ritual. But the question is, what chiefly affects us in the play? Is it the myth, as such indifferent to verbal form, serving as Sophocles' material, or his particular *composition* of it? The Oedipus myth has its own power, to be sure, but one must distinguish between this power and that of the dramatic embodiment the poet gave it. And by confusing these different powers the inflators of myth are able to credit it with properties that really belong to art.

Moreover, the mythic imagination is a believing imagination. Attaching no value to fictions, it envisages its objects as actually existing. Conversely, the imagination of art, a relatively late development in the history of human mentality, is marked above all by its liberation from the sheerly actual and material. Art achieves independence as it gradually detaches itself from myth. The poetic image, Cassirer notes, attains "its purely representative, specifically 'aesthetic' function only as the magic circle with which mythical consciousness surrounds it is broken, and it is recognized not as a

5. Susanne K. Langer, *Philosophy in a New Key* (New York: New American Library, 1948), p. 160 ff.

6. Susanne K. Langer, *Feeling and Form* (New York: Scribner's, 1953), p. 274 ff.

mythico-magical form, but as a particular sort of *formulation*." Then what is meant by
saying that not only the great epic and dramatic poets but even the best lyric poets
seem to be possessed by a kind of mythic power? Cassirer's reply is that in those poets
"the magic power of insight breaks forth again in its full intensity and objectifying
power. But this objectivity has discarded all material constraints. The spirit lives in
the world of language and in the mythical image without falling under the control of
either." Word and image, which once affected the mind as awesome external forces,
have now cast off effectual reality, becoming for the literary artist "a light, bright
ether in which the spirit can move without let or hindrance. This liberation is achieved
not because the mind throws aside the sensuous forms of word and image, but
because it uses them both as organs of its own, and thereby recognizes them for what
they really are: forms of its own self-revelation."[7]

This type of historical analysis of the relation between art and myth is unlikely to
interest the cultists. For what is the mind's recognition of its own creations if not an
advance toward freedom? But it is freedom which is refused by those who wish to re-
mystify the world through myth or dogma. This new-fashioned freedom is still largely
untried by the generality of men. Why not keep it so, thus saving them from its perils?
In literature this has prompted the endeavor to establish what might well be called a
poetics of restitution—restitution for the disenchantment of reality carried through by
science, rationality, and the historical consciousness. It is only natural that in such a
poetics, ruled by schematic notions of tradition, the liberation of art from the socio-
religious compulsions of the past should be taken as a calamity—a veritable expulsion
from Eden. And how is Eden to be regained? Inevitably some of the practitioners of
this poetics discovered that myth answered their purpose much better than tradition.
After all, the supra-temporality of myth provides the ideal refuge from history. To
them, as to Stephen Dedalus in *Ulysses*, history is a nightmare from which they are
trying to awake. But to awake from history into myth is like escaping from a nightmare
into a state of permanent insomnia.

But if the road back to genuine mythic consciousness is closed, what is still open is
the possibility of manipulating ideas of myth. And that is precisely the point of my
objection. For myth is not what its ideologues claim it to be. Though the common
matrix of both, it is neither art nor metaphysics. In fact, both art and metaphysics are
among those superior forces which culture brought to bear in its effort to surmount
the primitivism of myth. Dialectical freedom is unknown to myth, which permits no
distinction between realities and symbols. The proposition that "the world of human
culture . . . could not arise until the darkness of myth was fought and overcome"[8] is
no doubt historically valid. Witness the struggle against it in Greek philosophy, as
for instance in the animadversions on mythic tales in the *Phaedrus*. Socrates, walking
with his companion by the banks of the Ilissus, calls those tales "irrelevant things,"
declining to put his mind to them by reason of their uselessness in his search for self-
knowledge. Even if instructive in some things, the one thing they cannot impart is
ethical enlightenment: the question of good and evil is beyond myth and becomes

7. Ernst Cassirer, *Language and Myth* (New York: Dover, 1953), p. 97 ff.
8. Cassirer, *The Myth of the State*, p. 298.

crucial only with the emergence of the individual, to whom alone is given the capacity at once to assent to the gift of self-knowledge and to undergo its ordeal.

Individuality is in truth foreign to myth, which objectifies collective rather than personal experience. Its splendor is that of the original totality, the pristine unity of thought and action, word and deed. The sundering of that unity is one of the tragic contradictions of historical development, which is never an harmonious forward movement but "a cruel repugnant labor against itself," as Hegel described it with unequaled insight. It is the paradox of progress that humanity has proven itself unable to assimilate reality except by means of "the alienation of human forces." In order to recover the potency of myth civilized man would first have to undo the whole of his history; and when some literary intellectuals dream of this recovery they are manifestly reacting against the effects of self-alienation at the same time that they exemplify these effects with appalling simplicity. What Marx once called "the idiocy of the division of labor" must have gone very far indeed if people can so drastically separate their theories of life from their concrete living of it! (The "idiocy" results from the fragmentation of vital human functions, since, as Marx said, "together with the division of labor is given the possibility, nay, the actuality, that spiritual activity and material activity, pleasure and work, production and consumption, will fall to the lot of different individuals.")

It is not unimaginable that in the future the paradox of progress will be resolved and acting and thinking reintegrated. We can be certain, however, that a conquest so consummate will take place not within our civilization but beyond it, on the further shore of historical necessity, when man, at long last reconciling nature and culture within himself, will no longer be compelled to purchase every gain in freedom with the loss of wholeness and integrity. Admittedly that too is probably a dream, but it is at least a possible dream and so long as civilization lasts perhaps an indefeasible one. The fulfilment it promises is the hope of history—and its redemption. And inconceivable as that fulfilment may seem to us at present, it will be brought about through the real processes of history or not at all—never through the magic potion of myth.

I said above that the craze for myth is the fear of history. It is feared because modern life is above all an historical life producing changes with vertiginous speed, changes difficult to understand and even more difficult to control. And to some people it appears as though the past, all of it together with its gods and sacred books, were being ground to pieces in the powerhouse of change, senselessly used up as so much raw material in the fabrication of an unthinkable future. One way certain intellectuals have found of coping with their fear is to deny historical time and induce in themselves through aesthetic and ideological means a sensation of mythic time—the eternal past of ritual. The advantage of mythic time is that it is without definite articulation, confounding past, present, and future in an undifferentiated unity, as against historical time which is unrepeatable and of an ineluctable progression. The historical event is that which occurs once only, unlike the timeless event of myth that, recurring again and again, is endlessly present.

The turn from history toward myth is to be observed in some of the important creative works of this period, as Joseph Frank has shown in his remarkable essay "Spatial Form in Modern Literature." He quotes Allen Tate as saying that Ezra Pound's *Cantos* in their "powerful juxtapositions of the ancient, the Renaissance, and the modern worlds reduce all three elements to an unhistorical miscellany, timeless and without origin." Frank analyzes *The Waste Land, Ulysses, Nightwood* and other literary works along the same lines, establishing that while on one level they seem to be dealing with "the clash of historical perspectives induced by the identification of contemporary figures and events with various historical prototypes," in practice they make history unhistorical in that it is sensed as "a continuum in which distinctions of past and present are obliterated . . . past and present are seen spatially, locked in a timeless unity which, even if accentuating surface differences, eliminates any feeling of historical sequence by the very act of juxtaposition. The objective historical imagination, on which modern man has prided himself, and which he has cultivated so carefully since the Renaissance, is transformed in those writers into the mythical imagination for which historical time does not exist."[9] Frank offers no social-historical explanation of this retreat from history; he is simply concerned with it as an aesthetic phenomenon expressing itself in "spatial form."

Perhaps for that very reason he too readily assumes that the mythic imagination is actually operative in the writers he examines. But the supplanting of the sense of historical by the sense of mythic time is scarcely accomplished with such ease; the mere absence of the one does not necessarily confirm the presence of the other. For my part, what I perceive in Pound and Eliot are not the workings of the mythic imagination but an aesthetic simulacrum of it, a learned illusion of timelessness. We should not mistake historical retrospection, however richly allusive and organized in however "simultaneous" a fashion, for mythic immediacy and the pure imaginative embodiment of a perpetual present. In point of fact, the polemical irony which the poems both of Pound and Eliot generate at the expense of modern society in itself attests to a marked commitment toward history. Are not these poets conducting a campaign against history precisely in the name of history, which they approach, however, with mythic prepossessions, that is to say without either dynamism or objectivity, responding to its archaistic refinements while condemning its movement? The truth is that they are as involved in historicism as most contemporary writers sensitive to the "modern situation," but in their case the form it takes is negative. Willy-nilly they express the age, that few would deny is historicist through and through. As Eliot himself once wrote, if a poet is "sincere, he must express with individual differences the general state of mind—not as a duty, but because he cannot help participating in it." Eliot is plainly a more "sincere" poet than Pound, and he is also a religious man; and it is necessary to uphold the distinction between religion and myth. His religiousness, which has temperamental as well as deep social roots, hardly disallows the cultivation of historical awareness. This may well explain why he has always been able to curb his "mythicism," so that it is but one of the several tendencies in his work rather than its motive-power. As a literary critic he is seldom inclined to

9. Joseph Frank in *Criticism: The Foundations of Modern Literary Judgment*, edd. Mark Schorer, Josephine Miles, and Gordon McKenzie (New York: Harcourt, Brace & World, 1948), p. 392.

hunt for mythological patterns, whose task it seems to be to reduce the history of literature to sameness and static juxtaposition; more typically he searches for those alterations of sensibility that are historically illuminating and productive of significant change.

It is Pound who in his later phase is wholly in the throes of "mythicism." But, far from being a reincarnation of an ancient imaginative mode, it is really but another sample of modern ideology, applied to poetry with frenetic zeal in an effort to compensate for loss of coherence. In the *Cantos* time neither stands still as in myth nor moves as in history; it is merely suspended. As for Joyce's *Ulysses*, it seems to me that the mythological parallels it abounds in provide little more than the scaffolding for the structure of the novel; and only critics fascinated by exegesis would mistake it for the structure itself. Those parallels do not really enter substantively into the presentation of the characters. The manner in which Bloom is identified with Odysseus and Stephen with Telemachus is more like a mythic jest or conceit, as it were, than a true identification. To be sure, it reflects the somewhat scholastic humor of the author; but its principal function is that of helping him organize his material. In that sense it has more to do with the making of the novel than with the reading of it—for as readers we find both Stephen and Bloom convincing because they are firmly grounded in the historical actualities of Joyce's city, his country, and Europe as a whole. It is in *Finnegans Wake*, far more than in *Ulysses*, that the mythic bias is in ascendant, the historical element recedes, and the language itself is converted into a medium of myth.

Finnegans Wake is the most complete example of "spatial form" in modern literature. Joseph Frank's definition of that form is extremely plausible, yet I cannot agree that it is a mythic form in any but a very limited analogical sense. It is best understood, to my mind, as the aesthetic means devised for the projection of a non-historical or even anti-historical view of history. The most one can say of this form is that it reflects a mythic bias. But this bias is by no means independent of historicism, of which it is a kind of reactionary distortion or petrifaction.

There is a good deal of evidence supporting this conception of "spatial form." Thus in his book, *The Protestant Era*, Paul Tillich lists the main premises of the non-historical interpretation of history, and we find that one such premise is that "space is predominant against time; time is considered to be circular or repeating itself infinitely." What is the inner meaning of this spatializing of time? From Tillich's philosophical standpoint it means that time is being detached from history and yielded back to nature. In other words, the contradiction between history and nature is resolved in favor of the latter. Tillich defines time, in terms reminiscent of Schelling and Bergson, as the dimension of the dynamic, creative, and qualitative, whereas space he defines as the static and quantitative. If this contrast is valid, then one can only conclude that the attempt to respatialize time implies a defeatist attitude toward history, an attitude that in the long run makes for cultural regression.

Further premises of the non-historical interpretation of history are that "salvation is the salvation of individuals from time and history, not the salvation of a community through time and history," and that history is to be understood as "a process of deterioration, leading to the inescapable self-destruction of a world era." It is not difficult to recognize here some of the components of "mythicism." As an ideology "mythicism" is of course not to be equated at all points with its artistic practice. One must distinguish between the cultism of myth, which is primarily an ideological manifestation, and the literary works in which myth is made use of in one way or another. In Joyce the ideology is hardly perceptible, but you will find it in Eliot and a somewhat secularized version of it in Pound. Some critics write about Thomas Mann as if he too were enlisted in the service of myth. This is a mistake, I think. *Joseph and His Brothers* is not so much a mythic novel as a novel on mythic themes. In this narrative it is the characters, not at all the author, who confound past and present in their experience of that "pure time" which transcends both. Furthermore, in his recreation of myth Mann is heavily indebted to the Freudian psychology; and psychology is inherently anti-mythic. The Freudian method is a special adaptation of the historical method in general. Freud's early efforts to fit his theory into a biological framework were of no avail; and now it is clear, as W. H. Auden has so well put it, that Freud, "towers up as the genius who perceived that psychological events are not natural events but historical and that, therefore, psychology, as distinct from neurology, must be based on the presuppositions . . . not of the biologist but of the historian."

Not a few characteristics of "mythicism" are brought into Tillich's exposition under the heading of the "mystical" approach to history, against which he argues in the name of historical realism. This is a perspective that he evaluates as a creation of the West, especially in so far as it stands under Protestant influence. "For historical realism the really real appears in the structures created by the historical process," he writes. "History is open to interpretation only through active participation. We can grasp the power of historical being only if we are grasped by it in our historical experience."[10] His analysis, combining certain Marxist concepts with the religious variant of existential thought, repudiates all attempts to escape the present for the sake of the unreal past of archaism or the equally unreal future of utopianism. It is a view resistant to attitudes of religious pessimism toward the historical world and even more so to the mythic dissolution of it in the eternal past of ritual.

The fear of history is at bottom the fear of the hazards of freedom. In so far as man can be said to be capable of self-determination, history is the sole sphere in which he can conceivably attain it. But though history, as Tillich affirms, is above all the sphere of freedom, it is also the sphere in which "man *is determined* by fate against his freedom. Very often the creations of his freedom are the tools used by fate against him; as, for instance, today the technical powers created by him turn against him with irresistible force. There are periods in history in which the element of freedom predominates, and there are periods in which fate and necessity prevail. The latter is true of our day. . . ."[11] An analysis of this type, largely coinciding with the Hegelian-Marxist idea of historical tension and crisis, sufficiently accounts for the retreat from history toward myth. In our time the historical process is marked far more by loss and extremity than growth and mastery, and this fact is interpreted by the spokesmen of traditionalism as completely justifying their position. The mythic principle appeals to

10. Paul Tillich, *The Protestant Era* (Chicago: University of Chicago Press, 1948), p. 71 ff.
11. *Ibid.*, p. 186.

them because of its fixity and profoundly conservative implications. But the hope of stability it offers is illusory. To look to myth for deliverance from history is altogether futile.

In literature the withdrawal from historical experience and creativeness can only mean stagnation. For the creative artist to deny time in the name of the timeless and immemorial is to misconceive his task. He will never discover a shortcut to transcendence. True, in the imaginative act the artist does indeed challenge time, but in order to win he must also be able to meet *its* challenge; and his triumph over it is like that blessing which Jacob exacted from the angel only after grappling with him till the break of day.

In criticism the reaction against history is shown in the search for some sort of mythic model, so to speak, to which the literary work under scrutiny can be made to conform. The critics captivated by this procedure are inclined to take for granted that to identify a mythic pattern in a novel or poem is tantamount to disclosing its merit— an assumption patently false, for the very same pattern is easily discoverable in works entirely without merit. Implicit here is the notion that the sheer timelessness of the pattern is as such a guaranty of value. What is not grasped, however, is that the timeless is in itself nothing more than a pledge waiting for time to redeem it, or, to vary the figure, a barren form that only time can make fecund. And Blake said it when he wrote in his "Proverbs of Hell" that "eternity is in love with the productions of time."

Partisan Review, XX (1953), 635–648. Some of the reference notes have been omitted.

In contrast with Mr. Rahv's approach in the preceding essay, Wallace W. Douglas, whose special interest is the history of literary criticism, expounds the shortcomings of myth criticism through a scholarly consideration of the ways in which it uses the term "myth." He aims to reveal the underlying moral assumptions which, he contends, invalidate the aesthetic values and judgments of this critical mode. The merits of Mr. Douglas's arguments are perhaps best assessed when read in conjunction with the essays by Frye, Wheelwright, and Chase, all of whom he discusses.

THE MEANINGS OF "MYTH" IN
MODERN CRITICISM
Wallace W. Douglas

According to Professor Stallman, contemporary criticism reflects the spiritual disorder and incapacity of the age: its lost traditions, its lost conventions, its lost world order, and its lost belief in religion and myth.[1] This is perhaps an oversimplified description, but it does suggest one preoccupation of one group of critics who happen to be writing at the present time. And in the last term of the series, "myth," it is possible to find meanings which incorporate portions of meaning from all the other terms. Indeed at times "myth" seems to be the most important and inclusive word in modern criticism: a little magazine devoted a whole issue to it, the English Institute spent a meeting on its various aspects, and now critics, using the anthropological connotations of "myth," dignify criticism by extending it to a search for The Myth in the work of poets who have wanted to recreate The Myth. The word is used by critics of many sorts; and, since modern critics constantly deny that they form a single school, it can be expected to have almost as many meanings as critics who use it; as it turns out, the meanings are almost as many as the uses. The word is protean and its fate is procrustean, I would say, if an old-fashioned decorative mythological allusion is still permitted. But behind the many meanings lie the moral presuppositions that sanction some of the aesthetic values of modern critics, and an examination of the meanings and uses of the word "myth" may get at some of these presuppositions, which otherwise are lost in the brilliant linguistic and grammatical insights of modern criticism.

I

Occasionally "myth" can still be found, in its naïve or popular sense, as a synonym for "illusion," "legend," or false propaganda, or in an earlier literary sense of decorative or illustrative material. More often it occurs as a surrogate term for the fact that the characters and the actions of literary works have qualities that make them representative of types or classes or ideas. In one example of this use, the critic may have wanted

1. R. W. Stallman, "The New Critics," in *Critiques and Essays in Criticism, 1920–1948*, ed. R. W. Stallman (New York: Ronald Press, 1949), pp. 488–490.

to make something more of the word, for he also spoke of "myths or fairy tales or dreams, where again the people act under compulsion, toward fatally predetermined ends."[2] Presumably it is this representative quality that another critic refers to when he says: "Words open out into the larger symbolizations on all levels—for example, into archetypal symbol, ritual, and myth."[3] In a slightly more complex use "myth" becomes a heavy synonym for "belief" or sometimes "convention";[4] as when Shakespeare's themes of love, Christianity, and governance are described as "mythic."[5] This meaning very easily acquires connotations of value; for example, when the neutral idea of "belief" is changed into something like "the received forms, the symbolic versions of human wisdom,"[6] or when a myth is described as having "an archetypal meaning quite independent of any individual's conscious exploitation of it,"[7] or when it is made superior to philosophy and likened to "the blush of blood in the face," or when it is said to have a reality that lies far beneath "the words in which it happens to appear."[8]

Thus the spread in usage seems to be from "illusion" through "belief" to "higher truth." But before examining this last area of meaning, in which "myth" becomes a name, so far as I can tell, for revelation, I must mention the special way in which Mr. Hyman, Mr. Frye, and Mr. Fergusson are interested in the concept of myth. They all follow the Cambridge Hellenists in being more interested in the ritual, which, they hold, is explained by the myth, than in the myth itself; and they all accept the comparative method of the Cambridge school. According to Mr. Frye, "a purely structural approach has the same limitations in criticism that it has in biology. In itself it is simply a discrete series of analyses based on the mere existence of the literary structure, without developing any explanation of how the structure came to be what it was and what its nearest relatives are." Literary criticism, he says, needs a central hypothesis, which can be arrived at inductively from structural analysis by associating data and seeking larger patterns, or deductively by following out the consequences of what he regards as a necessary initial postulate of criticism, the postulate of the unity and total coherence of criticism. "Total literary history moves from the primitive to the sophisticated, and here we glimpse the possibility of seeing literature as a complication

2. Malcolm Cowley, "William Faulkner's Legend of the South," in *A Southern Vanguard*, ed. Allen Tate (New York: Prentice-Hall, 1947), p. 26.

3. Cleanth Brooks, "Foreword" in Stallman, *Critiques and Essays*, p. xix.

4. E. L. Hubler, "Three Shakespearian Myths: Mutability, Plenitude, and Reputation," *English Institute Essays, 1948* (New York: Columbia University Press, 1949), p. 97. Mr. Hubler's point is that, so far as he can tell, that is all that "myth" really means.

5. R. B. Heilman, "The Lear World," *English Institute Essays, 1948*, p. 36; Leslie A. Fiedler, "The Defense of the Illusion and the Creation of Myth," *English Institute Essays, 1948*, p. 76.

6. R. P. Blackmur, "Between Myth and Philosophy: Fragments of W. B. Yeats," *Southern Review*, VII (1942), 408.

7. Fiedler, "The Defense of the Illusion and the Creation of Myth," p. 76. Mr. Fiedler is talking about the play within the play, in *Hamlet* and in general, which he calls a "technical or structural myth." It is difficult to see here what other purpose is served by "myth" than that of allowing the critic to express approval of a convention which most modern audiences would find awkward and "unnatural."

8. Blackmur, "Between Myth and Philosophy," pp. 417–418.

of a relatively restricted and simple group of formulas that can be studied in primitive culture. If so, then the search for archetypes is a kind of literary anthropology, concerned with the way that literature is informed by pre-literary categories such as ritual, myth and folktale."[9] These critics differ, however, in the rituals to which they would reduce literary patterns: Mr. Fergusson, whose primary source seems to be in Aristotelian commentary, always finds in works of literature traces of an original dithyrambic ritual; Mr. Frye discovers signs of fertility rites; and Mr. Hyman expects the "monomyth" to be an elaboration of Van Gennep's famous *rites de passage*: "as students of myth we must separate from the world, penetrate to a source of knowledge, and return with whatever power or life-enhancement the truth may contain."[10]

As the quotation from Mr. Hyman suggests, these three critics are ultimately interested in some special knowledge and, in Mr. Hyman's case at least, also in power, *mana, orenda, virtú*, which they would discover in literature, if I understand their position, by following evolutionary anthropology, especially in its use of the theory of survivals, and examining modern works for traces of such things as "the lost collective rites that enabled the tribe to function." Thus, though in analyzing works they pay more attention to structure and form than most modern critics (and have a more systematic conception of literary forms), in the end they, too, come around to treating a literary work as a repository of truth, of racial memories, or of unconsciously held values; and to the extent that they do so, they are connected with the general school of mythical criticism.

In the simplest of the meanings that associate it with revelation or higher truth, "myth" is taken as a representation in fictional form of truths or values that are sanctioned by general belief: myth "tells the truth to the extent that people believe that it tells the truth";[11] it can be called "the lie as truth."[12] Sometimes in this view myth seems to be out-and-out rationalization created by an individual.* * * It may also mean a story in which historical, scientific, or metaphysical facts, regarded here as "true" but cold and uninteresting, are endowed with human values, or it may be a concept or system of concepts which are regarded as worthy of belief, "belief" being then defined as "an unquestionable basis for action, a mode of reality in which one lives."[13] In the most common variant of this class of meanings, "myth" becomes the sanctified and dogmatized expression, not necessarily in the form of literature, of basic social or class conventions and values, concepts which may be as inclusive as the "togetherness of the community mind," but which are more likely to be thought of as, for example, "the modern *daimon* of money" (as embodied somewhat anachronistically, it seems to me, in Fafnir) or the now sanctified assumptions of the Enlightenment, the Declaration of Independence, the French Revolution,

9. Northrop Frye, "The Archetypes of Literature," *Kenyon Review*, XIII (1951), 95, 99–100.

10. S. E. Hyman, "Myth, Ritual, and Nonsense," *Kenyon Review*, XI (1949), 455. (The connection with Van Gennep is my inference.)

11. Donald A. Stauffer, "The Modern Myth of the Modern Myth," *English Institute Essays, 1947* (New York: Columbia University Press, 1948), p. 23.

12. Fiedler, "The Defense of the Illusion and the Creation of Myth," p. 78.

13. Heilman, "The Lear World," p. 43.

and so forth. In all of these meanings there are traces of social or psychological functionalism.* * *

For obvious reasons such a functionalist definition cannot be very popular among critics oppressed by the spiritual disorder of the age and harried by regret for lost traditions and conventions; and most critics use "myth" to refer to truths that are inexpressible in discursive language, in other words, perhaps, as a synonym for "paraphrasable content," which, in their system of analysing the relations among the words of a poem, cannot be discussed unless disguised by some mystical name like "myth."

> The play virtually says that wisdom and insight must be sought by a denial of the ordinary sense and logic of the world and must be found in the intuitions of the especially gifted mind, the unusual mind, even the disordered mind. Here again, then, we find paradox asserting the Mystery, and the content of the play taking on a strongly mythical case.[14]

"Myth" legitimizes the heresy of paraphrase, in the first place, because it implies a whole series of antitheses that are important in modern criticism. Myth or myths are opposed to facts, to "cataloguable and manageable phenomena," to the logic of ordinary knowledge, to positivism, the empirical, the finite, to the logos, to the intelligence and will, and to the consciousness. "Myth" can be a sanctifying word, in the second place, because its content or form is said to originate in passionate, poetic, or intuitional views of reality; in the unconscious, the dream; in memories of the primordial, the Mystery, the primordial Mystery; in the world of spirit, of value, of an extra dimension; in the imagination; or in man's now suppressed or denied awareness of his sin. The line here seems to be that "myth" calls attention to the dark places in which this kind of truth originates, and it suggests the paradox and language of multiple reference in which it must be expressed: in fiction and myth "a typical human or folk character or landscape lives in an irrational image, that can only be described but not *explained* or referred back any farther than exactly that specific appearance and experience."[15] Myth being, then, a living embodiment of insights, any discussion of it will be descriptive, not analytical, and the terms of the discussion will be neither manageable words nor cataloguable phenomena, but semipoetic devices to call attention to the structural paradoxes, ironies, or tensions (depending on the critic) which partly suggest the nonrational and hence linguistically indescribable elements of experience which lie behind the myth that is being described. Thus whatever else he may be doing, the mythogogic critic is not at least constructing simplistic moral statements about what the poem says.

It is true that the critics occasionally seem to reduce myths to very simplistic meanings; indeed, one can sometimes come upon almost Renaissance phrasings. Thus one critic speaks of the myth of Penelope's farewell to Icarius: "Such was the Greek genius for embodying eternal truths in stories almost as eternal in their grace." And another critic says that the myths of Prometheus and Epimetheus record the classical "sense of the whole of life which must not be too quickly disturbed for the

14. *Ibid.*, p. 43.
15. *Ibid.*, pp. 41, 43.

prosecution of special scientific interests."[16] But more often (and this is the third way in which the concept of "myth" allows critics to talk about the content of a poem) myth is said to contain either the otherwise inexpressible insights or values of the individual or group unconscious or the projections of group or individual felt needs or values. The mythic is "what the French have traditionally called the 'merveilleux,' the lost world of dream and disorder and grotesquerie, without which our possibilities of freedom and power are impoverished."[17] Myth implies a belief in a "penumbral reality," which is both the "psychic extrapolation" of the collective representations of the primitive mind, and a recognition of an otherness that is "radically different [from man], awful, potentially hostile." Myth implies a prelogical mentality that is not bound by the law of contradiction but operates under the law of participation, according to which "objects and phenomena can be, though in a manner incomprehensible to us, at once themselves and not themselves." The mythic involves insights into the universal, or "commerce between the community and the mysteries," and undertakes a part of the ordering of experience.[18] Myth deals with the "fundamentals of our existence"; it is derived from "the word as the most ancient, the original account of the origins of the world"; it also imbeds a "complex of human problems" or carries "one of the archetypes from the collective unconsciousness of mankind" or "the timeless meaning" of an individual's psychic life. In what must be its widest senses, "myth in its union with logos, comprises the totality of human existence"; or, as "the myth," it is "the totality of all visions of truth which are untestable, non-demonstrable, non-empirical, non-logical."[19]

Perhaps the best way to conclude this description of modern mythogogy is to attempt a summary of the theories of Professor Chase, who is undoubtedly our most sedulous student of myth. He begins by assuming a mythopoeic mind or a mythopoeic psychology, which is superior to, or in its operation more inclusive than, rational or speculative reason. For such a mind, objects are not perceived "as such but as vehicles of efficacious activity analogous to and identifiable with the impersonal powers of the universe projected out of human emotions."[20] He then argues, asserting that "modern anthropologists" are in agreement with him, that primitive man lives in two worlds: the matter-of-fact world of the practical reason and the magico-religious world of the mythopoeic faculty. He argues also that civilized man lives "in the same world as the savages," by which he means not only that our experience is

16. F. L. Lucas, *Literature and Psychology* (London: Macmillan, 1951), p. 65. The interpretation of the Promethean myth is from Allen Tate, "To Whom is the Poet Responsible?" *Hudson Review*, IV (1951), 329.

17. Leslie A. Fiedler, "The Critic's Excluded Middle," *Kenyon Review*, XIII (1951), 689. Isn't this a somewhat extended meaning for the French word?

18. Lévy-Bruhl, as quoted by Philip Wheelwright, "Notes on Mythopoeia," *Sewanee Review*, LIX (1951), 577; Heilman, "The Lear World," p. 41, quoting Wheelwright.

19. Erich Kahler, "The Persistence of Myth," *Chimera*, IV (1946), 2–3; William Troy, "Postlude: Myth, Method, and the Future," *Chimera*, IV (1946), 83; Graham Hough, *The Last Romantics* (London: Duckworth, 1949), p. 112; Francis Fergusson, "The Pilgrim on the Threshold of Purgation," *Hudson Review*, IV (1952), 558; Herman Brock, "The Heritage of Myth in Literature," *Chimera*, IV (1946), 34; Heilman, "The Lear World," p. 32.

20. Richard Chase, *Quest for Myth* (Baton Rouge: Louisiana State University Press, 1949), p. 20.

similarly divided but also that "Our deepest experience, needs, and aspirations are the same, as surely as the crucial biological and psychic transitions occur in the life of every human being."[21] Of course, what Mr. Chase wants to do is to validate not only his concept of the double world but also his approval of the mythopoeic descriptions of the magico-religious experience of primitive man, as opposed to that of modern man. So he assumes pan-human needs and aspirations, which he grounds in the biological process of growth; then he can argue that modern man has arbitrarily limited experience to that portion subject to analysis by reason; and there is no health in him.* * *

On the basis of his anthropological analysis of myth as defensive projections of man's unconscious, Mr. Chase moves on to a definition of myth as "literature which suffuses the natural with preternatural efficacy (*mana*)."[22] The psychological function of myth is to fuse the perception of power with the perception of physical qualities. "If these observations are sound, any narrative or poem which reaffirms the dynamism and vibrancy of the world, which fortifies the ego with the impression that there is a magically potent brilliancy or dramatic force in the world, may be called myth."[23] Elsewhere he has said that myth is literature "functioning in a special way, achieving special modes of expression"; it is "literature operating in certain more or less definable ways which set it off from other kinds of literature."[24] But also it is a magical tale dealing with critical passages of life, and in several reviews Mr. Chase has written as if myth, rather than being a quality, were a thing contained in literature, a part of the material of literature.[25] Most often, though, Mr. Chase uses the word just about as Longinus used "the sublime," as a means of asserting his approval of various works.

II

In all of this mythogogic theorizing there are a good many parallels to the early Nietzsche of *The Birth of Tragedy*: not only, for example, such notions as that reason cannot explain all of experience, that art deals with the ineffably concrete and particular and that there is a "primordial contradiction and primordial pain in the heart of the Primal Unity," in itself a sphere "beyond and before all phenomena," but also the general world view—in Nietzsche's case a great melodrama of sin and destruction in which Socrates and Euripides, representing critical intelligence, accomplish the estrangement of man and nature and the subjugation of the latter to practical controls. For Nietzsche, at this stage, myths seem to have been legends revealing or embodying the folk wisdom of the Greeks. "The Greek knew and felt the terror and horror of existence. That he might endure this terror at all, he had to interpose between

21. *Ibid.*, p. 78.

22. *Ibid.*, p. 78.

23. Richard Chase, "Myth as Literature," *English Institute Essays, 1947* (New York: Columbia University Press, 1948), p. 11. But reaffirms how? By statement? In its form?

24. *Ibid.*, p. 10; "Myth Revisited," *Partisan Review*, XVII (1950), 885.

25. *Ibid.*, p. 890; cf. his review of Professor Howard's *Melville* in *Nation*, CLXXIV (1952), 255; "A Poet's Economy," *Hopkins Review*, V (1951), 37; and "Sense and Sensibility," *Kenyon Review*, XIII (1951), 688.

himself and life the radiant dream-birth of the Olympians."[26] This was the pre-Socratic Greek, who still—a little bit like Mr. Chase's pre-eighteenth-century man—felt a wonder which he expressed in myth, "the concentrated picture of the world, which, as abbreviature of phenomena, cannot dispense with wonder." Like contemporary critics, Nietzsche assumes a modern man essentially different in his modes of thinking and feeling from primitive man: he is "so broken up by the critico-historical spirit of our culture, that he can only make the former existence of myth credible to himself by learned means through intermediary abstractions." Without myth, any culture loses a "healthy creative power"; myth gives meaning to the foundations of the state and to the life of the individual.* * *

Nietzsche, again like contemporary critics, assumes an eternal conflict between what he calls the theoretic and the tragic world views. The dialectical desire for knowledge destroys man's power to receive myth, which is "a unique type of universality and truth towering into the infinite."* * *

III

I am not trying to establish *The Birth of Tragedy* as a source for contemporary mythogogic criticism. Instead I want to use it to suggest how, since 1871, such romantic speculation has been extended, strengthened, freshened, and provided with an apparently firm empirical foundation by evidence borrowed from psychology and anthropology, especially from the theorizing about the primitive mind, so-called. Of all anthropological theories, those of Lévy-Bruhl must have been the most persuasive to the critics who have sought to define "myth" in such a way as to provide themselves with "real" and extra-literary reasons for approving the various doctrines that from time to time they want to discover in literature. Whatever its intention, the effect of Lévy-Bruhl's work is to create a primitive mind, which, because it does not know the law of contradiction but only the "law" of participation, lives in a special and vitalizing relationship with the totality of nature. And in many places he seems to say that the primitive mind is richer and more complex than the civilized mind because it does not recognize any separation between images or ideas of objects and the emotions evoked by them; because it does not differentiate powers and qualities from things; because it does not have any concept of universal or abstraction; and because it does not operate according to conventional categories of causation or of abstract reasoning. To critics who presuppose an exhaustion of language and culture due either to a disruption of some primal connection between man and nature or to a dissociation of thought and emotion in men, the attractions of this concept are obvious, especially if the characteristics of contemporary primitive minds are used as evidence from which to infer the existence and characteristics of a general primitive mind comparable, in relation to the mental development of man, to the primitive horde in its relation to the social development of man. Furthermore, there would seem to be

---

26. Friedrich Nietzsche, *The Birth of Tragedy* in *The Philosophy of Nietzsche* (New York: Modern Library, 1937), p. 962.

involved in this speculation the idea of some great and total shift in the human way of thinking, a shift in which man's participation with and feeling of the greater forces of nature (expressed by the idea of *mana* or in animistic religions; concepts of great importance in nineteenth-century anthropology and in modern mythogogic criticism) were destroyed by the effects of the discovery of practical logic and physical causes: the postulation of such a change would be valuable to the antiscientism of modern criticism.

Behind these oddly assorted ideas, and holding them together to the extent that they can be held together, lie the assumptions of the Cambridge Hellenists, in whose work modern critics have found a most attractive idea, that of the ritual (i.e., religious, nonpractical, nonscientific) origin of literary forms. The first assumption is that there is a uniform pattern of cultural evolution, all societies passing through the same stages from a hypothetical primitive horde to the differentiated classes of a mature civilization. The stages of this evolution can be described by comparative study of the cultural forms in contemporary "primitive" societies, especially of the unintegrated forms, which are assumed to be survivals of earlier stages. The second assumption, derived from the first and controlling the literary theories of the critics, is that phenomena of civilized societies have the same basic values (functionally or symbolically) as apparently parallel phenomena in primitive societies, either those now existing or others the nature of which is determined by speculation on the evidence of monuments of quite mature civilizations; and that ultimate causes and true origins of contemporary phenomena can be determined by this backward tracing of the evolutionary pattern. The Cambridge school, of course, was most interested in establishing the ritual origin of Greek literary forms, and they stuck pretty close to the evidence of Greek monuments, drawing on the world-wide comparisons of scholars like Frazer only for confirmation. Contemporary literary critics have paid more attention to the confirmatory footnotes than to the body of the evidence. For them Br'er Rabbit "means" the same as an animal hero in a totemic culture, both being embodied in "animal stories." For them the shooting of an albatross by a presumably medieval sailor "meant" to an eighteenth-century audience and "means" to a modern high-school student or sophisticated literary critic precisely what the real event or its fictional representation would "mean" to a member of an albatross clan or totemic group, if any; or at least to a member of a totemically organized society—all killings of all animals, wherever, whenever, or however accomplished, sharing some or all of the characteristics of a violation of totemic taboo. This persistence of meaning is explained either by the theory of the survival of cultural forms or—perhaps in most cases it is *and*—some variant of the Jungian theory of racial memories, itself based, of course, on the theory of survivals. On the basis of these assumptions, critics are prepared to argue that the literature of Western civilization can be understood and evaluated by establishing its connection with, or similarity to, the religious rituals and the literature of an assumed world-wide primitive society and primitive mind, the last being the important idea, since it is assumed that the primitive or unspecialized mind has a greater contact with, a more complete view of, total reality than the modern mind.

None of these ideas helps much in discovering the formal literary characteristics of a myth; and, in general, "myth" seems to be less an analytical than a polemical term, calling attention rather to a critic's mood or moral attitude than to observed facts in the work under discussion. And this moral attitude is roughly similar among all critics who use the concept of "myth," in spite of variations and contradictions among their different descriptions of myth. It presupposes a radical dualism in man's experience. On the one hand is a material world, in which atoms blindly run, unaffected by man's needs and aspirations. This is the workaday world of ordinary logic. It is defined by scientific laws and described by abstractions. It is a world of facts, of things seen as members of classes rather than in their ineluctable reality, of phenomena treated as cataloguable and manageable. On the other hand is a magico-spiritual world, which is either the projection of man's needs and aspirations or the natural world viewed as a totality in which there are certain areas (the emotional, the ethical) so complex as not to be susceptible of scientific analysis, even though they possess a substantive reality similar to that of any natural fact. This is the world of emotion, value, and quality. It is a world of unique moments, of things seen as individuals. It is a world of felt truths, unverifiable, but none the less absolute. It is indefinable and can only be described by poetry.

It is not clear how the mind is related to these "worlds," though, on the whole, the critics seem to assume a parallel dualism of mind and matter. At any rate, they talk as if the mind had two functions or faculties, the speculative reason and the mythopoeic imagination, which correspond to the "world" of fact and the "world" of nonfact. This is the important assumption, for on it are grounded the moral attitudes that are the ultimate subjects of modern criticism. This view of the mind validates the critics' dramatization of modern history as a constant and furious struggle between these two aspects of mind, or more often between two kinds of mind, the predominantly rational and the predominantly mythopoeic. It also prepares for a whole series of antitheses, both moral and "critical": tradition and disorder, poetry and science, symbol and statement, convention and originality, the particular and the abstraction, metaphysical poetry and Platonic poetry, aristocratic order and democratic chaos, intension and extension, texture and structure, myth and logos—the list is infinite. The concepts of myth and of the mythopoeic mind and the anthropological evidence supporting them constitute a "pragmatic charter" for the beliefs, cravings, social attitudes, and standards of the critics. The word "myth" itself, whether used to refer to the assumed insights of primitive literature or to the content of modern literature, simply calls attention to the complex of ideas constituting this charter; it is, in other words, a sign by which critics can indicate their approval of the doctrine they find in whatever work they happen to be exploring. Somewhere in the background there is, perhaps, a valid literary problem: that of accounting for the continuing interest shown by men in the great classical works. And farther in the background may be the philosophical problem that was at least suggested by Hazlitt's dictum: "wherever there is a sense of beauty, or power, or harmony, as in the motion of a wave of the sea, in the growth of a flower ... *there* is poetry, in its birth." But, with the problem formulated as it is and with the discussion carried on as it is, the result has been to turn attention away from literature as literature and to import into criticism confusing terms and concepts drawn from a social science that is itself so insight-ridden as to be peculiarly agreeable to critics who in other contexts seem to feel that the sin without name is that of committing a social science.

Modern Philology, L (1953), 232–242. Some reference notes have been omitted; others have been shortened.

The contribution which concludes this group is from a scholar particularly interested in comparative modern literature. Mr. Block's essay, unlike the two preceding it, takes into account the merits as well as the defects accruing from contemporary literary absorption in anthropology. Thus, while he provides his own criticisms of underlying assumptions and problems of definition, Mr. Block also points out the useful ways of looking at literature afforded by a knowledge of anthropology. His essay may also be considered in the light of Stanley Hyman's, which opens Part Two, for both describe the rise of modern literature's interest in myth and its relevance to it.

CULTURAL ANTHROPOLOGY AND CONTEMPORARY LITERARY CRITICISM

Haskell M. Block

Roger Fry put the matter somewhat delicately when he wrote, "we have the possibility of infinitely diverse reactions to a work of art." The variety of principles and methods in contemporary literary criticism is perhaps not infinite, but we hear very little said about criticism as a common discipline following fixed and immutable laws. Over the gate to our critics' Paradise one may read "FAY CE QUE VOULDRAS," freely translated as "Anything Goes!" We have not method but methods, for criticism today is considered as limitless, as all embracing, as art itself. Long ago Alexander Pope could equate "Those Rules of old discovered, not devis'd" with "Nature," but we have since left off talking about "the critic's laws." To be sure, the subject-matter of criticism may be works of art, but the critic's principles and methods are more likely to be derived from history and biography, sociology and psychology, science and religion, philosophy and philology, and much besides. I say nothing of permutations and combinations, but it should not shock us when T. S. Eliot declares that even Shakespeare's laundry bills should not be too casually dismissed, "in the possibility that some genius will appear who will know of a use to which to put them."[1] I do not share Mr. Eliot's optimism, but it is at least understandable. The expansion of the boundaries of art, the attempt by writers to enlarge the magnitude of their work, to pack more and more into the printed page, has been accompanied by a parallel development in literary criticism. Today our critic is a would-be *uomo universale*, aiming at the total interpretation of the work of art and employing whatever means may serve to provide illumination.

The role of cultural anthropology in contemporary literary criticism is of special significance, not merely because of the ways in which critical values have been affected, but because anthropology provides an index to many of the preoccupations of the great creative thinkers of our time. The literary critic ought not to be thought of as a bleak and huddled figure in a darkened room, perpetually whispering to himself. He cannot help being moved by the stir and jostling of ideas around him, by attempts

1. T. S. Eliot, "The Function of Criticism," *Selected Essays* (London: Faber & Faber, 1934), p. 33.

in every area of experience to interpret and evaluate human activity. Thus it is important for the critic to know that investigations into the thought and action of so-called primitive peoples have shed not a little light on their descendants, that myth and ritual are not exclusively pre-historic phenomena. Out of an understanding of human behavior in times past we have come to know a good deal more about ourselves. And new interpretations of customs and beliefs have led to new ways of looking at literature. One has only to glance at an issue of any of our leading critical journals to see how boldly anthropological concepts and techniques have invaded literary criticism. I said invaded, not engulfed, for "Literature tills its crops in many fields," and our literary anthropologists are not strong enough to rule the land. But they have made headway to this extent, that with innumerable critics, committed or not to any particular point of view, the use of anthropological methods has come to be taken for granted.

The way in which this development took place has been explored in some detail by Messrs. Chase, Hyman, Frye, and others, and I have neither the time nor the desire to retrace well worn paths in so brief a survey. Vico, Herder, Schelling, Renan and Nietzsche have all been honored as progenitors. For my part, I find Renan's notion of philology as "la science des produits de l'esprit humain" particularly applicable to present-day critical trends. Renan conceived of philology as the vast synthesizing discipline, to embrace not only history, poetry, and philosophy, but also primitive mythology, ancient cults, comparative religion, and the ways in which all these subjects constitute part of the heritage of mankind. It may have been easy to make grandiose prophecies in 1848, but it is clear, I think, that since then, for good or ill, literary study has come at least part of the way toward fulfilling Renan's expectations. In the twentieth century the work of the so-called Cambridge School of Classical Anthropology has been especially influential. The meticulous and fascinating investigations of Sir James Frazer into almost every area of primitive rite were followed by the studies of Jane Harrison, F. M. Cornford, A. B. Cook, and Gilbert Murray, all applying the findings of comparative anthropology to the origins of Greek drama. These scholars showed conclusively that Greek drama developed out of ancient ritual and that expressions of ritual are preserved in the structure, characterization, theme, and even incidental details of many of the Greek plays which have come down to us. Nor has Frazer's influence been limited to the study of Hellenic literature. As early as 1903 Sir Edmund Chambers demonstrated the enormous relevance of *The Golden Bough* in helping us to understand medieval English drama. Jessie Weston's researches, culminating in *From Ritual to Romance* (1920), applied Frazer's methods to the legend of the Grail. More recently, in the same tradition, we have had Lord Raglan's provocative inquiry into the supposed historicity of heroic narrative (*The Hero*, 1936) and Miss E. M. Butler's investigation of patterns of heroic legend (*The Myth of the Magus*, 1948). All of this work has had fruitful implications, not only for anthropology and the social studies, but for much of the literary criticism of our time.

Now I am well aware that we cannot identify cultural anthropology with the Cambridge school. All the same, I do not share the attitude of our American anthropologists who decry Frazer's separation of ritual from its cultural constituent and sneer at literary critics who take his work seriously. Of course, I know that the present-day anthropologist is not interested in ancient Greek drama or in aught else that smacks of the Classical tradition, and that a trip to Melanesia is held in much greater esteem than an understanding of Frazer's work. What matters for us is not the inadequacy of the assumptions of Frazer and his followers so much as the ways in which their findings have affected literature and literary interpretation. To a large extent, literary critics have been compelled to recognize the value of anthropology in criticism because of the sheer inclusiveness of modern literature. Contemporary writers have cast a wide net indeed, and anyone familiar with the writings of Eliot, Yeats, Joyce, Mann, Lawrence, to list only a few, will understand at once how far reaching the effect of Frazer's work has been. I do not mean that Frazer and his successors have always exerted their influence apart from parallel developments in psychology, language, or social thought, but T. S. Eliot did not understate the case when he said, in 1924, that *The Golden Bough* is a work of no less importance than the writings of Freud and perhaps of greater permanence. Frazer, Eliot declared, "has extended the consciousness of the human mind into as dark and backward an abysm of time as has yet been explored." And Eliot went on to predict that the work of Frazer and other anthropologists "will not fail to have a profound effect upon the literature of the future."[2]

Indeed, by 1924 this effect was already apparent. Two years earlier critics were confounded by the publication of Joyce's *Ulysses* and Eliot's *The Wasteland*. I need not refer you to the notes which, I take it, serve to make Eliot's work the longest poem in the English language. The important point for us is that critical attention perforce was directed to the use of anthropological methods and materials in literature. Eliot himself summarized the new tendency in his review of *Ulysses*: "In using the myth, in manipulating a continuous parallel between contemporaneity and antiquity, Mr. Joyce is pursuing a method which others must pursue after him. They will not be imitators, any more than the scientist who uses the discoveries of an Einstein in pursuing his own, independent, further investigations. It is simply a way of controlling, of ordering, of giving a shape and a significance of the immense panorama of futility and anarchy which is contemporary history."[3] Whether or not we agree with Eliot's emphasis on the Homeric sub-structure in *Ulysses*, his horoscope was remarkably accurate. Let me call to your attention D. H. Lawrence's *Plumed Serpent* (1926). Now I would not "kidnap" Lawrence for the anthropologists. It is true that he pondered long over Tylor, Frazer, Harrison, and Murray, but as W. Y. Tindall points out, he also drew generously on Freud and Frobenius, Blavatsky and Pryse, Oriental mysticism and Aztec mythology, all part of his effort to bring life into direct contact with the elemental powers of the universe.[4] This qualification made, there can be no doubt of the value of anthropology in helping us understand Lawrence's novel. Quetzalcoatl, the plumed serpent, is very much in the traditional pattern of Frazer's

2. T. S. Eliot, "A prediction in regard to three English authors . . .," *Vanity Fair*, XXI (February, 1924), 29. Also see T. S. Eliot, "Euripides and Gilbert Murray," *Arts and Letters*, III (1920), 38.

3. T. S. Eliot, "Ulysses, Order, and Myth," in *James Joyce: Two Decades of Criticism*, ed. S. Givens (New York: Vanguard Press, 1948), p. 201. This essay first appeared in *The Dial* for November, 1923.

4. W. Y. Tindall, *D. H. Lawrence and Susan His Cow* (New York: Columbia University Press, 1939), pp. 97–98.

dying god, whose death is the fount of human spiritual revival. There are other examples of the conscious use of anthropology in literature. Among the richest are Edith Sitwell's *Gold Coast Customs* (1929), a savage celebration of the primitive and at the same time, a denunciation of contemporary civilization, clearly part of the "Wasteland" tradition, and Joyce's *Finnegans Wake* (1939), a mythical representation of the universal processes of creation, death, and re-creation. The researches of Campbell and others have but partially disclosed the remarkable extent to which Joyce pillaged the folklore, mythology, and fable of all cultures. The road to an understanding of such writers as Eliot, Lawrence, Sitwell, or Joyce is a tortuous one, but of this much we can be sure: in many instances, the structure of their works, the development of primary themes, the significance of even the most recondite allusions, all can be clarified to some extent by anthropological reference. Such analysis, let me add, often goes far beyond source hunting or philological exegesis; it drives at the central meaning of the work.

What, we may now ask, are the dominant assumptions of this new critical approach? First of all, it is almost a commonplace among a respectable number of critics that literature—or indeed any art—cannot be understood and appreciated as an isolated expression, cannot be limited to the working out of a pattern within the framework imposed by an art form, but rather must be viewed as part of the totality of human experience. Thus the simple separation of form and content, intrinsic and extrinsic values, or the like, falls away even for purposes of analysis—indeed, especially for such purposes. From this central assumption it is but one further step to assert that literature is part of a social situation and that literary works must be approached primarily as modes of collective belief and action. Myth and ritual, then, become essential qualities of literary expression. We have already seen examples which would support such a view, but the anthropological critic is not concerned merely with deliberate reference. Let me quote Colin Still, whose interpretation of mythical patterns in *The Tempest* is of seminal importance for modern practical criticism: ". . . genuine imaginative art is the result of an unconscious process whereby expression is given to perceptions of which the artist may or may not be conscious."[5] Thus we can see that any element or collocation of elements in a work may be considered an expression of recurring symbols basic in human experience, hence common to primitive and modern cultures. It is for this reason that Northrop Frye recently declared that *The Golden Bough* is primarily a study in literary criticism. Through it, Frye would insist, we can arrive at an understanding of the essential patterns—the archetypal images—of human experience, which must necessarily find expression in constant representational symbols.

I have stated the position as concisely as I can, without showing how particular modifications have affected individual practices. The disagreements in anthropology itself between the comparative, historical, and functional schools, the intrusion of Freudian and Jungian terminology, the ink that has been spilt over the relation of myth to ritual, these things need not concern us here. The disputes among anthropologically minded critics should not blind us to the more important fact that they

5. Colin Still, *The Timeless Theme* (London: Ivor Nicholson and Watson, 1936), p. 7.

have the same enemies and, within a spacious framework indeed, the same objectives.

In what practical ways has anthropology entered into literary interpretation? Let me begin with a simple illustration: the use of folklore in the elucidation of difficult passages. In the epilogue to *As You Like It* Rosalind declares, somewhat enigmatically for the modern reader: "If it be true that good wine needs no bush, 'tis true that a good play needs no epilogue. Yet to good wine they do use good bushes, and good plays prove the better by the help of good epilogues." The proverb of the wine and the bush refers to the vintner's practice of placing a tuft of ivy on the door of his shop, originally in order to curry favor with the wine god. Similar instances abound in early English literature, and I have no doubt that folklore can do a good deal more than it has in helping us to understand the writings of semi-literate peoples or in illuminating that shadowy no-man's-land between folk tradition and conscious art. Whatever objections one may have to Robert Graves' *The White Goddess*, there is no doubt that medieval Welsh and Celtic poetry owe much to primitive representations of "the birth, life, death and resurrection of the God of the Waxing Year."[6] Similarly, the early English Mummers' plays, in celebration of St. George, present vestiges of creation myths and fertility rites: the conqueror of dragon and Turk was also renowned for his ability to cure barrenness among women. It must be admitted, however, that in dealing with early folk drama we are on somewhat shaky ground; even the most careful investigators have had to rely heavily on analogy and conjecture.

I cannot pause to examine the study of anthropological material merely as part of the sources of a work. This is matter for scholarship; the materials of art can come from any area of human experience. More important is the conception of drama as ritual. Here the classical illustration is Sophocles' *Œdipus Rex*, but an equally good example would be Euripides' *Bacchae*, a mythical projection of fertility rite wherein a human sacrifice serves as the source of generative power, of group purification. In *The Bacchae* Pentheus, ruler of Thebes, attempts to observe the worship of Dionysus by spying on the Bacchants from a tree top. They discover him and, maddened with fury, uproot the tree, seize Pentheus, and tear his body to pieces. Bather, Murray, Dodd, and Thomson have shown that even seemingly insignificant details of the action point to the preservation of ancient ceremonial traditions. Like Œdipus, Pentheus is both king and scapegoat, the incarnation of the dying god. The power of ancient ritual is all the more impressive when we realize that in Euripides' day the deeper and more savage practices of Dionysiac worship had long been eliminated.

We are only beginning to understand the importance of ritual in more recent drama. Francis Fergusson's discussion of *Hamlet* in his brilliant *Idea of a Theater* demonstrates convincingly that a primary concern of Shakespeare's play is the welfare of the community, expressed in Hamlet's attempts to purify the state, to destroy the rottenness in Denmark. In this sense, the drama is not purely one of individual introspection. The stages of the development of the action are mirrored constantly in scenes of civic, military, or religious rituals. These ritual scenes, Fergusson declares, are all "ceremonious invocations of the well-being of society, and secular or religious

6. Robert Graves, *The White Goddess* (New York: Creative Age Press, 1948), p. 10.

devices for securing it."[7] At the same time, Fergusson points out that *Hamlet* is improvisation as well as rite, and much of the latter part of the play, from the players' scene on, is parody of ritual. One must not press analogies too hard, but it should be clear that Fergusson is insisting that the Elizabethan stage served a communal function resembling that of the theater of Sophocles and that this function adds an important dimension to Shakespeare's dramas. Similarly, in the case of *Macbeth*, it would not be difficult to show that the dénouement represents the purgation of evil and the triumph of the divine cosmic order. The green leaves of the branches of Birnam Wood symbolize the rebirth of the powers of goodness, the re-establishment of the health of the " body politic."

This view of drama as ritual does not deny the presence of conscious art, the role of artistic handling, of individual modification. Euripides and Shakespeare are no less poets for having ordered their material in accordance with ancient ritual, whether they did so deliberately or not, and there is still every reason to inquire why their plays continue to move us as they do. Yet we gain in understanding if we see how the formal elements of drama are at least sometimes arranged in conformity with a traditional rhythm of tragic action. I have no doubt that our insight into Greek and Elizabethan drama has been deepened by the application of anthropological methods.

When we come to the examination of more recent literature we are likely to discover vestiges of ancient ritual rather than direct expressions. Civilization has its price, not the least of which is the extinction of mystery and the impoverishment of wonder. Nietzsche was acutely aware of the rootlessness and isolation of modern man: "And now the myth-less man remains eternally hungering among all the bygones, and digs and grubs for roots, though he have to dig for them even among the remotest antiquities. The stupendous historical exigency of the unsatisfied modern culture, the gathering around one of countless other cultures, the consuming desire for knowledge—what does all this point to, if not to the loss of myth, the loss of the mythical home, the mythical source?"[8] Nietzsche's *Birth of Tragedy* (1872) is above all an attempt to re-establish a living relationship between myth and poetry, and it is this same attempt that animates much of contemporary criticism. For through an awareness of myth we can perhaps recapture the spirit of the now forgotten rites which lent passion and purpose to the most ordinary experiences of our forbearers. An understanding of myth has come to be a central concern of a large body of twentieth century thought.

There is no doubt that Myth is one of the most muddled and abused concepts in our critical vocabulary. It has been defined as a lie, a popular delusion, as mystical fantasy, as primitive science, as a record of historical fact, a symbol of philosophical truth, a reflection of unconscious motivations, indeed, any unconscious assumption. It is all very confusing and the anthropologists can offer little help. Myth has been feasted on for so long by the psychologist and the historian, the sociologist and the literary critic, that the anthropologist can do little more than pick at the bones. It

7. Francis Fergusson, *The Idea of a Theater* (Princeton: Princeton University Press, 1949), pp. 114 ff.

8. Friedrich Nietzsche, *The Birth of Tragedy*, tr. Haussmann (Edinburgh: T. N. Foulis, 1910), p. 175.

was with much irritation but, I suspect, even more restraint, that Malinowski insisted that myth, if it is to have any meaning at all, cannot be divorced from its social function; and it is no surprise to come across a sociological essay entitled "*Robinson Crusoe* as a Myth" in a quarterly dedicated to literary criticism.[9] Clearly, what matters in such an inquiry is not Defoe's novel but the use which society made of it. Richard Chase and those who agree with him that "Myth is literature" might not accept this notion of the term, but they offer no way out.[10] It is perhaps an important feature of our modern mythomania that its converts are willfully obscure. When any of them sets about defining his terms and clarifying his assumptions, we must be grateful.

We have not yet reached the point where we talk about the myth of the critic—though I do not doubt we will be there shortly—but we hear a good deal about the myth of the artist: Blake's myth, Joyce's myth, Kafka's myth, as though myth somehow existed apart from any social belief or collective function. Worse yet is the gratuitous use of primitive ritual as a source of mythical identification. William Troy is a sensitive reader of modern fiction, yet in his study, "Stendhal: In Quest of Henri Beyle," he tries to convert the author into the ceremonial scapegoat-hero through an easy identification with Julien Sorel.[11] Pressed into such purposes, anthropological analogues can serve only as themes and motifs—*Stoffgeschichte*—and ultimately break down into speculative biography. For further illustration, examine some of the recent critical studies of Melville and you will discover a full catalogue of initiation rites, fertility cults, myths, and ceremonies of every description, all too often finding support only in the mind of the critic.[12] It is especially disquieting to find Stanley Edgar Hyman, who knows as much about the subject of this paper as anyone, declare with aplomb that problems of action and motivation in Conrad's plots can be solved by the application "of such ancient tribal rituals as initiation, fertility, the totemic feast, purification, and expiation ceremonies, the killing of the god-king, etc."[13] Compare Hyman's bewildering picture of the ideal critic in the final chapter of *The Armed Vision* with this simplified reduction of Conrad's works. Too often, anthropological criticism has substituted the discovery of analogies for the examination of artistic structures. In this way, literature becomes for the critic little more than it is for the anthropologist: an artifact—an index of cultural behavior.

Some critics have gone far enough in their thinking to distinguish between mythical and non-mythical values in literature. Such a distinction does not depend on antique sources, primitive allusions, or the like. When operative as a controlling principle, as part of the organic unity of a work, mythical patterns are at the core of

9. Ian Watt, "'Robinson Crusoe' as a Myth," *Essays in Criticism*, I (1951), 95–119.

10. It should be noted that Mr. Chase has altered his position somewhat. Cf. "Myth Revisited," *Partisan Review*, XVII (1950), 885–891, in which he argues that myth is not all literature but a special kind of literature, hence subject to a separate mode of analysis.

11. William Troy, "Stendhal: In Quest of Henri Beyle," *Partisan Review*, IX (1942), 1–22.

12. Cf. Charles Olson, *Call Me Ishmael* (New York: Reynal and Hitchcock, 1947); Richard Chase, *Herman Melville* (New York: Macmillan, 1949); Newton Arvin, *Herman Melville* (New York: William Sloane, 1950), pp. 182–193.

13. Stanley Edgar Hyman, "The Critic as Narcissus," *Accent*, VIII (1948), 187–191.

aesthetic experience and cannot be neglected by criticism. I should add at once, however, that to explain such patterns as unconscious metaphors is to abandon all concern with the origin, structure, and function of art.

It should be clear that a good deal of literary anthropology takes no account of the uniqueness of individual works of art, or indeed, of the fact that the value of a work of art transcends its documentary function. The mere presence of anthropological material in a novel, play, or poem does not help us differentiate between masterpieces and drivel. Anthropological methods may convince us that the cow that jumped over the moon was a totem, but they cannot tell us how to distinguish poetry from fact. We may conclude that the use of anthropological concepts can contribute to an enlargement of artistic experience only in combination with an approach grounded in the aesthetic value of a work of art. The critic who feels that in anthropology he has found the key to the interpretation of literature will soon discover the loneliness of a darkened corridor. Apart from any specific conditions which may affect critical judgment, methodology is never enough. No method or combination of methods can mean anything in the hands of those who are insensitive or indifferent to art. These qualifications made, let us welcome the new approach but let us not cease to demand modesty and lucidity, as well as "that glimpse of truth" for which we may have forgotten to ask.

Journal of Aesthetics and Art Criticism, XI (1952), 46–54. Some of the reference notes have been omitted.

Part Three

MYTH AND CRITICISM

The selections in Part III cannot be reduced to simple categories; their subject-matter is diverse, their methods are different, and their purposes varied. Nevertheless, because of a broad similarity in orientation and interest, certain topics recur which serve both to interrelate and distinguish the essays, and which have suggested groupings. Viewed collectively, these twenty-one essays are impressive evidence of the variety and significance of the findings that reward serious attention to the literary uses of myth and ritual.

Definitions and Discriminations

The precise manner in which the critic can legitimately talk about the mythical aspects of a work of literature is a central consideration in the following group of four essays. In the interests of critical precision Herbert Weisinger ("The Myth and Ritual Approach to Shakespearean Tragedy") and Charles W. Eckert ("Initiatory Motifs in the Story of Telemachus") are especially concerned to discriminate between mythic and aesthetic dimensions, between ritual and thematic form. Francis Fergusson ("'Myth' and the Literary Scruple") suggests how terms like myth, legend, *and* fairy tale *(as defined by Malinowski) may help us to understand artists as diverse as Dante, Wagner, and Paul Valéry. Charles Moorman ("Myth and Medieval Literature : Sir Gawain and the Green Knight") similarly refines the critic's language by demonstrating Stanley Hyman's contention (pp. 47 ff.) that myth criticism is compatible with a variety of other approaches, including the historical and stylistic.*

"MYTH" AND THE LITERARY SCRUPLE

Francis Fergusson

"Myth" is one of those words which it has become almost impossible to use without apologetic quotation marks. Ill-defined for centuries, it is now used in many senses and for many purposes: to mean nonsense or willful obscurantism in some contexts, the deepest wisdom of man in others. One would like to be able to banish it to that pale Hades where "irony" and "ambiguity" have their impotent but pretentious afterlife. But unfortunately the student of literature cannot get along without "Myth." It is too evident that poetry, to say nothing of religion, philosophy and history, are akin to mythopoeia. Drama, the lyric and fiction live symbiotically with myths, nourished by them, and nourishing their flickering lives. Some of the inventions of poets—Kafka's *Metamorphosis*, Plato's tale of the charioteer with his white and his black horse—are modelled on myth. Some poetic works which we like—*Moby Dick*, Lorca's plays—have what we are pleased to call a "mythic" quality. Writers of all kinds use inherited myths in their own work. The student of literature cannot avoid talking about Myth; but how can he use the protean word with any decent rigor?

It was the early romantic poets and philosophers who started our modern cult of Myth. They sought in it some alternative to the narrow categories of modern rationalism, some defense of humane letters in a world created by applied science; often they felt it would replace formal religion. But in our time scientists and pseudo-scientists of every description—psychologists of several persuasions; archeologists, linguists, assorted varieties of anthropologists and sociologists—pronounce upon Myth with an imposing air of authority. And specialists in various fields have filled our books and our museums with countless mythic tales and mythic figures, not only from our own tradition but from every corner of the human time and space. In this welter of facts and theories the student of literature is in danger of losing his bearings altogether. For he cannot simply disregard the labors of countless savants on Myth; he must use them for his own purposes when they strike him as illuminating. On the other hand, he lacks the knowledge and the training to join the debates of specialists on their own terms. What he needs, I think, is a renewed sense of his own stake in Myth, plus a firmer reliance on the evidences in literature and on the methods and the criteria of literary analysis. For the point at which Myth concerns the student of literature is the point at which it is brought to life again in poetry, drama or fiction.

From this point of view it is evident that it is not realistic to talk about Myth-in-general, as though we had a generally agreed upon definition which would apply to all the instances of Myth in art and letters. And if one makes the all-important distinction between the second-hand, merely reported or summarized mythic tale, as we find it in Bulfinch or *The Hero with a Thousand Faces*, and the mythic tale as it actually lives in poetry or drama, it appears that we lack an unmistakeable example of even *one* myth. For the myth of Oedipus is one thing in *Oedipus Rex*, and something quite different in the dramas of Seneca or Dryden. Giraudoux, clearly recognizing this point, called his play *Amphytrion 38*. One of the most striking properties of myths is that they generate new forms (like the differing children of one parent) in the imaginations of those who try to grasp them. Until some imagination, that of a poet or only a reader or auditor, is thus fecundated by a myth, the myth would seem to exist only potentially. And if we cannot lay hands on even one myth prior to its imaginative embodiments, how can we hope to pin down myth-in-general in itself?

We must, I think, adopt an extremely ascetic regimen in our dealings with Myth. We must abandon hope of reaching any very plausible generalizations, and pay close attention to some of the many ways in which myths actually live in our literature. Of course the evidence, even when thus arbitrarily reduced, is almost endless, and very diverse. How can we rule out any of the living works which the narrative in the Christian Creed at one extreme, the lightest tale of Ovid at the other, have generated in the imaginations of artists in thousands of years? All one could hope to do is to choose rather haphazardly a few examples, as illustrations of what a literary approach to Myth might be.

Let us begin with a rough preliminary classification of the kinds of myths to be found in literature. The classification I wish to propose is taken from Malinowski's study of the Trobriand Islanders. He found three types of myth in that culture: Legends, which he defined as stories about the past which were believed to be true of the past, and which served to give the Islanders some significant conception of their history; Folk or Fairy Tales, told only for fun, without reference to truth, on occasions when the tribe was gathered simply for entertainment; and Religious Myths, which represented basic elements in the creed, the morals, and the social structure of that people. Malinowski based this classification on his observations of the Trobrianders, but it looks as though he had understood them by analogy with our own culture, for we can recognize the three types (or the three attitudes to Myth) in our art and literature. Some scientific anthropologists mistrust Malinowski precisely because he feels the kinship between the Trobrianders and us; but for me his value lies in his sympathy and his sense of the humane analogies between cultures. Let us claim him for the Humanities, and see how his classification may help us to understand our own heritage.

I think we should have to go back to Dante's Christianized Vergilian Legend of Rome to find a fully developed Historic Legend in Malinowski's sense. But the Fairy Tales, Little Red Riding Hood, the innumerable Greek tales of Arcady, of nymphs and shepherds, charming stories whose truth we never enquire into, have been common since the early Renaissance. Readers of Professor Douglas Bush's studies of literary myths will think of countless examples. It is easy to see why the Fairy Tale conception of Myth is quite at home in times of the most intransigent rationalism. If the myth makes no claim to truth in itself, but at most serves as pleasing illustration of some moral or political concept, we may enjoy it with a clear conscience. But the romantic and post-romantic cult of Myth is not content with these neoclassic attitudes. It seeks the Religious Myth, or tries to attribute metaphysical meaning to the myths it invokes. Most of the contemporary debates about Myth assume this religious intention on the part of the lovers of Myth, and so we have many interesting attempts (like Wheelwright's in *The Burning Fountain* or Campbell's in *The Hero with a Thousand Faces*) to defend Myth as a mode of knowing.

But the most natural view of Myth in the modern world (by which I mean our tradition since Dante defined the "allegory of poets") has been the Fairy Tale conception. And in the hands of Paul Valéry this way with Myth has turned out to have new vitality. No one could accuse Valéry of underestimating Reason, the usual complaint of users of myths in our time. He is the champion of *l'intelligence*, the emancipated but scrupulous mind, Reason at its most ambitious and austere: the ultimate reliance of modernists, from Socrates through Da Vinci to Valéry himself. And at the same time he is the high priest of pure poetry, "the representative poet of the first half of the 20th Century," as Eliot called him. His poetry should therefore be a crucial instance of the life of Myth in literature.

The first line of his *Fragments du Narcisse* announces the theme of that poem:

How you shine at last, pure end of my journey![1]

We are to imagine Narcissus bending over the pool, addressing his own shining reflection as the pure goal, now recognized at last, of his life's course. Then come the beautiful music and the Arcadian imagery of the *Fragments*: the reeds, the water, the quiet evening, the echoes and reflections which echo and reflect the inward focus of thought and desire. The poem has the magic suggestiveness, or call it the abstract allusiveness, of the finest *symboliste* achievements, and I do not therefore attempt to analyse it in detail. Suffice it to say that as we let the poem sink in we come to see that the first line is to be understood in more senses than one. It is not only Narcissus' address to his reflection, it is the poet's address to Narcissus, who illustrates the paradoxical goal of pure reason and also of pure poetry. Thus it is also the poet's invocation of his own spirit at that creative center of life where thought and poetic

1. *Que tu brilles enfin, terme pur de ma course!*

intuition both have their source. When the life of reason attains its highest abstraction its pleasure lies in contemplating itself in the act of contemplation. And when poetry is pure enough—approaching the abstractness of music, freeing itself from all attachment, whether to persons, things, or transcendent moral or religious goals—it becomes its own object. The best poems in Valéry's *symboliste* tradition are based on the sad delectation of poetry's self-love.

It is easy to see why Narcissus is addressed by Valéry as the very image of his own goal. Narcissus aptly represents Valéry's lifelong study: the mind's creative or formative power when it turns inward in search of itself. The perversity of the mythic figure, the futility of introversion even when most subtle, is part of the poet's gloomy meaning. And yet the question of the reality of Narcissus himself never arises. The poet is not interested in exploring the mythic narrative itself. He does not present the thwarted nymphs who beseech Narcissus in vain (except in Narcissus' vague fear of their interruption) nor the fight, nor the transformation of Narcissus himself into that pretty specimen of vegetable life, the Narcissus flower, which seems so suggestive in any realistic reading of the story. The figure of Narcissus is perhaps the "inspiration" of the poem, as a metaphor or even a word may be; but its value remains strictly poetic. In all of this Valéry accepts the Fairy Tale notion of Myth, handling it lightly, almost playfully, as though for entertainment only. His use of his myth is basically a more sophisticated version of the neoclassic convention: as a language, closely analogous to the endlessly worked-over but still iridescent words of French. Hence the deflated exactitude of the Valérian taste, the crystalline hardness one feels beneath the shimmer of his effects.

Valéry as *symboliste* represents a culmination of the romantic movement, its "classic" moment of complete self-awareness, as he himself would put it. He is concerned with the unique essence of poetry and its absolute independence; in his hands Myth serves poetry, not vice versa. Though he is the heir of the romantic poets he does not have a trace of their religious attitude to Myth. This is Malinowski's description of the Religious Myth—the "myth proper" as he calls it—among the Trobrianders:

> A special class of stories, regarded as sacred, embodied in ritual, morals and social organization. . . . These stories live not by idle interest . . . but are to the natives a statement of a primeval, greater and more relevant reality, by which the present life, fates and activities of mankind are determined, the knowledge of which supplies man with the motive for ritual and moral actions, as well as with indications how to perform them.

Valéry could accept none of this without betraying his faith in the independent formative power of the mind. But Malinowski's description applies by analogy to the narrative in the Christian Creed, the basis of European social and cultural order, and of much of European art, for a thousand years. And it applies also to what romantic poets seek vaguely, and more or less in vain, in the myths which they religiously invoke.

Wagner's *Tristan und Isolde* is the most perfect example I know of the romantic-religious cult of Myth. Thus Wagner opposes to Valéry's rationalist tradition, in which the mythic tales are told for fun or half-playfully allegorized, the Tristan narrative, in which he finds a "primeval, greater and more relevant reality" than that of reason and common sense. Valéry in *Narcisse* appeals to the individual intellect and its strictly poetic sensibility, but Wagner, basing all on the power of his music, reaches for a primitive, unindividualized mode of awareness in his hypnotized and mob-like audience. Valéry does not take the Narcissus story seriously except as metaphor or illustration, but Wagner makes the course of the Tristian narrative the very form, or "soul" of the opera. Each crucial episode: the drinking of the love-potion, the single night of love, the final *Liebestod*: has a ritual significance which perhaps reflects (as De Rougemont suggests) the rites of the half-forgotten cult of the Cathars. Valéry expects no result from his poem but the refined pleasures of the mind and the sensibility, but Wagner wants to effect an initiation or change of heart, and the final love-death seems to demand a momentary faith, at least, in a greater, unseen reality. We know that there is, in fact, a Wagnerian cult, which helped to nourish Hitler's attempt to create a German *Volk* by magic. One may even see in Schopenhauer, in Nietzche's *Birth of Tragedy*, and in Freud, with his death-wish and his boundless libido, a kind of theology for the gloomy-religious action of *Tristan*.

Wagner's treatment of the Tristan myth fulfills the requirements of Malinowski's definition of the Religious Myth. It also agrees with what Maritain has to say of "metaphysical myths" in his *Creative Intuition*: "The metaphysical myths are the organic signs and symbols of some faith actually lived. ... They are forms through which a conviction of the entire soul nourishes and quickens from within the very power of creative imagination. Such myths have no force except through the faith man has in them." Wagner must, I think, have worked upon *Tristan* with the faith which Maritain describes, for the creative power of the opera is unmistakeable. But unfortunately a faith may be desperate and deluded when one sees in "myth a source of higher teaching and ultra-spiritual insights, converting it into a magic mirror that reflects the heart's desire," as Philip Rahv says of the romantic cult of Myth. Wagner's religious acceptance of the Tristan myth is possible only at too great an expense: the rejection of the contemporary world along with all the achievements of reason, from morality to science. Those who see in the cult of Myth only willful obscurantism would find much in Wagner to support their thesis. And such reflections as these must throw some doubt on the faith which Wagner himself had in the "greater and more relevant reality" symbolized by *Tristan*; we know that he changed his mind about it later in his life.

The fact is that we are here in that dim and treacherous realm between firm religious belief on one side and make-believe on the other. Belief and make-believe have similar fertilizing effects upon human creativity. An actor must make-believe his role very deeply and with full concentration if he is to give more than a superficial performance, yet we do not attribute religious faith to him, even when we in the audience "believe" in the character he is presenting. And in our time we are more at home with make-believe than we are with belief—or perhaps we have simply lost the sense of the distinction. Even the truths of science begin to look like partial metaphors: necessary (though sometimes contradictory) hypotheses, which guide and nourish the scientific imagination for a time, not adequate and final truth. Thus the whole problem of the Religious Myth is on the edge of an even darker mystery: that of the nature, even the possibility, of real faith in our time.

That is one important reason why, in our attempt to collect the crucial evidences of poetry as it reincarnates myths, we must at this point remember Dante. For in the *Divine Comedy* we unmistakeably encounter the solidity of real belief. That poem, based on the Christian Creed, celebrates the faith and the moral, philosophic, and liturgical order which regulated Europe from the Dark Ages to the threshold of modern times: that "primeval, greater and more relevant reality" which Malinowski says the Religious Myth, the "myth proper," is supposed to embody. The *Divine Comedy* would, for this reason alone, be required reading for the study of the life of Myth in poetry.

Moreover the *Divine Comedy* contains all the kinds of Myth, and all the attitudes to Myth, which Malinowski describes, all in significant relation to each other and to the enlightened Reason of Dante's time. Thus Malinowski's "historic legend" is built into the framework of the poem: Virgil's legendary interpretation of Rome, which Dante combines with the historic drama of the Old Testament and places in the perspective of the Incarnation, wherein both the Hebrew and the Pagan traditions are fulfilled. This historical legend serves exactly the purpose Malinowski describes: based on the known facts of the past, which are accepted as true of the past, it gives Dante's generation its bearings in the historic sequence. What Malinowski calls Fairy Tales—the loot of Ovid and Lucan, more obscure tales from Arabic or Celtic sources— are alive again in every part of the *Comedy*. Dante takes them in a spirit akin to Valéry's: "my not-false errors" he calls them, when they inspire his imagination on the purgatorial stair. They provide much of the great poem's sensuous movement and variety; and when we look more closely we see that each has also its tropological meaning: they are visionary embodiments of the momentary experiences of the pilgrim spirit as the moral life unfolds. The ultimate meaning of the moral life, like that of the life of the race in history, is seen in the Incarnation and Sacrifice of Christ. It is that narrative, of course, which commands Dante's real belief and provides (quite apart from the question of *our* belief) the very pattern of the Religious Myth.

A real study of Dante's masterful way with his vast heritage of myths would require not minutes but years; and it would require a combination of erudition and tact which is not available. But one may get some slight sense of his virtuosity from almost any detail of the poem. Consider, for instance, what he does with the Siren in the dream which forms the opening sequence of *Purgatorio* XIX:

> Nell'ora che non può il calor diurno
>   intiepidar più il freddo della luna,
>   vinto da terra o talor da Saturno;
> quando i geomanti lor maggior fortuna
>   veggiono in oriente, inanzi all'alba,
>   surger per via che poco le sta bruna:
> mi venne in sogno una femmina balba,

negli occhi guercia e sopra i piè distorta,
  con le man monche, e di colore scialba.
Io la mirava: e come il sol conforta
  le fredde membra che la notte aggrava,
  così lo sguardo mio le facea scorta
la lingua, e poscia tutta la drizzava
  in poco d'ora, e lo smarrito volto,
  come amor vuol, così le colorava.
Poi ch'ell'avea il parlar così disciolto,
  cominciava a cantar sì che con pena
  da lei avrei mio intento rivolto.
"Io son," cantava, "io son dolce Sirena,
  che i marinari in mezzo mar dismago:
  tanto son i piacere a sentir piena.
Io volsi Ulisse del suo cammin vago
  col canto mio; e qual meco si ausa
  rado sen parte, sì tutto l'appago."
Ancor non era sua bocca richiusa,
  quando una donna apparve santa e presta
  lunghesso me per far colei confusa.
"O Virgilio, o Virgilio, chi é questa?"
  fieramente diceva; ed ei venia
  con gli occhi fitti pure in quella onesta.
L'altra prendeva, e dinanzi l'apria
  fendendo i drappi, e mostravami il ventre;
  quel mi svegliò col puzzo che n'uscia.

(At the hour when the heat of the day can no longer warm the cold of the moon, being overcome by earth or perhaps by Saturn;

When the geomancers see their *fortuna major* in the east, just before dawn, rising along a path which will not be dark for long:

There came to me in dream a stuttering woman, squint-eyed, twisted on her feet, with stunted hands, yellow in color. I gazed upon her, and as the sun comforts cold limbs which night weighs down, so my gaze made ready

Her tongue, and then in short time set her all straight, and her pale face, just as love wills, it colored.

As soon as her speech was loosened she began to sing, so that with difficulty I should have turned my attention from her. "I am," she sang, "I am that sweet Siren who bemuses sailors in the midst of the sea, so full I am of pleasure for them to feel.

"I turned Ulysses from his wandering way to this my song; whoever risks himself with me rarely departs, I satiate him so fully."

Her mouth was hardly closed when there appeared beside me a woman, alert and holy, to make that one confused.

"O Virgil, Virgil, who is this?" she was saying proudly, and he was coming, with his eyes fixed only on that honest one. He seized the other and opened her in front, ripping the clothes, and showed me the belly, which waked me with the stench that issued from it.)

Dante's treatment of the Siren in this passage is similar in several ways to Valéry's treatment of Narcissus: it is an example of Dante's "allegory of poets." Thus, like Valéry, he is more interested in the mythic figure than in her whole traditional story, and he uses her to get the sensuous immediacy and the subtle complexity of poetry. But she seems to have more reality than Valéry's conventional figure: if not a metaphysical entity in her own right, she is at least an ineluctable trope, the embodiment of one eternally-recurrent human experience. That is because the Siren has her place in a vaster vision which includes the perspectives of ethics and faith. Valéry's Narcissus, on the other hand, is presented as "pure" poetry.

Dante establishes the being and the meanings of his Siren by means of the context in which she appears: a certain point in the Pilgrim's spiritual growth, at a certain place on the Mountain, and toward the end of the second night of the purgatorial journey. By showing us the psyche in whose imagination the Siren appears, Dante includes several dimensions of mythopoeia which Valéry omits. We *see* the dreamer see his mythic enchantress, an image which at first says nothing to him. We then see him "believe" the image, and focus his attention and his unsatisfied desire upon it. Under that warmth and light the ancient myth, "colored as love wills," reveals some of the meanings she had held only potentially: in short, she is "brought to life." But the night in which she appears also helps us to understand her. In all three nights of the purgatorial journey the Pilgrim can rely neither upon his direct perception of the world, his moral will, or his reason. In the solitude and passivity of sleep he knows the call of many forms of love, including that irrational brute weight of desire which pulls, like gravitation, toward the bottom of the universe. In this passage the nocturnal chill that weighs limbs down presents this pull: the occasion for the Siren's appearance. The direction of love's movement thus indicated (night against reason and the day, the ambiguity of love and death) reminds one strongly of the motivation and the nocturnal imagery of *Tristan*. Dante may have seen at this point the object of Wagner's desperate faith.

But this is the *second* night of the purgatorial journey, and the Pilgrim has by this time acquired a certain moral awareness. After the Siren is warmed into beauty and song, at the very moment of pleasurable yielding, Virgil appears by that Grace which hovers over this region, and reveals the Siren's deathly aspect once more. Virgil represents reason and the accumulated wisdom of experience in the real world, and by this time his voice and presence are in a sense *within* the Pilgrim's spirit. In the dream he plays a role like that of the orthodox Freudian "superego," representative of moral truth. At this point in his development the Pilgrim (and the reader) can understand the mythic Siren from a moral point of view, and that suffices for escape.

But because of the sturdy realism which underlies the whole conception of the *Divine Comedy* the Siren, for all her moral meaning, is not reduced to the status of a moral allegory only. She retains some sort of being in her own right; she does not forfeit her status as one of the amoral figures of Myth, and that is characteristic of Dante's way with myths. Their visionary being is established first, their possible philosophical meaning for the Pilgrim, second; and when they disappear we do not feel that they have been rationalized out of all existence. The Siren first looks strange and evil, then she appears as infinitely attractive, then as dismaying and disgusting, but in all of these metamorphoses we never lose the sense that she was somehow *there*; and her power and mystery remain when we leave her.

If Dante can handle the figures of Myth with such subtle and flexible realism—that is, with respect both for the reality of the imagination in which they appear, and for the different reality of the figures themselves—it is because he understands them, not in conceptual terms, but by analogy with the Incarnation. The process whereby a myth is brought to life in a human imagination corresponds to that by which Christ lives again in the spirits of the faithful, through belief, concentration, love, and an imitative movement of spirit. The mythic forms which tempt the human spirit may in Dante's scheme be childish or deceptive. But their meaning for us, and the process whereby we reincarnate them in our own beings, are to be understood by analogy with the human figure, and the imitation, of Christ. Even Hell, where Dante endows so many evil forms with his own life and love, was made by Divine Power, Highest Wisdom and Primal Love. It is because Dante believes so completely in the reality of this basic Analogue that he can both share in the lives of many kinds of myths, and yet also pass beyond them, to consider their meaning in other terms and in relation to each other. His belief in the "primeval, greater and more relevant reality" of the Christian Narrative gives him a key to the heritage of Myth, makes him a master (probably *the* master) of the mythic modes of understanding.

The view of the world which Dante inherited, formed by the converging and age-long labors of Hebrew and Greek, has dissolved long since. His *modus vivendi* between Reason and Mythopoeia is no longer accessible to us. But if we are to consider the life of Myth in the poetry of our tradition, I do not see how we can continue to neglect the vast lore in the *Divine Comedy*.

One can sympathize with those numerous writers who use "Myth" to mean only wishful thinking or Machiavellian obscurantism. It would be nice to get rid of the term and its puzzles so simply. But that recourse is not available to those who stubbornly continue to be interested in Poetry, or indeed in any form of the Humanities. We cannot get rid of "Myth," but we can beware of it. We can remember some of the countless ways in which myths live in our literature from Homer to Faulkner. And we can study some of the forms this life takes with the respect for the unique individuality of play or poem which the masters of literature have taught us.

Sewanee Review, LXIV (1956), 171–185.

THE MYTH AND RITUAL APPROACH TO SHAKESPEAREAN TRAGEDY

Herbert Weisinger

* * * What I want to do in this paper is to describe the myth and ritual approach to literature as I understand it and to show what new light it can throw on Shakespeare's tragedies, and presumably to illuminate them afresh. For the purposes of this analysis, I take the myth and ritual pattern as fundamental and anterior to tragedy, and I pass Shakespeare's tragedies over this pattern, as tracings over the original drawing, in order to reveal his changes, modifications, and alterations of it; that is to say, I try to distinguish the uniquely Shakespearean from the generally tragic.* * *

Certainly I am not the first to suggest such a correlation; on the contrary, many critics have seen the connection and have in fact gone beyond the tragedies to the later plays in an effort to prove that the pattern of rebirth and reconciliation is fundamental to virtually the whole of Shakespeare's plays. But, while the myth and ritual pattern so used makes, if I may say so, a Christian Olympian out of Shakespeare, it does so only at the expense of the myth and ritual pattern and of the substance of the plays themselves. It is my contention that while the last plays of Shakespeare do indeed carry forward the tragic pattern established in *Hamlet, Othello, King Lear,* and *Macbeth,* they neither heighten nor deepen it but on the contrary reject and even destroy it. In fact, I would go so far as to argue that the tragic pattern in the tragedies themselves is scarcely maintained equally strongly over each of the plays. For, on the basis of a comparison between the myth and ritual pattern as I have described it in *Tragedy and the Paradox of the Fortunate Fall* and the tragedies, I think that Shakespeare's tragic vision, which he was able to sustain but tentatively in *Hamlet,* most fully in *Othello,* barely in *King Lear,* and hardly at all in *Macbeth,* failed him altogether in the last plays, and that this failure is manifested by the use of the elements of the myth and ritual pattern as mere machinery, virtually in burlesque fashion, and not as their informing and sustaining spirit. The instinct of the critics in applying the myth and ritual pattern to the plays has been sound, but their superimposition of the pattern on the plays has been inexact and, I suspect, prompted more by religious rather than by critical motives, with the result that both the method and the plays have been falsified.

I

If I begin with some diffidence, it is because I am always acutely aware that the myth and ritual pattern, upon which the myth and ritual approach to literature must be founded, is as uncertain in its origins as it is unrealized in actuality. I have tried to account for the persistence and power of the myth and ritual pattern by retracing it generally to that initial impact of experience which produced the archetypes of belief, and specifically, to the archetype of rebirth as crystallized out of the archetype of belief. Unfortunately no real proof of this process is possible, for the events which generated the primary shook of belief are now too deep and too dim in the racial memory of man to be exhumed by archeological means, though the psychoanalytic probings of Freud have cleared a path through this labyrinth, with reluctant confirmation coming from the anthropologists and classicists. Similarly, we must not forget that there is really no such thing as the myth and ritual pattern *per se*; at best, it is a probable construction of many varieties and variations of a number of beliefs and actions so closely related to each other that it is reasonable to construct—reconstruct would be a misleading word here—an ideal form of the myth and ritual pattern more comprehensive and more realized than any variations of it which we actually possess.

The myth and ritual pattern of the ancient Near East, which is at least six thousand years old, centers in a divine king who was killed annually and who was reborn in the person of his successor. In its later development, the king was not killed, but went through an annual symbolic death and a symbolic rebirth or resurrection. Starting out as a magical rite designed to ensure the success of the crops in climates where the outcome of the struggle between water and drought meant literally the difference between life and death, the pattern was gradually transformed into a religious ritual, designed this time to promote man's salvation, and finally became an ethical conviction, freed now of both its magical and religious ritual practices but still retaining in spiritualized and symbolic form its ancient appeal and emotional certitude. Because it begins with the need to survive, the pattern never loses its force, for it is concerned always with survival, whether physical or spiritual. So far as can be ascertained at present, the pattern had a double growth, one along the lines of the ancient civilizations of the Near East, the Sumerian, the Egyptian, the Babylonian, both South and North, the Palestinian—first with the Canaanites, and then with the Hebrews—and from thence into Christianity; the other along the lines of the island civilizations of the Aegean, from Crete to the mainland of Greece, from thence to Rome, and once more into Christianity, the two streams of development flowing into each other and reinforcing themselves at this crucial juncture.

Despite the differences between the religions of the ancient Near East (as, for example, between those of Egypt and Mesopotamia, and between that of the Hebrews and of the others), nevertheless they all possessed certain significant features of myth and ritual in common. These features, in their turn, stemmed from the common bond of ritual, characteristic (in one form or another) of all together, though, as I have said, none possessed completely all the elements, which varied in some degree from religion to religion. In this single, idealized ritual scheme, the well-being of the community was secured by the regular performance of certain ritual actions in which the king or his equivalent took the leading role. Moreover the king's importance for the community was incalculably increased by the almost universal conviction that the fortunes of the community or state and those of the king were inextricably intermingled; indeed one may go so far as to say that on the well-being of the king depended the well-being of the community as a whole. On the basis of the evidence covering different peoples at different times, we know then that in the ancient Near East there existed a pattern of thought and action which gripped the minds and emotions of those who believed in it so strongly that it was made the basis on which they could apprehend and accept the universe in which they lived. It made possible man's conviction that he could control that universe for his own purposes; and it placed in his hands the lever whereby he could exercise that control.

From an analysis of the extant seasonal rituals, particularly the new year festivals, and from the coronation, initiation, and personal rituals of the ancient Near East, it is possible to make a reconstructed model of the basic ritual form. Essentially the pattern contains these basic elements: 1. the indispensable role of the divine king; 2. the combat between the God and an opposing power; 3. the suffering of the God; 4. the death of the God; 5. the resurrection of the God; 6. the symbolic recreation of the myth of creation; 7. the sacred marriage; 8. the triumphal procession; and 9. the settling of destinies. We must remember, however, that the dying-rising-God theme constitutes but one illustration, so to speak, of the greater cycle of birth, death, and rebirth. The many and various rites connected with birth, with initiation, with marriage, and with death in the case of the individual, as well as the rites concerned with the planting, the harvesting, the new year celebrations, and with the installation ceremonies of the king in the case of the community, all these rites repeat each in its own way the deep-rooted and abiding cycle of death and rebirth. Not only do these rituals *symbolize* the passage from death to life, from one way of life to another, but they are the actual *means* of achieving the changeover; they mark the transition by which—through the processes of separation, regeneration, and the return on a higher level—both the individual and the community are assured their victory over the forces of chaos which are thereby kept under control.

The purpose of these rituals is by enaction to bring about a just order of existence in which God, nature, and man are placed in complete and final rapport with each other; they are both the defence against disorder and the guarantee of order. In the myth and ritual pattern, then, man has devised a mighty weapon by which he keeps at bay, and sometimes even seems to conquer, the hostile forces which endlessly threaten to overpower him. In the early stages of the development of the myth and ritual pattern, however, the best that man could hope for was an uneasy truce between himself and chaos, because the cycle merely returned to its beginnings; the God fought, was defeated, was resurrected, was momentarily triumphant, and thus ensured the well-being of the community for the coming year, but it was inevitable that in the course of the year he would again be defeated and would again have to go through his annual agony. Thus nothing new could be expected nor was anticipated, and year after year man could hope for no more than a temporary gain which he was sure would soon be turned into an inevitable loss. To achieve genuine faith, therefore, was an act of courage difficult and infrequent to attain, and it is no wonder that we detect in the myth and ritual pattern of the ancient Near East before the Hebraic-Christian tradition takes over, too strong a reliance on the mere machinery of ritual, ultimately leading not to faith but to superstition, as well as the melancholy notes of despair and pessimism. But the Hebraic-Christian tradition in the very process of adapting the pattern, transformed it, for by virtue of its unique and tenacious insistence on the mercy and judgment of its transcendent God, it introduced a new and vital element in the pattern, that of the dialectical leap from out of the endless circle on to a different and higher stage of understanding. The crucial moment in this transformation of the myth and ritual pattern comes when man, by himself, undertakes on his own to make the leap; to him remains the decision and his is the responsibility; by making the leap, he makes himself. The Hebraic-Christian tradition utilized the cycle of birth, life, death, and rebirth to conquer chaos and disorder, but it made its unique contribution to the pattern by giving man the possibility of defeating chaos and disorder by a single, supreme act of human will which could wipe them out at one stroke. In so doing it preserved the potency of the pattern and retained its ancient appeal and, at the same time, ensured its continued use by supplying the one element it had hitherto lacked to give it its permanent role as the means whereby man is enabled to live in an indifferent universe; it showed that man can, by himself, transcend that universe.

II

This, then, is the myth and ritual pattern as I understand it. What are its implications for tragedy? To start with, I would suggest that in the myth and ritual pattern we have the seedbed of tragedy, the stuff out of which it was ultimately formed. Both the form and content of tragedy, its architecture as well as its ideology, closely parallel the form and content of the myth and ritual pattern. But having said that, I must also say that the myth and ritual pattern and tragedy are not the same. Both share the same shape and the same intent, but they differ significantly in the manner of their creation and in the methods of achieving their purposes. The myth and ritual pattern is the group product of many and different minds groping on many and different levels over long and kaleidoscopic periods of time under the stimulus of motivations quite different from those which produce tragedy. I am not suggesting anything like the formerly accepted communal origin of the ballad, for we know that myth in its form as the complement to ritual must have been devised by the priest-astrologer-magicians of the ancient world. The intent of the myth and ritual pattern is control, its method that of mimetically reproducing the rhythm of birth, death, and birth again to gain that control. But imitation here means, not acting alike, as we think of the term—a parallel and similar yet at the same time a distinct and different attitude and behavior toward the thing imitated—but rather the interpenetration of and union with the imitator, the thing imitated, and the imitation, all three being one and the same thing.

Tragedy, on the other hand, is a creation compounded of conscious craft and conviction. If we describe the myth and ritual pattern as the passage from ignorance to understanding through suffering mimetically and at first hand, then we must describe tragedy as the passage from ignorance to understanding through suffering symbolically and at a distance. To speak of symbolic meaning is already to have made the leap from myth to art. In the myth and ritual pattern, the dying-reborn God-king, the worshippers for whom he suffers, and the action of his agony are identical; in tragedy, the tragic protagonist undergoes his suffering at an aesthetic distance and only vicariously in the minds of his audience. And for that reason does Aristotle tell us that tragedy is an imitation of an action. You participate in a ritual but you are a spectator of a play.

Moreover, tragedy reconstitutes the myth and ritual pattern in terms of its own needs. Of the nine elements which make up the myth and ritual pattern as I have described it, four have been virtually eliminated from tragedy, namely, the actual death of the God, the symbolic recreation of the myth of creation, the sacred marriage, and the triumphal procession; two elements, the indispensable role of the divine king and the settling of destinies, are retained only by implication and play rather ambiguous roles in tragedy; while the remaining three—combat, suffering (with death subsumed), and resurrection—now give tragedy its structure and substance. I have already noted that one of the characteristics of the myth and ritual pattern is its adaptability, its ability to change shape while retaining its potency, and we should therefore not be surprised to find the same process at work in its relation to tragedy. What is revealing, however, is the direction of change, for we find, first, that the theme of the settling of destinies which is the highest point in the myth and ritual pattern—the goal of the struggle, since without it the passion of the God would be in vain, and chaos and disorder would be triumphant—this theme, so elaborately explicated in the ritual practices of the ancient Near East, is no more than implied in tragedy, just as the correspondence between the well-being of the king and the well-being of the community, again so detailed in ritual, is only shadowed forth, as a condition to be aimed at but not to be achieved in reality.

Second, we discover that even greater emphasis is placed on the small moment of doubt in tragedy than in the myth and ritual pattern itself. In the rituals of the ancient Near East, at the point between the death of the God and his resurrection, all action is arrested as the participants fearfully and anxiously wait for the God to be revived. After the din of combat, this quiet moment of doubt and indecision is all the more awful, for there is no assurance that the God will be reborn: "For a small moment have I forsaken thee." "But," continues Isaiah, "with great mercies will I gather thee." It is no wonder that the small moment is followed in the pattern by creation, the sacred marriage, and the triumphal procession as the peoples' expression of joy that the death of the God has not been in vain and that for another year at least: "the earth remaineth, seedtime and harvest, and cold and heat, and summer and winter, and day and night shall not cease."

And, clearly spelling out the implications of the second change made by tragedy in the myth and ritual pattern is the third, the freedom of choice of the tragic protagonist and the responsibility for the consequences of making that choice. For in that small moment of doubt and indecision, when victory and defeat are poised in the balance, only the moral force of man wills him on in action to success. The tragic protagonist acts in the conviction that his action is right, and he accepts the responsibility for that action; for him to do less than that means the loss of his stature as a moral, responsible agent. The tragic occurs when by the fall of a man of strong character we are made aware of something greater than that man or even than mankind; we seem to see a new and truer vision of the universe.

But that vision cannot be bought cheaply. It cannot be bought by blind reliance on the mere machinery of the myth and ritual pattern, and it cannot be bought by fixing the fight, as Handel's librettist fatuously puts it:

> How vain is man who boasts in fight
> The valour of gigantic might,
> And dreams not that a hand unseen
> Directs and guides this weak machine.

Better the indifferent Gods of Lucretius than the busybody *deus ex machina* of Vine Street and Madison Avenue. Only the deliberate moral choice of the tragic protagonist confronted by two equal and opposite forces and fully aware of the consequences of his choice can bring off the victory, and then only at the expense of pain and suffering: "He is despised and rejected of men; a man of sorrows, and acquainted with grief." But suffering can be made bearable only when at the same time it is made part of a rational world order into which it fits and which has an understandable place for it. * * *

Tragedy therefore occurs when the accepted order of things is fundamentally questioned only to be the more triumphantly reaffirmed. It cannot exist where there is no faith; conversely, it cannot exist where there is no doubt; it can exist only in an atmosphere of sceptical faith. The protagonist must be free to choose, and though he chooses wrongly, yet the result of the wrong choice is our own escape and our enlightenment. Yet nothing less than this sacrifice will do, and only the symbolic sacrifice of one who is like us can make possible our atonement for the evil which is within us and for the sins which we are capable of committing. Nevertheless, in western thought, if man is free to choose, in the end he must choose rightly. He is free to choose his salvation, but he is punished for his wrong choice. Man is free, but he is free within the limits set for him by his condition as a man. So great is the emphasis placed on freedom of choice in tragedy that the settling of destinies, which in the myth and ritual pattern is the tangible reward of victory, recedes more and more into the background, and the messianic vision implicit in the settling of destinies is personalized and humanized in tragedy in the form of heightened self-awareness as the end of the tragic agony. In short, what I have been saying is that the myth and ritual pattern pertains to religion which proceeds by assertion, tragedy to literature which proceeds by assessment.

To sum up, then, the structure of tragic form, as derived from the myth and ritual pattern may be diagrammed in this way: the tragic protagonist, in whom is subsumed the well-being of the people and the welfare of the state, engages in conflict with a representation of darkness and evil; a temporary defeat is inflicted on the tragic protagonist, but after shame and suffering he emerges triumphant as the symbol of the victory of light and good over darkness and evil, a victory sanctified by the covenant of the settling of destinies which reaffirms the well-being of the people and the welfare of the state. In the course of the conflict there comes a point where the protagonist and the antagonist appear to merge into a single challenge against the order of God; the evil which the protagonist would not do, he does, and the good which he would, he does not; and in this moment we are made aware that the real protagonist of tragedy

last repudiates his wife: "She's like a liar, gone to burning hell." But this is for him the bottom of the pit, and by a supreme effort of will he purges the Iago from within him; and in that awful moment of self-awareness, he recreates himself as he might have been, he realizes his potential as a human being. Having by his rashness put the well-being of the people and the welfare of the state in jeopardy, as Brabantio had foretold, perhaps better than he knew,—

> Mine's not an idle cause. The Duke himself,
> Or any of my brothers of the state,
> Cannot but feel this wrong as 'twere their own;
> For if such actions may have passage free,
> Bond-slaves and pagans shall our statesmen be. (I. ii. 95–99)

—Othello is inevitably punished. And Iago is defeated by the one force which he is incapable of understanding, the power of principle. What he fails to see is that Othello's love for Desdemona is the symbol of Othello's faith in the goodness and justice of the world. What Othello seeks, therefore, when that faith is called into question, is not revenge, which is Iago's goal, but the cleansing of evil and the re-affirmation of goodness and justice: "It is the cause, my soul." From the depth of his self-awareness, bought at so dear a price, there emerges the theme of the settling of destinies, not embodied in the person of a successor, but filling as it were with its vision the entire stage, the sign of evil purged and the good restored, the image of man in his full stature as responsible man: "Speak of me as I am." "And when man faces destiny," Malraux writes, "destiny ends and man comes into his own."

IV

Both *Hamlet* and *Othello* possess three features in common which by contrast are not present in *Lear* and *Macbeth*. First, both *Hamlet* and *Othello* are for the Elizabethan audience contemporary plays laid in contemporary or nearly contemporary settings. No great historical distance separates them from their audience as it does in *Lear* and *Macbeth*, which are laid in pre-Christian England and Scotland. Second, both *Hamlet* and *Othello* operate within the Christian framework, recognized and apprehended as such by the audience for which they were written. But in *Lear* and *Macbeth* the pagan background is insistent. From the depth of their suffering Lear and Gloucester can appeal no higher than to the heathen gods: "As flies to wanton boys, are we to th' gods,/ They kill us for their sport" (IV. i. 38–39); and Edgar's wisdom is but cold comfort in the Stoic manner: "Bear free and patient thoughts" (IV. vi. 80). In *Macbeth*, the witches play the same role as do the gods in *Lear*:

> But 'tis strange;
> And oftentimes, to win us to our harm,
> The instruments of darkness tell us truths,
> Win us with honest trifles, to betray 's
> In deepest consequence. (I. iii. 122–26)

Finally, the theme of the settling of destinies—present directly in *Hamlet* and indirectly in *Othello*—fades away in *Lear* and disappears altogether in *Macbeth*. These changes reveal a significant shift in Shakespeare's use of the myth and ritual pattern and seem to be symptomatic of his increasing inability to bear the burden of the tragic vision. Having confronted the face of evil in *Othello* with an intensity unmatched even by the man staring at Death in Michelangelo's "Last Judgment," and having in the face of that evil been able to reassert the good, Shakespeare seems to have fallen back exhausted, so to speak, the effort of holding off evil weakening with each successive play.

Lear begins with the abdication of responsibility already accomplished; that a king could even contemplate, let alone achieve, the division of his kingdom must have struck an Elizabethan audience with fear and horror. By his own act, Lear deliberately divests himself of power and retains only the trappings of power, which in turn are one by one inexorably stripped from him until he stands naked on the heath in the rain. The waters of heaven give him wisdom, but his insight into the hypocrisy of this great stage of fools comes to him only in his madness, and he realizes at last that clothes—the symbols of his *hybris*—make neither the king nor the man. Having been purged of the pride of place, he sees himself as he is:

> I am a very foolish fond old man,
> Fourscore and upward, not an hour more nor less;
> And, to deal plainly,
> I fear I am not in my perfect mind. (IV. vii. 60–63)

But this moment of illumination, of heightened self-awareness, so like Othello's, occurs not at the end of Act V, where it would be normally expected, but at the end of Act IV. Having said "Pray you now, forget and forgive; I am old and foolish" (IV. vii. 85), what is left for Lear to say? Yet Shakespeare forces the action on to the shambles of the Grand Guignol of Act V, completely cancelling the calming and cleansing effect of the tragic vision already attained with Lear's self-awareness. The play ends not with the hope that this suffering has not been in vain, but with the defeatism of Kent's "All's cheerless, dark, and deadly" and Edgar's "The oldest hath borne most; we that are young/ Shall never see so much, nor live so long." The order of nature has been turned topsy-turvy; the old who cannot bear suffering have endured too much of it; the young who should be able to bear it are too weak.

But at least *Lear* gives us the consolation of the settling of destinies, mishandled and misplaced as it is. There is none in *Macbeth*. The action of the play begins with the figure of the bloody man and ends with the figure of the dead butcher, and nothing between mitigates the endless horrors of the progression from one to the other. Macbeth accepts the evil promise of the witches' prediction because they so neatly match the evil ambition already in him. Nor does his desire for the crown even pretend that it is for the well-being of the people and the welfare of the state, that excuse which gives some color to Bolingbroke's ambition: "I have no spurs/ To prick the sides of my intent," Macbeth confesses to himself, "but only/ Vaulting ambition." The country suffers under Macbeth's iron rule; "Things bad begun make strong themselves by ill" (III. ii. 55), says Macbeth, and Malcolm confirms him:

> I think our country sinks beneath the yoke;
> It weeps, it bleeds; and each new day a gash
> Is added to her wounds. (IV. iii. 39–41)

More—while Malcolm stands behind Macbeth as Fortinbras stands behind Hamlet, can we seriously accept him as the doctor who can "cast/ The water of my land, find her disease,/ And purge it to a sound and pristine health" (V. iii. 50–52)? What are we to make of a potential successor to the throne whose own ambivalence towards himself confounds even his strongest supporter? Is Macduff—are we—really persuaded that Malcolm is in fact capable of exhibiting "The king-becoming graces,/ As justice, verity, temp'rance, stableness,/ Bounty, perseverance, mercy, lowliness,/ Devotion, patience, courage, fortitude" (IV. iii. 91–94)? Surely his black scruples, coupled with his innocence and inexperience, bode ill for Scotland, whatever the outcome, so that when at last Malcolm is hailed King of Scotland, and, like Hal and Fortinbras, emerges as the symbol of the settling of destinies, our eyes do not see the vision of peace rising from suffering, and our ears hear only the echo—

> for, from this instant,
> There's nothing serious in mortality.
> All is but toys; renown and grace is dead;
> The wine of life is drawn, and the mere lees
> Is left this vault to brag of. (II. iii. 96–101)

—repeated in the dying close of Macbeth's reply to Seyton. The witches have indeed triumphed:

> He shall spurn fate, scorn death, and bear
> His hopes 'bove wisdom, grace, and fear;
> And, you all know, security
> Is mortals' chiefest enemy. (III. v. 30–33)

Man's security, for which he has fought so feverishly, the guarantee of rebirth, has at the very last moment been snatched away from him. Tragedy may be much more and much different from what I have been suggesting here, but one thing it cannot be and that is a tale signifying nothing. * * *

VI

The limitations of the subject of this paper prevent me from showing that the disintegration of the tragic pattern which we have seen take place in the major tragedies is paralleled in the three middle comedies, *Troilus and Cressida*, *All's Well That Ends Well*, and *Measure for Measure*, and comes to its culmination in the four last plays, *Pericles*, *Cymbeline*, *The Winter's Tale*, and *The Tempest*. Nevertheless, I think that the configuration of Shakespeare's thought was for the most part sympathetically conformable to the shape of the myth and ritual pattern. Yet having raised the pattern to the heights of its most moving and significant expression, Shakespeare was unable to hold it there for long. This does not mean that we must regard him as less than, say, Sophocles or Milton, neither of whom seems to have given way to doubt, nor does it mean that the myth and ritual pattern is inadequate either to its purposes or as a means of elucidating tragedy. On the contrary, the application of the pattern to Shakespeare's plays discriminates between them with nicety, it intensifies our awareness of the unique qualities of the individual plays, and it enables us to respond to Shakespeare on a most profound level of understanding. Recent critics of Shakespeare have enjoyed many a laugh at the expense of their predecessors who labored to box Shakespeare's plays under the neat labels "in the workshop," "in the world," "out of the depths," and "on the heights"—to use Dowden's terms—but I cannot see that they themselves have done anything more than to say the same thing in perhaps more fashionable language. But the myth and ritual approach converts a Progress into a Calvary.

Shakespeare paid for the cost of the tragic vision by its loss. He looked long and directly into the face of evil. In the end, he shut his eyes. Writing of another artist who found himself in the same dilemma, Sir Kenneth Clark says: "The perfect union of Piero's forms, transcending calculation, rested on confidence in the harmony of creation; and at some point this confidence left him." As it seems to me, at some point Shakespeare too lost his confidence in the harmony of creation. I do not know when Shakespeare reached that point, but I think that it perhaps came at the moment of his greatest expression of faith in the harmony of creation, in *Othello* when he realized that he had left Iago standing alive on the stage. When in the bottommost circle of Hell, Virgil steps aside from Dante and reveals to him that creature fairest once of the sons of light: "Behold now Dis!", the poet is moved to cry out: "This was not life, and yet it was not death." So in the end Iago: "Demand me nothing; what you know, you know./ From this time forth I never will speak word." The rest is silence.

Centennial Review, I (1957), 142–166. Part V has been omitted.

INITIATORY MOTIFS IN THE STORY OF TELEMACHUS

Charles W. Eckert

Critics of the *Odyssey*, from the Scholiast to Werner Jaeger, have frequently commented on the "educational" nature of Telemachus' voyage to Pylos and Sparta and the transformation from boy to man that occurs during the trip. The indecisive and mother-bound youth of the first books returns filled with the *menos* of the Homeric hero and joins in the cleansing of the house of Odysseus, more as his father's peer than as his son. Seen in this light, the story of Telemachus has a developed plot of its own and could be excerpted, if one chose, to form a separate work.

This common critical view has given direct support to the combined textual-critical arguments for the existence of a *Telemachia*, an independent poem which was wedded to a Voyage and Return of Odysseus to form the present *Odyssey*. The history of this argument is bound up with the almost two-hundred-year-old debate between the "Unitarians" and the "Separatists" and may be traced through a vast bibliography. But whether or not the *Telemachia* was once a separate work, it is substantially independent from the adventures of Odysseus and has always invited criticism in its own right.

To call the *Telemachia* the story of a young prince's education, however, is to define it somewhat imprecisely; the kind of education Telemachus undergoes is that known throughout the ancient world and modern primitive societies as *initiation*. The importance of rites of social initiation for Greek society has been frequently emphasized, notably by Jane Harrison (*Themis*, Cambridge 1912), Henri Jeanmaire (*Couroi et Courètes*, Lille 1939), George Thomson (*Aeschylus and Athens*, London 1941), and by most modern students of the Eleusiniana. Partly because of the prominence of initiation rites in the popular mystery cults, initiatory symbolism enters Platonic and Neoplatonic philosophy, alchemy, and mystical disciplines of many forms, and many initiatory rites or paradigms are employed in religion and literature until Renaissance times.

The real extent of the popularity of initiatory symbolism and the probable reasons for this popularity have not been sufficiently studied. The usual assumption made by students of religion and literature is that any group of initiatory motifs must be a "survival" from earlier social rituals practised in that particular society. The Cambridge school of myth-ritual study, under the influence of nineteenth-century theories of "cultural evolution," gave popularity to the belief that the resemblances between advanced religions and myths and primitive ritual (largely documented in modern societies) were to be explained genetically: prehistoric ritual must have given rise to the historical forms. There are several dangers in assuming this: first we cannot be certain that prehistoric rituals were the same as those documented among modern primitives; second, it is possible that initiatory symbolism arises psychogenetically or is borrowed from neighboring cultures; and third, the concentration upon hypothetical primitive sources takes our attention away from the advanced meanings which may be expressed through initiatory symbolism in higher cultures. Initiation is one of the constants of human society, not merely as a social ritual, but also as a symbolic system capable of expressing transition or transcendence from any polar state to its opposite. Just as initiation appears in social ritual wherever rites are employed to effect the transition from boy to man, so initiation as a symbolic system is employed universally to express such transcendental movements as ignorance to knowledge, secularity to sacrality, or life to death or immortality.

Whatever the importance of rituals of social initiation in the prehistoric Near East, the initiatory symbolisms found in historical religions and literatures must exist because of a *need* for this sort of symbolism and not merely as a survival of primitive social forms. Such a need existed, I believe, for Homer: the initiatory paradigm upon which the story of Telemachus is built gives the most apt symbolism for expressing the movement from boy to man which is at the heart of the *Telemachia*. This is, however, but one of a constellation of meanings which Homer derives from the paradigm; and many of these meanings are not prominent in primitive initiation ritual, as I shall attempt to demonstrate. The important point to be made at present is that the initiatory paradigm employed by Homer is probably not derived directly from ritual and cannot be adequately analyzed in terms of ritual analogues. In order to substantiate this statement I shall first give a brief description of initiation as a social ritual, then examine the initiatory elements in the *Telemachia* in detail, and finally examine the particular meanings Homer seems to derive from the initiatory paradigm.

Initiation rituals, usually called "puberty rituals" by ethnographers, are as widespread as rites concerned with crops or such major events as birth and death. The rites usually include killing an enemy or performing a sacrifice, or both; removal from the group to a hut, sacred ground, or unfrequented area; the endurance of ordeals and the performance of feats; instruction in the group myths, which include knowledge of origins, morality, the nature of deity, etc.; some rite of "marking" such as circumcision or scarification; and finally, investment with adult objects or clothing and a return to the group. The entire experience is extremely threatening because of the presence of the gods who usually "consume" or "kill" the initiates at some point in the rites so that they may return as those "reborn" to a higher status. The central symbolism of death and rebirth is well understood and is often ingeniously elaborated. Boys are frequently removed secretly and at night, and the mothers are told that the gods have stolen them and may kill them. This helps effect a break with the maternal world, since the boys' "death" is to a large degree a death to childhood and effeminizing influence. It is also, as Mircea Eliade has shown at length,[1] a death to the secular condition and to ignorance. The central rites of instruction give the boys the knowledge of the myths, moral codes and rituals—a knowledge which defines man in his religious and social roles and makes him a complete and responsible adult.

That such rituals were known to the Greeks in pre-Homeric times is highly probable, even if one argues only from the grounds that the vast majority of primitive societies

1. Mircea Eliade, *Birth and Rebirth*, tr. Willard Trask (New York: Harper, 1958). This is the best general study of both primitive and advanced religious initiation and contains a full bibliography.

employ initiation rites. This probability is increased by the fact that the Eleusiniana, the most popular cult of classical times, exhibits a clear initiatory structure: such rites as ablution and sacrifice, the journey from Athens to the sacred ground of the Telesterion at Eleusis in the company of a *mystagogos*, and the final *epopteia* or revelation of the sacred all have their analogues in social initiation. Greek education and the rearing of young men in general also recall initiatory practices at many points, especially in Sparta. But when we move from the social and religious spheres to those of myth and epic we move into a different dimension—one as large as the Near East itself, from which the early literature of the Greeks derives. It now seems an inescapable conclusion that the plot structures founded on the heroic quest, acts of purgation and regeneration, the slaying of chthonic demons, and the expiation of blood-guilt are rooted in the sacred myths of the Near East and are disseminated and transformed by singers. To look in each society for a specific ritual which may have given rise to a myth known to that society is to ignore the cosmopolitan and itinerant nature of recited story.

Albert Lord, who has studied at length the techniques of modern Yugoslavian epic singers, notes that stories are transmitted as complexes of motifs rather than as memorized texts (this is not true, of course, if a particular text has been fixed in writing and is considered inviolable). The motif is merely an act or situation—a murder, or marriage, or imprisonment—and the complex of motifs which makes up a "plot" may be all that is kept intact as a story is transmitted from region to region or transferred from hero to hero. Motifs may be variously rationalized, reordered, or dropped from the complex in favor of something more intelligible to the particular singer and his audience.

The initiatory paradigm at the heart of the *Telemachia* appears to be such a complex: it does not, of course, include all of Telemachus' activities; but it does include most of his important and many of his most puzzling actions. As stated before, initiation often begins with a nocturnal theft of the young boys by the older men (usually dressed as mythic beings) and the removal of the boys to a secluded place. Telemachus' voyage, undertaken at night and without Penelope's knowledge, is made in the company of Athena who, in the guise of Mentor ('teacher'), directs his initiation. The sacred ground to which the initiates proceed for the most critical of the rites may be a permanent sacred area, such as the Telesterion at Eleusis, or it may be an area especially marked out for the occasion.[2] Rites conducted on this sacred ground are believed to reactualize mythic events and mythic time (the time when the events were first performed), and the performers become the gods or demigods involved in these events.[3] For Telemachus, this sacred ground is the lower Peloponnese, the

2. The concept of "sacred space" is universal in primitive religious thought and has been extensively surveyed by Mircea Eliade, *The Sacred and the Profane*, tr. Willard Trask (New York: Harcourt, Brace, 1959).

3. The assumption of legendary roles by the officiators in primitive and ancient religious ceremonies is a universal custom. The role of hierophant at Eleusis was filled by members of the Eumolpidae, "descendants" of the mythical Eumolpus, the shepherd-god who brought the mysteries to Eleusis in the reign of Erechtheus, and Plutarch said that in his own day it was "Eumolpus" who initiated the Hellenes (*De Exilio* 607B).

ancient home of Mycenaean civilization, inhabited by two heroes of the Trojan War, Nestor and Menelaus. It is to Pylos and Sparta, far from his home, his mother, and all childhood associations, that Telemachus must go in order to receive the knowledge without which he cannot become a man.

During the second phase initiates usually endure periods of seclusion in a dark and threatening place and live in imminent fear of being destroyed by the gods. As Eliade states, "a considerable number of initiation rites reactualize the motif of death in darkness and at the hands of Divine Beings."[4] The psychological function of this is obvious, but its symbolic function, its implications of death for the boy and rebirth into a world of men, must be emphasized. The instruction that occurs during this phase is little more than a retelling of the myths which contain the knowledge without which one is not a man: the creation of the world and of the group, the early struggles of the divine founders with primal forces, and stories which embody the practical morality of the group usually make up the bulk of this "knowledge." The motifs of death in darkness and instruction are both prominent in the *Telemachia*. The threat of death comes, of course, from the suitors, who recognize that Telemachus has begun to mature and who determine to kill him upon his return by waylaying his ship; and both the voyages to and from Pylos are dangerous night voyages made under the close supervision of a supernatural being, Athena. The instruction that Telemachus receives is a recounting by Nestor and Menelaus of the most critical myth of his society, the story of the Trojan War and its aftermath. The fact that the Trojan War is for Nestor and Menelaus a matter of recent history does not diminish its importance as a source of heroic "knowledge," and I shall consider later the great significance of the Trojan story for Telemachus' personal development.

The third phase, which sometimes takes place on or near the sacred ground, sometimes at the place of seclusion, is that of physical initiation. Whatever rite is performed, whether it is as harsh and dangerous as subincision or merely scarification or piercing the septum of the ear, the alteration is less specifically sexual than it is the creation of an unalterable and conspicuous mark of adult male status. This phase is continuous with the fourth, which is often accompanied by the revelation of certain sacral objects and by long trips which retrace routes originally blazed by the mythical beings (as in the journey from Athens to Eleusis made by the Eleusinian initiates). Sometimes all four stages are passed while the men and boys travel an extensive, difficult route. Finally, the return of the initiates to the entire group often involves a mock rejection of the mother or a mock or real tyrannizing of women in general, a practice that may also occur earlier in the ceremony. In the *Odyssey*, the final battle in the hall fuses most of these motifs, including the scarification of Telemachus, the revelation (*epopteia*) of the totemic aegis of Athena to all present, and a real tyrannizing of women (the hanging of the twelve maidservants) by Telemachus. In both the generalized ritual and the *Telemachia* the essential symbolisms of travel, danger, instruction, physical alteration, the tyrannizing of women, and death and rebirth are readily apparent.

At this point it may be objected that some of the motifs, particularly the *epopteia*

4. Eliade, *Birth and Rebirth*, p. 9.

and the tyrannizing of women, are no part of the traditional *Telemachia* and might as well pertain to Odysseus. With this I am in full agreement: as has been frequently noted, the voyage of Odysseus includes many motifs found in initiatory myths and rituals.[5] It is not so "pure" an initiatory structure as is the voyage of Telemachus, but in Odysseus and Telemachus we do have a "doubled" father-son hero resembling those common in Near Eastern myth, and some of the final initiatory motifs may at one time have pertained to both heroes.

With this generalized pattern in mind, we may now look more closely at the activities of the major figures in the *Telemachia*. The first scene of the *Odyssey*, which pictures Zeus musing on the folly of Aegisthus whom Orestes was bound to slay as soon as he achieved manhood, becomes immediately significant for Telemachus when Athena announces her intention of going to Ithaca to counsel him to visit Pylos and Sparta. The real purpose of this visit, she states, is that he may earn repute among men and show that he is ready to put aside childishness and establish his authority with the suitors and his mother (1.271–302). Athena's true role in the *Telemachia*, of course, is that of a Kurotrophos—a term that in most modern commentaries is translated as "child-bearer" or "child-nurturer." Harrison and Nilsson,[6] however, have shown that *kouros* had the preclassical meaning of "young man just come to maturity," a definition which applies to the over 190 known examples of the kouros-type statue. As the Mentor to an initiate, Athena clearly resembles the *mystagogos* of the Eleusiniana and the older men of more primitive ritual.

With Athena's first visit concluded, Telemachus immediately begins his transformation by speaking sternly to his mother and to the suitors, calling forth the comment by Antinous that he has changed and that the gods must be helping him (1.384–7). The transformation continues during the great debate in Book 2, in which Telemachus tells the suitors of his plans and advises them that he will return to end their spoiling of his father's house now that he is "grown." Meanwhile, Athena (in the temporary guise of Telemachus) has secured a ship and a crew of twenty young men. When provisions have been taken aboard and night has fallen, the perilous trip begins. The combined motifs of darkness and enclosure in a womblike space (the ship) with a mythic being or beings in attendance are constants in initiatory rituals and myths. Jung has studied these motifs in many initiatory plots and has noted that the sea journey by night is a critical and decisive event in which the emphasis is not upon the "eternal recurrence" of the trip, but rather upon a "transformation into something higher."[7] No interpretation could be more appropriate to the journey Telemachus makes.

Upon their arrival in Pylos, Athena reassures the still timid Telemachus that his heart will prompt him to speak correctly in the presence of Nestor, and he approaches

5. See particularly Gabriel Germain, *Genèse de l'Odyssée* (Paris: Presses universitaires de France, 1954), pp. 78–86, 126–128, 131–132.

6. Harrison, *Themis* (Cambridge: Cambridge University Press, 1912), pp. 11–12; and M. P. Nilsson, *The Minoan-Mycenaean religion and its survivals in Greek religion*, 2nd ed. (Lund: C. W. K. Gleerup, 1950), p. 547, respectively.

7. Jolande Jacobi, *Complex, archetype, symbol in the psychology of C. G. Jung* (New York: Pantheon, 1959), p. 186.

the legendary hero, encountering first Nestor's son Peisistratus who henceforth remains his companion during his stay in Pylos and Sparta.[8] The details of Telemachus' conversations with the aged Nestor need not be recounted. Considered broadly, the conversations achieve the same two purposes as those held later with Menelaus in Sparta: they display the growing confidence and rhetorical ability of Telemachus and they transmit to him the "knowledge" without which he cannot be a complete man—the history of the Trojan War and the ensuing catastrophes that befell the Greeks. These myths free Telemachus from his childish past by establishing a new role for him in a higher reality. One remembers Telemachus' words to Antinous before leaving Ithaca: "I am old enough to learn from others what has happened and to feel my own strength at last" (2.314-5). The equation knowledge = strength seems implicit here. The story of Orestes is referred to by both Nestor and Menelaus, who underline its monitory significance for Telemachus and establish it as the particular segment of the "matter" of Troy which *defines* Telemachus in his new role as an adult. Now that the pattern of conduct is clear, Telemachus can act.

With the most important stage of his initiation concluded, Telemachus returns to Ithaca, again by night and under threat of death at the hands of the suitors. The long scenes in the hut of Eumaeus, where father and son are reunited, have no specific counterparts in initiation ritual, though they do reveal Telemachus' new maturity by demonstrating his resolute desire to prove his courage against the suitors and his ability to debate the plan of attack with so experienced a warrior as his father.

Perhaps the most interesting initiatory details, however, are found immediately before and during the final battle itself. A great deal has been written about the scene in which Athena leads Telemachus and Odysseus into the hall on the eve of battle in order to hide away the arms kept there (19.1-40). Athena precedes the two warriors bearing a golden lamp that sheds upon the walls and beams and pillars a blazing light and makes Telemachus exclaim at such a "great marvel." Pfeiffer has recently argued for a cultic significance in this scene. In terms of initiation, however, the scene recalls nothing so much as the reports of the final ceremonies inside the Telesterion at Eleusis which speak of the blaze of light that illuminates the hall when the initiates enter for the final rites.

With the hall prepared for battle, Odysseus waits for the sign from Zeus that will let him know that the gods favor his enterprise and will aid him. When the sign comes, the general battle begins; but it is soon interrupted by an extensive debate between Odysseus and the suitors and by the struggle in the storeroom between Melanthius, Philoetius and Eumaeus. Athena then sheds her guise of Mentor, assumes her most common and ancient epiphany, that of a bird, and flies to a roof beam from which she may survey the battle (22.239-40). Taking complete control, she directs the spears in their flights and tries the skill and courage of both heroes by withholding the strength they need to complete the slaughter. Then two curious things happen. First, Athena permits a spear thrown by Amphimedon to cut Tele-

8. Peisistratus resembles companions found in other initiatory myths (Orestes-Pylades; Heracles-Alcon; Theseus-Pirithous). Young men already initiated frequently accompany boys undergoing initiation.

machus near the wrist.[9] Immediately thereafter Athena lifts on high her "man-destroying" (*phthisimbroton*) aegis, throwing the suitors into a panic and sending them fleeing like kine.[10] Within the space of a dozen lines all but a few of the suitors are dead or dying. The motifs of scarification and the *epopteia* of the sacred symbol of the goddess all but complete the "rites" through which Telemachus has been transformed from a womanish boy to an heroic slayer of men. His final act is the hanging of the twelve maidens who had kept company with the suitors. This tyrannizing of women is a motif commonly found in European initiation scenarios, and is usually the direct consequence of the hero's acquisition of the *menos* or *ferg*—the overabundant heroic "furor" and strength—that the initiation rites have instilled in him and that must be burned out, so to speak, before he can return to normal society.[11] It also, of course, establishes his transcendence of the feminine ties of youth by displaying his absolute mastery over women.

The greatest danger in drawing parallels, as I have done, is that the validity of the argument may be thought to hinge upon the acceptability of all the detailed analogues suggested rather than upon the cumulative "proof" provided by the entire discussion. It is also important to note that Homer's use of an initiatory paradigm is in no way unique, but is rather very much *au courant*, not simply with respect to Greek social custom and religious ritual, but with respect to the Near Eastern literature of his era. If Greek myth did not come to us in such fragmented form, other examples of initiatory plots might be adduced: for instance, any composite version of the myths of Heracles, Theseus, Orestes, Erechtheus, or the Cretan Dionysus, to mention the best known, abounds with initiatory motifs. But the lack of a complete early text for any of these myths makes it impossible to say whether they at one time contained coherent initiatory patterns like that found in the *Telemachia*. The Hebrews, however, preserved more complete versions of their heroic stories, and very coherent initiatory patterns may be discovered in the stories of Moses, of the Exodus itself (a group initiation),[12] and of Jacob, Samson and David. The story of Moses, in particular, exhibits an almost pure initiatory structure and includes all the acts normally performed during social initiations. The priestly redactors of this story have transformed and rationalized some of the motifs, but on the whole they have preserved the pattern of initiation itself and have simply made it significant at the level of sacred history by reducing

9. Another spear wounds Eumaeus, but this fact does not alter the significance of what happens to Telemachus. Homer is not creating an initiatory plot; he is rationalizing one and in the process undoubtedly making additions of his own.

10. The revelation of sacral objects in initiatory rites is an event of such importance that it is fraught with danger even for the initiates. Its effects upon the uninitiated, should they accidentally observe the ceremonies, is universally regarded as disastrous. The terror of the suitors upon seeing the aegis of Athena is due to the sacral potency of the aegis, not to the mere presence of the goddess. In sculpture and art Athena's aegis is depicted with a gorgon's head in its center and a fringe of writhing serpents—as if to emphasize its fearful totemic power.

11. For an excellent discussion of this concept in European myth see Georges Dumézil, *Horace et les Curiaces* (Paris: Gallimard, 1942), pp. 11–33.

12. For initiatory motifs in the story of the Exodus see Theodor Reik, *Mystery on the Mountain* (New York: Harper, 1959).

Moses to an instrument of deity whose "initiation" attunes him to divine purpose instead of infusing him with autochthonous power.

The great value of the initiatory paradigm, as I have noted earlier, is that it can express a number of symbolisms equally well. The symbolism Homer derives from it can best be understood in the perspective of the shift from "myth to history" which Eric Voegelin and Mircea Eliade have sketched in broad outline and which occurred almost simultaneously in Greece and Israel. Earlier Near Eastern societies in their religious rituals and myths displayed a desire to live in an "eternal present" and to abolish history through repetitions of the creation and cyclical symbolisms of many sorts; but the new sense of living in history demanded new symbolisms of transition, linear movement, and transcendence which were elaborated in a new group of symbolic orders.

Among these orders (following Voegelin) were Greek epic, philosophy and drama, and the Hebrew conception of historical revelation. Each in its way makes a radical break with myth at the same time that it retains much of the content and some of the characteristics of myth. The initiatory paradigm becomes popular in cult and literature during the centuries when this major shift is occurring. The reason for this, I believe, is that initiation is peculiarly apt for expressing symbolisms appropriate both to myth and to history: the death and rebirth and the voyage and return of the initiate are perfect vehicles for the expression of repetitive and cyclical movements, while the change from boy to man and from ignorance to knowledge provide the potential for transitional and transcendental symbolisms. The range of meanings latent in initiation may be appreciated by comparing the myths of the initiations of Demophoon and Heracles (etiological for the founding of the Greater and Lesser Eleusiniana, respectively), in which initiation is little more than a rite of toughening or cleansing, with the education of Telemachus, and with the figurative initiation of the philosopher in Plato's *Phaedrus*. Plato's use of initiatory terminology drawn from popular cult sets an example followed by Platonists and Neoplatonists until the Renaissance (especially Plotinus and Ficino), and if we view the *Telemachia* in the context of this entire tradition, the analogues from primitive ritual become less significant and the advanced symbolism latent in the initiatory paradigm more apparent.

Perhaps the most striking difference between the initiations of Telemachus and those of such mythic heroes as Heracles or Theseus is that Telemachus is pictured as fulfilling an ideal pattern of conduct created by an earlier hero, Orestes. Myth lacks any perspective of historical depth, since it always deals with those who first performed certain actions—with the creators, so to speak, of the paradigms of conduct. But Homer creates the kind of historical perspective that makes for typological thought. To what degree Homer's myth of Orestes was initiatory is impossible to say, but according to the traditions known to the tragedians, Orestes underwent some sort of initiation before purging the House of Atreus. In the company of a tutor he spent a number of years at the sacred center of Delphi, where he must have been instructed in the history of the House of Atreus and his duty to avenge his father's death. Shortly before his return, an urn filled with his "ashes" was exhibited to Aegisthus, recalling the motif of the "death" of the initiate which precedes his rebirth. After purification by Apollo, Orestes returned to kill Aegisthus and his mother in a scene that in the *Choephori* is deliberately assimilated to the final ceremonies of the Eleusiniana. One should also note that the motifs of madness, self-mutilation, and extensive travel found in the *Oresteia* are commonplace in initiation scenarios.

If Homer knew the tradition containing all these specific analogues with their ritualistic overtones, he ignored most of it. The analogues he pursues are of a new order—the product of a shift from seeing traditional story as a sequence of acts to be understood in the context of ritual, to seeing the story as a general paradigm from which many meanings may be derived. Telemachus' voyage is not the ritualized fulfillment of a prophetic injunction, but a supervised quest for self-knowledge which reaches its goal in the realization that the House of Odysseus may become another House of Atreus unless he can imitate the courage and decisiveness of Orestes. This growth to maturity *through* paradigmatic knowledge, which is certainly the central symbolism of the *Telemachia*, differs from primitive instruction in the group myths by its emphasis upon the necessity for a personal decision on Telemachus' part. Knowledge is not given in an obligatory social rite; it must be sought, and, when found, accepted and converted into action. Telemachus' agon, compared to Orestes', is muted and distinctively human, yet its successful conclusion is the prelude to the reordering of the House of Odysseus and Telemachus' winning of *kleos* among men. His initiation, like those of Moses or David, has only its motif structure in common with the ritualized world of early myth. Homer has discovered a latent symbolism which accords with his historical perspective and has made "coming of age" an acquisition of the knowledge that makes for order and a discovery of the necessity for making decisions in a world which, as Zeus implies at the beginning of the *Odyssey*, is deterministic only for men who are weak of spirit. To this central symbolism Homer adds other conceptions not emphasized in primitive ritual, particularly Telemachus' growth in rhetorical ability and his associated mastery over the suitors, servants, and his mother upon his return.

The recognition that the *Telemachia* is founded upon an ordered paradigmatic structure should help answer those who have argued that the voyage of Telemachus is not substantive enough to stand as a separate work, or that the real purpose of the trip is to seek news of his father, or that the journey is an excuse to bring Nestor, Menelaus and Helen into the plot. Telemachus is both a major and an indispensable character, for upon his development, no less than upon the return of Odysseus, hinges the fate of Ithaca. One must remember that had not Odysseus nodded in warning, Telemachus would have strung the bow, and that he is ready to rule in Ithaca when Odysseus again leaves. Because Telemachus moves among the Herculean figures of Athena, Nestor, Menelaus and Orestes, his stature seems dwarfed and his agon of growth less dramatic than the sagas related to him by the reminiscing survivors of the battle of Troy. But in the *Telemachia* he is the hero, one whose human fears, youthful awkwardness and awe of the older heroes accentuates rather than detracts from the clear courage of his decision to confront the brutish suitors regardless of their numbers or strength. At the end of the *Odyssey* his shadow is as long as Orestes', not because it is also cast by the distant light from flaming Troy, but because he followed the advice to "think upon Orestes," and grew.

The Classical Journal, LIX (1963), 49–57. Some reference notes have been omitted.

MYTH AND MEDIEVAL LITERATURE:
SIR GAWAIN AND THE GREEN KNIGHT

Charles Moorman

It seems obvious that much of the current interest in the place of myth in literature, as manifested in an ever-increasing number of books and articles on the subject, stems from the fact that myth study can be said to be the logical successor, not in terms of literary influence, but of "intellectual fashion," to the New Criticism. It will be conceded that the New Critics have achieved their ends; they have succeeded in making even the most conservative academicians concentrate their efforts, both in print and in the classroom, toward bringing their peripheral studies of esthetics, sources, biography, and literary history to bear directly upon the illumination of a text in hand. The myth critics, on the other hand, bid fair to returning the serious study of literature to a point of view which the New Critics originally banded together to attack. These mythographers have forsaken that basic doctrine of the New Criticism which insisted on the integrity of the individual work of art, and have returned for inspiration to those sections of the library given over to myth, folklore, anthropology, psychology, and comparative religion.

A glance at the critical barrage directed at *Sir Gawain and the Green Knight*, and for that matter at almost any other place of medieval literature, which seems particularly susceptible to this sort of treatment, will show how the myth critic has shifted the focus of interest away from purely literary values and back again to the most sterile sorts of source hunting and parallel finding. Just as the typical nineteenth-century academician regarded *Sir Gawain and the Green Knight* only as a storehouse of information on medieval armor, architecture, and venery, so do the myth critics insist that the poem is only a repository of myth patterns and thus direct their efforts to elucidating Gawain's relationship to the British Jack-in-the-Green, the Celtic sun god, and the omnipresent vegetation god. A very brief review of two of these myth-minded critical treatments of *Sir Gawain and the Green Knight* should serve to demonstrate that, despite their pieties in theory, the myth critics have in practise shown that they believe that once they have discovered the myth pattern inherent in a piece of literature, they have illuminated and settled once and for all the critical problems presented by that particular work.

Our first critic, the late Heinrich Zimmer, is a follower of C. G. Jung, the disciple of Freud. The Jungian school takes as a point of departure Jung's concept of a "collective unconscious" in which mythological archetypes "correspond to certain *collective* structural elements of the human psyche in general, and like the morphological elements of the human body, are *inherited*." The Jungian critic thus first "circumscribes" the central archetype present in the work (which can never be exactly described because "it does not refer to any thing that is or has been conscious"), demonstrates its universality by bringing to light a number of parallel manifestations of the myth, and finally, by way of conclusion, states that in this particular poem we find an unconscious manifestation of the archetype. Professor Zimmer follows this general pattern rather closely in examining *Sir Gawain and the Green Knight* in the course of a volume entitled *The King and the Corpse*,[1] the unifying thesis of which is, as I understand it, that the hero's quest is essentially a psychiatric process by means of which the innocent hero, in undergoing the *rite de passage* which initiates him into the life of the whole man, gives up his conscious self and intellectual identity in order to be guided by his brute instincts to the bottom of his personality and there unite conscious and unconscious, intellectual and animal existences.

In his extended discussion of *Sir Gawain and the Green Knight*, Zimmer finds that the archetypal pattern which the poem reflects is that of the initiation of the hero, the *rite de passage*, which in turn involves the death-rebirth archetype: "Through the valley of death he [Gawain] is conducted to the aloof and lonely sanctuary of life renewed, and then, having withstood the trial, is reborn." But while no one would deny that the poem involves testing and initiation, it is difficult to understand in reading Zimmer's analysis just how this general statement of theme, applicable surely to a great many myths, is entirely and consistently relevant to a particularly finished and beautifully articulated fourteenth-century poem. For example, in order to superimpose his death-rebirth archetypal pattern on the poem, Zimmer states that the Green Knight represents Death and his wife Life. Zimmer bases these statements on the facts that (1) "in folklore and fairy tales the dead not uncommonly carry their heads under their arms . . . ," that (2) "pale green is the color of livid corpses," and that (3) Life is traditionally Death's bride. It seems evident to me that Zimmer goes too far afield in his speculations here. It would be wiser, and certainly more justifiable in terms of the poem, (1) to assume that the Green Knight picks up his head and tucks it under his arm because Gawain has just hacked it off and it is rolling about the hall, (2) to note that in English poetry (Zimmer cites Tibetan art at this point) the color green is traditionally associated with Life, if indeed it represents any one thing consistently, rather than with Death,[2] and (3) to object that the assignment of a symbolic role to Bercilak's Lady, not on the evidence of any personal characteristics, but simply on the grounds of her marriage, is at best a highly arbitrary business.

The rest of Zimmer's discussion consists not, as one would expect, of a detailed analysis of the progress of the romance, but instead of a helter-skelter examination of the myth pattern as it appears in the probable sources of *Sir Gawain and the Green Knight*. The reason for this retreat into the sources of the poem is evident: Zimmer states that "in the present version the point of the challenge, temptation, and trial is not made quite clear. The romance seems to miss something of its own suggested depth. . . . One cannot even be sure that the thirteenth and fourteenth century French and English poets . . . consciously intended the reading that inevitably emerges . . . ." In short, the poem and the myth do not agree. As an example of the *Gawain* poet's ignorance of his proper duties as myth recorder, Zimmer points out that the presence of Morgan le Fay in the poem may be attributed to the fact that "themes that must

1. Heinrich Zimmer, *The King and the Corpse* (New York: Pantheon, 1948).
2. Note that two pages later the "green girdle of death" mysteriously becomes the "talisman of rebirth."

once have been enacted on a higher mythical stage now appear obscured and encumbered with the trappings of chivalric pride and family intrigue." But it must be clear to even the most casual reader of the poem that since Morgan is, according to the poet, the instigator of the testing device and thus the prime mover of the plot-action, she cannot be done away with quite so easily and on grounds as tenuous as these without materially distorting the intent of the poet and the structure of the poem.

In short, Zimmer refuses to deal with the poem on its own terms; if Morgan le Fay, or if anything else for that matter, does not fit in with the myth and the archetype, then it is denounced as a late addition or put down as an example of the poet's failure to understand the myth involved, and so done away with as irrelevant to the proper study of the poem. This, it seems to me, is to underestimate gravely the skill, the understanding, and the intent of the poet and, worse than this, to ignore completely the literary qualities and the integrity of the text itself.

Our second critic, John Speirs, though offering a more carefully wrought analysis, makes the same mistake in emphasis.[3] Speirs begins his discussion of the poem by attacking those scholars and editors of the poem who have, according to him, "ignored its uniqueness" and deliberately refrained from examining the "object, the English poem as what it positively is." So far, nearly everyone would agree with Mr. Speirs' aims, if not with his language and tone. Yet what is the next point made in the analysis? Morgan le Fay is dismissed from serious consideration since she, as a character in the poem, is not "realized as Lady Macbeth is realized." What Mr. Speirs apparently cannot see is that none of the characters in the poem, including Gawain himself, is "realized as Lady Macbeth is realized"; since the *Gawain* poet is a medieval romancer, and not an Elizabethan dramatist, he quite naturally does not "realize" his characters as Shakespeare does. Had he done so, he would have violated every canon of the art which he so skillfully practised. Aside from this consideration, Mr. Speirs suffers, as did Professor Zimmer, from the mistaken notion that it is possible to add or subtract the parts of a poem regardless of all considerations of mechanical, much less organic, unity. In short, although Mr. Speirs states that he intends to look at the poem "as what in itself it is," he begins his analysis by deleting the character who motivates the entire action and in doing so eliminates the only explanation given us of what actually happens in the poem; Bercilak's statement of the meaning of the test becomes a "bone for the rationalizing mind to play with and be kept quiet with." Yet four lines later, Speirs speaks of the poem as a "great unified work of art."

Mr. Speirs next proceeds to more fertile matters of discussion. The poem is a "midwinter festival poem," and he immediately sends us away from the poem and off to the source books. The Green Knight is not Death this time but the "Green Man . . . the Jack in the Green or the Wild Man of the village festivals of England and Europe," who is in turn the "descendent of the Vegetation or Nature God of . . . almost universal and immemorial tradition whose death and resurrection mythologizes

3. John Speirs, "Sir Gawain and the Green Knight," *Scrutiny*, XVI (1949), 274-300.

the annual death and re-birth of nature . . . ."[4] This conclusion could have been fore-seen, since Mr. Speirs, judging from his outlook and from the sorts of evidence he brings forward and the authorities he cites, is a thorough-going ritualist, a disciple of the Cambridge school represented chiefly by Frazer, Miss Harrison, Cornford, Murray, and Miss Weston. Thus the long analysis which follows corresponds to the basic party line of the group, summarized by Stanley Edgar Hyman as the belief that myth is the "spoken correlative of a ritual, the story which the rite enacts or once enacted," and contains the usual Celtic mythologist talk about Gawain, none of which is particularly applicable here. For instance, we are told that Gawain's traditional role was that of "the hero, the agent who brought back the spring, restored the frozen life-processes, revived the god—or (in later versions) cured the king." How this can be said to illuminate the poem, I cannot see. In *Sir Gawain and the Green Knight*, Gawain is indeed the hero, but he unfreezes no life-processes (he himself is almost frozen, as a matter of fact), revives no god, cures no king.

The rest of Speirs' analysis is, for the most part, made up of strange attempts to find ritualistic backgrounds for details of the poem,[5] and Speirs goes on to make the usual and expected identifications: the old woman is the "old year" and Bercilak's Lady is the "new year." The hunts are "symbolically the doing-to-death of the qualities of the natural man which Courtesy has to vanquish" (this in spite of the fact that Speirs does not consider the poem to be about Courtesy and Chivalry at all), which symbolic hunts in turn are said to be related to "animal sacrifices of fertility rituals." The Green Chapel is the "secret source of life" (this in spite of the fact that it is the "corsedest kirk" that Gawain ever saw). And so it goes.

Mr. Speirs ends his analysis by reminding his readers how studiously he has avoided the "error of regarding it [the poem] simply as a recorded myth, the record of the story of a ritual." Yet it is hard to see that Speirs has in fact avoided such a pit-fall. He has certainly said nothing illuminative concerning the poem, except to cite as a general theme "a kind of adjustment, if not reconciliation between man and nature" and to add, lest this seem vague, that "in a more limited sense, the courtly order has been put to the test of nature." Yet even here it is hard to see just how this statement of theme fits the facts of the poem (the mixed nature of Gawain's success; the func-tion of Morgan le Fay in the action) and the facts of Speirs' own interpretation (the

4. It is always distressing to note these disagreements among the mythographers. Here Zimmer's death symbol becomes Speirs' life symbol. In the same way, Gawain's axe, a symbol of the primitive, pre-Christian nature of death in Zimmer's analysis, becomes a fertility symbol in Speirs' discussion.

5. For example, the lords and ladies of Arthur's court kick the Green Knight's head away as it rolls towards them not out of "cruelty" or "horror," but because the "head of the sacrificed beast in fertility rituals was believed pregnant with magical powers." Speirs offers as documentation for this statement a scholarly footnote relating the incident to the origin of football among primitive tribes. Speirs is so eager to connect everything in the poem with specific rituals and village festivals that he claims that Gawain's arms are described in great and glittering detail because Greek, Roman, and English dancers were so arrayed in festival dances; that medieval English knights might have been so arrayed he seems not to have considered. Having stated that the towers of Bercilak's castle are "as innumerable stalks thrust upward from the ground in spring" and that the castle is thus a fertility symbol, close to "the hidden source of life," Speirs adds a footnote remarking that "editors here interpose the red herring of 14th century architecture."

relation between the testing of the courtly order, the Old and New Year symbolism, and the vegetative god). I cannot understand how Mr. Speirs' analysis, for all its ingenuity and sincerity, accomplishes anything other than to repeat what essentially has always been said of the poem—that Gawain undergoes a series of tests and that this testing is the theme of the poem.

So might, with illustrations, run the case against myth criticism as currently practised. There is, however, a more sensible, and, I believe, a more productive attitude toward the place of myth in literature. Like these critics, I believe that the application of the fruits of myth study to literature furnishes the critic with a tool of interpretation by which he can arrive quickly and with great precision at the heart of a piece of literature. Yet I believe also that it is impossible to leave the problem, as do these critics, at the stage of identification; the myth is not the poem, and we must always remember that a definition must contain both *genus* and *differentia*, both identification and separation. In literary scholarship, it has never been sufficient to delineate a source; the scholar must show how that source is used in the work at hand, how it itself becomes a tool of creation. To be able to show how the poet uses myth and, in doing so, to concentrate not on the identity of the myth, but on its function, not on its closeness to the known pattern, but on the changes which the poet effects in that pattern, not on origin, but on use would seem to me to constitute the proper aim of the myth critic.

It would seem that any criticism following such a strategy must rest *ab initio* upon two major assumptions concerning the nature of myth itself: (1) that myth is in itself meaningful (the problem of myth origin); (2) that myth is used in literature, whether consciously or unconsciously, for a meaningful purpose (the problem of myth transmission). The first of these assumptions has been sufficiently examined to have become almost self-evident; no matter whether a critic holds to the ritual, the euhemerist, the Jungian, or to any variation of these doctrines, he will agree that myth is in some fashion and to some degree meaningful. Moreover, it seems to me that the critic has the right to hold to and use any reasonable theory of myth origin as long as the method of critical analysis which he raises on the structure of that theory is capable of throwing light upon a literary text.

The second of these two assumptions, that involving myth transmission, has a closer relationship to the problem of the function of myth in literary art. Here I would propose a distinction. I can understand very easily the use made of myth by modern artists who share our own ideas of the nature and composition of myth, by, for example, Yeats, Auden, Eliot, and Charles Williams. Theirs is a conscious and knowing use of myth; when Yeats speaks of a "Ledaean body" and Eliot of the "bloody wood," they hope by allusion to myth to bring to a poem, usually for purposes of identification and comparison, the whole context of the myth of which they refer. What Eliot wishes us to understand in that brief allusion to the "bloody wood" in *Sweeney among the Nightingales* and to apply to Sweeney's situation in the tavern is not simply the story of the ritual assassination of the priest-king at Nemi, but the consciousness of a whole complex of meaning which is itself represented by the murder of the priest-king and which takes on a still further relevancy and meaning when seen in relation to the complex of meaning, or lack of meaning, represented by Sweeney. In short, those modern writers who use myth use it consciously, with a clearly defined purpose, and, in the works of the men mentioned above at any rate, with good effect.

The writers of the Middle Ages present an entirely different problem, different not only in degree, but in kind, which has as yet not been sufficiently recognized, let alone dealt with. Here the use of myth seems to me to be in the great majority of instances unconscious. For example, we can say that the references to figures of the Christian myth (whether the *Gawain* poet would in fact consider these Old Testament characters "mythical" does not here affect the point) in the following passage from *Sir Gawain and the Green Knight* are designed to do little more than serve as ordinary metaphorical references, used here as "authorities" in typically medieval fashion to make a traditional antifeminist point about the nature of women:

> But yet it is no rare fault to be made a fool
> And through the wiles of women to be won to sorrow,
> For thus was Adam on this earth early beguiled,
> And Solomon with more than one, and Samson in his season—
> Delilah dealt him his fate—and David thereafter
> Suffered sorely from Bathsheba's sweetness and softness. (ll. 2414-2419)

But while the use of myth in this single passage is perfectly clear, can it be said that the ancient myth of initiation which underlies the poem as a whole is used consciously by the poet? John Speirs states, without evidence, that it is. I assert, using the same evidence, that it is not, and pending the discovery of concrete proof, I would maintain that mine is the more satisfactory point of view. Yet it is clear that the *rite de passage* pattern is repeated in essence, if not in detail, in *Sir Gawain and the Green Knight* and that some theory of transmission must be brought forward to explain the phenomenon.

I would at this point prefer to fall back upon what might be called common sense rather than upon metaphysics or psychology in suggesting a possible explanation. The *rite de passage*, in all its tremendously varied forms, would appear to represent an almost universal theme, appearing as it does over and over again in myth and in formal literature. It is not necessary, however, to be a follower of any school of myth interpretation to explain its universality. Certainly there would appear to be relatively few general literary themes which are of real importance to the human spirit. Of these, the passage of the soul through its difficulties to its triumph, *ad astra per aspera*, through the valley of the shadow of death on to the Celestial City, is constantly observable, clothed in an immense variety of forms, both in our own personal experience and in the vicarious experience of literature. The passage of the spirit, seen in its most articulate and naked form in the progress of the myth hero in the quest, is part of the general experience of being human. Thus, in the initiatory rites of savages, in the Holy Week of the Christian year, in the great myths of all peoples, this natural and omnipresent human problem and hope is elevated, by symbolic action, to universal and archetypal and, in most cases, religious heights. It seems entirely natural to me, therefore, that this theme should appear at all times and in all places and that it should appear in literary forms in which it would seem to be unconscious in that it is given a local habitation and a name instead of being transcribed in the broad and general terms which are natural to philosophy but alien to art. Myth therefore becomes, if nothing else, a touchstone useful in isolating and labeling the characteristics which this universal theme inherently assumes in art and useful also in defining the particular form, the nature of the *differentia*, which the pattern manifests in the work in hand.

In the Middle Ages, the prevailing use of the allegorical, rather than the symbolic, method would seem to bring nearer the surface of the literary work this unconscious mythic quality which to some degree underlies all literature. Thus it is that these myth patterns become comparatively easy to trace in the literature of this period. Here again I would suggest a further partition for purposes of analysis. It would seem to me that this general theme (called variously death-rebirth, initiation, withdrawal-return) appears in one dominant form in the literature of the Middle Ages—that of the journey. It is apparent that medieval literature is full of accounts of journeys: Dante travels through the realms of the dead; travelers find their way into the Celtic underworld; pilgrims "seken straunge strondes," and, most important of all, hundreds of knights traverse hundreds of fields and forests in quest of objects strange and high. That all of these journeys are variants of a single basic pattern—the pattern of the archetypal journey-initiation-quest—appears to me at this time to be a possibility. The application, therefore, of the journey myth, seen in terms of its initiatory, *rite de passage* aspect, to the specific journeys of medieval literature would be a useful task, provided always that the critic bear in mind that he must refrain from identifying myth and literature, that he must not neglect *differentia*, once he has established *genus*. No one would claim, of course, that such a line of action would further illuminate *The Divine Comedy*, where the pattern is revealed in such elevation and clarity as to render obvious its workings and its effects. But that this method of critical analysis should throw light on the works of Chrétien de Troyes, on *Pearl* and *Piers Plowman*, on Malory seems to me to be more than sufficient justification for undertaking the labors of the task.

This is, to say the least, a long preamble of a tale. Yet in demonstration I would attach at this point an analysis of *Sir Gawain and the Green Knight*. I would hope that this analysis will have two virtues in its favor: (1) that it attempts to treat myth, and more particularly this peculiarly important journey myth, in *Sir Gawain and the Green Knight* according to its function in the poem and (2) that it attempts to use myth as a tool, in conjunction with other tools of structure and imagery, in arriving at some statement of the theme of one of the most puzzling of all poems. We may very well begin with the structure of the poem.

The whole poem is very neatly enveloped by a framing reference to the noble Trojan ancestry of the British race and, more significantly, by the reveling at the court of King Arthur which begins and ends the poem. Thus, the narrative is enclosed within an envelope which brings the reader full circle from New Year's through the seasons to New Year's, and from Arthur's court to the Green Chapel to Arthur's court again. Gawain's adventure with the Green Knight is self-contained and so made to stand independently from the Arthurian material generally. *Sir Gawain and the Green Knight* can in no sense be said to be an episode in a longer chronicle concerning the history of the Round Table; it is a complete action in itself, containing as it does no references, either direct or indirect, to other incidents in the familiar Arthurian cycle. In this regard, the tone of the poem is also at least superficially alien to the tragedy and corruption which are a part of the kingdom's later history. It is, for the most part, a Christmas poem, filled with revelry and holiday celebrations in each of its four fits. The poem is dominated by the Christmas colors: the Green Knight, the white snow, the red and gold of Gawain's trappings. If we are to find in the poem any coherent theme, we must thus take into account first of all the facts (1) that the poem is self-contained and (2) that it is at least superficially a gay Christmas poem.

It will also be seen that, in each of the sections, the main action is surrounded and enveloped by a picture of Christmas revelry and courtly life which serves to make the poem an almost continuous Christmas celebration. Certainly the court scenes serve to link the fits together by maintaining parallel structure and by establishing thereby a remarkable consistency of tone. There are festal meals in each fit: Arthur's New Year's celebration in Fit I, the welcoming dinner which Bercilak gives to Gawain in II, the knightly dinners at Bercilak's castle in III, and Arthur's celebration at the return of Gawain in IV. There are also descriptions of the arming of knights in each fit: the Green Knight in Fit I, Gawain in II, the hunters in III, and Gawain again in IV. There are also many parallel incidents which serve to make connection backwards and forwards in the poem and so serve to keep the major action of the poem constantly before the reader. For example, the slaughtering of the captured animals suggests the beheading game; the exchange of gifts at the end of each day in the castle and the New Year's gift game at Arthur's court suggest the exchange of blows; each of Gawain's two journeys suggest the other by the repetition of the description of the terrain. These, like the descriptions of arms and dress, serve both to maintain structural unity and to establish the background of pomp and spendor upon which a great deal of the action takes place.

The elaborate nature descriptions, however, all of which are done on a gigantic scale—the three journeys of Gawain, "having wandered far from his friends" (l. 714), the hunting scenes, the description of the Green Chapel—contrast with the courtly scenes and so keep before the reader an atmosphere which shifts continually from the pleasant court life to the wild roughness of the world outside the court. We shall return to this point. Moreover, since so much of the poem (well over half) is taken up with this sort of descriptive detail, it, like the form of the poem, must be taken into account in any statement of the theme of the poem. For example, Professor Henry Savage has already pointed out the very close parallels which exist between the hunting descriptions and the temptation scenes in Gawain's bower. In the hunting scenes, it is clear that the nature of the hunted animal—the shy deer, the aggressive boar, the deceitful fox—suggests very powerfully the tactics which Gawain uses to put off the Lady's advances; he first attempts to put her off by evasion, then by demanding her intentions, and finally, to save his life, by accepting and hiding the green girdle. Such interpretation shows quite clearly that the balanced structure of the poem and the great abundance of balanced descriptive material—the feasting, arming, and nature passages—must be relevant to the theme of the poem.

The *Gawain* poet has also constructed a clear series of parallel incidents within the poem which serve to link the adventures of Gawain into a meaningful and balanced pattern. The function of many, if not all, of these parallel incidents is, I think, to establish for purposes of comparison two levels of courtesy and chivalry within the poem, that of Arthur's court and that of Bercilak's castle. It is at this point that we may best introduce the function of the initiation myth in the poem.

It is clear from the beginning that Gawain's task is spiritual rather than physical. It is usual to state, of course, that almost any given quest in the medieval romance is undertaken in behalf of a worthy cause and so has as its aim a non-physical and thus, in a sense, "spiritual" goal. But aside from such obvious exceptions as the Grail quest in the Arthurian cycle, the knightly quest is undertaken primarily in the service of the secular ideal of chivalric duty and not from any purely religious or spiritual motives. However, the quest of Gawain in this poem, although emanating from the chivalric virtue of loyalty to one's oath, is described in such terms as to transform it into a semi-religious quest for what can only be described as a spiritual object or set of values. Briefly stated then, the journey of Gawain to the domain of the Green Knight amounts, in mythical terms, to a *rite de passage* by which Gawain is initiated into a full understanding both of himself and of the values by which he lives and, by way of that knowledge (to return to the terms of the poem), to an understanding of the true nature of the chivalry of Arthur's court. Certainly the stages of the initiatory rite, as seen by Van Gennep and the other commentators, are reflected in the poem; Gawain, having received what Joseph Campbell designates a "call to adventure," journeys forth from his usual world (Arthur's court in the poem) and retires into a strange land, where he undergoes various tests (the assaults of the Lady) and receives a gift of great value to his people (the green girdle). He returns bearing this saving gift, but is scorned and so is unable to redeem his people by means of this curative device. The application of these general stages of the *rite de passage* to the poem will, I think, become clearer in detailed analysis.

Gawain's quest is plainly intended to be taken as a spiritual task. As Professor Denver Baughan points out, Arthur is not able to qualify for the adventure; he can only swing the Green Knight's axe wildly about, unable to strike with it. Gawain alone can deal the blow effectively. The element of magic in the poem reinforces this interpretation; the beheading game is from the beginning no ordinary chivalric adventure. Since this is true, it is likewise clear that Gawain's search for the Green Chapel becomes a spiritual quest; note that Gawain can find the castle of Bercilak only after he has prayed that he find "some lodging where [he] may devoutly hear a mass" (l. 755) and that he discovers the castle *immediately* upon ending the prayer with the words "Christ's Cross speed me" (l. 762). Gawain's journey becomes, in a sense, the journey of the individual towards a spiritual ideal higher than himself, made alone through the valley of the shadow "and no one but God to converse with on the way" (l. 696). Gawain's quest is also shown through imagery to be essentially religious in character. The pentangle device on Gawain's arms is described in great detail and in religious terms (ll. 620–669). He is said to undertake the journey "on God's behalf" (l. 692). Few people live in the wilderness through which Gawain rides "that praise either God or man with a good heart" (l. 702). Gawain prays to Mary on his journey (ll. 737–739), and it is clear that Gawain is under the Virgin's special protection (l. 1769) and that his fate is in the hands of God (ll. 1967, 2136 ff.). Gawain twice says that in keeping his tryst with the Green Knight he is obedient to God's will (ll. 2156 ff., 2208 ff.) and in his final interview with Bercilak, Gawain receives what sounds like religious absolution from the Green Knight (ll. 2390 ff.).

As I have said, the *Gawain* poet clearly contrasts the two courts. In the beginning, Arthur's company receives high praise:

> Full of courtly fun they bode in fellowship,
> The worthiest of warrior-knights under Christ's welkin,
> And the lovesomest ladies ever life beheld,
> And the comeliest king ever in keep or castle;
> For all this was a fair folk in their first free age,
>   in the hall. (ll. 50–55)

Guinevere is:

> The fairest, comeliest queen,
> Her gray eyes gleaming,
> That men had ever seen. (ll. 81–84)

There is certainly no sign of corruption or bad blood here. But when we compare these descriptions of Arthur's court with the later descriptions of Bercilak's court, it becomes apparent that Bercilak's court is just as elaborate as Arthur's and in several major respects closer to the courtly and chivalric ideal. First the lady of the castle:

> She was the fairest in the field in flesh and in feature,
> In compass and in color and in all other qualities
> *And goodlier than Guinevere, or so Gawain thought.*
>   (ll. 943–945; italics added)

Second, Bercilak's court boasts the finer hospitality. Compare Arthur's welcoming of the Green Knight, who has said that he comes in peace (see l. 266):

> . . . "Sir courteous knight,
> If battle is your pleasure,
> Here will fail no fight." (ll. 276–279)

with the Green Knight's welcoming of the armed Gawain:

> "Faith, while I live my fame will be the fairer
> That Gawain has been my guest at God's own feast."
>   (ll. 1035–1036)

Arthur, we note, is almost rude and certainly high-handed, since the unarmed Green Knight has said nothing about fighting and, in fact, carries the holly branch of peace. On the other hand, Gawain, armed to the teeth, is accepted as a guest and the modest court is delighted to have him.

It can be shown, moreover, that this contrast between the courtesy and chivalry of Arthur's court and that of Bercilak's furnishes the real motivation for the Green Knight's challenge. In his final explanation, Bercilak tells Gawain that he was sent to Arthur's court by Morgan:

> "To test your pompous *pride* and see if they were true,
> Those reports of renown about the Round Table."
>   (ll. 2457–2458; italics added)

He announces to Arthur upon his arrival at Camelot that he cannot remain long:

> But your kingly fame, my lord, is known far and fair,
> Your city and your knights said to be most excellent,
> Mightiest of men in armor, masters in the lists,
> Most modest and most manly in all this merry world,
> Cheeriest of champions at chevying or tilting,
> *And here are care and courtesy, kindliness and honor,*
> *And that has drawn men hither upon this dear day.*
>   (ll. 258–64; italics added)

Thus, since the testing of the courtesy and chivalry of the Round Table is the cause of the exchange of blows, the differences between the two courts, seen in conjunction with the spiritual nature of the quest, becomes of considerable importance in determining the theme of the poem.

In an important three-fold parallel, moreover, the Green Knight and his lady heap aspersions upon the courtesy and chivalry of Arthur's court by exposing it to irony. First, when none of the knights of the Round Table rises to meet his challenge, the Green Knight says:

> "What, is this King Arthur's court?" laughingly he cried,
> "Whose fame is forever and as far as men can travel?
> Where is now your pride, your pomp and your posturing,
> Your fierceness in fight and your chivalry and fame? (ll. 309–12)

Second, when Gawain is adamant in resisting the overtures of the lady, she doubts that the man before her is the courtly Gawain of whose *gentilesse* she has heard:

> "Now he that speeds each speech repay you for your sport!
> But, that you are the dashing Gawain, this I deeply doubt."
> . . . .
> "One so good as Gawain is greatly said to be,
> One in whom all courtesy cleanly is enclosed,
> Could not have lingered lightly so long with a lady
> But he had craved a kiss by his courtesy,
> By some light allusion let fall from his lips." (ll.1292–93; 1297–1301)

Third, when Gawain flinches at the Green Knight's first feint, Bercilak says:

> "Why, you're not Gawain, man!" he jeered, "of such high fame,
> He who never quaked or quailed in the clash of battle,
> For now you flinch in craven fear before you feel my steel!
> I never heard such cowardice ascribed to that great knight!"
>
> (ll. 2270–73)

It would seem that the Green Knight, like his lady, finds something wanting in the courtesy and the chivalry of the Round Table. In each case these ironical thrusts follow passages in which the Green Knight and his lady have heaped extravagant praise upon the Round Table and upon Gawain. Thus, it would seem that the difference between the two courts is further reinforced by having Bercilak and the lady first praise the chivalry of the court of Arthur and then, having tested it by their own standards, find fault with it.

In arriving at a statement of the probable theme of the poem, then, we must keep before us at least four major aspects of the form of the poem—the fact that the poem is a self-contained action, the fact that the poem follows in general outline the pattern of the hero's *rite de passage*, the poet's balanced use of court life and nature description, and the prevailing contrast between the court of Arthur and the court of Bercilak.

I have said that the self-contained form and Christmas tone of the poem belie any theory which places great emphasis upon the tragic later history of the court. Yet it is equally clear that even in the hey-day of the Round Table, as seen in *Sir Gawain and the Green Knight*, there are disturbing elements which it will be best to list for the sake of clarity:

1. The Arthurian court generally, and Gawain in particular, are subjected at crucial moments to a searching irony which they cannot answer except by raging (ll. 316–22, 2284–85).

2. Arthur is plainly incapable of responding to the Green Knight's challenge (ll. 330–31), and although Gawain is the only knight capable of undertaking the quest, yet even he only partly succeeds in resisting the temptations set before him and so returns to the court, his victory tainted with dishonor.

3. Guinevere is singled out for attack by Morgan (ll. 2456–58), and she clearly suffers by comparison with Bercilak's lady (ll. 943–45).

4. Most puzzling of all, Morgan le Fay, whatever her design, fails, since although Arthur is humiliated by his failure to strike the blow, Guinevere, whom Morgan wished to kill by fear, remains alive.

If we allow ourselves for a moment to hold the assumption that the *Gawain* poet knew the legend in its entirety, we will be able, I think, to fit these pieces of evidence into a meaningful pattern.

Morgan, a former mistress and student of the friendly magician Merlin (ll. 2448–51), is attempting to reform Arthur's court, to "test the pride" and the "renown" of the Round Table, by exposing it to the irony of a civilization, far more courtly and chivalrous, represented by Bercilak. Morgan's plan for reform takes the form of an exchange of blows, a knightly game, to be followed by a series of temptations designed to test the spiritual qualities of the company. Arthur, presumably because of his pride, cannot even qualify for the test, and only Gawain, because of his modesty the best of the knights (l. 354), can meet the challenge. Gawain, representing the best qualities of the court, embarks then upon an initiatory spiritual quest, a *rite de passage*, undergoes the necessary dangers and temptations, and returns bearing with him the green girdle which is a symbol both of his success and, ironically, of his failure. But even though Gawain's mission is not completely successful, it would seem that Morgan's plan had succeeded since Gawain has supplied the court with a strong object lesson in the value of chastity and faithfulness. Yet this is obviously not the case since Guinevere, whose death was an integral part of the plan, still lives. Then too, strangely enough, Gawain goes into an extended antifeminist harangue, presumably aimed at Bercilak's lady (ll. 2414–28). Yet we know that the responsibility for the failure of the mission lies solely with Gawain, that he accepted the girdle to save his own life, and that the Lady, far from being an evil temptress, was acting out a part written for her by Morgan and is, in fact, even more gracious than Guinevere. The antifeminist discourse must thus be aimed at Guinevere herself.

The point, I think, is this. The testing of Gawain is designed to warn the court of two potential dangers, sexual wantonness and unfaithfulness, which threaten its existence and which Morgan is attempting to remove. Wantonness is personified in the figure of Guinevere, who, we remember, is later to bring about the downfall of the court by her affair with Launcelot. Unfaithfulness, a breach in the chivalric code of loyalty, is manifested in the court itself, which later will indulge in the personal feuds which culminate in the treachery of Mordred. Thus, Morgan's plan fails on both counts because Arthur, though himself humiliated, is able to comfort and protect the queen (ll. 470–75), and Gawain, though able to resist the temptations of the Lady which are designed to test in him these two qualities, cannot keep complete faith with Bercilak. Both dangers remain in the court, and it is obvious from the knights' laughter (ll. 2513–15) that the court does not take seriously the green girdle, the gift of great value, which is a warning against both. Only the initiated Gawain perceives the danger.

The *Gawain* poet, I maintain, is presenting us, within a deliberately limited form, a microcosm, or better said, a semi-allegorical presentation of the whole history and meaning of the Round Table. Morgan attempts reform; Gawain fails in keeping faith with Bercilak; treacherous Guinevere remains alive. The form of the poem is thus quite consciously limited in time and in space in order to facilitate a unified and complete presentation of the progress of the Round Table; only in a single, complete adventure could the poet achieve any unified design which would reflect the whole of the tragedy. In this sense the poem is semi-allegorical in method in that we are not presented with a segment of the action, but with a miniature version of the whole action. The gay light tone, which reflects the ignorance and pride of Arthur's court, is maintained throughout the scenes which take place within the safe precincts of Camelot, but once the poem moves to the outside world, the tone changes radically. The journeys are always difficult and dangerous, the terrain rugged and foreboding. The scene of the final encounter, the Green Chapel, is, to Gawain, "the most accursed church" that he ever saw (l. 2195). Certainly, the prevailing tone is that of Christmas, but we must remember that the court is in "her first age" and tha: all the knights are ironically ignorant of Morgan's attempts to forestall the fate which will overtake them and ignorant also of the dangers outside the court which must be a part of any spiritual quest. Only the returned Gawain, who has himself made the initiatory journey, sees the imminent destruction which he expresses in his condemnation of women, and which he attempts to forestall by the institution of the green baldric.

Thus, the limited form of the poem, the gaiety of the court contrasted with the terrors of nature, the *rite de passage* and the prevailing contrast between the two courts all combine to give us the central theme. That some such purpose as this lies behind the romantic façade of the poem is further demonstrable by an examination of those features of the poem which the *Gawain* poet adds to his source materials. Professor Kittredge lists those elements which were "certainly added or greatly elaborated by the English author" as:

the learned introductory stanza summarizing the fabulous settlements of Western Europe . . .; the description of the Christmas festivities (i, 3) and that of the Green Knight (i, 7–9); the challenge (i, 12–13) and the speech of Gawain (i, 16); the highly poetical stanzas on the changing seasons (ii, 1–2); the very elaborate description of the process of arming a knight (ii, 4–6), with the allegorical account of the pentangle of virtues (ii, 7); Gawain's itinerary,—Logres, North Wales, Anglesea, Holyhead, the wilderness of Wirral (ii, 9); the winter piece (ii, 10); the justly celebrated account of the three hunts (iii, 1 ff.).[6]

The first of these additions, the introductory stanza, serves to introduce (1) the theme of treachery in the allusion to Antenor and (2) more importantly, the theme of change, of the alternation of happiness and sorrow in the history of England:

> Where war and woe and wonder
> At times have dwelt there
> And both joy and trouble often
> Have quickly alternated since then. (ll. 16–19)

This theme of the alternation of "joy and trouble" is immediately reinforced:

> And when this Britain was founded by this brave baron,
> Bold were the warriors bred there, battles they joyed in,
> Many the wonders they worked in that wild long-ago.
> Greater the glories they wrought in their gallant domain
> Than in any state in the sun men now sing of. (ll. 20–24)

In discussing Gawain's acceptance of the Green Knight's challenge, the poet says:

> Gawain was cheerful to have undergone that game,
> But wondered in his heart how heavy it might hang.

6. G. L. Kittredge, *A Study of Sir Gawain and the Green Knight* (Cambridge: Harvard University Press, 1916), pp. 129–130.

For though men be merry when the wine is in their midst,
A year speeds as swift as the skimming swallow's shadow,
And the gay beginnings seldom match the goal. (ll. 459-99)

Thus, at the very beginning of the poem, we can see the English poet adding to his source materials passages which emphasize the theme of change, the alternation of "joy and trouble" in the history of England. Moreover, when seen in the light of the whole history of Arthur's court, these remarks of the poet seem perfectly applicable to a poem which deals with the court in "her first age," ignorant of the treachery and civil war which will indeed change its "joy" to "trouble."

The "description of the Christmas festivities [at both courts] (i, 3) and that of the Green Knight (i, 7-9); the challenge [including the failure of Arthur] (i, 12-13) and the speech of Gawain" were necessary if the poet was to carry through his contrasting of the court of Arthur with that of Bercilak. For example, Christmas and New Year's Day, called by the poet a second Christmas (l. 65), would seem to be primarily social occasions at Arthur's court; while we have references to the singing of carols (l. 43) and to the "chanting in the chapel" (l. 63), there is no indication of the poem that the Christmas season has any special religious significance to Arthur's court; in fact, even Arthur's priests join in the general merriment (l. 64). On the other hand, we get a full description of the "devout" Christmas Evensong at Bercilak's castle including the observation that the knights "sat together soberly throughout the service" (l. 940). Moreover, Bercilak tells Gawain that he will be better off "that Gawain has been my guest at God's own feast" (l. 1036). In much the same way, the description of the Green Knight reinforces the contrast between the two courts by pointing out that Arthur immediately challenges the unarmed stranger to combat. Again, the challenge and Gawain's humble acceptance speech were added in order to point up Arthur's prideful attempt to deliver the blow and consequent failure and Gawain's humility in accepting and fulfilling the challenge.

The descriptions of the changing seasons may well have been added (1) as unifying and transitional devices and (2) as a means of supplying imagery of natural flux and change which would serve to remind the reader of the alternation of "blysse & blunder" which the poet had introduced at the beginning of the poem. The description of the arming of Gawain may serve to emphasize the contrast between the two courts by pointing up Bercilak's kindly welcoming of the armed Gawain. The description of Gawain's pentangle was almost certainly added in order to reinforce the spiritual quest theme of the poem. Finally, the descriptions of the journey and of winter emphasize the contrast between the warmth of the court and the wildness out of doors, and the hunting scenes furnish parallels and commentaries on the temptations of Gawain, who has remained home from the hunt.

Professor Kittredge states also that the *dénouement* of the poem, Gawain's return to Arthur's court, "shows plain traces of innovation." Gawain's return to the court, "full of shame," is "contrary to custom, for the old French poets are loath to let Gawain come off from any adventure without the highest credit." It would seem clear that the poet wished this obviously non-traditional conclusion to be regarded seriously. It is important to the poem as a whole that our final view of Gawain should be that of an initiated and matured penitent rather than of a stainless conqueror. The poet states that the king and the court laughed loudly at the king's decision that all the knights wear green baldrics (ll. 2513–14); we are not told that Gawain laughed with them. This ending also relates Gawain's adventure to the whole Arthurian court and so serves to reinforce the theory advanced here that the poet is writing not simply an isolated adventure of Gawain, but a highly compressed allegorical commentary on the entire Arthurian history.

What then is the relevancy of myth to *Sir Gawain and the Green Knight*? To begin with, whatever else it may be, the poem is not itself a vegetation or seasonal myth; it is first of all a highly sophisticated and skillfully wrought medieval poem. Thus it is of no critical value to say simply that *Sir Gawain and the Green Knight* is a record, or a manifestation, or a form of the *rite de passage* and let the matter rest with that identification. What the critic can say, I think, is that the myth of the hero's journey from innocence to knowledge underlies the poem and to a large extent determines its specific structure and theme. The critic can thus use myth both as a point of entrance and as a means of analysis; myth becomes (1) a means of coming directly and with dispatch to the structural and thematic core of a literary work and (2) a yard-stick by which the critic can measure the uses to which the poet puts the myth in terms of a specific metaphor and theme. In short, having discovered the myth core of a piece of literature, the critic must go on to examine in their own right the other literary aspects of the work, most of which he will find in turn to be determined by the central archetype. If I am right, the *Gawain* poet is using the myth of the hero's quest to develop a theme which lies at the core of medieval literature: that the tragedy of the Round Table, and of the secular society of which it is a symbol, was inevitable and that the seeds of that tragedy were present even in the "first age" of the youthful and joyous court at Christmas time.

Medieval Studies (Toronto), XVIII (1956), 158–172. Translations have replaced the Middle English quotations, and the majority of the reference notes have been omitted. In the main the translation follows that of James L. Rosenberg, *Sir Gawain and the Green Knight* (New York: Rinehart, 1959).

The Presence of Myth

The following three essays establish the presence of mythic elements in specific works. Richard P. Adams ("The Archetypal Pattern of Death and Rebirth in Milton's Lycidas") *and Reginald L. Cook ("Big Medicine in* Moby Dick") *show that readily apparent and long familiar elements in these works—for example, the use of classical mythology and magic—contribute significantly to their mythopoeic nature. Marvin Magalaner ("The Myth of Man: Joyce's* Finnegans Wake"), *in addition to sketching the various mythoi alluded to by Joyce, formulates what he regards as Joyce's own controlling "myth" or thematic pattern in* Finnegans Wake.

THE ARCHETYPAL PATTERN OF DEATH AND REBIRTH IN MILTON'S *LYCIDAS*

Richard P. Adams

It has been made increasingly evident by critics in recent years that the drowning of Edward King was the occasion, rather than the subject, of *Lycidas*. Milton's concern was generally with the life, death, and resurrection of the dedicated poet, and specifically with his own situation at the time. From this premise it follows that there are no digressions in the poem and that the form and traditions of pastoral elegy are entirely appropriate to its intentions.

Every serious poet must at some time come to an emotional realization of the length of art and the shortness of life. He, more than most men, desires immortality, which he tries to achieve in his works, to leave, as Milton said, "something so written to aftertimes, as they should not willingly let it die." It is an appalling thought that he may die himself before his work is done, and this thought may be most sharply imposed upon him by the death of a friend or acquaintance who is also a poet of some worth or promise. Such an event is likely to be felt as an impelling occasion to find some way of reconciling the desire for immortality with the certainty of death. Many poets, from Moschus (or whoever wrote the *Lament for Bion*) to Matthew Arnold, have used for this purpose the conventions of pastoral elegy as established by Theocritus in his *Lament for Daphnis*. They have made additions and modifications, but the continuity of the traditional form remains unbroken. Milton chose it because he considered it an appropriate vehicle for the expression of his feelings. The result renders any apology absurd.

The conventions of pastoral elegy were appropriate because they had been hammered out over the centuries by poets concerned, as Milton was, with the problem and the mystery of death. In the cultural medium of their origin, the Hellenistic world of the third century B.C., the most popular solutions of the problem of death were expressed in the rituals of various fertility cults. It is therefore not surprising to find that Adonis appeared in the *Fifteenth* and *Thirtieth Idylls* of Theocritus and that

Bion's pastoral elegy was a *Lament for Adonis*. Similarly, in the *Lament for Bion*, a long list of mourners was capped by the statement that "Cypris loves thee far more than the kiss wherewith she kissed the dying Adonis."[1] Analogies between the conventions of fertility ritual and those of pastoral elegy are numerous and obvious, and some of them at least were clearly seen by Milton, who used them to reinforce the imagery of *Lycidas*. He also used appropriate Christian materials and some references to medieval history and legend where they matched his pattern.

The result is a remarkably tight amalgam of death-and-rebirth imagery, drawn from a more than catholic variety of sources. It is far from being merely eclectic, however. Each individual image and reference has its immediate purpose and its relevancy to the form of the whole.

The emotional pattern of the poem consists of a two-fold movement. First it goes from the announcement of the friend's death downward through various expressions of sorrow to despair; then comfort is offered, and the sequence reverses itself until the conclusion is reached in heavenly joy. It is the conventional pattern of pastoral elegy, at least from the time of Virgil, and it is at the same time the pattern of Milton's feeling about death at the time he wrote *Lycidas*. There is no mystery or contradiction in the facts that *Lycidas* is one of the most richly traditional and conventional of all pastoral elegies, and that it is at the same time one of the most intensely personal in its expression of the poet's emotion. The two things do not conflict; they work together and reinforce each other. This effect can be demonstrated by an examination of individual images in relation to the overall pattern.

The opening invocation exposes a vein of death-and-rebirth imagery concerned with various forms of vegetation. The laurel, the myrtle, and the ivy are evergreens. Besides being emblems of poetry they are symbols of immortality generally, in contrast to deciduous plants. All of them have been held sacred to fertility gods and demigods. Adonis, in one version of his myth, was born out of a myrtle tree. The laurel was supposed to have been a sweetheart of Apollo transformed into a tree to escape his pursuit. The ivy was sacred to Dionysus.

The transformation by some deity of a mortal into a plant or flower was a favorite symbol of immortality in the classical myths. It is recalled in Milton's reference to "that sanguine flower inscrib'd with woe" (l. 106); that is, the hyacinth, which sprang from the blood of a young prince of Amyclae beloved and accidentally killed by Apollo, just as the rose (l. 45) was said to have sprung from the blood of Adonis and the violet (l. 145) from that of Attis, the fertility demigod of Phrygia. The amaranth (*Amaranthus*, l. 149) was also a symbol of immortality; its Greek root, coined for the purpose, meant "unfading." In *Paradise Lost* Milton spoke of it as

> Immortal Amarant, a Flour which once
> In Paradise, fast by the Tree of Life
> Began to bloom. . . . [III. 354–356]

These specific references are of course in addition to the general applications of the annual cycle of blighted and reviving vegetation. The ritual observances in the fertility

---

1. *Theocritus, Bion and Moschus*, tr. A. Lang (London: Macmillan, 1896), p. 200.

cults were designed partly to assist in the completion of the cycle, the revival of the demigod being accompanied by a sympathetic revival of fertility in plants and animals. In this connection the pathetic fallacy, one of the most persistent of the conventions of pastoral elegy, is no fallacy at all but a perfectly logical aspect of the ritual. In pastoral elegy, however, the application is often reversed, as it is in *Lycidas*, so that flowers, and vegetation generally, symbolize the promise of rebirth for the poet's friend as well as the mourning for his death.

The fact that King died by drowning perhaps fortuitously but nonetheless effectively opened up to Milton a much larger range of death-and-rebirth imagery, which he exploited with his usual thoroughness. No less than fifty lines, out of a total of 193, are concerned with water in one way or another. Water was of course a prime symbol of fertility in all the ancient cults, for reasons that Milton seems to recognize in connection with his flowers, which grow near "gushing brooks" (l. 137) and which "suck the honied showres" (l. 140). By the same association, the two friends had gone out "by fountain, shade, and rill" (l. 24), "Batt'ning our flocks with the fresh dews of night" (l. 29). He himself sang "to th'Okes and rills" (l. 186). Several references involving water are specifically to themes of death and rebirth, one of the most definite being the legend of Alpheus and Arethusa (ll. 132–133), to which Milton had referred in *Arcades* :

> Divine *Alpheus*, who by secret sluse,
> Stole under Seas to meet his *Arethuse*. . . . [30–31]

The nymph herself, transformed into a fountain, is a symbol of immortality in much the same sense as the rose, the violet, and the hyacinth. Milton's personification of Cambridge University as the River Cam (*Comus*, l. 103) is in harmony, and St. Peter as "The Pilot of the *Galilean* lake" (l. 109) is nearly related. This reference emphasizes the pattern of death and rebirth in two specific connections, the story of Peter's walk on the water, beginning to sink and being raised by Christ, and the fact that he was the keeper of the keys. The first item is reserved, while the second is developed immediately:

> Two massy Keyes he bore of metals twain,
> (The Golden opes, the Iron shuts amain) [110–111]

Milton goes to some length to show that water, the principle of life, is not responsible for the death of Lycidas. Triton ("the Herald of the Sea," l. 96) testifies that the winds were at home and that the Nereids ("Sleek *Panope* with all her sisters," l. 99) were attending to their duty as protectresses of ships and sailors. The blame is put finally on the man-made ship which, in defiance of the powers of nature, had been "Built in th'eclipse, and rigg'd with curses dark" (l. 101).

For some reason the descent into water which is often a feature of death-and-rebirth cycles is, if not often, at least sometimes associated with the dragon-fight theme, especially in North European mythology. Beowulf's fight with Grendel's mother in the cave under the mere is perhaps the most familiar example. Milton did not know *Beowulf*, but he paralleled the incident in *Lycidas*:

> Where thou perhaps under the whelming tide
> Visit'st the bottom of the monstrous world;
> Or whether thou to our moist vows deny'd,
> Sleep'st by the fable of *Bellerus* old,
> Where the great vision of the guarded Mount
> Looks toward *Namancos* and *Bayona's* hold. . . . [157–163]

The parallel is complete if the word "monstrous" is interpreted to mean "full of monsters."[2] There is no uncertainty about the references to Corineus, the slayer of Gogmagog, and to St. Michael, the dragon fighter par excellence of Christian tradition. The appeal to the dolphins to "waft the haples youth" (l. 164) follows naturally. It may refer to the story of Palaemon, whose body was carried ashore by dolphins, or to that of Arion, who was saved by them from drowning, or both. Ovid told a somewhat similar story of Bacchus, to which Milton referred in *Comus* (ll. 48–49).

The descent into and re-emergence from water is specifically related by Milton to the setting and rising of the sun as a symbol of death and rebirth.

> Weep no more, woful Shepherds weep no more,
> For *Lycidas* your sorrow is not dead,
> Sunk though he be beneath the watry floar,
> So sinks the day-star in the Ocean bed,
> And yet anon repairs his drooping head,
> And tricks his beams, and with new spangled Ore,
> Flames in the forehead of the morning sky:
> So *Lycidas* sunk low, but mounted high,
> Through the dear might of him that walk'd the waves. . . . [165–173]

Besides respecifying and reinforcing the reference to St. Peter's adventure (l. 109) this passage coordinates two accounts of the sun's journey from rising to setting. The first of these represents in parallel the life of the two friends at Cambridge (ll. 25–31), and the second represents the life of the surviving poet:

> Thus sang the uncouth Swain to th' Okes and rills,
> While the still morn went out with Sandals gray,
> He touch'd the tender stops of various Quills,
> With eager thought warbling his *Dorick* lay:
> And now the Sun had stretch'd out all the hills,
> And now was dropt into the Western Bay;
> At last he rose, and twitch'd his Mantle blew:
> To morrow to fresh Woods, and Pastures new. [186–193]

These passages render in a very striking way the pattern of life, death, and rebirth with which the poem as a whole is concerned.

The last quotation recalls the fact that Milton was expressing his own feelings in

2. *The Lycidas and Epitaphium Damonis* of Milton, ed. C. S. Jerram (London, 1897), p. 81.

Lycidas, and not any abstract or general or public sorrow. The personal note established in the first five lines is maintained throughout. It is struck again in the passage where he puts himself in the dead man's place (ll. 19–22), hoping that "some gentle Muse" will turn aside to confer on him the immortality which he is giving King. He deliberately takes to himself here the emotional experience of death and, at least by implication, of rebirth.

The nadir of the movement from life through death to resurrection follows logically by way of the reference to Orpheus, in which death is presented as final. The reference expands in at least three directions, two of which are exploited. Orpheus's descent into the underworld and not-quite-successful effort to rescue Eurydice is the most obvious, and perhaps for that reason the one that Milton neglects. The death of Orpheus at the hands of the Bacchanals, his dismemberment, and the journey of his head to Lesbos are the things that occupy Milton's attention first. The parallels between this event and the deaths of Adonis, Attis, Osiris, and other fertility demigods have been pointed out by modern scholars. The facts that he was a singer, i.e., a poet, that he died a violent death, that his head was thrown into the water, and that his mother Calliope, the muse of epic poetry, mourned his death made him sufficiently adaptable to the general pattern of pastoral elegy and to Milton's treatment. The third direction gives Milton, in the "digression" on fame, most scope for the expression of his personal feelings, both of despair and of hope. Identifying himself with Orpheus as before with King, he asks what is the use of casting his pearls before the swine by whom the god is killed, to whom he has paid his respects in *Comus* and whom he is about to attack in the passage on the corrupt clergy. Then Phoebus, the patron of Orpheus, representing Milton's patron Christ, promises him his final reward in Heaven.

Such are the means by which Milton in *Lycidas* interrelated elements from the fertility cults, the tradition of pastoral elegy, the Christian religion, and his own past with the purpose and most richly the effect of rendering his present emotion. Such, by the same token, is the meaning of the phrase "With eager thought," and such again is the promise of "fresh Woods, and Pastures new."

PMLA, LXIV (1949), 183–188. Some reference notes have been omitted.

BIG MEDICINE IN *MOBY DICK*

Reginald L. Cook

"There is magic in it." So Ishmael, solitary survivor of the Pequod's disastrous voyage in pursuit of the White Whale, discovers in the meditation of water. So Melville discloses in *Moby Dick*, his mythopoeic tale of the golden days of the whale fishery. For some readers the magic is in the symbolism and philosophy; for a few it is in the strange wonders of ceteological information; for many others it is in the spirited yarn, narrated in a sonorous, eloquent rhetoric, compounded of fun and fury.

Above all else, *Moby Dick* is a briny book. As soon as the land's behind, there is the feel of the ground-swell beneath stretched timbers, the curl of foam at the bows, the gurgle at the stern, ropeyards tingling, tall masts buckling, bowsprit plunging, and, for companions, nimble seamen who trim the yards, veteran harpooners who skilfully dart the barbed iron, and mates who have many times thrust the lance in the wide and endless waters from one side of the world to the other—tough, weather-ruddied, brawny hunters of whales with a windward look in their eyes. There is sea magic in the book—the yo-heave-o spirit of spreading sail on extended yards and halyards hard-strained through creaking blocks.

There is also a natural magic in the object of the chase—in the sperm whale with its immense head and comparatively small eye, its incredible power and remarkable propulsion. Who, among the whaling mariners, did not marvel at the breaching whale, rising vertically out of the water with such velocity that half its length is bared, or gaze in wonder at the whale suspended perpendicularly in the water, head downward, in the interesting motion known as peaking flukes! "Excepting the sublime breach . . . this peaking of the whale's flukes is perhaps the grandest sight to be seen in all animated nature." Melville surely speaks for himself when he says in *Moby Dick*: "Standing at the mast-head of my ship during a sunrise that crimsoned sky and sea, I once saw a large herd of whales in the east, all heading toward the sun, and for a moment vibrating in concert with peaked flukes. As it seemed to me at the time, such a grand embodiment of the gods was never beheld, even in Persia, the home of the fire-worshippers."

The whale's deep-diving—about two thousand feet—and its spouting are of the same order of natural magic. So also is its voracious appetite (to us), when we learn that the blue whale devours at one feeding the equivalent of six barrels of large shrimp-like crustaceans, called "krill," while the sperm whale feeds on cuttlefish, especially the giant squid. Moreover, Melville is quite as fascinated by its breeding habits, for doubtless he saw whales mating in tropical waters during the fall and winter, and doubtless he saw them following the veins in migrations, moving poleward to spend the summer in Arctic or Antarctic waters.

There is to-day another kind of magic beyond the scope of *Moby Dick*. It is the magic of mechanical enterprise where the big whaling vessels of Great Britain, Norway, Japan and Holland hunt in the Indian Ocean or off the coast of Peru or in the

Antarctic, completely equipped with mechanical gadgets that an inventive age has provided. Among the super-gadgets are planes, Asdic (sonic submarine detectors), radar and guns. Planes sight the whales; gunners follow the sounding whale on its dive by Asdic sonic beam; and radar spots the surfaced whale. The whaling guns, so important in making the kill, and efficiently unromantic, fire modern harpoons equipped with bombs that explode after contact. This is a "magic" that out-magics the skill that lent such splendor to "that wild Scandinavian vocation" of whaling in the golden age.

"I love all men who dive," Melville wrote Evert Duyckinck. He is himself a "thought-diver." It is not alone the whale who dives deep, sounding a thousand fathoms, as it is said, beneath light and air. In *Moby Dick* Melville dives deep and comes up with blood-shot eyes. It is the magic in this deep-diving that now interests us.

In *The Golden Bough* religion is represented as a belief in a conscious and personal power which controls and directs the course of nature and human life, and the practice of conciliating the higher power. Magic, on the contrary, assumes an order and uniformity in nature which is determined by immutable laws whose operation is foreseeable and calculable. While religion believes that through persuasion it is possible to induce the superhuman force that controls the universe to favor mankind, magic applies coercion. The magician arrogates more power than the religious devotee. He assumes that by spells, enchantments and ceremonies he can manipulate the impersonal force which controls all things. In the magician's arrogant authority the humble religious devotee sees "an impious and blasphemous usurpation of prerogatives that belong to God alone."

To the medicine man of primitive cults there were no elements of chance, caprice or accident in the course of nature. By following the laws of nature, as he understood them, the medicine man believed that he would be rewarded by success. When he failed to conform strictly to the rules of his art, his spell would be broken. Thus his power was not arbitrary and unlimited. Neither does Ahab assume that he is on the inside. He is not Supreme Dictator of the Universe although he gives the prescription for such a dictator. *Moby Dick* would have been far less credible had Melville endowed Ahab with superhuman power.

There is magic in *Moby Dick*. It is the magic of Ahab whose intent dictates the form and spirit of his quest. The ungodly Ahab is bent upon supernatural revenge. He forswears the Christian God of his fathers and celebrates a blasphemous ritual. In an ascendancy of egotistic will he vents his contempt on "ye great gods." "I laugh and hoot at ye, ye cricket-players, ye pugilists ... come forth from behind your cotton bags! Come, Ahab's compliments to ye; come and see if ye can swerve me." No suppliance here! No placative humility! Instead, the arrogance of the sorcerer who believes he can coerce the great gods. Yet Ahab proves to be mindful of the orthodox God when, on the eve of the final mortal encounter, he inquires: "Is it I, God, or who, that lifts this arm? But if the great sun move not of himself; but is an errand-boy in heaven; nor one single star can revolve, but by some invisible power; how then can this one small heart beat; this one small brain think thoughts; unless God does that beating, does that thinking, does that living, and not I."

There is a subtle consciousness in Ahab. He operates on two levels: sometimes on the Christian; more frequently on the primitive. Yet his ceremonial rituals are not aimed to influence either deity or devil. He hardly respects the power of either of them. He uses them only that the appropriate spells will inevitably produce the desired effect on his crew. There is no evidence that he believes in their efficacy in giving him ultimate power over Moby Dick, but they influence his men, and this is necessary to gain his bloody-minded end.

Ahab's magic does not follow the usual pattern of the primitive magician. He did not seek for supernatural power in a dream or vision, to be effected by fasting, stimulants or flagellant torture, as among the Plains Indian tribes of Western America, the African tribal groups, or the Melanesians. He does dream prophetically and fatefully of the hearses, and he prophesies that he will dismember his dismemberers, which subsequent events prove to be an erroneous prophesy. After the first fateful meeting with the White Whale at sea, he envisions his own greatness dramatically by exalting the egotistic will until his malaise is that of a megalomaniac paranoid. His behavior becomes strange and psychotic. He casts away his pipe, to be rid of serenity. He commands his men with overbearing looks and exaggerated actions. Yet there is comparatively little sadism and no masochism in his actions.

Ahab's reversion is important. It is linked with his personal misfortune. In the Christian world of rewards and punishments, salvation by faith, and the conciliation of powers superior to man, he is angered and puzzled by his personal fate. He is crazed by a loss which most mariners would accept as a vocational hazard. The aberrant Ahab is no ordinary mariner. In "The Quarter Deck" he states a personal quandary. Is the force which governs the world conscious or unconscious of human destiny? The orthodox mariner believes in a superhuman power that is conscious and personal. He considers deity susceptible to the insinuation of prayer and sacrifice. Ahab, victimized by an unreckoned force, asks: Is there an accountable God? He is aware of an invisible power, but he is unsure whether there is any intelligible meaning behind the inscrutable universe. All he knows is that the White Whale who has ripped his leg from his body is "outrageous strength, with an inscrutable malice sinewing it." This is what he will wreak his hate upon; this is the object of his fiery hunt. Seeing no particular efficacy in Christian conciliation of a force that permits evil to prevail, Ahab rejects the Christian way and turns by reversion to the forms of magic—"big medicine."

To solemnize the chase of the white-headed whale he calls for a heavily charged flagon of liquor "hot as Satan's hoof" and passes it round, rallying his men to take short draughts and long swallows. He orders his harpooners to detach the iron part of their harpoons and use them as goblets. He fills these ingenious goblets to the brim and ranking the mates opposite the harpooners, he focusses the fiery chase on Moby Dick until the White Whale spouts black blood and rolls fin out. In this exuberant ceremonial he unites the crew in an indissoluble league. "Death to Moby Dick! God hunt us all if we do not hunt Moby Dick to his death!"

Another example of "big medicine" is shown when Ahab's talismanic lance is forged. Its shank is made of rods from nail-stubs gathered from the steel shoes of racing horses welded together "like glue from the melted bones of murderers." The barbs were forged of Ahab's razors, sharp as "the needle-sleet of the Icy Sea," and tempered in the blood of the three heathen harpooners, initiates in the harpoon cult, aboard the Pequod. In the baptismal tempering of the barbs, Ahab utters a blasphemous incantation: "Ego non baptizo te in nomine patris, sed in nomine diaboli!"

The most sensational display of big medicine occurs when the typhoon lashes the Pequod. Ahab rises to tremendous height arrogating elemental power. It is a powerful magic that he exhibits, confounding some but not all of his men. At the base of the main-mast he holds aloft the lightning link in his left hand, placing his foot on the kneeling Parsee, and defyingly invokes the "clear spirit of clear fire" before the awed crew (although later Stubb disabuses the credulous Flask as to the actual risk in Ahab's seemingly dangerous act). The panic-stricken crew race to the braces to fix sail and turn homeward in awful fright when they see flames of "pale, forked fire" shooting from the naked barb of Ahab's specially forged harpoon in the whale-boat's bow. Ahab snatches the harpoon, waves it torch-like and swears to transfix the first man who casts loose a rope's end. He revitalizes in the crew its oath to hunt the White Whale, "and with one blast of his breath he extinguished the flame," to the terror of many of the men.

It is his belief that the elements do not destroy him when he defies them because he is one with them. Their right worship is not love or reverence but defiance—"defyingly I worship them," he exclaims as he holds the lightning rods aloft at the height of the typhoon. Extraordinary he is, for so sensitized is his physical organism that he reacts preternaturally to changes in environment not perceptible to grosser seamen. It is Ahab who first smells the presence of the White Whale. He is like a hound on a watery slot.

Those who have not been cowed stand in awe of his acts. Even the prudent and unconvinced Starbuck is constrained to obey Ahab's commands, rebelliously. When the needles in the binnacle compass demagnetize in the storm, Ahab takes lance-head, top-maul and the smallest of the sail-maker's needles, and with "strange motions" he magnetizes the needle from the lance-head and slips the needle over the compass card. Scornfully and triumphantly he awes the men with this show of magic, proving at least to his satisfaction that he is "lord of the level load-stone." Ahab is possessed of irrepressible histrionic abilities. Like Twain's Connecticut Yankee what he does has to be theatrical or he doesn't take any interest in it.

The final chapters of *Moby Dick* are a thoroughly documented representation of the fanatical passion of Captain Ahab in his attempt to infuse his will (through magic) upon his men and upon the elemental forces of the universe. And in a sense his magic is just as fundamental as its practice by the rudest aborigines of Australia or Africa. There are, we see, ceremonial rituals, the divinations of the Parsee and Ahab's dream, demonological connotations, harpoon cults, the masked god of the White Whale, the fetishistic death-lance, chant-like exclamations. In seventeenth century New England Ahab would be accused of wizardry and condemned as a sorcerer.

Aided by civilized qualities of intelligence and gifted with "high perception," Ahab knows how to appeal to the covetousness of his crew. He victimizes them with bribes and plies them with spirits, and effectively immobilizes them by strange ascendancies of megalomania through "sheer inveteracy of will." Ahab shows few gestures of mollification. He does lower for the chase when the White Whale is out of range, which tends to settle his men. He has studied the files of old log books and traced courses on large wrinkled yellowish sea-charts. He knows the set of tides and currents; he has calculated the driftings of the sperm whale's food; he has noted the tendency of the whale to swim in arbitrary veins; he will, therefore, hunt Moby Dick in particular latitudes and anticipate him in the Season-on-the-line.

Ahab's eventual defeat is attributable to a personal failure, not to the exaction of a lawful deity or higher power. After the second day of the chase, injured but unbeaten, he tells his first mate Starbuck, "I am the Fates' lieutenant, I act under orders." So he acted, for he thought the whole act was immutably decreed. He was ready; he asserted his desperate will; the immutable laws were acknowledged; the battle was joined; he fought heroically. Somewhere in between there was a slip. In perfect self-containment he finally addresses the whale. There is no trace of Christian submission or renunciation in his attitude. There is only the major chord of everweaning pride and arrogance, so typical of primitive medicine men. "Towards thee I roll, thou all-destroying but unconquering whale; to the last I grapple with thee; from hell's heart I stab at thee; for hate's sake I spit my last breath at thee."

His magic—the harpoon ritualistically forged, the crew shamanistically briefed, the contact vigilantly charted and planned—fail to destroy the force he opposes. Neither is the whale's attack unconditionally successful. In the mortal battle between the sentient Ahab and the inscrutable animate force incarnate in the White Whale, there is no clear-cut victory. If physical presence after mortal conflict is the only just measure of victory then inscrutability rules supreme over vulnerable sentience. If the spirit of man has not been conquered, and this Ahab believes when he refers to the "unconquering" whale, then victory is partial and limited, not unconditional and absolute for the whale. Ahab is physically destroyed but spiritually triumphant over adversity *sub specie aeternitatis*.

Ahab's equivocal defeat is, in a sense, the failure of magic as an effective force in the manipulation of natural forces. *Moby Dick* is not an apotheosis of magic. By inference, it is a confession of the inadequacy of magic as a means of control. Ahab is brave and proud, but in his reversion to magic he confesses human ignorance and in his physical defeat he betrays, not lack of skill but the limitation of all men before superior animate forces. Ahab's fallibility is a token of the inadequacy of magic. The inscrutable remains inscrutable, but its presence is more exactly defined. We know it for what it is: a terrifying power at the heart of things. Ahab possesses no enchantment, personal or derivative, that gives him the potency to penetrate the ultimate nature of things. His pent-up passion, his cunning and patient preparation, his exacting toil, his brilliant ingenuity, his frenzied bravado, all avail him little, actually.

There is also considerable big medicine in *Moby Dick* indirectly associated with Captain Ahab. The tattooed Queequeg worships a little hunchbacked glistening black ivory god called Yojo with guttural pagan psalmody. The Manx-man is popularly invested with abnormal powers of discernment. The impromptu ritual enacted when the Christian Ishmael "marries" the pagan Queequeg—together smoking the tomahawk pipe, pressing foreheads in embrace, dividing personal wealth and offering burnt biscuit to Yojo with salaams, are certainly evidences of "medicine." So, too, is the appearance of Fedallah: the tall, swart, black-jacketed, white-turbaned, protuberant-toothed Parsee who raises the Spirit Spout and prophesies Ahab's fate. Nor can we exclude the tattooed body of Queequeg, a perfect marvel of totemism, representing "a complete theory of the heavens and the earth and a mystical treatise on the art of attaining truth," as conceived by a prophet.

There are, moreover, correlative evidences of "medicine": Ahab's "brand," a cicatrice scoring him from head to toe, the result of his elemental strife at sea; his throne-like tripod of ivory bone on which he sits on the weather side of the deck; the vial of sand from Nantucket Soundings which Ahab carries with him like a fetish; and the red-billed savage sea-hawk stealing his hat. There are the ambiguous rumors: of the veiled prophecy of the squaw Tistig from Gayhead, the shrouded story of Ahab's scrimmage with a Spaniard before the altar in Santa, and the hinted desecration when Ahab spat in the silver calabash. Are the latter actual or imaginary events? Are they meaningful as the soothsaying Elijah's gibberish? At least they are just such rumors as would surround the sorcerer and lend credence to his supernatural power. Melville mentions the tendency of superstitious whalemen to indulge their fancies and their credulity. "The whaleman," he says, "is wrapped by influences all tending to make his fancy pregnant with many a mighty birth." The wonders of the deep (the wondrous cistern in the whale's huge head, the prodigy of his unhinged lower jaw, and the miracle of his symmetrical tail on the fabulous squid); and the heroics of the chase (Queequeg's "agile obstetrics" in rescuing Tashtego from the sinking Sperm Whale's head or jolly Stubb's exuberant chase of great whales), contribute perceptibly to the atmosphere of "big medicine" in *Moby Dick*.

Animism is touched circumspectly in the White Whale, and totemism is suggested in the whale as masked god. There are the forms and usages aboard ship as related to the mariner's tribal society—the harpooner clan—but there is no reference to taboo, unless Captain Boomer's attitude and the insane Gabriel's injunction are considered as such. Nor is there any eroticism, though one terrific orgy of Dionysian revelry and drunkenness takes place. Nor is there any exorcism of devils.

Melville has dealt carefully with the necromantic features of big medicine. Extended as the mythopoeic scenes are, Melville does not over-reach himself. He resolves the issues in his book by having Ahab remain true to himself. The nefarious Ahab neither renounces the fiery hunt nor recants his reversion to demonology. His Christian apostasy is unimpugnable; to the end his sorcery is virtuous if ineffective. Melville's handling of "big medicine" is reservedly romantic. He does not offer a well worked-out formula that begins with the practice of obtaining supernatural power in dream or vision, to be effected by continence, discipline, torture, fasting, alcohol or drugs, nor one which applies the technique of concentration until the "right" vision comes. This was not, of course, his aim. The "big medicine" is used to heighten the drama and to infuse the magnificent plangent poetry with strange imagistic overtones. It does, however, contribute to the intellectual content. It reinforces Melville's meaning and in its connotations gives Ahab's actions powerful significance.

Accent, VIII (1948), 102–109.

THE MYTH OF MAN: JOYCE'S *FINNEGANS WAKE*

Marvin Magalaner

Rebellion was the chief force in Joyce's life. Neither his religion nor his nation could subdue him. In his dealings with publishers and printers, he maintained an un-compromising attitude on questions of censorship. Nor would he compromise with his audience to the extent of simplifying or diluting a passage whose essential quality might have been lost through revision. Thoroughly misunderstood, unread except in smoke-filled reading rooms by furtive scholars, self-exiled from an Ireland too narrow to hold him and from a religion which had conflicted with his vigorous ego, maligned by a Shaun-type society which preferred amenable mediocrity to rebellious genius, James Joyce had greater need than most writers to construct for himself a myth which would offer some degree of stability in a disintegrating modern world.

Although worked out in intricate and complicated detail in the *Wake*, the framework of his "monomyth"[1] is plain, simple and sturdy. A disintegrating civilization, one in which, as Yeats says, "Things fall apart," because "the centre cannot hold . . . ," implies eventual destruction and complete oblivion, the negation of human progress. Joyce's means of escape from so negative a view of life lay in his skill in adapting to his peculiar needs the idea of cyclical history. If the final blotting out of our contemporary world be but the prelude to the flowering of a new civilization arising out of the ashes of the old, then despair may give way to the hope of affirmation, and the nervous sense of impending doom may be replaced by the resigned acceptance of the idea that from death will come renewed life. Or, as Joyce put it, "all that has been done has yet to be done and done again, when's day's woe, and lo, you're doomed, joyday dawns and, la, you dominate." (194)

No credit, of course, can be given to Joyce as the discoverer of the cyclical idea. It is at least as ancient as early Hindu culture, and its use in the construction of a pseudo-myth is as recent as Yeats' *A Vision*, which went even further than Joyce's plan in predicting the end of the present cycle of the world's development at the end of the twentieth century. But the explanation of cyclical history upon which Joyce drew most heavily for *Finnegans Wake* is that of the eighteenth-century Italian philosopher, Giambattista Vico.

Vico's conception of universal history, enunciated in his work, *La Scienza Nuova* (1725), would divide history into three great ever-recurring stages or cycles: the divine, the heroic, the human, with a smaller, chaotic interlude in which forces are set into motion which result in the reestablishment of the divine period and the repetition endlessly of the same cyclical movement. He had arrived at this rather arbitrary set of divisions as a result of his ambitious attempt to devise scientifically a system which would be able to account for apparently inexplicable similarities in language, custom,

---

1. James Joyce, *Finnegans Wake* (New York: Viking, 1939), p. 581. Subsequent references are indicated in the text.

and even personal traits, among peoples widely separated in space or time. In the words of Jules Michelet's engaging explanation of Vico's purpose:

> to trace the universal, eternal history that occurs in time under the form of particular histories, to descry the ideal circle in which the world turns: there is the aim of the new science. It is at once the philosophy and history of humanity.[2]

The wholeness of Vico's philosophy, its universal scope, appealed strongly to Joyce, at first for its own sake, and then for the ease with which its principles could be modified and adapted to his own plan of history. He saw that he could account for the shape of things to come by proving that history had followed a clearly discernible and consistent pattern in the past. Educated in the rigorous discipline of Jesuit scholastic exercises, Joyce naturally would find congenial to his temperament a view of history which, although all-embracing, was nevertheless capable of "exagmination" (497) in orderly, logical sections. He saw clearly the advantage of having ready to hand an established, public framework on which to build his private myth. He saw the pragmatic value for himself in the numerous parallels which Vico had drawn: the correspondence, for instance, between the ages, divine, heroic, human, and the pre-historic, fabulous (or mythological), and historical periods; or the parallel between Vico's ages and the development of language from hieroglyphic or sacred symbols of communication, through metaphorical or poetic expression, to the abstract language of our present "human" period. Specifically, he was attracted to the idea of social and political development from the age of blundering giants, propelled forward and upward by their animistic fear of, and reverence for, the thunder; to the age of patriarchs, with its heroic aristocracies (ancient Greece is a good example); and finally to the age of reasonable humanity living under monarchies and democracies until decay sets in and the resulting chaos and turbulence plant the seeds which will reproduce the three-fold cycle. To orientate his own position, and the plight of contemporary men in general, with respect to Vico's *cercle idéal* of human progress, but in terms of modern narrative projection, became Joyce's major job.

He did not try to obscure his purpose, and *Finnegans Wake* abounds in concrete statements of the theory, in the light of world history. "Gricks may rise and Troysirs fall . . . for in the byways of high improvidence that's what makes lifework leaving and the world's a cell for citters to cit in" (11) contains an essential statement of the proposition on which the book is based. Joyce hammered home his point again and again through the six hundred odd pages of his "cyclological" (220) novel. "The house of Atreox is fallen indeedust (Ilyam, Ilyum! Maeromor Mournomates!) . . . but deeds bounds going arise again." (55)

Although outward forms of things may change, governments may rise, decline, and be replaced by others, actually nothing is permanently lost in the history of the race: "Yet is no body present here which was not there before. Only is order othered.

2. The untranslated quotation is: tracer l'histoire universelle, éternelle qui se produit dans le temps sous la forme des histoires particulières, décrire le cercle idéal dans lequel tourne le monde réel: voilà l'objet de la nouvelle science. Elle est tout à la fois la philosophie et l'histoire de l'humanité.

Nought is nulled." (613) In this view, history becomes the tale of "one world burrowing on another," (275) and deriving from its predecessor primal changeless qualities which it, in turn, passes on intact to the next stage. The institutions of an age, its law courts and churches and literary criticism, may decay and disappear; but religion, married love, bodily disintegration, and hope of rebirth are deathless attributes of any and all ages.

Briefly and inadequately stated—for *Finnegans Wake* defies paraphrase—the narrative projection of cyclical history begins in the *Wake* with the giant Tim Finnegan, bricklayer, whose fall from a ladder and subsequent death bring the prehistoric age to an end. To supplant him, the heroic patriarch, father of us all, Humphrey Chimpden Earwicker (better known as HCE), arises from the debris of the earlier period. Even as the reader is introduced to Earwicker, however, the process of decay is already well advanced, and it is only a matter of time until HCE's twin sons, Shem and Shaun, will eclipse the father, rise in the human age to the ascendant position, to be overwhelmed in turn by the chaos which is inevitable as a prelude to the recommencement of the three cycles.

II

Although constantly berated, by those who do not take the time to read him, for his "private" frames of reference, actually Joyce appears to be straining to give his admittedly elaborate myth the support of as many established, traditional, publicly recognized writings as he can muster. Side by side, and often intertwining, the Christian story of Paradise lost and regained, the Irish myth of Finn MacCool and Diarmuid and Grania, the Celtic tale of the prankquean, the French romance of Tristan and Iseult, La Fontaine's fable of the Ondt and the Gracehoper—all have the function of helping the reader to get his bearings in unfamiliar territory by serving as guideposts along the "Vico Road." (452) Their use in this novel is not unlike the use which T. S. Eliot frequently makes of well-known snatches of verse. They put the reader in the proper mood, help to give him the mental set with which to approach the larger, more significant whole—Joyce's myth of man in history.

Traditional myths in *Finnegans Wake* serve another purpose too. To prove that through all ages "the same roturns," (18) Joyce needed more elemental, more vibrant evidence than the cold patterns of objectively recorded history. He needed heroes and heroines whose pattern of behavior was drawn from the well of the popular imagination. Here again Vico came to the rescue with his theory of the origin of mythical heroes. The hero, said Vico, is merely the projection of the ideal character of a people. A national or racial group has a tendency to place ideal types under proper names, and then to endow those proper names with personal attributes. This he illustrates by reference to Hercules. A man named Hercules once performed a brave deed. Primitive mentality, not able to grasp the abstraction of "*a* Hercules," simply called any brave man who seemed to fit the pattern, in later years, "Hercules." In short, to consider Hermes, Romulus, Athena as names for the expression of the national character of this or that country is to get close to the truth. This was Joyce's cue.

If the mythical heroes of a culture can come alive again in the shape of those who resemble the originals, then, in Joyce's myth, the Finn MacCool of heroic Ireland may return, and there is hope of Finn-again. "(lost leaders live! the heroes return!)" (74) If the patterns of mythical behavior are constant and may recur in modern dress, the way lies open for elaborate identification of the Earwicker household in contemporary Chapelizod with the deathless characters of medieval chivalry in the story of Tristan.

HCE is identified now with Tristan, the passionate lover, now with King Mark, the aging ruler with a fondness for a young, beautiful bride, Iseult. The latter is sometimes the wife of HCE, Anna Livia Plurabelle (ALP), and sometimes, in the incestuous by-ways of dream, their young daughter, Isabel. In general, there is very little direct equating of the original mythical characters to those of Joyce's myth. Much more subtly the contrast is drawn by hundreds of allusions to the Tristan story woven into the fabric of the *Wake*. Their appearance throughout the Earwicker saga, in the ordered profusion at the creation of which Rabelais and Joyce excel, points up the similarity implicitly. But the cumulative effect of the mighty outpouring, continually impinging upon the reader's consciousness, makes the desired conclusions inescapable —and much more effective than the mere telling.

The myth of Tristan and Iseult in *Finnegans Wake* acts as narrative expression for the idea that, in every age, the love of one human being for another forms a predictable and unchanging pattern. With us always we have the gallant hero-lover type—whether Tristan or HCE. The promiscuous, flirtatious Iseult, remains constantly inconstant from cycle to cycle. Nor is the third member of the triangle lacking in any age. The lustful King Mark of medieval legend, Earwicker the middleaged seducer of Irish Womanhood, the sugar-daddy of Peaches Browning fame—all are manifestations to Joyce of the pattern of history in one of its numerous facets. And his overwhelming insistence on telling and retelling in countless guises the plot of the Tristan story is simply his way of projecting into vivid narrative his belief that

> Those sort of things which has been going on onceaday in and twiceaday out every other nachtistag among all kinds of promiscious individuals at all ages in private homes and reeboos publikiss and allover all and elsewhere throughout secular sequence the country over and overabroad has been particularly stupendous. (66)

Probably to reinforce his argument that the outlines of the Tristan formula are not confined to national boundaries or particular periods, he introduced an analogue, the Celtic myth of Diarmuid and Grania. At times, one myth fades into the other, only to reappear on later pages distinct once more. In the Diarmuid-Grania myth, Finn MacCool is the equivalent of King Mark of the Tristan story. He wishes to marry Grania, but she places a "gaesa" or charm on Diarmuid, the man of her choice, compelling him to elope with her. Iseult, in the French version, attains the same end by tricking Mark's faithful retainer, Tristan, into drinking a love potion which binds him forever to her in unreasoning passion. In both myths there is wild pursuit of the offending lovers by the aging monarchs and eventual capture in the woods. In both, the hero refrains, through a sense of loyalty, from consummating a marriage undertaken under shady pretensions; Tristan shuns the second Iseult, his legal wife, while Diarmuid refuses Grania the attentions of a husband out of respect to Finn.

If any one mythical character may be said to dominate the *Wake*, and Joyce's thinking, then purely on the number of times he is invoked, the nod goes to Finn MacCumhal—pronounced Finn MacCool. A careful comparison of *Finnegans Wake* with Chapter XIII of John A. Macculloch's book, *Celtic* (in *The Mythology of All Races*), is enough to convince the reader that Joyce was more than superficially interested in the warrior-giant of that period of Irish history which is shrouded in hazy speculation. In Finn, Joyce undoubtedly saw a legitimate ancestor for his modern hero, Humphrey Chimpden Earwicker. The title which Joyce gave to his book, arrived at very deliberately and only after years of rumination, is an indication of the importance which the author placed upon the Finn-Earwicker parallel.

Like Finn, Earwicker is half Norse, an invader from the mainland who becomes a staunch defender of the soil of Ireland against foreign attack. Finn means "white" or "fair"; and Earwicker's son, the embodiment of his father, is given the name of Kevin, which means "Fairborn" in the Irish tongue. Both Finn and HCE live close to Dublin and are connected with activities on the river Liffey. Both are involved in adventures in *Tir fo Thiunn*, Land under Waves, Finn when he enters the heavenly region as a God, Earwicker when he finds himself imprisoned beneath Lough Neagh at the conclusion of his trial, a significant difference when one considers that Finn lived in the happy days of an earlier, heroic cycle while the humpbacked bartender of Chapelizod is the representative of our present dying age. "One tradition," says Macculloch, "alleged that, like Arthur, Fionn [Finn] was still living secretly somewhere, within a hill or on an island, ready to come . . . in the hour of his country's need . . ." It is easy to see why Joyce, "self exiled in upon his ego," (184) "Irish emigrant the wrong way out," (190) should have used Finn as the symbol of a happier Ireland. "Once it happened, so it may again." (625)

From his storehouse of obscurities, Joyce selected the Irish legend of Jarl van Hoother and the prankquean (21) to enrich his myth. Apparently the narrative of Grace O'Malley's three-time kidnapping of the sons of the Earl as repayment for a supposed snub by that lord of the castle, and the subsequent wild but fruitless pursuits of the mischievous kidnapper, was carefully chosen for its associative values. The incident, first of all, stresses the ritual aspect of myth, especially important in the cyclical context of *Finnegans Wake*. Three times the prankquean appears at the gate of the castle; three times she propounds her riddle and is rebuffed. Each time, until the last one, she snatches up one of the earl's children in her anger, and leads the anguished earl a merry chase, eludes him, only to reappear after forty years to repeat the ritual. The legend, in other words, rehearses on a small scale the cyclical movement of Joyce's myth. Even the thunder, coming at the end of the third cycle to usher in a new round, is present in the sound of the slamming door.

Going one step further, the prankquean episode contains in microcosm numerous mythical forces which receive their full development later on in the *Wake*. In the two pages which Joyce allots to the incident, most of the major characters of his "Pageant of Past History" (221) pass in review. Adam and Eve set the time of the occurrence. The gay young prankquean who seized the child and "started to rain and to rain," (21) is Anna Livia Plurabelle, river-wife of HCE. Hilary and Christopher, the "jiminy" whom she abducts at regular intervals, are Kevin and Jerry, the twin sons of ALP and Earwicker, another incarnation of Jarl van Hoother. But this is just the beginning. In an attempt to introduce the analogy of Tristan and Iseult, Joyce's ingenuity works overtime. After kidnapping Hilary, "she provorted him to the one-certain allsecure and he became a tristian." (22) Following the episode through on this level, we find that other obscurities become clear. The prankquean prefaces each statement of her riddle with "Mark the Wans," "Mark the Twy," "Mark the Tris." Van Hoother-Earwicker-Mark is undoubtedly King Mark, whose close relative, Hilary-Jerry-Tristan, has been seduced by the woman in the case, Prankquean-Anna Livia-Iseult. The reader is not allowed to forget the Diarmuid-Grania parallel either, for the narrator's favorite oath resolves itself every time into a distorted anagram of the name Diarmuid ("be dermot," "be redtom," "be dom ter.") It would be hard to imagine another passage of comparable length which compressed as many relevant associative variations on a theme as does the episode of the prankquean. Nor has this sketchy examination exhausted the possibilities of the legend. For if we look at *Finnegans Wake* as the great, sprawling dream of everybody, each of its episodes acquires deeper, fresher meaning.

III

Finnegans Wake is the dream of H. C. Earwicker, tavernkeeper, on a warm evening. After carrying to artistic completion in *Ulysses* a description of an ordinary day in the life of ordinary Mr. Leopold Bloom, Joyce decided to turn his talents to the much more difficult job of depicting just as completely the mind of an average citizen of modern Ireland in sleep. His close friend, Eugene Jolas, tells us that Joyce was "an intensely conscious observer of the unconscious drama . . . was always eager to discuss them [dreams], because they interested him as images of the nocturnal universe." Living much of his adult life in Zurich and other European capitals, he was close to the excitement surrounding discoveries relating to dreams and the unconscious mind. Freud and Jung were more than names to him.

And while Freud and Jung may have disagreed in matters of detail concerning the relation of dream to myth, Joyce's genius for extracting from any system what suited his special needs allowed him to build his "Eyrawyggla saga" (48) on elements from both which, to the mind of the lay reader, would not appear to conflict.

In explaining his race psychology in *Totem and Taboo*, Freud declares that "we base everything upon the assumption of a psyche of the mass . . ." and later that "a continuity in the emotional life of mankind" is necessary to the holding of his theory. As an example of what he means by these abstractions, he cites the "sense of guilt" which may survive for many generations after the act which gave rise to the original emotion in the ancestors of the race. No layman would find difficulty in reconciling these statements with those of Freud's disciple, Jung, who broke with the master over the interpretation of the unconscious. Jung denies that the unconscious is personal in its deeper levels. At least one layer of it is not derived from personal experience. This part, universal in its manifestations, is called the collective unconscious. The contents of this collective unconscious he calls "archetypes," ancient and primordial images impressed upon the minds of early men. When these archetypes become conscious and are converted into traditional formulae, the result is myth, a conscious form, handed on relatively unchanged over long centuries. What interested Joyce in all this was the fact that dreams were a primary means of bringing to the surface myth-ical archetypes or patterns. Keeping in mind the Viconian idea of the recurrence of the hero type, and the concept of cyclical history, Joyce saw with what ease the psycho-analytical idea of myth could be accommodated to the larger myth of man. He saw how smoothly the definition of the scientist Abraham would fit his own pattern: ". . . myth is a fragment of the infantile soul life of the race and the dream is the myth of the individ-ual." The skill with which Joyce worked out the pattern is worth noticing.

Freud contends that "dreams are (disguised) fulfilments of a (suppressed, re-pressed) wish." In *The Interpretation of Dreams*, he points out that the distortion which often accompanies dreams is simply an act of censorship performed by the mind to protect the dreamer from the shock of the naked wish. Applying this formula to the sleeping Earwicker, Joyce managed to solve it through recourse to myth. Earwicker's age is creeping up on him. He feels that he is no longer the dashing lover he once was. Things have not been going well for him: he has lost a local election campaign, and gossip accuses him of unspecified, scandalous conduct. Worst of all, his fair young bride, Anna Livia, has grown old and ugly at his side until he has reached the point at which his feeling for her will become one of cold neutrality. The waning passion for his wife is gradually being replaced by a socially unsanctioned, incestuous interest in their daughter, Isabel. Thoroughly conventional in his waking conduct, quick to feel hurt by the opprobrium of his peers, Earwicker has been able to repress his dangerous wish. But sleep and dream are no respecters of convention. The "dislocated reason" (189) of night logic will out. Yet the mental censor of Ear-wicker's dream will not allow a shocking, straightforward presentation of the wish, lest the sleeper awake. So from that part of the collective unconscious which resides in the innkeeper's mind, Joyce drew upon the archetypal pattern of the Tristan myth, the ever-present human situation of eternal triangle. The dream distorts the relation-ships out of focus, but, at the same time, it allows the psychic energy of the unconscious wish to be dissipated. Earwicker becomes—what he secretly longs to be—the very model of an amorous knight wooing and winning the fair lady Iseult, in real life his own daughter. It is even possible to imagine old Anna Livia, minus her once-powerful sex-appeal, as the King Mark of the myth, impotent and deserted.

In the "no placelike no timelike" (609) atmosphere of dream, which seems to put "Allspace in a Notshall," (455) there is no need to observe the unities of logical behavior. Therefore the reader is not surprised to find the Tristan pattern fading into the analogical archetype of Diarmuid and Grania. Here, Earwicker is reborn as the blue-eyed, fair-haired youth, Diarmuid, who is in a position to find himself sought after by the Grania-daughter figure of the Irish myth. The scene may shift again to reveal the lovely prankquean-daughter image hotly pursued by Earwicker in his role of Earl van Hoother. Over all the book flows what to Jung is the commonest and perhaps the most powerful symbol of the unconscious: Water. For the leading female character of the *Wake*, the symbolic mother of us all, is the river Liffey,

Anna Livia Plurabelle, a figure which represents to Jung "an experience of woman far older than that of the individual," an embodiment of the eternal feminine.

An even more obvious case may be made for the presence of the Oedipus archetypal myth in *Finnegans Wake*. If we accept Freud's supposition that the beginnings of society are rooted in the Oedipal situation, the killing of the hated, arrogant father by the band of rebel sons, then his conclusions certainly merit consideration. In *Totem and Taboo*, he points out that this "removal of the primal father by the band of brothers must have left ineradicable traces in the history of mankind . . . in mythology." Freud continues with the comment that when this basic situation is portrayed in literature

> the hero must suffer. He has taken upon himself the so-called "tragic guilt," which is not always easy to explain; it is often not a guilt in the ordinary sense. Almost always it consisted of a rebellion against a divine or human authority . . . .

Even a casual reader of the *Wake*—if such there be—might well feel that Freud had personally aided Joyce in writing the book, so closely is the substance of his statements followed in the projection of Joyce's myth. The hero of the *Wake*, Here Comes Everybody, is at bottom just such a tragic figure, the All-Father of the race. For a hazy, indefinable indiscretion, he is the butt of his immediate society, the patrons of the tavern and the gossips of the town, who "want to hear all/about" (196) his sin. What the guilt is is never discovered although a profusion of rumors keeps the issue alive. It is not even certain that the crime is HCE's, and thus the prosecutors often blend with the defendant, the accusers change places with the accused in bewildering confusion. Perhaps this is further explained by Freud's remark that

> He had to suffer because he was the primal father, the hero of that primordial tragedy the repetition of which here serves a certain tendency, and the tragic guilt is the guilt which he had to take upon himself in order to free the . . . [accusers] of theirs . . .

In much the same way as Christ suffered the jeers of the populace, Earwicker in his tavern submits to the insults of the tipsy customers. Actually it was not he, the hero, who was any more guilty than his tormentors. But in the tragic figure is concentrated the feeling of sin which the rest are able to transfer from themselves. "Thus the tragic hero, though still against his will, is made the redeemer . . ."

IV

In projecting his narrative, Joyce was faced with problems of linguistic expression which, after the experience with words gained in writing *Ulysses*, he was extremely well-equipped to handle. To his friend Jolas, he confided, "I have discovered that I can do anything with language I want . . ." What he wanted was to get away from bare, bald, denotative words of conventional, logical, expository prose—a deadening medium for a modern artist who had become as sensitive to sound as the almost-blind Joyce. But there was more to the change than that.

For "this nonday diary, this allnights newseryreel" (489) of the *Wake*, the language of day was particularly inappropriate. A dream is not logical, by waking standards, nor can the effect of dream be communicated effectively by the worn out words of day logic, the language of this chapter. To express his dream-myth, he had to invent a language not dependent for its meaning solely on the logical order of its words in space and time. The words had to be mixed up, both in their order and in their organic structure so that they would convey, when unscrambled consciously or unconsciously, not only their "logical" day meaning, but, much more important, the wealth of associative values which resulted from their very ambiguity. In this respect, the language resembled in function the language of poetry, offering to the careful reader layer upon layer of rich, associative meaning. The rejuvenated words, unbelievably enriched, must bear the responsibility in the *Wake* which the vivid images, flashing in illogical order before the eye of the dreamer, bear in the dream. And since Joyce in *Finnegans Wake* is concerned with the mythical element of the collective unconscious in dream, his word coinages serve the additional purpose of infusing fresh vitality into the traditional myths. His treatment of myth in the language of dream is best illustrated by reference to the Tristan theme.

Hundreds—perhaps thousands—of puns on the names of characters in the Tristan story are spinkled through the pages of the *Wake* to keep the motif constantly alive. Where the motif dominates, the page bristles with veiled and obvious references. Here is a case in point:

> . . . The new world presses. Where the old conk cruised now croons the yunk. Exeunc throw a darras Kram of Llawnroc, ye gink guy, kirked into yord. Enterest attawonder Wehpen, luftcat revol, fairescapading in his natsirt. Tuesy tumbles. And mild aunt Liza is as loose as her neese. Fulfest withim inbrace behent. As gent would deem oncontinent. So mulct per wenche is Elsker woed. Ne hath his thrysting. Fin. (387–388)

Obviously, to those who have been conditioned to Joycean verbal fireworks, the excerpt is simply one more link in the chain of evidence that world history is cyclical. In this instance the Tristan theme is the concrete example chosen. The clues to the passage are the inverted names: "Kram of Llawnroc" is Mark of Cornwall, the cuckolded husband of "Tuesy," or Yseut (Iseult). The key words of the phrase "Wehpen . . . in his natsirt," when inverted, yield "Nephew . . . tristan." The actors of the myth are now revealed. But why the hocus-pocus of inversion in the first place? Is Joyce seeking merely to fascinate puzzle addicts or to flaunt his disdain of direct communication in the language of men in the face of his readers? A reading of the Tristan-Iseult myth should shatter that conclusion. In the original narrative, Tristan is forced by the dangerous circumstances of his activities to conceal his true identity behind an alias. He invariably adopts an anagram of his own name, calling himself most often Tantris (or Tremtriss). Evidently Joyce has seen here a natural opportunity to alter the organic constitution of the words, not arbitrarily but within the framework of the public and almost universal myth.

But the twisting of key words here serves also the purpose of associative enrichment. Thus Mark is a "gink," the four letters carrying the double meaning of king and, in modern slang, a fool. Perhaps there is implicit here a contrast between the nobility of the past and the tawdriness of the present cycle. Similarly, "Wehpen, luftcat revol" means "Nephew, tactful lover," since Tristan was Mark's nephew as well as being the cagey lover of Mark's bride. On another level, however, the words in the context of the passage quoted here may stand for "weapon, lifted revolver," a phrase which would have a surface, as well as a phallic, significance. Again "revol" may have here the additional connotative force of "rebel" or "revolt," since Tristan is bucking royal authority by "fairescapading in his natsirt" with the queen. "Fairescapading" too has its associations. From the French "faire," "to make," the word takes on the meaning of "to make an escape." Since Tristan's meeting with Iseult in the present cycle of the world's development take place in one-night cheap hotels, the word has the additional meaning of "fire-escape" escapades, in which the hero makes a sudden, "tactful" withdrawal through the window.

Inasmuch as the episode from which this extract is taken describes the honeymoon voyage of Tristan and Iseult aboard the dream ship, it is natural that the new world, Tristan, should press, having supplanted the old, King Mark. Mark and his alias, Kram, have been gotten rid of, so the Shakespearian stage directions proclaim their departure: "Exeunc throw a darras" the king. It will be noted that "Exeunt," the stage direction indicating the exit of characters from the scene, has been distorted in Earwicker's dream to "Exeunc," which conveys the same meaning but has the additional force of its comic connotation, "Exit-unc (les)" Mark and/or Kram. The ejection is forcible, "throw a darras" (through an arras); (and those who know Joyce will not lightly let pass a possible, though far-fetched, allusion to "Theodorus," a bishop in Antioch at the time of the Roman Empire, whose writings were rejected by the church). At any rate, Mark is "kirked into yord," kicked into the yard. But "kirk" is the Scotch word for church, so that the latter phrase may also be translated by "churchyard." The incident occurs on a ship, however, and Joyce must provide a reasonable means for disposing of the unwanted Mark. Again word distortion plays its part, for "yord" may be anagrammed as "dory," the small boat usually tied to the stern of a ship, for the use of the crew in an emergency. A possible inference would be that the king was kicked into the dory, symbolically of course, while the unsanctioned love affair was taking place on the honeymoon ship. With the king out of the way, the passage continues, "Tuesy tumbles," passion is unabated, "Ne hath his thrysting. Fin." The last line is richly ambiguous, for "thrysting" may mean in this context "thirsting" or "trysting," and, at the same time, it obviously stands for "Tristan." The line may therefore be read: "Nor had Tristan's thirsting and/or trysting an end."

When one considers that this brief and incomplete analysis has attempted merely to mention several of the highlights of fewer than seven lines of *Finnegans Wake*, leaving numerous associations untouched for fear of overwhelming the reader in details, the complexity and profuse richness of Joyce's dream-myth language become apparent. When one further remembers that to each reader additional associations may present themselves in the distortion of conventional words and phrases, some idea of the advantage of using such a linguistic system in assembling a myth of Everyman is inescapable. Purely from a practical standpoint, such a system had to be worked out if

Joyce was to satisfy the scientific description of the collective unconscious and the Freudian representation of dream. Frederick J. Hoffman, in *Freudianism and the Literary Mind*, points out clearly that the condensation, displacement, and distortion of dream images, required by Freud's interpretation, had somehow to be approximated in language if they were to be recorded faithfully. In the telescoping of words ("Exeunc" for "exit, uncles"), in his distortion of language ("Enterest" or "entereth" or "interest"), in his puns all through the *Wake*, Joyce makes an admirable leap from image to word.

V

"Was it worth doing?" is the question most frequently asked in connection with *Finnegans Wake*. Were the seventeen years which Joyce spent building up his system worth the effort? It is by now one of the trite ironies of our world that, in proportion as Joyce succeeded in the task of reducing his myth to the only expression capable of exposing it fully, the number of readers who were prepared to puzzle out the result diminished. His difficulties with a conventional and mentally slothful public had prepared him for this reaction. "Please stop if you're a B. C. minding missy, please do. But should you prefer A. D. stepplease." (272) He realized that his apparent obscurity would alienate a public suspicious of what it did not understand; he expected to be scorned for "his root language." (424) "the whacker his word the weaker our ears for auracles who parles parses orileys." (467) It is to Joyce's credit that he chose to abjure popularity if it had to be bought at the expense of weakening the all-embracing dream of the race. Perhaps a sensible approach to a satisfactory answer is to decide just what he accomplished in those seventeen years.

He succeeded in verbalizing in literature levels of consciousness and unconsciousness which had hitherto appeared inexpressible. Susanne K. Langer, in *Philosophy in a New Key*, defines the relation of dream to myth:

Myth begins in fantasy, which may remain tacit for a long time; for the primary form of fantasy is the entirely subjective and private phenomenon of *dream*.

The lowest form of story is not much more than a dream narrative.

The plan of writing this "dream-narrative" in order to get below the surface emptiness of ordinary prose and ordinary, trite audience appeal was daringly conceived and executed. To have novelized the Viconian idea of history alone would not have been enough; to have written a dream-narrative on a trivial theme would have indicated a degree of virtuosity. But to do what Joyce did, to treat an epic theme in a technique designed to pierce the shabby cloak of channelized language and feeling through recourse to the "private phenomenon" of dream made public—that is enough to demand of one man in one lifetime.

He was able, in addition, to reconcile, and often to fuse, numerous conceptions of myth into a greater whole, his own myth of man. Freud and Jung, irreconcilable in their personal careers, are tapped for their contributions to the study of myth, and, under Joyce's skilled hand, both yield fruitful material. HCE suffers dismemberment in his dream, reliving the ordeal of Osiris in the Egyptian myth and acknowledging the influence of Frazer. The obscure Viconian stab at defining the origin of myth in language takes its place beside the traditional, archetypal myths. Yet the reader does not feel, upon reading *Finnegans Wake*, that he is being asked to swallow a myth sandwich, layer upon layer of unrelated writings stuffed between the two covers of a book. Perhaps it is the atmosphere of dream—or that created by the language of the dream-narrative—which accounts for the reader's willingness to suspend his disbelief in the presence of such an unlikely blend. Whatever the reason, the juxtaposition of a great mass of logically incongruous mythical material seems just as natural to the reader as do disconnected images in a dream to the dreamer. That, in itself, is no mean literary accomplishment.

In terms of cyclical history, he was able to explain the wasteland atmosphere of his time. The present cycle of the world is fast decaying; it is almost ready to give way to the new era. Its inhabitants are sterile:

> Who are the component partners of our societate, the doorboy, the cleaner, the sojer, the crook, the squeezer, the lounger, . . . the bleakablue tramp . . . who are latecomers all the year's round by anticipation, are the porters of the passions in virtue of retroratiocination . . . who crunch the crusts of comfort due to depredation, drain the mead for misery to incur intoxication, condone every evil by practical justification and condam any good to its own gratification, who are ruled, roped, duped and driven . . . ?
> Answer: The Morphios! (142)

But the new cycle will bring good.

Joyce waited for this good with patience and resignation born of long disappointment and disillusion: "such is manowife's lot of lose and win again . . . So what are you going to do about it? O dear!" (117)

Now, ten years later, the world is still waiting for the answer.

University of Kansas City Review, XVI (1950), 265–277.

The Imaginal Design

One of the most significant achievements of modern criticism has been the demonstration of the importance of imagery to literary understanding. In the hands of Caroline Spurgeon, G. Wilson Knight, and their counterparts among the new critics, studies of imagery generally concentrated on patterns unique to the work of the author. In the following group of essays Peter B. Murray ("Myth in The Blithedale Romance*"), John E. Hart ("The Red Badge of Courage* as Myth and Symbol*"), and Robert Harrison ("Symbolism of the Cyclical Myth in* Endymion*") take a further step: they trace the archetypal lineaments of imagery and thus establish concrete links between individual works of art and human experiences that are at once primordial and perennial. As a result, their essays have marked affinities with those of Joseph Campbell (pp. 15 ff.) and Andrew Lytle (pp. 99 ff.).*

MYTH IN *THE BLITHEDALE ROMANCE*

Peter B. Murray

Nathaniel Hawthorne put his profound understanding of mythology to its most significant use in *The Blithedale Romance*. Miles Coverdale, the fictional narrator, is a minor poet with an intensely mythopoeic imagination, and as he interprets the action of the *Romance*, Hawthorne uses the quality of his interpretation to define his character. Coverdale's story and vision are based on many of the same perceptions about life as are the Greek season myths, and he employs the actions, metaphors, and symbols of those myths to give his work its structure, to characterize his people, and to describe human relations. Coverdale has not merely reformulated old myth; he creates a new myth relating man to nature and to the deity and dramatizing the mystery of life and death. Blithedale, like the Brook Farm of real life, is an experiment in communal living whose founders hope to establish a perfect society. Coverdale's mythopoeic narrative suggests that the Utopian's dream of static perfection is false because the human condition is one of ceaseless change, of inexorable growth and decay.

Even Coverdale's more abstract statements about the human condition are usually made in terms of natural decay and the passing of the seasons. Thus when he recovers from his illness, he says "it was like death. And, as with death, too, it was good to have gone through it," for otherwise he had been unable to fling aside his old flesh like an "unseasonable garment; and after shivering a little while," to reclothe himself "much more satisfactorily than in my previous suit."[1] As the summer passes, the people at Blithedale regard their life there hopefully, "as if the soil beneath our feet had not been fathom-deep with the dust of deluded generations, on every one of which, as on ourselves, the world had imposed itself as a hitherto unwedded bride" (p. 466). Later, when Priscilla says she hopes "there might never be any change, but

1. Nathaniel Hawthorne, *The Complete Works*, ed. G. P. Lathrop (Boston: Houghton Mifflin, 1883), V, 388–389. Subsequent references are indicated in the text.

one summer follow another, and all just like this," Coverdale promptly rejoins, "No summer ever came back, and no two summers ever were alike. . . . Times change, and people change; and if our hearts do not change as readily, so much the worse for us" (pp. 482–483).

At the crucial moment just after Hollingsworth has broken with Zenobia, Coverdale symbolically stumbles over a pile of firewood which has decayed "from autumn to autumn" until only a "green mound" remains, and he thinks of the long-dead woodman returning and trying to light a fire with it. As a result of the scene that follows, Zenobia kills herself, and at the conclusion of the *Romance* Coverdale writes:

> But, all this while, we have been standing by Zenobia's grave. I have never since beheld it, but make no question that the grass grew all the better, on that little parallelogram of pasture-land, for the decay of the beautiful woman who slept beneath. How Nature seems to love us! And how readily, nevertheless, without a sigh or a complaint, she converts us to a meaner purpose, when her highest one—that of a conscious intellectual life and sensibility—has been untimely balked! While Zenobia lived, Nature was proud of her, and directed all eyes upon that radiant presence, as her fairest handiwork. Zenobia perished. Will not Nature shed a tear? Ah, no!—she adopts the calamity at once into her system, and is just as well pleased, for aught we can see, with the tuft of ranker vegetation that grew out of Zenobia's heart, as with all the beauty which has bequeathed us no earthly representative except in this crop of weeds. It is because the spirit is inestimable that the lifeless body is so little valued. (pp. 595–596)

At the beginning of the next chapter, Coverdale describes how, in the years that have "darkened" around him since, he has thought of their high hopes "in that first summer" for the establishment of a new order, and he goes on to describe the sad decay of Blithedale over the years into Fourierism and then death: "Where once we toiled with our whole hopeful hearts, the town-paupers, aged, nerveless, and disconsolate, creep sluggishly afield" (pp. 597–598).

It is only Coverdale who integrates the decay of humans and their institutions with natural decay. Hollingsworth and Zenobia have, of course, strikingly individual ideas about human perfectibility; Priscilla thinks time can pass without change; and Westervelt can say of Zenobia after her death, with unconscious irony, that "she had life's summer all before her" (p. 591).

As Coverdale shapes the narrative, the seasons are organically related to the destinies of the characters and their relations to one another. The story begins with the coming of spring and ends with autumn. Coverdale hikes to Blithedale on a mid-April day which, though it ends in a foreshadowing blizzard, is mild and even balmy in the forenoon. That night Hollingsworth brings Priscilla to Blithedale. Priscilla is described in terms connecting her with the myth of Persephone, the Queen of the Underworld who returns to the earth each spring. She is of a wan hue, indicating "seclusion from the sun and free atmosphere, like a flower shrub that had done its best to blossom in too scanty light" (p. 350). She is sent by "Providence" to be "the first-fruits of the world," who will "begin to look like a creature of this world" if properly cared for (pp. 354–355). Often in the early chapters Priscilla is referred to as having been closed up somewhere, or as a plant which had been growing in the shade. In a belated May Day ritual of spring, Zenobia and Priscilla gather flowers together, and Zenobia decks Priscilla out in blossoms. Priscilla is then described as "the very picture of the New England spring," and Zenobia says, "The best type of her is one of those anemones," a flower connected with the theme of natural mortality in Greek myth (p. 386). And as time passes, Priscilla "still kept budding and blossoming" as "Nature [was] shaping out a woman before our very eyes" (p. 402).

The season-based structure of the *Romance* continues through Coverdale's withdrawal from the "sunburnt and arid aspect of our woods and pastures, beneath the August sky" and from the fiery ire of Hollingsworth immediately following their open break, the major crisis in the *Romance* (p. 477). The midsummer crisis divides the book exactly in half; the first half is dominated by spring, the second half by autumn.

The seasonal symbolism and structure reach their climax as the catastrophe approaches. In Chapter XII Coverdale had described his forest retreat and anticipated the "surprise of the Community, when, like an allegorical figure of rich October, I should make my appearance, with shoulders bent beneath the burden of ripe grapes, and some of the crushed ones crimsoning my brow as with a blood-stain" (p. 432). When he returns to Blithedale from town on a "breezy September forenoon," the ripe breath of autumn is in the air, which is like "ethereal wine" (pp. 551–552). When in town, he had thought of the impending disaster as an atonement for evil. Earlier he had remarked that someone would have to sanctify by death their way of life. Now, possessed by the mythic significance of harvest, Coverdale has a presentiment that evil is coming, just when he feels closest to the red clay of the farm where he had earned his bread and eaten it—the farm that was his home and might be his grave: "I could have knelt down, and have laid my breast against that soil" (p. 554). When he climbs into his forest retreat, he finds the grapes ripe and longs for their wine to stimulate "bacchanalian ecstasies." He then comes on the Blithedale folk "full of jollity [like] . . . Comus and his crew . . . holding revels" (p. 557). Leaving the revels, Coverdale finds Zenobia, Hollingsworth, and Priscilla at Eliot's Pulpit. Zenobia has already been tried and condemned and, dressed as the queen of the festival with a leafy crown, she awaits her fate. Her suicide follows soon after and the summer at Blithedale is at an end. As the queen of the festival was sacrificed in other times, here Zenobia atones for evil through her death.

And so the *Romance* begins with the coming of Priscilla and spring to Blithedale, reaches its mid-point and major crisis in searing mid-August, and concludes with the coming of autumn and decay. The mythic symbolism of the seasons divides the *Romance* into two balanced parts: spring and early summer in which life and relationships develop and seem to approach fruitfulness, and mid-summer and autumn with their paradoxically inseparable ripeness and decay. At the middle of the book the people are split apart, not to be reunited until the final crisis. In each half of the book there is a journey to Blithedale described, a symbolically important story within the story, a seasonal ritual, a rescue of Priscilla by Hollingsworth, and a climactic scene at Eliot's Pulpit. Significantly, one half begins with the coming of Priscilla to Blithe-dale, and the other half ends with the departure of Zenobia from life.

At the beginning of the *Romance* and through most of it, Priscilla, and not Zenobia, seems likely to be "sacrificed" at the end. It is Priscilla who is weak and sickly, and it is Zenobia who seems to be loved by Hollingsworth, a fact that makes Priscilla droop. This leads to an examination of the very important flower and vine symbols relating Zenobia to Priscilla and Priscilla to nearly everyone else. The complex symbolic texture here suggests that we are dealing with a myth which reflects the duality of deity and of human nature: in many ways the action and the symbols suggest that Zenobia and Priscilla are partial people, two aspects of the feminine personality.

Zenobia is described as always wearing an exotic flower in her hair, and Coverdale says this is more indicative of her proud character than a great diamond would be. Coverdale decides that Zenobia's nature is suited to spreading fresh flowers and reviving faded ones. This is just before Priscilla, the pale flower, joins the group at Blithedale to be revived by Zenobia, sometimes symbolized as a rosy flower. Through-out the book Coverdale reminds us of the exotic flower in Zenobia's hair, which toward the end of the book is symbolically replaced by an artificial imitation. During a sickness shortly after his arrival at Blithedale, Coverdale bursts out that "Zenobia is an enchantress! . . . She is a sister of the Veiled Lady. That flower in her hair is a talisman. If you were to snatch it away, she would vanish, or be transformed into something else," which partially explicates the symbol (p. 371). Once, when Zenobia saw that her ornamental flower had drooped, "she flung it on the floor" (p. 344). This gesture of flower-flinging relates the flower symbol to both Zenobia and Priscilla, for though Zenobia flings away Priscilla as a flower, it is herself she finally flings into the river after giving her talisman to Coverdale for Priscilla. Referring to Priscilla, Westervelt tells Zenobia to "fling the girl off" (p. 438). Shortly afterward, at the conclusion of the first scene at Eliot's Pulpit, when Zenobia subtly expresses her love for Hollingsworth, she is tremulous, like her flower, and Priscilla immediately droops. To Coverdale, Priscilla then appeared to be "carelessly let fall, like a flower they had done with" (pp. 462-463). And again, at the end of Moodie's tale, Coverdale writes that on that very evening "Priscilla—poor, pallid flower!—was either snatched from Zenobia's hand, or flung wilfully away" (p. 539). It is deeply ironic that when all is lost to her, Zenobia should remark that Hollingsworth "has flung away what would have served him better than the poor, pale flower he kept" (pp. 573-574). To Cover-dale, the daily death of her exotic flower symbolizes Zenobia's ultimate fate: each day is for the talismanic flower what the summer is for Zenobia. And Priscilla, the pale flower, is related to Zenobia through the flower symbols: as the fortunes of Zenobia rise, Priscilla seems to droop, and the ambiguity of reference of the flower leaves us uncertain which of them the catastrophe will befall.

The importance of the vine as a symbol lies not alone in its connection with the festival of autumn. As Moodie tells Coverdale his story, he speaks of how he described the beautiful Zenobia to Priscilla, and "Priscilla's love grew, and tended upward, and twined itself perseveringly around this unseen sister; as a grape-vine might strive to clamber out of a gloomy hollow among the rocks, and embrace a young tree standing in the sunny warmth above" (p. 531). When Coverdale wants to gain perspective on the Blithedale drama and pierce to the heart of the mystery, he retreats to his "hermit-age, in the heart of the white-pine tree" (p. 555). When he first describes this "vine encircled heart of the tall pine" (p. 495), he writes:

> It was a kind of leafy cave, high upward into the air, among the midmost branches of a white-pine tree. A wild grape-vine, of unusual size and luxuriance, had twined and twisted itself up into the tree, and, after wreathing the entanglement of its tendrils almost around every bough, had caught hold of three or four neighboring trees, and married the whole clump with a perfectly inextricable knot of polygamy. ... A hollow chamber of rare seclusion had been formed by the decay of some of the pine branches, which the vine had lovingly strangled with its embrace, burying them from the light of day in an aerial sepulchre of its own leaves. (p. 431)

The intense vitality of Coverdale's symbolism is nowhere more evident. We see, for example, how Priscilla affects her hosts—Coverdale is soon to think of her as a "gentle parasite" to Hollingsworth as well as to Zenobia—and how Coverdale in his hermitage virtually sits in the heart of the mystery of his friends, and, applying the figure again, in his own heart. The symbolic terms interact even further as Coverdale tells us this hermitage symbolized his individuality, and that he sat there owl-like, able, like Pallas Athene, to see all "those sublunary matters in which lay a lore as infinite as that of the planets" (p. 432). From his hermitage Coverdale hears Zenobia say that Priscilla "clung to me from the first," and a few lines later add ambiguously, with potential reference to both Priscilla and Westervelt, "With what kind of a being am I linked? ... If my creator cares aught for my soul, let him release me from this miserable bond! ... It will strangle me, at last!" (p. 438). The flower dies, and the vine lives on; each is subject to the seasons, but whereas the parasitic choker only *sleeps* in winter, the flower must return to earth. The vine, though a parasite as it chokes, may bind sunlit trees together, even against their will, and may, after throttling them, lash them together in an upright position, preserving a semblance of life in them through its own green leaves and crimson-staining fruit.

In addition to the images already mentioned that indicate the cold darkness from which Priscilla comes to Blithedale, there are other passages which reveal how, Persephone-like, she comes from captivity in the household of a king of the underworld. Her life as the Veiled Lady with Westervelt is described in terms emphasizing its deathly aspects. Her veil "was supposed to insulate her from the material world, from time and space, and to endow her with many of the privileges of a disembodied spirit" (p. 326). In her legend, Zenobia says that Priscilla's life as the Veiled Lady lacked reality, and hesitates even to call it life. Moodie tells Coverdale that the young Priscilla was thought of as a "ghost-child" lacking "earthly substance" and so subject to Westervelt, who is characterized in part as follows: "The boundaries of his power were defined by the verge of the pit of Tartarus on the one hand, and the third sphere of the celestial world on the other." Westervelt was "perhaps a mechanical contrivance, in which a demon walked about" (p. 534). Coverdale rarely saw Westervelt that he did not remark the demonic and unreal quality of the man. This interpretation of Westervelt is consistent with Coverdale's perception of his character as expressed in other terms, for his "cold scepticism smothers . . . our spiritual aspirations," and he is "miserably incomplete on the emotional side, with hardly any sensibilities. . . . No passion, save of the senses; no holy tenderness" (pp. 435–436). And climactically, when Zenobia is buried, Westervelt is the first to throw a clod of dirt into the open grave, symbolizing his claim on her as the sacrifice, the new prisoner of the under-world. It is then that Coverdale thinks, "Heaven deal with Westervelt according to his nature and deserts!—that is to say, annihilate him. He was altogether earthy, worldly, made for time and its gross objects, and incapable . . . of so much as one spiritual idea" (p. 592).

If Westervelt suggests the demonic and death-bearing aspect of deity, Hollingsworth suggests the Messianic. His tenderness during Coverdale's illness reminds Coverdale of "God's own love." But Hollingsworth channels all his love into the "spectral monster" that is his philanthropic theory. All his relations with others he forces to "minister, in some way, to the terrible egotism he mistook for an angel of God" (p. 382). Coverdale thinks of Zenobia and Priscilla as the "disciples" of Hollings-worth. Hollingsworth is one of those who act as "high-priest" to make "sacrifices" to a "false deity" that "is but a spectrum of the priest himself" (p. 400). Like Jesus, Hollingsworth says "be with me . . . or be against me! there is no third choice for you (p. 474). At Eliot's Pulpit Hollingsworth is first the passionate preacher and later the terrible judge who condemns Zenobia.

Hollingsworth is also figured forth as Vulcan or Hephaistos, the god of the forge who can use his art to create living human beings. When Hollingsworth first joins the group at Blithedale, Coverdale describes him as a former blacksmith with features of iron. Later Hollingsworth says of himself, "I have always been in earnest. . . . I have hammered thought out of iron, after heating the iron in my heart" (p. 396). Through this symbol Hollingsworth is related to Zenobia: "As for Zenobia, there was a glow in her cheeks that made me think of Pandora, fresh from Vulcan's workshop, and full of the celestial warmth by dint of which he had tempered and moulded her" (p. 347). The transformation of Zenobia into a work of art through the agency of Hollingsworth is not completed until much later, however, when Zenobia returns to town, driven by her desire to have Hollingsworth all for herself, and arranges with Westervelt to deliver Priscilla back into bondage as the Veiled Lady. Zenobia then replaces the living flower in her hair with a jewelled one, imparting "the last touch that transformed Zenobia into a work of art" (p. 506). The motif is tragically completed when Zenobia ironically becomes "the marble image of a death-agony" (p. 586). There is irony in this final description of Zenobia partly in the cold contrast it affords with the fire images used by Coverdale to suggest the warmth of her character. She and Hollingsworth are both characterized through images suggesting that they are sources of heat and light, just as Priscilla and Westervelt are described as cold and dull.

The situation in the *Romance* also suggests a connection between Priscilla and Pandora, and the Pandora myth thus serves as another pattern of images linking Zenobia and Priscilla. Zeus, angered that man had been given fire, ordered Hephaistos to make Pandora a source of trouble for man, and carry her to where he could see men sitting about their fire. So in the *Romance* Moodie, the father, sends Priscilla with

Hollingsworth to the fireside at Blithedale. In the description of his first day at Blithedale Coverdale makes much of the significance of the warm hearth to the people gathered there and to anyone passing outside. The "outer solitude . . . like another state of existence" looked "into the little sphere of warmth and light" (p. 362). "There is nothing so pleasant and encouraging to a solitary traveller, on a stormy night, as a flood of firelight seen amid the gloom. These ruddy window-panes cannot fail to cheer the hearts of all that look at them. Are they not warm with the beacon-fire which we have kindled for humanity?" (p. 348). A moment later there is a rap at the door and Priscilla, the Pandora-like bringer of trouble, arrives at Blithedale.

As Hollingsworth and Westervelt participate in the myth of the *Romance* as contrasting aspects of deity, so the action and the symbols seem to suggest some connection between Zeus-Hades and Moodie. We have just seen a parallel between Moodie and Zeus in the myth of Pandora. Also, as the one who makes Westervelt release Priscilla, Moodie is like Zeus winning the release of Persephone from Hades. The name of his daughter Zenobia means "one whose life derives from Zeus." Moodie tells Coverdale his life history: how he was Fauntleroy ("the little lord") and had a home that "might almost be styled a palace; his habits, in the ordinary sense, princely. His whole being seemed to have crystallized itself into external splendor." If he loved Zenobia, "it was because she shone" (p. 527). But when his gold was gone "being a mere image, an optical delusion," he vanished "into the shadow of the first intervening cloud" (p. 528). He called himself Moodie and "skulked in corners, and crept about in a sort of noonday twilight, making himself gray and misty, at all hours, with his morbid intolerance of sunshine" (p. 530).

Thus Fauntleroy-Moodie is in part a dramatization of the ambivalence of deity, having the brightness of Zeus and the darkness of Zeus' brother or shadowed alterego, Hades. Coverdale thinks of Moodie as an invisible idol, connecting him with Hades, the invisible god, and he thinks the world to be dull spiritually and dead for Moodie, as it is for Westervelt. As Moodie, Fauntleroy moved into the abandoned mansion of a former governor. Here Priscilla was born, and during her childhood never stirred "out of the old governor's dusky house" (p. 533). When Zenobia comes to visit Moodie there, near the end of the *Romance*, he warns her to love Priscilla, and reflects that "in Zenobia I live again! . . . Were I to reappear, my shame would go with me from darkness into daylight. Zenobia has the splendor, and not the shame. Let the world admire her, and be dazzled by her, the brilliant child of my prosperity! It is Fauntleroy that still shines through her!" (p. 539). Moodie is the father of both Zenobia and Priscilla, and each is a natural product of the state in which she was born, Zenobia in a bright, princely palace, Priscilla in the darkness of the former governor's mansion.

Zenobia, because of her physical beauty, because of the relationship to Zeus suggested by her name, and because she is perhaps symbolized by a dove at one point in Coverdale's narrative, may be partially identified with the love goddess, Aphrodite. This indicates that for some of the purposes of the *Romance* the love rivalry of Zenobia and Priscilla for Hollingsworth is comparable to the life-versus-death conflict between Aphrodite and Persephone for Adonis.

The archetypal conflict between the creative and the deathly may be seen in every element of the book's structure. Spring, Zenobia, Hollingsworth, and Fauntleroy, varieties of the potential, the bright, or the vital, are set against autumn, Priscilla, Westervelt, and Moodie, varieties of the denial of life. The tragic view that in this conflict the warm and vital must give way to the cold and spiritless is dramatized through the seasonal structure of the *Romance*, with its resolution in the autumnal surrender of Zenobia and Hollingsworth. The fiery, consuming loves of Hollingsworth are energetically and even dangerously creative, but they are tamed by decay. At the end Westervelt can throw dirt on Zenobia's coffin, and Hollingsworth is only supported in the airy sepulcher of the world by the climbing tendrils of the vine of Priscilla. Fire is hot, exotic flowers are luxuriant, and a summer may be full of life, but autumn and decay are inevitable.

Coverdale's mythopoeic narrative projects his own internal conflict. Its dualism reflects the division in his own soul between the desire to live and have love and the belief that he must remain aloof and live vicariously in order to be a creative artist. Zenobia accuses him of "groping for human emotions in the dark corners of the heart" (p. 562), and he is aware that he is in danger of "unhumanizing" his heart through prying into the hearts of others. But he regards himself as the "Chorus in a classic play, which seems to be set aloof from the possibility of personal commencement," and so feels "impelled . . . (often against my own will, and to the detriment of my own comfort) to live in other lives, and to endeavor—by generous sympathies, by delicate intuitions, by taking note of things too slight for record, and by bringing my human spirit into manifold accordance with the companions whom God assigned me—to learn the secret which was hidden even from themselves" (pp. 430, 502).

In the final chapter Coverdale confesses his failure to find love. As he does so he emphasizes loss and decay in the cycle of nature: "The whole soil of our farm, for a long time afterwards, seemed but the sodded earth over [Zenobia's] grave" (p. 597). He sums up a good deal when he says: "As regards human progress . . . , let them believe in it who can, and aid in it who choose" (p. 598). He does not deny that the life of nature will renew itself, however. I have already quoted the passage in which he lingers over the grass that rises from Zenobia's grave, but as this example shows, his personality makes him stress the contrast between the "tuft of ranker vegetation" and her spirit, which was "inestimable" partly because it was *unique*. Since Coverdale is aloof from human society, he is denied the hope that goes with the mythic vision of comedy, which sees renewal for the life of the group if not for the individual in the coming of a new spring. Such a hopeful vision is implicit in the myth of the seasons just as the tragic vision is, but Coverdale's mythopoeic imagination is governed by the loneliness of his own life.

PMLA, LXXV (1960), 591–596. Originally titled "Mythopoesis in *The Blithedale Romance*." Revised and retitled by the author. Some reference notes have been omitted.

THE RED BADGE OF COURAGE
AS MYTH AND SYMBOL

John E. Hart

When Stephen Crane published *The Red Badge of Courage* in 1895, the book created an almost immediate sensation. Crane had had no experience in war, but in portraying the reactions of a young soldier in battle, he had written with amazing accuracy. As one way of re-examining *The Red Badge of Courage*, we would want to read it as myth and symbolic action. Clearly, the construction of the story, its moral and meaning, its reliance on symbol follow in detail the traditional formula of myth. Crane's main theme is the discovery of self, that unconscious self, which, when identified with the inexhaustible energies of the group, enables man to understand the "deep forces that have shaped man's destiny." The progressive movement of the hero, as in all myth, is that of separation, initiation, and return. Within this general framework, Crane plots his story with individual variation. Henry Fleming, a Youth, ventures forth from his known environment into a region of naturalistic, if not super-naturalistic wonder; he encounters the monstrous forces of war and death; he is transformed through a series of rites and revelations into a hero; he returns to identify his new self with the deeper communal forces of the group and to bestow the blessings of his findings on his fellow comrades.

Whatever its "realistic" style, much of the novel's meaning is revealed through the use of metaphor and symbol. The names of characters, for example, suggest both particular attributes and general qualities: the Tall Soldier, whose courage and confidence enable him to measure up to the vicissitudes of war and life; the Loud Soldier, the braggart, the over-confident, whose personality is, like Henry's, transformed in war; the Tattered Soldier, whose clothes signify his lowly and exhausted plight; the Cheery Man, whose keenness and valor prevent his falling into despair. Likewise, the use of color helps to clarify and extend the meaning. Red, traditionally associated with blood and fire, suggests courage, flag, life-energy, desire, ambition. Black, traditionally associated with death, implies "great unknown," darkness, forests, and, by extension, entombment and psychological death. The whole paraphernalia of myth-religions and sacrificial rites—the ceremonial dancing, the dragons with fiery eyes, the menacing landscape, the entombment, the sudden appearance of a guide, those symbols so profoundly familiar to the unconscious and so frightening to the conscious personality—give new dimensions of meaning to the novel.

What prompts Henry to leave his known environment is his unconscious longing to become a hero. In a state of conscious reflection, he looks on war with distrust. Battles belonged to the past. Had not "secular and religious education" effaced the "throat grappling instinct" and "firm finance" "held in check the passions"? But in dreams, he has thrilled to the "sweep and fire" of "vague and bloody conflicts"; he has "imagined people secure in the shadow of his eagle-eyed prowess." As the wind brings the noise of the ringing church bells, he listens to their summons as a proclamation from the "voice of the people." Shivering in his bed in a "prolonged ecstasy of excitement," he determines to enlist. If the call has come in an unconscious dream-like state where the associations of wind, church bells, ecstasy, heroism, glory are identified with the "voice" of the "group," Henry, fully "awake," insists on his decision. Although his mother, motivated apparently by "deep conviction" and impregnable ethical motives, tries to dissuade his ardor, she actually helps him in the initial step of his journey. She prepares his equipment: "eight pairs of socks," "yer best shirts," "a cup of blackberry jam." She advises him to watch the company he keeps and to do as he is told. Underlining the very nature of the problem, she warns that he will be "jest one little fellow amongst a hull lot of others."

It is this conflict between unconscious desire and conscious fear that prevents Henry from coming to terms with his new environment. Consciously concerned with thoughts of rumored battle, he crawls into his hut "through an intricate hole that served it as a door," where he can be "alone with some new thoughts that had lately come to him." Although his apparent concern is over fear of battle, his real anxiety is that of his individuation. As far as his relationship to war is concerned, he knows "nothing of himself." He has always "taken certain things for granted, never challenging his belief in ultimate success, and bothering little about means and roads." Now, he is an "unknown quantity." If his problems merge into that of whether he will or will not run from an "environment" that threatens to "swallow" his very identity, he sees that it cannot be solved by "mental slate and pencil." Action—"blaze, blood, and danger"—is the only test.

In giving artistic conception to Henry's conflict, Crane relies on a pattern of darkness and light, but adapts such traditional machinery to his particular purpose. As we have seen, Henry achieves courage and strength in the "darkness" of his tent, where his unconscious mind faces the problems of his new surroundings openly and bravely. As he peers into the "ominous distance" and ponders "upon the mystic gloom" in the morning twilight, he is eager to settle his "great problem" with the "red eyes across the river"—eyes like "orbs of a row of dragons advancing." Coming from the darkness towards the dawn, he watches "the gigantic figure of the colonel on a gigantic horse." They loom "black and pattern like" against the yellow sky. As the "black rider," the messenger of death lifts "his gigantic arm and calmly stroke[s] his mustache," Henry can hardly breathe. Then, with the hazy light of day, he feels the consciousness of growing fear. It seems ironic that his comrades, especially the Tall Soldier, should be filled with ardor, even song—just as he was in the darkness of his room at home. With the "developing day," the "two long, thin, black columns" have become "two serpents crawling from the cavern of night." These columns, monsters themselves, move from darkness to light with little fear, for they move, not as so many individuals, but as group units. Clearly, if Henry is to achieve his ambitions, he must "see" and "face" the enemy in the light of day without fear, as well as "perceive" his relationship to the group, which is, in a sense, a "monster" itself.

Henry's growing concern is not for his comrades, but for himself. Although he must march along with them, he feels caught "by the iron laws of tradition." He considers himself "separated from the others." At night, when the campfires dot the landscape "like red peculiar blossoms" (as communal fires which impregnate the landscape with "life" and "vitality," they suggest the life energy of the group), Henry remains a "few paces in the gloom," a "mental outcast." He is "alone in space," where only the "mood of darkness" seems to sympathize with him. He concludes that no other person is "wrestling with such a terrific personal problem." But even in the darkness of his tent he cannot escape: the "red, shivering reflection of a fire" shines through the canvas. He sees "visions of a thousand-tongued fear that would babble at his back and cause him to flee." His "fine mind" can no more face the monster war than it can cope with the "brute minds" of his comrades.

Next day as Henry, with sudden "impulse of curiosity," stares at the "woven red" against the "soft greens and browns," the harmony of landscape is broken when the line of men stumble onto a dead soldier in their path. Henry pauses and tries to "read in the dead eyes the answer to the Question." What irony it is that the ranks open "to avoid the corpse," as if, invulnerable, death forces a way itself. He notes that the wind strokes the dead man's beard, just as the black rider had stroked his mustache. Probing his sensations, he feels no ardor for battle. His soldier's clothes do not fit, for he is not a "real" soldier. His "fine mind" enables him to see what the "brute minds" of his comrades do not: the landscape threatens to engulf them. Their ardor is not heroism. They are merely going to a sacrifice, going "to look at war, the red animal— war the blood-swollen god." Even if he warned them, they would not listen. Misunderstood, he can only "look to the grave for comprehension." His feeling is prophetic, for it anticipates the death and transformation of personality that is about to occur.

Before he actually runs from battle, Henry experiences a moment of true realization. Impatient to know whether he is a "man of traditional courage," he suddenly loses "concern for himself," and becomes "not a man but a member." "Welded into a common personality" and "dominated by a single desire," he feels the "red rage" and "battle brotherhood"—that "mysterious fraternity born of the smoke and danger of death." He is carried along in a kind of "battle sleep." He rushes at the "black phantoms" like a "pestered animal." Then, awakening to the awareness of a second attack, he feels weak and bloodless. "Like the man who lost his legs at the approach of the red and green monster," he seems "to shut his eyes and wait to be gobbled." He has a revelation. Throwing down his gun, he flees like a "blind man." His vision of "selflessness" disappears; in this "blindness" his fears are magnified. "Death about to thrust him between the shoulder blades [is] far more dreadful than death about to smite him between the eyes." Impotent and blind (without gun and "vision"), he runs into the forest "as if resolved to bury himself." He is both physically and psychologically isolated from the group and hence from the very source of food and energy, both material and spiritual, that impels heroic achievement.

In the language of myth Henry's inability to face the monsters of battle in the "light," to identify himself with his comrades (both acts are, in a sense, identical), and thus to give up his individual self, which is sustained only in "darkness and in isolation," so that his full self can be realized in the light of communal identification symbolize a loss of spiritual, moral, and physical power, which only a rebirth of identity can solve.

Only by being reborn can he come to understand that man's courage springs from the self-realization that he must participate harmoniously as a member of the group. Only then can he understand the "deep forces" from which his individual energy and vitality spring. Thus, Henry's entombment in the forest is only preliminary to the resurrection that will follow. Without his full powers, his transformation cannot be effected by himself, but requires the necessity of ritualistic lessons and the aid of outside forces or agents. His own attempts to expiate his feeling of guilt by logic only leave him lost and confused in the labyrinth of his limitations.

After the burial of himself in the forest, it is his unconscious awareness of the nature of death that restores the strength and energy he had felt in his dreams at home. As he pushes on, going from "obscurity into promises of a greater obscurity," he comes face to face with the very "act" from which he is running. It is a dead soldier covered with "black" ants. As he recoils in terror, the branches of the forest hold him firm. In a moment of blind fear, he imagines that "some strange voice . . . from the dead throat" will squawk after him in "horrible menaces," but he hears, almost unconsciously, only a soft wind, which sings a "hymn of twilight." This aura of tranquility, produced in a "religious half light"—the boughs are arched like a chapel—transfixes Henry. He hears a "terrific medley of all noises." It is ironic that he should be fleeing from the black rider only to encounter death and "black ants." His ego is deflated. Did he ever imagine that he and his comrades could decide the war as if they were "cutting the letters of their names deep into everlasting tablets of brass?" Actually, the "affair" would receive only a "meek and immaterial title." With this thought and the song of the wind comes a certain faith. "Pictures of stupendous conflicts" pass through his mind. As he hears the "red cheers" of marching men, he is determined: he runs in the direction of the "crimson roar" of battle.

Although Henry's old fears have not been completely overcome, his meeting with the Tattered Man clarifies the need and method of atoning for his guilt. Having joined the marching soldiers, Henry is envious of this mob of "bleeding men." He walks beside the twice-wounded Tattered Man, whose face is "suffused with a light of love for the army which [is] to him all things beautiful and powerful." Moving in the "light of love," the Man speaks in a voice as "gentle as a girl's." "Where yeh hit?" he repeatedly asks Henry. "Letters of guilt" burn on the Youth's brow. How can he defend himself against an agency which so pitilessly reveals man's secrets? How can he atone for his guilt? His wish that "he, too, had a wound, a red badge of courage" is only preliminary to the fulfillment of atonement, just as in the rites of some primitive tribes or as in Christ's crucifixion on the cross, "blood" plays an essential part in the act of atonement and in the process of transformation.

If the Tattered Man's questioning reveals the need and nature of atonement, meeting the Tall Soldier shows the quality of character needed to make the sacrifice. Justifying the "tall" of his name by his "supreme unconcern" for battle, Conklin accepts his role as part of the group with coolness and humility. Because he realizes the insignificance of self, he has no fear of a threatening landscape. Sleeping, eating, and drinking afford him greatest satisfaction. During meal time, he is "quiet and contented," as if his spirit were "communing with viands." Now, fatally wounded, he is at his rendezvous with death; his actions are ceremonial, "rite-like." He moves with "mysterious purpose," like "the devotee of a mad religion, blood-sucking, muscle-wrenching, bone-crushing." His chest heaves "as if an animal was within," his "arms beat wildly," "his tall figure [stretches] itself to its full height" and falls to the ground—dead. His side looks "as if it had been chewed by wolves," as if the monster war had eaten him and then swallowed his life. This "ceremony at the place of meeting," this sacrificial ritual of placating the monster has enabled him to find the ultimate answer to the Question, but it has consumed its victim in the process.

It is the receiving of the wound, a kind of "magic" touch, whatever its irony of being false, that actually enables Henry to effect atonement. As the army itself retreats, he is truly "at one" with the group ("at one" and atone have similar functions as the very words imply), for both are running from battle. Actually, Henry is not "conscious" of what has happened. Clutching boldly at a retreating man's arm, he begs for an answer. Desperate at being restrained, the man strikes the Youth with his rifle. Henry falls. His legs seem "to die." In a ritual not unlike that of Conklin's dying (it is Henry's "youth," his immature self dying), he grabs at the grass, he twists and lurches, he fights "an intense battle with his body." Then, he goes "tall soldier fashion." In his exaltation, he is afraid to touch his head lest he disturb his "red badge of courage." He relishes "the cool, liquid feeling," which evokes the memory of "certain meals his mother had cooked," "the bank of a shaded pool," "the melody in the wind of youthful summer." The association of blood with that of food suggests the identical function of each. Just as food is nourishment to the body, so blood is nourishment to his spiritual and moral self. Because the monster has "eaten" of him and thus destroyed his fears, he has achieved a moral and spiritual maturity, even, as his going "tall" implies, sexual potency. He feels the tranquility and harmony that has always characterized his dream state. But his wound is an actual fact, and the achieved atonement is not quite the same as in a "pure" dream state. Yet it is still achieved under the ægis of "dusk," and can only be fully realized in the full "light" of group identification.

Henry is further assisted in his transformation by an "unseen guide." Wandering in the darkness, he is overtaken by the Cheery Man, whose voice, possessing a "wand of a magic kind," guides him to his regiment. Thinking of him later, Henry recalls that "he had not once seen his face."

It is important to note here what part food and eating play in Henry's atonement and rebirth. As we have seen, food has both physical and spiritual significance. From the first, Henry has observed that "eating" was of greatest importance to the soldiers. After the Tall Soldier's death, he has speculated on "what those men had eaten that they could be in such haste to force their way to grim chances of death." Now, he discovers that he has "a scorching thirst," a hunger that is "more powerful than a direct hunger." He is desperately tired. He cannot see distinctly. He feels the need "of food and rest, at whatever cost." On seeing his comrades again, he goes directly towards the "red light"—symbol of group energy. They fuss over his wound and give him a canteen of coffee. As he swallows the "delicious draught," the mixture feels as cool to him as did the wound. He feels like an "exhausted soldier after a feast of war." He has tasted of and been eaten by the great monster. By the wound (the being eaten), he has atoned for his guilt with blood. In eating and drinking with his comrades (the communal feasting), he has achieved both literal and spiritual identification with the group. Through his initiation, he has returned as a "member," not an isolated individual. By "swallowing or being swallowed," he has, through atonement and re-birth, come to be master of himself and, henceforth, to be master of others. The Loud Soldier gives up his blankets, and Henry is, in sleep, soon "like his comrades."

In the language of myth, Henry has become a hero. When he awakes next morning from a "thousand years'" sleep, he finds, like Rip Van Winkle, a new "unexpected world." What he discovers has happened to the Loud Soldier is actually the same change that has come over him. For the first time Henry is aware that others have been wrestling with problems not unlike his own. If the Loud Soldier is now a man of reliance, a man of "purpose and abilities," Henry perceives in imagery that recalls the "blossoming campfires" of his comrades that

a faith in himself had secretly blossomed. There was a little flower of confidence growing within him. He was a man of experience.

Again like the Loud Soldier, he has at last

overcome obstacles which he admitted to be mountainous. They had fallen like paper peaks, and he was now what he called a hero. He had not been aware of the process. He had slept and, awakening, found himself a knight.

Having overcome the obstacle of self, Henry has at last discovered that the dragon war is, after all, only a gigantic guard of the great death.

If the hero is to fulfill the total requirements of his role, he must bring back into the normal world of day the wisdom that he has acquired during his transformation. Like the "knight" that he is, Henry is now able to face the red and black dragons on the "clear" field of battle. He performs like a "pagan who defends his religion," a "barbarian," "a beast." As the regiment moves forward, Henry is "unconsciously in advance." Although many men shield their eyes, he looks squarely ahead. What he sees "in the new appearance of the landscape" is like "a revelation." There is both a clarity of vision and of perception: the darkness of the landscape has vanished; the blindness of his mental insight has passed. As with the wound and the coffee, he feels the "delirium that encounters despair and death." He has, perhaps, in this "temporary but sublime absence of selfishness," found the reason for being there after all. As the pace quickly "eats up the energies of the men," they dance and gyrate "like savages." Without regard for self, Henry spurs them forward towards the colors.

In the language of myth, it is woman who represents the totality of what can be known. As "life," she embodies both love and hate. To accept her is to be king, the incarnate god, of her created world. As knower (one who recognizes her), the hero is master. Meeting the goddess and winning her is the final test of the hero's talent. Curiously, it is the flag that occupies the position of goddess in the story. The flag is the lure, the beautiful maiden of the configuration, whose capture is necessary if Henry is to fulfill his role as hero. Crane writes:

> With [Henry], as he hurled himself forward, was born a love, a despairing fondness of this flag which was near him. It was a creation of beauty and invulnerability. It was a goddess, radiant, that bended its form with an imperious gesture to him. It was a woman, red and white, hating and loving, that called him with the voice of his hope. Because no harm could come to it he endowed it with power. He kept near, as if it could be a saver of lives, and an imploring cry went from his mind.

As Henry and his comrade wrench the pole from the dead bearer, they both acquire an invincible wand of hope and power. Taking it roughly from his friend, Henry has, indeed, reached heroic proportions.

In his role as hero, Henry stands "erect and tranquil" in face of the great monster. Having "rid himself of the red sickness of battle," having overcome his fear of losing individual identity, he now despises the "brass and bombast of his earlier gospels." Because he is at-one with his comrades, he has acquired their "daring spirit of a savage religion-mad," their "brute" strength to endure the violence of a violent world, the "red of blood and black of passion." His individual strength is their collective strength, that strength of the totality which the flag symbolizes. As Crane says:

> He felt a quiet manhood, nonassertive but of sturdy and strong blood. He knew that he would no more quail before his guides wherever they should point. He had been to touch the great death, and found that, after all, it was but the great death. He was a man.

At last he has put the "somber phantom" of his desertion at a distance. Having emerged into the "golden ray of sun," Henry feels a "store of assurance."

Following the general pattern of myth with peculiar individual variations, Crane has shown how the moral and spiritual strength of the individual springs from the group, and how, through the identification of self with group, the individual can be "reborn in identity with the whole meaning of the universe." Just as his would-be hero was able to overcome his fears and achieve a new moral and spiritual existence, so all men can come to face life, face it as calmly and as coolly as one faces the terrors, the odd beings, the deluding images of dreams. If it is, as Campbell points out, the "unconscious" which supplies the "keys that open the whole realm of the desired and feared adventures of the discovery of self," then man, to discover self, must translate his dreams into actuality. To say that Henry accomplishes his purpose is not to imply that Crane himself achieved the same kind of integration. Whatever the final irony implied, he certainly saw that the discovery of self was essential to building the "bolder, cleaner, more spacious, and fully human life."

University of Kansas City Review, XIX (1953), 249–256. The reference notes have been omitted.

SYMBOLISM OF THE CYCLICAL MYTH IN
ENDYMION

Robert Harrison

The Genius of Poetry must work out its own salvation in a man : It cannot be matured by law and precept, but by sensation & watchfulness in itself. That which is creative must create itself—In Endymion, I leapt headlong into the Sea, and thereby have become better acquainted with the Soundings, the quicksands, & the rocks, than if I had stayed upon the green shore, and piped a silly pipe, and took tea & comfortable advice. (Letter to Hessey, Oct. 9, 1818)

In an explication of *Endymion*, one of the first problems the critic must face is that of structure. He must explain (or explain away) the book-divisions of the poem. For obvious reasons, the latter alternative is easier both to propose and to defend; one need only assert, "His mind was like a pack of scattered cards," and thereby put an end to the questioning. One may contend that in each of the four books Keats merely tallied up his thousand lines as per schedule, put up his pen, and called it a day. This argument, by offering nothing, risks nothing. To say that *Endymion* is nothing more than a more or less poetical accumulation of 4000 lines is to evade the poem itself; it is to deny its existence. Because *Endymion* is, it is something, and moreover it is something meaningful. There are no psychic accidents, no "just as wells." Even nothing is significant psychologically, because it represents the absence of *something*.

On the other hand, critics who have tried to point out the significance of the poem have been compelled at the outset to defend its structural divisions as meaningful. And this has been their first stumbling block. Claude Lee Finney, for example, in claiming that each book of *Endymion* corresponds to a stage of the "Pleasure Thermometer," is forced to locate the Cave of Quietude somewhere in the domain of spiritual (Neo-Platonic) love. And Middleton Murry, while avoiding the pitfalls of such a Procrustean interpretation by confining his arguments to the most general terms, must move by leaps from one "significant passage" to the next and thereby ignore a great deal of the poem.[1]

Interpretations such as those of Finney and Newell Ford may be strained and unnatural, insofar as the meaning of the poem is concerned, but they are attempts at analysis.[2] James Caldwell and E. C. Pettet have done thoroughgoing jobs of pointing out the flaws in a Neo-Platonic interpretation of *Endymion*, but each of them offers in its place a variation of the "pack of scattered cards" argument.[3] They have demonstrated a greater interest in explicating the state of Keats's mind at the time he wrote

1. Claude Lee Finney, *The Evolution of Keats's Poetry* (2 vols., Cambridge: Harvard University Press, 1936); John Middleton Murry, *Keats* (New York: Noonday Press, 1955).
2. Newell Ford, *The Prefigurative Imagination of John Keats* (Stanford: Stanford University Press, 1951).
3. James R. Caldwell, *John Keats' Fancy* (Ithaca: Cornell University Press, 1945); E. C. Pettet, *On the Poetry of Keats* (Cambridge: Cambridge University Press, 1957).

Endymion than in explicating the poem itself. And their arguments are formidable—as far as they go. In criticizing Finney's analysis, Caldwell points out that *Endymion* reflects not the consistent metaphor of an allegory, but rather the "personal symbolizing of a dream."[4] Then he veers away to suggest that Keats was consciously writing poetry of the unconscious, in accordance with the theory of the association of ideas. Pettet shows us how a poem such as *Endymion* could have been written by a man such as Keats. In other words, both Pettet and Caldwell have presented valuable commentary on the psychic and physical forces which made it possible for Keats to write *Endymion* instead of, say, *Howl*. But a shift of interest from the poet to the poem is desirable—some explanation of what the poem is, rather than why it was.

This is what Ford and Finney have tried to do, with regrettable insistence on "divine essences" and the like. But regardless of their errors in interpretation, their method is praiseworthy. The poem must be examined as an artistic entity as well as a projection of the man John Keats.

And the first step is to look for a thematic function in the structure of the poem. Assuming that Caldwell is correct in stating that *Endymion* reflects (in a sense) the "personal symbolizing of a dream," we must now ask: What is the personal symbolizing of a dream, and how personal are dream symbols?

In *The Hero with a Thousand Faces* Campbell defines a dream as "personalized myth," and goes on to say that "both myth and dream are symbolic in the same general way of the dynamics of the psyche."[5] And a step further: if we accept the inverse of Campbell's statement, that myth is generalized or universal dream which uses the same symbols for the same ends, we should expect to find some sort of correlation between the "personalized" symbols in *Endymion* and the generalized, unspecified symbols of mythology. The link here may be found in Carl Jung's theory of the "collective dream." In the collective dream certain archetypal symbols appear as predispositions in the mind which arrange the material of the unconscious in identifiable patterns.[6] These archetypal symbols pervade mythology, and their patterns show an amazing consistency of recurrence. The cosmogonic cycles of the Hindus and the Aztecs, the descent of such heroes as Jonah, Heracles, and the Eskimo trickster, Raven, into the belly of a whale—all these show similarities that can hardly be explained by any theory of *Völkerwanderung*.

One of the archetypal patterns of mythology is that of the cyclical myth. It recurs in religion, in fairy tales, in epics diverse as the *Aeneid* and the Welsh legend of Gurion Bach. The cyclical myth may be described as a spiralling motion in which the hero experiences a descent (*kathodos*) and an ascent (*anodos*), emerging not at the point of outset, but at a higher level. The basic movements in this eccentric circle are: the Call to the Quest (for it is a quest, though not a Neo-Platonic one), Acceptance and Descent into the Underworld (time of trials), Fulfilment of the Quest, and Return, often apotheosized by some sort of sacred marriage.

I intend to show that each book of *Endymion* corresponds to a stage or movement

---

4. Caldwell, *Keats' Fancy*, p. 124.
5. Joseph Campbell, *The Hero with a Thousand Faces* (New York: Meridian, 1956), p. 19.
6. Carl G. Jung, *Symbols of Transformation* (New York: Pantheon, 1956), p. 102.

of the cyclical myth, and to suggest that Keats's headlong leap into the sea, with its quicksands and rocks, may refer to something more than technical experimentation in a new poetical form.

I. THE CALL TO THE QUEST

Keats moves leisurely into the poem, beginning with a formal induction in which he states his relationship to it (the "thing of beauty" is the poem itself) and his purpose in writing it. Then he sets the scene—and immediately an ominous note is struck.[7] We find Mount Latmos described as a land of "gloomy shades, sequestered deep, / Where no man went," (67–68) a place where lambs often disappear, never to be seen again. The countryside is beautiful, to be sure, but not with the lush, domesticated beauty of a Palma Vecchio landscape. It is rather a beauty of light and shadow, of pleasure and terror, and in it we see more than a little of the sinister beauty of Dante's dusky wood. And rightly so, for the topography must prepare us for the descent of the hero.

But before the hero appears, before any movement takes place, we are introduced to Pan through his votaries. Since Pan forms a sort of anagogical backdrop to the first book, giving to it a textural framework, some explanation of his significance must be attempted. First, his rôle as a fertility god cannot be overemphasized. Keats's description of the procession is packed with fertility imagery: milk-white vase, lilies, Leda's love, boar-spear, prickly furze budding lavish gold, cup of honey—and almost every word in the hymn to Pan indicates that he is to be regarded as the sponsor of generation. But he is also the "strange ministrant of undescribed sounds" (285) and "Dread opener of the mysterious doors / Leading to universal knowledge." (288–289) Here Pan assumes another level of meaning; he guards the doors to knowledge beyond nature, and in this capacity he is the "lodge / For solitary thinkings; such as dodge / Conception to the very bourne of heaven." (293–295) His body (the pine) unites the dome of heaven with the four corners of earth, thus squaring the mystical circle; he is the link to the collective unconscious, but he is also the protecting deity whose duty it is to shield its intolerable knowledge from the uninitiated; his votaries wisely and humbly make no effort to venture beyond him.[8] They acknowledge their place in nature (the conscious); the wonders of nature are the uttermost bound of their comprehension; they desire no more, for no more has been made visible to them. Endymion alone has been summoned to the quest, and he alone cannot be satisfied with Pan.

This is made quite clear in the assembly of the shepherds. One by one they rehearse their conceptions of the afterlife; one speaks of reunion with his "quick gone love" (375), another with his "rosy child" (379), one with "fellow huntsmen" (386) and so on—except for Endymion, who sits motionless with grief. For he has been permitted a glance into that universe beyond (or within) Pan, a universe unknown to his companions. The world can no longer please him.

7. *The Poetical Works of John Keats*, ed. H. W. Garrod (London: Oxford University Press, 1956), p. 63. Hereafter, numbers in parentheses will indicate line numbers in this text.
8. Campbell, *The Hero*, p. 81.

Soon Peona appears and leads him away to a "bowery island," (428) where she lulls him to sleep. Certain actions and images may be observed here which explain Peona's rôle and suggest relationships of which Keats himself may have been unaware. She persuades him to suffer "A yielding up, a cradling on her care," (411) she leads him away "like some midnight spirit nurse," (413) "guarding his forehead," (416) to a shallop which "lightly dipt, and rose, and sank, / And dipt again, with the young couple's weight." (425-426) She steers toward a bowery island, where she "him laid / Under her favourite bower's quiet shade, / On her own couch." (436-438) It should be obvious by now that Peona is more than a sister to Endymion; her meaning is not yet fully apparent, for it expands later in the poem and is augmented by the appearance of Phoebe and the Indian Maid. But for the moment we can say that Peona is a mother-image, and that as Endymion's protectress she tries to dissuade him from leaving her "bower" and setting forth on his quest. She has led him to an arbor "overwove / By many a summer's silent fingering" (431-432) and lulled him into a Lethean sleep. Although "bower" is a slippery image in Keats's poetry, it is safe to assume that it is never wholly distinct from the womb.

Endymion's dream (453-464) links him temporarily with the Lotus Eaters and escape. Here his frequent napping may be seen as a regression to the infantile ego. Endymion is sealed in by the walls of childhood; the parent-image (here Peona) stands as a threshold guardian, blocking his way to the quest in the same manner that Pan insulates humanity in general.

And for the moment Peona is successful. Endymion responds to her lullaby—the comparison with "Dryope's lone lulling of her child" (495) is apt—but he cannot forget the call. He tells her of his dream in the bed of poppies.

Under the opiate influence of the magical poppies Endymion has been given a preview of his quest. Phoebe appeared to him in forms celestial and terrestrial, conveyed him briefly through the heavens and then to the underworld, allowed him to sample the ultimate consummation. But then he fell into a dreamless sleep and awoke to the sound of "Faint fare-thee-wells" (690) and

> all the pleasant hues
> Of heaven and earth had faded: deepest shades
> Were deepest dungeons; heaths and sunny glades
> Were full of pestilent light; our taintless rills
> Seem'd sooty, and o'er-spread with upturn'd gills
> Of dying fish; the vermeil rose had blown
> In frightful scarlet, and its thorns out-grown
> Like spiked aloe. (691-698)

Campbell points out that this is a normal result of refusing the call to the quest:

Often in actual life, and not infrequently in the myths and popular tales, we encounter the dull case of the call unanswered; for it is always possible to turn the ear to other interests. Refusal of the summons converts the adventure into its negative. Walled in boredom, hard work, or "culture," the subject loses the power of significant affirmative action and becomes a victim to be saved. His flowering world becomes a wasteland of dry stones and his life feels meaningless.[9]

And from another source:

> Because I have called and ye refused ... I also will laugh at your calamity; I will mock when your fear cometh; when your fear cometh as desolation, and when your destruction cometh as a whirlwind; when distress and anguish cometh upon you. (Proverbs I. 24–27)

Peona, in her rôle of protectress, casts about for some way to prevent Endymion from setting out on his quest. She thinks to herself, "*Shame | On this poor weakness!*" (717–718) and tells him with maternal chiding

> how light
> Must dreams themselves be; seeing they're more slight
> Than the mere nothing that engenders them! (754–756)

Although Endymion gives in for the moment, he finally manages to shake free from the restraining hand of Peona and express the theme of the quest. He has always wanted material glory, but now he sees that "there are / Richer entanglements, enthralments far / More self-destroying." (797–799) Intuitively he has grasped the essential meaning of the quest; it is to be a voyage into self-destruction, into dissolution of the conscious trappings of identity and geography and time, and its goal is yet "A hope beyond the shadow of a dream." (857)

Endymion's second dream vision presents the formal challenge to the quest. He is in a "deep hollow" (864) where vestal primroses grow in the "gaps and slits / In a mossy stone" (876–877) and where he would "bubble up the water through a reed." (880) The imagery here hardly requires commentary. He sees the Cupid cloud (889) and follows it to the well in which he sees Phoebe's face.

Quite often the call to the quest is seen as an apparent blunder, the accident of a dream. But there are no accidents in dreams. And once the gauntlet is dropped, there can be no peace for the hero until he takes it up. As Campbell says,

> Whether dream or myth, in these adventures there is an atmosphere of irresistible fascination about the figure that appears suddenly as guide, marking a new period, a new stage, in the biography. That which has to be faced, and is somehow profoundly familiar to the unconscious—though unknown, surprising, and even frightening to the conscious personality—makes itself known; and what formerly was meaningful may become strangely emptied of value ... Thereafter, even though the hero returns for a while to his familiar occupations, they may be found unfruitful. A series of signs of increasing force then will become visible until ... the summons can no longer be denied.[10]

9. Campbell, *The Hero*, p. 59.
10. Campbell, *The Hero*, pp. 55–56.

II. ACCEPTANCE AND DESCENT

Once having traversed the threshold, the hero moves in a dream landscape of curiously fluid, ambiguous forms, where he must survive a succession of trials. This is a favorite phase of the myth-adventure. It has produced a world literature of miraculous tests and ordeals. The hero is covertly aided by the advice, amulets and secret agents of the supernatural helper whom he met before his entrance into this region. Or it may be that he here discovers for the first time that there is a benign power everywhere supporting him in his superhuman passage. (Campbell, p. 97)

Keats opens Book II with an expository declaration of the quest theme. We may note here that each book of *Endymion* is introduced by a non-dramatic statement by Keats *qua* poet on the subject of the poem itself. There is something of the "camera eye" technique in these introductory commentaries; in each of the books the movement is from exposition to narration, from thought to feeling, from external observation to intuition.

In line 44 we return to the narrative body of the poem. Endymion, sitting "by a shady spring, / And elbow-deep with feverous fingering / Stems the upbursting cold." (53–55) A butterfly appears (the butterfly, normally symbolic of the psyche, is here his mystagogue) and conducts him to "a splashing fountain's side . . . near a cavern's mouth." (84–85) It may be observed in passing that the recurrent image of the fountain in *Endymion* is closely related to the World Omphalos, the symbol of continuous creation, the mystery of the maintenance of the world through the miracle of regeneration.[11] Thus the fountain-image is, in one sense, an emanation of Pan. But it is also the vehicle of Endymion's quest and the link between Pheobe and the Indian Maid.

The butterfly suddenly becomes a nymph, and amid a mélange of erotic imagery (lilies, crystal coffer, shells, pearly cup) she announces the challenge, telling Endymion:

> on this day
> I've been thy guide; that thou must wander far
> In other regions, past the scanty bar
> To mortal steps, before thou cans't be ta'en
> From every wasting sigh, from every pain,
> Into the gentle bosom of thy love. (122–127)

Endymion, still undecided, ponders the challenge for a moment, then accepts it:

> I can see
> Naught earthly worth my compassing; so stand
> Upon a misty, jutting head of land—
> Alone? No, no; and by the Orphean lute,
> When mad Eurydice is listening to't;

11. Campbell, *The Hero*, pp. 40–46.

I'd rather stand upon this misty peak,
With not a thing to sigh for, or to seek,
But the soft shadow of my thrice-seen love,
Than be—I care not what. (161–169)

The challenge formally accepted, Endymion now receives his instructions. A voice from the cavern thunders out "Descend, / Young mountaineer!" (202–203) and counsels him to boldness. "He ne'er is crown'd / With immortality, who fears to follow / Where airy voices lead: so through the hollow, / The silent mysteries of earth, descend!" (211–214)

At this point, according to Pettet, Endymion succumbs temporarily to the death-wish. In a sense this is true, but a comparison with the themes of the *Fall of Hyperion* and *Hyperion* suggests that Endymion's death-wish is no simple yearning for oblivion, but rather a death-wish in that he will die into life; by passing through the "hollow" (womb) he will unite the conscious with the unconscious and become a part of both worlds. As Endymion said in Book I, the chief intensity may be gained only through a process of self-destruction. Compare with this the statement of Ananda Coomaraswamy: "No creature can attain a higher grade of nature without ceasing to exist."[12] and Jung: "That the highest summit of life can be expressed through the symbolism of death is a well-known fact, for any growing beyond oneself means death."[13]

So Endymion, to avoid madness, accepts the challenge and dives into the underworld. It is a strange, fabulous world—gloomy, bejewelled, with paths outshooting like meteorites, angry lightnings, silver grottos, floods of crystal—and here are all the things he has seen and known all his life, but they are now transfigured; i.e., the "mimic temple, so complete and true / In sacred custom, that he well nigh fear'd / To search it inwards." (257–259) This is the realm of the collective unconscious, wherein are hoarded all the rejected or undeveloped elements of Endymion's mind. As Campbell points out:

> The unconscious sends all sort of vapors, odd beings, terrors, and deluding images up into the mind—whether in dream, broad daylight, or insanity; for the human kingdom, beneath the floor of the comparatively neat little dwelling that we call our consciousness, goes down into unsuspected Aladdin caves. There not only jewels but also dangerous jinn abide; the inconvenient or resisted psychological powers that we have not thought or dared to integrate into our lives . . . They are fiendishly fascinating too, for they carry keys that open the whole realm of the desired and feared adventure of the discovery of the self. Destruction of the world that we have built and in which we live, and of ourselves within it; but then a wonderful reconstruction, of the bolder, cleaner, more spacious, and fully human life—that is the lure, the promise and terror, of these disturbing night visitants from the mythological realm that we carry within.[14]

The impact of the underworld on Endymion has been great, but still not great enough

12. As quoted in Campbell, *The Hero*, p. 92.
13. As quoted in Campbell, *The Hero*, p. 285.
14. Campbell, *The Hero*, p. 8.

to jar him free from his tenacious ego. Consciousness gradually returns (275) and with it the "fog-born elf" (277) of selfhood. But the first step has been taken, although he does not yet recognize its significance: the challenge has been accepted and, since Endymion is pre-eminently hero-material, success will come with time.

But for the present, Endymion must experience what Jung calls the "perils of the soul." Bewildered and unable to cope with the overwhelming recognition of the collective unconscious, he returns to the shrine of Diana (his link with the world of nature and consciousness) and complains of his solitude, of the breaking of the cord which has bound him to the earth and nature. He is not yet fully prepared for a direct revelation of the collective unconscious:

> Within my breast there lives a choking flame—
> O let me cool't the zephyr-boughs among!
> A homeward fever parches up my tongue—
> O let me slake it at the running springs! (317–320)
> Deliver me from this rapacious deep! (332)

And suddenly his prayer is granted; magic flowers spring up through the slabs (cf. Book I, l. 900, where the same boon is granted) and offer Endymion temporary respite, giving him a "flowery wreath" with which to bind himself to earth. And before long another mystagogue appears and leads him to the myrtle-walled chamber of Adonis. In Adonis, Endymion meets the successful Grail Knight. As a cherub announces,

> For 'tis the nicest touch of human honour,
> When some ethereal and high-favouring donor
> Presents immortal bowers to mortal sense. (436–438)

Maternal fertility associations are here almost overpowering: intertwined tendrils, ivy mesh with its Ethiop berries, the bugle-blooms of woodbine, convolvulus in streaked vases—every image in the bower of Adonis pertains to rebirth. But perhaps the most impressive of these is the coronal above Adonis' head: four lily stalks joined. In addition to the obvious sexual connotation, the concentric quaternity is a *mandala*, a symbol recognized as representative of order forged from chaos and the individuated self (the "complete man"). Thus Venus and Adonis evidently form an image of perfection—the ultimate boon of the psyche (Venus) linked to continuous creation (Adonis). Here then are the chief deities in the realm of Pan.[15]

Encouraged by the hopeful words of Venus, Endymion sets out on the quest once again and walks along the banks of a subterranean stream where, apparently by accident, he dips his spear into the water, and at the splash

> those spouting columns rose
> Sudden a poplar's height, and 'gan to enclose
> His diamond path with fretwork, streaming round
> Alive, and dazzling cool, and with a sound,
> Haply, like dolphin tumults. (606–610)

15. Jung, *Symbols of Transformation*, p. 433.

Here, for the first time, we see that Endymion is no mere mortal; he is capable of performing a gratuitous act of creation. And the act itself is significant in showing the intimate relationship between water and creativity.

But lest Endymion become vain in his new-won gift, and experience the bliss of the apotheosis without learning its sorrow, he is shown the terrible spectre of Cybele; as Pettet remarks, Keats probably realized that Cybele was a goddess of fertility connected with spring festivals, and that her lover, Attis, was a god of vegetation.[16] Here then is the obverse of the medal: Cybele and Attis are the opposite numbers of Venus and Adonis. It is essential that Endymion learn through Cybele the dark side of the mother-goddess. So, for the time, he dips into a bower of asphodel, where sleep finally rescues him.

Endymion's dream in the jasmine bower is a prothalamium to his union with the goddess. The imagery here suggests (as it must, to be true to the psychological implications of rebirth) that Phoebe is a composite female figure or *anima*. She is to Endymion mother, sister, mistress, and bride. She is Venus, Brynhild, Dornröschen, the fairy godmother—but at the same time she is also Cybele, La Belle Dame Sans Merci, Lamia, the old sow that eats her farrow.

Endymion does not realize this. In her present emanation she is a queenly lover who gives herself to him and promises to instruct him in "Lispings empyrean"; (819) he does not hear her allusion to the opposites that she represents. (823–824) When Endymion wakes up from his dream in the jasmine bower, he has passed beyond violence; he is now nearing that supreme control that will be necessary if he is to survive the knowledge of the Cave of Quietude, where he is to pass into the body of the mother. He pauses in a grotto of "fish-semblances" (884)—no longer the "up-turn'd gills of dying fish" since he has accepted the quest—and thinks back on his earlier life. He realizes that a transformation is taking place, that he can never return to the same identity. So with doubt and trembling, he devotes himself to the quest once more:

> How long must I remain in jeopardy
> Of blank amazements that amaze no more?
> Now I have tasted her sweet soul to the core
> All other depths are shallow: essences,
> Once spiritual, are like muddy lees. (902–906)

When Alpheus and Arethusa glide by he speaks to his mystagogue, interceding on behalf of the twin springs—and immediately he is removed from the earth once more and sees "the giant sea above his head." (1023) Here the elements of creativity and transformation are united, and here Endymion is to fulfil his quest.

III. THE QUEST FULFILLED

After the opening diatribe on the assumptions of mundane power and ambition, Keats addresses Phoebe and definitely identifies her as the lady of the quest. She is the

16. Here we see the disastrous aspect of reunion with the mother-image. As the son/lover of Cybele, Attis was driven mad and forced to castrate himself in penance for having broken the incest-taboo.

creative principle, for her "silver lip" (56) kisses dead things to life and she is the reason for Endymion's journey. "Wherever beauty dwells . . . thou pointest out the way, and straight 'tis won." (93, 96) We know now that Endymion is to be a successful quester—but first he must prove himself. He wanders over the ocean floor, in the hollow vast of

> Old rusted anchors, helmets, breast-plates large
> Of gone sea-warriors; brazen breaks and targe;
> Rudders that for a hundred years had lost
> The sway of human hand; gold vase emboss'd
> With long-forgotten story. (123–127)

These images dredged up from the collective unconscious fill Endymion with awe but, aided by Diana, he moves on toward his goal. As Nietzsche has observed:

> In sleep and in dreams we pass through the whole thought of earlier humanity . . . What I mean is this: as man now reasons in dreams, so humanity also reasoned for many thousands of years when awake; the first cause which occurred to the mind as an explanation of anything that requires explanation was sufficient and passed for truth . . . This atavistic element in man's nature still manifests itself in our dreams, for it is the foundation upon which the higher reason had developed and still develops in every individual.[17]

In the hymn to Phoebe, Endymion reveals that she is identified with every object of his desire; she has always been his patroness and the author of his existence—"in my boyhood, every joy and pain / By thee were fashion'd to the self-same end." (160–161) He knows now that he was born to the quest.

Soon the final test is offered to Endymion: he meets Glaucus, and now he must consummate his new-won power.

In Glaucus we encounter once more a stock figure of the cyclical myth pattern. Pettet hints at his identity, but errs in assuming him to be parallel to Adonis and Attis.[18] We must not forget the words of the cherub: "'Tis the nicest touch of human honour, when some ethereal and high-favouring donor presents immortal bowers to mortal sense." Attis and Adonis have achieved (to opposite ends, of course) the supreme boon, the sacred marriage. Glaucus, on the other hand, has met with total failure. He is the unsuccessful Grail Knight, the fisher-king; like his counterparts in other myths, he is a sterile, impotent old man; frequently, like Tiresias, he is androgynous. Through some fault in his character he has failed to elude one of the many pitfalls on the journey. Like the unsuccessful suitors of Dornröschen, Glaucus has fallen through a lack of recognition: he has failed to recognize and avoid the perils of Circe. Like Tiresias and the unfortunate Sibyl, he knows everything and can do nothing; he must be rescued by the hero. As he points out, Endymion has been sent here "for great enfranchisement" (299)—by virtue of the creative power which is his, he can restore life to all the victims of love.

---

17. *Human, All-Too-Human*, tr. H. Zimmern (New York: Macmillan, 1909), I, 23, 25.
18. Pettet, *On the Poetry of Keats*, p. 183.

In the story of Glaucus' misadventures we see once more the significance of water. Glaucus was a child of the sea; dolphins were his playmates, and sea-monsters his companions. Then as he matured he felt the summons to the quest and "plung'd for life or death." (380) He deserted the safety of his watery paradise (childhood) and pursued Scylla, his Phoebe. But, despairing too soon at her reluctance to submit, he tried to win her by unfair means, by securing the aid of Circe. And this was his downfall. For Circe, who is symbolic of both the love-death and the eternal round of womb and tomb, charmed him and took him as her lover. So instead of ascending to the ultimate boon of the quest, Glaucus found its opposite in the service of Circe— bestiality. Unable to face the grotesqueries of Circe's hell, he tried to flee, but was caught and doomed to a thousand years of life-in-death. Glaucus' tragic flaw has obviously been that of trying to short-cut the necessary hazards of the quest, and his punishment is a millennium of sterility. Scylla (love) is dead to him, and his only hope lies in wisdom and faith; he must store up the bodies of all drowned lovers and await the hero, who will consummate the prophecy of the scroll.

Now Endymion faces the supreme test of his power. In fulfilling the prophecy and becoming a guardian deity of lovers, he makes himself eligible to receive the love of Phoebe. As Campbell says, "The effect of the successful adventure of the hero is the unlocking and release again of the flow of life into the body of the world."[19] Through a symbolic ritual he enacts the death of Glaucus and his subsequent rebirth, now purged of the flaw which made him yield to Circe; then, in like manner, Endymion restores all the drowned lovers.

The rest of Book III points toward the assumption of Endymion. Here love and creation are united—Venus and Cupid are together with Neptune in his sea-palace. Once again Venus has words of good cheer for Endymion; she says that he is progressing nicely, although he has "not yet / Escap'd from dull mortality's harsh net," (906–907) and she hints that fulfillment is not far away. The love-feast in Neptune's palace continues with hymns to the trinity of love—Neptune, Venus, and Cupid. Then the Titans arrive and Endymion faints; he has not yet achieved the equanimity of a god, and the sight of them is too much for him. But in his dream Phoebe tells him he has succeeded in the quest. He has proved himself. "'Tis done— / Immortal bliss for me too hast thou won." (1023–1024)

Now, like Adonis, he is to be a god of love and generation, a seasonal lover of Phoebe.

IV. APOTHEOSIS AND RETURN

Of the four books of *Endymion*, the final one is both the most difficult to reconcile with the general scheme of the poem and the most interesting because of the indecision and conflict that it reveals. All the elements of the cyclical myth are present, but they are no longer linked in a single-minded progression toward apotheosis of the hero and his triumphant return to humanity. Campbell outlines the final movement of the heroic cycle as

19. Campbell, *The Hero*, p. 40.

the return and reintegration with society, which is indispensable to the continuous circulation of spiritual energy into the world and . . . is the justification of the long retreat.[20]

At this stage in the myth the hero has died as an individual, but as eternal man—timeless, unspecified, universal man—he is reborn. And his final task is to return to the earth with the life-giving boon of his knowledge and teach to mankind the lesson he has learned. But in Book IV we are confronted with a puzzling diversion: the Indian Maid. Almost incongruously she disturbs the normal flow of the narrative, the assumption of Endymion and his return as a transfigured mortal. At first we might take her to be the familiar figure of the temptress, an equivalent of Circe; we might expect her to stand as a stumbling block in the hero's path. But it soon becomes apparent that she is not a demonic counterpart to Phoebe. Indeed, she differs from Phoebe more through an abundance of humanity than through a lack of spirituality. She is pre-eminently desirable, but since she is in competition with Phoebe for the love of Endymion, she must somehow represent an antithesis to the boon of divine love, i.e., the death of the spirit. Endymion identifies her with the death-wish: "Thou art my executioner" (111) and "dying I shall kiss thy lily hand." (118) He feels that to love her is to give himself up to oblivion.

In the usual pattern of the cyclical myth, the rôle of the Indian Maid would be played by the stock figure of the lamia. But she is no lamia; and she is no more carnal than the Phoebe we saw in the jasmine bower. Her only error has been to wander too far from home on a love quest. In order to understand the Indian Maid, we must move from the pattern of the universal myth to the particular; we must acknowledge her as a personal symbol, a symbol somehow suggestive of indecision. The conflicts suggested by the juxtaposition of the Indian Maid and Phoebe are many, but it may be assumed that the Indian Maid is the lesser vehicle. First, she is a mortal and cannot offer Endymion any boon beyond mortal love. Second, she comes to Endymion gratis; he need perform no deeds of valor in order to win her love (in fact, proximity seems to have dictated the whole affair; she would have been quite willing to accept Hyacinthus as a lover, had he been nearby). Third, love for the Indian Maid will inevitably return Endymion to his old station as a shepherd-king, and the spiral of the cyclical myth will flatten into a simple Viconian round.

These are only hints at her meaning. All that must be said here is that she represents a pleasant but infinitely lesser achievement for Endymion than that offered by Phoebe. And Endymion, recognizing this fact, feels that to accept her is to accept sensual oblivion.

At any rate, Endymion sadly gives himself up to her and forsakes the quest. But immediately Phoebe calls him back and sends Mercury to rescue him. Once again he is given a dream-preview of the sacred marriage, and once again he dedicates himself to her. " 'Tis she, / His very goddess: good-bye earth, and sea, / And air, and pains, and care, and suffering; / Good-bye to all but love!" (430–433) But as soon as he wakes, he is once more torn between human and divine love.

20. Campbell, *The Hero*, p. 36.

Then, with no decision reached, Endymion dies.

The Cave of Quietude is a commonplace in the cyclical myth; in one sense it is the kingdom of death, but only that sort of death which presupposes rebirth; in the various levels of consciousness it is the realm of dreamless sleep, beyond grief and joy alike. Here, as we might expect, Endymion experiences his final trial before the sacred marriage and atonement with the goddess; here he should pass beyond the trappings of time and place to understanding; here he should be transformed into a god. Yet there is always the nagging insistence that he is here also to do penance for the Indian Maid.

Then, with the sudden ascension into the empyrean which leads to the bestowal of the boon, Endymion enters into the sacred marriage with Phoebe. Here we expect a long, majestic processional leading up to the ceremony and epithalamium; we expect an expanded and more intense version of the scene in Neptune's palace; we expect hymns and odes to love and, finally, the apocalyptic coronation of Endymion. But there is none.

There is, instead, a sudden break in the narrative; the climax topples before it arrives, and the Indian Maid crowds back onstage. The movement is now personal—for some reason Keats did not allow Endymion to pursue the normal course of the hero, the end toward which the first three books have pointed. Within the space of three lines he is torn from heaven and set down on earth with a jar that "went nigh to kill." (614)

From here on the narrative falters. For better or worse, the Indian Maid has usurped the place of the goddess and Endymion stands impotent, halfway between two worlds. Again he chooses the *Liebestod*:

> Let us aye love each other; let us fare
> On forest-fruits, and never, never go
> Among the abodes of mortals here below,
> Or be by phantoms duped. (626–629)

This is obviously a second choice for Endymion, a nepenthe for his lost goddess. He says regretfully:

> I have clung
> To nothing, lov'd a nothing, nothing seen
> Or felt but a great dream! (636–638)

and he vows to forsake the quest forever. In his declaration to the Indian Maid (624–721) we see a congeries of erotic images formerly associated with the realm of Pan. Endymion has now devoted himself to simple mortality and the life of the senses: "one gentle squeeze, / Warm as a dove's nest among summer trees, / And warm with dew at ooze from living blood!" (665–667) But with a sort of annoying perversity the Indian Maid now admits the sovereignty of Phoebe and refuses Endymion; she has become an agent of the goddess.

Whatever the Indian Maid signified previously, she has now changed for the worse. The logical climax of *Endymion* has been aborted and now Keats is forging mechanically toward an end. And the poem shows it. Keats anticipates the reader's reaction when he says,

> it nigh grieves
> Me to behold thee thus in last extreme. (770–771)

But there are still two hundred lines to go. First Peona is wheeled back in, where she bustles about, planning the wedding of Endymion and the Indian Maid (now estranged). Then in desperation the "spirit-blow / Was struck, and all were dreamers." (899–900) Peona and the Indian Maid drift away. Endymion prepares to die, having given up both divine and worldly goals. The Indian Maid returns, becomes Phoebe, and announces that Endymion has succeeded in the quest and is now a deity. And Peona, like the reader by this time,

> went
> Home through the gloomy wood in wonderment. (1002–1003)

In the last two hundred lines of *Endymion* we find the most cogent argument for reading the poem as a cyclical myth. We see that it is only when the thread of the universal myth is lost, only when Keats begins to write poetry from the top of the head, that the significance vanishes and the symbols become unintelligible and contradictory to all but the psychoanalyst. So long as Keats followed his own precept,

> The Genius of Poetry must work out its own salvation in a man: It cannot be matured by law and precept, but by sensation & watchfulness in itself. That which is creative must create itself,

he was on firm ground. But with the appearance of the Indian Maid the spell is broken and the poem degenerates into a welter of indecision and impotence, rather hastily patched together at the end by an apologetic *dea ex machina*.

Texas Studies in Literature and Language, I (1960), 538–554. Some of the reference notes have been omitted, others modified.

The Critical Analogy

The creative possibilities of analogical thinking are recognized by psychologists, logicians, and many others. On numerous occasions literary criticism has illuminated hitherto unnoticed or misunderstood aspects of a work by using an analogical approach. We attain a new perspective if we think of a Lawrence novel as a dramatic poem, The Waste Land *as a condensed epic, or* The Ox-Bow Incident *as a Platonic dialogue. This is the critical strategy employed in the following group of three essays. By treating the works under consideration as like—but not necessarily identical with—certain classical myths, primitive rites of nature, or fairy tales, Joseph L. Blotner ("Mythic Patterns in To the Lighthouse"), John Lydenberg ("Nature Myth in Faulkner's The Bear"), and Shirley Grob ("Dickens and Some Motifs of the Fairy Tale") simultaneously delineate individual structural features and suggest motifs that can be used in future comparative studies.*

MYTHIC PATTERNS IN *TO THE LIGHTHOUSE*

Joseph L. Blotner

I

The impulses and convictions which gave birth to *Three Guineas* and *A Room of One's Own* carried over into Virginia Woolf's fiction. Their most powerful expression is found in *To the Lighthouse*. But something, probably her strict and demanding artistic conscience, prevented their appearance in the form of the intellectual and argumentative feminism found in the first two books. In this novel Virginia Woolf's concept of woman's role in life is crystallized in the character of Mrs. Ramsay, whose attributes are those of major female figures in pagan myth. The most useful myth for interpreting the novel is that of the Primordial Goddess, who "is threefold in relation to Zeus: mother (Rhea), wife (Demeter), and daughter (Persephone)." One of the major sources of the myth is the Homeric "Hymn to Demeter," in which the poet compares Rhea with her daughter Demeter, and makes it clear that Demeter and her daughter Persephone "are to be thought of as a *double figure*, one half of which is the ideal complement of the other."[1] This double figure is that of the Kore, the primordial maiden, who is also a mother. Also useful in interpreting the novel is the Oedipus myth.

In using myth as an approach to a work of literature, the critic can make one of two assertions: the artist knowingly used myth as a basis for his creation; or, all unaware, he used it as it welled up out of the subconscious layers of his psyche where it resided as forgotten material, as an archetypal pattern or a fragment of the collective or racial unconscious. But one of these assertions leads to a dilemma when it is applied to *To the Lighthouse*, and the other is fundamentally unsound for either fruitful criticism or

1. C. G. Jung and C. Kerényi, *Essays on a Science of Mythology*, trans. R. F. C. Hull (New York: Pantheon, 1949), pp. 25, 152.

243

sound scholarship. First, Virginia Woolf's diary shows that she read Greek, and "On Not Knowing Greek" shows that she venerated it. And, even had she not read Jung, Freud, and Frazer prior to 1927,[2] she would have known about them through other members of the Bloomsbury Group. However, there is no direct evidence that she consciously used myth in the writing of this novel. Therefore, to assert that she did would be only speculation. Second, because of the relatively large number of these patterns as presented by Frazer, Jung, and Freud, and because of the enormous number of variations into which they can be differentiated by particular cultures, one is able to find some sort of referent in them for major elements of many novels. Then, any parallel between the mythic pattern and the work of art, by virtue of invoking the supposedly forgotten, or the archetypal patterns in the artist's unconscious, is argued as sufficient basis for claiming that a causative relationship exists. Virginia Woolf in her diary reiterated the role of her "subconscious" in the germination of a novel and noted "how tremendously important unconsciousness is when one writes." However, this proposition is susceptible of neither proof nor disproof. These myths may well have risen from Virginia Woolf's subconscious to form the framework of her novel, but this can be shown by neither critic nor psychologist. There is, however, a third position. When meaningful, coherent, and illuminating parallels are discerned, the work may be interpreted in terms of the myth. Often what appears fragmentary or only partly disclosed in the work may be revealed as complete and explicit through the myth.

This method is used from the outside, so to speak. It is not an interior approach asserting that myth was present at the conception and execution of the work; it rather asserts that myth may be brought to the work at its reading. It is like laying a colored transparency over a sheet covered with a maze of hues to reveal the orderly pattern which otherwise resides within them unperceived. Thus, in *To the Lighthouse* the myths of Oedipus and the Kore, superimposed momentarily upon the novel, provide a framework within whose boundaries and by virtue of whose spatial ordering the symbolic people, passages, and phrases of the book can be seen to assume a relationship to each other which illuminates their reciprocal functions and meanings. But since one key may open several doors in a house while leaving several more still unlocked, the mythic approach will not be urged as a Rosetta Stone for fathoming all the meanings of *To the Lighthouse*. However, this interpretation has several advantages. It shows that this is not, as has often been asserted, a novel which is poetic but plotless. The poetry is certainly there but so is the plot, if one reads the novel with all its striking parallels against these myths which are so strong in plot. This is not to suggest that Mrs. Woolf is consciously or unconsciously indebted to *The Golden Bough*, Bulfinch's mythology, or the sources of these works for her plot, but rather that the mythic approach helps to show that this novel has in fact a clear and coherent narrative beneath its enchanting poetry and evocative prose. In this interpretation Mrs.

2. *A Writer's Diary: Being Extracts from the Diary of Virginia Woolf*, ed. Leonard Woolf (New York: Harcourt, Brace, 1954). Leonard Woolf, in a recent letter, informs me that he doubts that Virginia Woolf ever read any of Freud's works, but that he (Woolf) had discussed them with her, having read them as he published them in England under the imprint of the Hogarth Press.

Ramsay is not merely Goodness* * *, nor light, spirit, and spell* * *. She is more than this and more than the mainspring of the novel: she is the meaning of the novel. This interpretation also relates this work, Virginia Woolf's finest as an artist, to her fundamental convictions as a woman.

Although it has been suggested that *To the Lighthouse* can be explained in terms of Christian myth, there is much evidence, both external and internal, which argues against this interpretation. Virginia Woolf's agnosticism appears on many pages of her diary. And Christian symbolism is quite as inappropriate for Mrs. Ramsay. When the phrase, "We are in the hands of the Lord," enters her mind, she rejects it: "instantly she was annoyed with herself for saying that. Who had said it? Not she; she had been trapped into saying something she did not mean."[3] This has been "an insincerity slipping in among the truths . . ." (98). The beam from the Lighthouse sweeps over her, "purifying out of existence that lie, any lie" (97). If there is a place in the novel for a male deity, he is not Christ, but Zeus. This deity would appropriately be he, linked with the hidden malevolence Mrs. Ramsay sometimes senses in life, for Zeus was the god who connived with Hades in the abduction of Persephone, and was himself the bridegroom by violence of Demeter.

That Mrs. Woolf's characters are symbolic is quite clear. Mrs. Ramsay and her husband stand watching their children when suddenly a meaning descends upon them, "making them representative . . . made them in the dusk standing, looking, the symbols of marriage, husband and wife" (110–111). But Mrs. Ramsay is a symbol of much more than this. She is a symbol of the female principle in life. Clothed in beauty, an intuitive and fructifying force, she opposes the logical but arid and sterile male principle. Her influence works toward the mating of men and women, toward their becoming fruitful like herself. Her function is the same on the intellectual level, for she gives her protection and inspiration to both art and science. To Lily Briscoe the painter she gives stimulus and understanding; to Carmichael the poet she gives haven from squalor and a shrewish wife; to Ramsay the philosopher she supplies love, comfort, and reassurance; to Tansley the graduate student she offers protection for a personality rubbed raw by insecurity; to Bankes the botanist she renders affection and respite from a widowed life and priestlike devotion to science. "Indeed, she had the whole of the other sex under her protection; for reasons she could not explain . . . finally, for an attitude towards herself which no woman could fail to feel or to find agreeable, something trustful, childlike, reverential . . ." (13).

II

Comparing her feelings upon completing *The Waves* with those she had when she finished *To the Lighthouse*, Virginia Woolf wrote that "What interests me in the last stage was the freedom and boldness with which my imagination picked up, used and tossed aside all the images, symbols *which I had prepared* [italics mine]. I am sure that this is the right way of using them—not in set pieces, as I had tried at first coherently, but simply as images, never making them work out; only suggest. Thus

3. Virginia Woolf, *To the Lighthouse* (New York: Harcourt Brace Modern Classics, 1927), p. 97. The pages from which further quotations are drawn are indicated in the text.

I hope to have kept the sound of the sea and the birds, dawn and garden subconsciously present, doing their work under ground" (*Writer's Diary*, p. 165). This penetrating introspection gives the keynote for interpretation of Virginia Woolf's use of image and symbol. One must not expect a point-for-point correspondence between symbol and referent, and, by implication, no exact parallel between character and plot on the one hand and mythic personage and mythic pattern on the other. However, there are surprisingly strong correspondences between the two.

Rhea was the oldest of the gods, the child of Gaea, Mother Earth, and Ouranos, Father Heaven. When her brother Cronos overthrew Ouranos, Rhea became Cronos' wife and queen of the universe. Since Gaea was not actually a divinity, however, nor ever separated from the earth and personified, her daughter Rhea is the primal pagan goddess antedating the male gods. Although Cronos was said to have brought in the Golden Age in Italy when he fled there from the victorious Zeus, he cuts a poor figure beside Rhea. Having attained power by mutilating and dethroning his father, he attempted to keep it by swallowing his children. This he did with each of the first five Rhea bore him, attempting to thwart the prophecy that one of his children would overthrow him. By contrast, Rhea is the completely good and loving mother. Wrapping a stone in swaddling clothes and substituting it for Zeus, she has the child spirited to Crete. It is he who later delivers his brothers and sisters by forcing Cronos to disgorge them.

Whereas Rhea has six children, three boys and three girls, Mrs. Ramsay has eight, four boys and four girls. Like Cronos, Mr. Ramsay was sometimes "like a lion seeking whom he could devour . . ." (233). He has power and authority: "Let him be fifty feet away, let him not even speak to you, let him not even see you, he permeated, he prevailed, he imposed himself. He changed everything" (233). In each family the youngest child, a male, is the one who opposes the father. Zeus, alone in his exile on Crete, might have reflected like James, "I shall be left to fight the tyrant alone" (250). As Rhea protected Zeus from physical harm, so Mrs. Ramsay tries to guard James from psychological wounds. When Mr. Ramsay declares that the weather will not permit the trip to the Lighthouse which James so passionately desires, Mrs. Ramsay tries to induce her husband to modify his pronouncement. She reflects that children never forget; "she was certain that he was thinking, we are not going to the Lighthouse tomorrow; and she thought, he will remember that all his life" (95).

Mrs. Ramsay has many of the physical attributes of a goddess. To Lily's eyes she seems to wear "an august shape . . ." (80). She has a "royalty of form . . ." (47). Lily perceives that Mr. Bankes "worshipped" Mrs. Ramsay (75). When Mr. Bankes hears her voice, he visualizes her as "very clearly Greek" (47), and feels that "the Graces assembled seemed to have joined hands in meadows of asphodel to compose that face" (47). Augustus Carmichael bows as if to do her "homage" (167). When Charles Tansley glimpses her standing motionless, a picture of Queen Victoria behind her, he realizes that she is "the most beautiful person he had ever seen" (25). He visualizes her "stepping through fields of flowers and taking to her breast buds that had broken and lambs that had fallen; with the stars in her eyes and the wind in her hair . . ." (25). And her glance comes from "eyes of unparalleled depth" (77).

Even as he speaks of prosaic things, "one would be thinking of Greek temples, and how beauty had been with them there in that stuffy room" (291). Even her bearing is regal: "like some queen who, finding her people gathered in the hall, looks down upon them, and descends among them, and acknowledges their tributes silently, and accepts their devotion and their prostration before her ... she went down, and crossed the hall and bowed her head very slightly, as if she accepted what they could not say: their tribute to her beauty" (124).

Mrs. Ramsay's psychic qualities are also those of a goddess. She is possessed of an intuitive knowledge and wisdom, and exercises a dominion over those around her, seeming almost to cast a spell upon them. Lily Briscoe, particularly sensitive to this aspect of her character, struggles with ambivalent feelings. She sees Mrs. Ramsay as "unquestionably the loveliest of people ... the best perhaps" (76), yet she chafes at her imperiousness. Lily laughs at her, "presiding with immutable calm over destinies which she completely failed to understand" (78). But at the same time she divines, in the heart of this woman "like treasures in the tombs of kings, tablets bearing sacred inscriptions, which if one could spell them out, would teach one everything ..." (79). When Mrs. Ramsay exercises her powers, her domination, Lily is moved to reflect that "there was something frightening about her. She was irresistible" (125). Her perceptions are clearly psychic: "She knew then—she knew without having learnt. Her simplicity fathomed what clever people falsified. Her singleness of mind made her drop, plumb like a stone, alight exact as a bird, gave her, naturally, this swoop and fall of the spirit upon truth ..." (46). Her grey eyes seem to penetrate the thoughts and feelings of others. Her domination pulls them all together, makes them interact as she wants them to do. But, "directly she went a sort of disintegration set in ..." (168).

III

If Mrs. Ramsay resembles Rhea, she appears almost an incarnation of Demeter. This divine being, the Goddess of the Corn, was the daughter of Cronos and Rhea and the sister of Zeus. But unlike him and the other Olympians, she was, with Dionysus, mankind's best friend. Hers was the divine power which made the earth fruitful. It was she "who was worshipped, not like the other gods by the bloody sacrifices men liked, but in every humble act that made the farm fruitful. Through her the field of grain was hallowed, 'Demeter's holy grain'."[4] Even when the originally simple rites in her honor evolved into the Eleusinian Mysteries, their effect was still beneficent. The quality of these observances survived even the decline of Greece and the rise of Rome, for Cicero wrote that "among the many excellent and indeed divine institutions which ... Athens has brought forth and contributed to human life, none, in my opinion, is better than those mysteries. For by their means we have been brought out of our barbarous and savage mode of life and refined into a state of civilization, and as the rites are called 'initiations,' so in very truth we have learned from them the beginnings of life, and have gained the power not only to live happily, but also to die with a better hope."

Symbols of fruitfulness cluster around Mrs. Ramsay. She plants flowers and sees

4. Edith Hamilton, *Mythology* (Boston: Little, Brown, 1942), p. 54.

that they are tended. The others, thinking of her, associate flowers with her instinctively. She adorns herself with a green shawl. Running throughout the book, through her own stream of consciousness, is an almost obsessive concern that the greenhouse shall be repaired and preserved. Many of the figures of speech used to describe her relate to nature. Concentrating, "she grew still like a tree . . ." (177). In solitary meditation she reflects "how if one was alone, one leant to inanimate things; trees, streams, flowers; felt they expressed one; felt they became one; felt they knew one, in a sense were one . . ." (97). At times she even thinks in terms of myth. Contemplation of a cornucopia-like dish of fruit "made her think of a trophy fetched from the bottom of the sea, of Neptune's banquet, of the bunch that hangs with vine leaves over the shoulder of Bacchus . . ." (146).

She is an ardent matchmaker, giving Paul Rayley the impetus and encouragement to propose to Minta Doyle, determining to marry Lily Briscoe to William Bankes. She insists that "Minta must, they all must marry . . . an unmarried woman had missed the best of life. The house seemed full of children and Mrs. Ramsay listening . . ." (77). And her attitude toward marriage seems more pagan than Christian. The elaborate dinner over which she presides, coming immediately after Paul's successful proposal to Minta, gives her mixed feelings, a sense "of celebrating a festival, as if two emotions were called up in her, one profound—for what could be more serious than the love of man for woman, what more commanding, more impressive, bearing in its bosom the seeds of death; at the same time these lovers, these people entering into illusion glittering eyed, must be danced round with mockery, decorated with garlands" (151). And this mockery is not at all inconsistent with the character of Demeter. Kerényi writes that in the figure of the Kore "There is, for instance, the strange equation of marriage and death, the bridal chamber and the grave. Marriage in this connexion has the character of murder; the brutal ravisher is the god of death himself. On the other hand, marriage retains its proper and primary meaning as the union of man and woman. But not only does it call forth the lamentations of the celebrants, it also calls forth obscene speech and laughing at obscene actions" (pp. 179–180).

An important characteristic of Mrs. Ramsay in her Demeter aspect is her complete femininity. As Demeter was worshipped more by men than women, as the sacrifices to her were humble and restrained rather than fierce and bloody like those of men, so Mrs. Ramsay in all her aspects is feminine and opposed to that which is undesirable in masculinity. When she gives to Mr. Ramsay the sympathy and reassurance he begs, the action is symbolic: "into this delicious fecundity, this fountain and spray of life, the fatal sterility of the male plunged itself, like a beak of brass, barren and bare" (58). By this act, Mr. Ramsay is "taken within the circle of life . . . his barrenness made fertile . . ." (59). This characteristic is not exclusively Mr. Ramsay's: "she felt, as a fact without hostility, the sterility of men . . ." (126). With her quick intuition, her special knowledge, she is at the opposite pole from them. Although she does not possess their analytical reasoning powers, she is far more perceptive than they. "How much they missed, after all, these very clever men! How dried up they did become, to be sure" (150). There is little doubt that these sentiments are inherent in Virginia Woolf's feminism. In Mrs. Ramsay's thoughts one finds an echo of those of her creator, who wrote, "the egotism of men surprises and shocks me even now," who found that "the male atmosphere is disconcerting to me . . . I think what an abrupt precipice cleaves asunder the male intelligence, and how they pride themselves upon a point of view which much resembles stupidity" (*Writer's Diary*, pp. 135, 12). Jung concludes his essay on the psychological aspects of the Kore with the comment that "Demeter-Kore exists on the plane of mother-daughter experience which is alien to man and shuts him out. In fact, the psychology of the Demeter cult has all the features of a matriarchal order of society where the man is an indispensable but on the whole disturbing factor" (p. 245).

Even the story of the Fisherman and His Wife, which Mrs. Ramsay reads to James, reflects this attitude. To perceive it, however, one must do what Virginia Woolf did in *Orlando*: change the sex of the principal character. In *To the Lighthouse* the individual who makes the insatiable demands is not the wife but the husband. Mr. Ramsay, the philosopher, has driven himself to the Q of mental effort and understanding. He is plunged into melancholy despair at his inability to reach Z. He is described as standing desolate in darkness on a narrow spit of land, the black seas nearly engulfing him. It is his wife who is content with that which they have already received, who accepts their portion and cherishes their gift of love.

The figures of Demeter and Mrs. Ramsay are linked in another important way. They are characterized not only by fruitfulness, but by sorrow as well. This element also serves to point up the transition from the Demeter to the Persephone component of this multiple myth. Demeter's sorrow is caused, of course, by her loss of Persephone. Mrs. Ramsay's sorrow is neither so continuous nor so specifically focused as that of Demeter. But when she falls prey to it, her sorrow is genuine and pervasive, and highly suggestive of that of the goddess: "Never did anybody look so sad. Bitter and black, half way down, in the darkness, in the shaft which ran from sunlight to the depths, perhaps a tear formed; a tear fell; the waters swayed this way and that, received it, and were at rest. Never did anybody look so sad" (46). And this is not a simple *weltschmerz*, but a genuine reaction to a frightening vision of a real antagonist, for "she felt this thing that she called life terrible, hostile and quick to pounce on you if you gave it a chance" (92). Another of Mrs. Ramsay's interior monologues might be that of the goddess implored to make the earth fruitful again: "Why, one asked oneself, does one take all these pains for the human race to go on? Is it so very desirable" (134)?

IV

In the familiar story, Demeter's only child Persephone was abducted by Hades and spirited down to the underworld to reign with him over the souls of all the dead. In her anguish for her daughter, the Goddess of the Corn "withheld her gifts from the earth, which turned into a frozen desert. The green and flowering land was icebound and lifeless because Persephone had disappeared" (Hamilton, p. 57). Finally compelled to intervene, Zeus sent Hermes to Hades with the order that Persephone must be released. Hades complied, but first forced her to eat a pomegranate seed, whose magical properties would insure her return to him for a third of each year. Zeus also sent Rhea to Demeter to tell her that Persephone would be released and to ask

Demeter to make the earth fruitful again. Demeter, of course, complied. Edith Hamilton writes:

> In the stories of both goddesses, Demeter and Persephone, the idea of sorrow was foremost. Demeter, goddess of the harvest wealth, was still more the divine sorrowing mother who saw her daughter die each year. Persephone was the radiant maiden of the spring and the summertime. . . . But all the while Persephone knew how brief that beauty was; fruits, flowers, leaves, all the fair growth of the earth, must end with the coming of the cold and pass like herself into the power of death. After the lord of the dark world below carried her away she was never again the gay young creature who had played in the flowery meadow without a thought of care or trouble. She did indeed rise from the dead every spring, but she brought with her the memory of where she had come from; with all her bright beauty there was something strange and awesome about her. She was often said to be "the maiden whose name may not be spoken" (pp. 53–54).

Many allusions in *To the Lighthouse* suggest the Persephone-Mrs. Ramsay correspondence. Barely nine pages into the novel one reads that she had "in her veins the blood of that very noble, if slightly mythical, Italian house, whose daughters, scattered about English drawing rooms in the nineteenth century, had lisped so charmingly, had stormed so wildly, and all her wit and bearing and her temper came from them . . ." (17).

Early in the novel Mrs. Ramsay has premonitions, foreshadowings of her departure from the green and flowering loveliness of the Isle of Skye, of her descent into the world of shades. As she sits in the gathering dusk, she looks out upon her garden: "the whitening of the flowers and something grey in the leaves conspired together, to rouse in her a feeling of anxiety" (93–94). Her mood deepens until "all the being and the doing, expansive, glittering, vocal, evaporated; and one shrunk, with a sense of solemnity, to being oneself, a wedge-shaped core of darkness, something invisible to others" (95). Yet at times these depths are briefly pierced by shafts of light. The sound of the waves on the beach "seemed of some old cradle song, murmured by nature, 'I am guarding you—I am your support'" (27). It is as if Persephone, sensing the imminence of her rape and abduction, divined also that her salvation would come from her who had sung a cradle song, her mother Demeter, the goddess so close to nature.

Mrs. Ramsay's death is communicated to the reader with shocking suddenness and brevity, as though it were not the event itself which was important, but rather its consequences. In Lily Briscoe's reflections in "The Lighthouse" section of the novel, however, the reader is given Lily's special vision of Mrs. Ramsay's departure. And, of course, it is Lily who is most sensitive to Mrs. Ramsay, to her essence and her function. As Lily paints, the images sweep in on her mind: "It was strange how clearly she saw her, stepping with her usual quickness across fields among whose folds, purplish and soft, among whose flowers, hyacinths or lilies, she vanished. It was some trick of the painter's eye. For days after she had heard of her death she had seen her thus, putting her wreath to her forehead and going unquestioningly with her companion, a shade across the fields . . . all had been part of the fields of death"

(269–270). When Persephone had wandered away from her companions, thus isolating herself for Hades' attack, she had been attracted by banks of narcissus, hyacinths, and lilies (Frazer, p. 36). As she was abducted, she dropped the lilies she had gathered.[5] Thirty pages later in the novel, Lily's vision of Mrs. Ramsay's departure is resumed: "She let her flowers fall from her basket, scattered and tumbled them on to the grass and, reluctantly and hesitatingly, but without question or complaint . . . went too. Down fields, across valleys, white, flower-strewn . . . the hills were austere. It was rocky; it was steep. The waves sounded hoarse on the stones beneath. They went, the three of them together . . ." (299). The identity of the third figure is problematical. The daughter to whom Mrs. Ramsay is closest, the lovely Prue, follows her mother in death.[6] It may be that Lily's unconscious mind has joined Prue to her mother in this symbolic vision. Since the unity of the two divine persons is central to the concept of the Kore, this is a workable hypothesis for this interpretation.[7] But in terms of the myth, Mrs. Ramsay's failure to question or complain does not seem apt. In view of the other detailed correspondences—the falling flowers, the rocky steepness so clearly suggestive of the chasm out of which Hades rose to seize his prey—this is perhaps one point upon which one might invoke Virginia Woolf's avowed intention of making her symbols work "not in set pieces . . . but simply as images, never making them work out; only suggest" (*Writer's Diary*, p. 165).

The very first pages of "Time Passes," the middle section of the novel, may be seen as symbolic of the transformation of the earth when Demeter withheld her gifts: "a downpouring of immense darkness began. Nothing, it seemed, could survive the flood, the profusion of darkness . . ." (189). There is not only darkness, but also dissolution as "fumbling airs" creep into the house; "wearily, ghostlily . . . they . . . blanched the apples . . . fumbled the petals of roses . . ." (191). "Divine goodness" displays the treasures which might be given to men if they deserved them, but "it does not please him; he covers his treasures in a drench of hail, and so breaks them . . . the nights are now full of wind and destruction . . ." (193).

Then, as this section of the novel progresses, vegetation springs up in the solitude as time passes. But there is a horror beneath this growth, now blind, purposeless, and even destructive: "the flowers standing there, looking before them, looking up, yet beholding nothing, eyeless, and so terrible" (203). The house becomes a moldering shell, in the process of dissolution. Finally, "If [a] feather had fallen, if it had tipped the scale downwards, the whole house would have plunged to the depths to lie upon the sands of oblivion" (209). This once pleasant place, now reft of the force which had made it beautiful, "would have turned and pitched downwards to the depths of darkness" (208). The time of catastrophes, private and public, has come; Andrew is

5. "In ancient art Demeter and Persephone are characterized as goddesses of the corn by the crowns of corn which they wear on their heads and by the stalks of corn which they hold in their hands" (J. G. Frazer, *The Golden Bough* [3rd ed.; London: Macmillan, 1912], VII, 43).

6. Prue's death had come as a result of childbirth. This in itself suggests the inextricable connection of birth and death in the Kore myth.

7. Kerényi and Jung (note 1, above) describe versions of the Persephone myth in which Demeter, as well as her daughter, was a victim of rape (pp. 170, 197, 251). Thus, in another version, Mrs. Ramsay and her daughter would signify Demeter and her daughter.

killed by a piece of shrapnel; Prue dies in childbirth; and the first World War sweeps across the face of Europe.

V

The reappearance of Persephone has its symbolic equivalent in the novel in the return of the force which Mrs. Ramsay represented. Mrs. McNab receives orders to have the house restored. The predominant activity in the last section of the book is the expedition to the Lighthouse, upon which Mr. Ramsay is determined almost as if it were a rite of propitiation toward Mrs. Ramsay's spirit. And clearly, her spirit has a profound effect upon Lily. In this, Virginia Woolf may have been influenced by *A Passage to India*, the novel of her intimate friend, E. M. Forster. This book, which she felt represented Forster in "his prime," appeared three years before *To the Lighthouse*. The central female figure in Forster's novel is Mrs. Moore, an old Englishwoman. Through her influence, felt returning after her death, some of the wounds inflicted during the conflict between the British and the Indians in Chandrapore are healed. Earlier in *To the Lighthouse* Mrs. Ramsay has performed an act symbolic of Demeter's role in the rescue of Persephone. Going to the nursery, she has covered the boar's skull which has kept her daughter Cam awake until eleven o'clock at night—covered the skull with her own green shawl. The symbol of death is banished and obliterated by the symbol of fertility. In Lily's first night in the house after her return, she reflects that "peace had come" (213). If the guests were to go down to the darkened beach, "They would see then night flowing down in purple; his head crowned; his sceptre jewelled; and how in his eyes a child might look" (213). This dark and kingly deity, whose symbol had earlier frightened a child from sleep, has now been disarmed. The feminine principle, the Kore, has triumphed over the dark underworld with her release from it.

As the day passes, Lily invokes Mrs. Ramsay, fruitlessly at first. But then she feels her imminence. "'Mrs. Ramsay! Mrs. Ramsay!' she repeated. She owed it all to her" (241). At times Lily's longing is so intense that "she called out silently, to that essence which sat by the boat, that abstract one made of her, that woman in grey, as if to abuse her for having gone, and then having gone, come back again. It had seemed so safe, thinking of her. Ghost, air, nothingness, a thing you could play with easily and safely at any time of day or night, she had been that, and then suddenly she put her hand out and wrung the heart thus" (266).

But finally, of course, as the boat reaches the Lighthouse and the rapport is achieved between James, Cam, and Mr. Ramsay, Lily completes her picture, becomes, in this individual work, fruitful as an artist. Just as Mrs. Ramsay's spirit has been the force which brings about the consummation of the trip to the Lighthouse, so her spirit brings about Lily's epiphany. In that famous passage, "With a sudden intensity, as if she saw it clear for a second, she drew a line there, in the centre. It was done; it was finished. Yes, she thought, laying down her brush in extreme fatigue, I have had my vision" (310). The return of Persephone is thus twofold. Mrs. Ramsay, in the Persephone aspect of the Kore, has returned as an almost palpable presence to the Isle of Skye from which she had been snatched by death. Persephone has also returned through Lily's final achievement of the artistic vision and triumph denied her ten years earlier.[8] As clear as the existence of the relationship between Mrs. Ramsay and Lily is the function of this relationship: "Demeter and Kore, mother and daughter, extend the feminine consciousness both upwards and downwards. They add an 'older and younger,' 'stronger and weaker' dimension to it and widen out the narrowly limited conscious mind bound in space and time, giving it intimations of a greater and more comprehensive personality which has a share in the eternal course of things" (Jung, p. 225). Both the mother figure and the daughter figure are united in that they are artists—the one in paints and the other in human relationships—and in that they are bound to each other by psychic bonds which remain firm even beyond death. Demeter has effected the liberation of Persephone.

VI

Sigmund Freud's interpretation of the Oedipus myth is almost as famous as the myth itself. This pattern, Freud says, dramatized in the legend of the Greek youth who unwittingly kills his father, marries and begets children with his mother, and then blinds himself in atonement, is fundamental in human experience. It is so basic that "the beginnings of religion, ethics, society, and art meet in the Oedipus complex." We are moved by Sophocles' play, Freud says, by the consciousness that Oedipus' fate "might have been our own. . . . It may be that we were all destined to divert our first sexual impulses toward our mothers, and our first impulses of hatred and violence toward our fathers; our dreams convince us that we were."[9]

That the relationship between James, Mrs. Ramsay, and Mr. Ramsay reflects this pattern is so clear as to be almost unmistakable. The intense adoration which James cherishes for his mother has its opposite in an equally strong hatred for his father, "casting ridicule upon his wife, who was ten thousand times better in every way than he was (James thought) . . ." (10). Virginia Woolf says of Mr. Ramsay that "his son hated him" (57). This emotion is thoroughgoing: "Had there been an axe handy, or a poker, any weapon that would have gashed a hole in his father's breast and killed him, there and then, James would have seized it" (10). Mrs. Ramsay is solicitous and fearful for James as Jocasta might have been for the young Oedipus: "what demon possessed him, her youngest, her cherished?" (43).

James's jealousy and feelings of rivalry with his father are intensified by his perhaps unconscious knowledge of the sexual aspect of the relationship between his parents. He is made acutely aware of it in the episode early in the novel in which Mr. Ramsay comes to his wife for the sympathy and reassurance he demands. The imagery used to describe this action is patently sexual. James, standing between his mother's knees, feels her seem "to raise herself with an effort, and at once to pour erect into the air

8. There is another factor which confirms Lily's role as a Persephone figure in this interpretation. Mrs. Ramsay's characterization of her as prim and old-maidish is nothing more than emphasis and re-emphasis of a characteristic of Persephone, "whose salient feature was an elemental virginity" (Kerényi and Jung, p. 207).

9. *The Basic Writings of Sigmund Freud*, ed. and trans. A. A. Brill (New York: Modern Library, 1938), p. 308.

a rain of energy ... and into this fountain and spray of life, the fatal sterility of the male plunged itself, like a beak of brass, barren and bare" (58). Then James feels shut out when, the demand complied with, "Mrs. Ramsay seemed to fold herself together, one petal closed in another, and the whole fabric fell in exhaustion upon itself, so that she had only strength enough to move her finger, in exquisite abandonment to exhaustion ... while there throbbed through her, like a pulse in a spring which has expanded to its full width and now gently ceases to beat, the rapture of successful creation" (60–61).

Into the third section of the novel, across the space of ten years, James carries these same emotions undiminished in intensity. Of his mother he thinks, "She alone spoke the truth; to her alone could he speak it" (278). Contemplating his father, James realizes that "He had always kept this old symbol of taking a knife and striking his father to the heart" (273). The pattern is so strong that now James and his father compete in another triangle in which Cam has been substituted for Mrs. Ramsay. The two children have made a compact to resist their father's tyranny, but James feels that he will lose to him again just as he had before. As Mr. Ramsay begins to win Cam over, James acknowledges his defeat. "'Yes,' thought James pitilessly ... 'now she will give way. I shall be left to fight the tyrant alone'" (250). An instant later, the antecedent of the present experience is dredged up out of the recesses of his memory: "There was a flash of blue, he remembered, and then somebody sitting with him laughed, surrendered, and he was very angry. It must have been his mother, he thought, sitting on a low chair, with his father standing over her" (251).

Freud writes of the ambivalence the child feels toward his father, the conflict between tenderness and hostility. He concludes that unless the child is successful in repressing the sexual love for the mother and hostility for the father, while concomitantly allowing the natural affection for the father to grow, neurosis will be the result. Significantly, at the end of the finally accomplished journey to the Lighthouse, James experiences his rapport with Mr. Ramsay. Cam addresses herself silently to James: "You've got it at last. For she knew that this was what James had been wanting ... He was so pleased that he was not going to let anybody share a grain of his pleasure. His father had praised him" (306).

VII

The Oedipus myth is consonant with the Persephone myth in its application to *To the Lighthouse* and both are reflections of fundamental patterns of human experience. The two old antagonists testify to this judgment of their importance, Freud to the former and Jung to the latter. Appropriately, the symbol for one section of the novel, "The Window," is female, and that for another section, "The Lighthouse," is male. Exalting the feminine principle in life over the masculine, Virginia Woolf built her novel around a character embodying the life-giving role of the female. In opposition, she shows the male, both in the father and son aspect, as death-bearing—arid, sterile, hateful, and "fatal" (58). The female principle in life is exalted in all its aspects of love which are opposed to the harsh and critical aspects of the male principle, of fertility with its pattern of triumph over death in rebirth. What, then, becomes of the single obvious central symbol, the Lighthouse? Its use is simply this: in its stability, its essential constancy despite cyclical change which is not really change at all, this symbol refers to Mrs. Ramsay herself. This meaning is revealed to the reader explicitly: Mrs. Ramsay "looked up over her knitting and met the third stroke and it seemed to her like her own eyes, searching as she alone could search into her mind and heart . . . She praised herself in praising the light, without vanity, for she was stern, she was searching, she was beautiful like that light" (97). And just as there are three persons combined in the Primordial Goddess, so there are three strokes to the Lighthouse beam, and "the long steady stroke, the last of the three . . . was her stroke . . ." (96).

As Mrs. Ramsay gives love, stability, and fruitfulness to her family and those in her orbit, so the female force should always function. It serves to ameliorate or mitigate the effects of male violence, hate, and destructiveness. And should the physical embodiment of this force pay her debt to the world of shades, this is not an ever-enduring loss, for it returns through those whom it has made fruitful and thus drawn into the rebirth pattern. Or it may be sought, found, and embraced as, in their separate ways, James, Cam, and Mr. Ramsay experience it at the end of their ritual and symbolic voyage to the Lighthouse.

PMLA, LXXI (1956), 547–562. Some of the reference notes have been omitted.

NATURE MYTH IN FAULKNER'S *THE BEAR*

John Lydenberg

William Faulkner's power derives in large part from his myth-making and myth-using ability. The mythical aspects of this work are twofold. One type of Faulkner myth has been widely recognized and discussed. Probably the best exposition of this appears in the introduction to the Viking *Portable* selections, in which Malcolm Cowley shows how Faulkner's vision of a mythical South informs and gives unity to the bulk of his best work. His characters grow out of the dense, lush fabric of Southern society. But they are not realistic exemplars of aspects of the South. The most notable of them are larger than life and carry with them an obvious, if not always clear, allegorical significance. Men like Sutpen or Hightower or Joe Christmas or Popeye—to suggest only a few of the many—are more-than-human actors in the saga of the mythical kingdom of Yoknapatawpha, the Mississippi county that symbolizes Faulkner's South.

But of course his stories are not merely about the South; they are about men, or Man. Here appears the other type of myth: the primitive nature myth. Perhaps one should not say "appears," for the myth lies imbedded in Faulkner's feeling about human actions and seldom appears as a readily visible outcropping, as does his conception of the mythical kingdom. Faulkner feels man acting in an eternity, in a timeless confusion of past and future, acting not as a rational Deweyan creature but as a natural, unthinking (but always moral) animal. These men do not "understand" themselves, and neither Faulkner nor the reader fully understands them in any naturalistic sense. Sometimes these creatures driven by instinct become simply grotesques; sometimes the inflated rhetoric gives the characters the specious portentousness of a gigantic gray balloon. But often the aura of something-more-ness casts a spell upon the reader, makes him sense where he does not exactly comprehend the eternal human significance of the ritual activities carried out by these suprahuman beings. They are acting out magical tales that portray man's plight in a world he cannot understand or control. They are Man, the primordial and immortal, the creator and protagonist of myth.

This dual myth-making can best be demonstrated in the short story "The Bear." "The Bear" is by general agreement one of Faulkner's most exciting and rewarding stories. Malcolm Cowley and Robert Penn Warren have both shown its importance for an understanding of Faulkner's attitudes toward the land, the Negro, and the South. Warren referred to it as "profoundly symbolic," but refrained from examining its symbolism except as it relates to Faulkner's Southern mythology. No one—so far as I know—has sought to explain just what makes it so powerful and moving, what gives one the feeling that it is more than a superb hunting story and more than an allegory of man's relation to the land and to his fellow man. The source of this power can be discerned if we see that beneath its other layers of meaning, the story is essentially a nature myth.

"The Bear," in its final version, can be summarized briefly. When Ike McCaslin is ten, he is first taken with a group of men on their yearly hunting trip into the wilderness of Sutpen's hundred. He quickly learns to be a good hunter under the tutelage of the old half-Indian, half-Negro guide, Sam Fathers. The routine hunting has an added goal: the killing of Old Ben, a huge and sage, almost legendary bear, who always defies capture. Sam Fathers maintains that none of their dogs can bring Old Ben to bay, and that they must find one stronger and braver. Finally he gets what he needs, a wild dog named Lion. When Ike is sixteen, the last chase occurs. Hunters shoot in vain, hounds are killed as they try to hold Ben. And then Lion rushes in, followed by Boon, the quarter-Indian retainer, who charges like the dog, directly upon the bear, to make the kill with his knife. Lion dies from his wounds the next day. Sam Fathers drops from exhaustion and dies shortly thereafter. The story proper is then interrupted by Part IV, a section as long again as the rest. Part V is a short epilogue, telling of Ike's sole return to the scene of his apprenticeship, his visit to the graves of Lion and Sam Fathers, and his meeting with Boon.

On one level the story is a symbolic representation of man's relation to the land, and particularly the Southerner's conquest of his native land. In attempting to kill Old Ben, the men are contending with the wilderness itself. In one sense, as men, they have a perfect right to do this, as long as they act with dignity and propriety, maintaining their humility while they demonstrate the ability of human beings to master the brute forces of nature. The hunters from Jefferson are gentlemen and sportsmen, representing the ideals of the old order at its best, the honor, dignity, and courage of the South. In their rapport with nature and their contest with Old Ben, they regain the purity they have lost in their workaday world, and abjure the petty conventions with which they ordinarily mar their lives. But as Southerners they are part of "that whole edifice intricate and complex and founded upon injustice"; they are part of that South that has bought and sold land and has held men as slaves. Their original sins have alienated them irrevocably from nature. Thus their conquest of Old Ben becomes a rape. What might in other circumstances have been right, is now a violation of the wilderness and the Southern land.

Part IV makes explicit the social comment implied in the drama of Old Ben. It consists of a long and complicated account of the McCaslin family, white and mulatto, and a series of pronunciamentos by Ike upon the South, the land, truth, man's frailties and God's will. It is in effect Ike's spiritual autobiography given as explanation of his reasons for relinquishing and repudiating, for refusing to own land or participate actively in the life of the South. Ike discovers that he can do nothing to lift or lighten the curse the Southerners have brought on themselves, the monstrous offspring of their God-given free will. The price of purity, Ike finds, is non-involvement, and he chooses purity.

Thus Part IV carries us far beyond the confines of the story of the hunt. It creates a McCaslin myth that fits into the broad saga of Faulkner's mythical kingdom, and it includes in nondramatic form a good deal of direct social comment. The rest of "The Bear" cannot be regarded as *simply* a dramatic symbolization of Ike's conscientious repudiation. Its symbolism cannot fully be interpreted in terms of this social myth.

One responds emotionally to the bear hunt as to a separate unit, an indivisible and self-sufficient whole. Part IV and Old Ben's story resemble the components of a binary star. They revolve about each other and even cast light upon each other. But each contains the source of its own light.

II

It is the mythical quality of the bear hunt proper that gives the story its haunting power. Beneath its other meanings and symbolisms lies the magical tale enacted by superhuman characters. Here religion and magic are combined in a ritual demonstration of the eternal struggle between Man and Nature. A statement of the legend recounting their partial reconciliation would run somewhat as follows:

Every fall members of the tribe make a pilgrimage to the domain of the Great Beast, the bear that is more than a bear, the preternatural animal that symbolizes for them their relation to Nature and thus to life. They maintain, of course, the forms of routine hunts. But beneath the conventional ritual lies the religious rite: the hunting of the tribal god, whom they dare not, and cannot, touch, but whom they are impelled to challenge. In this rite the established social relations dissolve; the artificial ranks of Jefferson give way to more natural relations as Sam Fathers is automatically given the lead. The bear and Sam are both taboo. Like a totem animal, Old Ben is at the same time sacred, and dangerous or forbidden (though in no sense unclean). Also he is truly animistic, possessing a soul of his own, initiating action, not inert like other creatures of nature. And Sam, the high priest, although alone admitted to the arcana and trusted with the tutelage of the young neophyte, is yet outside the pale, living by himself, irrevocably differentiated from the others by his Negro blood, and yet kept pure and attuned to nature by his royal Indian blood.

This particular legend of man and the Nature God relates the induction of Ike, the natural and pure boy, into the mysteries of manhood. Guided by Sam Fathers, Ike learns how to retain his purity and bring himself into harmony with the forces of Nature. He learns human woodlore and the human codes and techniques of the hunt. And he learns their limitations. Old Ben, always concerned with the doings of his mortals, comes to gaze upon Ike as he stands alone and unprepared in a clearing. Ike "knew that the bear was looking at him. He never saw it. He did not know whether it was facing him from the cane or behind him." His apprehension does not depend on human senses. Awareness of his coming relation to the bear grows not from rational processes, but from intuition: "he knew now that he would never fire at it."

Yet he must see, must meet, Old Ben. He will be vouchsafed the vision, but only when he divests himself of man-made signs of fear and vanity. "*The gun*, the boy thought. *The gun.* 'You will have to choose,' Sam said." So one day, before light, he starts out unarmed on his pilgrimage, alone and helpless, with courage and humility, guided by his newly acquired woodlore, and by compass and watch, traveling till past noon, past the time at which he should have turned back to regain camp in safety. He has not yet found the bear. Then he realizes that divesting himself of the gun, necessary as that is, will not suffice if he wishes to come into the presence. "He stood for a moment—a child, alien and lost in the green and soaring gloom of the markless wilderness. Then he relinquished completely to it. It was the watch and the compass. He was still tainted."

He takes off the two artifacts, hangs them from a bush, and continues farther into the woods. Now he is at last pure—and lost. Then the footprints, huge, misshapen, and unmistakable, appear, one by one, leading him back to the spot he could no longer have found unaided, to the watch and the compass in the sunlight of the glade.

Then he saw the bear. It did not emerge, appear; it was just there, immobile, fixed in the green and windless noon's hot dappling, not as big as he had dreamed it but as big as he had expected, bigger, dimensionless against the dappled obscurity, looking at him. Then it moved. It crossed the glade without haste, walking for an instant into the sun's full glare and out of it, and stopped again and looked back at him across one shoulder. Then it was gone. It didn't walk into the woods. It faded, sank back into the wilderness without motion as he had watched a fish, a huge old bass, sink back into the dark depths of its pool and vanish without even any movements of its fins.

Ike has seen the vision. That is his goal, but it is not the goal for the tribe, nor for Sam Fathers who as priest must prepare the kill for them. They are under a compulsion to carry out their annual ritual at the time of "the year's death," to strive to conquer the Nature God whose very presence challenges them and raises doubts as to their power.

The priest has first to make the proper medicine; he has to find the right dog. Out of the wilds it comes, as if sent by higher powers, untamable, silent, like no other dog. Then Sam, magician as well as priest, shapes him into the force, the instrument, that alone can master Old Ben. Lion is almost literally bewitched—broken maybe, but not tamed or civilized or "humanized." He is removed from the order of nature, but not allowed to partake of the order of civilization or humanity.

Sam Fathers fashions the instrument; that is his duty as it has been his duty to train the neophyte, to induct him into the mysteries, and thus to prepare, in effect, his own successor. But it is not for the priest to perform the impious and necessary deed. Because he belongs to the order of nature as well as of man—as Ike does now— neither of them can do more than assist at the rites. Nor can Major de Spain or General Compson or other human hunters pair with Lion. That is for Boon, who has never hit any animal bigger than a squirrel with his shotgun, who is like Lion in his imperturbable nonhumanity. Boon is part Indian; "he had neither profession job nor trade"; he has "the mind of a child, the heart of a horse, and little hard shoe-button eyes without depth or meanness or generosity or viciousness or gentleness or anything else." So he takes Lion into his bed, makes Lion a part of him. Divorced from nature and from man—"the big, grave, sleepy-seeming dog which, as Sam Fathers said, cared about no man and no thing; and the violent, insensitive, hard-faced man with his touch of remote Indian blood and the mind almost of a child"—the two mavericks live their own lives, dedicated and fated.

The "yearly pageant-rite" continues for six years. Then out of the swamps come the rest of the tribe, knowing the climax is approaching, accepted by the Jefferson aristocrats as proper participants in the final rites. Ike, the young priest, is given the post of honor on the one-eyed mule which alone among the mules and horses will not shy at the smell of blood. Beside him stands the dog who "loved no man and no thing." Lion "looked at him. It moved its head and looked at him across the trivial uproar of the hounds, out of the yellow eyes as depthless as Boon's, as free as Boon's of meanness or generosity or gentleness or viciousness. They were just cold and sleepy. Then it blinked, and he knew it was not looking at him and never had been, without even bothering to turn its head away."

The final hunt is short, for Old Ben can be downed only when his time has come, not by the contrived machinations of men, but by the destined ordering of events and his own free will. The hounds run the bear; a swamper fires; Walter Ewell fires;[1] Boon cannot fire.[2] Then the bear turns and Lion drives in, is caught in the bear's two arms and falls with him. Ike draws back the hammers of his gun. And Boon, like Lion, drives in, jumps on Ben's back and thrusts his knife into the bear's throat. Again they fall. Then "the bear surged erect, raising with it the man and the dog too, and turned and still carrying the man and the dog it took two or three steps towards the woods on its hind feet as a man would have walked and crashed down. It didn't collapse, crumple. It fell all of a piece, as a tree falls, so that all three of them, man dog and bear, seemed to bounce once."

The tribe comes up, with wagon and mules, to carry back to camp the dead bear, Lion with his guts raked out, Boon bleeding, and Sam Fathers who dropped, unscathed but paralyzed, at the moment that Ben received his death wound. The doctor from the near-by sawmill pushes back Lion's entrails and sews him up. Sam lies quiet in his hut after talking in his old unknown tongue, and then pleading, "Let me out, master. Let me go home."

Next day the swampers and trappers gather again, sitting around Lion in the front yard, "talking quietly of hunting, of the game and the dogs which ran it, of hounds and bear and deer and men of yesterday vanished from the earth, while from time to time the great blue dog would open his eyes, not as if he were listening to them but as though to look at the woods for a moment before closing his eyes again, to remember the woods or to see that they were still there. He died at sundown." And in his hut Sam quietly goes after the bear whose death he was destined to prepare and upon whose life his own depended, leaving behind the de Spains and Compsons who will no longer hunt in this wilderness and the new priest who will keep himself pure to observe, always from the outside, the impious destruction of the remaining Nature by men who can no longer be taught the saving virtues of pride and humility. They have succeeded in doing what they felt they had to do, what they thought they wanted to do. But their act was essentially sacrilegious, however necessary and glorious it

---

1. In "The Old People," the story preceding "The Bear" in *Go Down, Moses*, Faulkner says that Walter Ewell never misses. Thus mention of his shooting and missing at this particular time takes on added significance.

2. Boon explained that he could not fire because Lion was too close. That was, of course, not the "real" reason; Boon could not kill Ben with a civilized gun (to say nothing of the fact that he couldn't hit anything with his gun anyway).

may have seemed. They have not gained the power and strength of their feared and reverenced god by conquering him. Indeed, as human beings will, they have mistaken their true relation to him. They tried to possess what they could not possess, and now they can no longer even share in it.

Boon remains, but he has violated the fundamental taboo. Permitted to do this by virtue of his nonhumanity, he is yet in part human. He has broken the law, killed with his own hand the bear, taken upon himself the mastery of that which was no man's to master. So when the chiefs withdraw, and the sawmills grind their way into the forests, Boon polices the new desecrations. When Ike returns to gaze once more upon the remnants of the wilderness, he finds Boon alone in the clearing where the squirrels can be trapped in the isolated tree. Boon, with the gun he could never aim successfully, frenziedly hammers the barrel against the breech of the dismembered weapon, shouting at the intruder, any intruder, "Get out of here! Don't touch them! Don't touch a one of them! They're mine!" Having killed the bear, he now possesses all the creatures of nature, and will snarl jealously at the innocent who walks peacefully through the woods. The result of his impiety is, literally, madness.

III

That, of course, is not exactly Faulkner's "Bear." But it is part of it, an essential part. If a reading of the story as myth results in suppressions and distortions, as it does, any other reading leaves us unsatisfied. Only thus can we answer certain crucial questions that otherwise baffle us. The most important ones relate to the four central characters: Why can Ike or Sam not kill the bear? Why can Boon? Why are Boon and Lion drawn precisely so? And why does Sam Fathers die along with Old Ben?

Ike has developed and retained the requisite purity. He has learned to face nature with pride and humility. He is not tainted like de Spain and Compson by having owned slaves. According to Faulkner's version of the huntsman's code, Ike should be the one who has the right to kill Old Ben, as General Compson feels when he assigns him the one mule that can approach the bear. Or it might be argued that Sam Fathers, with his unsurpassed knowledge, instinct, and dignity, rightly deserves the honor. If Old Ben is merely the greatest of bears, it would seem fitting for either Ike or Sam to demonstrate his impeccable relationship to nature by accomplishing the task. But Faulkner rules differently.

Lion and Boon do it. At first glance that may seem explicable if we consider Old Ben's death as symbolizing man's destruction of the wilderness. Then the deed cannot be performed by Ike or Sam, for it would be essentially vicious, done in violation of the rules by men ignorant or disrespectful of the rules. Thus one may think it could be assigned to Boon, "the plebeian," and that strange, wild dog. But actually neither of them is "bad," neither belongs to a mean order of hunters. Boon and Lion are creatures set apart, dehumanized, possessing neither virtues nor vices. In their actions and in his words describing them, Faulkner takes great pains to link them together and to remove from them all human traits.[3]

Thus the killing of the bear cannot be explained by a naturalistic interpretation of

3. In "The Old People," Boon is referred to as "a mastiff."

the symbolism. Old Ben is not merely an extraordinary bear representing the wilderness and impervious to all but the most skilfull or improper attacks. He is the totem animal, the god who can never be bested by men with their hounds and guns, but only by a nonhuman Boon with Lion, the instrument fashioned by the priest.

Sam Fathers' death can likewise be explained only by the nature myth. If the conquest of Old Ben is the triumphant culmination of the boy's induction into the hunting clan, Sam, his mentor, would presumably be allowed a share in the triumph. If the bear's death symbolizes the destruction of the wild, Sam's demise can be seen as paralleling that of the nature of which he is so completely a part. But then the whole affair would be immoral, and Sam could not manage and lead the case so willingly, nor would he die placid and satisfied. Only as part of a nature rite does his death become fully understandable. It is as if the priest and the god are possessed of the same soul. The priest fulfils his function; his magic makes the god vulnerable to the men. He has to do it; and according to human standards he wins a victory for his tribe. But it is a victory for which the only fit reward is the death he is content to accept. The actors act out their ordained roles. And in the end the deed brings neither jubilation nor mourning—only retribution, tragic in the high sense, right as the things which are inevitable are right.

A further paradox, a seeming contradiction, appears in the conjunction of the two words which are repeated so often that they clearly constitute a major theme. Pride and humility. Here conjoined are two apparently polar concepts: the quintessence of Christianity in the virtue of humility; and the greatest of sins, the sin of Satan. Though at first the words puzzle one, or else slip by as merely a pleasant conceit, they soon gather up into themselves the entire "meaning" of the story. This meaning can be read in purely naturalistic terms: Faulkner gives these two qualities as the huntsman's necessary virtues. But they take on additional connotations. Humility becomes the proper attitude to the nature gods, with whom man can merely bring himself into harmony as Sam teaches Ike to do. The pride arises out of the individual's realization of his manhood: his acquisition of the self-control which permits him to perform the rituals as he should. Actually it is humanly impossible to possess these two qualities fully at the same time. Sam alone truly has them, and as the priest he has partly escaped from his humanity. Ike apparently believes he has developed them, finally; and Faulkner seems to agree with him. But Ike cannot quite become Sam's successor, for in acquiring the necessary humility—and insight—he loses the ability to act with the full pride of a man, and can only be an onlooker, indeed in his later life, as told in Part IV and "Delta Autumn," a sort of Ishmael.

In conclusion, then, "The Bear" is first of all a magnificent story. The inclusion of Part IV gives us specific insights into Faulkner's attitudes toward his Southern society and adds another legend to the saga of his mythical kingdom. The tale of Old Ben by itself has a different sort of effect. Our response is not intellectual but emotional. The relatively simple story of the hunting of a wise old bear suggests the mysteries of life, which we feel subconsciously and cannot consider in the rationalistic terms we use to analyze the "how" of ordinary life. Thus it appears as a nature myth, embodying the ambivalences that lie at the heart of primitive taboos, rituals, and religions, and the awe we feel toward that which we are unable to comprehend or master. From strata buried deep under our rationalistic understanding, it dredges up our feeling that the simple and the primitive—the stolid dignity and the superstitions of Sam Fathers—are the true. It evokes our terrible and fatal attraction toward the imperturbable, the powerful, the great—as symbolized in the immortal Old Ben. And it expresses our knowledge that as men we have to conquer and overcome, and our knowledge that it is beyond our human power to do so—that it is necessary and sacrilegious.

American Literature, XXIV (1952), 62–72. Some of the reference notes have been omitted.

DICKENS AND SOME MOTIFS OF THE FAIRY TALE

Shirley Grob

Dickens' confession in an 1853 issue of *Household Words* that he entertained "a very great tenderness for the fairy literature" of his childhood is not likely to come as much of a surprise to his readers.[1] Casual references to this literature—particularly to the Arabian Nights—brighten the pages of almost every novel and testify concretely to his belief that in "an utilitarian age, of all other times, it is a matter of grave importance that fairy tales should be respected."[2] More importantly, both character and plot in Dickens owe something to this primitive form of fiction. Critics unresponsive to the magic of "story" and interested only in clinical reactions describe Dickens' good and bad characters as "monsters"[3] of virtue and villainy, but countless readers have happily recognized that Mr. Pickwick, as he sets out "walking to the end of the world,"[4] or Little Nell, as she makes her way "untouched and unstained"[5] through the perils of the enchanted wood, retain some likeness to the prince and princess of the fairy tale. Dickens deliberately generates the greatest amount of external conflict possible by following the simple fairy-tale formula of pitting the smallest boy against the greatest giant or the gentlest girl against the wickedest witch. Similarly, his plots are ordered with a felicity and completeness found only in the fairy world. Just as the grateful fox who was spared by the kind young hero reappears at the end of the fairy tale to assist the hero in delivering the castle from an evil spell, so the seemingly unrelated elements in Dickens' plots eventually come together in the way most likely to please the reader.

This kind of hidden relatedness is also characteristic of the plot of many eighteenth-century novels and Elizabethan plays and romances, but Dickens' novels are particularly close to the spirit of the fairy tale in their concern for the underdog. In the fairy tale it is always the younger brother who wins the fortune, the ugly duckling who becomes the swan, and the poor goose girl who marries the prince and lives happily ever after. To Dickens these victories against impossible odds are always moral victories, and in his article on the fairy tale in *Household Words* he claims that

> It would be hard to estimate the amount of Gentleness and Mercy that has made its way among us through these slight channels. Forbearance, Courtesy, Consideration for the Poor and Aged, Kind Treatment of Animals, Love of Nature, Abhorrence of

---

1. "Frauds on the Fairies," *Household Words*, VIII (1853), 97.
2. *Ibid.*
3. Eugene Goodheart, "Dickens' Method of Characterization," *The Dickensian*, LIV (1958), 35.
4. G. K. Chesterton, *Charles Dickens: The Last of the Great Men* (New York: Readers Club, 1942), p. 67.
5. Edgar Johnson, *Charles Dickens: His Tragedy and Triumph* (New York: Simon & Schuster, 1952), I, 325.

Tyranny and Brute Force—many such good things have been first nourished in the child's heart by this powerful aid.[6]

This is undeniably a somewhat idealized impression of the fairy tale, as any adult who returns to them for the first time since childhood can affirm, but it is central to an understanding of Dickens' use of this material to recognize that this *is* his impression. Actually the same fairy tale is likely to contain elements from savage tribes, barbaric civilizations, and Christian societies; so that shockingly cruel customs, Eastern magic, and Christian virtues may be inextricably intertwined. Thus the underdog hero of the fairy tale may succeed, as Dickens suggests, by virtue of his moral superiority; but he may also succeed by luck, magic, physical strength, or even by cunning (as in the Puss-in-Boots cycle where the hero obtains riches by fraud and lying).

At any rate, Dickens particularly delights in such morally edifying fairy-tale favorites as "the ill-treated child," "the wicked step-parent," "the proud princess," and "the good bear," but the type which I should like to consider in the most detail is that of the man or woman who has some of the attributes and performs some of the functions of the benevolent fairy godmother. Such characters are present in Dickens all the way from *The Pickwick Papers* to *Our Mutual Friend*, but Dickens is not, of course, a static artist and the use he makes of this type changes correspondingly as his vision darkens and his methods mature. Moreover, the "fairy godmothers" are related to the running conflict in Dickens between self-responsible work and elective grace as the most desirable means of fulfilling "great expectations"; but they have not been discussed in any very systematic way or with much attention to their fairy-tale ancestry. I have no "expectations" of arriving at any very original conclusions regarding Dickens' changing beliefs, but I should like to suggest the "fairy godmother" as one convenient, and sometimes illuminating, perspective from which to view these changes. And in *Our Mutual Friend* we shall see how Dickens' partial return to his earliest manner in the handling of fairy-tale motifs contributes to the lack of intellectual and artistic unity in the novel.

The Good Rich Man who cheers his corner of the world by the simple expedient of distributing gold at the end of the novel is primarily a phenomenon of Dickens' early optimistic period. This generous *deus ex machina*, represented by such figures as Pickwick, the Cheerybles, old Chuzzlewit, and Scrooge, is compositely described by Orwell as a "superhumanly kindhearted old gentleman who 'trots' to and fro, raising his employees' wages, patting children on the head, getting debtors out of jail, and, in general, acting the fairy godmother."[7] "Acting the fairy godmother" is an accurate description of the function of such characters, but Dickens has not yet begun to make much use of their fairy-tale associations. Indeed, old Martin Chuzzlewit is reminiscent of the "crusty old man with heart of gold" common in eighteenth century novels.

It is not until *David Copperfield* that Dickens begins to exploit the fairy tale. "The ill-treated child who runs away from his stepmother"(fairy-tale fathers invariably

6. "Frauds on Fairies," *Household Words*, p. 97.
7. George Orwell, "Charles Dickens," *A Collection of Essays* (New York: Doubleday, 1954), p. 59.

make appalling mistakes in choosing their second wives) and "the young man who seeks his fortune" are two basic fairy-tale situations which are often fused in the novel, particularly in the so-called novel of education. David Copperfield then has some resemblance to all the sensitive young men who, as Trilling has put it, inevitably go through a "Tunnel of Horrors" in early life but, almost as inevitably, "come out safely at the other end."[8] But David's story is more closely related to the fairy tale than to the usual *Bildungsroman*, for young David sees the world as a place of ogres and good fairies, and, more importantly, he has a private fairy godmother who helps him out of the "tunnel."

Dickens is particularly skillful at giving a sense of the way the world looks to a child. One of his devices is the repeated use of fairy-tale imagery to suggest the intensity of childhood impressions. Children seldom see people as commonplace, so that somewhat uncommon persons become in their eyes exaggeratedly so. David consoles himself, while living under the Murdstone tyranny, by "impersonating" his favorite adventure story and fairy-tale characters and by "putting Mr. and Miss Murdstone into all the bad ones."[9] David himself is generally Tom Jones, Roderick Random, or Captain Somebody, but he sees the people he loves and hates as fairy-tale figures. Mr. and Miss Murdstone are obviously the "ogres" of the piece, the schoolmaster is a "giant in a story-book," (89) Rose Dartle is a "cruel princess," (667) Uriah Heep is an "ugly and rebellious genie," (747) and Mrs. Heep is an "ill-looking enchantress." (571) Little Emily, Dora, and Agnes are all fairies or good spirits. Although the fairy-tale imagery decreases as David grows older (Agnes, for example, comes more and more to be his "good Angel"), (367) it reappears abundantly, even tiresomely, in connection with David's infatuation for the incurably childish Dora. Dora is an enchanting "Fairy," (390) being in love with Dora is like being "in Fairyland," (396) and speaking seriously to Dora makes one either "Blue Beard," (636) or a "Monster who had got into a Fairy's bower." (543)

The description of David's birth on the first page of the novel immediately introduces the themes of luck and enchantment. The baby is born at a late hour of a Friday night, an hour which augurs that he may be unlucky in life but that he will be privileged to see spirits; while, on the other hand, he is born with a lucky caul. The grown-up David claims to have seen no actual spirits, but he admits that his great-aunt, Miss Betsy Trotwood, reminds him of "one of those super-natural beings whom it was popularly supposed I was entitled to see." (12) The suddenness of Miss Betsy's first appearance, the imperiousness of her manner, and the abruptness of her departure are unmistakable signs of Miss Betsy's kinship with the fairy people. David's mother sits weeping before the fire like Cinderella at the hearth when, lifting her eyes, she sees through the window a strange lady who is touched by the glow of the setting sun. (4) With all the quaint unpredictability of such creatures, Miss Betsy peers in at the window before entering, makes the odd request that David's mother take off her cap so that she can see her, and announces that she intends to be the new baby girl's

---

8. Lionel Trilling, *E. M. Forster* (Norfolk: New Directions, 1943), p. 79.

9. *David Copperfield*, p. 56. All quotations from the novels are from *The New Oxford Illustrated Dickens* (London: Oxford University Press, 1948–   ).

godmother. The new baby is a boy, and Miss Betsy silently puts on her bonnet and walks out of the house never to return, vanishing "like a discontented fairy." (12) Miss Betsy is certainly discontented, but she is not revengeful like the uninvited fairy in "Sleeping Beauty," who makes a wish that the infant Princess "shall prick herself with a distaff in her fifteenth year and fall down dead." Indeed there is a hint, in the best story-book manner, that Miss Betsy is very likely to turn out to be the good fairy. As David's mother sits hanging her head and weeping during the visit, she has "a fancy that she felt Miss Betsy touch her hair, and that with no ungentle hand; but looking at her, in her timid hope, she found that lady sitting with the skirt of her dress tucked up, her hands folded on one knee, and her feet upon the fender, frowning at the fire." (5) Later in the novel it is this "fancy," of which his mother had told him, that gives some faint encouragement to David in his desperate resolve to run away from the countinghouse of Murdstone and Grinby. The ragged runaway has no sooner been put to rest on his aunt's sofa than there is a repetition of this kind of moment:

> It might have been a dream, originating in the fancy which had occupied my mind so long, but I woke with the impression that my aunt had come and bent over me, and had put my hair away from my face, and laid my head more comfortably, and had then stood looking at me. The words, "Pretty fellow," or "Poor Fellow," seemed to be in my ears, too; but certainly there was nothing else, when I awoke, to lead me to believe that they had been uttered by my aunt, who sat in the bow-window gazing at the sea. (196)

It is an almost symbolic touch—the blessing of the good spirit, the wand of the fairy godmother. David remains anxious about what will be done with him, but it is all over for the reader, who knows quite well that Aunt Betsy is going to use her powers (which are really the resources of a good heart) to vanquish the wicked step-parents of the ill-treated child. The Murdstones loom gigantic to a frightened child, but when they appear in Miss Betsy's parlor "their physical strength, their awful visages, their hypocritical assumptions of respectability, are no match for the goodness and direct-ness of one brave frail old woman."[10]

Later in the novel David's aunt temporarily loses her money, but by this point David is no longer an ill-treated child. If he is a fairy-tale figure at all, he is the young man who must perform impossible tasks for the hand of his fairy princess. On being faced with the necessity for earning money, David thinks of himself rather romantically as setting out to clear his way through the "forest of difficulty," (520) cutting down trees one by one until he shall come to Dora. The difficulties of shorthand become one "gnarled oak" (545) in the forest. The prince and princess do not quite live "happily ever after," but Dora obligingly leaves David to Agnes, with whom he does live happily. Indeed the only fully ironic play on the conventions of the fairy tale occurs when Miss Mowcher, skeptical of the disinterestedness of Steerforth's criticisms of Emily's

10. E. K. Browne, "David Copperfield," *Yale Review*, XXXVII (1948), 659.

suitor, answers slyly, "Quite a long story. Ought to end 'and they lived happily ever afterward,' oughtn't it?" (334)

With the exception of *Our Mutual Friend*, Dickens' tendency after *David Copperfield* is toward an increasingly ironic use of the fairy tale. Esther Summerson, for example, begins her narrative in *Bleak House* with the comment that she had been brought up "like some of the princesses in the fairy stories" (15) by her godmother; but this godmother, far from sending Esther to the ball in a golden coach, keeps her home from the birthday parties of other children with the comment "It would have been far better, little Esther, that you had had no birthday; that you had never been born." (17) But at least the discovery of her disgrace—the illegitimacy of her birth—liberates her, as J. Hillis Miller points out, from false expectations and "forces her to assume full responsibility for her own life."[11]

Jarndyce is in some ways like the good rich man of the earlier novels, but he prefers helping his young charges into congenial professions to rescuing them from the necessity of earning a living. More importantly, if they persist in clinging to flimsy expectations, he is powerless to help them. Richard Carstone restlessly abandons surgery, the law, and the army, one after another, because "his blood is infected" (492) by the prospect of easy money from the settlement of "Jarndyce versus Jarndyce." Dickens is satirizing Chancery, of course, but he does not exonerate Richard from lack of self-discipline. Martin Chuzzlewit, it will be remembered, had also "been bred up from childhood with great expectations," (93) and, like Richard, is unable to make a go of his profession; but as soon as he learns a lesson in unselfishness, he is rescued and rewarded by the rich old man who has been anxiously watching over him. The biographical basis of *David Copperfield* makes one hesitate to call this novel the turning point in Dickens' attitude toward self-responsible work versus elective grace (good rich men, fairy godmothers, wills, etc.) as the most desirable means of getting money, but there is some change in the latter part of the novel, for the grown-up David lectures on the value of "steady, plain, hard-working qualities" (606) while his aunt commends him for coming out of their trial "persevering, self-reliant and self-denying." (776) Richard's trial, on the other hand, ends only with his death, and his whole career is a depressing process of mental and physical deterioration.

Great Expectations is both Dickens' most serious exploration of the theme of "expectations" and his most ironic (and sophisticated) use of the conventions of the fairy tale. Modern commentators have justly praised the discipline which Dickens exercises in this novel in subordinating everything to the central theme of innocence, false expectations, selfishness, disillusionment, and redemptive suffering. Similarly, in his use of fairy-tale material, Dickens exercises rigorous selection, and one of the minor ways he reworks some of the materials of *David Copperfield* is to eliminate all merely decorative or incidental fairy-tale images. The three or four fairy-tale references in *Great Expectations* are carefully selected to provide highly ironic commentary on the theme of "expectations."

Young Pip soothes his wounded feelings and thwarts the vulgar curiosity of his

11. J. Hillis Miller, *Charles Dickens: The World of His Novels* (Cambridge: Harvard University Press, 1959), p. 332.

sister and uncle by telling extravagant lies about his visit to Satis House, but he has seen for himself that Miss Havisham has some mysterious connection with death. Although his first impression was of richness and splendor, he had seen, after a moment, that everything in the room was faded and withered, "that everything had stopped, like the watch and the clock, a long time ago." (55) Pip finds Miss Havisham "perfectly incomprehensible"; (61) but, on his second visit, when he is taken to see the cobwebby bridal cake inhabited by splotchy spiders, he finds a name for her out of the fairy-tale books. He calls her "the Witch of the place." (79) Pip can not yet know the accuracy of his designation, for Miss Havisham's neurotic desire to mold a heartless beauty who will break the hearts of the men who love her is only a refinement of the traditional witch practice of bewitching children in order to eat their hearts; but at least he recognizes that she is bad. After Pip acquires his "expectations," his moral values deteriorate so that he is not able, or does not want to be able, to tell good from bad. On his way to London to take up his new station in life, Pip stops at Satis House to say good-by to Miss Havisham. She is again leaning on her crutchstick, but this time Pip sees it, not as the stick of a witch, but as the wand of a fairy godmother. In painful contrast to his restrained parting from Joe and Biddy, Pip goes down on his knees to kiss Miss Havisham's hand:

> She stretched out her hand, and I went down on my knee and put it to my lips. . . . She looked at Sarah Pocket with triumph in her weird eyes, and so I left my fairy godmother, with both her hands on her crutchstick, standing in the midst of the dimly lighted room. (149)

A comparison of Betsy Trotwood and Miss Havisham as fairy godmothers is a good measure of Dickens' tighter control over his materials and his greater interest in theme. Miss Betsy has a past, but it is not very important to her role as a fairy godmother (except in so far as we would *not* expect her to help David). It is not very important in explaining her character, for it may have bearing on her outward abruptness of manner but surely has no connection with her other eccentricities like her fear of fire or her objection to donkeys. Indeed, Miss Betsy's past does not come to light until she has ceased to be important as a character, and it is used primarily as an illustration of the theme of the "undisciplined heart" (661) which dominates the latter part of the novel. Miss Havisham, fantastic as she may be, is all of a piece, for every detail of her character takes its meaning from the most shattering event of her past. She is half-mad, but her madness has made her an artist, for in fashioning Estella into a breaker of hearts and in making her own life into an unrelieved "reproach"[12] to the man who jilted her, she is an inspired creator and a brilliantly false fairy godmother.

But the deepest irony of the novel comes not from the false fairy godmother, but from the true one. Miss Havisham, judged as a fairy godmother, simply reverses the fairy tale by seeking to frustrate the wishes of others; but Abel Magwitch, as a socially

12. *Ibid.*, p. 258.

unacceptable "fairy godmother" creates a problem foreign to fairy-tale literature.[13] In this primitive form of fiction the swineherd of natural nobility may become king by a stroke of good fortune with no questions asked. In "The Golden Goose," for a typical example, a mistreated youngest son shares his cake and wine with a little old gray man he meets in the wood. As a consequence of his good deed, he receives a golden goose, which eventually enables him to marry the king's daughter and inherit the kingdom. The old man's identity is not important. Pip, on the other hand, loses his natural goodness when he moves up in society, and he is snobbishly horrified when he learns that his "golden goose" was sent to him by a crude convict in gratitude for some wine and a pork pie. It is not, of course, until Pip learns to love the convict, accept the limitations of his place in society, and assume full responsibility for his own life that he becomes a gentleman in the true sense.

Our Mutual Friend I should like to consider in somewhat more detail, for the full extent of Dickens' use of fairy-tale motifs in this novel has not, I think, been commented on. The novel has been described both as Dickens' Wasteland and as his Indian summer, as the "darkest and bitterest"[14] of his novels and as a return to his "merrier and more normal manner."[15] Surely it is something of both, for the characters who compose the two main lines of plot—(1) Bella Wilfer-John Harmon-Noddy Boffin, and (2) Lizzie Hexam-Eugene Wrayburn-Bradley Headstone—are denizens of two different and really irreconcilable worlds. The theme of materialism, brought out most clearly perhaps in a third group of characters who bear the brunt of the social satire (Mr. Podsnap, Lady Tippins, Fledgeby, the Lammles, the Veneerings), is common to both strands of plot, but the treatment and implications are quite unlike. Recent critics tend to emphasize the darker side of the novel, the vision of vulturism. Society, from the slimy scavengers of the Thames underworld to the parasites of high society, is a swamp of "crawling, creeping, fluttering and buzzing creatures, attracted by the gold dust" (209) of the Harmon mounds. But muddy water does not trickle through all the pages of the novel, and the Bella-John-Boffin story is treated, with a surprising absence of irony, in the manner of the fairy story. Thus, elements from both Dickens' early and his late visions of society and the world are present in the novel, but I can not see that there is what has been called an intellectual and artistic "synthesis of his developing insight throughout a lifetime."[16]

Noddy Boffin does not perhaps look much like a fairy godmother, but as the agent responsible for raising Bella from "rags to riches," he fulfills something of this function. He might, of course, be called a final example of the Good Rich Man who appeared in some of the earlier novels, but, although he does not seem to be based on a specific fairy-tale figure (both he and Bella are composite types), the plot lines, the stock incidents, and the imagery suggest that he is of fairy-tale ancestry. Boffin's title immediately suggests the gold motif common to the fairy tale, but the "Golden Dustman"

13. Harry Stone, in an admirable analysis of the mythical elements of "Fire, Hand, and Gate in 'Great Expectations,'" *Kenyon Review*, XXIV (1962), 676–677, suggests that Magwitch fulfills not only the role of fairy godmother but that of the beast in "Beauty and the Beast."
14. Johnson, *Charles Dickens: His Tragedy and Triumphs*, II, 1043.
15. Chesterton, *Charles Dickens: The Last of the Great Men*, p. 168.
16. Johnson, *Charles Dickens: His Tragedy and Triumph*, II, 1041.

is no descendant of King Midas, for he knows too well the difference between the tarnished gold of misers and the "true golden gold" (773) of the generous heart. Mr. and Mrs. Boffin formulate two plans for doing good with their inheritance. They will adopt an orphan child (they have wished for a child "like the Kings and Queens in the Fairy Tales," (103) and they will try to bring true the "wishes" (112) of the girl who was disappointed of her riches.

Bella is often praised by commentators as a refreshing change from such monsters of virtue as Florence Dombey, Agnes Wickfield, and Esther Summerson, and so she is; but her portrait does not seem to me to have the psychological depth which distinguishes Bradley Headstone as a change from the usual monster of villainy. Her greediness is a "given" of the story which is as easily rooted out as the flaw in the character of any beautiful fairy-tale princess. Her initial selfishness has been intensified by her position in the will of old John Harmon, but her greediness is seldom put in a social context and she does not really impress one as trying "to keep up with" the Podsnaps, the Lammles, and the Veneerings. She longs for "money, money, money" (460) but the few times her longings take concrete form they are of an exotic nature— as when she thinks of sailing along coral reefs in the company of an Indian prince who has emeralds blazing on his turban. (319) The unmistakable fairy-tale touch, however, is Bella's tendency to ask questions of her looking glass like the proud queen in "Snow White and the Seven Dwarfs," who asks her magic mirror "Looking glass upon the wall / Who is the fairest of us all?"

Certainly there is a strong element of the incredible in the stratagem devised by Mr. Boffin and John Harmon for curing Bella of her greediness. Posing as a "regular brown bear" or "grisly old growler," (773) Mr. Boffin is somewhat reminiscent of all the tales like "Beauty and the Beast" or "Snow-White and Rose-Red" in which the hero is freed of his beast- or bear-covering when the heroine exhibits the requisite virtue. John, who has been posing all along as a poor man in order to test whether Bella can love him for himself, is more closely related to such stories as "The Swineherd" or "King Thrushbeard." In the latter, for example, the father of a haughty, but beautiful, princess, who scorns all her suitors, decides that his daughter shall marry the next beggar who knocks at the door. The beggar, who is really one of her old suitors in disguise, forces her to do the dirty work of the kitchen and to sell crockery in the marketplace. When the princess learns to regret her old pride and haughtiness, the beggar reveals himself as King Thrushbeard and explains, "for love of you I disguised myself . . . all this I did to bend your proud spirit and to punish you for the haughtiness with which you mocked me." The princess now feels she is not worthy to be his wife, but the King answers, "Be Happy! Those evil days are over. Now we will celebrate our wedding." Surely it is in such a spirit that we must read Bella's story if we are to believe that Bella does not mind having been deceived by her husband during her courtship, engagement, and the entire first year of her marriage, or that she does not mind having been subjected to an elaborate character test. Indeed, the whole episode of Bella's married life savors of the mysterious marriage taboo of primitive societies which have been preserved in fairy tales. Bella, for example, does not know her husband's real name and must never ask the reason of anything he does. One of the most famous of the fairy tales based on a primitive taboo, this time the religious taboo of the sacred enclosure, is "Bluebeard," and John admits that he does have a "secret chamber" (745) but that Bella must demonstrate perfect faith in him.

Moreover, the fairy-tale atmosphere of the Bella-John-Boffin story is reinforced by a quantity of fairy-tale imagery almost as great as in *David Copperfield*, where it is used to suggest the child's viewpoint. The little engagement supper celebrated by Bella, John, and Mr. Wilfer in the countinghouse of Chicksey, Veneering, and Stobbles is described three times as a supper of "three nursery hobgoblins at their house in the forest." (609) The wedding party, on the other hand, is somewhat more exotic with golden drinks from the Golden Age and fish from the *Arabian Nights*. (668) And, appropriately, the only anxiety of the wedding party had been the thought that perhaps Bella's mother might suddenly appear "like the spiteful Fairy at the christening of the Princesses, to do something dreadful to the marriage service." (665) But Bella's marriage is not jinxed and she assures John that his tender regard means as much to her "as the wishes in the fairy story that were all fulfilled as soon as spoken." (680) Even concrete objects, in keeping with the general atmosphere, hint delicately of the fairy tale—the rich dresses left behind when Bella flees down Boffin's great staircase, (601–602) the shoes that are a full size too large for Bella's little feet, (681) the lock of hair given to her father. (662)

But perhaps the most telling distinction between the atmosphere of Bella's romance and the atmosphere of Lizzie Hexam's romance is the more romantic handling of social status. Bella is raised *up* by the Boffins but it is hard to say what she has been raised up to. Mr. Boffin considers Henrietta Boffin to be a "high-flyer at Fashion" (55) and Lady Tippins leaves a card, but it requires quite an act of the imagination to think of the Boffins as really belonging to any social class. Even John Harmon's social status is not as clear as that of Eugene Wrayburn and it is reckoned in golden coins and sparkling jewels rather than family and visiting cards. Lizzie, of course, is raised from a much lower position than Bella to a higher one; but, as she has a kind of natural nobility, this in no way precludes a more romantic treatment of her story. She is, however, treated realistically. As the uneducated Cinderella of an unidealized world, she finds it somewhat painful to leap from class to class. She is eventually married to Eugene and in the final distribution of nosegays receives even the blessing of Eugene's "Reverend Father," but there is certainly considerable indication, as Boll points out in an article on the plotting of the novel,[17] that Dickens has geared the story for an unhappy ending with the death of Eugene. At any rate, love cannot silence the voice of Society, stupid as that voice may be, and Eugene has to become something of a hero, resolutely turning his back on the idea of taking his wife out to the colonies to escape the sneers of Podsnap and Lady Tippins.

The conclusion of the novel shows Dickens at his least responsible, for he does not seem able to resist showering riches on everyone in sight. Bella has been primarily the haughty princess who loses her false values and repudiates the golden coach of the Golden Dustman to walk with the muddy street sweeper, (599) but Dickens has been eagerly waiting to make her Cinderella again. Compared to Esther's new cottage at the

17. Ernest Boll, "The Plotting of 'Our Mutual Friend,'" *Modern Philology*, XLII (1944), 101.

end of *Bleak House*, Bella's new house is Aladdin's palace. Indeed there are echoes of the *Arabian Nights* in the description of the ivory casket of jewels on Bella's toilette table or the "charming aviary, in which a number of tropical birds, more gorgeous in color than the flowers, were flying about; and among those birds were gold and silver fish, and mosses and water-lilies, and a fountain, and all manner of wonders." (767) John, far from being a street sweeper (or a secretary or a China House employee for that matter), is again a rich man through the generosity of Mr. Boffin. The money seems rightfully his, of course, but the delight Dickens takes in dissolving the China House forever is an indication of the way Dickens appears, in this strand of the novel, to have returned full circle to his earliest position on the related matters of work, money, and expectations. But the passage which seems almost like self-parody on Dickens' part is the one in which John and Bella, having taken over the fortune from Mr. Boffin, play at being fairy godmothers themselves and bestow money on every underdog remotely associated with them:

> In tracing out affairs for which John's fictitious death was to be considered in any way responsible, they used a very broad and free construction; regarding, for instance, the dolls' dressmaker as having a claim on their protection, because of her association with Mrs. Eugene Wrayburn, and because of Mrs. Eugene's old association, in her turn, with the dark side of the story. It followed that the old man, Riah, as a good and serviceable friend to both, was not to be disclaimed. Nor even Mr. Inspector, as having been trepanned into an industrious hunt on a false scent. (803)

There is, however, one place in the novel where the grim world of the Thames waterside and the golden world of the fairy tale make contact, for there is yet a third "Cinderella" in the person of Miss Jenny Wren. The little dolls' dressmaker does not look at first glance like Cinderella, for she is a queer little person of indeterminate age with a deformed body and a drunken father. Moreover, she is not an angel of patience, and Dickens does not shrink from revealing the bitterness and sharpness which the circumstances of her life have created in her. But Jenny has another side which these realities have not been able to crush completely, a side represented visually by her long golden hair, and mentally by her shining visions of a better world where children are never chilled, anxious, ragged, or in pain. In his working notebook for *Our Mutual Friend*, Dickens sums up these two sides of the dolls' dressmaker as "her earthy side and her imaginative side."[18] Jenny does not escape from this life. She works incessantly and meets her responsibilities with all the resources of her deformed body, but the secret of her endurance, of her ability to cope with the grimness of her life, is her "imaginative side." One of the first things we learn about her is that her real name is Fanny Cleaver but that "she had long ago chosen to bestow upon herself the appellation of Miss Jenny Wren." (234) Similarly, she chooses to think of herself as her father's parent rather than as his neglected child, because in choosing the situation and accepting the responsibility for it, she can live with it. As Miller points out,

18. *Ibid.*, p. 107.

the act of changing a situation into "an imaginative version of itself is a way of dealing with it."[19]

It is some such consolation and encouragement which Jenny and the gentle Jew, Riah, derive from referring to each other as "Cinderella" and "fairy godmother," a ritual which prevents their best selves from being totally submerged in their material environment. The fairy tale, Dickens claims in *Household Words*, helps "keep us, in some sense, ever young, by preserving through our worldly ways one slender track not overgrown with weeds."[20] *Our Mutual Friend* lacks artistic unity because it tries to fuse two worlds which are governed by different laws, but the pleasure which Jenny takes in regarding her crutch-stick (the sign of her infirmity) as the wand of her fairy godmother (434) suggests that Dickens has not lost sight of the value of the type of novel which he began his career by writing. It is, of course, a more limited kind of literature than the dark complex novels of Dickens' last phase, but there is something eternally refreshing to the human spirit in the ritual fairy-tale triumph of the hero and heroine over the forces of darkness.

Texas Studies in Literature and Language, V (1964), 567–579. One reference note has been omitted.

19. Miller, *Charles Dickens: The World of His Novels*, p. 308.
20. "Frauds on the Fairies," *Household Words*, p. 97.

Mythic Themes and Forms

*The next three essays extend the concern with structural form developed in the two pre-
ceding groups. The critical focus in this group, it will be noted, is less on myth as image
patterns or as analogy than on its capacities for conditioning kinds of narrative and
embodying peculiarly universal themes. Specifically, James M. Cox ("Remarks on the
Sad Initiation of Huckleberry Finn") stresses the initiatory nature of Mark Twain's
themes; Louis Crompton ("The Sunburnt God: Ritual and Tragic Myth in* The Return
of the Native) *the interplay of myth and genre in Hardy's novel; and John B. Vickery
("Myth and Ritual in the Shorter Fiction of D. H. Lawrence") the structural relevance
of specific myths as well as the kinds of use to which Lawrence puts myth in general in
his short stories.*

REMARKS ON THE SAD INITIATION OF HUCKLEBERRY FINN

James M. Cox

The Adventures of Huckleberry Finn is one of those rare books which are at once
acceptable to the intelligentsia and to that celebrated American phenomenon, the
average citizen; it is a book which even anti-literary children read and enjoy. Even if
the language of the book should eventually be lost or, worse still, replaced by convenient
abridgements, the memory of Huck Finn would still survive among us like some old
and indestructible god. In the popular imagination, however, Huck Finn does not
exist by himself, but is accompanied by Tom Sawyer, his other half. These two figures
are not imagined as individuals; they are conceived as identical twins who roam about
the earth stealing jam, beating up sissies, playing hooky, and raising hell in general.
Furthermore, the Tom-Huck image exists in terms of Tom Sawyer; the real Huck
Finn who floated down the Mississippi with Nigger Jim has been shuffled under the
rather trivial aegis of the Bad Boy.

Yet there is a grim logic behind this discomforting shift, for if Huck stands un-
comfortably next to Tom Sawyer at least he has been there before. Indeed he even
adopted Tom Sawyer's name during those rather flat final chapters of *Huckleberry
Finn*. After Huck reached his unknown destination, the Phelps farm, the only terms
on which he could exist were Tom's terms, and, driven to distraction by the hemming
forces which threatened to annihilate him, he gave up his freedom to be free. In order
to save himself, the fugitive played the part of Tom Sawyer and in playing it he
completed his long, arduous, and disillusioning initiation. The characters, the implications, and the art of this initiation can be fully realized by beginning with the work
behind *Huckleberry Finn, The Adventures of Tom Sawyer*.

The most striking aspect of *Tom Sawyer* is its almost total lack of plot in the conventional sense of that word. There is little or no transition between episodes; continuity results from appearance and reappearance of the same characters. The most obvious defense of this lack of causal sequence—plot as machinery—is that it reinforces the pervasive determinism of Tom Sawyer's world. Although Tom reacts to the daily occurrences which confront him and although he makes belated attempts to meet his fate, he is quite powerless to initiate the action.

The real unity of Tom Sawyer arises not so much from the underlying determinism as from the insistent rhythm of the novel, a rhythm based upon repetition and variation of central motives. The violence and terror which are just beneath the surface of the boys' world regularly erupt into it. After the pleasures of the schoolroom comes the dark and unknown night, bringing with it fear and death. Even on Jackson's Island, the idyllic innocence of the afternoon is overtaken by a night thunderstorm which almost rips the island apart. Often this repetition is executed in much more subtle terms, providing submerged links between the episodes. Thus in one episode Tom and Joe Harper play Robin Hood in the dark woods, pretending to kill each other. The following night, in another scene, Tom and Huck witness the brutal murder in the graveyard. This effect is repeated when Muff Potter begs Injun Joe to swear secrecy in the matter of the killing, a scene followed by the one in which the boys, who have witnessed the crime, also swear to reveal nothing of what they have seen. They attempt to make their oath "real" by creating careful rituals which they religiously enact. The innocent rituals of the children are performed with grotesque reality by the adults. The chief characters of the book sense the fundamental dangers which confront them after the sun goes down, and they fall back on ritual and superstition to protect themselves from the inscrutable powers which lurk at the edge of the clearing.

The absence of formal transition, the constant rhythm of the action, the double exposure effect arising from the superimposition of one episode upon another all coordinate to give a kind of dream structure to the novel. The presence of characters is often unexplained and their disappearance unaccounted for. Becky Thatcher and Joe Harper fade out of the action toward the end of the novel; the doctor's appearance in the graveyard remains a mystery as does his motive for hiring the grave robbers. Characters slip in and out of their identity by wearing deliberate disguises (disguise and mistaken identity are favorite devices of Mark Twain which he uses brilliantly in *Huckleberry Finn* and interestingly in *A Connecticut Yankee, The Prince and the Pauper, Tom Sawyer Detective,* and *Pudd'nhead Wilson*); episodes drift into each other; sometimes, as with the Robin Hood game, an entire episode serves as a mask for another incident. The unity of the novel can be perceived only by looking *through* one scene into another.

Adding to this rhythmic structure and reinforcing the unity is, of course, the central character of Tom. Walter Blair, a Mark Twain specialist who attempted a conventional explanation of the structure of *Tom Sawyer,* contended that the novel deals with a boy's growth, but instead of analyzing the psychology of that growth he wandered away from his fertile suggestion and divided the novel into rather useless structural units. The novel is indeed about growing up. Appearing first merely as a Bad Boy,

Tom, as Mr. Blair points out, develops into a character of real interest. His humor has been much discussed, its sources have been thoroughly examined, but the psychology behind it has often been neglected. Tom's repeated death fantasies are nowhere scrutinized by the scholars who have so painstakingly provided a "background" for the novel, yet these very fantasies give Tom's character depth and complexity. Time after time the rhythm of the novel is expressed in terms of this death wish. Tom retires into solitude envisioning the mourning of the village when its inhabitants realize that he is no more. The culmination of the Jackson Island episode is the triumphal return of Tom and his two cronies to witness their own funerals. Even when death closes in on Tom and Becky in the darkness of the cave, Tom awaits it with a certain pleasure.

But there is another death, a death brutal and ghastly, lurking just beyond the boys' world and constantly impinging on it; it is the death in the graveyard and the death of Injun Joe—instead of warmth and protection this death is informed with terror. To see it as a brutal fact waiting in the adult world is to look with wistful eyes at that other death. The cave episode, fantastic from a "realistic" point of view, is oddly appropriate because it embodies the paradox of death and isolation; it is in the cave that Tom, in the very arms of the warm shadow, manages to find the will to force his way to light and safety, but it is also in the cave that Injun Joe meets one of the most violent and horrifying deaths in our literature. The two images of death are united in the cave, and it is hardly pure coincidence that Injun Joe, the demon who has haunted Tom's dreams, lies dead at the sealed doorway of the abyss from which Tom has escaped. Tom has, albeit unconsciously, experienced what Hans Castorp more consciously experienced in the snowstorm; he has glimpsed the sheer terror at the center of his childhood image of death. His immediate return to the cave to seize the treasure suggests his inner triumph.

The discovery of the treasure, significantly hidden under Injun Joe's cross, enables Tom to enter heroically the ranks of the respectable. Of course, he has been slyly respectable all along. Even when he breaks the law he does so with the intimate knowledge that he is expected to break it. His acute dramatic sense enables him to see the part he is to play, and he is therefore constantly aware of his participation in sacred social rites. This awareness results in a kind of compulsive badness in his nature; he achieves the Frommian ideal of wanting to do what society expects him to do. As the curtain drops there is triumphant confirmation of Tom's membership in the cult of the respectable. He is even trying to sell the club to Huck, cautioning him to remain a member of society because if one is to belong to Tom Sawyer's Outlaw Gang one must, paradoxically, obey the law:

> *Huck:* Now Tom, hain't you always ben friendly to me? You wouldn't shet me out, would you, Tom? You wouldn't do that, now, *would* you, Tom?
> *Tom:* Huck, I wouldn't want to, and I don't want to—but what would people say? Why, they'd say, "Mph! Tom Sawyer's Gang! pretty low characters in it!" They'd mean you, Huck.

The implications of Tom's entrance into society illuminate the differences between

Tom and Huck and also throw Mark Twain himself into much sharper focus. Van Wyck Brooks in his *Ordeal of Mark Twain* took the events of Twain's life and tried to see the books as repetitions of his life troubles, attempting to prove that Olivia Langdon and William Dean Howells thwarted Mark Twain's artistic development. Although his contention that Mark Twain never grew up is convincing, his approach is extremely questionable. Bernard De Voto has done much to dispel Brooks' theory that Mark Twain was thwarted, and for all his windiness, De Voto has seen that Twain himself was the prude as much as Olivia Langdon or Howells. A thorough analysis of Mark Twain's work will corroborate De Voto. He actually sought out Olivia Langdon, knowing full well she was a semi-invalid and a puritan. The picture of this "bad boy" coming east to roost is fraught with irony, and certainly his complete trust in Howells' judgment can hardly be blamed on Howells. He was perfectly content with the nickname, "Youth," by which Olivia called him, and he addressed his friend Mrs. Fairbanks as "mother" while his own mother was still very much alive. One scarcely has to be a Freudian to perceive that like Tom Sawyer he sought the authority and protection of respectability. In view of Twain's own quest it is quite remarkable, yet paradoxically inevitable, that *Huckleberry Finn* ever saw the light of day.

The Adventures of Huckleberry Finn is a conscious continuation and extension o *Tom Sawyer*. As he begins his own story, Huck carefully recounts the events of his immediate past. After mentioning the discovery of gold he goes on to say:

> The Widow Douglas she took me for her son, and allowed she would sivilize me; but it was rough living in the house all the time, considering how dismal regular and decent the widow was in all her ways; and so when I couldn't stand it no longer I lit out. I got into my old rags and my sugar-hogshead again, and was free and satisfied. But Tom Sawyer he hunted me up and said he was going to start a band of robbers, and I might join if I would go back to the widow and be respectable. So I went back.

Here is the argument of the entire novel—all that follows revolves around this major theme, Huck's initiation into respectable society. The tragic irony of the novel is Huck's inner awareness that membership in the cult will involve the dissolution of his character and the denial of his values.

Huck is hardly situated comfortably at the Widow Douglas' where Miss Watson plies him with frontier puritanism on the one hand and Tom Sawyer confronts him with bourgeois romanticism on the other, when his ruthless father suddenly appears demanding Huck's money which is happily drawing interest, having been shrewdly invested by Judge Thatcher. Pap's onslaught is momentarily halted by the young judge who, fresh from the East, attempts to reform the outcast drunkard. In a chapter significantly entitled "Pap Starts in on a New Life" the whole initiation and rebirth theme is launched on a tragi-comic note. The beautiful spare room in the judge's home is opened to Pap and great is the celebration by the judge's family as Pap jubilantly begins the new life, but during the night he slips out of the beautiful room, trades his new coat which they have given him for a jug of "forty-rod," and climbs back into the room, gets terribly drunk, finally falls off the porch roof into the yard—"and when they come to look at that spare room they had to take soundings before they could navigate it." After this fearful fall from respectability, Pap seizes Huck, whom he considers as property suddenly become valuable, transports him to a log hut up the river, and imprisons him. He treats Huck so violently that Huck finally stages a mock murder of himself in order to escape. This fake murder is probably the most vital and crucial incident of the entire novel. Having killed himself, Huck is "dead" throughout the entire journey down the river. He is indeed the man without identity who is reborn at almost every river bend, not because he desires a new role, but because he must re-create himself to elude the forces which close in on him from every side. The rebirth theme which began with Pap's reform becomes the driving idea behind the entire action.

Coupled with and inseparable from the theme of rebirth is the central image of death. Huck has hardly assumed the role of outcast when he meets Jim, who is also in frantic flight (interestingly enough, Jim is considered in terms of property too; his motive for escaping was fear of being sold down the river for $800.00), and the two fugitives watch the house of death float by on the swollen Mississippi. When Jim carefully covers up the face of the dead man in the house, the second major image of the novel is forged. These two images, rebirth and death, provide a frame for all succeeding episodes of the arduous initiation. As Huck and Jim move down the river, an oncoming steamboat crashes into their raft, forcing the two outcasts to swim for their lives. From this baptism Huck emerges to enter the new life at the Grangerfords under the name of George Jackson. His final act in that life is to cover the dead face of Buck Grangerford much as Jim had covered Pap's face in the house of death. When the Duke and King come aboard, their unscrupulous schemes force Huck and Jim to appear in new disguises; but the image of death is never absent. It confronts Huck in the little "one-horse town" in Arkansas where Colonel Sherburn shoots the drunken Boggs in cold blood. When the townspeople lift Boggs from the street and take him to the little drug store, Huck peers in through the window to watch him die. The Peter Wilks episode involves the same central images. The Duke and the King disguise themselves as foreign kinsmen of the deceased Wilks and they force Huck to play the role of an English valet. The final scene of the episode takes place in the graveyard where the mob of townsmen has gathered to exhume the buried Wilks in an effort to discover whether the Duke and King are imposters. A flash of lightning reveals the dead man with the gold on his breast where Huck had hidden it. The man who has Huck in charge forgets his prisoner in his zeal to see corpse and gold; Huck takes full advantage of the moment and runs out of that world forever.

Finally, at the Phelps farm the initiation is completed. Huck is reborn as Tom Sawyer and this time no image of death appears. The Duke and the King are far back in his past and the wheel has indeed come full circle. Jim is imprisoned in a cabin much like the one in which Pap locked Huck; Tom Sawyer himself comes to the rescue in the role of Sid Sawyer; the entire household, though not the same as the one in which the novel began, is related to it through strong blood ties. The full import of this initiation becomes more clearly evident when the differences between Huck and Tom Sawyer are examined.

All of Tom Sawyer's world has been imported into this novel, but with the addition of Huck as narrator and protagonist and Jim as his companion, Tom's world is seen in sharp perspective. Huck and Jim may have to live in that world but they are not of it, and their very detachment creates a larger and deeper universe of which Tom Sawyer's values are but a part. True, Huck is finally overtaken by the society represented by Tom, but his heroic flight and his inner resistance give dignity to his submission. Huck is, after all, incorruptible and though his body is finally captured by the society which "wants" him so, it has not got his name affixed to it; as the novel ends, the real Huck who cannot die is ready to "light out for the territory," to continue his restless flight from "sivilization." Tom Sawyer's initiation had been routine, had merely confirmed his membership in a society to which he already latently belonged; Tom's whole attitude toward his initiators was, as I pointed out, one of self-consciousness, even affectation. Huck's initiation, on the other hand, is forced upon him; his drama is different in that it is drama, not play; everything is at stake in an elemental conflict where the values of one world are pitted against the values of another. And Huck's humor is deeper and greater because it is underlain by the pathos and tragedy of his situation.

Huck is, in the deepest sense, an outcast. Although Tom is an orphan, he at least has relatives who recognize his credentials and have adopted him. Huck has only Pap, the drunkard, the outcast himself, whose eyes shine through his tangled, greasy hair "like he was behind vines." Pap attains intense symbolic stature in his brief but violent pilgrimage:

> ... There warn't no color in his face where his face showed; it was white; not like another man's white, but a white to make a body's flesh crawl—a tree toad white, a fish-belly white. As for his clothes—just rags, that was all.

There is in this description a supernatural quality which links Pap to Melville's whale. His ways are not so much evil as they are inscrutable; he has somehow gotten consumed by the very nature he set out to conquer and out of the dark union between himself and the River the divine Huck has sprung; Huck certainly belongs more to the river than to the society along its banks, but this in no way makes of him a Rousseauistic child of nature. His lineal descendancy from Pap removes him from the garden of innocence, but if it implies his connection with violence and terror, it also puts him in touch with the deeper human forces which cannot be neatly filed under sociological headings. He has "connections" which, though they do not enable him to get ahead in an acquisitive society, give him a depth and a reality which far surpass anything Tom Sawyer has dreamed of.

Both boys fall back on a world of superstition, but Huck's rituals are naturally inherited while Tom's are appropriated from books. Tom's whole life is an imitation of the romances he has read or heard in the middle class society of which he is a part. The drab and empty life of St. Petersburg forces Tom's mind into an irretrievable past and he pathetically attempts to revive dead chivalry in blighted prairie air. Huck's whole code is, on the contrary, part of him, and he reacts sensitively to life about him. Instead of importing life and law from outside worlds, he invests the objects and people of his world with a life of their own. The difference between Tom Sawyer and Huckleberry Finn is the difference between the primitive and the effete imagination. Tom's drive to dominate his companions, the quality which marks him a devotee at the shrine of William James's bitch goddess, arises from the imitative aspect of his mind. The artificial application of a foreign code demands its strict inflexibility. When Tom organizes his gang at the beginning of the novel he is helpless before the independent machinery of his code; even when the machinery obviously will not work, he insists on its use. In his desire to free Jim according to "the rules," Tom displays utter disregard for him as a human being. The ultimate irony emerges when Huck discovers Tom has known Jim was legally free all the time. This discovery explains the deep mystery to Huck who has been wondering all along why Tom Sawyer would "lower hisself" by helping a runaway slave. Through Huck's apparently innocent eyes we get an intimate glimpse into the soul of Tom Sawyer and we see an appalling relationship between Tom and Colonel Sellers, George Babbitt, and, I suppose, Willy Loman.

It is inevitable that Tom should assume Sid Sawyer's role when he reappears at at the end of the novel. Sid, Tom's half brother, was the Good Boy of *Tom Sawyer*; he was the eternal prude, the darling of a puritan Sunday School. Yet for all Tom's apparent romantic revolt, his values are Sid's values and though he retains illusions of himself he shows unmistakably that he really is Sid's half-brother. In the closing chapters of the novel Tom's very words become "respectable" and "principle," "regular" and "duty."

> ... The thing for us to do is just to do our *duty*, and not worry about whether anybody *sees* us do it or not. Hain't you got no principle at all?

Huck's relationship to Tom is much more distant. True, there are times when he attempts to emulate Tom Sawyer. Even when he stages his own murder he is conscious that Tom Sawyer would think it was right proud. He sometimes treats Jim the way Tom might treat him. He puts the rattlesnake in Jim's bed and sees the terrifying results. When the two of them board the *Walter Scott*, Huck consciously plays the role of the adventurous Tom much to the dismay of Jim. After Huck and Jim become separated in the fog, Huck attempts to deceive Jim into believing that the separation is a product of Jim's fertile imagination, but Jim humiliates him in the famous passage which ends:

> Dat truck dah is trash; en trash is what people is dat puts dirt on de head er dey frens en makes 'em ashamed.

Most of the time, however, Huck is living on too thin a margin to afford Tom's luxurious romances. His motives, arising from his struggle for survival, allow him to indulge in no impracticalities, but he knows the fugitive must rely on magic and superstition to propitiate the inscrutable powers which confront him. The wedding of the practical and the magical gives Huck's character a mobility in the constricting circumstances which envelop him. But all his mobility is not enough, for the forces which pursue him are as relentless as the Mississippi's current. They appear in the forms of the Duke and King, the Grangerfords and Shepherdsons and their feud, Judith Loftus, even Jim. Every living thing becomes a source of danger to the lost boy without a name. Huck's remarkable observation upon first seeing the Duke and King coming toward him at a run reveals the terror of his plight:

> ... Just as I was passing a place where a kind of a cowpath crossed the crick, here comes a couple of men tearing up the path as tight as they could foot it. I thought I was a goner, for whenever anybody was after anybody I judged it was *me*—or maybe Jim.

Because Huck completely lives his rituals, because he participates to the tips of his fingers in a struggle for survival, and because his whole world and all its values are at stake, he transcends the empty rituals of Tom Sawyer's universe and achieves mythic significance.

When he wearily walks into the Phelps yard and is once more faced with the inevitable proposition of creating himself, he feels his string playing out. At Judith Loftus', at the Grangerfords', before the King and Duke, Huck, the man without identity, had been able to choose his disguise from a vast store of verbal masks which he kept ready at hand; but at the Phelps home even his name has been chosen and he bewilderingly attempts to discover who he is. As he stands before Aunt Sally trying to solve the riddle of his identity, he feels so tight and uncomfortable that he almost wishes he were dead:

> ... Well, I see I was up a stump—and up it good. Providence had stood by me this fur all right, but I was hard and tight aground now. I see it warn't a bit of use to try to go ahead—I'd got to throw up my hand. So I says to myself, here's another place where I got to resk the truth.

The swirl of events never allows him to "resk the truth" (the phrase itself suggests the ironic plight of Huck's position throughout the novel): Uncle Silas Phelps arrives at this precise moment and Huck finds to his delight and amazement that he is supposed to be Tom Sawyer. The very language Huck uses at this point suggests the myth behind the humor:

> By jings, I almost slumped through the floor! But there warn't no time to swap knives; the old man grabbed me by the hand and shook, and kept on shaking. . . . But if they was joyful, it warn't nothing to what I was; for it was like being born again, I was so glad to find out who I was.

There is bitter irony in Huck's assumption of Tom's name because the values of Tom Sawyer are so antithetical to the values of Huck Finn; in the final analysis, the two boys cannot exist in the same world. When Huck regains his own identity at the very end of the novel he immediately feels the compulsion to "light out for the territory" because he knows that to be Huck Finn is to be the outcast beyond the paling fences. From Mark Twain's point of view in this novel, Tom Sawyer civilization involves obedience, imitation, and is directly opposed to a dynamic and creative frontier imagination. In Tom Sawyer's triumph, the hard core of Mark Twain's later disillusion and pessimism is already evident. Although Huck Finn may escape to the territory, the whole outline of the frontier is receding westward before the surge of small town culture, and it is indeed doomed country into which Huck must retreat.

Huck Finn cannot be reduced to historical proportions, however, even though there is much in the novel for the historian. The territory to which Huck refers is more than a diminishing area in nineteenth century America. It is a metaphoric equivalent of the broader and deeper vision which Huck and Jim represent. To be in the "territory" is not to be in heaven, for the wilderness and waste places have their perils for the sojourner, as Pap's presence fearfully testifies, but it is to escape the dehumanizing forces of the little towns; it is to be stripped of the pride encouraged by a sterile respectability and to feel absolute humility in the face of the awful unseen powers. Huck and Jim are the only real human beings in the novel—they are human because they can still feel and because they possess a heightened sensitivity to the promises and terrors of life. The characters whom they encounter, with the exception of the young and innocent, have an angularity and rigidity which mark them as grotesques. The blind spots of the eminently respectable become proving grounds for the avaricious; the pretentious righteousness of one group merely encourages the brutal sensationalism of another. Only Huck and Jim possess wholeness of spirit among the horde of fragmentary personalities which parade through the novel. The society which hotly pursues Huck and Jim knows that they possess the real secrets—that is why it so desperately wants to "own" them.

And if Tom has taken Sid's role and Huck has been forced to take Tom's in this rather discouraging progression, who is left to take Huck's place? Fifteen years later Mark Twain could not answer the question, for his imagination had been consumed by what Bernard De Voto calls the symbols of despair. There is someone, however, to take Huck's place in this novel; he is, of course, that primitive of primitives, Jim. He stands in relation to Huck in this novel much as Huck stood in relation to Tom in *Tom Sawyer*, and is in many ways the central figure of the book. It is to Jim that Huck retreats as if to a savior; he it is who mothers Huck as they travel down the big river; and he it is who, knowing secretly that Huck's Pap is dead forever, takes Huck to his own bosom to nourish him through the ordeal of being lost. Acting as Huck's foster father, Jim brings to that role a warmth and gentleness which Huck had never known under the brutal masculinity of his real father. Near the end of the novel, after Jim has accompanied and protected Huck on their perilous journey, how appropriate it is that he should be led back to the Phelps plantation, following his temporary escape with Tom, arrayed in the dress which the boys had stolen from Aunt Sally. The incident points up the ambivalent nature of Jim, emphasizing his role of motherly father to Huck. Leslie Fiedler, looking at the novel as an American myth of love, has searchingly explored this ambivalent relationship.

Jim is also one of the two great human forces in the book. By means of his truth and sincerity, the fraud and hoax of the world along the river banks are thrown into sharp relief. Probably the finest example of Jim's function as a moral norm occurs on the raft just before the King and Duke meet the country boy who unwittingly directs them into the Peter Wilks exploit. Huck awakens at daybreak one morning to see Jim grieving to himself. Jim finally tells him that a whacking sound he heard on shore reminded him of the time he disciplined his little daughter for not obeying a command. Upon repeating his command to no avail, Jim finally struck the child down, only to find that her recent attack of scarlet fever had left her deaf and dumb:

> Oh, Huck, I burst out a-crying en grab her up in my arms, en say, 'Oh, de po' little thing! De Lord God Almighty forgive po' ole Jim, kaze he never gwyne to fogive hisself as long's he live!' Oh, she was plumb deef en dumb, Huck, plumb deef en dumb—en I'd ben a-treat'n her so!

Immediately after this burst of genuine remorse, the Duke and the King launch their expedition to rob the Wilks daughters of their inheritance by pretending to be Peter Wilks' foreign kinsmen. The Duke poses as a deaf mute. By employing the same device he used so successfully in *Tom Sawyer*, Twain establishes a subtle and exquisite relationship between the two episodes. Through Jim's sensitivity the entire Wilks episode is thrown into much more precise focus. Indeed, Jim is the conscience of the novel, the spiritual yardstick by which all men are measured. As the two fugitives move down the river, Huck's whole moral sense grows out of and revolves around the presence of Jim, and his ability to measure up signifies his worth. Huck's whole sense of wrong, his feeling of guilt are products of his intimate association with Jim—his companionship with the runaway slave makes possible his moral growth.

Many critics, intent on seeing Jim as a symbol of the tragic consequences of slavery, have failed to see that he is much more than this. He is that great residue of primitive, fertile force turned free at the end of the novel at the very moment Huck is captured. That Mark Twain recognized in the Negro a new American protagonist is evident not only in his creation of Jim, but in his interesting return to the whole problem of slavery in *Pudd'nhead Wilson*. Certainly Jim and Thomas à Becket Driscoll stand solidly behind Faulkner, Robert Penn Warren, and Richard Wright. Having been thrown from his secure place within the social structure, Jim will be the new fugitive which the bourgeoisie will, with a great deal of hesitation, wish to make respectable.

There is an inexorable and crushing logic inherent in the ending of *Huckleberry Finn*. T. S. Eliot, in his remarkable introductory essay to the Cressett Library edition of the novel, remarked the inevitability of the final chapters, but failed to enlarge upon the generalization. Most critics agree that the ending is much weaker than the rest of the book, as indeed it is, but often they mistakenly gauge that weakness. Certainly Tom's reappearance itself does not weaken the ending. Any comprehensive vision of the book will, it seems to me, consider Tom's presence at the end not only vital but inevitable. The flatness of the ending results from Tom's domination of the action and the style. As soon as he appears, his whole aggressive spirit bids for position, and although Mark Twain attempts to use Huck to exploit the ironies of the situation, Tom's seizure of the style damages the tenor of the novel. It is a stylistic rather than a structural flaw, a failure in taste rather than in conception.

Mark Twain's failure in taste at this particular juncture bears further consideration. *Huckleberry Finn* is without question his greatest work, and diametric opposition of

Tom and Huck is eminently clear. The substitution of Tom's humor for Huck's vision indicates that Mark Twain, though aware of the two sets of values, could not keep a proper balance between them because of his fascination with Tom Sawyer. In turning over the narration to Huck Finn he had turned to the incorruptible part of himself which was not for sale and could not be bought. The opening paragraph of the novel indicates that he was not entirely unaware of what he was about:

> You don't know about me without you have read a book by the name of *The Adventures of Tom Sawyer*; but that ain't no matter. That book was made by Mr. Mark Twain, and he told the truth, mainly. There was things which he stretched, but mainly he told the truth.

"Mainly he told the truth." In this novel Mark Twain tried to tell the whole truth through Huckleberry Finn. Although Tom Sawyer makes his presence too much felt at the end of the novel, Mark Twain saw his whole truth with supreme vision. Because of the deeply human values which are at stake, neither the satire nor the humor is tainted by the scoffing disillusion and the adolescent cynicism in which he finally foundered. The unobtrusive formal perfection allows the novel to retain the primitive power and immediacy of the myth which it recreates; its impact strikes us in the profoundest areas of our consciousness, and we are reminded of the darkness and the terror and the violence which stalk the virgin forest where the American dream lies waiting, aware and unaware.

Sewanee Review, LXII (1954), 389–405.

THE SUNBURNT GOD: RITUAL AND TRAGIC MYTH IN *THE RETURN OF THE NATIVE*

Louis Crompton

The writer of prose fiction has, in general, three courses open to him. He may write prose romance, in which case the setting of his story is usually fabulous and its imaginary world either pleasanter than real life or more sinisterly mysterious. Alternatively he may, as in the case of Fielding or Jane Austen, imitate epic or dramatic forms of the tightly plotted sort that Aristotle analyzes in the *Poetics*. Or, again, he may regard himself as a social scientist, and base his novel not on romantic myth or rationalized plot but on some psychological or social theory.

Criticism has, in its turn, tended to align itself with these three modes in placing its emphasis on one or the other: on the analysis of archetypes, on characterization and dramatic probability, or on the novelist's social vision. Partisanship, one notes, has not been unknown. Social realists—Zola, for instance—have usually seen the three modes as an entelechy, romance being a kind of embryo, and dramatic form (now decried as "theatrical") merely a further stage on the way to modern realism. At the moment the social realists are somewhat in retreat, and archetypal critics have gained ground. But have we not formulated the critical problem too crudely in assuming that these readings of fiction are mutually exclusive? There may, rather, be some advantage in aiming at increased breadth of response in the reader quite apart from what we may call the "party lines" of literary criticism.

Take, for instance, *The Return of the Native*, a novel often relegated, with the rest of its author's writings, to the category of "transitional fiction," with the implication that we are here faced with a monstrous mixture of Victorian theatricalism and scientific modernism. Since Hardy is a novelist with a manifestly superb sense of formal unity, such a judgment ought to leave us uneasy. Perhaps the solution lies not in dismissing the book as, formally, a weird hybrid but rather in seeing it as a work of fiction in which the writer is using all three modes simultaneously as part of a carefully wrought whole. Since the first, or romantic, aspect of Hardy's art has up to now received least attention, the aim of what follows is to illuminate this romantic element, but the reader who has always read the book realistically will do well to keep his "realistic" interpretation firmly in mind. The purpose of this essay is not to replace a story of "real events" by "pure" mythology but to show how the two interpenetrate each other.

The Return of the Native is unusual among the run of Victorian novels in that it contains, on however small a scale, a messianic hero. Such a type is a natural link between romance and tragedy. It is rare in Renaissance tragedy, with its cult of king and courtier, and is probably best represented in English literature by such religious dramas as *Samson Agonistes* and *Saint Joan*. Since the English novel developed in a period largely hostile both to romance and to religious enthusiasm, its central male characters are usually the heroes who are no heroes, *hommes moyens sensuels* like

289

Tom Jones or the young men in Dickens and Thackeray. The religious figures, on the other hand, are most often the hypocrites and fools appropriate to comic art.

The Return of the Native is, of course, a double tragedy with two main characters, Clym Yeobright and Eustacia Vye. But we may perhaps best understand the structure of the book by looking first at Hardy's male protagonist. The first thing we notice is that he has something of the sense of mission shared by both Joan and Samson. He is both a hero with tragic stature and (more surprisingly, in view of Hardy's agnosticism) a figure in a religious ritual. His character contains the fatal imbalance of the tragic hero at the same time that it raises him above the mob of mediocrities. "Was Yeobright's mind well-proportioned?" Hardy asks:

> No. A well-proportioned mind is one which shows no particular bias; one of which we may safely say that it will never cause its owner to be confined as a madman, tortured as a heretic, or crucified as a blasphemer. Also, on the other hand, that it will never cause him to be applauded as a prophet, revered as a priest, or exalted as a king.[1]

Clym is a sanguine idealist who plans a revolutionary educational scheme. His youthful naïveté is so much insisted upon that it comes as a shock to learn (in the epilogue) that he is past thirty. There is a touch of the young Milton about him, and like Milton he chooses a ridiculously inappropriate mate for his scholarly undertaking. The natural symbols for such a character would suggest altruism, youth, enlightenment (ironically qualified by hints of blindness), pride, and soaring aspiration. His name conveys the first three of these, "Clym" being short for "Clement," and the *yeo-* in "Yeobright" an archaic form of "young." When Hardy tells us that, "As is usual with bright natures, the deity that lies ignominiously chained within an ephemeral human carcase shone out of him like a ray" (168), he evidently wishes us to associate Clym with suffering heroes like Prometheus and disguised gods like Apollo. The peasant bonfires that precede his arrival celebrate the death and rebirth of the Teutonic sun-god, Balder:

> Moreover to light a fire is the instinctive and resistant act of man when, at the winter ingress, the curfew is sounded throughout Nature. It indicates a spontaneous, Promethean rebelliousness against the fiat that this recurrent season shall bring forth foul times, cold darkness, misery and death. Black chaos comes, and the fettered gods of the earth say, Let there be light. (19)

Hardy several times describes Clym's hair as a golden halo, lit by the sinking rays of the winter sun. In view of these facts we should not be surprised that after one of the most elaborate preparations in English literature, Hardy has Clym make his appearance exactly at the moment of the winter solstice. Or rather, that this is the first of two "first" appearances, since Eustacia only hears his voice on this occasion. She does not actually see him till Christmas Day. The year's time in which the action of the novel

---

1. *Return of the Native* (New York: Harper, 1899), pp. 212–213. Subsequent page references in the text are to this, the Wessex, edition.

takes place thus serves a triple purpose. Hardy seems to have considered it an equivalent to the twenty-four hours of classical tragedy. Ruth Firor, in her fascinating study of Hardy's folklore, has pointed out that it corresponds to the Celtic year, which is based on a vegetation cycle, and has its chief festivals in November and May. But we have also a parallel with the Christian church year, since the book begins with an "advent" leading to the Christmas epiphany and ends with a tragic crisis which occurs on a night "as dark as Gethsemane."

The account of any effort to realize a romantic or messianic ideal of heroism in real life is likely to be hedged with more than a little irony. The would-be hero may be shown up as a likeable but misguided idiot, as in *Don Quixote*, or the whole force of the association may lie in the contrast, as in T. S. Eliot's use of heroic myth to expose a debased and vulgarized present. Hardy's use of heroic archetypes is partly serious and partly ironic, his characters appearing at one moment comparable to their heroic models, at other times ludicrously smaller and weaker. Clym is at the same time the shining hero of romance, the flawed hero of classical tragedy whose *hubris* leads to his downfall, and the diminished hero of modern realism.

Full-fledged heroic romance begins with the hero's birth, as in the Siegmund-Sieglinde portion of the *Ring*. Hardy has preferred to concentrate on what Frye in the *Anatomy of Criticism* has called the secondary, or initiatory, stage of romance. This part of the cycle generally describes the hero's induction into some cult, religious or secular (as in the case of knighthood) and his temporary withdrawal from the world. The eligibility of Egdon as a place of retreat is obvious. It is in real fact the desert against whose ignorance and isolation Clym must struggle. In the famous set-piece with which the novel opens, Hardy compares the heath successively to the classical Tartarus, to Dante's Limbo, and to the wilderness of Genesis 21. Such a cluster of analogues may seem to load the symbolism rather heavily, but each makes its point: Tartarus is the prison of the exiled Titans (and of that bored Olympian, Eustacia), Limbo is the abode of spiritual darkness from which Christ rescues men on Easter Saturday, and Ishmael's desert brings to mind both Venn and Yeobright in their roles as social outcasts.

In the archetypal romance, the hero's withdrawal is traditionally a period of probation in which he gains knowledge for his coming mission. Hitherto untried, he now undergoes a series of ordeals of which the commonest are temptations to wealth or sexual pleasure. Examples would be the testing of Guyon in Book II of the *Faerie Queene* or of Parsifal in the Grail legends. (Milton is sufficiently aware of the parallels between the tests facing the romantic hero and the temptations of Christ that he pauses, in *Paradise Regained*, to explain the difference.) Failure at this point is felt to be particularly ignominious and usually results in the hero's regression to a state of servitude, called "effeminacy" in Spenser and symbolized in *Samson Agonistes* by physical blindness.

Unlike the hero, whose messianic pretensions we are likely to regard quizzically, the witch is a romance figure that has survived into modern fiction relatively unchanged, her most dangerous powers having always been largely sexual anyway. Within the tradition of nineteenth-century realism, Eustacia Vye is a spoiled neurotic whose imagination, fed on popular novels and romanticized history, has bred dreams doomed to frustration by her marriage to an unambitious husband. Anyone who attempts to read the book only on this level, however, will probably be baffled by a number of points, particularly her frequent disguises. These can be understood only if one realizes that part of Hardy's purpose is to gather around her the sinister suggestions which surround the witch of romance: hence her reputation for necromancy, the "crooked sixpence" (a witch's charm) with which she pays Johnny for watching the bonfires, and her comparison of herself on another occasion to the witch of Endor.

Perhaps the most curious scene in *The Return of the Native* is Eustacia's appearance in the mummers' play. Her transvestitism sounds like an echo of Shakespeare or Gautier; the meaning of the episode, however, most likely lies in its ritual significance. The mummers' play in which she takes part originally consisted of a combat between Winter and Summer, in which Winter is killed and then revived by the Leech. The engrafting of the St. George legend upon this rite is a late development. Eustacia's part, the "Turkish Knight" who is St. George's antagonist, is a descendant of the original Night-Winter figure. (Hardy elsewhere remarks of Eustacia's hair that "a whole winter did not contain darkness enough to form its shadow: it closed over her forehead like nightfall extinguishing the western glow" [77].) The dénouement, in which St. George is magically restored to life, is an interesting adumbration of the novel's action. Hardy points up the analogy by excerpting from the text the lines that tell of the Saint's marriage to a mysterious dark southerner, "the King of Egypt's daughter." This last detail reminds us that Hardy has already explicitly compared Eustacia to one eastern temptress, Cleopatra, and indirectly to another, Nausicaa, when he makes her father a Corfiote, from "Alcinous' isle."

The great fictional studies of the pathology of the romantic imagination are, of course, *Don Quixote* and *Madame Bovary*, and Hardy, by pairing a starry-eyed idealist with a dissatisfied neurotic, is attempting variations on the themes of Cervantes and Flaubert. But the use of realism to satirize romanticism generates an irony that is double-edged. Commentators not infrequently turn satires on romance upside down and exalt the Don Quixotes over their humdrum neighbors. If realism makes romance look absurd, romance has a way of making real life look absurd, too, when it protests against its dullness and compromises. Consequently we should not be puzzled if both Clym and Eustacia appear to us as simultaneously sympathetic and perverse.

There is a difference, however, between Clym and Eustacia as romantic dreamers. The difference is, indeed, crucial, and lies in the fact that Clym's imagination is essentially pure while Eustacia's is corrupted. Both are at odds with their environment, both are blinded by hopeful illusions, but where Clym suffers from nothing worse than naïve ignorance of the world and women, Eustacia is disastrously egotistical. Diggory Venn's selfless devotion to Tamsin is incomprehensible to her, and she is equally baffled by Clym's disgust with the business of diamond-selling. With superb irony Hardy makes the climax of Clym's courtship the scene in which Eustacia wrests from her unwilling lover a description of the play of lights on the jewels in the Apollo Gallery of the Louvre.

She dreams of herself as a Sultana at the side of a strong-willed emperor, indulging her desire for "music, poetry, passion, war" (351). When Hardy says that Eustacia was "not entirely unlovable" he can hardly mean more than that she inspires the pity we feel for selfish people, weak rather than tyrannous or cruel, whose schemes come to nothing. Moreover, though she dreams of inspiring a grand passion, she is peculiarly cold herself. Despite the hints of banked erotic fires, Hardy, in the celebrated passage in which he calls her a goddess in Cimmerian exile, compares her to Artemis, Hera, and Athena, not to Aphrodite, who would seem to be the obvious choice. Eustacia is able to persuade herself, temporarily, that she is in love with Clym but only so long as she thinks he can realize her dream of a knight in silver armor who will rescue her from the heath.

Eustacia's natural affinities, Hardy tells us, are for "dark" kings like Saul or for worldly sophisticates like Pontius Pilate, both of whom are chiefly notable as antagonists of messianic heroes. Wildeve, however, falls as far short of her ideal as Clym; his lack of aggressive strength so diminishes him in Eustacia's eyes that she comes to prefer suicide to escape with him. As the opposite of an Apollonian figure he is identified with darkness, confusion, and night, and Hardy fixes him in the world of romance by giving him a face shaped like a Gothic shield. "Wildeve" suggests a sabbath of warlocks and witches and Eustacia, appropriately enough, conjures him up on three successive Fifth of Novembers.[2] Wildeve's archetype is the lonely knight of Keats' ballad, wandering on the barren heath under the enchantress' spell. Alternatively, in a realistic sense, he is to Mrs. Yeobright the awful example of a professional man gone wrong through some woman's influence. Hardy describes him as petulant, gloomy, and masochistic, and compares him, fittingly enough, to Rousseau, whose description of himself as just this kind of nympholept has been shocking moralists for two hundred years.

Diggory Venn is a rather more difficult character to place. "Diggory" is a name of Cornish origin. It appears most notably in the medieval tale of *Sir Degarre*, but by the nineteenth century it was used chiefly for rustics and servants. Venn seems to belong with a special group of fictional archetypes, the Ishmaels or outsiders, young men out of luck in fortune or love who stand aside from the main action but occasionally start it off in some new direction. His role is like Edgar's in *King Lear*: both are "pseudo-bogeymen" and both show considerable eligibility as heroes, the mixture of stoicism and chivalry they represent being pretty irresistible. The problem for the author is to keep such characters in their secondary billing, since there is always a lively popular demand that he forget about the tragedy and find this man a nice sympathetic girl to settle down with, as Tate did in his revision of *Lear* and Hardy had to in his "Aftercourses."

Everyone has noted that the characters in romance are either all white or all black. Hardy varies this scheme by making his characters black or red, a less radical departure from convention than would at first appear. The dark characters, Wildeve and Eustacia, both suffer from depression of spirits, or as Hardy somewhat grandiloquently calls it, "hypochondriasis." Eustacia's odd accoutrements of watch, hourglass, and telescope recall the paraphernalia of the brooding housewife in Dürer's "Melencholia 1," an important icon for nineteenth-century representations of despair. The

2. The Walpurgis Night aspect of the Celtic New Year is preserved in the modern Hallowe'en.

complement of black in the spectrum of humors is red. Tamsin's red hair symbolizes her sanguine temperament, but the chief connotations of red in the novel seem to be humility and rusticity, the heath-cutters reddish colored leggings being a sign of their social rank. ("Russet," for this reason, means both "red" and "clownish" in Shakespeare and Milton.) Eustacia, who is chagrined at Clym's loss of his "golden halo," is particularly enraged that he should look like a laborer after his eyesight fails:

> Ah! you don't know how differently he appeared when I first met him, though it is such a little while ago. His hands were as white and soft as mine; and look at them now, how rough and brown they are! His complexion is by nature fair, and that rusty look he has now, all of a colour with his leather clothes, is caused by the burning of the sun. (349)

Diggory Venn's redness is also a social stigma.

Romance deals with legendary heroes, high tragedy with kings and rulers, modern realism with people who often give the impression of being smaller and dingier than the average. Hardy relates his characters to myth through his romantic archetypes, and solves the problem of the tragic hero's social elevation by underscoring the Vyes' and Yeobrights' sense of superiority to the general ruck of peasants and small farmers who make up the closed society of the heath. As a naturalist we should also expect him to turn the telescope around and show the characters in reduced scale as insignificant figures in a landscape. He does this in the furze-cutting scenes where Clym is compared to "a mere parasite of the heath, fretting its surface in his daily labor as a moth frets a garment" (343).

The entomological details of the book remind us that the imagery of naturalist fiction is remarkably fixed, as conventional in its own way as the dragons and steeds of chivalry. Steinbeck's turtle, Hemingway's ants, and the rabbits and wounded pheasants of *Tess* are all related symbols of human impotence. In the grim scene of Mrs. Yeobright's death in the August heat, Hardy draws the reader's attention to the plight of the "obscene creatures" wallowing under the half-baked mud and the helplessness of the wasps drunk on the fermented fruit in the orchard.

In romance the hero is free, his story an extended exercise in wish fulfillment; in tragedy he is subject to fate and moral judgments and in modern realism to biological and economic laws which seriously limit any sense of human responsibility. Certainly, *The Return of the Native* is nearer to the tragic norm than the economic and psychological determinism of *Tess*. When Hardy, in the love scenes, describes the heath as overlaid with a purple mask that hides its harshness, he is indulging in the kind of irony that Schopenhauer would have appreciated, but in general the characters seem to be less the victims of some inexorable natural law than of the play of chance and the operation of a free, and even perverse, human will.

The large number of disastrous accidents have led critics to complain, somewhat irrelevantly, of Hardy's "pessimism." Pessimism is, indeed, less a matter of chance than of a belief in inexorable laws that make for human misery. True, there is a hint of some such fatalism in Clym's marriage. Clym and Eustacia have exactly opposite aspirations, but their characters and situations make it all but inevitable that they should misjudge each other. Eustacia's melancholy and her persecution appeal to Clym's chivalry at the same time that his infatuation makes him blind to the "idle voluptuary" Mrs. Yeobright sees. Nevertheless, there is an element of hubristic wilfulness (Hardy's phrase for this is "pride of life") and even something paradoxically perverse in the steely reserve which underlies his sympathetic and self-sacrificing nature.

This combination of pride and idealism is an instinctive bond between Clym and his mother at the same time that it separates him from her. Mrs. Yeobright is thus reduced to the pathetic role of a Cassandra who foresees tragedy but is helpless to prevent it. Nevertheless it is possible to argue that her relationship with her son is the emotional center of the book. Certainly, her journey across the heath as a suppliant for his love is one of the most poignant scenes in English fiction. It is connected with another study of parent-child estrangement, *King Lear*, through several details: the setting, the serpent sting which causes her death, and the boy who accompanies her. But the boy is not an ironic commentator on the action like Lear's fool. Hardy emphasizes his childish self-absorption as a subtle way of underlining Mrs. Yeobright's sense of alienation from her son. His rhythmical questions ("Dó you álways dráw your bréath like thát?" [356]) imitate the tragic ballad, which also often takes the form of a dialogue between a sufferer and a coolly detached interlocutor.

Clym's reaction to his mother's death is violent in the extreme. Reaction from a siren is likely to produce a flight to a protective mother-figure; Clym is about to seek out his mother when he finds her prostrate on the heath. The result is a tremendous accession of guilt feelings. Hardy makes him re-enact Oedipus' story when he has him search out the "riddle" of his mother's death in spite of the warnings of the heath-dwellers, and his face, he tells us, resembles the mask of Oedipus when he finds out the truth from Johnny. But his intensely felt remorse is neither Greek nor heroic. There is something childishly histrionic in his outbursts: "I sinned against her, and on that account there is no light for me" (384); "If there is any justice in God let Him kill me now. He has nearly blinded me, but that is not enough" (385–386). The desire to return to a world of darkness is clear enough. In the last section Clym lives shut up in the back rooms of his mother's house. Hardy was, indeed, very astute in choosing the Oedipus myth as the counterpoint to the dénouement of his romance. The mood of "Aftercourses" is that of *Oedipus at Colonus*. The tragic hero who has caused the death of the two women he loved most has become the half-blind prophet. Clym is a crippled Christ whose ministry comes after his passion. His Prometheanism past, he preaches on what Hardy ironically calls "morally unimpeachable subjects," his favorite text being the passage in 1 Kings 2 in which Solomon defers to his mother Bathsheba.

Faced with the problem of marrying Tamsin to Diggory in the epilogue, Hardy handles his task with remarkable tact. Clym has become the puppet-like projection of his dead mother's will, at first planning to marry Tamsin himself in accordance with her wishes, then repeating her objections to Diggory. By introducing the Maypole revels (which he calls "homage to nature, self-adoration, frantic gaieties, fragments of Teutonic rites to divinities whose names are forgotten" [479]) Hardy completes another ritual pattern. These are the "comic" counterparts of the November bonfires, their polar opposites in the ritual year, just as the "pride of life" which finds expression in these festivals is the comic analogue of tragic *hubris*. Grandfer Cantle and Christian now assume their natural roles as rustics in a kind of "As You Like It," providing a comic frame for the serious male characters, Grandfer's excess of wilfulness and Christian's humorous will-lessness making them humorous counterparts of Clym and Wildeve.

Frye remarks that in many tragedies the hero makes his first appearance as a "semi-divine figure, at least in his own eyes, and then an inexorable dialectic sets to work which separates the divine pretence from the human actuality."[3] In Eustacia's case, as in Clym's, the movement of the novel is from mythological romance to tragic suffering. She, too, appears first as a glamorous demi-god and ends as a struggling human, bound upon the wheel of fate. With her death we have moved from the world of ritual and romance to the psychological realism of Flaubert and Ibsen.

But if Eustacia's story touches myth at one point and case-history at the other, she has also some of the fascination of a queen of high tragedy. Perhaps we can best understand her if we take a cue from Hardy and compare her to Cleopatra. Like her, she is pleasure-loving, self-indulgent, quick to shift with the winds of fortune, and expert at varying her moods to captivate the men she wants. She, of course, is candid enough to warn Clym that her love for him may not outlast their marriage, but this candor has its roots in a fatalism that robs her of all moral scrupulosity. She lays the blame for each unfortunate turn of events on "some indistinct, colossal Prince of the World, who had framed her situation and ruled her lot" (369). In this view of life she resembles Merimée's Carmen.

Behind all this, however, we feel a powerful romantic malaise and self-destructiveness. In the MS version of the novel, Hardy described her features as a blend of those of Byron and Marie Antoinette. She is a Rousseauist in her disdain for convention and in her eternal dissatisfaction: she wants only what she does not have. She is saved from the vulgarity of Emma Bovary's excesses only by her unfailing dignity.

A natural queen without realms to rule, she can only look as if she had lost them. If this air of having accidentally mislaid a kingdom strikes the reader as slightly absurd, and makes us think of the actress who is always a little too good for her part, no one needs to be reminded that the sense of discrepancy between the ideal image of one's self and actuality is not only one of the most common of human emotions, but also one of the most painful. Her death is, consequently, a kind of Byronic protest against the very nature of things, against the fact that the world does not offer her any of the images of glory of which she has dreamed. She is, like Kafka's circus performer, a "hunger artist," who refuses to come to terms with reality. In her death she both acknowledges her defeat and asserts her freedom.

Hardy has written a double classical tragedy and a double case-history; in so doing he helps us to realize that literature is intensely conservative in its forms at the same time that it is capable of making radical conquests of new material. This is what

3. Northrop Frye, *Anatomy of Criticism* (Princeton: Princeton University Press, 1957), p. 217.

Hardy meant in his essay, "The Profitable Reading of Fiction," when he urges that we should read novels with the widest range of imaginative reference and in terms of our total literary experience:

> Good fiction can be defined here as that kind of imaginative writing which lies nearest to the epic, dramatic, or narrative masterpieces of the past. . . . New methods and plans may arise and come into fashion, as we see them do; but the general theme can never be changed, nor (what is less obvious) can the relative importance of the various particulars be greatly interfered with.[4]

Such a statement ought to stand as a warning to readers who think that Hardy's value, for better or for worse, lies all in his iconoclasm. In endorsing or decrying the message, they fail to realize how deeply rooted in tradition Hardy's art is, and consequently fail to bring to the reading of his novels the same imaginative effort one brings, say, to the reading of Joyce or Eliot. But this is exactly what *The Return of the Native* asks of us: any lesser response fails to do justice to its depth and complexity.

Boston University Studies in English, IV (1960), 229–240. Some of the reference notes have been omitted.

4. Thomas Hardy, *Life and Art* (New York: Greenberg, 1925), p. 61.

MYTH AND RITUAL IN THE
SHORTER FICTION OF D. H. LAWRENCE

John B. Vickery

This essay approaches the subject of myth and ritual in D. H. Lawrence's work in two ways: first, through a sketch of his extensive use of material from anthropology and comparative religion; and second, through the analysis of three stories, *England, My England, The Virgin and the Gipsy*, and *The Fox*. These last were deliberately chosen from those tales less obviously possessed of mythico-ritualistic elements in order better to dramatize the extent of Lawrence's use of such elements while at the same time demonstrating a critical technique for the illumination of structure, theme, and motives.

Of all the stories in *The Tales of D. H. Lawrence* barely half a dozen contain no allusions whatsoever to primitive beliefs, habits of thought, or behavior. The rest through image, scene, action, or allusion embrace virtually every major notion concerning myth and ritual to be found in *The Golden Bough*. The point here is not that Frazer's great study constitutes Lawrence's only source, though it is undeniably one of the most important, but that it is the most encyclopedic treatment of primitive life available to the English-speaking world and the one that lies behind the bulk of current literary interest in the subject. As such it is the most convenient touchstone for gauging Lawrence's interest in anthropology and comparative religion.

Lawrence's stories, like *The Golden Bough*, are filled with a number of different kinds of creatures possessing essentially human forms. Unequivocally anthropological are the names of Isis, Osiris, Adonis, Dionysus, Astarte, Bacchus, Pan, Venus, Persephone, Baal, Ashtaroth, Artemis, Cybele, and Balder. All of these are leading characters in Frazer's drama of the dying and reviving god and his wife-mother-lover so that their frequent mention in stories such as *The Ladybird, St. Mawr*, and *The Man Who Died* make this drama one of Lawrence's major *leit-motivs*. Nor does he confine himself simply to the major deities and fertility cults of the Semitic, Egyptian, Greek, and Scandinavian worlds. The nature and temperament of his characters are continually being defined with reference to maenads, dryads, fauns, and satyrs, out of whose coalescence the greater deities emerged. Indeed, it is in just such references that we see the anthropological dimension with which Lawrence's concept of the spirit of place is endowed. Thus, in *St. Mawr* the New England woman and Louise Carrington feel that the landscape lives and that it possesses a spirit which senses the sacred nature of the female sex. And in this conviction the spirit of place embodies the interrelation of vegetative and human fertility and the primitive worship of both found in *The Golden Bough*.

Neither Lawrence nor Frazer confines his attention solely to the objects of human veneration and respect. Intensification of mood, clarification of character, and deepening of theme, all are achieved by invoking such creatures as devils, demons, and ghosts. Sometimes they are mentioned only casually, but other times they become central to the story as with the title image of *The Captain's Doll* which is not only magical but is regarded by the Captain as a male devil arousing both fascination and repulsion. In *St. Mawr* Frazer's point about the variety of forms possessed by supernatural beings is illustrated by associating demons, devils, and ghosts with human beings, animals, and vegetation. While many of these metaphoric identifications are of vicious, unpleasant persons, there are others which suggest that Lawrence shares Jane Harrison's view of the spiritual worth of the chthonic powers of the underworld. For Frazer and Lawrence both, they reflect one of man's deepest impulses and one which is fundamentally religious in character. Thus, there is a world of difference between the sadistic Pauline of *The Lovely Lady* or the diabolic Ethel Cane of *None of That* and a representative miner like Mr. Pinnegar in *Jimmy and the Desperate Woman*. In this connection, it is particularly interesting to note how often Lawrence's miners—the perfect image of the contemporary underworld—possess that inexpugnable quality of life and personal power that Frazer and Miss Harrison attributed to chthonic deities.

In addition to the miner as chthonic power, Lawrence's stories possess many other characters who function as archetypes. One of the most important of these is the stranger who, as in *The Golden Bough*, is a disturbing figure because of his aura of fertility and his apparently magical powers to influence others. Such stories as *Odor of Chrysanthemums*, *Samson and Delilah*, *The Fox*, and *The Border Line* testify both to the importance of this figure and also to the variety ascribed to it by Lawrence. The same is true of such anthropologically symbolic figures as the virgin (*The Virgin and the Gypsy* and *The Princess*), the witch or magician (*Wintry Peacock* and *Mother and Daughter*), the hanged man (*The Thorn in the Flesh*, *A Fragment of Stained Glass*, and *The Man Who Died*), and the scapegoat (*England, My England* and *The Princess*). And back of these figures, bulking large in *The Golden Bough* too, are the warriors, hunters, farmers, peasants, and primitive savages whose social and personal needs give rise to the myths and rituals found in Lawrence and Frazer. Indeed, in *The Man Who Loved Islands* there is even a satiric portrait of the sort of person who was one of Frazer's earliest and most avid readers.

Densely populated as Lawrence's stories are with the figures of comparative religion, this is not their only affinity with the primitive world of *The Golden Bough*. Time and time again the characters exhibit those mental phenomena, those modes of thought and belief that Frazer chronicled with such a wealth of illustration. Levels of consciousness from the rational to the most intuitive are as graphically presented in stories like *Glad Ghosts*, *St. Mawr*, *The Rocking-Horse Winner*, and *The Blind Man* as they are in *The Golden Bough*. Particularly striking in this connection is the idea of spells and magic in general. Lawrence probably describes more characters as "spell-bound" and does so more repeatedly than any other writer of recent times. Through their recurrent use, especially in contexts of great dramatic intensity and mythopoeic overtones, he refurbishes such time-worn phrases and invests them with some of their original potency. *Daughters of the Vicar*, *The Captain's Doll*, and *The Border Line*, all have characters who exercise and react to spells both deliberately imposed and the casual by-product of the individual's impact as a personality on another human being. These spells usually exist between a man and a woman who are aware of one another as desirable but unknown and therefore dangerous, but they also obtain between parent and child as in *The Christening* and *England, My England*. Other aspects of magic used in Lawrence's stories to reveal character relationships as well as the incalculable nature of the human mind are talismans, images, second sight, trances, mediums together with all the other apparatus of spiritualism, and sinister physical transformations.

Nor are their physical and mental qualities all that Lawrence's characters share with Frazer's primitive peoples. Lawrence's work, like *The Golden Bough*, possesses a deep and persistent interest in those human actions whose importance derives as much from their being performed by the majority of people as from their being essential to human existence. Death, marriage, fornication, initiation, dancing, sacrifice, departure and arrival, and many other actions are focused on by Lawrence not merely because the conventions of fiction demand a kind of loose realism but because they are performed, consciously or not, in ritualistic fashion. The very manner of their performance testifies to their connection with the sacred existence, that is, the order in which the mysterious potency of life itself resides. Typical of Lawrence's use of ritual actions are those stories revolving around death or sex. In *The Prussian Officer*, for example, the struggle between the two men parallels the ritual combat in the grove at Nemi in which victory entails a new and unknown life that leads to a final defeat. Even more deliberately ritualistic is the sacrificial death undergone by the central figure in *The Woman Who Rode Away*, while *The Last Laugh* shows the swift retribution visited upon the man who penetrates the mystery of the god's existence and approaches too close to the divine but dangerous power.

Nor is this power limited to the gods. From the behavior of many of Lawrence's characters it is apparent that they would agree with Ernest Crawley's remark in his study of primitive marriage *The Mystic Rose* that "all persons are potentially dangerous to others, as well as potentially in danger, in virtue simply of the distinction between man and man." *Daughters of the Vicar*, *Second Best*, and *The Horse Dealer's Daughter* develop with considerable power this feeling of the danger inherent in love and entrance into the marriage state. On the other hand, stories such as *The Shades of Spring* and *Sun* reflect Frazer's emphasis on the beneficent custom of human beings miming the rite of the Sacred Marriage in which male and female fertility deities guarantee the perpetuation and flourishing of all forms of life. Similarly, extra- or pre-marital fornication regarded as a sacred rite rather than a social or moral sin is central to both *The Ladybird* and *The Man Who Died*, thereby dramatizing *The Golden Bough*'s accounts of women who have considered it an honor and religious obligation to serve the god through participating in sexual relations with him.

Not all the ritualistic actions of Lawrence's characters, however, are of such an unusual order; many are concerned with human behavior in the face of practical problems in daily life. Perhaps the best example of this is the miner's method of cleaning himself after a day under ground. The practice of kneeling on the hearthrug, stripped to the waist, and washing in a large basin is one to which Lawrence often refers. *Daughters of the Vicar*, *A Sick Collier*, and *Jimmy and the Desperate Woman* chart both its recurrence and Lawrence's own developing comprehension of its ritualistic character. The first two stories stress the habitual, unconscious movements involved, the feelings of awe and fear aroused, and the underlying phallic core of object and attitude; while the last emphasizes the hypnotic fascination it generates and defines its anthropological role by repeatedly calling it a ritual.

Complementing the mythic and ritualistic qualities possessed by Lawrence's characters and their actions is their physical background, the natural phenomena with which the author invests their world and to which they respond. Their associations with the fertility deities of the ancient world are accentuated by the images of vegetative fertility which run through many of the tales. In *The Prussian Officer* the woman, the golden wheat, and the green corn coalesce into an image reminiscent of Frazer's Corn Goddess. The gradual revival and awakening of the woman in *Sun* is described in terms of ripening grapes and gourds, while her retreat is guarded by a single cypress tree, which Frazer describes as sacred to the healing god's sanctuary. Similarly, pine trees, which are central to the rites of Attis and Osiris, appear as mythopoeic vegetative forms in *St. Mawr*, *The Border Line*, and *The Man Who Died*. Equally sacred to primitive Europeans and even more numerous, according to Frazer, are oak trees, which in both *A Fragment of Stained Glass* and *The Shades of Spring* Lawrence associates with the hyacinth, the flower of the divine king. The same sort of symbolic background is provided by recurrent references to anemones, almond blossoms, hyacinths, and ivy, all of which *The Golden Bough* shows to be vegetative signs and representatives of the great fertility deities like Adonis and Dionysus. On the animal level, this mythic dimension of the stories is conveyed through the weight of significance given to such creatures as the horse, the snake, the fox, the rat, the scarab, the pigeon, the dove, the mole, the lamb, and the cock, each of which figures in the myths, rites, and superstitions explored by Frazer. The same sort of stress is placed on the mythical nature and magical properties of such phenomena as the sun, moon, water, and fire. In stories like *Sun*, *The Horse Dealer's Daughter*, *The Ladybird*, *The Woman Who Rode Away*, and *The Man Who Died* they become central to the meaning of the story and to the behavior of the characters who see in them not so much objects as omens, talismans, ritual modes, and mythical beings that lead them to a further and deeper participation in the drama of existence.

The foregoing sketch suggests that Lawrence's stories contain a wealth of material drawn from anthropology and comparative religion. Needless to say, however, certain myths and rites play a more important part than others in shaping the theme and structure of the stories. Thus, at the risk of oversimplification we can resolve Lawrence's shorter fiction into six main categories which constitute a progression from the obvious and apparent to the subtle and hidden presence of myth and ritual. At one end of the scale, representing a concealed anthropological dimension, is a story such as *England, My England*, which is based on the myth of the scapegoat and the rites of passage leading to his expulsion. Equally interesting is the use to which Lawrence puts these beliefs and observances. Lawrence's penchant for social, cultural, historical, and spiritual jeremiads on modern life, especially that of the middle and upper classes, is as well known as it is important, but not much notice has been taken of the way in which, as in *England, My England*, he employs myth as a way of emphasizing his major criticisms. For him myth functions as a satiric device by offering not only a contrast between the mythico-ritualistic life of ancient man and that of contemporary man which is profane because commonplace and ordinary but also a sense of the continuity between the two worlds that shows how the one may be both a degeneration and an adaptation of the other.

The second category deals with myths of the Andromeda type in which a virgin faces a sacrificial death and attains a salvation which, as Lawrence would insist, is only partly secular. The central rites are those of purification and revivification by water and fire, a point made clear by the most obvious representatives of this type, *The Virgin and the Gypsy* and *The Horse Dealer's Daughter*. In such stories Lawrence's use of myth and ritual is primarily structural: the myth serves as a concealed pattern which organizes the narrative into a ritual sequence. The third category reveals the presence of myth more directly and also fuses the two uses to which it has been put in the earlier categories. Both *St Mawr* and *The Fox* exemplify Lawrence's treatment of the animal or totemic myth, whose strangeness has, unfortunately, largely kept it from being taken seriously as an integral part of the tale. In *St. Mawr* the myth is more nearly satiric or critical in function, while in *The Fox* it operates as a concealed pattern, though, to be sure, there are elements of both in each.

With the fourth category, which includes stories like *The Ladybird*, *The Princess*, and *Sun*, myth is neither concealed nor employed as critical instrument. Instead it operates as a kind of second story, almost a double plot which illuminates the basic story by suggesting a link with man's earliest forms of belief and behavior. The relevant myth is that of the Sacred Marriage, while the rites of initiation, taboo or prohibition, and fecundation present serve to define the central characters' reaction toward the myth itself. Consequently, we find here instances of Lawrence's using ritual as mythic reenactment, as a method of telling a past story through what is now being done. A related but distinct use of myth and ritual occurs in the fifth category, where stories like *The Man Who Died* and *The Woman Who Rode Away* deal directly and as part of the narrative with the myth of the reviving god and his worship through rites of separation, initiation, propitiation, and ordination. Lawrence treats myth in these instances as a new version of an old story, a technique that links these stories to Graves's *King Jesus*, Mann's *Joseph* series, Gide's *Theseus*, and Faulkner's *A Fable*. In every case the author takes a well-established myth or legend and in the process of retelling it fleshes it out with his own imaginative extrapolations so that the final product is both a new tale and a commentary on the old one.

While in one sense these last stories represent the fullest development of myth and ritual in Lawrence's shorter fiction, there is also a sixth category which is important but stands a little to one side of the others. It embraces stories like *The Last Laugh*, *Glad Ghosts*, and *The Rocking-Horse Winner* that focus on the myth of a supernatural world populated by spirits of the dead, ghosts, and invisible divinities and coped with by human beings through magical rites of propitiation and prediction as well as the hocus-pocus of spiritualism. In these myth is again used to underscore a point, most frequently that of the mystery of existence, though as a by-product there are some satiric asides on human ignorance. Ritual, on the other hand, is equated primarily with contemporary habit patterns and as a result becomes, as it were, a satiric view of itself; for modern man's attempt to deal with the unknown is shown to be largely silly or disastrous. In effect, these "ghost" stories demonstrate a concomitant of the other tales' insistence on the importance of myth and ritual: these show that it is too vital a subject with which to trifle or dabble.

II

In *England, My England* the gradual transformation of the passionate idyll of Egbert's and Winifred's marriage into a savage combat that culminates with World War I and Egbert's death is Lawrence's version of the myth of the dying god and the rites of expulsion that accompany the scapegoat. He takes great pains at the beginning of the story to stress the ancient, primitive character both of the scene and of the protagonists. Crockham, where the newlyweds settled, "belonged to the old England of hamlets and yeomen" and "it lay there secret, primitive, savage as when the Saxons first came." It is one of those places where "the savage England lingers in patches." Into this bygone world come Winifred and Egbert to reflect its sense of the past: "She, too, seemed to come out of the old England, ruddy, strong, with a certain crude, passionate quiescence and a hawthorn robustness. And he, he was tall and slim and agile, like an English archer with his long supple legs and fine movements." Egbert enhances this affinity by having "a passion for old folk-music, collecting folk-songs and folk-dances, studying the Morris-dance and the old customs."

The connection with the past demonstrated in the setting, the appearance, and the interests of the characters culminates in their marital behavior. Though the desire is their own, it is intensified by and derives from their immediate physical setting: "The flame of their two bodies burnt again into that old cottage, that was haunted already by so much bygone, physical desire. You could not be in the dark room for an hour without the influences coming over you. The hot blood-desire of bygone yeomen, there in this old den where they had lusted and bred for so many generations." In celebrating so triumphantly what Arnold van Gennep calls the fecundation rites of marriage, the couple not only fuse modern individuals with the medieval world of the yeoman but also suggest the truly primitive character of that world. One of the central rites of ancient times that persisted into more recent ages among the European peasantry is the mimetic observance by human beings of the Sacred Marriage of the god and goddess. It is just such an imitative rite that Egbert and Winifred are unconsciously involved in, as Lawrence intimates by juxtaposing the images of their union and the flourishing vegetation and garden which Egbert is said to have "recreated." Further support for this is found in Winifred's being regarded as "a ruddy fire into which he could cast himself for rejuvenation" since *The Golden Bough* emphasizes the procreative and purificatory powers of fire and its employment in conjunction with the Sacred Marriage ritual.

Lawrence, however, is writing a story of savage irony and despairing anguish, and hence he focuses not on the joyous celebration of renewed life that normally follows the ritual marriage but on the expulsion and death of the protagonist. This is ironically prepared for in the midst of the ritual of erotic ecstasy by the intrusion of the author's mock invocation "Ah, that it might never end, this passion, this marriage!" That it will end is certain not only because Egbert and Winifred prove to be incompatible personalities but also because they are unconsciously miming the ritual existence of the fertility deity who suffers a cyclic rejection and demise. And in the same scene an image of the impersonal yet necessary cruelty inherent in the mythic world is revealed in the snake's endeavor to swallow a frog who is uttering "the strangest scream, like the very soul of the dark past crying aloud." Nor is it accident that this ritual of self-preservation should have been witnessed by Winifred, who is to take the lead in Egbert's expulsion from the marriage, the family, and life itself.

In connection with the growing alienation that develops between Egbert and Winifred it is important to notice that the strain between them is not derived from the contrast of Egbert's indolent dilettantism to her passion for responsibility and duty nor even from his habit of sponging off her father. These are, at the most, contributory factors. The genuine source of their estrangement lies in a virtually inevitable change in the structure of their world. Instructive here is van Gennep's point, made in *Les Rites de Passage*, that the life of the individual passes through certain successive stages and that this is achieved through the intermediary of ceremonies calculated to make the transition a safe one. These *rites de passage* are threefold, consisting of those which van Gennep calls "*séparation, marge, et agrégation.*" The crucial change in the world of the two characters comes when they enter the state of parenthood. Here is the beginning of the ritual of separation, of detachment from the old world and the old life. Winifred finds in her child "a new center of interest" so that "without anything happening, he was gradually, unconsciously excluded from the circle." Then, following their second child, she begins to resent and despise that physical love which has already become of secondary importance to her in the role of dutiful and responsible mother. To provide a conscious justification for this attitude, she turns to the issue of money and his failure to earn a living. Having thus articulated her sense of critical detachment from her husband, she at length formulates what it is that really separates them: "It was that he stood for nothing."

With this we come to the central antithesis in the story, that between her husband and her father. The basic desire of the former is "to hold aloof. It was not his season." The latter, on the other hand, plunges into the struggle of existence with "an acrid faith like the sap of some not-to-be-exterminated tree. Just a blind acrid faith as sap is blind and acrid, and yet pushes on in growth and in faith." The "stoic and epicurean" husband confronts the hardy vegetative father and succumbs, in the last analysis, because he lacks the father's "will-to-power, . . . the single power of his own blind self." Their struggle, however, is not direct but operates through and in the person of Winifred. For her, the basic familial unit is comprised of her parents, herself, and her child; in it she finds the core of life, "the human trinity for her." She does so because her father has maintained "a certain primitive dominion over the souls of his children, the old, almost magic prestige of paternity. There it was, still burning in him, the old smoky torch of parental godhead. . . . Fatherhood that had life-and-death authority over the children." The only thing that could have supplanted her father would have been Winifred's finding in her husband a greater male power and authority. But since Egbert does not possess this power, Lawrence ironically inverts the mythic formula which calls for the young ruler or deity to succeed the old one. Egbert rejects the possibility of his own divinity as a human being replete with power and becomes in contrast to the father a taboo-figure, "the living negative of power." And what he taboos by his very presence is Winifred's attempt to exercise "her dark, silent, passionate authority," "the old blood-power," "the old dark magic of parental authority." To this end he uses his own form of magic and witchcraft not only to transform her parental authority into "a sort of tyranny" but also to steal the children (the image is Lawrence's) from her. His magic is that which most completely captures children, namely, the exercise of complete license in behavior: "They could do as they liked with him."

Out of the two men's indirect struggle for the role of father has come the ritual of separation celebrated by Winifred in her increasing sexual reticence and by Egbert in his denial of her parental authority coupled with his own rejection of responsibility. This, however, is but the first stage in the rites of passage, that of detachment from the old life. It is followed by what van Gennep calls the "*rite de marge*," the behavior that marks the interim stage between the old and the new modes of life. In *England, My England* this is reflected in the incident of the first-born child's being lamed as a result of falling on a sickle left in the grass by Egbert. With this the antithesis between Winifred's passion for duty and authority (a worship of hierarchy) and Egbert's rejection of responsibility and power (a belief in liberty and self-determination) is projected into the visible and external world so forcefully that husband and wife are seen to be completely separated, to be living in different worlds. In the weeks that follow the accident, both are moving toward their new and distinct modes of existence. As a period of physical, emotional, and spiritual transition it is "a dark and bitter time" for all.

Yet this incident and its repercussions are not significant solely as a rite of transition from marriage to legal separation. For in the early part of the story Egbert has been identified as a representative and worshipper of phallic potency who like the primitive divine king rules only so long as he can demonstrate his power as a fertility figure. When Winifred denies him this, she makes him "lock up his own vivid life inside himself" and thereby reduces him to virtual impotence. Both Egbert and the divine king react in the same way: through a sacrifice of the first-born, man may continue to live as he has, to retain a wife as well as a throne, to prolong a marriage as well as a reign. Clearly, such a rite could not be deliberately embarked upon by a member of the civilized world for whom it would be a monstrously evil act. But as Lawrence seems to indicate, it would be quite possible to desire this in the subconscious where the primitive and savage impulses of man linger even yet. Thus, the contemporary consciousness registers this longing for sacrifice literally as "a wicked look" and metaphorically as Egbert's having "seven devils inside his long, slim, white body."

Similarly, Egbert himself, immediately after the accident, seeks to assuage his deep sense of guilt by insisting on the accidental character of the event. What is at the core of this guilt, however, is not his own superficial carelessness but rather his profound and abiding responsibility. In times of great calamity, *The Golden Bough* tells us, it was customary to sacrifice the first-born. And for Egbert there could be no greater calamity than losing Winifred, for, as has been suggested, it is through her that his spirit of fertility is released and his rejuvenation effected. By indirectly attempting to sacrifice the child, Egbert is seeking to acquire a new lease of life, to atone for his sins (especially the denial of parental authority's divinity), and to demonstrate that he, like Winifred's father, "had kept alive the old red flame of fatherhood, the fatherhood that had even the right to sacrifice the child to God, like Isaac." That Egbert is using the child as a substitute for himself is further suggested by the weapon's being a sickle, the instrument employed in harvest rituals to sacrifice the fertility deity. Even more striking is the fact that, according to Frazer, "the corn-spirit is conceived as a child who is separated from its mother by the stroke of the sickle."

It is part, however, of Lawrence's ironic intention that this effort at prolonging a state of existence regarded as fruitful and idyllic should be thwarted. He is concerned not with the revival but with the death of human society and its protagonists. This is borne out by the sacrifice of the child, which as a ritual of transition proves to be "an agony and a long crucifixion." The irony appears in that the sacrifice is not complete, the child does not die, and so the father cannot restore the marriage to its sacred status. A further irony follows from the fact that the ultimate ritual sacrifice is made by Egbert as a result of his being the scapegoat in the accident. It is with his assumption of this role that the final stage of the "*rite de passage*" is reached. Following the marginal, transitional observance there is the absorption into a new world and a new mode of life. For Winifred the child's injury completely ends her passionate attachment to Egbert. The existence into which she is drawn is that of institutional religion, the Roman Catholic Church. Here she finds an alternative to the life of passion, sensuality, and distraction she has known with Egbert.

It is from this that Egbert's own ritual of absorption or assimilation follows. When Winifred becomes "purely the *Mater Dolorata*," he finds that for him "she was closed as a tomb, ... the tomb of his manhood and his fatherhood," an image which both adumbrates his fate and reveals the degree of her responsibility. Like the primitive scapegoat, he finds that he is shut out forever from the community he has known, compelled "to turn aside," to wander "hither and thither, desultory," possessed of "no real home." Even clearer evidence of his assumption of the role of ritual outcast from society is the hatchet-like cleft in his brow developed since the accident which he bears as his Cain-like "stigma." It is this together with his relation to her and her family that gives him for Winifred "the Ishmael quality." But the scapegoat is not simply the creature who wanders in lonely isolation until overtaken by death. It is also representative of the divinity whose death is preordained as an elaborate ritual of sacrifice. Egbert's divinity is revealed by his appearing to Winifred's now nun-like soul as "an erect, supple symbol of life, the living body" and to her Christianized eyes as "Baal and Ashtaroth," "a supple living idol" that "if she watched him she was damned."

To her he appears godlike, but to himself he is the object of sacrifice. Thus, in the landscape bits of vegetation seem to him "like a sprinkling of sacrificial blood."

And from this his imagination comes to be dominated by "the savage old spirit of the place: the desire for old gods, old, lost passions, the passion of the cold-blooded, darting snakes that hissed and shot away from him, the mystery of blood-sacrifices, all the lost, intense sensations of the primeval people of the place, whose passions seethed in the air still, from those long days before the Romans came."

The opportunity for the blood-sacrifice of the scapegoat is provided by the war into which he is projected by his wife and father-in-law. With his enlistment the various rites associated with the scapegoat are performed. The customary inversion of the social hierarchy is reflected in Egbert's awareness that joining the army meant "he was going to put himself into the power of his inferiors. . . . He was going to subjugate himself." Similarly, Winifred's being "so ready to serve the *soldier*, when she repudiated the man" (Lawrence's italics) mirrors the scapegoat's being permitted sexual intercourse with a woman usually forbidden him. And finally, Egbert's being wounded twice before his death approximates the custom of beating and wounding the scapegoat before putting him to death. By these rites he is confirmed in his role; now he is not simply expelled from his family, he has "gone out of life, beyond the pale of life." Nor is it without significance that Lawrence should present Egbert under the image of "a man who is going to take a jump from a height," for the scapegoat commonly met his fate by being hurled from a cliff. Out of these rites comes a feeling of participation in an inescapable experience that sustains him through even his death agonies and permits him to will the completion of the scapegoat ritual by which the myth of the dying god is enacted.

III

The Virgin and the Gypsy elaborates the myth of the virgin whose salvation follows from her exposure to a sacrificial death. Central to this salvation is her meeting the stranger, the gypsy who focuses her resistance to her narrow, hypocritical family and its "rectory morality." When instead of concealing or ignoring "the dark, tremulous potent secret of her virginity" she accepts its power to arouse desire, she is capable of accepting the challenge of the outcast which is none other than to become an outcast oneself, to dare to go one's own way.

The steps by which Yvette comes to this awareness are all designed to underscore the mythical and ritualistic character of the narrative. Thus, the first meeting between the young people and the gypsies is described in only partly ironical fashion as occurring between Christians and pagans. Emerging from her private palm-reading session with the gypsy woman, Yvette maintains a "witch-like silence," a manner that is intensified later at a dance when she suggests a "young virgin *witch*" (Lawrence's italics) who "might metamorphose into something uncanny." This quality appears only after her meeting with the stranger, a figure traditionally thought to cast spells and perform other magical feats. And significantly enough, Lawrence twice repeats that the gypsy-stranger's desire exercises a spell-like power over her. As a result of this, too, she finds her soul stolen from her body and drawn to the world of the gypsies.

Nor is the gypsy simply the stranger as magician; he is also the stranger as the representative of the fertility spirit. This is borne out not only by the sexual power Yvette perceives in him and by his being linked with a kindling fire but also by Yvette's being likened in his presence to a flower about to blossom, an act for which he is responsible. His absorption with "the mysterious fruit of her virginity," Mrs. Fawcett's insistence that for Yvette to have a love affair with him would be prostitution, and Mr. Eastwood's declaration that "'he's a resurrected man,'" all combine to identify him as the fertility figure who appears as a stranger to assist in the ritual defloration of unmarried girls.

Strikingly enough, this ritual itself does not seem to take place in the story, though some readers may feel that the ending of Section IX is discreetly ambiguous on this score. Instead, like Mabel, Yvette participates first in a watery sacrifice of her life and then in a divestiture before a fertility figure that restores her to a full sense of life's significance. Her encounter with the water is both a ritual of purgation or purification and protection. The first of these is borne out not only by the usual purificatory qualities attached to water but also by the presence of the larch and laurel trees, both of which are sacred and one of which forms a part of traditional ceremonies of purification. Yet from its being a raging torrent to which Yvette is exposed, it is clear that this rite is more than baptismal in character. It is also the ritual sacrifice that precedes the baptismal introduction into a new existence. The Andromeda aspect of the story is subtly brought out by the image of the water as "a *devouring* flood" (my italics). This image together with the attendant descriptions suggests that the threat to which Yvette is exposed is both that of the folklore monster (it is described as "a shaggy, tawny wave-front of water advancing like a wall of lions") and the universal flood that represents a return to chaos.

As stories like *Daughters of the Vicar* make clear, however, chaos in itself is not an unrewarding prospect for Lawrence. It represents that dissolution of the old existence without which no new life can come into being and acquire form. Thus, when Yvette feels "as if the flood was in her soul," we see that it is a psychological dissolution of universal proportions as well as a terrifying natural event. As a ritual of protection, the torrential stream is linked to flood sagas such as in the Bible. The central point here is that the flood functions as a judgment and punishment whereby only the righteous are preserved from destruction. The death by water of the Mater signifies the final assessment of her evil nature. In effect, then, the scene recapitulates Wundt's point that the universal flood (*Sintflut*) develops into a sin flood (*Sündflut*).

With the removal of Yvette's dress, a "death-gripping thing," her purgation of the old, death-like existence of the family is complete, and as prophesied by the gypsy woman, she comes into contact with the dark man who stirs the flame warming her heart. Her understanding of what he has done for her is seen in her acquiescence to his subsequent departure. Like the fertility figure of myth, he lives the cyclic existence of the nomad so that his disappearance is as inevitable as his appearance. Pointing up this parallel is the comment on the letter from "some unknown place": "And only then she realized that he had a name." By her belated discovery of the gypsy's name, Lawrence emphasizes the archetypal nature of the entire story. Essentially, then, the two leading characters participate in what T. H. Gaster's *Thespis* regards as the true function of myth, namely, the translation of "the punctual into terms of the durative, the real into those of the ideal." As Yvette Saywell and Joe Boswell, they are characters, human beings; as the virgin and the gypsy, they are archetypes with associations that extend far beyond the rectory and village of Papplewick.

IV

A quite different kind of myth is employed by Lawrence in *The Fox* and *St. Mawr*, namely, the animal or totemic myth. In totemism an intimate relation is assumed between certain human beings and certain natural or artificial objects, the latter being called the totems of the former. The outlines of the totemic myth are most apparent in *The Fox* partly because it is shorter and partly because it is a much less complex story than *St. Mawr*. *The Fox* deals with the development and resolution of a romantic triangle involving two girls and a man. Through the use of psychological associations and prophetic dreams the story gradually brings out its totemic form. At the outset Nellie March and Jill Banford are gentlemen farmers who are rather consistently unsuccessful because of a combination of their disinclination for hard work and of their unfortunate circumstances, the most notable of which is a marauding fox that carries off their hens. The first stage in the development of the totemic myth occurs when Nellie encounters the fox one evening, for as a result "she was spellbound—she knew he knew her. So he looked into her eyes, and her soul failed her." The depth of the impression made on her by this meeting is indicated in part by Lawrence's repetition of the image of the spell and possession five times in the two pages following. Ultimately "it was the fox which somehow dominated her unconsciousness, possessed the blank half of her musing," a state that continues from August to November.

The second stage of the myth is reached with the arrival of Henry Grenfel in search of his grandfather, the former owner of the farm and now dead. The stage of confrontation is succeeded by one of identification. Nellie first finds herself "spellbound" by Henry just as by the fox; then she sees the man as quite literally the animal. This identification is due first to his physical appearance and later to his basic form of behavior, that of a fox-like secret watcher. With this stage the totem moves into her consciousness from her unconscious; with the animal-man "in full presence" she accepts the spell that hitherto has been imposed on her and abandons the attempt "to keep up two planes of consciousness." Now "she could at last lapse into the odor of the fox," for the strangeness of her attraction has been modified by the appearance of the man.

The story then enters on the third or prophetic phase of the myth. For the very night of Henry's arrival Nellie dreams of herself and the fox: "It was the fox singing. He was very yellow and bright, like corn. She went nearer to him, but he ran away and ceased singing. He seemed near, and she wanted to touch him. She stretched out her hand, but suddenly he bit her wrist, and at the same instant, as she drew back, the fox, turning round to bound away, whisked his brush across her face, and it seemed his brush was on fire, for it seared and burned her mouth with a great pain." The prophecy immediately begins to work itself out next morning when Nellie notices that "something about the glint of his khaki reminded her of the brilliance of her dream-fox."

It is fulfilled a fortnight later when Henry declares his love to Nellie and asks her to marry him, for as she is about to join Jill upstairs, "quick as lightning he kissed her on the mouth, with a quick brushing kiss."

While prophetic concerning their ultimate relationship, the dream is also revelatory about the nature of the fox and, by extension, Henry. To anyone familiar with *The Golden Bough*, the above description of the fox suggests that he is to be identified with the primitive fertility deity or, more specifically, with Dionysus as the corn-spirit. Significantly enough, during harvest season the man who hits the last corn with his sickle is called the Fox and during the evening dances with all the girls. Thus, in Frazer as well as Lawrence fertility figure, man, and animal are all connected. Nor is it irrelevant that at the beginning of the story, before confronting either the fox or Henry, the two girls regard the fox as "a demon." He moves from devil to god as Nellie becomes increasingly aware of what he represents and of what she desires. At the same time, in its appearing to Nellie that "his brush was on fire," the dream hints too at the fate of the fox. This image recalls the custom of fastening burning torches to foxes' tails as punishment for having destroyed the crops in the past. In this there is perhaps an oblique foreshadowing of the fox's death at the hands of Henry and his gun.

The prophetic phase adumbrates the phallic relation of Nellie and Henry, the death of the fox, and, in a second dream of Nellie's, the death of Jill. In the last stage of the myth, that of the sacrificial action, these events are made real. The story's problem, of course, centers on the human triangle; though Nellie is drawn to Henry, Jill stands resolutely between them, threatening the success of his pursuit. The only resolution can be the removal of Jill herself in some swift, irreversible fashion. Preparatory to this, however, Henry slays the fox, an action that is too heavily empha-sized to be merely gratuitous plot embroidery. In point of fact, this reflects that part of the totemic myth in which the divine animal is solemnly sacrificed as part of an annual ritual.

A clue to the most important reason for Henry's slaying of the fox is Frazer's remark that totemism "appears to be mainly a crude, almost childlike attempt to satisfy the primary wants of man," an attempt that operates through the magical creation of that which is sought. For what Henry clearly wants is Nellie, and to this end he eventually attempts the removal of Jill. What he creates is, in short, the absence of Jill, an event that is magical in the sense that it is apparently uncaused and yet follows from the concentrated will of Henry. The slaying of the fox is both a rehearsal and a primitive adumbration of the human death insofar as it demonstrates Henry's resolve in the face of the sacrificial slaying of the creature most sacred to the society. To observe the totemic sacrifice of the fox is to be able to perform it in connection with the totem of modern society, namely, another human being.

In carrying out this twin sacrifice, Henry employs what van Gennep calls "*le rite positif*" in which the individual's wish is translated into an act. Central here is the ability to focus one's spiritual and emotional energies on a single end: "In his heart he had decided her death. A terrible still force seemed in him, and a power that was just his. If he turned even a hair's breadth in the wrong direction, he would lose the power." This rite of separation by sacrifice is identical with that of assimilation by which Henry draws Nellie to him. In both cases the act is first mimed in the imagination as a magical guarantee of its physical success. Like Frazer's savages, Henry believes that the central feature of the hunt resides in the conquest of the soul: "First of all, even before you come in sight of your quarry, there is a strange battle, like mesmerism. Your own soul, as a hunter, has gone out to fasten on the soul of the deer, even before you see any deer. And the soul of the deer fights to escape. Even before the deer has any wind of you, it is so. It is a subtle, profound battle of wills which takes place in the invisible." And it is in this spirit that Henry stalks, in turn, Nellie, the fox, and finally, Jill.

These rites, however, are not simply isolated events performed for immediate practical ends; they are also the behavioral concomitant of Henry's character and the culmination of his prototypical social function. For just prior to Jill's death Henry is likened to "a huntsman who is watching a flying bird." That this is more than a casual simile is suggested by Jill's having been described as a bird on more than one occasion. Even more important is the scene that inaugurated the hunt motif, the scene in which Henry first thinks of marrying Nellie. Lawrence here emphasizes Henry's basic nature: "He was a huntsman in spirit, not a farmer, and not a soldier stuck in a regiment. And it was as a young hunter that he wanted to bring down March as his quarry, to make her his wife." With this, we find a broader perspective on the totemic myth and ritual, one which links it to a way of life characteristic of the society itself. Frazer formulates this pattern clearly when he observes that although totemism "probably always originated in the hunting stage of society, it has by no means been confined to that primitive phase of human development but has often survived not only into the pastoral but into the agricultural stage." And as we have seen, in *The Fox* the survival of totemism and the mingling of the two stages of society are both present: in the midst of the agricultural life of the two girls appears both the totemic respectful awe of the fox felt by Nellie and the "stranger-youth" who is a hunter.

Just as the totemic myth and ritual underlies the narrative development, so it also defines the relationships of the characters. For Nellie, Henry is the totem animal to be revered and respected; for Jill, whose own totem is the bird, he is the sinister antagonist, a natural enemy to be feared. For Henry, Nellie March is the game he seeks, while Jill is a bothersome creature whose intrusive demands and influence on Nellie ultimately overcome the taboo on man-slaying. Thus, in a sense, both women are objects of the hunt, the one because she is desired, the other because she is not. Mediating between them is the fox who is also overcome by the hunter. In the case of Jill, as already noted, the fox slaying is a rehearsal for the human death. Nellie, on the other hand, is won over completely following the death of the fox. What is contingent and fortuitous in the realism of the narrative pattern becomes necessary and inevitable in terms of the totemic myth. For Nellie, the fox, her totem, contains what Frazer calls the external soul, that projection of one's life drives into the objective world which keeps one in contact with reality and so alive as an individual. With the slaying of the fox Henry has acquired her soul and so can sway her to his will, an achievement symbolized by her changing from breeches, "strong as armor," to a dress in which she is "accessible." From all of this it is apparent that if, as Malinowski says in *Magic, Science, and Religion*, totemism is "a mode of social grouping and a religious system of beliefs and practices," then it is central to the meaning of *The Fox*. The various attitudes toward the fox obviously produce conflicting groups within the society as a whole. At the same time, Henry's drive to marry Nellie qualifies as religious in Malinowski's sense, that is, as expressing the desire "to control the most important objects" in man's surroundings.

Modern Fiction Studies, V (1959), 65–82.

The Psychological Dimension

The particular emphasis in the following group of essays is on the psychological (Freudian-Jungian) ramifications of myth and ritual in literature. From Claire Rosenfield ("An Archetypal Analysis of Conrad's Nostromo*") to Harry Slochower ("The Use of Myth in Kafka and Mann") there is also a rough kind of progression from a microscopic to a macroscopic concern with the text. This reflects an underlying shift from individual psychology to what in Freud's case has been called metapsychology. Hence, where Miss Rosenfield concentrates on* Nostromo's *themes and characters, Mr. Slochower views Kafka and Mann as mythically identified cultural symptoms or symbols. William Bysshe Stein ("Walden: The Wisdom of the Centaur") mediates between these two approaches by a close examination of the centaur motif in* Walden *from which he derives conclusions with broad implications for American literature and culture.*

AN ARCHETYPAL ANALYSIS OF CONRAD'S
NOSTROMO

Claire Rosenfield

During and after the writing of *Nostromo* Joseph Conrad's letters reflect his feelings of frustrated failure caused by too intense, too prolonged effort. In a letter to William Rothenstein he wrote, "I am not myself and shall not be myself till I am born again after *Nostromo* is finished";[1] and after his "rebirth" he confessed to having written it in "the tenacity of despair."[2] That the completed product made him despair can be seen in two letters to R. B. Cunninghame Graham: "I feel a great humbug";[3] and, again, "For in regard to that book I feel a great fraud."[4] Seven years after the event *A Personal Record* recalls the intensity of his authorial involvement and, in a typical Conradian parenthesis, the very conscious creation required by such an edifice. "All I know, is that, for twenty months, neglecting the common joys of life that fall to the lot of the humblest on this earth, I had, like the prophet of old, 'wrestled with the Lord' for my creation, . . . (there was not a single brick, stone, or grain of sand of its soil I had not placed in position with my own hands)."[5] And, he records, the novel "is still mentioned now and again, and indeed kindly, sometimes in connection with the word 'failure' and sometimes in conjunction with the word 'astonishing.'"[6]

And, indeed, both these adjectives describe this novel's unique greatness: it is an "astonishing failure." *Nostromo* is essentially two imperfectly integrated stories, each

1. *Joseph Conrad, Life and Letters*, ed. G. Jean-Aubry (Garden City: Doubleday, Page, 1927), I, 330.
2. *Ibid.*, p. 336.
3. *Ibid.*, p. 337.
4. *Ibid.*, p. 338.
5. Joseph Conrad, *A Personal Record* (New York: Harper, 1925), pp. 98–100.
6. *Ibid.*, p. 98.

with its particular hero, each with a "felt" life of its own. And the author has separated the life of each hero into the rituals, the recurrent symbolic acts, that unite him to the community and the dreams by which he idealizes his individual existence as a man. Authorial detachment provides irony; authorial sympathy, tragedy. At many points the two never fuse within the characters of the men who assume the burdens of the symbolic quests.

The first story is the *historical* one which deals with the Costaguana past, the events of the Montero rebellion, and the attempts of the Republic of Sulaco to separate from the rest of Costaguana. Once we accept the fictional world of the Conradian vision, we accept the life within that world as factual; the imaginative recreation of history becomes more real than the newspaper accounts which deal with actual worlds, but worlds that the reader has never visited. No mere visitor could be confronted by such an abundance of information so dramatically and thoroughly evoked. However, as Lord Raglan says, "all history depends . . . upon chronology, and no real idea of chronology can be obtained except by seeing the facts tabulated in chronological sequence."[7] Within the fictional reality of *Nostromo* chronology does exist. Or rather the chronology existed within the mind of the author who must have had some coherent story prior to his artistic and temperamental violation of the temporal sequence. And although the disruptions of time are often baffling, although precise events often cannot be measured exactly in days or months or years, an ordered pattern can be reconstructed from the accounts of the characters. As if the memories of the characters were not sufficient record, Conrad has provided the reader with a written authority for events of the fictional past—an unpublished work by the late Don José Avellanos called "History of Fifty Years of Misrule." Again, this written source, like the events which it records, exists only within the framework of the novel. The presence of a "source" helps to support the historical nature of one of the plots; for history, after all, is a form of knowledge which "depends upon written records."[8] And "Fifty Years of Misrule" supplies the exact chronology of Costaguana affairs.

Don José is not the only historian of Sulaco. The unimaginative Captain "Fussy Joe" Mitchell, "having spent a clear thirty years of his life on the high seas before getting what he called a 'shore billet,' was astonished at the importance of transactions (other than relating to shipping) which take place on dry land. Almost every event out of the usual daily course 'marked an epoch' for him or else was 'history.'"[9] He recalls the "epoch" marked by the days between Nostromo's ride to Cayta and the final separation of Sulaco from the Occidental Province; he is "penetrated by the sense of historical importance of men, events, and buildings." Yet if we use Lord Raglan's standard for the historian,[10] Captain Mitchell is not a true one because his narrative within the fictional frame is oral. The captive listener, confused by the surfeit of

---

7. Lord Raglan, *The Hero: A Study in Tradition, Myth, and Drama* (New York: Vintage, 1956), p. 5.
8. *Ibid.*, p. 8.
9. Joseph Conrad, *Nostromo* (Garden City: Doubleday, Page, 1925), pp. 112–113. Subsequent page references appear in the text.
10. Raglan, *The Hero*, p. 5.

names and events and information, is much like the audience at any factual or complicated fictional narrative. He remembers little or distorts what he has heard. Were
he to relate the events to another he would turn history, the record of facts in a timed
world, into tradition or myth, which is timeless. This superintendent of the "Oceanic
Steam Navigation Company (the O.S.N. of familiar speech)" is a true historian only
because the author has made him one, has created a written record of the former's
oral account of "cosas de Costaguana" as his fictional reality. The storyteller, the
novelist, is the only actual historian of Sulaco.

The history of the fictional Sulaco can be constructed, though that reconstruction
requires an attentive and involved reader. Some time in the recent past the fifteen-year
tyranny of Guzman Bento, the "Citizen Savior of his Country," dominated the political
sphere of this recorded world. Both Don José Avellanos and Dr. Monygham experienced the hatred of this ruler, the former because he was an aristocrat, a "Blanco,"
the latter because the old tyrant imagined a conspiracy to overthrow him. After the
death of Guzman Bento, the mine was confiscated when the miners "incited to revolt
by the emissaries sent out from the capital, had risen upon their English chiefs and
murdered them to a man." (52) Then Charles Gould's father was given the perpetual
concession of the ruined mine in full settlement for forced loans by the fourth
Costaguana government in six years. The constant use of such phrases as "the epoch
of civil wars whence had emerged the iron tyranny of Guzman Bento of fearful
memory" or "the barbarous ill-usage under Guzman Bento" or a parenthesis assuring
us that Guzman Bento was called the "Citizen Savior of the Country"—all these
reinforce the narrator's position that he is recording the history of an area which is
civilized and corruptible.

As if the abundance of detail were not enough, Conrad gives further validity to the
"historical" events by juxtaposing the creatures of his imagination with actual
historical personages. Giorgio Viola, the Italian innkeeper, is an old companion of
and cook for Garibaldi, an "austere republican" whose divinities are "liberty and
Garibaldi," and whose personal devil is Cavour, the "arch intriguer." The contempt of
this man of the people for the rebellious populace is simply a belief that his present
life (a fictional reality) is devoid of the idealism which permeated a particular moment in
actual historical time. The square of Sulaco is dominated by the statue of a European
ruler, Charles IV, whose marble ineffectuality reminds us of the real Rey of Sulaco,
the stony presence of Charles Gould. Nor does this statue of a real emperor possess a
greater significance than the plaques celebrating the events of the "third of May"
and the Separation of Sulaco from the rest of the Occidental Province, plaques which
Captain Mitchell points out to his privileged but captive listener. Indeed, the equestrian
statue is removed because, as the historically minded Captain Mitchell tells us, "'it
was an anachronism.'" The irony of such a phrase is apparent; yet the word "anachronism" can have no meaning except in a world possessing a sense of the linear progression
of time.

The historical narrative, then, deals with the actual events within a fictional but
thoroughly visualized physical setting. It involves activity relating to the formation
of a nation, events which are very much a part of a temporal pattern. That the method-

ical record of actions, time as a "continuous causal chain,"[11] is violated does not mean that a concern with time does not exist. Rather, the violations of the linear progression of time enables us to become more thoroughly involved in the historical events.

Unlike the world of political events, which is within time, there is another world in *Nostromo*, a traditional one where the motions of the clock have no meaning. The silver—and treasure in general—dominates this second story. Some of the characters do recognize the distinction between history and tradition. Charles Gould confronts Pedro Montero with the fact that he will destroy the San Tomé mine rather than let the Montero government confiscate it: "But since the San Tomé mine had developed into world-wide fame his threat had enough force and effectiveness to reach the rudimentary intelligence of Pedro Montero, wrapped up as it was in the futilities of historical anecdotes. The Gould Concession was a serious asset in the country's finance, and what was more, in the private budgets of many officials as well. It was traditional. It was known. It was staid." (402–403) In spite of the changes of the revolutionary governments the mine itself is changeless, seeking to be above worldly considerations. Pedro, intellectually nourished on "historical works, light and gossipy in tone," finds himself in Sulaco in a ravaged building. Facing Charles Gould, "that stony fiend," he finds that his imagination is "subdued by a feeling of insecurity and impermanence." The Intendencia which houses the government can be destroyed; the mine, in any state, is a force, a symbol not only of abstract justice, but also of permanence, of some Absolute.

A dominant characteristic of the world of men is liability to corruption; of the world of immutable values, incorruptibility. Because Nostromo throughout possesses the name and reputation of "Incorruptible," he is entrusted with the saving of the store of silver from the political factions. When the Italian boatswain finally leaves Decoud and the silver upon the Great Isabel, he reminds the latter that there is no necessity for speed or for revealing the hiding place of the silver. "'And always remember, señor, before you open your lips for a confidence, that this treasure may be left safely here for hundreds of years. Time is on its side, señor. And silver is an incorruptible metal that can be trusted to keep its value forever . . . An incorruptible metal.'" (299–300) The final three hundred pages reveals that Nostromo, flesh, is corruptible in every sense of the word, but that the silver, apparently lost forever, does, indeed, have time on its side.

The mine and the silver, then, present the reader with larger motifs which help to define and control the changing human experience of the Conradian universe. The petty quarrels of the political scene derive an absolute sanction from the mythic world of the silver. Everything which surrounds the treasure—superstitions, guardians, landscape, images used to describe it or to link it with the natural world—reveals figurations which have existed in folklore, fairy tale, myth, and legend. The artist appropriates from the heritage of his cultural life and from the experiences to which all men are subject an universal conventional alphabet[12] that can enlarge the most

11. Georges Poulet, *Studies in Human Time*, tr. Elliott Coleman (Baltimore: Johns Hopkins University Press, 1956), p. 32.

12. See Northrop Frye, *Anatomy of Criticism* (Princeton: Princeton University Press, 1957), pp. 131–239.

provincial or particular experience. In his fictional presentation of the San Tomé mine and the influence which it exerts over the imagination shaping history, Conrad employs—either consciously or unconsciously—this controlling alphabet.

To extend this distinction between history and tradition, one need only relate both to the concepts of a perfect and of a fallen world. Sulaco, though its orange groves and isolation suggest Eden, is very different from our conception of paradise. It is inextricably part of the fallen world. Though most of its people are very primitive, a decadent Spanish aristocracy exists to remind us that the equality of Eden has long since been forgotten. Or perhaps we might say that this is a microcosm of the fallen world, possessing within its natural barriers all sorts of evil. The Golfo Placido which leads to it grows so dark that it hides from the "eye of God Himself" the work of man's hand. Although the "luxuriant beauty of the orange gardens bears witness to its [Sulaco's] antiquity," although it had once found "inviolable sanctuary from the trading world," this paradisiacal state could not continue. It now has access to Europe through the steamships of the O.S.N. company, whose ships "disregard everything but the tyranny of time."

On the other hand, the mine is a "paradise of snakes." When Mrs. Gould reflects upon the influence which the mine exerts after its reconstruction, she speaks of "'having disturbed a good many snakes in that Paradise.'" And Gould answers, "'It is no longer a Paradise of snakes. We have brought mankind into it, and we cannot turn our backs upon them to go and begin a new life elsewhere.'" (209) What Conrad presents is a demonic paradise, a parody of the Eden of GENESIS in which the only change was the daily rhythms of darkness and light. This "paradise of snakes" is a prophecy of the future, of the constant threat of corruption over the Conradian universe, of the evil influence of the traditional in the political affairs of the area. The jumbled and tangled natural setting which greets Charles and Mrs. Gould—the Adam and Eve who first yield to the temptations of power—represents the irrational of the individual or the prehistory of the new race born of material interests. Unlike our first parents, who were driven from paradise to found the race of man in time, Charles brings his new race into a demonic Eden.

That early landscape, which in its greenery suggested the Biblical paradise, contained "the thread of a slender waterfall" that "flashed bright and glassy through the dark green of the fronds of tree-ferns." But this waterfall, normally a symbol of regeneration, becomes changed by the activities of the concession:

> The waterfall existed no longer. The tree-ferns that had luxuriated in its spray had dried around the dried-up pool, and the high ravine was only a big trench half filled up with the refuse of excavations and tailings. The torrent, dammed up above, sent its water rushing along the open flumes of scooped tree-trunks striding on trestle legs to turbines working the stamps on the lower plateau—the *mesa grande* of the San Tomé Mountain. Only the memory of the waterfall, with its amazing fernery, like a hanging garden above the rocks of the gorge, was preserved in Mrs. Gould's water colour sketch. (106)

That the symbol of rebirth has simply been corrupted by mechanization is now apparent. Conrad describes the silver as it descends the mountains as a "stream of silver." The metaphor indicates that the phenomenal world has become charged with a new meaning, because of its association with material interests. By means of the conventional imagery of myth, Conrad reveals how these men who idealize and spiritualize the material give their actions the sanction which Greek or Shakespearean tragedy invested in an orderly but unknown cosmos. After the mine is place in working order, "Security seemed to *flow* [italics mine] upon the land from the mountain gorge." The half-wild Indian miners are like primitive tribes who attribute a human soul to objects of nature and so make little distinction between the human and sub-human and superhuman. Their animism is as much a part of their religious lives as their Catholicism. "They invested it [the mine] with a protecting and invincible virtue as though it were a fetish made by their own hands."

This special world can be seen from Sulaco at night, for it is situated on the side of a mountain. This superior height recalls the tendency of Biblical and classical humanity to situate religious shrines in high places. And its lights make it seem outside the spatial considerations of those who are tied to earth; it seems "suspended in the dark night between earth and heaven." Such description contributes to the ambiguity surrounding this traditional force. On the one hand, its paradise is demonic; it destroys the natural. On the other hand, it casts a light in the darkness—whether that darkness be the literal darkness of nature, the darkness representing the indifference of the universe, the symbolic darkness which is ignorance or the irrational in historical events, or the darkness of a world under a curse. Again, it is nearer heaven than hell. So the question remains: What kind of a force is this mine? Can it order by its very presence the chaotic, disorderly history of Sulaco? Or is the hope it seems to offer simply a parody of divine grace?

Even the human guardians of the silver gain a unique distinction when archetypal patterns attempt to reveal the divine within particular men. The man whose capital helps to finance reconstruction, Mr. Holroyd, is a kind of God figure. (The temptation to point out the similarity of this name to *Holy rōd* is overwhelming.) Or he claims an equal share of divinity because he regards God "as a sort of influential partner." Like God, dispensing justice to humanity, Holroyd distributes his time with regard to geographical importance. Sulaco receives twenty minutes a month of his undivided attention. But the engineer-in-chief of the railroad reminds us that, where material interests are spiritualized, time is of no consequence: "'To be a millionaire, and such a millionaire as Holroyd, is like being eternally young. The audacity of youth reckons upon what it fancies as unlimited time at its disposal; but a millionaire has unlimited means in his hand—which is better. One's time on earth is an uncertain quantity, but about the long reach of millions there is no doubt.'" (317) This god is, after all, but a self-deceptive idealist who attempts to justify his hopes of absolute power by "a pet dream of a purer form of Christianity." But such "'Food for vanity,'" as Dr. Monygham—cynic, sceptic, and himself a self-deceptive idealist—reminds us, "'makes the world go round.'"

Motifs from fairy tales or Märchen also become associated with the mine, enhancing its traditional role in the narrative. Unlike a fairy tale, however, Conrad's story does not divide the characters so easily into black and white, evil and good. The burden of proof shifts from one side to the other. Charles's father, a man well read in "light literature" became so obsessed with the mine that he regarded it as the "Old Man of the Sea fastened upon his shoulders. He also began to dream of vampires." His correspondence to his son takes on the "flavor of a gruesome Arabian Night's tale." Unfortunately the son, like the father, has "fallen under the spell of the San Tomé mine."

Finally, all Charles's actions are dominated by his awareness of the mine; his idealism takes the form of a "moral romance." As Decoud explains to Mrs. Gould, he "'could not believe his own motives if he did not make them first a part of some fairy-tale.'" Decoud, arguing for Separation, Decoud the politician and journalist of Sulaco who both records and shapes historical events, says again in comparing Charles and himself, "'Life is not for me a moral romance derived from the tradition of a pretty fairytale.'" Even the engineer-in-chief, who claims that the railroad has no practical hobby-horse to ride, and who wishes to establish his neutrality in the up-heavals of Sulaco, claims that Charles is in the position of the "'goose with the golden egg.'" The firmness of this position in the imaginative life of mankind is then em-phasized. Decoud's plan of Separation may fail or may not fail. Ribierism has col-lapsed because it was "merely rational," based on predictable historical laws. But the fairy tale has a logic based upon association, which is part of the imaginative life of the race. "'The tale of killing the goose with the golden eggs has not been evolved for nothing out of the wisdom of mankind. It is a story that will never grow old.'" (315)

To insure success the world of the mine has its benevolent, protecting feminine presence. Mrs. Gould is described again and again as fairy-like, as resembling "a fairy posed lightly before dainty philtres dispensed out of vessels of silver and por-celain." In one of the reader's last pictures of her she is sitting alone in the "Treasure House of the World." "Small and dainty, as if radiating a light of her own in the deep shade of the interlaced boughs, she resembled a good fairy, weary with a long career of well-doing, touched by the withering suspicion of the uselessness of her labors, the powerlessness of her magic." (520) Many of the affairs of the mine, as well as her good deeds, are conducted in her boudoir, blue and white, approximating the colors assigned by liturgical art to that Christian "good fairy," the Virgin Mary. That she keeps a statue of The Queen of heaven in a niche in her home reinforces this identi-fication between her benevolence and that of the mother of Christ.

We can imply from the irrationality of the political narrative that history is the story of man's unsuccessful attempts to cope with his fallen state. In the name of security he replaces one imperfection by another equally imperfect. The epoch of civil war is followed by the iron tyranny of Guzman Bento (who at least maintains peace), which is followed by several revolutions and "fatuous imbecility, plenty of cruelty and suffering still," which is followed by the benevolent tyranny of Don Vincente Ribiera, "a man of culture and of unblemished character," which is followed by the revolutions led by men like General Montero, his brother, Pedro, and Colonel Sotillo. Martin Decoud dies in the cause of Separation; in the last few pages rumors abound of Sulaco's wishing to extend peace to the rest of Costaguana by means of union.

History is, at once, the story of individual men who want to realize or idealize their ambitions, dreamers who delude themselves that they are democrats, that they are concerned with the people; and it is perpetual cycle whereby every human situation will always be repeated. Politics is a constant round of mental and moral failure. The traditional sphere of the mine, the language and iconography derived from myth and fairy tale, must make individual endeavor meaningful within this constant cycle or give men's actions a moral justification. But, as we have already seen, the description of the mine implies a value judgment; the area around the mine changes as a result of the endeavors of the Gould Concession. The "slender waterfall" no longer exists in the gorge. "The tree-ferns that had luxuriated in its spray had died around the dried-up pool, and the high ravine was only a big trench half filled up with the refuse of excavations and tailings." (706) Now the silver from the mountain is the only stream; it has replaced natural phenomena. The primitive miners have work and a measure of security; they are, however, herded into three anonymous villages—numbered rather than named. Individual freedom has disappeared.

Not only is the mine's influence over nature destructive, but also its influence over its owner is dehumanizing. The relationship between Gould and his wife disintegrates as a result of the enchantment of his opportunity. No children are born to this marriage. If not actually, Emilia is symbolically virginal. She dreads the mine as if it were another woman! "'Don Carlos' mission is to preserve unstained the fair fame of his mine. Mrs. Gould's mission is to save him from the effects of that cold and over-mastering passion, which she dreads more than if it were an infatuation for another woman.'" (245) Nor can Gould's failure in the realm of love be attributed to the author's own temperamental inability to deal with love between the sexes. As Thomas Moser suggests,[13] Conrad found that subject of love uncongenial; but in Charles Gould he reveals the successful characterization of a man unable to love for reasons which were congenial to Conrad. He is attempting to be faithful to an image of himself; he is a romantic like Lord Jim. Like Lord Jim he allows his egoism to isolate him completely from other human beings. This man who attempts to sentimentalize his actions is simply another portrait of a type which Conrad successfully created again and again— the self-deluded idealist. His role within the novel parallels that of the Fisher King in traditional story, the ruler whose wounds, either actual or symbolic, cause the wasting of his lands; he is the redeemer turned destroyer. In truth, Mrs. Gould is Conrad's only successful characterization of a woman, but this is so because she does not present the usual problems of a woman in love. Although she is still young, this fact is hard for the reader to realize because of her good works and because of Monygham's attachment to her. Although she loves, she does not manifest that love in a demonstrative passion; rather, she is simply there—loyal, passive, unobtrusive. Her unhappiness is stressed once—at the end, where it cannot destroy our firm impression of her. Finally, she too is an idealist; she sentimentalizes her husband's actions.

Nor is the mine a stabilizing influence over the affairs of Sulaco. It finances Don Vincente Ribiera, lures Colonel Sotillo's support for the Monterists, and nourishes

13. Thomas Moser, *Joseph Conrad: Achievement and Decline* (Cambridge: Harvard University Press, 1957), pp. 50–130.

Pedro Montero's dreams of grandeur. "'The real objective of the revolted garrison of Esmeralda is the San Tomé mine itself . . . otherwise the Occidental Province would have been, no doubt, left alone for many weeks.'" (244) Dr. Monygham makes the last pessimistic statement concerning the future of the Concession as a moral and practical force: "'No!' interrupted the doctor. 'There is no peace and no rest in the development of material interests . . . Mrs. Gould, the time approaches when all that the Gould Concession stands for shall weigh as heavily upon the people as the barbarism, cruelty, and misrule of a few years back.'" (511)

Just as *Nostromo* is two stories—a historical one and a traditional one—so it possesses two heroes who together make the composite hero of the novel. The traditional hero is Nostromo, the Genoese sailor, whose early life is a parody of the characteristics which Otto Rank and, after him, Lord Raglan, assign to the hero myth. His parentage and childhood are unknown. The only certain fact about his youth is that he suffered brutalities at the hands of a cruel uncle "who (he firmly believed) had cheated him out of his orphan's inheritance." The exposure myth whereby the elected infant child, born in unusual circumstances, is committed to the waves by the man who represents the father in authority if not in fact, is here in changed form. Nostromo escapes the cruel relative at fourteen, flees across the traditional body of water to a strange land, Sulaco, where he simply "came ashore one evening," and then finds the equivalents of both the kind stepparents *and* strange adventures. Old Giorgio, the Genoese Garibaldino, compares Nostromo's age to that of his dead son. Dona Teresa, his wife, constantly claims the prerogatives of a mother. "He was escaping from her, she feared . . . she railed at his poverty, his exploits, his adventures, his loves and his reputation; but in her heart she had never given him up, as though indeed, he had been her son." (254) When he relates his great mission to her as she is dying and receives only her indignation, he himself admits her claims: "'What angry nonsense are you talking, mother?'" His final refusal to fetch a priest for her weighs heavily upon him, for he "had been orphaned so young that he could remember no other woman whom he called mother." Dr. Monygham pronounces a judgment which reflects the classic Oedipal situation: "'women are so very unaccountable, in every position and at all times of life, that I thought sometimes she was, in a way, don't you see? in love with him—the Capataz.'" (319)

Again and again there is evidence that a reputation for supernatural exploits has gathered around the name of this Italian sailor, just as popular report endowed the heroes of every age with miraculous deeds. He has a special talent for appearing "whenever there is something picturesque to be done." At the moment of gravest danger he saves President Ribiera from the mob; he appears at the inn of old Viola as the enraged populace turn their guns upon it; his mere presence is enough to quell the people. He alone is cited for the task of removing the silver; Captain Mitchell mourns his supposed death because only he is capable of achieving the desperate ride to Cayta. And his vanity thrives on the adulation of both aristocrat and democrat. He is not only Nostromo, the "boatswain," he is *Nostro uomo*, "our man," which abbreviated in Italian becomes *Nostr'uomo*.

Though he presents a physical appearance above the ordinary and though his actions reveal heroic potentiality, Nostromo still does not possess the stature of a hero. For all his extraordinary ability he is only a man of the people, a captain of the cargadores. The cargadores themselves are an "outcast lot of very mixed blood, mainly negroes, everlastingly at feud with the other customers of low grog-shops in the town." (14) And Nostromo serves as their aloof and condescending taskmaster, superior to them in ability and vanity but not in origin.

The deficiencies which are present in the capataz are corrected in the person of Martin Decoud, the Journalist of Sulaco. This young man, born in Costaguana of a family later settled in Paris, is an aristocrat, a dilettante, and, like Gould, a self-deceptive idealist. He luxuriates in his position as spectator, in his indifference, his lack of faith, his scepticism. But he deceives himself because he is neither indifferent nor uncommitted. Conrad often uses the word "imagined" when speaking of De-coud's lack of self-knowledge. "Martin Decoud . . . imagined himself to derive an artistic pleasure from watching the picturesque extreme of wrong-headedness into which an honest, almost sacred conviction may drive a man." (200) "He imagined himself Parisian to the tips of his fingers." That he believes he is a man without faith and principles is apparent from his letter to his sister; that he is capable of intense passions is also apparent from his earnestness in carrying out his initial mission to Sulaco, from his deep love for Antonio Avellanos, from his editorials in *Povenir* (for which he is marked for execution when the Monterist faction takes Sulaco), from his mission to accomplish Separation, and from his final suicide. Conrad always treats Decoud's pose of "idle cumberer of the earth" with irony. But in Decoud's passionate moments—in his isolation and uncertainty—we can see many of the author's major concerns. Nostromo is the romantic hero, the simple naïve man who sees events in terms of good and evil, the hero by temperament. Decoud, on the other hand, is capable of the tragic vision, the awareness of ambiguity and irony in life. He alone possesses the exquisite sensibility which realizes that he is part of an immense indifference of things. He is the hero by birth, Aristotle's "type ennobled," the man who can fall from a superior height because the superior height is his rightful social position.

Moreover, the hero is traditionally and historically a national figure, who is willing to subordinate his individual concerns for the larger good of the community. At the outset he is a free agent, who either by choice or special election, is gradually caught up in a chain of causality. He must assume the burden of the quest through which he meets and conquers the dragon that oppresses and blights the land. The regeneration of civilization may be the result of his success.

Sulaco approximates the fallen world of myth; its symbolic curse is expressed in the image of the burden from which no man is exempt. The landscape is often described as being under the weight of clouds or of shadows. The "burdened Indians," the people "all under burdens," accept their lot with patience and silence; their actual loads are representative of the weight of the past which is intangible. By Separation Decoud expects to free the land so that the rest of Costaguana cannot hang "like a millstone round our necks," so that Sulaco may be freed from the stupidity of the past. Nor does Decoud's expectation of Antonia's love negate the selflessness of his actions.

We can see in her presence the guiding feminine symbol by means of which Decoud must overcome his own physical limitations, the virgin princess of myth and fairy tale whose hand is the final reward for all successful action in the social sphere. Nostromo, too, regards his quest—the removal of the silver—as an attempt to promote the common good. In accepting the quest, he realizes that he is accepting a curse. And the rewards are in reality insignificant—an incorruptible reputation—compared with the dangers involved. Dr. Monygham pricks his vanity by saying that "'for taking the *curse of death* [italics mine] upon my back, as you call it, nothing else but the whole treasure would do.'" (259) Moreover, the curse of the silver does involve a symbolic death and recalls the curse of Dona Teresa's "lost soul."

Neither Decoud nor Nostromo—the first accepting the call to adventure of the historical narrative; the other, the call of the traditional story—has yet confronted the possibilities of his own nature. Neither man has been sufficiently alone to look inward in order to make the discoveries which will enable him to understand himself and, perhaps through understanding of his own identity, to aid his fellow men. The moment these two set themselves adrift in the lighter with its cargo of silver, they are more alone than either has ever previously been. Their withdrawal from human society is the first step in the complete cycle of the hero's adventure into the unknown. Moreover, the journey by sea in a lighter suggests the hero's journey into the interior regions of the mind. What we have in the novel are external referents which are symbolic translations of internal events.

That Conrad has unconsciously blurred the boundary between the real voyage and and the interior journey of the psyche becomes apparent as soon as the two men leave the shore. The standards of the visible world lose their meanings as soon as the night-sea is encountered. "The effect was that of being launched into space." In the last eleven pages of Chapter VII, images and metaphors suggesting sleep, dream, and unreality increase in number. To Decoud the stillness affects his senses "like a powerful drug"; he begins to lose his belief in his own individuality and at times doesn't know "whether he were asleep or awake." The past, as well as the present, seems betrayed by the indifference of the dream. "All his active sensations and feelings, from as far back as he could remember, seemed to him the maddest of dreams. Even his passionate devotion to Antonia into which he had worked himself up out of the depths of his scepticism, had lost all appearance of reality." (267) Such intense silence approximates death. "In this foretaste of eternal peace they floated vivid and light, like unearthly clear dreams of earthly things that may haunt the souls freed by death from the misty atmosphere of regrets and hopes." (262)

The irrationality of the whole situation provides a superb example of man's fate in an irrational world. They find both sense experience and intellect useless in floating in impenetrable darkness. Unable to determine whether or not they are moving, they yet cannot control their direction. Symbolizing the wider theme of the *bateau ivre*, the rudderless (literally, "drunken") boat, their actions externalize in fictional form the experience of all mankind in an indifferent nature. "'This is a blind game with death,'" says Nostromo—but so, too, is life. When Hirsch, the hide merchant, is discovered hidden upon the lighter, his fate also remains "suspended in the darkness of the gulf, at the mercy of events which could not be foreseen." (275)

That darkness and shadow suggest the unconscious, the buried life, is made very explicit. At the moment Nostromo snuffs the candle Decoud realizes the uniqueness of his position. "Intellectually self-confident, he suffered from being deprived of the only weapon he could use with effect. No intelligence could penetrate the darkness of the Placid Gulf." (275) He has begun to confront the interior world of his existence in this dreamlike setting. So jealous is the capataz of his reputation that Nostromo resents a situation in which courage is not good enough. "'I have a good eye and a steady hand; no man can say he ever saw me tired or uncertain what to do; but, *por Dios*, Don Martin, I have been sent out into this black calm on a business where neither a good eye, nor a steady hand, nor judgment are any use.'" (275–276)

In myth, as I have noted, the hero must undertake a night-sea journey into an ambiguous region either in the dark interior of the earth or below the waters of the sea. This is a symbolic death that occurs that he may encounter the forces of evil, the monsters that blight the world of natural cycle; he descends, so to speak, into the belly of the whale or into the mouth of the dragon. In overcoming the monster which is death, he experiences the peace of paradise and a knowledge of the unity of existence. But he must be reborn in order to bring his special truth back to a fallen world, in order to redeem mankind. On a personal level, the ritual quest symbolizes the journey into the self, into the dark interior landscape of the dream which approximates the still waters of the womb. After conquering the dragon that is the Ego, the individual is reborn better able to endure the continual flux of life because he has gained a new knowledge of the self, a new sense of identity.

The collision with the troop ship, the burial of the treasure, and Nostromo's final swim back to the mainland—all these can be equaled with the mythic journey into the underworld, the death and rebirth of the capataz. As a result of the report forced from the frightened Hirsch, who is miraculously saved, Nostromo and Decoud are considered dead. The man whose reputation depends upon saving the silver has purportedly "saved" it at the cost of his own life. Yet the truth is that the freighted boat does not sink, but is with difficulty conveyed to the small island. Nostromo, after burying the silver and leaving Decoud, himself sinks the lighter, destroys all evidence of his own survival, and swims to the shore in order to return to Sulaco.

His emergence from the dark sea where the lighter is "hardly distinguishable from the black water upon which he floated," reveals the figure of a man who has passed through several worlds. First of all, he reaches land before dawn and sleeps the entire day until after sunset. Sleeping for fourteen hours, he loses his sense of the linear passage of time in the historical world. The site he chooses reflects the corruption caused by death; it is the quadrangle of an old fort among "ruined bits of walls and rotting remnants of roofs and sheds." As he sleeps, the entire area possesses the ambiguity present between the spiritual or internal world of the dark gulf, the world revealed in sleep or death, and the real world where man is required to act. He lay "as if dead," "as still as a corpse." A rey-zamuro watches his body "from a hillock of rubbish" for "signs of death and corruption." The capataz sleeps through the "white blaze of noon" and only wakes after darkness has again descended. He is thrust back into the world in which ambiguity and irrationality must be confronted by the knowledge gained from an irrational and ambiguous experience. Only after Nostromo awakes does the bird fly away—and then reluctantly, as if aware of the invisible corruption within or aware that this man has just been reborn from the peace of a symbolic death. And because this man has been "reborn," because he is now without those externalities necessary to his sense of personal identity, he is not fully equipped to handle the exigencies of his situation. Rather, Conrad uses the images of the child just born or of an animal, a regression to the primitive in the individual life or to the prehuman state. He awakes "with the lost air of a man just born into the world." With a "growling yawn" he appears "as natural and free from evil in the moment of waking as a magnificent and unconscious wild beast."

But the world into which Nostromo is reborn is a world which believes that he is dead. So this man, whose faithfulness and worth is based upon an exaggerated concern for public reputation, finds his new life dreamlike. As he enters Sulaco, the town seems unreal. "The thought that it was no longer open to him to ride through the street, recognized by every one, great and little, as he used to do every evening on his way to play *monte* in the posada of the Mexican Domingo; or to sit in the place of honor, listening to songs and looking at dances, made it appear to him as a town that had no existence." (414–415) Obsessed by a feeling of betrayal, he rushes to the custom-house "like a pursued shadow" to be greeted by another unreality—the shadow of Hirsch's hanging dead body. When Dr. Monygham relates recent events, Nostromo listens "as if in a dream," feeling "himself of as little account as the man." Even the ride to Cayta must be undertaken without the support of an admiring audience. It is the achievement of a ghost, or of a man unable to meet the world he once knew on his his own terms.

Nostromo as hero, then, has undergone many aspects of the ritual adventure. He has withdrawn temporarily from mankind in order to fulfill the requirements of his task. His withdrawal into the unknown takes the form of the journey by night-sea, a region where the unconscious may project its fantasies without the hindrance of time and space. The darkness of the gulf represents that world beyond the boundaries which sense imposes. His entire adventure upon the gulf is his descent into the belly of the whale, into the peace of death. Although little more than twenty-four hours have elapsed, Conrad has artistically created the illusion of time held in suspension. His images suggest an immutable world. Having technically won his victory by saving the silver, Nostromo is reborn, supposedly able to redeem the fallen world with his new presence.

But, as we have been told, the mythic journey is within; the gulf is the "realm we enter in sleep. We carry it within ourselves forever."[14] What has been demanded of Nostromo is that he annihilate his ego in order to save Sulaco. When he enters the peace of the gulf, he for the first time faces the possibility of his own failure. Though Decoud is his companion in the adventure, he is at last entirely, profoundly isolated. The perfect logic of his very simple character breaks down in a situation which cannot

14. Joseph Campbell, *The Hero with a Thousand Faces* (New York: Meridian, 1956), p. 17.

be controlled by "a good eye nor steady hand nor judgment." Like the revolutionary Colonel Sotillo he has never realized "the limitations put upon human faculties by the darkness of night," by the repressed within one's own nature. And he resents having to face the threat of corruption over all humanity in the Conradian scheme of things and over all flesh in the fallen world of myth. He thinks he has been betrayed by the Blancos, the aristocrats who use him, although his own ego destroys him. He resents, finally, any human truth which denies the reality of his past actions. Certainly the awareness of failure and the inevitability of death, the "intimate impressions of universal dissolution," cause the collapse of his vanity.

What Nostromo cannot do when he returns is "survive the impact of the world"[15] as the successful hero should. He cannot readjust himself to the society whose admiration he requires. After his symbolic rebirth, he cannot bridge the gap between the two worlds—the logical simple world he has created for himself and the dark world of the unknown. His new life begins the moment he awakens on the mainland, for he must live at once concealed himself and concealing the hiding place of the silver. Decoud's death merely intensifies his own secret life. The disappearance of both the ingots and Decoud causes an "irrational apprehension." Decoud's leaving the spade near the treasure, an act which reveals the hiding space, denotes "utter carelessness or sudden panic," conduct which confounds Nostromo's consistent nature. His simplicity does not embrace a knowledge of the irrational.

Changes take place in him over the years. His public life as Nostromo has ceased, existing only in the memory of those who participated in the fight for Separation. (Several of these, however, are dead.) He has made another public existence for himself as Gian' Battista Fidanza: his real name is first used, ironically enough, when he discovers that Decoud is dead and the four ingots of silver are gone. Now he is "unpicturesque, but always a little mysterious." The name which meant "boatswain" or "our man" is replaced by a surname which denotes reliability. But his new public life is only appearance; the real life is hidden. The confidence he inspired can exist only in memory or as a lie. His position as *capataz de cargadores* is assumed by Ramires, a starving waif grown to manhood and a suitor of Giselle Viola. By stealing the silver, Nostromo grows rich slowly. The world believes Captain Fidanza has a profitable business. He becomes betrothed ostensibly to Linda Viola, but secretly courts Giselle, who he feels will accept his crime. When he is shot, he lies to Giselle about the motive of his return to the Great Isabel. "'It seemed as though I could not live through the night without seeing thee once more—my star, my little flower.'" (554)

As Nostromo's secrets grow, so his isolation from the community grows. The town for which he undertook the quest is forgotten. In his own eyes, however, he is still Nostromo, still "Incorruptible." He refuses to admit the "soft spot, the place of decay"[16] within, denies the evil in himself and so symbolically denies it in all mankind. And in denying his personal evil, he proves that he cannot transcend the limitations of his own ego. At last he dies, admitting the truth only once to Emilia Gould. To him-

15. *Ibid.*, p. 226.
16. Joseph Conrad, *Lord Jim: a Romance* (Garden City: Doubleday, Page, 1925), p. 13.

self and the world he had denied, he has "lived his own life on the assumption of unbroken fidelity, rectitude, and courage!"

But the successful hero is the whole man, a creature who realizes that both guilt and innocence, corruption and purity, are mixed inevitably in the human sphere. Nostromo's fault is that he is a man "who, satisfied with his own appearance, presumes to consider himself right and whole, a hero, a king in the seat of judgment."[17] The silver, once given him as an actual task and a symbol of his hero's quest, now becomes the measure of his guilt. Like the king of the folktale who must bear on his back the gruesome corpse of an unknown criminal—a corpse whose ghostly voice propounds riddles for the king to answer—Nostromo must bear the symbolic weight of the treasure. In the tale the decaying corpse represents the dead body of the past, "another one of our egos";[18] the ghostly voice within it which prods the king is "still another, the strangest ego of all. It dwells behind, beyond, within the kingly 'I' that we consciously consider ourselves to be, and, making its voice echo from the dead forms around, threatens sudden death to us should we refuse to obey its whims. It sets us tasks and pricks us to and fro, involving us in the hideous game of life and death."[19] The king, after his strange initiation, becomes aware of his complicity in mankind's guilt as well as in mankind's innocence, and so completes his task. After Nostromo is "reborn" and returns unknown to Sulaco, he, "deprived of certain simple realities, such as the admiration of women, the adulation of men, the admired publicity of his life, was ready to feel the burden of sacrilegious guilt descend upon his shoulders." (420)

The symbolic weight of the buried silver makes him feel enslaved. The references to weight become gradually combined with images of a man in fetters. At all times he is "as if he had been chained to the treasure." To Nostromo these unreal chains have an almost visible and audible force. It angers him because Giselle cannot hear "the clanking of his fetters—his silver fetters—from afar." But her love for Nostromo does not bind her as Linda's does; for the latter wants to share her lover's guilt, carries her love "like an increasing load of shameful fetters." Symbolically burdened by the treasure, he dies actually bearing it. When he is shot by a senile Viola, he is creeping out of the foliage "loaded with silver." Even as he is dying, however, he has but one moment of personal doubt. True to his vision of himself, he dies proclaiming that he has been betrayed.

Again, the knowledge that the whole man combines reason and lack of it, guilt and innocence, binds the archetypal hero more closely to the community which he has saved. His vision of the eternal has confirmed him in his communal role. In this novel Nostromo's denial of the irrational world and his conscious refusal to accept his guilt (although he unconsciously bears it) isolate him. Again, the silver destroys any meaningful personal relationships which he might establish. Dying, Dona Teresa, the symbolic mother, the nourishing, all-protecting feminine presence in the universe,

17. Heinrich Zimmer, *The King and the Corpse*, tr. & ed. Joseph Campbell (New York: Pantheon, 1956), p. 224.

18. *Ibid.*, p. 223.

19. *Ibid.*

predicts his failure. "'Your folly shall betray you into poverty, misery, starvation.'" This is the curse upon his whole venture. After he has grown rich on the treasure, he transfers his affections to the blond Giselle from the dark Linda, who was to have been his wife. "Linda, with her mother's voice, had taken more her mother's place." To old Viola she is "like a daughter and wife in one." Linda is rejected by Nostromo because he realizes she would not condone his actions. In the mythical counterpart of this fictional episode the reward for the hero's victory is the beautiful woman at once mother, virgin, sister. Linda, as adopted sister of Nostromo's second family, as symbolic replacement for Dona Teresa—wife to old Viola and mother to Giselle for whom she feels "maternal tenderness"—and as betrothed for Nostromo, fulfills this role.

But this role is traditionally filled by the blond woman, the innocent, the representative of the world of reason. According to Mario Praz, the dark woman usually is the temptress, the vampire, the creature who, whether through her own volition or because of something beyond her control, has a pact with the devil for the destruction of the hero.[20] And Linda does partake of this irrationality. She is passionate rather than submissive. When she suspects Giselle's duplicity, she behaves like a vampire; she flings "herself upon the chair in which her indolent sister was lying and impressed the mark of her teeth at the base of the whitest neck in Sulaco." (549) Yet with typical Conradian irony the pattern is again reversed. Linda does reveal a depth of emotion consistent with her characterization as the daughter of the woman who was herself a little in love with Nostromo yet who places a curse upon his actions. But she is also the lighthouse keeper. She watches the light, which stands on the Great Isabel and shines over the treasure, the dark spot in Nostromo's life. The light, like the candle lit in the gulf, seems to represent reason, appears as a symbol of communication. It has an important function in guiding the members of the community back to shore. Ironically, although with poetic justice it beams over the silver, it cannot penetrate or reveal the burial place of the treasure. As a force of isolation the silver remains stronger than the light of communication.

Giselle, on the other hand, appears innocent. In truth, her very submissiveness, her indolence, is "seductive." She attracts him not only because of her difference from Linda, but because her hair is "like gold" and because her voice, unlike Linda's reminds him of the "tinkling of a silver bell." Admittedly his love-making is embarrassing to the reader. But it is embarrassing not only because Conrad found the subject matter uncongenial, but also because Giselle never becomes a real woman. She is always a symbol of a traditional but dehumanizing force.

Like Charles Gould, whose mine becomes the substitute for a woman, Nostromo's final isolation is from his hero's reward, from the woman he loves. Gradually the inanimate silver is what he yearns "to clasp, embrace, absorb, subjugate in unquestioned possession." He cannot tell Giselle where the treasure is buried because the "spectre of the unlawful treasure arose, standing by her side like a figure of silver, pitiless and secret with a finger upon its pale lips." (542) Finally, this figure of silver, not the human Giselle, draws him back to the island to meet his death.

20. Mario Praz, *The Romantic Agony*, 2nd ed., tr. Angus Davidson (New York: Oxford University Press, 1956).

Nostromo achieves a dubious type of immortality in the end. Refusing to get a priest for the dying Teresa Viola, and thus denying her her hope of salvation, he speaks of his own dangerous mission. Should he die, he bequeaths his silver buttons to one of his pretty Morenita girl friends for her next lover. Then, with a phrase which fulfills its early promise as ironic foreshadowing, he says, "'. . . the man need not be afraid I shall linger on earth after I am dead, like those Gringos that haunt the Azuera.'" (258) While floating upon the gulf Nostromo juxtaposes the dangers of the adventure and a possible search for the legendary "devils and ghosts" of the other treasure. A slave of the buried silver while he lives, he becomes when he is dead its perpetual guardian: ". . . the genius of the magnificent Capataz de Corgadores dominated the dark gulf containing his conquests of treasure and love." Meaning at once "an extraordinary power" and "a spirit presiding over a person or place," the word "genius" describes the immortality of Nostromo; he is a memory which depends upon Linda's love and the lives of those involved in the historical events of Sulaco, and a spirit of sinister unrest which in popular lore hovers over forbidden treasure. Ironically, he had shunned the love of Linda when he was alive, and no one knows of that unrest when he is dead.

Ultimately our lack of identification with Nostromo affects our conception of him as an ideal hero. That his very human self-deception does not enlist our sympathy can, I think, be attributed to the detachment with which Conrad himself seems to view him. Too simple in intellect and too consistent in behavior, his characterization does not reveal any tension between the active world and the inner, personal one. When he begins to question himself, he manages to shift the burden of his self-doubt onto another. "The silences of his personal despair"[21] do not exist. Before the incident on the lighter, we have only isolated glimpses of a man who, purportedly magnificent in appearance, uncomplex by nature, enormous in vanity, arrives at the right place at the right time. These superficial moments in no way prepare us for a man who is capable of any depth of emotion or suffering. His persistent posing in public—especially the rather absurd incident with the Morenita—tends to be ludicrous and immature, a characteristic of the egocentric folk hero rather than the universalized and communal tragic hero. Once the hero of popular report and illiterate societies evolves into a literary character, whether in drama or in a novel, he demands a complexity which Nostromo reveals only in isolated moments. Nor does Conrad's failure to make his courtship of Giselle believable help us to appreciate this man of the people. This courtship—although couched in clichés consistent with this sailor's lack of education—is, indeed, a perfect example of the author's inability to cope with a love relationship. Conrad did not use those clichés because he felt they were in character; rather, he used them because he could not handle this type of scene artistically.

Nostromo's greatest advocate in the fictional world of Sulaco further alienates the reader; for this advocate is a fool. Pompous, unimaginative, talkative—all these words describe Captain Mitchell of the O.S.N. And through Captain Mitchell's point of view and in his tedious prose we first hear of Nostromo. Thereafter, the admirable captain's opinion (no less dull for being admirable) pursues the Capataz. He suggests

21. Campbell, *The Hero with a Thousand Faces*, p. 391.

his boatswain for every unusual venture; when another character—Decoud or Mrs. Gould—wishes to praise the Genoese, they do so on Captain Mitchell's recommendation. The reader, then, is unfavorably influenced by a character whose greatest admirer is essentially comic. Certainly Captain Mitchell's standing up to Sotillo is courageous; but somehow the manner in which it is done is primarily humorous. Nor does the gold chronometer which the Captain almost dies for—inscribed though it may be—seem a worthy object for an obsession. Or perhaps this obsession merely reveals how much Captain Mitchell is part of the timed universe of historical events.

Yet the final reason for Nostromo's failure as a hero is that he simply lacks status; unlike Legett, or Marlow, he is not a "Conway boy." He is only a sailor and the men he dominates are mainly Negroes. Because they are traditionally symbols of the unknown —and by extension, evil—in Western culture, the dark races or the darker members of the white race reflect the irrational areas within ourselves which have been repressed by civilization. Conrad's own attitude toward the revolutionaries can be seen by the fact that many of the populace possess Negroid characteristics: Pedro Montero and his brother, the General, "were very much alike in appearance, both bald, with bunches of crisp hair above their ears, arguing the presence of some negro blood." (286) The *Negro Liberalism* of the Monterist press frightens Señor Avellanos. Both Decoud and Hirsch regard the insurgents as "negro Liberals," a term manifesting Conrad's own conservative bias. In a sense Nostromo repudiates the revolutionaries by acting for the aristocratic Blancos, the whites, the reasonable men who are living in "indolence" rather than in "mental darkness" like the lower classes. But he eventually feels that the Blancos have betrayed him, a "man of the people."

Moreover, in our childhood fantasies and in our dreams we become princes and princesses. If we deign to consider ourselves boatswains, we always manage to elevate ourselves in the end to a royal or divine stature. This never happens to Nostromo, who moves from capataz to captain, but never to a position high enough for Blanco's respect.

Perhaps Nostromo would engage our sympathies if Decoud were not compared with him. Whereas we watch Nostromo too often through the eyes of Captain Mitchell, we see Decoud chiefly through two points of view—his own and his author's. As Albert Guerard points out,[22] on the one hand, we have the man who denies his own commitment, proclaims his indifference; on the other, the man of action who, while protesting his innocence, does act. He realizes his responsibility and so involves himself. The man who claims to regard himself with ironic detachment receives Conrad's sympathy. The author may judge his pose adversely, but never denies him sympathy. Moreover, his "love affair" with Antonia, because it is expressed in heroic actions rather than the words of romance, does succeed. That he assigns his motives to his love for her does not diminish either these motives or his love. Rather, it proves the extent of his commitment.

Precisely because Decoud is more actor than spectator his final suicide is convincing. Once adrift on the gulf with Nostromo, he is affected by the belief that this silent darkness is a "foretaste of eternal peace" and that he is freed by "death from

22. Albert Guerard, *Conrad the Novelist* (Cambridge: Harvard University Press, 1958), pp. 201–202.

the misty atmosphere of regrets and hopes." The complete loss of all sense of reality, makes him "the prey of an extremely languid but not unpleasant indifference." How much greater is the peace of the Great Isabel after Nostromo leaves, where no birds visit and where silence becomes "like a tense, thin cord to which he hung suspended by both hands." A reasonable and intelligent man who had before understood the motives of other men, he beholds "the universe as a succession of incomprehensible images." Everything—including his own individuality—merges into the mindless natural world. Nor is he now supported by that activity in which "we find the sustaining illusion of an independent existence as against the whole scheme of things of which we form a helpless part." (497) One acts on behalf of other men because one anticipates a future good based on human rationality. But the total silence challenges Decoud with a vision of complete irrationality and brute nature. Solitude dispels man's "sustaining illusion." The symbolic language of the mountains changes. When he wished to push his political schemes, they cried to him, "Separate." Now Higuerota hovers above, an image of a silent cosmos indifferently viewing man's puny, corrupt struggles.

Decoud decides to kill himself because his vision of total evil has become overwhelming. This acute recognition of irrationality takes the classic form of the hero's refusal to return to the troubled life he has left. His suicide, then, is not an admission that something has value but rather a denial of responsibility because of the belief in all-pervasive evil. Conrad, while he agrees with the vision, does emphasize man's duty toward his fellows. So Decoud's denial is understandable but inexcusable. It is the crime which is the breach of faith with all humanity; it is Lord Jim's jump from the *Patna*; it is the individual isolation of each member of the *Narcissus* as a result of misdirected pity for the evil Negro James Wait. Yet somehow the very intensity of Decoud's despair, the anguish which his inward voyage reveals evokes our sympathy— and from the excellence of the prose rhythms and language, the author's as well. Of such anguish new myths are made.

In this refusal to return to the life of action can be seen many figurations of myths and dream. Decoud is left temporarily upon a small island in a gulf which seems to deny the visible world; and "Numerous indeed are the heroes fabled to have taken up residence forever in the blessed isle of the unaging Goddess of Immortal Being."[23] Ironically, his isle is hardly blessed and is soon to be haunted by Nostromo. Again, Decoud moves from a symbolic to an actual death. "He pulled straight towards the setting sun." Myth usually assigns the unknown, the land of death, to the west; for the limitations of our senses make such spatial imprecision necessary. We must relate what we cannot see or know to an area which we cannot reach, yet which our perceptions can encompass. Finally, piling significant image upon significant image, Conrad has the Journalist of Sulaco shoot himself. He falls back into the sea, which itself is the nothingness of death or the body of water which separates the dead from the living. He has weighted his body with four bars of the San Tomé mine; he carries his burden of inherited guilt with him into the world of silence and death.

Decoud, as complex hero, has based his life upon a belief in his own rationality.

23. Campbell, *The Hero with a Thousand Faces*, p. 193.

Nostromo, as simple hero, has also lived his twenty-four years upon a consistent pattern which, given his premises of existence, is no less rational. The apparently timeless world presents Decoud with a completely irrational universe, in which the pose of scepticism ceases to be a pose and the actions of a reasonable man are revealed for what they are—useless. Nostromo, too, fails because he refuses to admit that he can behave irrationally. Neither emerges from the quest a whole man aware both of the good and evil, reason and lack of it—the one because his vision overwhelms mere rationality; the other because he refuses to admit personal evil, refuses to annihilate his own ego for the community. Each undergoes rites of initiation designed to create the true hero, the self-effacing man whose deeds are a constant reminder of the timeless beyond the world of forms, of the oneness between the individual and the society of which he is only a part. But the obsessive sense of isolation and fragmentation of each reveals that the tragedy of the composite hero of *Nostromo* is a tragedy of modern man's loss of identity. Nostromo's two names and the ambiguity of his nickname reveal this same lack of unity. Perhaps the fact that there are two heroes—or four— shows the extent of modern man's dismemberment of personality.

What Joseph Campbell calls the "mythologically instructed community"—that community which "translates the individual's life-crises and life-deeds into classic, impersonal forms"[24]—does not exist in Sulaco—nor, indeed, in modern society. Instead, Conrad has used images of a world in which myth possessed a vital force, but has skillfully applied these images to the Gould Concession, the world of "material interests" that dehumanizes and is demonic in order to make an ironic statement upon the failure of his own society. The myths which Jerome Bruner calls the "treasure of an instructed community"[25] are replaced by the treasure which forms a new myth of a capitalist society. Nor does this treasure, given a validity by universal patterns, help to form the cohesive society which was the usual result of the hero's quest and the ritual acts as initiation. Rather, it simply supports the decay already apparent in the timed world of historical events. The cycle of political acts is contaminated by the evil inherent in the myth created around the silver in particular, and money or material interests in general. Unlike the magic sword wielded by the successful hero, it is a "weapon of wealth, double-edged with the cupidity and misery of mankind, steeped in all the vices of self-indulgence as in a concoction of poisonous roots, tainting the very cause for which it is drawn." (305)

Texas Studies in Literature and Language, III (1962), 510–534. Some reference notes have been omitted.

24. *Ibid.*, p. 383.
25. Jerome S. Bruner, "Myth and Identity," *Daedalus*, XCI (1959), 357.

WALDEN: THE WISDOM OF THE CENTAUR

William Bysshe Stein

Such virtues only as admit excess,
Brave, bounteous acts, regal magnificence,
All-seeing prudence, magnanimity
That knows no bound, and that heroic virtue
For which antiquity hath left no name.
But patterns only, such as Hercules,
Achilles, Theseus.

It is a mistake, I think, to read *Walden* as an historical work. It belongs to the nine-teenth century only through the accident of having been written in time. Similarly it is not, except adventitiously, concerned with Thoreau the man in any contemporary sense. I mean by this that the book must be read on the ground and in the terms of its world: which is to say, (I use the phrase only because no other will serve) the myth it embodies. To read it as autobiography, social criticism, or philosophy is to discount the transfiguration which the original materials of the journals undergo. Of course, I do not deny that *Walden* can be approached in this way, but it seems to me that the journals themselves invite this kind of valuation, not their imaginative transformation. This latter product demands the Jamesian attention which Thoreau long before him called for: "To read well, that is, to read true books in a true spirit, is a noble exercise, and one that will task the reader more than any exercise which the customs of the day esteem." Since *Walden*, as its critics would have it, is a true book, why is it read with an inflexible orientation on the nineteenth century? This in my opinion is unimagin-ative reading. I am sure that Mahatma Gandhi did not read *Walden* in this light. He read it as it "speaks to the intellect and heart of mankind, to all who [could] *understand* him." He is the one student of *Walden* who bothered to heed the pun on "*understand*," interpretively to stand under the pragmatic deception of the dollars-and-cents report of life on the pond—Thoreau's flippant ridicule of man's obsession with materialistic income. This one word encourages the search for the pattern of "that heroic virtue" of the poem. (I might observe that no critic has paid any attention to this excerpt from the complemental verses to the first chapter, even though Thoreau himself anticipates its citation by stating his definition of the absolute virtue for which every individual should seek: "His goodness must not be a partial and transitory act, but a constant superfluity, which costs him nothing, and of which he is unconscious.") It deplores infatuation with the merely existential, the "transient occasion." It points towards those patterns of antiquity to be found "understanding" Thoreau's blatant ironies.* * *

I

Thoreau's journal writings are full of impressions of an existence out of time and out of space. Within himself he felt those strange agitations of otherness that momentarily obliterated the historical man. In virtual *participation mystique* with nature he believed himself haunted by mythic memories that rendered his nineteenth-century ego anonymous:

> I am glad to remember to-night, as I sit by my door, that I too am at least a remote descendant of that heroic race of men of whom there is tradition. I too sit here on the shore of my Ithaca, a fellow wanderer and survivor of Ulysses. How symbolical, significant of I know not what, the pitch pine stands here before my door!

Out of such experiences, one would think, ought to have come the appropriate apothegm, the inevitable truism of the Transcendentalist who perceives the harmony of microcosm and macrocosm. None came. In these intervals he was not the Thoreau who parroted his master. He was the awe-struck initiate who stood on the threshold of the unaccountable mystery of life. But in later meditation upon the connection of modern man with the ancient myths, he began to discern the latter as vehicles of a *philosophia perennis*:

> The hidden significance of these fables which has been detected, the ethics running parallel to the poetry and the history, is not so remarkable as the readiness with which they may be made to express any truth. They are the skeletons of still older and universal truths than any whose flesh and blood they are for the time made to wear. It is like striving to make the sun and the sea signify. What signifies it?

But even in this passage there is doubt. He has not yet realized that this knowledge is a pattern of living, not the abstract formulation of the ethical code.

Perhaps Thoreau would never have extended his apprehension to the function of myth beyond this intellectual synthesis if he had not after his return to civilization, acquainted himself with Thomas Carew's poem (the complemental verses from which I have quoted). The lines which open this essay, I contend, brought to conscious awareness the intuitive truths which eluded him on the shores of Walden Pond. Beyond the rational assumptions of what he lived for in his self-exile from society, he descried in Carew's "heroic virtue" the instinctive motivation behind his conduct. As a consequence he spent seven years rewriting his journals in order to give them the "signifying" form that would recapture the mythic implications of his transformative experiences in the woods.

The epiphany of the poem defies casual interpretation. It hinges, of course, upon familiarity with the myths of Hercules, Achilles, and Theseus, with their underlying spirit (as Gandhi found it in *Walden*) not with the obvious details of their trials and ordeals. Thoreau, it seems to me intuited the one common feature of all of them which controls their ultimate meanings and discloses the universal ethic subsuming their apparent exaggerations. At the same time he saw that this common element was the single parallel to the myth he himself had lived. This was the perception that each of the heroes had been educated by the centaur Chiron. This may seem a trivial detail, but the fact remains that every hero myth is based upon the presupposition that its protagonist will achieve his ultimate goal only after he comes to terms with his own centauric nature, which is fatefully compounded of animal instincts and human virtues. Chiron is the teacher of the sons of the gods because he is the archetypal figure of the wise man. Half man and half animal, his external appearance attests the balance of animal and human traits, the two sources of total wisdom, the instinctive and the intellectual in mutual harmony. To attain this equipoise is to achieve selfhood. It presupposes the conscious direction of the instincts towards moral ends. It involves the recognition of the sacred role of the "lower" man. This is to say that one must always trust his animal nature, for the dark side of the total human personality, essentially indifferent to any distinctions between good and evil, must be accepted and brought under the control of those discerning faculties of the mind which can channel its energies towards virtue. Under these conditions the individual (the hero) reconciles the centauric division within himself. Such a transformative experience is the basis of Thoreau's formulation of the "higher laws" which operate in the conduct of man:

> I caught a glimpse of a woodchuck stealing across my path, and felt a strange thrill of savage delight, and was strongly tempted to seize and devour him raw; not that I was hungry then, except for that wildness which he represented. . . . while I lived at the pond, I found myself ranging the woods, like a half-starved hound, with a strange abandonment, seeking some kind of venison which I might devour, and no morsel could have been too savage for me. The wildest scenes had become unaccountably familiar. I found in myself . . . an instinct toward the higher, or, as it is named, spiritual life, as do most men, and another toward a primitive rank and savage one, *and I reverence them both*. (italics mine)

This surrender to the instincts, one ought to take note, is not attended by any deprecation of the intellect. Rather Thoreau here acknowledges not only his centauric character but his need to enact the centauric myth in order to achieve the full virtues or total wisdom which he calls in the same chapter, "a wisdom clarified by experience." But, as I will show later, this is an inevitable development, part of the imaginative form in which he shaped *Walden*.* * *

III

* * * Let me begin by repeating again that *Walden* cannot be read profitably as a form of autobiography. It is *sui generis* an original product of the imagination, and it must be read in these terms. His activities in the woods are not to be classified as the practical measures of sustaining life. Such a factual reading is for those whom he baits with the teasing practicalities of economic existence in the opening pages of *Walden*. His labors are not designed to satisfy mere physical needs. His labors are heroic—Herculean. No task is performed for itself, that is, for the material end which it consummates. Rather each one, progressively, severs his connection with historical time, harmonizing his activities with the rhythms of nature which are, eternally, a manifestation of mythic timelessness. For, on the human plane of existence, he executes those important acts of life which were revealed *ab origine* by gods, heroes, and ancestors (and here we cannot forget the epiphany of his kinship with the Homeric

heroes). These, then, are exemplary and paradigmatic gestures, the mythic precedents upon which he bases his reliving of the pattern of heroic virtue.

In condensing the journal writings of some two years into the sacred period of a year, he clearly enunciates this purpose since he gives his book the consecrated form of ritual. This deliberate alteration of time is also reflected in beginning his adventure in the spring of the year (actually he moved out of his hut in July). In this modification of fact he simply acknowledges that the seasonal calendar, as it coincides with the religious, celebrates in the space of a year the cosmogonic miracles which took place *ab origine*. The sacred year reiterates the Creation: man is made contemporary with cosmogonic and anthropogonic beginnings because ritual projects him into this mythical past. All this is comprehended in the physical renewal of spring, for in this phenomenon we bear witness to the release of those mysterious potencies of nature which are also innate in man. As the world is born again, so is man. Hence we can understand why Thoreau exults: "man's capacities have never been measured." He could not say less as he further proclaims that he is standing "on the meeting of two eternities."

But to initiate the transformation into the original unity of man, nature, and god requires an awareness of mythic precedent and an adherence to the ritual which commemorates it. And when Thoreau builds his hut, he repeats the cosmogonic act which, in the myths of construction, constitutes the laying of the foundation of the world. In imitating this event he dissolves into the mythic time of the beginning *in illo tempore*. Indeed he anticipates the enactment of this ritual in his parable of new clothes: another Eden must have another Adam:

> I say, beware of all enterprises that require new clothes, and not rather a new wearer of clothes. If there is not a new man, how can the new clothes be made to fit? If you have any enterprise before you, try it in your old clothes. All men want, not something to *do with*, but something to *do*, or rather something to *be*. Perhaps we should never procure a new suit . . . until we have so conducted, and so enterprised or sailed in some way, that we feel like new men in the old, . . . Our moulting season, like that of the fowls, must be a crisis in our lives. The loon retires to solitary ponds to spend it. Thus also the snake casts its slough, and the caterpillar its wormy coat, by an internal industry and expansion.

This sense of rebirth is echoed in his feeling of satisfaction after his structure is completed. In it he sees his own growth towards a mysterious unity of being, a fulfillment of self:

> What of architectural beauty I now see, I know has grown from within outward, out of the necessities and character of the indweller, who is the only builder,—out of some unconscious truthfulness, and nobleness, without ever a thought for the appearance and whatever additional beauty of this kind is destined to be produced will be preceded by a like unconscious beauty of life.

Here Thoreau's perspective embraces three of the planes of reality on which myth manifests itself. The hut, biologically, is the house of flesh; spiritually, the house of the soul; and, cosmically, the house of the universe. Steadfastly he moves towards the complete identification of himself with mythic otherness, a complete severance with the encumbering world of time and history.

But to become a hero involves labors, repetitions again of the ordeals and tests which prepare a Theseus, a Hercules, or a Perseus for the influx of the self-knowledge that is Chiron's wisdom. It is no surprise, therefore, to find Thoreau thinking of his tasks in the heroic terms of myth: "To enjoy these advantages I was ready to carry it on; like Atlas, to take the world on my shoulders." As he cultivates the virginal forest lands, merely hoeing his beans, he has titillating intuitions of a new identity:

> What was the meaning of this so steady and self-respecting, this small Herculean labor, I knew not. I came to love my rows, my beans, though so many more than I wanted. They attached me to the earth, and so I got strength like Antaeus. But why should I raise them? Only Heaven knows.

In the sly negation of the last sentence, he actually expresses the motivation behind his farming. All planting, cultivating, and harvesting in their connection with the regeneration of time presuppose precedents *in illo tempore*, and of these he is aware. *Sub specie aeternitatis* he follows the commands of the divine—Heaven indeed does know! Of considerable interest at this point in this focus of Thoreau's "labors" is the use of the word itself in *Walden*. If one were to attempt a distinction between the book and the journals, discounting form alone, he would, I believe, invoke the texture of the style as the chief difference. By this I mean the analogical matrix, as Mark Schorer uses the term. Only in the revised product does Thoreau view human endeavors in the common denominator of mythic labor, work directed towards inward enlightenment. And to dramatize this precise meaning of the word, he invariably associates it with some aspect of Hercules' life or lineage. It is as if Carew's poem acts like an incantation.

IV

But the myth of Hercules (and of course all of his mythical counterparts) is a controlling inspiration in another way. In it Thoreau finds the clearest parallel to his own spiritual labors on Walden Pond. I am not suggesting that he emulates Hercules' destruction of the Nemean lion or the Ceryneian hind; however, he comes to an understanding of his animalistic tendencies under a similar mythic discipline. His devotion to this Greek hero is determined by still another factor, one also of extreme importance. It is only Hercules whose transcendence of his centauric imbalance is an essential movement in the mythic pattern. The latter's accidental crime of murder is basically a human one, even though we might say that the gods ordain it to test his mettle. For in his atonement of this outrage he gains the admiration of the Olympian gods. This may seem like a paradox, if not ludicrous overstatement, when one considers the repeated intervention of the gods to help him accomplish his ends. Yet this is not so. The aid he receives from supernatural helpers in the language of myth simply illustrates the growth of divine virtue in the hero (I might add that this motif is a recurrent one in fairy tales also). His willingness to undertake the various ordeals insures the influx of the extra-human powers of divinity.

Thoreau himself is brought to the realization that sheer animal strength and courage, even when fortuitously expended in heroic accomplishment, are insignificant unless they are attended by moral insight. His intercourse on the pond with the Canadian woodchopper incites this awareness, for this huge and graceful workman, though "a true Homeric or Paphlagonian man," has "dull sleepy blue eyes." His soul has not yet been awakened. And when Thoreau looks at him, conscious of his innocence and friendly disposition, one cannot help thinking of Hercules before he was wakened to the realization that heroic virtue presupposes spiritual sensitivity:

> In him the animal man chiefly was developed. In physical endurance he was cousin to the pine and the rock. . . . But the intellectual and what is called the spiritual man in him were slumbering as in an infant. He had been instructed in that innocent and ineffectual way in which Catholic priests teach aborigines, by which the pupil is never educated to the degree of consciousness, but only to the degree of trust and reverence, and the child is not made a man, but kept a child.

As Thoreau surveys his own plight, it is the antithesis of the Canadian. He is predominantly the intellectual man who has lost rapport with his instincts. This information is conveyed in a highly elliptical fashion, even facetiously. Yet the statement of his predicament, I would wager, has teased many an attentive reader of *Walden* with all the fascination of the Sphinx before its secret was read. (At this point I wonder whether Oedipus really penetrated its secret as it applied to himself, for its animal-human form is what he forgets about himself in his later arrogance.)

Almost irrelevantly, at least in context, Thoreau in one spot announces:

> I long ago lost a hound, a bay horse, and a turtle dove, and am still on their trail. Many are the travellers I have spoken concerning them, describing their tracks and what calls they answered to. I have met one or two who heard the hound, and the tramp of the horse, and even seen the dove disappear behind a cloud, and they seemed anxious to recover them as if they had lost them themselves.

If one takes this literally, it is nonsense. Yet one cannot pass over it with impunity. An interpretation must be attempted, for Thoreau means exactly what he says on a certain level of reality. And he is unequivocal about this matter in immediate context: "You will pardon some obscurities, for there are more secrets in my trade than in most men's." I will risk the opinion that this image triad is the key to the understanding of the myth of the centaur which is unfolded in *Walden*. Not until he discovers "the way" of the lost animals (the bird is a surrogate) will he be able to pursue "the Way" to the knowledge of the heroic virtue. In effect, his instincts and intuitions have deserted him because he has denied their sacredness; his intellect has attempted to usurp their function. Not until his encounter with the woodchuck does he attain the reconciliation of his centauric polarity.

But let me now explicate the significance of the image triad, preliminary to my explanation of how Thoreau recovers communication with the hound, the bay horse, and the turtle dove. The hound, in an analogy with the supernatural helpers of Hercules, is the hunting dog of extraordinary powers. He scents out, chases, corners, or trees. He is never off the trail. He is the ideal "pointer," for he is infallible in his ability to point "the way." Symbolically he is the embodiment of instinctive wisdom and awareness. His quarry, as he serves man, is the elusive relationship with the ground rhythms of nature which Thoreau, as a civilized (?) man, has lost, the ability to "live simply and wisely" and "to suck out all the marrow of life, . . . to drive life into a corner, and reduce it to its lowest terms." Similarly the bay horse cannot be permitted to wander at will, for then the horse is the rider and not the mount. The animal in his integral connection with man represents the centauric character of the human personality. The horse is the purely instinctive aspect of man's command of conflicting virtues. If the bay horse retains his freedom, then his owner, who should guide him with his will power, his moral sense, and his reason, will forever be controlled by nature's chaotic forces. On the other hand, should he once more gather the reins in his hand, he will penetrate to the dark secrets of the primordial foundation on which cosmic truth lies. This is naked reality, what Thoreau calls "the essential facts of life."

With these "lower" aspects of his total being mastered he is ready to listen to the oracular voice of the turtle dove. The bird is the voice of the wilderness untouched by human culture. It is directly a part of nature, unlike the hound and the horse. Its cooing song is an invitation to share the secret of the forest in which it lives; and, in its flights into the clouds, it prophesies that "the way" of nature (the instincts) is "the Way" to the intuition of divine knowledge.

V

In the permutations of myth the order of initiation into a higher state of illumination constantly changes. Only the final goal is important. Similarly the nature and the severity of the ordeals which the hero undergoes also alter in shape as if calling to one's attention the diversity of human experience. Let me therefore schematize the pattern of the centauric myth which Thoreau lived. The first seven chapters of *Walden* exhibit the hero's necessary impatience with the world in which he lives. He demonstrates in this portion of the book his intellectual apprehension of the deficiencies of his culture. He invokes fact after fact to argue its sterility and stagnation until finally the reader, like him, is compelled to admit that this is the vision of a sick and dying society, the recurrent Waste Land of myths. But underlying this objective criticism of the external world is a secret dissatisfaction with himself. This inner discontent is objectified in a reiteration of the mythic precedents which primitive cultures followed to regenerate time. Finally in chapter eight, after a return from the village and after wandering through "the vastness and strangeness" of the forest (in myth the forest always serves as a place of initiation, for here lurk the demonic presences, the ancestral spirits, the untamed forces of nature), he borrows a repetitious precedent in myth: in losing himself he finds himself. He denies the reality of the village from which he has come, performing, as Huck Finn does when he simulates his own murder, the rite of severance. He dies to the old self which once found its identity in the village:

> Not till we are lost, in other words not till we have lost the world, do we begin to find ourselves, and realize where we are and the infinite extent of our relations.

The only place in which one can find the total integration of all the cosmic forces is in a world reborn in all of its newness and innocence, in its entelechy, completely actualized, all potentialities fulfilled. Thoreau, though he is able to envision this existence in mythic time, must still, like any initiate into higher truth, prepare himself for its realization through the performance of certain acts of preparation, purificatory in nature, before he is ready to achieve centauric discipline.

As his myth unfolds, it next takes shape in the ritual blessing of waters. In the enactment of this sacrament, equivalent on different planes of reality to Christ's blessing of the waters on Epiphany and to its extension into baptism (new birth), Walden Pond ceases to be merely a topographic location in the world. It is transformed into a prototypal model, an archetype of the celestial pools of the land of fairy:

> . . . On that spring morning when Adam and Eve were driven out of Eden Walden Pond was already in existence, . . . covered with myriads of ducks and geese, which had not heard of the fall, when still pure lakes sufficed them. Even then it had commenced to rise and fall, and had clarified its waters and colored them the hue they now wear, and obtained a patent of Heaven to be the only Walden Pond in the world and distiller of celestial dews. Who knows in how many unremembered nation's literatures this has been the Castalian Fountain? or what nymphs presided over it in the Golden Age? It is a gem of the first water which Concord wears in her coronet.

His sense of purity upon the repetition of this ritual of cleansing leads him to celebrate the event in a hymn of worship:

> It is no dream of mine,
> To ornament a line;
> I cannot come nearer to God and Heaven
> Than I live to Walden even.
> I am its stony shore,
> And the breeze that passes o'er;
> In the hollow of my hand
> Are its waters and its sand,
> And its deepest resort
> Lies high in my thought.

In its relation to the previous passage, especially in the allusion to the Fall of man, it posits salvation through nature, not through the redemptive act of a redeemer. The poem, then foreshadows Thoreau's renunciation of the institutional machinery of salvation, an inevitable development in his dedication to the mythic gods.

Significantly this experience is almost immediately followed by his formulation of the "higher laws" of being. And consistent with the growth of centauric wisdom, he recognizes the necessity of a stage of wholly instinctive existence: "the embryo man passes through the hunter stage of development." In this statement Thoreau implies that no individual can ever become perfect without understanding from within the quality of the savage and the inhuman. To shed blood is part of the initiation into higher knowledge. By assimilating the implications of this ruthlessness to human conduct, he learns the meaning of mercy, pity, and justice. He becomes capable of controlling the demonic forces of darkness which reside within him. Lest I be accused of reading meaning into an innocuous observation, let me point out that Thoreau conceives this self-education to be the influence which, phylogenetically and onto-genetically, rehearses the development of man from a savage into an intellectual and spiritual being:

> There is a period in the history of the individual, as of the race, when the hunters are the "best men," as the Algonquins called them. We cannot but pity the boy who has never fired a gun; he is no more humane, while his education has been sadly neglected.

And next, in even more precise terms, he proceeds to acknowledge the inextinguishable primitive which lurks in every human breast, in centauric imagery affirming the need of every man to keep the savage within him under the control of conscious virtue:

> He is blessed who is assured that the animal is dying out in him day by day, and the divine being established. Perhaps there is none but has cause for shame on account of the inferior and brutish nature to which he is allied. I fear that we are such gods or demigods only as fauns and satyrs, the divine allied to beasts, the creatures of appetites.

And what is this but the sign of man's coming into wisdom, knowing what he is not, hence knowing what he must do.

VI

And in his intercourse with his "brute neighbors" on the shores of the pond, Thoreau finally begins to overtake the hound, the bay horse, and the turtle dove which he had lost in his enchantment of intellect. To be sure, one cannot expect to find these supernatural creatures in their past forms. They are always incarnations of the needs of the moment. Embodiments of whatever instinct that will serve man best, they appear with all the suddenness of a jinni out of a bottle, waiting only to lead their discoverer to the secrets of the treasures of living. And with the typical illogicality of myth, since order is of no consequence in timelessness, the surrogate of the turtle-dove, the young of the shyest bird of all, the partridge, invades his retreat to whisper to him the answer to the riddle of centauric equipoise. If I may translate Thoreau's message from them into mythic language, they inform him, like Carew's poem, that virtue grows out of active involvement in the affairs of life, keeping innocence in balance with the stress of experience. This, at any rate, is what Thoreau reads in their eyes:

> They are not callow, like the young of most birds, but more perfectly developed and precocious even than chickens. The remarkably adult yet innocent expression of their open and serene eye is memorable. All intelligence seems reflected in them. They suggest not merely the purity of infancy, but a wisdom clarified by experience. Such an eye was not born when the bird was, but is coeval with the sky it reflects.

Surely this intuition, in the most concrete terms, takes him back to that instantaneous moment of mythic creation when man was in total harmony with himself, with nature, and with God. In the obvious sense of the passage, the eye of the partridge is a celestial archetype of the heavens. And Thoreau himself comments, "the woods do not yield another such gem." Here, then, is the turtle-dove in another guise, still an integral part of nature and of God. And again this lost component of his self announces that the instincts are "the way" to an understanding of "the Way" of heroic virtue.

While one perhaps may carry mythic shape-shifting to extremes, one can, I think, argue that in *Walden*, with all its invocations of animal wisdom, virtually hundreds of surrogates obtrude to serve Thoreau in his quest for a new identity. The numerous creatures which serve as harbingers of spring might appear to be, in this light, inevitable counters of proof in the line of argument. However, these latter belong to the culmination of Thoreau's enlightenment rather than to the preliminary steps which make it possible. Thus in seeking the totem counterpart of the bay horse, I choose his experience with the fox as the one which best illustrates his growing conviction that the primal instincts are sacred in their own right, chthonic energies looking forward to the advent of creative form and differentiation. And here the emergence of cosmos from chaos intrudes as the archetypal precedent. A similar intuition dictates Thoreau's response to hungry foxes prowling the woods for food. He is not frightened or appalled by their chilling cries; rather he associates their bestiality with a search for domestication:

> Sometimes I heard the foxes as they ranged over the snowcrust, in moonlight nights, in search of a partridge or other game, barking raggedly and demonically like forest dogs, as if laboring with some anxiety, or seeking expression, struggling for light and to be dogs outright and run freely in the streets; for if we take the ages into our account, may there not be a civilization going on among brutes as well as men? They seemed to me to be rudimental, burrowing men, still standing on their defense, awaiting their transformation.

These are not scientific speculations; they are simply intuitions into his own transformative experience viewed on the level of reality which portends the new center of gravity of his own personality. And if one pursues still further the implications of his feeling in regard to the foxes, one cannot forget that in the ritual dances of the American Indians the fox has often served as a symbolic focus, projecting the desire of man to acquire the sly and cunning traits of the animal, those instincts which might serve him efficiently in his struggle to survive in the jungle of nature. For is it not the ability of man to assimilate savage virtues to the needs of human reason that has enabled him to counterbalance the primordial anger of the demonic world? Thoreau would not think otherwise.

After this atavistic reconciliation it seems to follow that his terminal insight into the primitive should come in a vision of the august and regal magnificence of nature. Ritualistically this inflow of serene wisdom comes when the land is bound in the paralysis of winter. With the springs of life under the spell of the debilitating sickness of the Waste Land, he perceives that the regenerative powers of the biocosmic world are enduring. Appropriately the incitation stems from an impulse of compassion for one of the petty members of the animal kingdom, a bedraggled and frightened hare caught in winter's traces:

> One evening one sat by my door two paces from me, at first trembling with fear, yet unwilling to move: a poor wee thing, lean and bony, with ragged ears and sharp nose, scant tail and slender paws. It looked as if Nature no longer contained the breed of nobler bloods, but stood on her last toes.

But this appearance of nature, as he is soon to discover, is only one of her careless reflexes. For behind this deceptive image of the moribund lurks the flashing, resurgent energy of life engaged to life:

> I took a step, and lo, away it scud with an elastic spring over the snow crust, straightening its body and its limbs into graceful length, and soon put the forest between me and itself,—the wild free venison, asserting its vigor and the dignity of Nature. Not without reason was its slenderness. Such then was its nature. (*Lepus, levipes*, light-foot, some think.)

And in running into the forest, the hare, like the partridge and the fox, points "the way" to centauric enlightenment. In the dark maze of the woods lie all the secrets of the soul's adventure. It holds the answer to all the forbidden lore of blood and terror that the mind in its egocentric orientation devaluates. But to penetrate into this heart of darkness is to approach the mystery of life. When this light dawns everything in nature declares itself to be sacred. And it is on wings of this intuition that Thoreau pronounces the immortality of the hare and the partridge. They too spring from the archetypal darkness of the dim past:

> They are among the most simple and indigenous animal products; ancient and venerable families known to antiquity as to modern times; of the very hue and substance of Nature, nearest allied to leaves and to the ground, and to one another; it is either winged or legged. It is hardly as if you had seen a wild creature when a rabbit or partridge bursts away, only a natural one, as much to be expected as rustling leaves. The partridge and the rabbit are still sure to thrive, like true natives of the soil, whatever revolutions occur.

With this deification of the earth and its creatures, Thoreau admits the sanctity of the primitive and the instinctual. This prepares him for the centauric theophany which the coming of spring heralds. In body and spirit he is in complete harmony with nature as she was in the instant of Creation: "so the coming of spring is like the creation of Cosmos out of Chaos and the realization of the Golden Age." This is the ritual conclusion of *Walden*, the fulfilled journey of the spirit in its search for the heroic virtue. Encompassing the breadth of the year, from spring to spring (in defiance, I submit, of the factual journal writings), it figures Thoreau as Hercules, Theseus, Perseus, or Achilles.

VII

This myth of the hero, as I have indicated, contrasts with the premises of its adaptation by contemporary and later writers of American fiction. In Hawthorne and Melville*** the hero lives in a world whose own centauric split is the condition of his soul. He cannot redeem the Waste Land from its sickness because its inhabitants will not admit the existence of the condition. The culture lacks the self-knowledge, inward and outward, which is the presupposition of salvation. This self-complacency of the present is the enemy of the redemptive truth of tradition since in this perspective the moment at hand is the culmination of all human development. No *philosophia perennis* is permitted to speak. Hence the hero, blind to the ideal of an entelechy, feeds upon the delusions of his ego until this self-cannibalism erupts into the curse of the incurable wound.

When one considers Twain's *Huckleberry Finn* in this same light, he is confronted by the miracle of transformative experience that is wisdom. The young hero's instincts metamorphose into conscious knowledge as soon as he assimilates the implications of the chthonic secrets of the snake skin on Jackson Island. The wisdom of the serpent, as in the myths of all primitive peoples, becomes the medicine of the soul, healing the strife between his inner and outer self. After he surmounts all the temptations of the Huck Finn that he destroyed on the banks of the rising spring river in the simulated murder (the willing sacrifice), he is challenged by the specter of the false hero just as he stands on the verge of self-fulfillment. By his silence at the indignation which Tom Sawyer's behavior arouses in his mind, he surrenders his heroic virtue to this posturing exemplar of middle class self-satisfaction. Perhaps this treason to his own nature is inevitable, symbolic of Mark Twain's identical surrender to a world which he hated. In any event, Huck is ultimately tainted by the blight of his own culture.

Of course, Hemingway's Jake Barnes in *The Sun Also Rises* is a reincarnation of Huck Finn, a half century later, in the shambles of middle class civilization, the cancer of the Gilded Age in the full power of its malignancy. The hero, in his sexual impotency, reflects the sterility of this culture. Cut off thereby from the instructive levels of human wisdom, he seeks in the outward violence of the world the regenerative miracle that will make him whole again. But his surrender to these forces, especially at the bullfight with its remnants of ritual discipline, exhibits him as cause and agent of the lost generation's submission to instinctual anarchy. As exemplar of the defeated manhood of his culture, he cannot channel his derelict energies towards moral ends. Infatuated with the illusion of reality, Jake Barnes is doomed to a life of empty gestures (ritual without purpose). Though he attempts, like Nick Adams in "Big

Two-Hearted River," to rejuvenate himself in nature, he fails because he has pro-faned her too much. One cannot, as he did, prostitute the sacred emotions. One must discipline them to the requirements of the spirit, aspiring for the intuition of self-knowledge that enables Nick Adams to conquer the temptations of the river, the swamp, and the forest. For the latter, as the blatant imagery of the short story suggests, is preparing himself for the role of the Grail hero. In his self-conquest of inward fears, he redeems himself from the paralysis of will of which Jake Barnes is a passive victim.

In the preordained circle of destiny that closes in upon Joe Christmas, Faulkner exploits an identical pattern of the false hero. The protagonist's delusion of negro blood is a surrogate image of the curse of Hemingway's Waste Land, for it projects his capitulation to the primitive darkness of his emotions, by extension his default from the light of August, the zodiacal symbol of the Virgin whose redemptive qualities are ironically shifted to the magdalene-earth-mother archetype in the figure of Lena. Without interpretive exaggeration, one can say, I think, that the chief motif of the novel is the search for the lost mother, psychologically the woman from whom he was traumatically separated in his infancy, spiritually the Virgin Mother (or how else is one to explain Faulkner's name symbolism). Either can provide the sense of relatedness upon which his salvation depends. Or, to put it another way, the one is the other, the expression of selfless love. But the hero's centauric cleavage is absolute. His conscious outlook on life has been irrevocably masculinized by his ritual destruction of the sheep. It therefore drives him inexorably towards his fate of castration. The perform-ance of the emasculation permanently separates him from the feminine which he scorns. This event, however, has been predestined by the instincts whose feminine holiness has been defiled by his warped reason. They offer him as a willing sacrifice to the composite goddess whom they serve. Joe's destiny, of course, figures the cata-strophic direction towards which our culture drifts, for his nihilistic individualism, contemptuous of emotional and moral values, reflects the spiritual sickness of the twentieth century. This is to say that the Christ of our Christianity no longer mediates the life-goals which we pursue. In the eyes of Faulkner his purely feminine com-passion, as symbolized in the Virgin spiritually and in Lena earthfully, has degenerated into the eunuch logic of science, militarism, and historical progressivism.

At this juncture Faulkner's judgment of modern man converges with the dis-illusionment which incited Thoreau to abandon the village for a sojourn on Walden Pond. The latter, in fact, prophesies the doom of culture envisioned in *Light in August* (and I am not overlooking the comic redemption of Byron Bunch). The myth of the centaur which he lived is a protest against the compromises that materialism has forced upon Christianity. In its failure to sustain the value structure of the spirit he advocates a return to the *philosophia perennis* out of which it grew. By this I mean that he counsels a new relationship with nature, one which Christianity perhaps too arbitrarily devaluated, thus uprooting man from the sources of his being in the maternal earth. It is this secret that Byron Bunch discovers in his barefoot Magdalene.

ELH, XXV (1958), 194–215. Part II has been omitted.

THE USE OF MYTH IN KAFKA AND MANN

Harry Slochower

A study of the great literary classics shows that their themes are organically inter-woven with mythic and religious motifs. The interconnection is more intimate in the eastern and primitive myths, in the mythopoesis of Greece and Rome, and, of course, in the Catholic myth of Dante. But myth and religion also find their way into modern classics, such as Racine's *Phèdre*, Rabelais's *Gargantua*, Goethe's *Faust*, Wagner's *Ring*, Melville's *Moby Dick*, and the poetry of William Blake. Even in our secular twentieth century, we find that the outstanding writers are preoccupied with them. To mention some: André Malraux, James Joyce, the Danish writer Nexö, and, above all, the two men with whom we are concerned in this chapter, Franz Kafka and Thomas Mann.

I

Myth and religion, along with other cultural forms, are at one in their common attempt to get at basic reality seen in symbolic transformation. However, what differentiates myth and religion, particularly from science and philosophy, is their anthropomorphic approach. Whereas science and philosophy focus on the cosmos as a whole, the special interest of myth and religion is the subject of *man*. A second element which unites the two is their *normative* perspective. Both approach the problem of man, not in terms of neutral objectivity, but apply selected value judgments.

Another feature which connects myth and religion is their view of the human drama as having a *communal* origin and destiny. And these are seen as undergoing a *dramatistic* process: the primary communal stage is followed by a mediate phase, in which the individual loosens himself from his social matrix. This defection is called his crime or sin. It results in his "Cain"-journey, in his suffering and crucifixion. However, in the course of the dramatic development, the crime may become transfigured into "the blessing." This becomes possible to the extent that the individual recognizes the supra-individual element within his ego, and seeks to reintegrate it with his commune on a higher level.

Both myth and religion are concerned with ultimate reality. But myth is distinguished from religion in that it presents reality as an *immanent* mode. The form of the myth is the story or picture—that is, its universal prototypes are presented through concrete, particularized imagery, and are embodied in individual characters and specific situations. Moreover, its sensuous presentation of reality also takes account of the temporal historic situation in which man is placed.

As a result of its stress on the immanent and the particular, the myth can do greater justice to the *mediate* stage of individual defection or revolt. In the myth, the crime of the hero appears as a *necessary* act, *through* which he can become transformed. And while the hero comes to recognize that his revolt has been in excess, and experiences fear and trembling, he never fully surrenders or recants. It follows that in the mythic

349

process, there is no complete redemption as in religion—no eschatology or paradise. Even as the individual is reintegrated with his commune, the element of individuation, of experience, and of revolt, continues as a moment calling for a new revolt aiming at a higher re-recreation.

In sum, the myth contains two basic categories: *Creation*, which relates to the pattern, the prototype, the beginnings and ends of things; and the *Quest*, which refers to the critical questioning of the old tradition aiming at a *futuristic* tradition. In Aristotle's *Rhetoric*, we have the three categories of Logos, Ethos, and Pathos. Generally speaking, we might say that the myth of Creation is concerned with Logos, the myth of the Quest with Pathos or emotion and with Ethos or the character of the individual— always seeking a new Logos whenever the existing law takes on a closed hierarchical form.

We have observed that myth and religion offer a communal standard of behavior. This standard is conditioned by social and political historic factors. Even as history and culture live by the myth, they, in turn, affect the form, content, and direction of the myth. It follows that the all human standard inherent in the myth may be distorted by the "ideology" of the myth, serving partisan and special interests. This opens the way toward the misuse of the myth. And, in the course of history, the myth has been often employed toward inhuman purposes. In our own twentieth century— the era of Kafka and Mann—we are confronted with a plethora of false and manufactured myths. Let me mention two in particular which are relevant to Kafka and Mann: the racial "folk," masquerading as a human commune, and the technological "one world," giving the illusion that the power of mechanical gadgets, such as the atomic bomb, can replace the power of man.

The works of Franz Kafka and Thomas Mann present the menace in the false and dead myth. But they also suggest—Kafka somewhat hesitantly, Mann more confidently —the possibility of a "breakthrough" and the reemergence of the living myth, of one human world.

II

When we look over the life and works of Franz Kafka, we are impressed with the fact that they reveal fear, fear and loneliness, alienation from the world, from the public commune in which he lived. He was a Jew, an alien, in an alienating world, Kafka's commercialized world, the semi-feudal, semi-bourgeois bureaucracy of the old Austro-Hungarian Empire. And we find that he also felt estranged from his father and even partly from his mother, estranged from his country, estranged from his profession, estranged from women, and in fear of marriage. Finally, there is his fear and alienation from his potential reading public, as manifested in his request to his friend Max Brod that Kafka's manuscripts be burned.

Franz Kafka, a Jew and an alien, had a particularly difficult problem in finding the mythic reference in the past. Job could do it. He was near enough to his God, and Sophocles has a certain mythic reference in Moira. The difficulties became greater with Hamlet, Faust, and Ahab. By the twentieth century, especially for those such as

Kafka who were Jews in name only, there is an even greater difficulty of finding a reference backwards.

What has become of Job's God in Kafka's world? What has become of the Mosaic Law? What has become of the Judges? They are reduced to bookkeepers. God and the Judges are readers of legal briefs and manuscripts. And the Prophet, the Klamm, this "all" figure has become a fat, middle-aged bureaucrat. This is the form in which Logos and God now appear. This is the communal reference which Kafka finds in his world. Documents which cover lives and aspirations, documents and numbers, have replaced the idea of the law.

We have here the Evil One in modern form. The Devil is Society, this particular Society, Society characterized by impersonality. It is the Fiend, whom you cannot see, a faceless, dehumanized something which accuses you and does not tell you what you are accused of, a kind of bureaucratic version of original sin.

This is the one Devil. The other resides within the individual who has been reduced to this facelessness himself and who remains indifferent to the outrage of evil. This "hero" is not a protesting, passionate, fiery Job, or a Prometheus, or an Oedipus, or even a Dante; he is an orphan, a bachelor, vermin—in the story, "Metamorphosis," a cockroach. And the only way in which he revolts, in Kafka's *The Trial*, is simply by a kind of passive, non-conscious self-arrest. More than that, he is guilty even over this "revolt," guilty because he does not feel the power in him to replace the commune, to replace the father—an echo of Hamlet. Yet, Hamlet is still quite active in his inaction. But Joseph K.'s inactivity, in comparison, is nearer to a man such as Swann in Proust's work or Castorp in *The Magic Mountain*.

And so we find that Kafka's heroes do not reenact the Oedipus theme. They do not revolt against their fathers. Rather, they reverse the Oedipus pattern and the sons sacrifice themselves for the fathers. In the story, "The Judgment," the son commits suicide, whereupon the energy and vitality of the father's house are enhanced. In the story, "Metamorphosis," the hero wakes up one morning and finds he is a cockroach, whereupon the father's fortunes begin to increase.

Yet Kafka's work contains the suggestion of a third stage, the stage of reintegration. But in Kafka, this phase which we find in *The Castle*, the *Great Wall of China*, is much more of a prayer than a hope. *The Castle* is the omnipotent structure of judges and lawyers that become more remote, the more you try to approach it. As such it reminds one of Socrates's saying, "The more I know, the more I find out that I don't know"; of Dante's theology, that knowledge leads to the realization of man's deep ignorance; and of the idea of the Law which shows man to be utterly corrupt.

The Castle is omnipotent, on the one hand, a taboo not to be violated; on the other hand, it is decadent, as was the Austro-Hungarian castle of Kafka's time. Yet, we have here a more positive attempt to reach the Law. In *The Trial*, Joseph K. begins with a certain militance, but, as the novel proceeds, his revolt is nearly crushed. In *The Castle*, "K." demands a job as a surveyor, holding that he has *a right* to work. And even though he does not get entrance into the Castle, there is a suggestion which Kafka sketched that in time he was to be permitted at least to live in the village.

In this novel, Kafka rejects two approaches; the approach of Amalia, the anarchic rebel, the individual who will have nothing to do with the judges; and the alternative way of the Pepis (in the last part of *The Castle*, which is not translated, unfortunately, in the Knopf edition), who live huddled together in the underground. This way of submerging the ego, K. cannot accept either. When Pepi begs of K.: "Just stay with us until Springtime," the only answer K. makes is, "When does Springtime come?" Yet the feeling we get is that the individual K.'s must first go underground to the Mothers, to the Pepis, to start at the bottom, and work their way through.

But the greater promise lies in man's insatiability and rebellious quest, as suggested in the sermon in *The Trial*. It is the sermon about the legend of the gatekeeper who stands at the gates and will not allow the individuals to pass through. In the end, Joseph K. learns that the gate was kept open only for him. He alone could go through, but Joseph K. is a simpleton. He is called, in German, "*Ein Mann vom Lande*." In other words, he was too simpleminded to try to go through, to defy the gatekeeper.

This defiance is necessary. It is the duty of the individual to defy the gatekeeper, and, having done so, he might be allowed to pass through. We can say, then, about Kafka, that in the main his is the myth of the quest, with very little confidence and hope in the myth of creation; but this quest, this seeking, this critique, is also a certainty which the K.'s cannot give up.

To be sure, the negative elements seem to abound in Kafka's work. It abounds in metaphors, such as air which stifles, incurable wounds, castration symbols (injuries to knees and thighs), the cage, etc.—metaphors which suggest the closed circle. Yet, Kafka is to be distinguished from most of his followers who have taken up these negative aspects and erected them into a system of negativism and of critique, for there remains in Kafka a consuming yearning for the law and the truth. He does not end in a Kierkegaardian "either/or," and he does not end with submission or surrender. The quest in Kafka is also an inevitable and persisting feature of man's way. In its persistence lies the promise of the quest.

III

When we turn to Thomas Mann, we have a man who lacks many of the personal burdens from which Kafka suffered. In Mann's case we, therefore, have a more positive voice, possibly also because he has taken a longer and deeper look backward toward a mythic reference. In him we do find the preoccupation with and the emphasis on the myth of creation. Myths abound in all of Thomas Mann's works, Egyptian, Hebraic, Christian, and Germanic.

But this positive voice in Thomas Mann is not one which ignores the ideology of the myth mentioned before. As a matter of fact, in most of his works we find a warning against two kinds of myth: against the dead myth—the dual symbol for that is the Egyptian mummy—and the German Magic Mountain *Kultur*, an inactive idealism or romanticism. That is the myth as stasis, disporting itself in music, philosophy, and dreams.

The other danger, equally great, and bound up with the first, is the myth as up-rooting dynamics, the myth as the devouring father and mother. It, too, appears in two forms. It may be *Kultur* itself, where the transcendent dynamic, while confined to the realm of the idea or the spirit, is a form of imperialism, an esthetic imperialism which may—as shown in *Doctor Faustus* and suggested in earlier works—be translated into the imperialism of the body, the cannibalism of Lidice and Auschwitz.

These are the dangerous myths. Mann encountered them by a living myth which has its roots in a living God, a God Who combines both creation and the quest, the God Who *calls for* the individual quest, as Job's God Who condones Job, at least partly because Job has rebelled against Him, whereas He does not condone the three friends who did not show this critical quest.

The earlier Mann was only groping for this living God and this living myth. In his works through *The Magic Mountain*, we find the presentation of a false creativeness. It is conditioned by the German and European commercialized commune, similar to that in which Kafka's characters were entangled. This false communal base necessarily shapes the false quest of the hero.

When we think of *The Magic Mountain*—and we might also, at this point, think of Mann's much later work, *Doctor Faustus*—our story, in terms of the three stages, unfolds somewhat like this: in both cases, you might say with Hamlet, "The time is out of joint." The flatland of Castorp and the birthplace of Leverkühn, the hero of *Doctor Faustus*, embody a commercialized collective which they consciously or unconsciously reject. The two heroes then proceed to disport themselves in aloneness, Doctor Faustus much more so than Castorp. Both secede from this commune, Castorp seven years above the flatland to the mountain, Leverkühn to the valley—his Nietzschean Sils Maria. And here they practice transcendence, ideological, musical transcendence.

But even as they think they have freed themselves from the compulsion of the material base, we find that their ideology is a counterpart, the spiritual counterpart of their mephitic, commercialized collective. To be sure, it is not identical with it. Something is saved, but the vapors from below invade the heights above, or descend to the depths below, so that when Castorp goes to his tertiary stage, at the end of the seven years, and realigns himself with his "comrades," it is not the high commune of Job or Oedipus or Dante, it is Germany in the First World War. Castorp thinks it is Schubert he is fighting for, but we know, and Mann knows by 1924, that Castorp is fighting for Thyssen and Krupp. Similarly, the reintegration of the work of Leverkühn at the end turns out to be in continuity with the Esau collective of Nazism.

Between *The Magic Mountain* and *Doctor Faustus*, with their false myth, we have the human myth of living creation, the Joseph story, where Mann leaves the bourgeois world to penetrate deep into the human—a kind of international folk song and an attempted answer to the nationalistic howling of the time. It was begun approximately with the ascent of Nazism. Its origin-reference is a God Who appears in the threefold form of the spirit of Abraham, the physics of Isaac, and the human father, Jacob, who combines the two; in psychological terms, the super-ego of Abraham, the id of Isaac, and the integrated ego of Jacob. Joseph would reconcile his three fathers, would unite them all. Not only them. He also reenacts Osiris, Tammuz, Adonis. His is the mediating function of the artist—he is a "between" character, and the word "between," in Hebrew, I understand, has the same root as the words, "knowing" and "insight." Knowledge and insight appear as mediating categories. Joseph's "blessing" consists in the mediation between beauty and wisdom and in his *Geist*, the questing, seeking spirit, but always with reference to his commune, Jacob, the Father—God.

But his is also the hybris of individual revolt, in his notion that all must love him, and more than they love themselves. However, in the third stage, when he comes to Egypt, he returns to his father-brother collective. Yet the story also contains the epilogue of the myth, which prevents a final redemption. For the Egypt-commune is a eunuch civilization. There is a question as to whether Joseph's social reforms are a public or a private collectivism. Hence, he loses the blessing, which is given over to Judah, the suffering man. The blessing is taken away from Joseph, whose figure has developed from the Adonis to the Hermes figure, that is, to the worldly leader, the businessman.

Let me now turn to Mann's work of 1948, on which I touched before. In 1924, as we saw, Castorp rejoins a false commune. The Joseph story would correct Castorp's error, which led to the Fascist commune in the nineteen hundred and thirties. The Joseph story deals with the potentialities and possibilities of man in the future. But, in the meantime, the world was in the death grip of Fascism. Hence the story of Doctor Faustus with the background of the Hitler-band, on the one hand—an echo of the earliest Hun barbarism—and, on the other hand, the alternative commune of Bach and Dürer, which also gave birth to the Faust figure. Leverkühn leaves his heights for the valley, but he is much more esthetic than Castorp ever was. Castorp at least met one human personality, Peeperkorn, and associated with lesser figures as well. Leverkühn disports himself in complete isolation to practice transcendence. He transcends by indulging himself in theology and music. This esthetic imperialism is his pact with the Devil.

The pact with the Devil has a dual aspect. It is the pact of the German intellectual with pure spirit which is divorced from politics, from society, from the people. This apartness means that it cannot have love or warmth, but only coldness or heat. The embrace of the pure spirit leads to the embrace of the impure body—the Esmeralda episode in Leverkühn's story, this promiscuous "*Freudenmädchen*" to whom the most solitary is drawn.

Mann is saying here that we must not separate the good from the bad Germany. There is only one Germany, and the good Germany has contributed toward the bad Germany, although they are not identical. The pact has taken place long before Hitler. Hell means the inability to love, somewhat in the manner in which Zossima defines it in *The Brothers Karamazov*. The price Leverkühn pays for his creation is precisely the price of removal from women and people and from friends and the world. At the end he calls the commune to him, and makes his confession. He confesses that his work has been the product of the Demon, and should be rejected. But Mann, the writer, the historian, the Apollonian observer of the German Dionysian personality, would partly redeem Leverkühn's musical effort. Music has been the pact with the Devil, but music is the most universal language. The problem, however, is to bring music back to the folk, to make it communal without making it common. The cancer in the German *Kultur* music of Leverkühn is that it was produced in isolation, away from people.

IV

Let me, in conclusion, state that Kafka and Mann show us that the choice we face is that between the individual ego, on the one hand, lost in an anonymous public collective which today we think of as "the East." The other danger is that the ego might be choked by the Western private power collective. It is too late to go back to the Eastern primitive collective; but it would be myopic to disregard the Eastern momentum, calling for a supraracial, supranational, supraindividual fraternity. We cannot and must not choose between the Western ego and the Eastern commune. This, it seems to me, is what Mann, in particular, is saying. While both warn against the danger within the existing commune, they both know that the idea of man is not exhausted by historical coordinates. Through him flow eternal currents, prototypes, recurrent motifs, which give meaning to the words, "man" and "one world." There is the possibility of the ego to fulfil itself, not to be choked or destroyed, but to fulfil itself in a public collective, confined to the material realm, and allowing for cultural, for ego differentiations.

This is the promise of the human myth. The fulfilment of this promise depends, to be sure, on a human historic situation, one which might be created by the awakened powers which slumber in man.

Spiritual Problems in Contemporary Literature, ed., Stanley Romaine Hopper (New York: Harper, 1953), pp. 117–126.

From Mythological to Mythopoeic

The two essays in this concluding group—"Tennyson's Mythology: A Study of Demeter and Persephone*" by Robert Stange and "Prophetic Myths in Zola" by Philip Walker— concentrate on explicit mythological allusions and demonstrate their esthetic relevance to theme and form. By restricting the concept of myth more nearly to the older sense of classical mythology, Mr. Stange and Mr. Walker perform two notable services. First, they show us some of the ways in which nineteenth-century literature exploited classical and Christian mythology and thereby helped prepare the way for the exploration and redefinition of myth that has taken place in our time. Second, by drawing attention to the importance of these mythic materials they suggest avenues of investigation for critics concerned with more extended mythopoeic interpretations. Out of such studies might well emerge a new and fruitful view of Tennyson and Zola, estheticism and naturalism, and ultimately of nineteenth-century literature as a whole.*

TENNYSON'S MYTHOLOGY: A STUDY OF *DEMETER AND PERSEPHONE*

G. Robert Stange

Our present image of Tennyson's poetic career is well established; the pattern, in its broad outlines, is of a youthful burst of subjective lyricism followed by a half-century of suppression, propriety and worldly success. As Harold Nicolson has ingenuously put it, Tennyson "was intended to be a subjective poet, and was forced by circumstances into fifty years of unnatural objectivity." If we disregard its obvious inaccuracies such a view has much to recommend it. The reader of our time, influenced by the Aesthetic movement, nourished on the works of the French poets and novelists, is clearly more at home with a Tennyson who belongs to the band of *poètes maudits* than he would be with the Victorians' apotheosized Laureate. And since no total impression of a poet's life, no dramatic construction of his career, is ever likely to be accurate, we might well content ourselves with this image of Alfred Tennyson and be grateful to its originators for having made at least a small place for him in the modern pantheon.

But though we hold to the image of Tennyson as a poet of tortured sensibility, the voice of an ineffable despair, we must not permit this interpretation to be chronologically limited. The detached and almost hermetic qualities of the early poems did, it is true, give way to a tendency toward homely didacticism, and it is easy to assume that the Tennyson of the middle and later years found himself as a "public" poet. The final fifty years, however, were not given over to an "unnatural objectivity"; the tensions—and the richness—which mark Tennyson's early work can be found at the end as well as at the beginning of the collected poems.

Tennyson's poems, of whatever date, which seem to the modern reader efficient and expressive tend to display what can only be called the Tennysonian complex. They are ambiguous in tone; they exhibit the dialogue of the mind with itself; they circle round the anguished perception of the oppositions that rend the poet and his world. Tennyson's most typical conflict centers on his confusion as to the function of poetry. Throughout his career he sought to justify the saving power of poetry and expressed the ambivalence of the nineteenth century artist, rejected by the world, who at one moment rejoices in his isolation, and at another struggles to assert himself as *sacer vates*.

Underlying this conflict is the poet's combined hatred for and acceptance of his age. He described it as "an age of lies, and also an age of stinks," yet he felt that the sober, energetic Victorian world somehow marked the threshold of a glimmering new existence in which all irreconcilables would be fused and faith and light have their day. Intermixed with these attitudes was the poet's characteristically Victorian religious conflict. Here too all was doubt and division. It was impossible for him to believe in conventional Christianity, yet that faith represented the only belief worth having. In this sphere Tennyson, as every reader of *In Memoriam* knows, attempted to affirm the value of doubt itself, to celebrate a weak faith in the "one far-off divine event,/To which the whole creation moves."

Such a web of velleities and confusions would seem to offer the material not of great poetry, but of a poetry of passive suffering, of a wayward and individual despair. Tennyson nevertheless managed to create a body of great verse out of apparently defective materials. His achievement does not rest on an objectification or dramatization of his conflicts, nor on the strategies of ironic detachment and acute intellectual analysis. His tendency was rather to surround his personal subjects with the rich trappings of myth and legend, to suffuse them with a noble and melodious melancholy, to align his psychic ambivalences with the permanently affecting oppositions of the life of man and nature.

Stéphane Mallarmé, in trying to sum up his sense of Tennyson's nobility, had recourse to a comment of Villiers de l'Isle-Adam: "In effect, literature properly so called no more exists than does pure space—what reminds one of a great poet is the impression of sublimity he has left with you through his work rather than the work itself."[1] The impression of sublimity that Tennyson's poetry communicates does not, of course, exist independent of the work itself. He was above all a workman, and a close reading of his work would call attention not only to the peculiar climate of his poetry, but to the range of his interests and techniques, to the unexpected flexibility of his poetic instrument.

I intend to examine a very late poem of Tennyson's in the light of these generalizations. *Demeter and Persephone* recommends itself as a complex work which deals with the question of spiritual estrangement, which incorporates the poet's concern with his age and with religious belief, and which has the further interest of anticipating the

1. "En effet, la littérature proprement dite n'existant pas plus que l'espace pur—ce que l'on se rappelle d'un grand poète, c'est l'impression dite de sublimité qu'il vous a laissée, par et à travers son œuvre, plutôt que l'œuvre elle-même."

reinterpretation of mythology which has informed some of the most distinguished poetry of our century.

Tennyson, who was eighty when *Demeter and Persephone* was published (in 1889), spoke of it afterwards in a pleasantly off-hand way. It is reported that his son Hallam suggested the subject because, he said, "I knew that my father considered Demeter one of the most beautiful types of womanhood." And the poet answered, "I will write it, but when I write an antique like this I must put it into a frame—something modern about it. It is no use giving a mere *réchauffé* of old legends." He would cite as an example of the "frame" the lines in which Demeter envisions a coming race of "younger kindlier Gods," and iterates Tennyson's notion of the "one far-off divine event." The frame of modernism involved first a penetration of the essential meanings of the Greek legend, conceived not as allegory or symbol, but in the terms of myth itself, and then an assimilation of those meanings to the Christian hope of a New Jerusalem. The most striking achievement of the poem is the consistency with which the language of myth is used to include reflections on the nature of artistic creation, on the condition of the age, and on religious doctrine.

Tennyson derived his legend from the Homeric *Hymn to Demeter* and, except in the conclusion to his poem, was faithful to the spirit of the Greek original. However, the nature of his selection and variation of emphasis is in itself expressive. The expansive detail and the typal quality of the hymn are rejected in favor of a dramatic emphasis on the situation of the goddess and her daughter. Tennyson omitted the ritualistic background of the original; Zeus and Pluto appear only as symbols of the polarity of existence. The narrative is compressed to fit the exacting demands of the dramatic monologue form, and events are altered so that the scene of both Demeter's soliloquy and the reunion with her daughter is the Vale of Enna, from which Persephone was originally abducted.

With all these rearrangements, one discovers that the myth, though it retains its identity, has become a Tennysonian subject. Attempts have often been made to distinguish the "classical" poems from Tennyson's other work and to find in them a firmer tone, an elevated impersonality. But the fact is that every Greek or Roman theme that the poet chose to treat became in his hands a symbolic narrative of separation, either from an object of love or from the natural course of life. Such dissimilar classical poems as *Oenone*, *Ulysses*, and *Tithonus* share this central theme. In each case the subject offered an opportunity for a figurative expression of personal concerns, and the pattern of situation that emerges in the classical idylls is very little different from that of the poems based on history, medieval legend, or original narrative.

In a manner which is significant to the history of English poetry, Tennyson's reinterpretation of the myth of Demeter has affinities with that modern view of myth which is derived from the research of Sir James Frazer. The first volume of *The Golden Bough* was published in 1890, a year after Tennyson's *Demeter*. In the seventh volume of his study Frazer said:

... we do no indignity to the myth of Demeter and Persephone—one of the few myths in which the sunshine and clarity of the Greek genius are crossed by the shadow and mystery of death—when we trace its origin to some of the most familiar, yet eternally affecting aspects of nature, to the melancholy gloom and decay of autumn and to the freshness, the brightness, and the verdure of spring.[2]

Tennyson's center of interest in Demeter is the scheme of related antinomies from which the imagery of the poem develops, and which are inherent in the myth. The poem's basic design is one of oppositions between brightness and gloom (compare Frazer's shadow and brightness). This pattern reflects the contrast between Persephone's joyful life on earth and her imprisonment in the underworld, and includes the antitheses of decay and fertility; of the ruling principles of life: God, "the Bright one," and "the Dark one," his brother; and finally the underlying duality of life and death.

Frazer interpreted the two goddesses as personifications of the corn in its double aspect—Persephone as the seed and Demeter as the ripe ear. Though Tennyson followed the nineteenth century tradition of regarding Demeter as the Earth Mother,[3] his imaginative construction of the myth reveals the same insights as Frazer's scholarly study:

> Above all, thought of the seed buried in the earth in order to spring up to new and higher life readily suggested a comparison with human destiny, and strengthened the hope that for man too the grave would be but the beginning of a better and happier existence in some brighter world unknown. This simple and natural reflection seems perfectly sufficient to explain the association of the Corn Goddess at Eleusis with the mystery of death and the hope of a blissful immortality.[4]

Throughout his poem Tennyson stressed the theme of regeneration and related it to other threads of his imagery. The episodes are ordered and the change of emotions punctuated by the progression of the seasons—we follow Demeter through the phases of the year, from the melancholy of autumn, through the despair of winter, to the lightening hope of spring. The opening lines state some of the main motifs:

> Faint as a climate-changing bird that flies
> All night across the darkness, and at dawn
> Falls on the threshold of her native land,
> And can no more, thou camest, O my child,
> Led upward by the God of ghosts and dreams,
> Who laid thee at Eleusis, dazed and dumb
> With passing thro' at once from state to state,
> Until I brought thee hither, that the day,
> When here thy hands let fall the gather'd flower,
> Might break thro' clouded memories once again
> On thy lost self.

2. J. G. Frazer, *The Golden Bough* (3rd ed.; London, Macmillan, 1912), VII, 91.

3. Frazer found no justification for this identification either in the rites of Demeter or in the artistic representation of the two goddesses.

4. Frazer, *The Golden Bough*, VII, 90.

The passage exhibits the poem's characteristic quality of multiple suggestion and controlled ambiguity. The simile of the "climate-changing bird" is typical; Persephone, like a bird, comes back *with* the spring, but she is mythically the changer of the climate, and her return *is* the spring. The darkness and the dawn represent not only the days of the bird's flight and the passage from the gloom of hell to the light of earth, but more profoundly, the birth of a new day and a new season, symbolized by Persephone's emergence from the underworld. The return to the native land is the first suggestion of a succeeding discrimination among three states of being; Hades marks one undesirable extreme and Heaven the other; the earth, or more particularly, the Vale of Enna, symbolizes the middle state, the good place—but I shall have more to say of this later.

It is implied that Persephone's abduction involved a losing of the self; she is "led upward" by Hermes out of the land of death and carried by her mother to the place where the return of day will bring her former self to light. In the lines that follow, Persephone's rebirth is expressed by images of light:

> A sudden nightingale
> Saw thee, and flash'd into a frolic of song
> And welcome; and a gleam as of the moon,
> When first she peers along the tremulous deep,
> Fled wavering o'er thy face, and chased away
> That shadow of a likeness to the king
> Of shadows, thy dark mate, Persephone!
> Queen of the dead no more—my child! Thine eyes
> Again were human-godlike, and the Sun
> Burst from a swimming fleece of winter gray,
> And robed thee in his day from head to feet—
> 'Mother!' and I was folded in thine arms.
>
> (Lines 11–22)

The nightingale's song of welcome which partly dispels the shadow of death, Persephone's likeness to her "dark mate," may be thought of as the greeting of nature. But Persephone does not again become the child of Demeter until the day has fully dawned. We are not allowed to forget that though the spirit of fecundity may be reunited to her mother, the earth, she is married to the god of darkness. In the second section of the poem this double allegiance is more fully developed; Persephone has been permanently altered and to some extent estranged by what she has seen in hell:

> Child, those imperial, disimpassion'd eyes
> Awed even me at first, thy mother—eyes
> That oft had seen the serpent-wanded power
> Draw downward into Hades with his drift
> Of flickering spectres, lighted from below
> By the red race of fiery Phlegethon;

> But when before have Gods or men beheld
> The Life that had descended re-arise,
> And lighted from above him by the Sun?
> So mighty was the mother's childless cry,
> A cry that rang thro' Hades, Earth, and Heaven!
>
> (Lines 23-33)

When we come to examine the third section of the poem we shall see that the place of reunion, the Vale of Enna, closely resembles certain recurrent scenes in Tennyson's poetry, locations which are symbolic of the proper home of the spirit. Anticipating this interpretation, one might examine this section of the poem to see if it reflects any of the poet's personal concerns. Persephone is clearly the personification of fertility, but it is possible that she may also express the principle of poetic creativity. The journey to the underworld has frequently served as a figurative expression of a poet's experience. The myth of Orpheus is the most notable example of such an application; but early in his career Tennyson used the figure of Ulysses (who had visited the underworld and returned) to stand for the poet who had lived more fully than other men and had consequently estranged himself from them. Tennyson also, and in this T. S. Eliot has followed him, found in the myth of Tiresias an analogy to the suffering the poet must undergo as a result of the preternatural vision the gods had granted him. Both Tennyson and Eliot presumably based their interpretations on Homer, who accorded to Tiresias a special position in the underworld as the only shade that retained integrity of judgment and knowledge after death.

The description of Persephone's transformation, which is original with Tennyson, bears some resemblance to his treatment of mythical poet-figures. The changes that the "human" goddess has suffered reflect the traditional conception of the terrible effects of visions that are not meant for earthly eyes. In the fires of hell she has seen revealed the secrets of death; she has become "imperial"—that is, regnant over the spirits of the underworld—and "disimpassioned"—remote from ordinary emotion. She is a "human-godlike" personage who has become estranged from our life by the intensity of her dark experiences.

Tennyson was obsessed by the theme of penetration to secret wisdom. The seer— Tiresias, Lucretius, Merlin, the Ancient Sage—is vouchsafed a vision which is accompanied by both powers and dangers. The descent and resurrection of Persephone is related to this theme; one aspect of her legend conveys Tennyson's sense of the poet's penetration of the realm of the imagination, of the forbidden region of shadows which must be entered before the highest beauty or the highest meaning of experience may be perceived. Since the story of Persephone is a myth of generation, the poet includes in his treatment of it not only the fertility of the soil and the creation of new life, but his definition of the attributes of the artist—imperial, disimpassioned, who moves between divided and distinguished worlds.

Related to all the implications of the Persephone myth is the notion that only through union with the earth can the principle of creativity find its self. Demeter laments the change Persephone has suffered, but rejoices that her daughter has risen again; the experience is likened to the feeling of the sun's warmth, and conveyed by images that are instinct with the sense of vegetable growth. The idea of rebirth is emphasized by Demeter's "childless cry," which recalls Persephone to earth. This is, of course, explicitly the wail of a deprived mother, but it suggests the pains of labor, and may be thought of as the Earth Mother's cry of agony as she brings forth new life from the world of death.

The third section celebrates the precarious triumph of life and fertility over death:

> So in this pleasant vale we stand again,
> The field of Enna, now once more ablaze
> With flowers that brighten as thy footstep falls,
> All flowers—but for one black blur of earth
> Left by that closing chasm, thro' which the car
> Of dark Aïdoneus rising rapt thee hence.
> And here, my child, tho' folded in thine arms,
> I feel the deathless heart of motherhood
> Within me shudder, lest the naked glebe
> Should yawn once more into the gulf, and thence
> The shrilly whinnyings of the team of Hell,
> Ascending, pierce the glad and songful air,
> And all at once their arch'd necks, midnight-maned,
> Jet upward thro' the midday blossom.
>   No!
> For, see, thy foot has touch'd it; all the space
> Of blank earth-baldness clothes itself afresh,
> And breaks into the crocus-purple hour
> That saw thee vanish   (Lines 34–51)

The passage, I think, intentionally echoes some famous lines from Milton's description of the Garden of Eden:

>   Not that faire field
> Of *Enna*, where *Proserpin* gathring flours
> Her self a fairer Floure by gloomie *Dis*
> Was gatherd, which cost *Ceres* all that pain
> To seek her through the world . . .
> . . . might with this Paradise
> Of Eden strive.

This passage of *Paradise Lost* (Book IV, lines 268 ff.) is one that Tennyson frequently read aloud, and the parallel both indicates the traditional background of his description and suggests the conception of the Vale of Enna as the earthly paradise.

Imaginary places analogous to the Eden garden are abundant in Tennyson's poems; they usually suggest a refuge from active life, a retreat to the past (as in *The Hesperides* and *Maud*), or a sacred bower of poetic inspiration (as in *The Poet's Mind*). In Tennyson's poetry both heights and depths suggest danger and death; the valley, the sheltered plain, represent the fruitful life. The secluded valley of Enna is reminiscent of the enclosed, shadowy gardens, or the tropical islands of the other poems.

An account of Demeter's long search for Persephone follows and contrasts with the description of the pleasant vale. The subject is the kind for which Tennyson felt a peculiar sympathy: an elevated spirit deprived of the sources of its power, wandering shelterless through a desolate landscape. The world through which Demeter moves is one that has lost its power of generation; without abandoning the mythical treatment, Tennyson expresses his characteristic melancholy and presents a vision of an age deprived of the principle of life and creativity.

The poet described himself in *In Memoriam* as "a child crying in the night"; Demeter expresses the same sense of hopeless despair. She called her daughter's name to the midnight winds and heard voices in the night; she peered into tombs and caves, and after following out "a league of labyrinthine darkness," she saw a vision of the Fates, who could not tell her of her daughter since she was not mortal. All the images of this fourth section evoke blackness, desolation, and death.

> . . . I stared from every eagle-peak,
> I thridded the black heart of all the woods,
> I peer'd thro' tomb and cave, and in the storms
> Of autumn swept across the city, and heard
> The murmur of their temples chanting me,
> Me, me, the desolate mother!
>   'Where?'—and turned,
> And fled by many a waste, forlorn of man,
> And grieved for man thro' all my grief for thee,—
> The jungle rooted in his shatter'd hearth,
> The serpent coil'd about his broken shaft,
> The scorpion crawling over naked skulls;—
> I saw the tiger in the ruined fane
> Spring from his fallen God, but trace of thee
> I saw not.   (Lines 67–80)

This wasteland is both a concrete extension of the mood of the bereaved Demeter and the image of a society without faith or hope. "Evil," said Tennyson in 1887, "will come upon us headlong, if morality tries to get on without religion." In this ruined world beasts swarm over the relics of civilization; the tiger springs from man's fallen God. The Moerae know nothing of the universal fate beyond them, which can be anticipated only when Demeter and Persephone are re-united.

The description of the search is the most "Tennysonian" passage in the poem. It is in keeping with the original myth, yet it bears the weight of Tennyson's psychic, social, and religious concerns. It exemplifies what the poet, in another connection, called a "parabolic drift." The figure of Demeter is analogous to the sensitive mind searching for creativity. It is implied that there must be union between the mother and daughter before fecundity can be achieved; like the poet, Demeter wanders through endless deserts and dark places, crying out, demanding to know the secrets of nature, in order that she may summon Persephone back to life and to the dying world.

The lowest point of Demeter's despair is reached when she is greeted by the ghost of her daughter, which tells her:

> 'The Bright one in the highest
> Is brother of the Dark one in the lowest,
> And Bright and Dark have sworn that I, the child
> Of thee, the great Earth-Mother, thee, the Power
> That lifts her buried life from gloom to bloom,
> Should be for ever and for evermore
> The Bride of Darkness.'   (Lines 93–99)

Demeter learns that the two highest and opposite powers are related, and that both are heedless of the life of earth. The Earth Mother bears the same relation to the extremes of God and the king of the underworld that the Vale of Enna bears to heaven and hell; her power is the source of terrestrial life. She curses the cold and complacent gods of heaven:

> I would not mingle with their feasts; to me
> Their nectar smack'd of hemlock on the lips,
> Their rich ambrosia tasted aconite.
> The man, that only lives and loves an hour,
> Seem'd nobler than their hard eternities.
>   (Lines 101–105)

The goddess' grief brings on the death of vegetation, and fall gives place to winter; the course of the seasons is again a reflection of Demeter's emotions.

Then the god, "who still is highest," relents, and decrees that Persephone may dwell,

> For nine white moons of each whole year with me,
> Three dark ones in the shadow with thy king.

And the narrative of Demeter's search is concluded by a Keatsian description of the return of fertility to the earth:

> Once more the reaper in the gleam of dawn
> Will see me by the landmark far away,
> Blessing his field, or seated in the dusk
> Of even, by the lonely threshing-floor,
> Rejoicing in the harvest and the grange.
>   (Lines 121–125)

Here, insofar as the poem is an adaptation of a Greek myth, it may be considered to end. The cycle of the year is rounded and the season of fertility has returned. The concluding section of the poem is a bold attempt to extend the meanings of the classical myth by grafting on to it a hopeful vision of the future which embodies Tennyson's conception of the gentle humanism of Christian faith. Demeter proclaims the working of a "Fate beyond the Fates" which is impenetrable to the Olympian gods. This universal fate decrees the eventual triumph of "younger, kindlier Gods" who will bear down the Olympians even as they conquered the Titans. Will not the new Gods come, Demeter asks,

> To quench, not hurl the thunderbolt, to stay,
> Not spread the plague, the famine; Gods indeed,
> To send the noon into the night and break
> The sunless halls of Hades into Heaven?
> Till thy dark lord accept and love the Sun,
> And all the Shadow die into the Light,
> When thou shalt dwell the whole bright year with me.

(Lines 131–137)

Tennyson was quite right in conceiving this section as the "something modern" with which he surrounded the old legend. As an attempt to augment the implications of a vital myth the passage is in the great tradition of Spenser, Milton, and the Shelley of *Prometheus Unbound*. In its synthesis of the myths of more than one culture it anticipates the interpretation of mythology which later enriched the poetry of Yeats and Eliot. But what was "modern" to Tennyson is Victorian to us, and it is this conclusion to *Demeter and Persephone* which now seems most dated.

The difficulty Tennyson faced was that of presenting a vision of the triumph of life and love without having the belief that would make that vision ring true. In stating his affirmation Tennyson lacked the assurance that one finds in such poets as Dante or George Herbert. For Tennyson the dream of faith soon reduces itself to a faint trust in "the larger hope." With so inadequate a base the poet was perhaps inevitably tempted to push his assertions farther than was appropriate. It is instructive to compare Tennyson's uplifting message with the modified hope expressed at the end of Eliot's *Waste Land* (which also attempts a fusion of disparate mythologies), or with the vision of the future presented by Yeats' *Second Coming*. Tennyson's desire for certainty, when he felt none, mars the last lines of *Demeter*, and though they are gorgeously colored, they seem quite static. Demeter addresses her daughter:

> . . . thou that hast from men
> As Queen of Death, that worship which is Fear,
> Henceforth, as having risen from out the dead,
> Shalt ever send thy life along with mine
> From buried grain thro' springing blade, and bless
> Their garner'd autumn also, reap with me,
> Earth-Mother, in the harvest hymns of Earth
> The worship which is Love, and see no more
> The Stone, the Wheel, the dimly-glimmering lawns
> Of that Elysium, all the hateful fires
> Of torment, and the shadowy warrior glide
> Along the silent field of Asphodel.

The myth of Persephone has been reinterpreted as an anticipation of the story of Christ. The conception of an unchanging life and a continual earthly fruition is, however, not entirely consistent with the notion of a union of opposites imaged by the buried grain. It is curious, too, that the best lines of the poem describe the Elysium that is to be abolished. The success of Tennyson's reinterpretation is not, I think, an unqualified one.

Whatever may be the flaws of *Demeter and Persephone*, they are not of the sort one finds in minor poetry. The poet may not have entirely succeeded in making his myth bear the modern implication, but of the creative energy and poetic skill he brought to his task there can be no doubt. Beneath the poem's elegant diction and its sharp, almost Pre-Raphaelite outlines one perceives the action of the sad, shadowy drama which is typical of Tennyson's poetry. The poem skirts the edge of excessive self-pity, of railing at the age, of pious reflection on faith and doubt, of the bathos which ruined many Victorian poems. But Tennyson's core of toughness saves him. His extraordinary insight into the nature of myth, his ability to relate a private or social distress to the radical dualities of human experience, makes a poetic triumph out of a personal despair.

ELH, XXI (1954), 67–80. Some of the reference notes have been omitted.

PROPHETIC MYTHS IN ZOLA

Philip Walker

I

Certain myths exerted an extraordinary hold on Zola's imagination, as one may see not only in *La faute de l'abbé Mouret* (1875) but also in at least two of his greatest works, *Germinal* (1885) and *La débâcle* (1892). These latter novels were written in a period overshadowed by the idea of decadence—the period described by Mario Praz in the last chapter of *The Romantic Agony*—when Wagner's *Götterdämmerung* and Schopenhauer's philosophy were the rage in France and such representative authors as d'Aurevilly, Verlaine, and Huysmans gave voice to a gloomy premonition that the Dies Irae of the West—decadent Latin civilization in particular—was at hand. Zola's *La joie de vivre* (1884), with its setting suggestive of legendary *villes englouties*, came out the same year as Elémir Bourges' novel *Le crépuscule des dieux* and the first volume of d'Aurevilly's *La décadence latine*; and the next year, the year *Germinal* was published, saw the foundation of the *Revue Wagnérienne*. It is not surprising that nearly all the myths appearing in Zola's novels at this time reflected this widespread mood of cosmic catastrophism. Yet even where he used the same mythological themes (for example, Sodom and Gomorrah) as some of the decadents and did so in the same historical frame, the sharp differences in their approaches to history clearly emerge. For where the decadents were almost exclusively obsessed with the theme of decline and fall and a sense of "delicious death agony" (to borrow a phrase from Praz), Zola, without being indifferent to this, was predominantly concerned with the theme of cultural regeneration. Significantly, nearly all the myths evoked in the novels we have mentioned are myths of catastrophe and death but also, at the same time, of redemption and rebirth.

In this respect, Zola was nearer to the mood of the present age, what Carl Jung calls "the mood of world destruction and renewal" symbolized in much contemporary art. This is not quite the same as the decadents' romantic pessimism and monotonous *routine du gouffre*, just as their premonition that they were living in the "twilight of the gods" is not exactly the same as our own shadowy suspicion that we are living in, to quote Jung, "what the Greeks called the 'right time' for a metamorphosis of the gods—that is, of the fundamental principles and symbols."[1]

Something of this metamorphosis (which Jung ascribes in part to the might of modern technology and science) is to be seen in Zola's treatment of mythology even more dramatically than in many of the original poetic symbols that complement and inform the factual realism of his works. It is here, in the violence he did to these images still so deeply colored for most of us with Christian, humanistic meanings, that may be perceived the full sharpness of his break with the past (with which most of the decadents still identified themselves). In his mythological and other symbols he went far beyond the "scientific" statements of his materialism in *Le roman expérimental*

---

1. C. G. Jung, "God, the Devil, and the Human Soul." *Atlantic Monthly*, CC (Nov. 1957), 63.

and elsewhere in the direction, for example, of the dehumanization of art, of unanimism, irrationalism, nihilism; or of an erotic mystique with affinities to D. H. Lawrence; or of a theory of history analogous, as Guy Robert has pointed out, to Nietzsche's "myth" of Eternal Return, or, again, of a cult of violence (including war) as a potentially redemptive force of nature.

The process involved is thus in some ways prophetic. It is not so much a matter of using myths for literary embellishment (which would have been against the grain of Zola's naturalistic esthetics) as it is of consciously or unconsciously transforming myth into an expression of a new *Zeitgeist*. This prophetic quality is especially evident in such deliberately prophetic historical novels as *Germinal* and *La débâcle* with their apocalyptic endings, but is already discernible in Zola's development of the story of Adam and Eve (and of the larger theme of man's fall and redemption) in *La faute de le'abbé Mouret.* * *

II

* * *Along with Zola's quasi-religious eroticism, unanimism, paganism, and along with his tendency toward an irrational, poetic cult of primitive natural forces, there is also a lurking hint of nihilism in *La faute de l'abbé Mouret*. This modernized version of the myth of Adam and Eve may be a paean to nature, a wild hymn to life; nevertheless, there is a threatening darkness in the philosophical background: Jeanbernat, the guardian of Paradou, indicates the whole horizon, earth and sky. "Nothing really exists, nothing at all. . . . If you blew out the sun, that would be the end of everything," he says in Part I, and he repeats the same fear toward the end of the book: "Well, I was right, nothing really exists, nothing at all. . . . It was just a hoax."[2]

III

These conscious or unconscious tendencies are more radically symbolized in *Germinal*, where there is a discreet, yet significant, application of Christian, Celtic, and Greco-Roman mythology.

It was perhaps inevitable that myths should find their way into this novel (which Henry James and Havelock Ellis regarded as one of Zola's two or three works most likely to survive and which André Gide selected in 1946 as one of the ten greatest French novels). The subject is not only epic, but prophetic—even apocalyptic—in scope. The strike in the coal mines, as Zola's notes and letters prove, is a frame through which he can portray the history of modern class warfare while prophesying the shape of things to come. "That's the important thing about this book: I want it to predict the future," he wrote in the first paragraph of his Ebauche, "to bring up the problem that's going to be the most important problem of the twentieth century."[3]

2. Emile Zola, *La faute de l'abbé Mouret* (Paris: Charpentier, 1875), pp. 52, 417. "Il n'y a rien, rien, rien . . . Quand on soufflera sur le soleil, ça sera fini" (p. 52); "Allez, j'avais raison, il n'y a rien, rien, rien . . . Tout ça, c'est de la farce" (p. 417).

3. Bibliothèque Nationale (Paris), MS, Fonds français, Nouvelles acquisitions, 10307, fol. 402. Zola's working notes for *Germinal* are contained in MSS. 10307, 10308. Subsequent references are indicated in the text.

This could not be done without indicating his subjective vision of history, and this required a use of intensely suggestive symbols of the sort that myth provides.

Even where it was not a matter of adapting specific myths from the past, his imagination in writing *Germinal* was unmistakably mythopoeic. As a careful examination of the novel and voluminous working notes shows, his method of composition was here almost precisely the method he suggested to Céard, soon after the publications of *Germinal*, in a letter on the subject of the synthesis that existed in practice, if not theory, between his realism and his poetry. The secret of his art, he implied, was to be discovered in the "mechanism" of his "Mensonge," his manner of imposing his inner vision on his objective imitation of reality. This fictional "lie," as he said—or *fictio*—was to give the impression that he was a scientifically objective portrayer of documentary facts, whereas factual details were for him primarily a "tremplin"—or springboard—from which he could mount toward poetic symbol. As he suggested in the same letter, this movement was in the direction of a more effective expression of reality than factual description alone could provide: "Now, I may be wrong, but I keep on thinking that my particular sort of lie works in the direction of truth. I have a hypertrophy for the true detail, the leap to the stars from the springboard of exact observation. Truth rises with one beat of the wing all the way to the symbol."[4] There is no doubt that this is a more exact description of Zola's art during his best creative period than *Le roman expérimental*. His fiction is not, in practice, so much the result of any application of the scientific experimental method (and where Zola tried hardest to be a scientist he was at his poorest as an artist) as it is the product of the peculiarly modern tension between the modern scientific mind and the primordial mythopoeic mind, each of which has its own manner of discovering and representing truth. His art, in *Germinal*, is par excellence the art of an era in which myth and science are in theory opposed, but tend, in practice, to assume at times each the form of the other.

As examples of the mythopoeic forms taken by Zola's imagination in this novel, his tendencies, already observed in *La faute de l'abbé Mouret*, to turn men into animals, give beasts human traits, and personify physical objects might be mentioned. Winds cry famine; clouds flee in horror; industrial structures assume the shapes of enormous man-devouring beasts or of titanic giants struggling against death as they are swallowed up by the trembling earth. The old mine horse Bataille is referred to as a sage, a "philosophe" (I, 65; II, 195), and does indeed dream, like a Platonic philosopher in his cave, of a symbolic sun. Human characters, on the other hand, are given animalistic names like "Chaval" and are described as ants, snakes, cats, sheep, dogs, wolves, and so on. And they are given bestial or nonhuman traits—La Maheude, the symbol of proletarian motherhood, with her canine breasts and breath that streams like a panting dog's, Mouquette with her gigantic buttocks, and the like. Another, La Brûlé, Zola wrote in his notes, was to be made into a demoniac—"une énergumène" (MS 10308, fol. 43), and Bonnemort was to be "une chose" (MS 10308, fol. 32). Zola's vision of collective humanity in *Germinal* is no less mythopoeic than his portrayal of individuals

4. Emile Zola, *Correspondance, Les œuvres complètes*, ed. Maurice Le Blond (Paris: Bernouard, 1927-29), II, 637.

—an expression of a biologically oriented, unanimistic materialism which has little place for either the Christian or humanistic concept of *humanitas*. No one has described this vision better than Lemaitre: "Men appear, like waves, on a sea of shadows and unconsciousness: this is the very simple philosophical vision which one may find at the core of the drama."[5] Where Lemaitre showed his Christian, humanistic bias, however, was in calling this pessimistic, for, underlying as it does almost the whole of modern materialism, it has by no means always been taken as a pessimistic vision of man by materialists themselves, who, on the contrary, have sometimes been curiously exalted by it.

The myths, symbols, and images expressing Zola's intuition of man, nature, and history in *Germinal* are nearly all involved in his development of its two principal metaphorical themes, the Underworld and the Deluge. The idea of comparing the setting of a proletarian novel to hell is in itself, of course, hardly less banal than the analogy between social upheaval and a catastrophic storm, but Zola succeeded in constructing out of these admittedly prosaic inspirations intensely poetic and expressive symbols of his revolutionary modern thought. In doing so, he revived two of the most universal archetypes of myth with something coming very close to their original force. It is not a matter of scattering here and there a few random images, but of weaving into the basically realistic fabric of the novel a multitude of analogies and metaphors arranged in a manner which is not at all haphazard, whether consciously intended by Zola or not. The progress of the storm theme, for example, may be followed from its foreshadowing in the overturelike first chapter—in the sea-tempest imagery and crying winds sweeping "the blinding spray of shadows" across the road, which "stretched out with the straightness of a pier"[6]—to the approach of the storm in the imagery of the hectic, explosive description of the miners' summer festival in Part III, Chapter ii, and from here on through two great climaxes—the human flood thundering across the plain in Part V and the catastrophic, apocalyptic descriptions of the inundated mines in Part VII—to its last traces in the fleeing little red clouds perceived by Etienne as, startled by the loud song of a lark, he looks up at the prophetic sunrise of a new Age of Gold. Although the hasty reader may be no more consciously aware of the storm theme than the average cinema goer may be of the background music of a film, a study of Zola's development of the theme will show that he had in mind no ordinary storm, but a vast, cosmic upheaval reminiscent of the Great Flood of Genesis or of the earthquakes and fiery, watery disasters that recur in early Greek mythology in the wars between the Titans and the early reign of Zeus. In short, one is very far here from a merely artistic analogy, or romantic parallel, between man and nature; nor can one speak properly here of the pathetic fallacy, which can hardly exist as such in Zola's unanimistic philosophy, in which everything alike is a force of a single nature endowed with a single life. It is a storm which includes the blood and

5. "Les hommes apparaissant, semblables à des flots, sur une mer de ténèbres et d'inconscience: voilà la vision philosophique, très simple, dans laquelle ce drame se résout. . . ." Quoted in the appendix of *Germinal*, ed. Maurice Le Blond (Paris: Bernouard, 1927-29), p. 576.

6. Emile Zola, *Germinal* (Paris: Charpentier, 1885), I, 1. Subsequent references are indicated in the text.

tears of men quite as much as rain and snow. And nature in *Germinal* does not simply reflect the social drama; earth and heaven intervene in the human struggle, like Homeric gods. Which is it, for instance, that exerts the more compelling force upon the mob of strikers, described in terms of a steadily mounting stormy tide, during the midnight strike meeting in the forest—the self-appointed leaders, who themselves flash in the shadows like lightning, or the large, white moon that slowly rises through-out the chapter until its apotheosis (at what would have been the exact center, or pivot, of the book if Zola had not belatedly added Part VII) in the final sentence of the chapter? And, opposed to the moon, symbol of the mad violence of the strike, there is the sun, which slowly rises in the last chapter of the book as a symbol of the sane force of nature that will ultimately bring forth the new Golden Age as surely as the sun itself brings back spring. And it is here, in the final pages, that Zola presents a vision of nature as earth-mother bringing forth, as in the myth of Deucalion and Pyrrha, a new and hardier race of men springing up from under the growing wheat— an autochthonous race well adapted to labor and the struggles that will result in the return of paradise. The storm theme is thus, as Zola has developed it, a major expression of his thought—and particularly of his vision of history. Beside sym-bolizing his materialism and unanimism, it suggests—especially since the progress of the storm parallels and reflects the sequence of the seasons—already something of the cyclical view of history that Guy Robert has detected in *La terre*. It also suggests the tendency on Zola's part, concerned as he is with the problem of social death and regeneration, to regard catastrophe and violence as potentially beneficent forces of nature. Like the great floods of mythology, the flood of *Germinal* is at once destructive and reconstructive, and it is principally through it that the setting of the novel is transformed from a Dantesque vision of the underworld into the spectacle of a new world in the full throes of creation.[7]

Myths from the old world are borrowed to help express the birth of the con-temporary world. This includes Christian myths and symbols, for just as Dante and Milton, whom Zola admired, subordinated pagan myths to Christian ones, Zola, representative of the new mentality, reversed the process and incorporated Christian symbols into a neopagan mode of thought. This appears in his symbolic treatment of the setting, which he had told himself in his notes to make into "un véritable enfer" (MS. 10307, fol. 420). The novel begins with what is, at least metaphorically, a descent into the underworld. It is undeniable that much of the imagery employed in this section and in the description of the interior of the Jean-Bart pit in Part V, Chapter ii, is strongly reminiscent of traditional Christian conceptions of the infernal— in, for example, Zola's heavy use of the colors red and black, his treatment of the super-structure of the Voreux mine as a sort of *gueule d'enfer*, his depiction of the receiving

---

7. Zola's fascination with the theme of world destruction and renewal goes back long before the *fin de siècle* and antedates his own naturalism. His 1869 prospectus of the Rougon-Macquart series for Lacroix indicated that he would study "des lueurs troubles du moment, des convulsions fatales de l'enfantement d'un monde" (see the appendix of *La fortune des Rougon*, ed. Maurice Le Blond [Paris: Bernouard, 1927–29], p. 354). This was already a major theme, however, of Zola's youthful projected epic poem "La genèse."

shed as an infernal church with suggestions of the Black Mass, his repeated applications of the serpent image (become, in *Germinal*, a symbol apparently of the capitalist system), his descriptions of bestiality, vice, and torture in the mines, his evocation of smoke, flames, the extremes of heat and cold, the "sixième voie, dans l'enfer" (I, 38), and so on.

Toward the end of the novel, however, Christian imagery of hell gives way to allusions suggestive of medieval Celtic myths of the underworld (II, 200, 208, 220)—tales of engulfed towns and cathedrals, of the sort that also fascinated the symbolists. It is perhaps the significance of these stories that the dead are separated by only the very thinnest of veils from the living and that the simplest act of interest and generosity on the part of the latter could bring the former back to life. In the most dramatic of this type of allusion in *Germinal*, a young engineer, Négrel, has bravely had himself lowered in a basket deep down into the broken shaft of the Voreux in order to inspect the damage. Having passed through a shifting subterranean water deposit called the "torrent," "this subterranean sea with its unknown storms and wrecks," he hears far below him under the flooding waters frantic cries for help, and, "far off in the great shifting shadows," he seems to see "streets, squares of a devastated city."[8] It is Négrel's suddenly acquired feeling of solidarity with the working class that helps more than anything else to bring out the dramatic rescue of the hero—a prophetic scene culminating in a moving fraternal embrace between Etienne and Négrel, suggestive of the utopian social order that might result from social cooperation.

Greco-Roman mythology is, nevertheless, more strongly suggested than either Christian or Celtic symbolism in *Germinal*. With one or two exceptions, all the explicit mythological allusions scattered throughout the novel are classical: Furies, Ceres, the Golden Age, Tartarus, and so on. The peculiarity of these allusions is that they all suggest not just any Greco-Roman myths but particularly stories of the Creation and the War of the Gods: the primordial cosmic struggles between Uranus and Cronus, Cronus and Jupiter. The Furies leaped into being from the blood of Uranus after he had been grievously wounded by Cronus' iron sickle. The golden-haired Ceres was, like her father Cronus, connected with the golden harvest and, like her daughter Proserpine, associated with rites of death and of the lower world. She was also connected by the Eleusinians with ceremonies representing the alternation of life and death in nature and, apparently, the resurrection and immortality of man. The mention of Ceres in *Germinal*, where the same themes are developed, is therefore curious, to say the least (especially since *Germinal* is one of Zola's most minutely planned, carefully written novels). Again, Tartarus was the profound abysm of the earth where Uranus thrust his fearful children the Hecatonchires and Cyclops, who were released by Jupiter at the advice of their mother, the earth-mother Gaea, to take part in his war against Cronus. It was here, also, that after ages of struggle the Titans were consigned in their turn, making of Tartarus a symbol of the destructive revolutionary forces that eternally exist deep within the earth itself. Undoubtedly, these and other subjects referred to by Zola from the same bodies of myth were of a sort particularly

8. "cette mer souterraine aux tempêtes et aux naufrages ignorés . . . très loin dans le jeu des grandes ombres mouvantes . . . des rues, des carrefours de ville détruite" (II, 200).

adaptable to the expression of his own philosophy of history and of nature. And there is every indication that his allusions to them are, whether consciously deliberate on his part or not, more than superficial. If, for instance, the ironic analogy is made between the capitalistic era and the Golden Age, it is not surprising that he should have compared Mme Hennebeau, the mine director's barren wife and the richest character in the book, to Ceres (I, 223). Nor is it surprising that here, as seven years later in *La débâcle*, he should have compared proletarians to the Furies (II, 87). The analogy between the gulf of Tartarus and the ancient burning mine Tartaret has, furthermore, been given an extended development (II, 11–12). Just as Tartarus was the abode of the Titans, Tartaret is, according to the local legend of the mining region, the abode of a terrible giant, the *Homme noir*; and, just as the dreadful children of Uranus were called up by Gaea to fight their elder brother Cronus, the proletarians, whom Zola described collectively as "une force de la nature" (II, 66), well up out of the depths of the earth about Tartaret to wage revolutionary warfare on capital. Moreover, if at times there is a strong possible analogy to be made between Zola's concept of a revolutionary nature, always on the side of her children against their fathers, and Gaea, there is perhaps an even more obvious analogy between Zola's *Dieu inconnu*, a personification of capital and one of the most recurrent images in the novel, and Cronus— especially since, among other things, both are shown as devourers of their children (the proletariat being the product of capitalistic society). Again, while the metaphorical flood of *Germinal* may remind one in some respects of the Biblical Deluge, the violence of the strike may be even more reminiscent of the catastrophes of the war between Cronus and Jupiter. Indeed, Zola's description of the destruction of the mines in Parts V and VII strongly recalls mythological images of the defeat of the Titans. The Voreux mine superstructure in Part VII is personified as a giant resting on a powerful knee. Then, as the earth trembles below it, the knee bends, the giant stands up and breaks into a staggering march as he fights against death and is at last dragged down into the gaping void below (Pt. II, pp. 206–207). There are, in addition, such an impressive number of analogies between the Greco-Roman mythical cosmos and the setting of *Germinal* (Oceanus and the Torrent, the Elysian Fields and Catherine's dying hallucination, the Vale of Enna and Côte-Verte) that it is almost impossible not to believe that Zola had classical mythology more or less in mind and that consciously or unconsciously he was tempted to conceive of the historical cataclysms of the modern world in terms of these ancient myths that have to do with the cyclical succession of the ages and with the metamorphosis of primitive gods. In fact, the central symbol of the novel would seem to lie in his placing Côte-Verte, a vale of eternal spring with its green grass and flowers blooming even in the harsh northern winter, over Tartaret (Tartarus). Over the symbol of death, violence, eternal revolution—and dependent on it—is the symbol of regeneration and eternal life.

IV

* * *This mystique of history, cult of violence, overwhelming catastrophic sense of time, mingled fear and hope, dehumanization of man, unanimism, irrationalism,

hint of nihilism, predilection for the archaic, the primitive—all discernible in Zola's metamorphosis of myth—may have its roots in eighteenth- and nineteenth-century thought, but is already very much in the spirit of the contemporary age. In Zola's use of myth one may see, above all, a symbolic expression not only of an awareness that the Christian, humanistic world is passing away but also a desire to see it go—to "destroy in order to destroy," as he writes in *La débâcle*, "to bury old rotten humanity beneath the ashes of a world, in the hope that a new society would spring up again, happy and innocent, in the terrestrial paradise of the primitive legends!"[9]

PMLA, LXXIV (1959), 444–452. Some of the reference notes have been omitted.

9. Emile Zola, *La débâcle* (Paris: Charpentier, 1892), II, 331: "détruire pour détruire . . . ensevelir la vieille humanité pourrie sous les cendres d'un monde, dans l'espoir qu'une société nouvelle repousserait heureuse et candide, en plein paradis terrestre des primitives légendes."

A SELECTIVE BIBLIOGRAPHY

ARBOIS DE JUBAINVILLE, HENRY D'. *The Irish Mythological Cycle and Celtic Mythology.* Tr. by R. I. Best. Dublin: Hodges, Figgis & Co., 1903.

ARVIN, NEWTON. *Herman Melville.* New York: William Sloan, 1950.

BARBER, C. L. *Shakespeare's Festive Comedy.* Princeton: Princeton University Press, 1959.

BIDNEY, DAVID. *Theoretical Anthropology.* New York: Columbia University Press, 1953.

BLOOM, HAROLD. *Shelley's Mythmaking.* New Haven: Yale University Press, 1959.

BODKIN, MAUD. *Archetypal Patterns in Poetry.* Oxford: Oxford University Press, 1934.

BUTLER, E. M. *The Myth of the Magus.* Cambridge: Cambridge University Press, 1948.

CAILLOIS, ROGER. *Man and the Sacred.* Tr. by Meyer Barash. Glencoe, Ill., Free Press, 1959.

CAMPBELL, JOSEPH. *The Hero with a Thousand Faces.* New York: Bollingen, 1949.

——. *The Masks of God.* 4 vols. New York: Viking, 1959.

CASSIRER, ERNST. *Essay on Man.* New Haven: Yale University Press, 1944.

——. *Language and Myth.* Tr. by Susanne Langer. New York: Harper & Bros., 1946.

——. *The Myth of the State.* New Haven: Yale University Press, 1946.

——. *The Philosophy of Symbolic Forms.* 3 vols. Tr. by Ralph Manheim. New Haven: Yale University Press, 1955.

CHASE, RICHARD. *Quest for Myth.* Baton Rouge: Louisiana State University Press, 1946.

——. *Herman Melville.* New York: Macmillan, 1949.

COOK, A. B. *Zeus.* 3 vols. Cambridge: Cambridge University Press, 1914–40.

CORNFORD, F. M. *The Origin of the Attic Comedy.* London: Edward Arnold, 1914.

——. *Thucydides Mythistoricus.* London: Edward Arnold, 1907.

——. *From Religion to Philosophy.* Cambridge: Cambridge University Press, 1912.

——. *The Unwritten Philosophy.* Cambridge: Cambridge University Press, 1950.

COULANGES, FUSTEL DE. *The Ancient City.* Tr. by W. Small. Boston: Lee & Shepard, 1874.

DURKHEIM, ÉMILE. *The Elementary Forms of the Religious Life.* Tr. by Joseph Ward Swain. London: Allen & Unwin, 1915.

ELIADE, MIRCEA. *The Myth of the Eternal Return.* Tr. by Willard R. Trask. New York: Pantheon, 1954.

——. *Birth and Rebirth.* Tr. by Willard R. Trask. New York: Pantheon, 1958.

——. *Myths, Dreams, and Mysteries.* Tr. by Philip Mairet. New York: Harper, 1960.

ELLIOTT, ROBERT C. *The Power of Satire.* Princeton: Princeton University Press, 1960.

FARNELL, L. R. *The Cult of the Greek States.* 5 vols. Oxford: Oxford University Press, 1896–1909.

———. *Greek Hero Cults and Ideas of Immortality.* Oxford: Oxford University Press, 1921.

FERGUSSON, FRANCIS. *The Idea of a Theater.* Princeton: Princeton University Press, 1949.

FONTENROSE, JOSEPH. *Python; a Study of Delphic Myth and its Origins.* Berkeley: University of California Press, 1959.

FRANKFORT, HENRI *et al. The Intellectual Adventure of Ancient Man.* Chicago: University of Chicago Press, 1946.

FRANKLIN, H. BRUCE. *The Wake of the Gods : Melville's Mythology.* Stanford: Stanford University Press, 1963.

FRAZER, SIR JAMES G. *The Golden Bough.* 12 vols. London: Macmillan, 1907–1915.

———. *Folk-lore in the Old Testament.* 3 vols. London: Macmillan, 1918.

———. *The Worship of Nature.* London: Macmillan, 1926.

FREUD, SIGMUND. *Totem and Taboo.* Tr. by A. A. Brill. New York: Moffat, Yard & Co., 1918.

FROMM, ERICH. *The Forgotten Language.* New York: Rinehart, 1951.

FRYE, NORTHROP. *Anatomy of Criticism.* Princeton: Princeton University Press, 1957.

GASTER, T. H. *Thespis : Ritual, Myth and Drama in the Ancient Near East.* New York: Schuman, 1950.

GENNEP, ARNOLD VAN. *The Rites of Passage.* Tr. by Monika B. Vizedom & Gabrielle L. Caffee. London: Routledge & Kegan Paul, 1960.

GRAVES, ROBERT. *The White Goddess.* New York: Farrar, Strauss & Cudahy, 1948.

———. *The Greek Myths.* 2 vols. Baltimore: Penguin, 1955.

HARRISON, JANE. *Prolegomena to the Study of Greek Religion.* Cambridge: Cambridge University Press, 1903.

———. *Themis.* Cambridge: Cambridge University Press, 1912.

———. *Ancient Art and Ritual.* London: Home University Library, 1913.

———. *Epilegomena to the Study of Greek Religion.* Cambridge: Cambridge University Press, 1921.

HARTLAND, EDWIN SIDNEY. *The Science of Fairy Tales.* London: Walter Scott, 1891.

———. *The Legend of Perseus.* 3 vols. London: D. Nutt, 1894–96.

HERSKOVITS, MELVILLE AND FRANCIS S. *Dahomean Narrative.* Evanston, Ill., Northwestern University Press, 1958.

HOCART, A. M. *Kingship.* Oxford: Oxford University Press, 1927.

———. *The Life-Giving Myth,* ed. Lord Raglan. London: Methuen, 1952.

HOFFMAN, DANIEL G. *Form and Fable in American Fiction.* New York: Oxford University Press, 1961.

HOOKE, S. H., ED. *Myth and Ritual.* London: Oxford University Press, 1933.

———. *The Labyrinth.* New York: Macmillan, 1935.

———. *Myth, Ritual and Kingship.* Oxford: Oxford University Press, 1958.

HYMAN, STANLEY EDGAR. *The Tangled Bank.* New York: Atheneum, 1962.

JAMES, E. O. *Christian Myth and Ritual.* London: J. Murray, 1933.

JAMES, E. O. *Myth and Ritual in the Ancient Near East.* London: Thames & Hudson, 1958.

———. *The Cult of the Mother Goddess.* London: Thames & Hudson, 1959.

———. *The Ancient Gods.* New York: Putnam, 1960.

JONES, ERNEST. *Essays in Applied Psycho-Analysis.* London: Hogarth Press, 1951. Vol. 2.

JUNG, C. G. *Symbols for the Transformation.* Tr. by R. F. C. Hull. New York: Pantheon, 1956.

———. *The Archetypes and the Collective Unconscious.* Tr. by R. F. C. Hull. New York: Pantheon, 1959.

JUNG, C. G. AND K. KERÉNYI. *Essays on a Science of Mythology.* Tr. by R. F. C. Hull. New York: Pantheon, 1949.

KRAPPE, A. H. *The Science of Folklore.* London: Methuen, 1930.

LANG, ALEXANDER. *Custom and Myth.* London: Longmans, Green & Co., 1904. (1st ed. 1884)

———. *Myth, Ritual and Religion.* 2 vols. London: Longmans, Green & Co., 1913. (1st ed. 1887)

LANGER, SUSANNE K. *Philosophy in a New Key.* Cambridge: Harvard University Press, 1942.

LEVY, G. R. *The Gate of Horn.* London: Faber & Faber, 1948.

———. *The Sword from the Rock.* London: Faber & Faber, 1953.

LÉVY-BRUHL, LUCIEN. *Primitive Mentality.* Tr. by Lilian A. Clare. London: George Allen & Unwin, 1923.

———. *How Natives Think.* Tr. by Lillian A. Clare. London: George Allen & Unwin, 1926.

———. *The "Soul" of the Primitive.* Tr. by Lilian A. Clare. London: George Allen & Unwin, 1928.

———. *Primitives and the Supernatural.* Tr. by Lilian A. Clare. New York: E. P. Dutton, 1935.

MACCAFFREY, ISABEL GAMBLE. *Paradise Lost as "Myth."* Cambridge: Harvard University Press, 1959.

MALINOWSKI, BRONISLAW. *Myth in Primitive Psychology.* London: K. Paul, Trench, Trubner, 1926.

———. *Magic, Science and Religion.* Glencoe: Free Press, 1948.

MARETT, R. R. *Psychology and Folk-Lore.* London: Methuen, 1920.

———. *Faith, Hope and Charity in Primitive Religion.* Oxford: Clarendon Press, 1932.

———. *Sacraments of Simple Folk.* Oxford: Clarendon Press, 1933.

———. *Head, Heart and Hands in Human Evolution.* London: Hutchinson, 1935.

MOORMAN, CHARLES. *Arthurian Triptych.* Berkeley: University of California Press, 1960.

MURRAY, GILBERT. *The Rise of the Greek Epic.* 4th ed. London: Oxford University Press, 1934. (1st ed. 1907)

———. *The Classical Tradition in Poetry.* Cambridge: Harvard University Press, 1927.

MURRAY, HENRY A. ED. *Myth and Myth-making.* New York: Braziller, 1960.

OESTERLEY, W. O. E. *The Sacred Dance*. Cambridge: Cambridge University Press, 1923.

OLSON, CHARLES. *Call Me Ishmael*. New York: Reynal & Hitchcock, 1947.

PHILPOTTS, BERTHA S. *The Elder Edda and Ancient Scandinavian Drama*. Cambridge: Cambridge University Press, 1920.

PRESCOTT, FREDERICK C. *Poetry and Myth*. New York: Macmillan, 1927.

RADIN, PAUL. *Primitive Religion*. New York: Viking, 1937.

———. *The Trickster*. New York: Philosophical Library, 1956.

RAGLAN, LORD. *Jocasta's Crime*. London: Methuen, 1933.

———. *The Hero*. London: Methuen, 1936.

———. *Death and Rebirth*. London: Watts, 1945.

RANK, OTTO. *The Myth of the Birth of the Hero*. New York: Journal of Nervous and Mental Disease Publishing Co., 1914.

RANSOM, JOHN CROWE. *God Without Thunder*. New York: Harcourt, 1930.

REIK, THEODOR. *Ritual*. Tr. by Douglas Bryan. New York: W. W. Norton, 1931.

———. *Myth and Guilt*. London: Hutchinson, 1958.

———. *Mystery on the Mountain*. New York: Harper, 1959.

———: *The Creation of Woman*. New York: Braziller, 1960.

———. *The Temptation*. New York: Braziller, 1961.

———. *Pagan Rites in Judaism*. New York: Farrar, Strauss, 1964.

RHYS, SIR JOHN. *Lectures on the Origin and Growth of Religion as Illustrated by Celtic Heathendom*. London: Williams & Norgate, 1888.

———. *Celtic Folklore, Welsh and Manx*. 2 vols. Oxford: Clarendon Press, 1901.

RICHARDS, I. A. *Coleridge on Imagination*. London: Routledge & Kegan Paul, 1926.

ROBERTSON, J. M. *Christianity and Mythology*. 2nd ed. London: Watts, 1910.

RÓHEIM, GÉZA. *Animism, Magic, and the Divine King*. London: Kegan Paul, 1930.

———. *The Riddle of the Sphinx*. London: Hogarth Press, 1934.

———. *The Eternal Ones of the Dream*. New York: International Universities Press, 1945.

———. *The Origin and Function of Culture*. New York: Nervous and Mental Disease Monographs, 1943.

———. *Psychoanalysis and Anthropology*. New York: International Universities Press, 1950.

———. *The Gates of the Dream*. New York: International Universities Press, 1952.

ROUGEMONT, DENIS DE. *Love in the Western World*. Tr. by Montgomery Belgion. New York: Pantheon, 1956.

SCHMIDT, WILHELM. *The Origin and Growth of Religion: Facts and Theories*. Tr. by H. J. Rose. New York: Lincoln Macveagh, 1931.

SEBEOK, T. A., ED., *Myth: A Symposium*. Bloomington: Indiana University Press, 1958.

SEIDEN, MORTON I. *William Butler Yeats: The Poet as Mythmaker*. East Lansing: Michigan State University Press, 1962.

SEWELL, ELIZABETH. *The Orphic Voice*. New Haven: Yale University Press, 1960.

SHUMAKER, WAYNE. *Literature and the Irrational*. New York: Prentice-Hall, 1960.

SIMPSON, WILLIAM. *The Buddhist Praying-Wheel.* London: Macmillan, 1896.

——. *The Jonah Legend.* London: Grant Richards, 1899.

SLOTE, BERNICE, ED., *Myth and Symbol.* Lincoln: University of Nebraska Press, 1963.

SMITH, HENRY NASH. *Virgin Land: The American West as Symbol and Myth.* Cambridge: Harvard University Press, 1950.

SMITH, WILLIAM ROBERTSON. *Lectures on the Religion of the Semites.* 3rd ed., ed. Stanley A. Cook. London: A. & C. Black, 1927. (1st ed. 1889)

SPEIRS, JOHN. *Medieval English Poetry.* London: Faber & Faber, 1957.

SPENCE, LEWIS. *An Introduction to Mythology.* London: G. G. Harrap, 1921.

——. *The Outlines of Mythology.* New York: Fawcett, 1961.

STILL, COLIN. *Shakespeare's Mystery Play.* London: C. Palmer. 1921.

——. *The Timeless Theme.* London: Nicholson & Watson, 1936.

THOMSON, J. A. K. *The Art of the Logos.* London: Allen & Unwin, 1935.

TINDALL, WILLIAM YORK. *Forces in Modern British Literature.* New York: Vintage, 1956.

TYLOR, SIR E. B. *Primitive Culture.* 2 vols. London: J. Murray, 1920. (1st ed. 1871)

URBAN, WILBUR M. *Language and Reality.* London: Allen & Unwin, 1939.

WATTS, ALAN. *Myth and Ritual in Christianity.* New York: Vanguard, 1953.

WATTS, HAROLD H. *Hound and Quarry.* London: Routledge & Paul, 1953.

WEISINGER, HERBERT. *Tragedy and the Paradox of the Fortunate Fall.* East Lansing: Michigan State University Press, 1953.

——. *The Agony and the Triumph: Papers on the Use and Abuse of Myth.* East Lansing: Michigan State University Press, 1964.

WESTON, JESSIE L. *The Quest of the Holy Grail.* London: G. Bell & Sons, 1913.

——. *From Ritual to Romance.* Cambridge: Cambridge University Press, 1920.

WHEELWRIGHT, PHILIP. *The Burning Fountain.* Bloomington: Indiana University Press, 1954.

——. *Metaphor and Reality.* Bloomington: Indiana University Press, 1962.

ZIMMER, HEINRICH. *The King and the Corpse,* ed. Joseph Campbell. New York: Pantheon, 1948.

ACKNOWLEDGMENTS

For help in the preparation of this book I am greatly indebted to a number of people. My wife has patiently discussed problems in the planning, selection, and presentation of materials in this collection. For their courtesies I am also grateful to the librarians of Purdue University, the University of Illinois, and the University of California at Riverside and at Los Angeles. My thanks also go to the authors, editors, publishers, and author's agents listed below for their permission to reprint the specified material in whole or in part.

J. B. V.

In Part One:

"Myth, Symbolism, and Truth" by David Bidney. Reprinted from *Myth: A Symposium*, edited by Thomas A. Sebeok, Indiana University Press, 1965. Originally published by *Journal of American Folklore*. Reprinted by permission of Indiana University Press.

"Bios and Mythos: Prolegomena to a Science of Myth" by Joseph Campbell. This selection reprinted from *Psychoanalysis and Culture*, edited by G. B. Wilbur and W. Muensterberger, International Universities Press, 1951. Copyright 1951 by International Universities Press and used with the permission of the publisher and Russell and Volkening, Inc.

"Myth and Folk-Tale" by Géza Róheim. Reprinted by permission of the editors of *American Imago*.

"Myths and Rituals: A General Theory" by Clyde Kluckhohn. Reprinted by permission of the publishers from *Harvard Theological Review* XXXV (1942), Cambridge, Massachusetts: Harvard University Press.

In Part Two:

"The Ritual View of Myth and the Mythic" by Stanley Edgar Hyman. Reprinted from *Myth: A Symposium*, edited by Thomas A. Sebeok, Indiana University Press, 1965. Originally published by *Journal of American Folklore*. Reprinted by permission of the author and Indiana University Press.

"Notes on Mythopoeia" by Philip Wheelwright. Reprinted by permission of the author and *The Sewanee Review*.

"Notes on the Study of Myth" by Richard Chase. Reprinted by permission of Frances W. Chase and *Partisan Review*.

"Myth and Drama" by Harold H. Watts. Reprinted by permission of the author and *Cross Currents*.

"The Archetypes of Literature" by Northrop Frye. Reprinted by permission of the author and *Kenyon Review*.

"The Working Novelist and the Mythmaking Process" by Andrew Lytle. Reprinted from *Myth and Mythmaking*, edited by A. H. Murray, George Braziller, Inc.,

384   ACKNOWLEDGMENTS

1960. Originally published by *Daedalus*. Reprinted by permission of the author and George Braziller, Inc.

"The Myth and the Powerhouse" by Philip Rahv. Reprinted from *The Myth and the Powerhouse* by Philip Rahv by permission of the author and Farrar, Straus & Giroux, Inc. Copyright 1953, 1965 by Philip Rahv. Originally published by *Partisan Review*.

"The Meanings of 'Myth' in Modern Criticism" by Wallace W. Douglas. Reprinted from *Modern Philology* by permission of the University of Chicago Press. Copyright 1953 by The University of Chicago.

"Cultural Anthropology and Contemporary Literary Criticism" by Haskell M. Block. Reprinted by permission of the author and the *Journal of Aesthetics and Art Criticism*.

In Part Three:

"'Myth' and the Literary Scruple" by Francis Fergusson. Reprinted from *The Human Image in Dramatic Literature* by Francis Fergusson, Doubleday Anchor Books, 1957. Originally published by *The Sewanee Review*. Reprinted by permission of *The Sewanee Review*. Copyright 1957 by Francis Fergusson.

"The Myth and Ritual Approach to Shakespearean Tragedy" by Herbert Weisinger. Reprinted by permission of the author and *Centennial Review*.

"Initiatory Motifs in the Story of Telemachus" by Charles W. Eckert. Reprinted by permission of the author and *Classical Journal*.

"Myth and Medieval Literature: *Sir Gawain and the Green Knight*" by Charles Moorman. Reprinted by permission of the author and *Medieval Studies*.

"The Archetypal Pattern of Death and Rebirth in Milton's *Lycidas*" by Richard P. Adams, "Mythopoesis in *The Blithedale Romance*" by Peter B. Murray, "Mythic Patterns in *To the Lighthouse*" by Joseph L. Blotner, and "Prophetic Myths in Zola" by Philip Walker. Reprinted from *PMLA* by permission of the authors and Modern Language Association.

"Big Medicine in *Moby-Dick*" by Reginald L. Cook. Reprinted from *Accent* by permission of the author.

"The Myth of Man: Joyce's *Finnegans Wake*" by Marvin Magalaner and "*The Red Badge of Courage* as Myth and Symbol" by John E. Hart. Reprinted by permission of the authors and the *University of Kansas City Review*.

"Symbolism of the Cyclical Myth in *Endymion*" by Robert Harrison, "Dickens and Some Motifs of the Fairy Tale" by Shirley Grob, and "An Archetypal Analysis of Conrad's *Nostromo*" by Claire Rosenfield. Reprinted by permission of the authors and the editors of *Texas Studies in Literature and Language*.

"Nature Myth in Faulkner's *The Bear*" by John Lydenberg. Reprinted by permission of the author and *American Literature*, published by Duke University Press.

"Remarks on the Sad Initiation of Huckleberry Finn" by James M. Cox. Reprinted by permission of the author and *The Sewanee Review*.

"The Sunburnt God: Ritual and Tragic Myth in *The Return of the Native*" by Louis Crompton. Reprinted by permission of the author and *Boston University Studies in English.*

"Myth and Ritual in the Shorter Fiction of D. H. Lawrence" by John B. Vickery. Reprinted from *Modern Fiction Studies* by permission of the Purdue Research Foundation.

"*Walden*: The Wisdom of the Centaur" by William Bysshe Stein and "Tennyson's Mythology: A Study of *Demeter and Persephone*" by G. Robert Stange. Reprinted by permission of the authors and *ELH.*

"The Use of Myth in Kafka and Mann" by Harry Slochower. Reprinted from *Spiritual Problems in Contemporary Literature*, Torchbook edition, edited by Stanley Romaine Hopper. Copyright 1952, 1957 by the Institute for Social and Religious Studies. Reprinted by permission of Harper & Row, Publishers.

INDEX